Beginning C# Web Applications with Visual Studio .NET

Daniel Cazzulino
Victor Garcia Aprea
James Greenwood
Chris Hart

Wrox Press Ltd. ®

Beginning C# Web Applications with Visual Studio .NET

First Printed November 2002

Published by Wrox Press Ltd
Arden House, 1102 Warwick Road, Acock's Green, Birmingham, B27 6BH, UK
Printed in the United States
ISBN 1-86100-732-9

Trademark Acknowledgments

Wrox has endeavored to provide trademark information about all the companies and products mentioned in this book by the appropriate use of capitals. However, Wrox cannot guarantee the accuracy of this information.

Credits

Authors
Daniel Cazzulino
Victor Garcia Aprea
James Greenwood
Chris Hart

Additional Material
Ian Nutt

Technical Reviewers
Martin Beaulieu
Carl Burnham
Daniel Cazzulino
Mitch Denny
Robin Dewson
Damien Foggon
Mark Horner
Don Lee
Scott Robertson
Ken Slovak
David Schultz
Tobin Titus

Technical Editors
Mankee Cheng
Chris Hart
Ian Nutt

Commissioning Editors
Paul Jeffcoat
Mankee Cheng
Ian Nutt

Managing Editors
Viv Emery
Joanna Mason

Series Editor
John Collin

Project Managers
Emma Batch
Darren Murphy

Author Agent
Nicola Phillips

Production Coordinator
Neil Lote

Cover
Natalie O'Donnell

Index
John Collin

Proofreader
Chris Smith

About the Authors

Daniel Cazzulino

Daniel Cazzulino is a senior developer who discovered C# and the .NET Framework very early in the beta process. He has been working for many years in distributed solutions based on Windows DNA, COM/COM+ and Visual Basic, and is now dedicated full time to the new platform. He runs his own company, DEVerest, in Buenos Aires, specializing in .NET technologies. He's also a fairly regular contributor to Wrox publications and sites. He's a big fan of computers, the W3C, and everything related to XML and the Internet (for work, learning, and fun).

When he's not coding furiously, he's dreaming up innovative techniques for rediscovering the wheel and some day will eventually come up with a fairly original idea. The open source movement caught his interest too, and he manages a SourceForge project called NMatrix, which also honours the best movie he has seen in his entire life (he's seen it countless times) (Reloaded and Revolutions aren't out yet!). He might seem crazy, but his hobby is... COMPUTERS! From time to time, he tortures his friends playing paddle, bowling, pool, paintball, and even chess with some them!

You can reach Daniel at dcazzulino@users.sf.net, or though his company's web site at http://www.deverest.com.ar.

To my friends, who understood my absence, and were so supportive even if I didn't deserve it. To my wife, who patiently stands by me, understands my work, and forgives me for working late at night from time to time. But most important for both of us are our children, even if we don't have any yet, because everything we do is for them. This book is for you kids, and I hope you know that we loved you long before you were born. – DHC

Victor Garcia Aprea

Victor Garcia Aprea works as a CTO for Obies Technologies (http://www.obies.com), a .NET development and consulting firm. He has been involved with .NET since the very early bits, and was recently recognized by Microsoft as a Most Valuable Professional for ASP.NET technologies. He is currently leading the development of a large ASP.NET application for the biggest entertainment company in Argentina.

When he's not writing code, he likes to be hanging around with friends, fighting with his cat, swimming, and practicing Kung Fu (in that order).

You can contact Victor at vga@obies.com.

To my father, who has been the greatest model to follow in life. I'm working hard to become someday half the man he was. I miss you, ol' man.

Thanks are also due to my editors, Ian and Mankee, for the amazing job they did in turning my gibberish into prose.

And last (but not least!) a huge thanks goes to Catalina, for her endless patience and understanding; to Marta, for always being there; and to Antonio, for sharing his incredible talent. Nothing I do would be possible without their help.
– VGA

James Greenwood

James Greenwood is a technical architect and author based in West Yorkshire, England. He spends his days (and most of his nights) designing and implementing .NET solutions from Government knowledge-management systems to mobile integration platforms, all the while waxing lyrical on the latest Microsoft technologies. His professional interests include research into distributed interfaces, the automation of application development, and human-machine convergence.

When he can be prized away from the keyboard, James can be found out and about, indulging in his other great loves – British sports cars and Egyptology.

You can reach James at jsg@altervisitor.com.

Chris Hart

Chris Hart is currently an editor and part-time in-house author at Wrox Press. She lives in Birmingham (UK, not Alabama), in a house full of computers. After gaining a BEng (Hons) in Mechanical Engineering at university, she moved into network administration and end-user training for a while. A move to Wrox re-awakened her love of programming, and in the three and a half years since joining, Chris has been working for the most part with ASP and ASP.NET and associated technologies.

In her spare time, Chris can be found down at the gym, or playing with code, or looking for obscure cabling at computer fairs. Chris authored chapters in *Beginning ASP.NET 1.0* under her maiden name, Chris Goode. She recently married Java and Visual Basic .NET author James Hart.

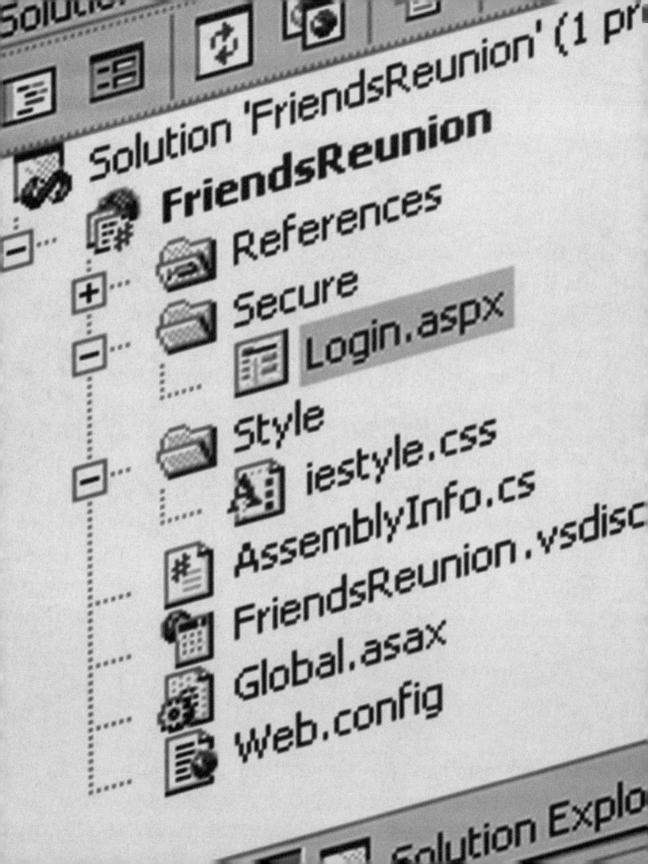

Solution 'FriendsReunion' (1 pr

Solution 'FriendsReunion

FriendsReunion

References

Secure

Login.aspx

Style

iestyle.css

AssemblyInfo.cs

FriendsReunion.vsdisc

Global.asax

Web.config

Solution Explo

Table of Contents

Table of Contents

Table of Contents

Table of Contents

Table of Contents

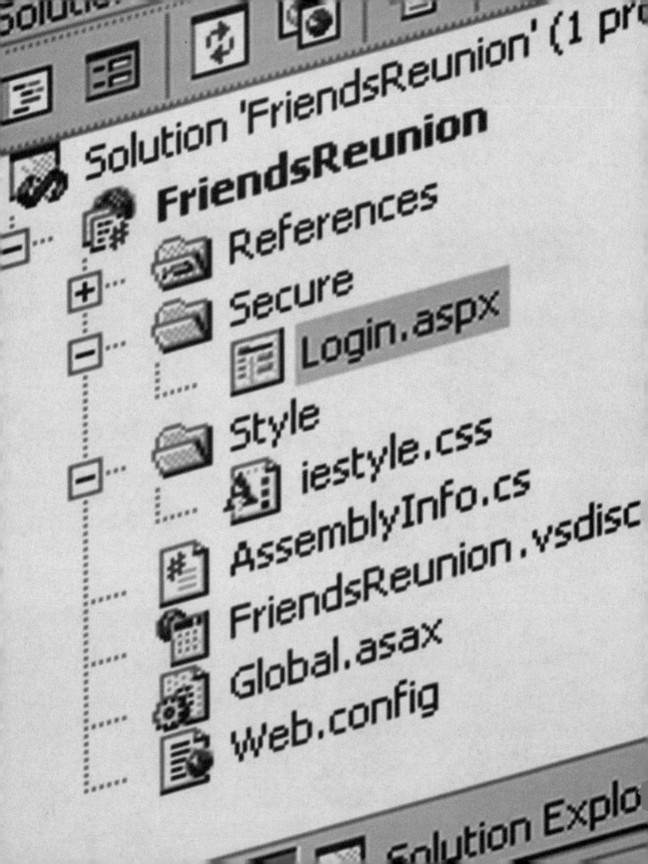

Introduction

The introduction of .NET has blurred the lines between previously distinct programming disciplines, and it has done so to great effect for developers. With so much functionality encapsulated by the .NET Framework class library, some diverse tasks have gained a common programming interface.

One area in which this change is particularly striking is that of **web development**. Before .NET, web application programming "the Microsoft way" was all about ASP. At the time, ASP was new, accessible, and exciting – but it was also script-based and inefficient, and the IDEs were disjointed. Microsoft has channeled the lessons it learned from ASP into its .NET Framework. Now, with ASP.NET (the .NET web development technology), we can create efficient, interactive Internet applications using the same languages that we would use for Windows desktop applications.

In Visual Studio .NET, Microsoft has taken this idea a stage further; not only does the *code* look similar, but the *GUI* looks similar too. Visual C# .NET's familiar form-based interface is used for development of web applications *as well as* for desktop programs. If you want to, you can create a web application without ever seeing a line of HTML code, and you can take advantage of all the facilities for testing and debugging that Visual Studio .NET provides to programmers of all disciplines.

The structure of class libraries in the .NET Framework is such that the methodology we use is the same – regardless of whether we're developing desktop applications or web applications. ASP.NET is really just a series of classes in the .NET Framework, in exactly the same way as the Windows Forms classes. From this perspective, the move from desktop application development to web development shouldn't be too much of a leap.

Yet there *are* some major differences that we need to consider when move to web development. We are no longer talking about applications installed and running on individual machines; instead, we're talking about hosting an application on a central server, ready to be accessed by hundreds or thousands of remote clients every hour. The problem domain is now quite different, and more concerned with performance and scalability issues to ensure that the end user's experience is as smooth as possible.

In this book, we'll set out to understand the issues involved in the web development paradigm, and how they're different from those we're used to in desktop application development. With these principles clear in our minds, we can then consider how to set about building our applications; and beginning at Chapter 3, we'll build a feature-rich, interactive web application called *Friends Reunion* using C#, ASP.NET, and Visual Studio .NET.

The emphasis is on learning by practice. Every single example in the book is described step by step, and we'll outline and explain every single stage in the development, debugging, and deployment of the *Friends Reunion* application. The source code for the application is available online at http://www.wrox.com.

Who Is This Book For?

This book is predominantly targeted at developers who have some experience in the C# language (perhaps through practical application of the language, or simply from a C# tutorial book). These developers may fall into one of two groups:

- ❑ Readers who have little or no web development experience, have gained their C# experience mostly in the context of desktop applications, and are seeking to apply this C# expertise in web development in .NET

- ❑ Readers who have gained some web development experience using ASP, PHP, or other technologies, and are seeking to move into web development using .NET and their favored C# programming language.

This book does not assume that you have programmed for the web environment before; but it does assume that you have some familiarity with the C# programming language. Previous experience of the Visual Studio .NET integrated development environment (IDE) is not essential, but would be helpful. Similarly, we assume no previous experience of HTML, XML, databases, or any of the other technologies mentioned in this book – though a little background knowledge does no harm.

What Does This Book Cover?

The first two chapters of this book are introductory. They'll set out the preliminary material that enables us to begin work on the *Friends Reunion* web application in Chapter 3.

Each of the remaining chapters (from 3 to 13) examines a different aspect of web application development using C# and ASP.NET. In each chapter, we study an aspect both in general terms and within the context of the *Friends Reunion* application. Over the course of these eleven chapters, we will build, test, debug, and deploy a rich interactive web application – and you'll see every single step.

Here's a summary of the chapters in this book:

❏ **Chapter 1** is an introduction to the web environment. It discusses the similarities and differences between web applications and desktop applications, and explains what happens behind the scenes when a user employs a browser to request a web page. The intention is to give a clear insight into the issues that influence the way we design applications for the Web, and to set the scene for the remainder of the book. We also set up the web server here, and create a couple of simple examples to get things started.

❏ In **Chapter 2**, we move on to create some basic ASP.NET **web forms** using Visual Studio .NET. We look at how web forms are processed and the life cycle of a page, and we demonstrate it all by walking through our first ASP.NET application.

❏ **Chapter 3** is all about the **server control**. The server control is the core part of any web form – it's at the heart of the development of dynamic, interactive web sites in .NET. Visual Studio .NET allows us to drag and drop server controls onto our web forms in exactly the same way that we insert Windows Forms controls into a Windows desktop application; and we can add code to our forms to interact with these controls in much the same way, too.

❏ In **Chapters 4 and 5** we turn our attention to **data**. Most interactive web applications rely on the existence and manipulation of data of some form or other, and on storage of that data (either in a full-scale database or some other format). In Chapter 4 we use **ADO.NET** to access and manipulate data. In Chapter 5 we see how **data binding** techniques make it easy to display data on our pages in a user-friendly manner; we also see how to apply templates to our web forms to alter the look and feel of our data-bound controls.

❏ **Chapter 6** is about **applications**, **sessions**, and **state**. By nature, the web is a stateless medium – when you request a web page, the web server delivers it and then forgets about you. If we want our web applications to recognize a user when they make multiple page requests (for example, as they browse an e-commerce application adding items to a shopping basket) then we need to know about the different techniques we can use to retain state across pages, or for a session, or across an application.

❏ **Chapters 7 and 8** focus on **XML** – a topic that has become very important as widespread Internet connectivity becomes the norm. In Chapter 7 we look at the concept of markup and how it is widely relevant to data-driven applications, and we create our own XML language by way of an XML schema. In Chapter 8, we explore how we can use that XML schema to facilitate a data transfer feature – exploiting XML's nature as the perfect vehicle for data transfer across the Internet.

❏ In **Chapter 9** we turn briefly away from web sites, to learn about a different type of web application – the **web service**. Web services enable us to expose our application's functionality to other "client" applications – these applications make requests using standards and protocols over the Internet. This also means that we can use other people's web services in our code as if they were components on our own system – even though they are only accessible across the Internet. We'll examine both how to create our own web services and how to consume existing services.

❏ **Chapter 10** is about ASP.NET **authentication**, **authorization**, and **security**. The role of security in an application is motivated by the need to restrict a user's (or application's) access to certain resources, or their ability to perform certain actions. For example, we may want to include administrative tools in our web application, and to prevent access to these admin pages for all but authorized users. This chapter looks at the tools available to us in ASP.NET for authenticating and authorizing users of our applications.

❑ **Chapter 11** tackles two distinct but related subjects: **debugging** and **exception handling**. Debugging is much easier when we understand the different types of bugs that can occur, and easier still with the array of debugging tools and techniques made available by Visual Studio .NET and the .NET Framework – so we'll study all that in the first half of the chapter. In the second half, we use the .NET exception mechanism to handle some potential input errors that could occur at run time, and prevent the application from crashing in a heap.

❑ In **Chapter 12** we tackle two more different but related subjects: **performance** and **caching**. We set out to understand what we mean by "good performance", and we demonstrate a number of techniques we can use to analyze our application in realistic conditions. We put the application under stress to see what happens, and we identify and fix a number of different bottlenecks. We understand the issues related to caching, and employ a number of different caching techniques to save our application some processing effort and hence optimize use of our server's resources.

❑ Finally, in **Chapter 13**, we see how to prepare our application for **deployment**. Visual Studio .NET provides us with some easy-to-use tools that enable us to build our own deployment wizards. We demonstrate how to prepare the application for deployment – web site, database, and all – by wrapping it all up into an easy-to-use installation wizard.

There are two appendices. Appendix A contains a brief overview of the structure and functionality of the *Friends Reunion* web application. Appendix B contains more information about the setup of the IIS 5.x web server and the MSDE data engine, and it also contains a preview of Microsoft's new web server software, IIS 6.0.

What You Need to Use This Book

The following is the list of recommended system requirements for running the code in this book:

❑ A suitable operating system. Either **Windows 2000 Professional, Server** or **Advanced Server Edition** (at the time of writing, the latest service pack is SP2), or **Windows XP Professional Edition**.

❑ **Internet Information Server** (**IIS**) **5.0 or 5.1**. This is shipped with the operating systems listed above. **IIS 6.0** is not released at the time of writing, but will be suitable alternative web server software.

❑ The **.NET Framework SDK**.

❑ **Visual Studio .NET** (or **Visual C# .NET**) **Standard Edition** or higher.

❑ The **SQL Server Desktop Engine** (also known as **MSDE**), or **Microsoft SQL Server**.

> *MSDE is shipped with the .NET Framework SDK, and also with Visual Studio .NET and Visual C# .NET. To install it, execute the file InstMSDE.exe (which is found in the \Program Files\Microsoft.NET\FrameworkSDK\Samples\Setup\MSDE folder). MSDE does not offer the same admin tools as SQL Server, but there are some useful command-line utilities detailed in the file \Program Files\Microsoft.NET\FrameworkSDK\Samples\Setup\ html\ConfigDetails.htm. Moreover, note that Visual Studio .NET provides a useful UI to any SQL Server or MSDE database.*

Note that Windows XP Home Edition does *not* come with IIS, and cannot run IIS. For ASP.NET web development on Windows XP Home Edition, you may consider the ASP.NET Web Matrix tool, available for free download from http://www.asp.net. This tool offers limited ASP.NET web server functionality, but you won't be able to run web projects in Visual Studio .NET on this version.

This book assumes that you have at least some familiarity with desktop application programming in a Visual C# .NET environment. We'll cover other technologies (such as ASP.NET, ADO.NET, XML, and SQL) in sufficient detail as we progress through the book – although a little prior knowledge never goes amiss.

Style Conventions

We have used certain layout and font styles in this book that are designed to help you to differentiate between the different kinds of information. Here are examples of the styles that are used, with an explanation of what they mean.

As you'd expect, we present code in two different ways: in-line code and displayed code. When we need to mention keywords and other coding specifics within the text (for example, in discussion relating to an `if...else` construct or the `System.Web` namespace) we use the single-width font as shown in this sentence. If we want to show a more substantial block of code, then we display it like this:

```
<asp:TextBox id="txtNameBox" runat="server" />
<asp:Button id="btnSubmit" onclick="btnSubmit_Click"
                        runat="server" Text="Click Here!" />
```

Sometimes, you will see code in a mixture of gray and white backgrounds, like this:

```
private void Page_Load(object sender, System.EventArgs e)
{
   HeaderIconImageUrl = Request.ApplicationPath + "/Images/winbook.gif";
   HeaderMessage = "Informative Page";
}
```

In cases like this, we use the gray shading to draw attention to a particular section of the code – perhaps because it is new code, or it is particularly important to this part of the discussion.

Advice, hints, and background information come in this type of font.

> **Important pieces of information come in boxes like this.**

Bullets appear indented, with each new bullet marked as follows:

❑ **Important Words** are in a bold type font.

❑ Words that appear on the screen, or in menus like File or Window, are in a similar font to the one you would see on a Windows desktop.

❑ Keys that you press on the keyboard like *Ctrl* and *Enter*, are in italics.

5

Customer Support and Feedback

We value feedback from our readers, and we want to know what you think about this book: what you liked, what you didn't like, and what you think we can do better next time. You can send us your comments, either by returning the reply card in the back of the book, or by e-mail to feedback@wrox.com. Please be sure to mention the book's ISBN and title in your message.

How to Download the Source Code for the Book

When you visit the Wrox site, http://www.wrox.com/, simply locate the title through our Search facility or by using one of the title lists. Click on Download in the Code column, or on Download Code on the book's detail page.

When you click to download the code for this book, you are presented with a page that has three options:

❑   If you are already a member of the Wrox Developer Community (if you have already registered on ASPToday, C#Today, or Wroxbase), you can log in with your usual username and password combination to download the code.

❑   If you are not already a member, you have the option of registering for free code downloads. By registering, you will be able to download several free articles from Wrox Press. It will also enable us to keep you informed about updates and new editions of this book.

❑   The third option is to bypass registration completely and simply download the code.

Registration for code download is *not* mandatory for this book. If you *do* register for the code download, your details will not be passed to any third party. For more details, you can review our terms and conditions, which are linked from the download page.

When you reach the code download section, you will find that the files that are available for download from our site have been archived using WinZip. When you have saved the files to a folder on your hard drive, you will need to extract the files using a de-compression program such as WinZip or PKUnzip. When you extract the files, the code is extracted into chapter folders. When you start the extraction process, ensure your software (WinZip, PKUnzip, etc.) is set to use folder names.

Errata

We've made every effort to make sure that there are no errors in the text or in the code. However, no one is perfect and mistakes do occur. If you find an error in one of our books, like a spelling mistake or a faulty piece of code, we would be very grateful for feedback. By sending in errata you may save another reader hours of frustration, and of course, you will be helping us provide even higher quality information. Simply e-mail the information to support@wrox.com, where your information will be checked and, if correct, posted to the errata page for that title, or used in subsequent editions of the book.

To find errata on the web site, go to http://www.wrox.com/, and simply locate the title through our Advanced Search or title list. Click on the Errata link, which is below the cover graphic on the book's detail page.

Technical Support

If you would like to make a direct query about a problem in the book, you need to e-mail support@wrox.com. A typical e-mail should include the following things:

❑ In the Subject field, tell us the **book name**, the **last four digits of the ISBN** (7329 for this book), and the **page number** of the problem.

❑ In the body of the message, tell use your **name**, **contact information**, and the **problem**.

We *won't* send you junk mail. We need these details to save your time and ours. When you send an e-mail message, it will go through the following chain of support:

1. **Customer Support** – Your message is delivered to one of our customer support staff – they're the first people to read it. They have files on most frequently asked questions and will answer anything general about the book or the web site immediately.

2. **The Editorial Team** – Deeper queries are forwarded to the technical editor responsible for the book. They have experience with the programming language or particular product, and are able to answer detailed technical questions on the subject. Once an issue has been resolved, the editor can post the errata to the web site.

3. **The Authors** – Finally, in the unlikely event that the editor cannot answer your problem, they will forward the request to the author. We do try to protect the author from any distractions to their writing; however, we are quite happy to forward specific requests to them. All Wrox authors help with the support on their books. They will mail the customer and the editor with their response, and again all readers should benefit.

> Note that the Wrox support process can only offer support to issues that are directly pertinent to the content of our published title. Support for questions that fall outside the scope of normal book support is provided via the community lists of our http://p2p.wrox.com/ forum.

p2p.wrox.com

For author and peer discussion join, the **P2P mailing lists**. Our unique system provides **programmer to programmer**™ contact on mailing lists, forums, and newsgroups, all *in addition* to our one-to-one e-mail support system. Wrox authors and editors and other industry experts are present on our mailing lists.

At p2p.wrox.com you will find a number of different lists that will help you, not only while you read this book, but also as you develop your own applications. Particularly appropriate to this book are the aspx and aspx_professional lists in the .NET category of the web site.

To subscribe to a mailing list just follow these steps:

1. Go to http://p2p.wrox.com/

2. Choose the appropriate category from the left menu bar

3. Click on the mailing list you wish to join

4. Follow the instructions to subscribe and fill in your e-mail address and password

5. Reply to the confirmation e-mail you receive

6. Use the subscription manager to join more lists and set your e-mail preferences

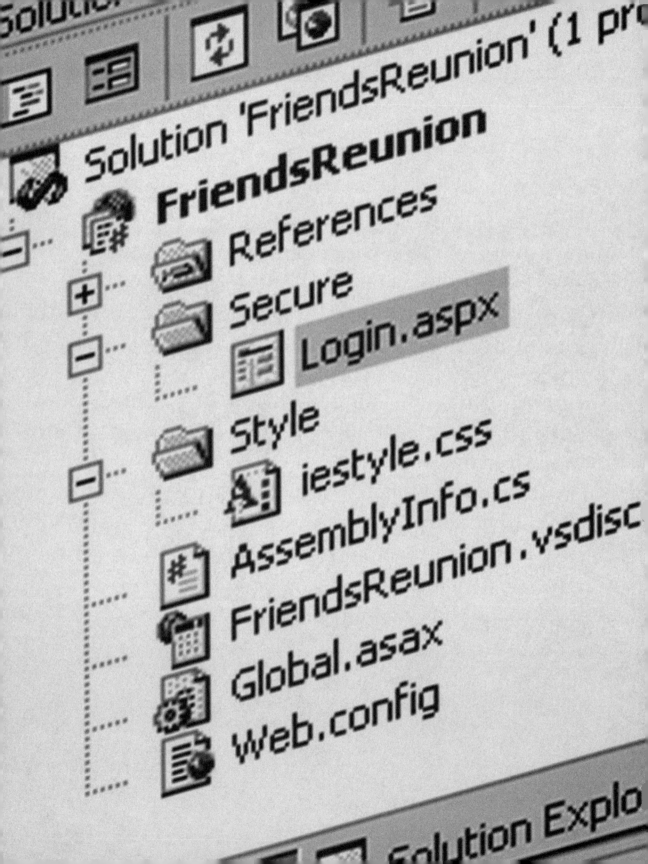

Environment and Architecture

There are any number of differences between Windows desktop applications and web applications, but one difference seems to be fundamental. This difference lies in the relative locations of the *application* itself and its *user interface*:

❑ When we run a Windows desktop application, the user interface appears on the screen of the machine on which the application is running. Messages between the application and its user interface are passed through the operating system of the machine. There's just one machine involved here, and no network.

❑ When we run a web application, the user interface can appear in the browser of *any* machine. Messages between the application and its user interface must also pass across a network, because typically the web application and its user interface are on two *separate* machines.

This single difference in architecture manifests itself in many ways. If you're used to writing desktop applications and you're coming to web applications for the first time, it brings many new issues for you to consider. Arguably the most significant advantage is that the end user doesn't have to be on the same machine that the application's running on – they don't even have to be in the same country! But there are many other technical, practical, and design considerations. For example:

❑ Messaging. Since a running web application must communicate with its user interface across a network, there needs to be a way of passing messages between the two that is 'network-proof'.

❑ Manipulating the user interface. How can a web application tell its browser-based user interface what buttons, text, labels etc. to show, and how to arrange and style them?

❑ Security. If a web application is available across a public network, we need to prevent unwelcome users from accessing the application, or from tapping in on authorized users.

❑ Multiple users. A web application can be executed via a remote machine, so it can (in principle) be executed by two or more users at the same time.

❑ Identification and state. How does a web application identify a user for the first time, and recognize that user when they come back?

If you're migrating from desktop application development to the web, then these are just a few issues that derive from the simple fact that an executing web application is (usually) physically separate from its user interface.

We'll see the answers to some of these questions in this chapter, and we'll see answers to all of them over the course of the book. In this chapter in particular, we're going to focus on the web environment and on the architecture of web applications, inspired by a need to understand the implications of having an application and its user interface on different machines.

In this chapter, we'll look at:

❑   How the web works – from the time the user requests a page to the time they receive the response

❑   What a web application is and how it is composed

❑   The purpose of HTTP, and its role in the request/response interaction between a browser and the web application server

❑   The role of the web server in hosting a web application, and of virtual directories in organizing web applications

❑   The difference between static content and dynamic content

❑   How client-side code and server-side code bring different effects to the world of dynamic content

We'll start by taking a look at how the web works, and how our requests for web pages get processed.

The Web Model

We can take advantage of the web to set up an application that runs in one central location, and can be accessed by users located anywhere in the world – through just a browser and an Internet connection. The earliest web applications weren't really "applications" in the functional sense, but they took advantage of this basic concept to host documents in single a central location and enable users to access these documents from distant places.

With the global explosion of interest in the Internet, developers all over the world are now creating web applications that are much more functionally rich in their design. Web applications no longer exist just as a central resource for shared documents; now, they're still a central resource but we use them interactively to buy groceries, to calculate our taxes, and to send and receive e-mail, while our children use the web as an exciting interactive learning experience!

We're now using web applications to perform all those interactive tasks that were previously only in the domain of the desktop application. We don't need to install the software anymore – we just need to point the browser across the Internet to the application.

Desktop Applications and Web Applications

If you've built a Windows desktop application in a language like C#, then it's not too difficult to sit down and write a C# *web* application that looks and feels quite similar to it. You can design the forms in the user interface (UI) to be similar, and you can have them react to mouse-clicks and button-presses in a similar way, and you can make the back-end processing of the two applications quite similar:

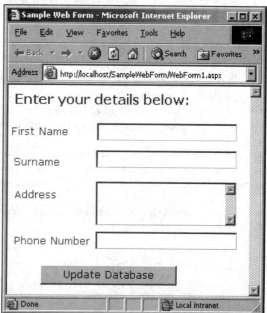

To use the desktop version of this application, you'd need to install it on a machine and then sit at that machine while you use it. Your mouse-clicks and key-presses will be detected by the operating system, and passed to the process in which the desktop application is running. The application interprets these messages, does whatever processing is necessary, and tells the operating system what changes should be made to the UI as a result. All the communication between the application process and the UI is done via the operating system of that machine.

To use the web version of this application, you'd need to use a web browser. You type a URL into the web browser, which tells it where to find the machine on which the application is running. The browser arranges for a message to be sent across a network to this other machine. When the message is received by that machine, it's passed to the application – which interprets the message and decides what the UI (a web page) should look like. Then it sends a description of that web page back across the network to the browser.

There are far more players involved in the use of the web application than the desktop application, but the advantages of this remote-access concept are nothing short of phenomenal. To build an effective web application, it's really worth understanding these interactions between browser and web application in finer detail, because they shape the whole way we write web applications.

Web Servers and Web Clients

We all know that, by entering a URL into the address bar of a browser window, we can surf and navigate to a web site. But what actually happens, behind the scenes, when we hit *Enter* or click a Go button to submit that URL?

To look more deeply into this, it helps if we first make a clear distinction between the different machines and messages involved. So:

❑ We tend to refer to the machine on which a browser is running as a **web client**, while the machine on which the web application is running is called a **web server**.

❑ When a user types a URL into a browser and hits Go, or clicks on a link in a web page, the resulting message sent from the browser to the web server is called a **request**. The message containing the contents of a web page (which is sent by the web server to the browser in reaction to receiving the request) is called a **response**.

In fact, the request and response are the vital components of this communication process. From the point of view of a web application, they're critically important: it's the request that tells the web application what to do, and the response that contains the fruits of its labors.

With those concepts clearly defined, let's examine the process that takes place when a user employs a browser to request a web page:

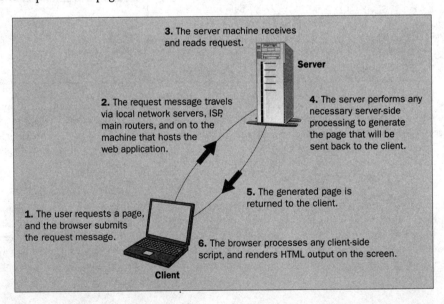

As you can see from the diagram, it's all about exchange of messages – the request message and response message – and we'll expand on this in the following explanation of the diagram.

Step 1: The Client Request

In this stage, the user clicks on a link, or types a URL into a browser, or performs some similar action that initiates a request. The request is a message that must be sent to the web server.

In order to send any request (or response) message, the browser needs to do three things:

❑ First, it needs to **describe** the message in a standard way so that it can be understood by the web server that receives it. For this, it uses **HyperText Transfer Protocol** (**HTTP**). This is the protocol used by the Web to describe both requests and responses. The described request message is called the **HTTP request**, and it has a very particular format that contains information about the request plus the information required to deliver it to the web server.

❑ Second, it needs to **package** the message so that it can be safely transported across the network. For this, it uses the **Transmission Control Protocol** (**TCP**).

❑ Third, it needs to **address** the message, to specify indicate the place to which the message should be delivered. For this, it uses the **Internet Protocol** (**IP**).

> *TCP and IP are often grouped together and referred to as TCP/IP. When you hear someone talking about TCP/IP, they're talking about packaging and addressing Internet messages.*

So, when the browser has described the message, packaged it, and addressed it, then the request is ready to by dispatched across the network towards its intended target – the web server.

Step 2: Routing the Request

Thanks to the HTTP, TCP, and IP protocols, the request message is formatted in a such a way that it can be understood by each of the machines involved in **routing** the request (that is, passing the request from one machine to another as it finds its way from the web client to the web server).

The web server machine will be connected to the Internet (either directly or via a firewall), and will be uniquely identified on the Internet by its **IP address**. An IP address is a set of four numbers, each of which ranges between 0 and 255.

However, the original request probably didn't contain an IP address – more likely, it was made using a URL that began with a named web site address (this is usually something more memorable, like http://www.wrox.com/). The link between an IP address and its named equivalent is mapped using **Domain Name Service** (**DNS**). For example, DNS currently maps the URL http://www.wrox.com/ to the IP address http://204.148.170.145/ – so requests for web pages at the URL http://www.wrox.com/ are directed towards the web server whose IP address is http://204.148.170.145/.

> *The set of four numbers in an IP address enables us to address almost 4.3 billion machines uniquely. IP version 6 is starting to emerge as a new version of the protocol that allows for many more unique addresses by employing eight sets of four hexadecimals (so that each set of four is between 0000 and FFFF). Despite the fact that 4.3 billion sounds like a lot, the invention of portable devices with "always on" Internet connections, such as mobile phones connecting over GPRS, mean that we will eventually run out of today's IP addresses. This is why IPv6 was created.*

One address we'll be seeing a lot of in this book is http://localhost/. This is a special address that resolves to the IP address http://127.0.0.1/. Any computer recognizes this address as referring to itself. It's the IP address for the local machine, known as a **loop-back address**.

Step 3: Receiving and Processing the HTTP Request

The standardized format for web requests is defined by HTTP, so when the HTTP request arrives at its destination, the web server knows exactly how to read it.

In HTTP, there are two principle types of request that a web client can make of a server:

- ❑ The client can ask the server to send it a resource such as a web page, a picture, or an MP3 file. This is called a **GET** request, because it 'gets' information from the server. This is a commonly-used method, for example, when developing a search facility on a web site, where the same request will be made on more than one occasion. It's also how we request simple web pages and images.

- ❑ The client can ask the server to perform some processing in order to generate a response. This is called a **POST** request, because the client posts the information that the server must process, and then awaits a response. This method is more likely to be used, for example, when submitting personal data in an on-line shopping site, or in any other situation where we are sending information to the server.

Step 4: Server Processing

The web server is the place where the application is running. It is responsible for ensuring that any necessary server-side processing takes place in order to complete its task and generate a response.

If the HTML request contains a request for a simple HTML page, then the web server will locate the HTML page, wrap it into an HTTP response, and dispatch it back to the client. By contrast, if the request is for an ASPX page, the web server will pass the request to the ASP.NET processor, which takes care of processing the page and generating the HTML, before the web server wraps that newly-generated HTML into an HTTP response ready to be sent back to the client.

The HTTP response consists of two parts – the header and the body. The header contains information that tells the browser whether the request was successful, or whether there was an error processing the request. For example, if the web server received the request but was unable to locate the requested page, then the header will contain an HTTP 404 (file not found) error code. The response body is where a successfully requested resource (such as a block of HTML) is placed.

Step 5: Routing the Response

The HTML page, generated at the web server, has been described in terms of an HTTP response message, and is packaged and addressed using TCP/IP. The return address is an IP address, which was included in the HTTP request message sent in Step 1.

The HTTP response message is routed back across the network to its target destination – the web client that made the original request.

Step 6: Client-Side Processing and Rendering

When the HTTP response reaches the web client, the browser reads the response, and processes any client-side code. This processed code is now displayed in the browser window.

So now we know what goes on when we request a page, it's time to start using some code. We need to install and configure a web server so that we can host web pages, so let's start with some configuration.

Configuring Your System for Web Development

The best way to appreciate all this in practice is to create some web pages and look at them from the perspective of both end user and web server. We'll begin to do this shortly (and we'll do plenty during the course of the book!); but before we can start, we need to install and configure a web server, which we'll use to host our web applications.

If you are running Windows 2000, Windows XP, or even Windows .NET Server, you will be able to use Microsoft's own web server – **Internet Information Server (IIS)** – to host your applications. Other web servers are available for Windows and for other development platforms (notably Apache, which can be installed on Windows machines, Linux machines, and now even comes pre-installed on Mac OS X machines). For this book, we'll use IIS to host our web applications because in order to properly host ASP.NET applications, we need IIS installed on a compatible operating system.

Different versions of IIS are supplied as part of different versions of the Windows operating system:

Operating System	IIS version supplied
Windows 2000 Professional or higher	IIS 5.0
Windows XP Professional	IIS 5.1
Windows .NET Server	IIS 6.0

IIS 5.0 and IIS 5.1 are very similar (in fact, IIS 5.1 is just a minor update of IIS 5.0). IIS 6.0 is a more substantial revamp of the IIS architecture; at time of writing, IIS 6.0 is still a release candidate as part of Windows .NET Server, due to launch early 2003.

Having said that, the front-end interface for all of these versions is very similar; therefore, the configuration process we describe in this chapter works equally well on all of these IIS versions. For the remainder of the book, we'll limit our discussions mainly to the features available to IIS 5.x developers. We've included an overview of IIS 6.0 in Appendix B.

Setting up Your Web Server

The IIS installation process itself is a fairly painless operation. If you haven't installed any of the necessary software yet, then we recommend that you install IIS *before* either the .NET Framework or Visual Studio .NET, because the installation of the latter configures the former so that it is able to deal with the ASP.NET files that are central to web applications in .NET.

Try It Out – Installing and Configuring IIS for .NET Web Applications

If you *have* already installed the .NET Framework and/or VS.NET, you could proceed by uninstalling VS.NET, then the .NET Framework (via the Add/Remove Programs group in your Control Panel); then install IIS (as described is Step 1 below); and finally reinstall VS.NET. But this is an aggressive (and time-consuming) process, so we recommend that you try the built-in fix tool described in Step 2, and only use the uninstall/reinstall method as a last resort.

1. To install IIS, open up your system Control Panel, and head to Add/Remove Programs. In the dialog that appears, select Add/Remove Windows Components. In the list of components that appears, select Internet Information Services (IIS):

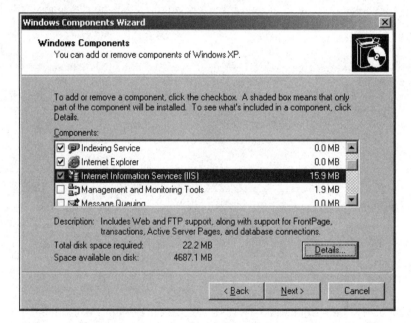

Accept all the default settings, and the installation process will commence.

2. If you have not yet installed the .NET Framework, or VS.NET, then you can go ahead and install them now.

   If, by contrast, you had installed the .NET Framework and VS.NET *before* you installed IIS, you need to perform one of the following in order to 'repair' the .NET Framework:

   ❑ If you own the Visual Studio .NET DVD, insert the DVD, then select Start | Run. In the dialog that appears, type the following command (on one line):

```
<Drive>:\wcu\dotNetFramework\dotnetfx.exe
                /t:c:\temp
                /c:"msiexec.exe
                /fvecms c:\temp\netfx.msi"
```

❑   If you own the Visual Studio .NET CDs, insert the Visual Studio .NET Windows Component Update CD, and again select Start | Run. In the dialog, type the following command (on one line):

```
<Drive>:\dotNetFramework\dotnetfx.exe
                /t:c:\temp
                /c:"msiexec.exe
                /fvecms c:\temp\netfx.msi"
```

IIS Administration

Once it has completed, you can check that your installation was successful by viewing the **Internet Services Manager** (**ISM**). The ISM is the key administration tool that you will use to configure your IIS web server software.

To run the console, select Start | Run, type inetmgr into the box, and click the OK button. Alternatively you can use the Internet Services Manager shortcut in the Administrative Tools group in your control panel (if you are running Windows XP, this link is named Internet Information Services). You should see something like this:

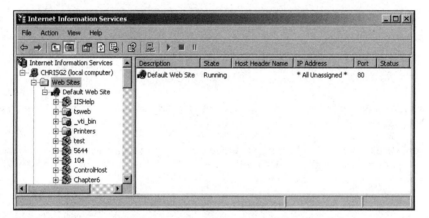

Creating Virtual Directories

In the folder list you will notice that several of the folders are marked with a strange icon. This icon indicates that the folder is a **virtual directory**, which is also configured to be a root location for a web application. IIS maps each **virtual directory** to a **physical directory** on the web server machine:

❑   The virtual directory structure is the structure that the end user sees when they browse the pages of the web site though a browser.

❑   The physical directory structure is the *actual* folder structure that is used on the web server's hard disk for organizing and storing the pages and resources of the web application.

Thus, the web developer can use this mapping of virtual directories to physical ones to place the web application's source files in the most convenient place on their server, and to hide their server's physical organization from end users (each virtual directory is just the 'alias' of a physical directory). Let's see how this works, and examine the process in more detail in an example.

Try It Out – Creating a Virtual Directory

In this example, we'll use the **Internet Services Manager** to create a virtual directory that points to a physical folder on our system. We'll write a simple HTML page and place it inside the physical directory, so that it will be possible to use a browser to browse to that page via HTTP, using the virtual directory "structure" we created.

1. Use Windows Explorer to create a directory called `BegCSharpWeb` anywhere on your drive, and then create a sub-directory called `Chapter1Examples` within it – so that you finish up with a physical directory structure like `C:\BegCSharpWeb\Chapter1Examples`.

2. Fire up a text or code editor such as Notepad. (We'll be using VS.NET in every other example in the book, but for this example it's really not necessary.) Enter the following simple HTML code into a new file:

```html
<html>
  <head>
    <title>Beginning C# Web Applications - Simple Test HTML Page</title>
  </head>
  <body>
    <h2>A Simple HTML Page</h2>
    <p>Hello world!</p>
  </body>
</html>
```

3. Save this file as `HelloWorld.htm` in the `\BegCSharpWeb\Chapter1Examples` directory that you just created.

4. Now we'll create a virtual directory. Open up the IIS management console (select **Start | Run** and type `inetmgr`). Right-click on the **Default Web Site** node, and select **New | Virtual Directory** from the context menu:

At this point, an introductory dialog will appear. Just click Next to continue.

5. In the first dialog of the Wizard proper, you'll be prompted for the name that you want to give to your virtual directory. This is the name that an end user will see in the Address box of a browser when they request the page. Let's call our directory Wrox7329Ch01 (the numbers 7329 are the last four digits of the ISBN of this book), and click Next:

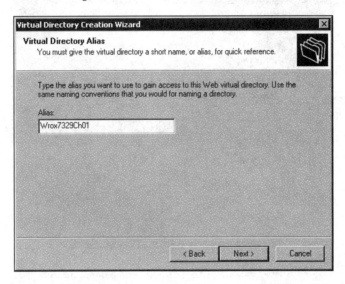

6. In the next dialog, browse to the Chapter1Examples physical directory (or just enter the directory path into the textbox), and then click Next again:

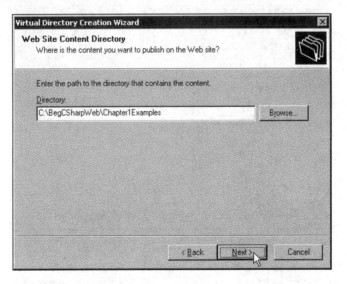

7. The penultimate dialog presents a number of options relating to the permissions enabled on resources contained within this virtual directory. By default, users will be able to read files and run script-based programs. For now, we're going to leave the default settings, so click on **Next** to continue:

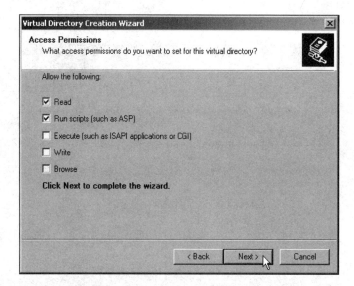

8. The last dialog confirms that the virtual directory has been created successfully. Click **Finish** to close the Wizard. Our new virtual directory then appears in the directory list in the IIS console window:

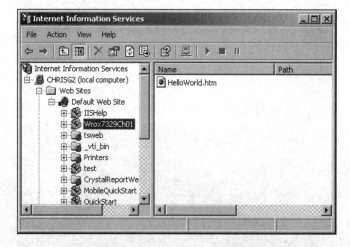

It's also possible to create a virtual directory using Windows Explorer. To do that, you would right-click on the physical directory in question (C:\BegCSharpWeb\Chapter1Examples in our case), and select Properties from the context menu; then select the Web Sharing tab and select the Share this folder radio button. Finally, type the virtual directory (alias) name into the Alias textbox:

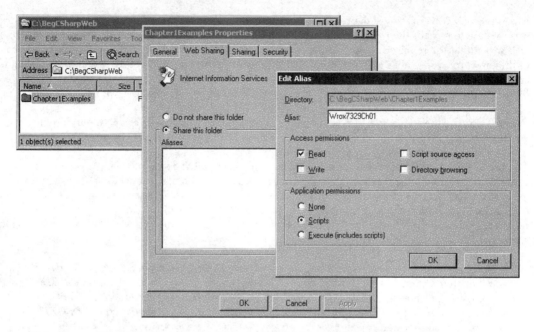

It's also possible to create virtual directories using Visual Studio .NET, as we'll see later.

9. Whichever method you've used to generate the virtual directory, the result will be the same. You can now run the example by opening up your web browser and entering http://localhost/Wrox7329Ch01/HelloWorld.htm into your address bar. You should see the following:

How It Works

At the end of the example, we play the part of the end user, by typing a URL into the Address box of the browser and sending the request. The direction of the request is determined very quickly by examination of the first part of the URL – http://localhost/. The machine name localhost very quickly resolves to the loop-back IP address, http://127.0.0.1/ – so the request is sent to the web server software (the IIS installation) that exists and is running on the local machine.

When the web server receives the request, it reads and processes it. To establish exactly what resource was requested, it reads the remaining part of the URL – /Wrox7329Ch01/HelloWorld.htm. This tells the web server that the required resource is the HTML page, HelloWorld.htm, and that it should be located in the directory whose alias is /Wrox7329Ch01. The web server knows that this virtual directory alias corresponds to the physical directory, C:\BegCSharpWeb\Chapter1Examples, so it is able to fetch the .htm file from that location. All this processing is invisible to the end user who requested the page.

When it's ready, the web server sends the required output back to the requestor. In our case, the request was for a simple HTML page, and the HTML is sent back to our browser.

The browser 'understands' HTML, and knows what to do with it. The simple HTML page in this example is designed to display a simple page on the browser. HTML is a **markup language**, constructed using plain text, and we didn't need any fancy tools to create it. The browser interprets the HTML that it received, and renders the page on-screen (by putting the contents of the <title> element into the title-bar, rendering the contents of the <h2> element as a level-2 heading, and so on). We'll discuss the subject of markup languages in more detail in Chapter 7.

Finally, you've probably noticed that if you double-click on an .htm file in Windows Explorer, then (by default) it appears in a web browser. It looks the same as requesting it in HTTP, but it's not. The file is opened in a browser because, by default, the operating system is configured to open .htm files in a browser. As you can see in the Address box of the screenshot, this page is not the result of an HTTP request, so it was generated locally by the operating system, not by the web server:

It's the web server, not the operating system, that is responsible for arranging that any necessary server-side code is executed, and it's HTTP that allows the requests to be carried between web client and web server machines in a network. For a web application to work, requests must be made using http:\\ URLs and virtual directories, not through physical directories.

If you want, you can add more HTML pages and other web resources to the physical directory C:\BegCSharpWeb\Chapter1Examples, and they'll be accessible via a browser in the same way, by browsing to the virtual directory http:\\localhost\Wrox7329Ch01\....

Configuring Virtual Directories

When we were setting up the virtual directory in the example above, we chose to accept the default access settings. Of course, it's possible to influence the amount of access users have to our applications by adjusting these settings after the virtual directory has been created. You can alter the settings for your virtual directory by right-clicking on the virtual directory in the ISM, and selecting **Properties**:

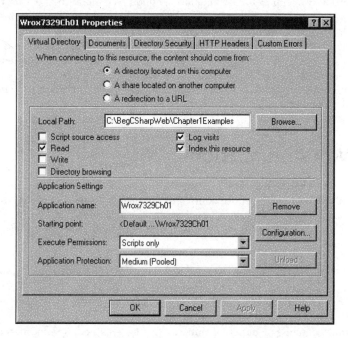

In the dialog, you can see a collection of six checkboxes – these relate to basic permissions. We can alter these as required, but note that we always need to have the **Read** checkbox enabled if anyone is to view any of the pages in our directory! Out of the other available options, you will find the following two to be the most useful:

❑ **Write**: this needs to be set if the user is to be allowed to update files within the virtual directory.

❑ **Directory browsing**: this is a useful permission to enable when you're developing a web application by hand, because it allows you to examine the contents of the virtual directory through a web browser by browsing to that virtual directory. (You can try this out. Select the checkbox, hit OK, then browse to http:\\localhost\Wrox7329Ch01 on our web server – you'll see a **Windows Explorer**-like display of the contents of the corresponding physical directory.) It's recommended that you disable this permission for production web applications, though, because it exposes potentially sensitive information about your file listing to anyone who cares to try it out.

There are more security settings we can apply to our virtual directories to further control access to pages, which are discussed in a bit more detail in Appendix B; and we'll also discuss security controls set at the ASP.NET level in Chapter 10.

If we choose to do so, we can create multiple virtual directories on our web server, with each one pointing to a different physical location. We can even create multiple aliases for the same physical directory, each with different permissions and settings.

Virtual Directories and Web Applications

Also in this dialog box is a section for **Application Settings**. We mentioned earlier that the icon in the ISM represents a virtual directory that is configured to be the root location for a **web application**.

This is a concept that is very important to .NET web application programming with ASP.NET. In particular, ASP.NET requires a web application's configuration files and components to be stored in a specific location relative to the web application root. We don't need to worry too much about configuring directories as applications in this book, because Visual Studio .NET will handle it all for us at the time it creates the web application.

Dynamic Web Applications

One of the things about the `HelloWorld.htm` HTML page is that, no matter how many times you look at it, it's always the same. The entire content of the page is contained in that one file. In fact, the contents of that page don't need to be generated at all. The web server throws the HTML out of the `.htm` file straight into the HTTP response and back to the browser, and the browser renders the HTML straight onto the screen.

Content like this is called **static content**. Static content doesn't need to be generated at the time it is requested, because it has already been generated *before* the request was made. (That's why it's the same each time.)

It's fine to store your content as a bunch of static `.htm` files – indeed, if your content is static then it's unlikely to be a great burden to your web server when someone requests it. But static content alone doesn't make for an interactive web experience. If you want your web users to be able to read data stored in a database, or write to a database, or if you want you web application to react to the user's actions, or make calculations at the time the request is made, then your web pages need to be backed up with the processing code that can perform those actions – and you need that processing code to be executed on request. The result is a more interactive web application involving a certain amount of **dynamic content**.

Pros and Cons of Dynamic Content

So, the main difference between static content and dynamic content is simple: static content is pre-generated *before* the request is made, dynamic content is generated *after* the request is made. We gain two clear advantages by generating the content after the request is made:

❑ First, the web application can tailor the content it generates according to values submitted as part of the request. For example, if you're using an e-commerce web site and you submit your username and password, then the next page you'd expect to see is a dynamically generated page containing information about your personal account.

❑ Second, the web application can tailor the content it generates according to the most recent information available. For example, there are plenty of sites around that include a little display of the number of users currently using the site. That display is generated using 'up-to-the-minute' information taken at exactly the moment the request is received by the web server.

The main disadvantage of dynamic content is that it takes processor power to generate it. If you have a web server that serves web pages to many consecutive users, then your web server must be able to support the server-side processing for all those users. If you have content that rarely changes, then it's better to store it statically and save your server's resources. We'll talk about performance issues in much more detail in Chapter 12, but suffice to say that static content *does* have its place in web application development.

Client-side Processing and Server-side Processing

There are two ways in which we can create a dynamic, interactive feel to our web applications – through server-side processing and client-side processing. This book is largely about the former, and the two certainly play very different roles within the request-response process.

Client-side Code

We can design our web pages to include client-side code that is passed to the browser, along with HTML, as part of the HTTP response. This code executes on the browser, after the response is finished (Step 6 of the diagram we saw earlier in the chapter), and is an effective way to give pages a more lively and interactive feel.

Client-side code can take the form of JavaScript, Java Applets, and even Flash applications. As we said, it's the browser that processes this code – it is often code that is intended to give an instant reaction to button-clicks and keyboard presses within the browser. Most modern rich browser clients support JavaScript scripting; to view something like a Flash movie, the browser is likely to need the appropriate plug-in. These days, most modern browsers come with Flash pre-installed, but this doesn't mean that *all* browsers come with Flash pre-installed.

Placing large amounts of client-side code in a page does come at a cost. It increases the size of the page, and that makes it slower to load. Moreover, not all browsers can handle client-side code (some users disable client-side scripting to eliminate annoying features like pop-up adverts; others use stripped down browsers to speed up browsing times), and every different type of browser handles client-side code differently.

Server-side Code

The server-side processing takes place much earlier in the request-response process (Step 4 of the figure). It's here that the web application can react to data passed up as part of the HTTP request, query databases, and perform other processing as necessary, and generate the page content (HTML plus client-side code) to be sent back to the browser.

The server-side code is the place where our application can react to user input and respond with customized results. For example, if you search the Amazon web site for the latest CD by your favorite artist, Amazon's web server executes server-side code to search its datastores for the relevant item. It sorts any items that match the search according to whatever sort criterion you may have specified (perhaps by album name, or artist name, or release date), and uses this information to generate HTML that is returned to your browser for display.

As well as generating HTML, we can also use server-side code to generate client-side code to be sent back to the browser for execution there. This is the sort of feature that ASP.NET has built-in to some of its server controls (a subject that we'll cover in depth in Chapter 3).

Although server-side code is powerful, it isn't the perfect solution to every requirement. There are plenty of features that are better coded using client-side code, and often we can reduce the overall load on the web server with a little judicious application of some client-side code. (For example we can use client-side techniques to validate a registration form before it's submitted to a server; and we should certainly never use server-side code to handle mouse rollover events!)

Ultimately, a good, interactive, efficient web application is the right blend of dynamic server-side code, client-side code, and static content.

It's time for an example. The simple HTML example that we used earlier didn't use any dynamic elements at all, so let's look at an example that contains some server-side and client-side functionality in an ASP.NET web page.

Try It Out – Creating a Dynamic Page

We'll use Visual Studio .NET to create our first dynamic example, using both server-side code and client-side code. In the next chapter, we'll look at the Visual Studio .NET environment and creating ASP.NET applications in more detail. In this example, we'll concentrate on a simple example, constructed with a minimum of fuss.

1. Open up Visual Studio .NET and create a new Visual C# project – an ASP.NET Web Application using the address http://localhost/ClockExample, as shown below:

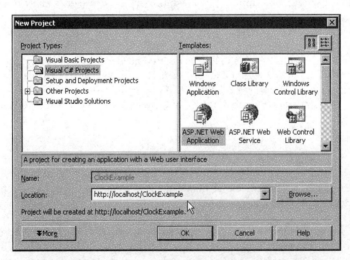

2. Once the blank application has been created (this may take a while) you will be presented with a design-time view of a web form. Click on the HTML button at the bottom of the form to take us to the HTML view of our page:

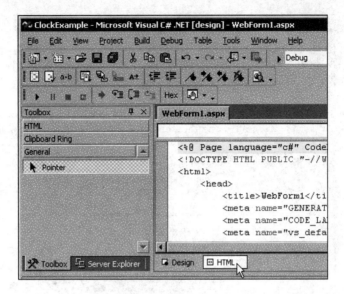

3. In the main window with our HTML source code, adjust the code as shown in the following highlighted lines:

```
<%@ Page language="c#" Codebehind="WebForm1.aspx.cs"
         AutoEventWireup="false" Inherits="ClockExample.WebForm1" %>
<!DOCTYPE HTML PUBLIC "-//W3C//DTD HTML 4.0 Transitional//EN" >
<html>
   <head>
     <title>What's the time?</title>
     <meta name="GENERATOR" content="Microsoft Visual Studio 7.0">
     <meta name="CODE_LANGUAGE" content="C#">
     <meta name="vs_defaultClientScript" content="JavaScript">
     <meta name="vs_targetSchema"
content="http://schemas.microsoft.com/intellisense/ie5">
   </head>
   <body>
     <form id="Form1" method="post" runat="server">
       <p>The time (according to the web server) is:
          <%= System.DateTime.Now %>
       </p>
       <p>What's the time on the web client?
         <input onclick="alert('Web client time is now ' + new Date());"
                type="button" value="Client Time"/>
       </p>
     </form>
   </body>
</html>
```

4. Run the application by pressing *F5*, or clicking the Start button on the toolbar:

When the application runs, you should see the time at which the page was loaded on your web server. Wait a few seconds, and then click the button, and a window should pop up:

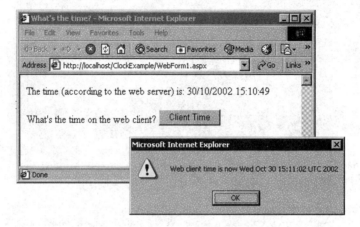

How It Works

The server-side processing and client-side processing occur at different stages in the overall request-response process, as described in the six-stage diagram earlier in the chapter. The screenshot above shows what happened when I ran this example.

When I made the request, the browser packaged it up into an HTTP request and sent it off towards the web server. When the web server received the request, it examined the URL to find out what resource was requested. In this case, it's the web page called WebForm1.aspx, located in the physical directory whose alias is ClockExample.

Now, this time we didn't create the ClockExample virtual directory ourselves. Instead, VS.NET did it for us when we first created the ClockExample web application. By default, VS.NET creates a virtual directory for each new ASP.NET web application, and it creates a corresponding physical directory as a subfolder of C:\Inetpub\wwwroot\ (assuming that C: is the local hard drive on the web server).

So, the web server reads the virtual resource location /ClockExample/WebForm1.aspx, and searches its hard drive for the resource at C:\Inetpub\wwwroot\ClockExample\WebForm1.aspx.

The resource it finds there is an .aspx file, containing the code we saw in Step 3. This code is a mixture of HTML, server-side code, and client-side code. More importantly, the web server uses the suffix of the file to decide how it should process the file. Notice that it's not an .htm, like the static page in the previous example. Rather, it's an .aspx file. If we've installed IIS and the .NET Framework correctly on our web server machine, then the IIS web server software will know that it needs to send .aspx files to the ASP.NET processor for server-side processing.

The ASP.NET processor examines the content of the .aspx file, looking for server-side code to process. In fact, it finds only two fragments of server-side code here. The first is a Page directive:

```
<%@ Page language="c#" Codebehind="WebForm1.aspx.cs"
        AutoEventWireup="false" Inherits="ClockExample.WebForm1" %>
```

This directive describes how ASP.NET should interpret and process the server-side code in the file. We'll touch on attributes of the Page directive throughout the book; for now, you just need to know that the ASP.NET engine uses this information to process the page, and does not send it to the browser.

More interesting to us right now is the second fragment of server-side code:

```
<p>The time (according to the web server) is:
    <%= System.DateTime.Now %>
</p>
```

The server-side fragment is the section flanked by <% and %> tags, and surrounded here by a couple of lines of HTML. The ASP.NET engine recognizes this as a fragment of server-side code, and processes it. In fact, it evaluates the Now property of the System.DateTime object, which returns a string containing the current date and time. When my web server processed this line in reaction to my page request, the time (according to the web server) was 15:10 and 49 seconds – so the ASP.NET processor generated the following HTML here:

```
<p>The time (according to the web server) is: 30/10/2002 15:10:49</p>
```

There isn't any more server-side code in this .aspx file; so with this action, the ASP.NET processor has done it's job. The resulting HTML and client-side code is sent to the browser and rendered on the screen. To see what the web server sends to the browser, we can just use View | Source (or a similar option) on the browser:

Most of this is HTML, and there's one little bit of client-side script. In the HTML, we have a <head> element that contains the title of the page, and a few elements of metadata (information about how the page was created, and so on). We also have a <body> element that contains the stuff we see on the page. It consists of a <form> containing:

❑ A hidden <input> element. (This is named _ _VIEWSTATE, and contains encoded information that is generated by ASP.NET and used when working with forms. It's related to the concept of maintaining **state** in applications, which is a subject we'll introduce in the next section and revisit as we progress through the book.)

❑ A <p> paragraph element containing the time info created by the server.

❑ Another <p> paragraph element, which itself contains more text and an <input> element of type button.

It's the button that arouses our interest now. Let's look at that <input> tag more closely:

```
<input onclick="alert('Web client time is now ' + new Date());"
       type="button" value="Client Time"/>
```

When the user clicks this button, the onclick event is fired, and the alert() method runs on the browser, producing a message box. This is client-side processing, and the time and date reported are the time and date as calculated by the browser, not the web server:

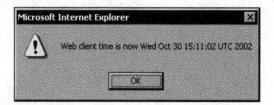

Maintaining State

When we request a resource from a server, using GET or POST, the server responds to our request and returns the appropriate data. After the HTTP response has been sent back to the client, the server then forgets all about the client. HTTP is known as a **stateless** protocol. This means that state (that is, information relating to the connection and who's at the other end of it) is not retained from one request to the next.

If we were to accept this limitation as unavoidable, it would certainly restrict the usefulness of web applications. Being able to 'remember' a user is necessary in all kinds of situations. For example:

❑ Imagine using a site that requires you to log in, and being forced to log in for every single page! It would be much easier if you could log in once and have the web server recognize you when you make subsequent requests.

❑ Consider the problems of an e-commerce site with shopping baskets, in which the web application must remember what each user has ordered as they make their make their way through the pages of the site.

To counter this problem, there are two important techniques available to us:

❑ We can instruct our application to store state on the server in an object of some type – we could store selected information about the client in a temporary location that exists for as long as the user is browsing the site. The server can then remove this temporary data when the user navigates out of scope of the application, or closes their browser.

❏   We can store selected information about the client on the client's machine, and there are two
    methods of doing this too:

    ❏   We can place the data in a small file called a **cookie**. We can use cookies to store small
    amounts of data, such as general preferences or login details, and each time a user
    navigates to our site, those nuggets of data can be passed up as part of the request and
    used by the web application to achieve an "automatic login" or to personalize the interface

    ❏   We can place data in a hidden <input> field within the HTML for the page – this is
    known as **viewstate**, and we saw it briefly in the example above. We'll learn more about
    viewstate, and how we can use it, in Chapters 2 and 6, and we'll learn about how it affects
    performance in Chapter 12.

State management is a fundamental aspect of dynamic web applications. We'll have more to say on the
subject of statelessness, and strategies for dealing with it, in Chapter 6.

Web Application Architecture

A web application is more than just a collection of web pages. For example, a web application can
contain configuration files, stylesheet files (that control the visual appearance of the site), and files that
link to a database server to retrieve information. Let's take a look how a basic web application fits together:

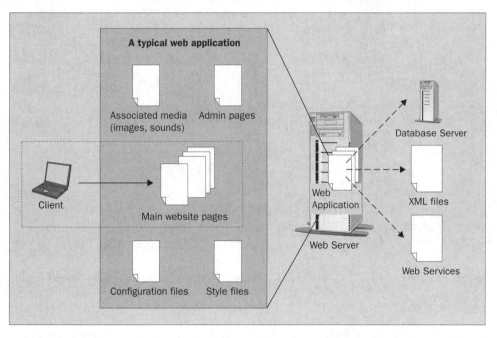

The web client (that is, the machine employed by the end user browsing to the web application) can
only see the main web site pages. This main site can itself link to images, music files, or pictures that are
displayed on the main pages. The site can use separate style files to customize the appearance of the
site. The site's configuration can be controlled by individual configuration files, and we can administer
our site by using custom administration pages if we want.

33

The application can draw on information stored in databases, XML files, and even web services. Within a web application scenario, there are plenty of client-server relationships.

ASP.NET Web Applications

As we will see in later chapters, ASP.NET web applications follow this model very well. Compared to older technologies like ASP 3.0, ASP.NET web applications can separate out each part of the application into a separate file. The architecture of ASP.NET lends itself to **encapsulation** and **reuse**, which means that it's much easier to modularize our applications and avoid reams of repeated code.

When we create an ASP.NET application, we split up our application into the following pieces:

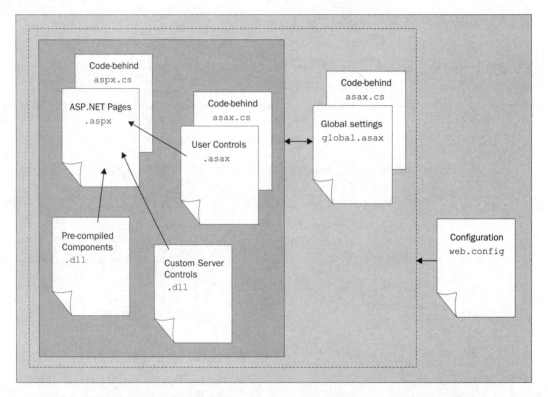

At the core of an application is the ASP.NET page, which has an associated **code-behind** page. This page can use functionality and presentation elements from user controls, pre-compiled components, and custom server controls:

❏ User controls contain presentation code that is intended to be reused across many pages, and can even be cached to improve loading times. An example would be to create a header control that contained links to other parts of our site. We'll see an example in Chapter 3.

❏ Components contain application code that can be reused as required by compiling it into classes that can be used in our ASP.NET pages.

❑ Custom server controls are similar to pre-compiled components, with the exception that they are designed for providing reusable visual elements that can be placed on our ASP.NET pages. There is a rapidly-growing market for professional compiled custom server controls for user interface elements such as toolbars, menus, and so on, which can be downloaded, installed, and then deployed in your own applications.

We also have a **global settings file**, `global.asax`, which can provide application-level support, such as session management, application-level events, storage of information that we can use throughout the application or for the duration of a session, and so on. Finally, the web application's files are governed by a **configuration file**, `Web.config`, which controls exactly how our application operates; for example, the security settings in place on our application, and settings such as how long each session should last.

In Chapter 2, we'll start to learn more about the core ASP.NET components, and how an ASP.NET application is constructed. We can gain a lot of insight into the construction of ASP.NET web applications just by using the Visual Studio .NET environment, which can create basic template files for us that are ready for us to extend and customize as appropriate.

Summary

Windows desktop applications and web applications can be made to behave in similar ways, but under the covers they are fundamentally very different. A desktop application must be installed and executed on the user's machine. By contrast, a web application runs on a machine that could be anywhere else in the world, and the user interacts with it remotely through a web browser.

The physical separation of a web client machine and a web application machine means that we need a network-proof set of protocols to allow them to communicate. Each interaction takes the form of a request message and a response message. The web uses HTTP to describe a message, TCP to package it, and IP to address it. At the client end, the user interacts with the web application through a browser or similar piece of software; at the server end, the web application is hosted by web server software (such as IIS).

There are two types of web content. Static content is generated *before* the user requested it, while dynamic content it is not generated until *after* the request arrives at the server. Web content can be made to be more interactive by means of dynamic techniques, specifically server-side processing and client-side processing. Most web applications consist of some combination of static content, server-side code, and client-side code.

Typically, a web application is made up of many client-server relationships. For example, a user triggers a browser to request a page from the web server. For the web server to respond, it may in turn have to make requests of server-side components, databases, file systems, and other services.

.NET's answer to the problems of web application programming is **ASP.NET**. We've seen a little of how ASP.NET makes it easy for us to design applications in a modular way, to get good organization of our application, and to encourage encapsulation and reuse. In Chapter 2, we'll examine the task of creating ASP.NET web applications in more detail, and we'll explore the Visual Studio .NET web development environment and the ASP.NET architecture. Then, in Chapter 3, we'll be ready to start work on the *Friends Reunion* web application!

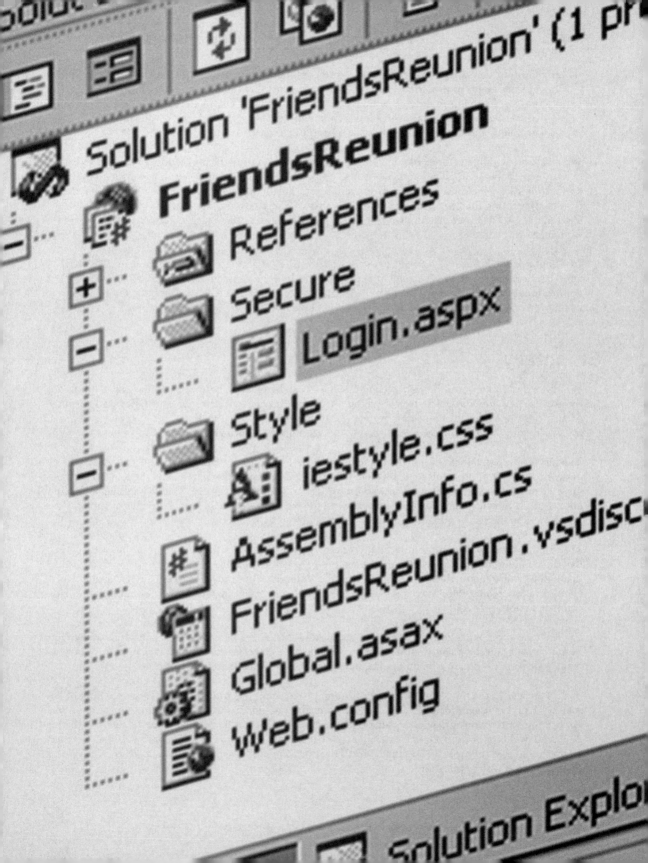

Solution 'FriendsReunion' (1 pr

FriendsReunion
- References
- Secure
  - Login.aspx
- Style
  - iestyle.css
- AssemblyInfo.cs
- FriendsReunion.vsdisc
- Global.asax
- Web.config

Solution Explo

Web Development in .NET

In this chapter, we're going to build on our understanding of the architecture of the Web by looking specifically at how *ASP.NET* web applications work, and how we can create them. We'll start looking at the structure of a page and the elements of a page, and we'll put together some very simple pages that demonstrate some basic techniques. All this will help to get you ready to start building the *Friends Reunion* application in Chapter 3.

Along the way, we're also going to be making good use of the Visual Studio .NET integrated development environment (IDE), and we'll start to discover some of the VS.NET tools that will feature a lot in the web application development in this book.

We don't *have* to use VS.NET when developing ASP.NET web applications in C#. Whatever development tools you choose to use for developing web projects, the problems you come across (in areas like security, usability, maintainability, upgradeability, debugging, error-handling, etc.) are likely to be problems that all other web developers encounter too. Different IDEs will help you to tackle these problems in different ways. Microsoft has learned a lot of big lessons from the limitations of its pre-.NET IDEs, and has applied them effectively to VS.NET. The result is a highly usable and integrated IDE, which is why we choose to use it in this book.

In this chapter we'll learn more about:

- ❑ The features available when developing web applications in .NET
- ❑ Building C# web applications using Visual Studio .NET
- ❑ What goes on behind the scenes of an ASP.NET application, and how .NET applies the object-oriented design paradigm to web applications
- ❑ What happens when a user requests an ASP.NET page, and how server-side code results in client-side content

ASP.NET is at the center of web application development in .NET, so let's start by understanding more about that.

An Introduction to ASP.NET

As we saw in Chapter 1, a large-scale web application can be a complicated thing, which takes advantage of many different technologies. If we write our application using the .NET Framework, then the technology at center of it all, pulling everything together, is **ASP.NET**.

So what is ASP.NET? Here's a definition that summarizes the key characteristics:

> **ASP.NET is an event-driven, control-based architecture that generates content and dynamic client-side code from server-side code using functionality described in the `System.Web` classes of the .NET Framework.**

There is plenty to digest in this definition, and some of the terms used here will perhaps be more familiar than others. Let's unravel this statement, so that we can get a better understanding of all the implications of this definition, and of how ASP.NET is important to us:

- ❑ *ASP.NET generates content and dynamic client-side code...* In Chapter 1, we saw that when a web server receives a web page request, it performs any necessary processing to generate the page response before sending that response back to the browser. ASP.NET is the technology at the center of that processing.

- ❑ *ASP.NET generates [responses] from server-side code...* ASP.NET works on the web server. It takes the page request, and executes the necessary server-side code to generate the web page that is sent back to the browser in the response.

- ❑ *ASP.NET is event-driven...* ASP.NET pages fire **events**, and we can write code to react to those events. These events include user-input actions (such as when a user clicks on a button or selects an item from a drop-down list in the page), and events that occur as part of the lifecycle of the page (like the `Page_Load` event, which fires when a page is loaded).

- ❑ *ASP.NET is control-based...* ASP.NET relies heavily on reuse of elements of visual functionality known as **server controls**. In this chapter we'll look at server controls in generic terms, and in Chapter 3 we'll learn about the different *types* of server controls, how they work, and how they're used.

- ❑ *ASP.NET uses functionality described in the `System.Web` classes of the .NET Framework...* ASP.NET achieves all this using a comprehensive set of .NET Framework classes contained within the `System.Web` namespace and the 16 other namespaces that begin `System.Web.*` (these are sometimes called the **ASP.NET classes**). It includes functionality for simple ASP.NET pages, web forms, web services, controls, etc. We'll meet all of these over the course of this book.

ASP.NET Pages and Web Forms

In all this, there are two more terms that we should cover right now:

- ❑ An **ASP.NET page** is a web page that contains server-side elements written using ASP.NET classes. An ASP.NET page has a file extension of `.aspx`.

❑ A **web form** is a type of ASP.NET page that contains an interactive form.

You've probably come across the HTML <form> element, and it's important to note that a web form is *not* the same as an HTML <form> element. Rather, a web form is an ASP.NET page that has a <form> element within it. Since many ASP.NET pages contain forms, the terms *web form* and *ASP.NET page* are often used interchangeably.

Building Web Forms in Visual Studio .NET

If you're familiar with the process of building Windows forms in Visual Studio .NET or in Visual Basic 6.0, then you're probably already comfortable with the way in which these IDEs allow you to:

❑ Use a drag-and-drop technique to add different controls (such as textboxes, labels, drop-down boxes, buttons, etc.) to your forms

❑ Double-click on a control in order to add an event-handler to the control, allowing your application to respond to events.

In Visual Studio .NET, Microsoft has worked hard to create a web development environment that is similar in look and feel to the Windows development environment you're already used to. So, VS.NET makes the same drag-and-drop techniques available for creating web forms, and provides a very similar experience whenever you need to code an event-handler for your web form.

Visual Studio .NET also gives us control over the positioning of our form elements, and a Property browser that allows us to assign features and properties to our controls, and so on. As we've said, VS.NET is not the *only* tool available for coding .NET web applications (for example, you can use the ASP.NET Web Matrix, which is a free tool available from http://www.asp.net; it's even possible to code everything using Notepad). But the VS.NET IDE is familiar in look-and-feel, and offers us lots of help (shortcuts, wizards, code-generation) when developing applications for the Web.

The Structure of a Web Form: Presentation and Processing

In Chapter 1, we saw a very basic example of a web form. It consisted of some HTML code and some in-line C# code; when a user requests this web form, the server runs the simple C# process to work out the current time on the web server, and sends a page to the browser that has the web-server's time (at that instant) displayed on the browser.

Looking back at that code, you'll see that all the presentation code and server-processing code is mixed together in the page:

```
<body MS_POSITIONING="FlowLayout">
  <form id="Form1" method="post" runat="server">
    <p>What's the time on the web server?
       The time is: <%= System.DateTime.Now.ToString() %></p>
    <p>What's the time on the client?
       <input onclick="now = new Date(); alert('The time is ' + now);"
              type="button" value="Client Time"/></p>
  </form>
</body>
```

For a simple page such as this one, that's not too much of a problem. But it's good practice to separate these two different parts of code. The standard method for doing this in ASP.NET is to use two different files:

❑ The first file has an `.aspx` extension, and contains all of the **presentation code**, including the HTML and server controls.

❑ The second file has an identical name, but has an `.aspx.cs` file extension. This file contains all the **functional code**, and is known as a **code-behind** file. It contains only the language-specific (in our case, C#-specific) code in which our classes, methods, and event-handlers are coded.

When we create a web form or ASP.NET page, VS.NET automatically creates both the `.aspx` file and the `.aspx.cs` file for us.

Keeping the presentation and "code behind" separate in this way is a great way to organize code. It makes the code much more maintainable, and even allows a web page designer and a C# developer to work side by side on different elements of the same page.

In addition to these two files, and the automatically-generated code contained within them, VS.NET also creates many other files that relate to configuration and setup of our web application. We'll look at these in more detail as we build up the main example in this chapter. We'll begin that example now.

Try It Out – Controlling the Presentation Elements on a Web Form

The best way to see all this in action is in an example. So here we'll create a new C# ASP.NET web application, and with a single web form. We'll concentrate on the basic presentational elements of the web form for now; we'll work on the style (and other) properties and functionality of this web form later on in the chapter.

1. First, open the Internet Services Manager (from the Administrative Tools dialog in the Control Panel) and use it to ensure that your default web site is Started. (If you see the word Stopped next to the web site name, right-click to start it.)

2. Now open Visual Studio .NET. Create a new C# ASP.NET Web Application – call it `Chapter2Examples` by typing http://localhost/Chapter2Examples into the Location box. Then click OK.

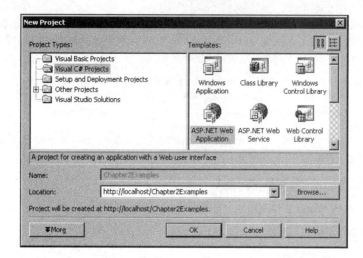

3. Now wait a few seconds while VS.NET creates a new web application. During this time, VS.NET is performing all the necessary file creation and configuration of the new web application on your local machine (since you specified localhost as the machine name). You should now see the following screen:

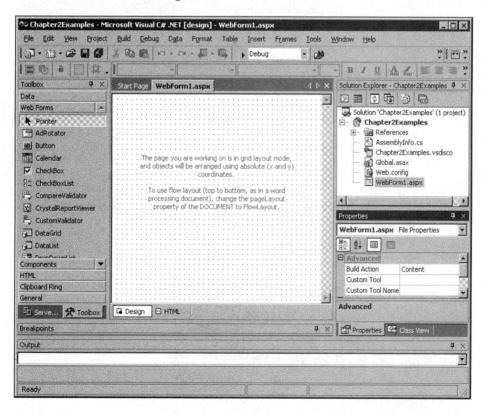

4. Now we can start to build our web form. As it happens, VS.NET has created a web form, `WebForm1.aspx`, already. We'll delete this web form and create one that has a name of our own choosing.

So, go to the Solution Explorer pane (which is shown at the top-right of the screenshot above – if you can't see it, type *Ctrl+Alt+L* to make it appear). Then select WebForm1.aspx, and delete it. VS.NET will warn you that `WebForm1.aspx` will be deleted permanently: just hit OK.

5. Now we can create a web form of our own. Right-click on the Chapter2Examples project in the Solution Explorer, and select Add | Add Web Form from the context menu:

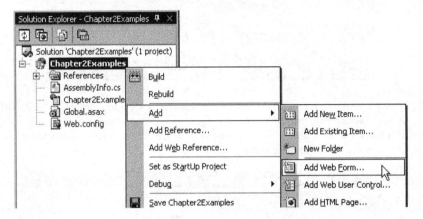

In the Name field of the resulting dialog, type the name of our new ASPX page (we'll call it Ch2WebForm.aspx), and click OK.

6. Now wait a couple more seconds while VS.NET creates the two files for this web form: the design file (`Ch2WebForm.aspx`) and its associated code-behind file (`Ch2WebForm.aspx.cs`). You'll see a new entry for Ch2WebForm.aspx in the Solution Explorer. VS.NET will open this file for you, in Design view, so it's ready for you to start work on it.

7. Click once anywhere within the grid on the page designer. Then go to the Properties pane, find the pageLayout property, and set its value to FlowLayout:

Then return to the **Design** view of the page, and you'll see that the grid marks have disappeared.

8. Now we can start adding visual elements to the page. Place your cursor in the **Design** view of the page, and start typing text so that it looks like this:

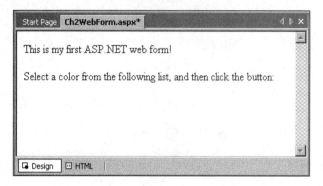

Make sure you press the *Enter* key at the end of each line of text, so that when you've finished, the cursor is below the second line of text.

9. Now look at the toolbox on the left of the IDE (press *Ctrl+Alt+X* if it's not already visible). Select the **Web Forms** tab, and add a **DropDownList** control to the page (either double-click the **DropDownList** item in the toolbar, or drag-and-drop it from the toolbar onto the page).

Next, add a **Button** control to the page in the same way, so that it is positioned just after the **DropDownList**. Then position your cursor at the end of the line, and press *Enter* to create a new line.

Finally, add a **Label** control to the new line, in the same way you added the other two controls. The **Design** view for `Ch2WebForm.aspx` should now look like this:

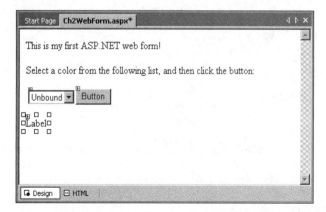

10. Have a look at the presentation code that you've generated by adding these items to the page. To do this, click the **HTML** button at the bottom of this view. We'll discuss this code in more detail in a moment:

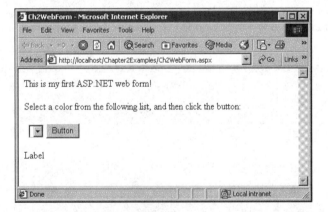

```
Start Page   Ch2WebForm.aspx*                                                    ◁ ▷ ✕
Client Objects & Events              ▾   (No Events)                      ▾  ═|═
   <%@ Page language="c#" Codebehind="Ch2WebForm.aspx.cs" AutoEventWireup="false" Inherits="(
   <!DOCTYPE HTML PUBLIC "-//W3C//DTD HTML 4.0 Transitional//EN" >
   <html>
       <head>
           <title>Ch2WebForm</title>
           <meta name="GENERATOR" content="Microsoft Visual Studio 7.0">
           <meta name="CODE_LANGUAGE" content="C#">
           <meta name="vs_defaultClientScript" content="JavaScript">
           <meta name="vs_targetSchema" content="http://schemas.microsoft.com/intellisense/i(
       </head>
       <body>
           <form id="Ch2WebForm" method="post" runat="server">
               <p>This is my first ASP.NET web form!
               </p>
               <p>Select a color from the following list, and then click the button:</p>
               <p> 
                   <asp:dropdownlist id="DropDownList1" runat="server"></asp:dropdownlist>
                   <asp:button id="Button1" runat="server" text="Button"></asp:button></p>
               <p>
                   <asp:label id="Label1" runat="server">Label</asp:label></p>
           </form>
       </body>
   </html>
◁                                                                                  ▷
 ⌨ Design  ⊟ HTML
```

11. You can run the project at this stage. To do this, first go to Solution Explorer, right-click on
Ch2WebForm.aspx, and select Set As Start Page. Then press *F5*, to build the project and run
it in debug mode. This will start up a new browser window, with the page displayed like this:

```
 Ch2WebForm - Microsoft Internet Explorer                          _ □ ✕
  File   Edit   View   Favorites   Tools   Help
 ⇐ Back  ▾  ⇒  ▾  ⊗  ▣  ⌂  ⊘ Search  ☀ Favorites  ⊕ Media  ⊘  ▤ ▾  ⊜   »
 Address ⌠⊘ http://localhost/Chapter2Examples/Ch2WebForm.aspx    ▾  ⇒ Go  Links »

 This is my first ASP.NET web form!

 Select a color from the following list, and then click the button:

 ▢ ▾  Button

 Label

 ⊘ Done                                         ⬚ Local intranet
```

How It Works

The first thing you'll notice is that the page displayed in the browser doesn't do very much. There are
no entries in the drop-down box and nothing happens when you click the button. We'll add this
functionality at a later stage, but first let's look at what we've done so far.

The first interesting thing we did was change the page's pageLayout property from GridLayout to
FlowLayout. **Grid layout mode** is useful for absolute positioning of elements, but it uses a technique that
is not compatible with all browsers. **Flow layout mode** is a more natural approach to layout; it assumes a
top-down, left-right approach and reduces the clutter in the design view of our pages in the IDE.

In the remaining few steps, we created the content that we see on the page. We have a couple of lines of text, and three controls. By adding this text and these controls to the page, we've generated a number of new tags in the presentation code in Ch2WebForm.aspx – you mat have noticed that in Step 10, when you looked at the HTML view of the Ch2WebForm.aspx file. Let's examine some aspects of that code more closely.

The first line is a page directive:

```
<%@ Page language="c#" Codebehind="Ch2WebForm.aspx.cs"
        AutoEventWireup="false"
        Inherits="Chapter2Examples.Ch2WebForm" %>
```

This contains information that ASP.NET uses when it executes the page to generate output for the browser. In particular, note that it indicates that the code-behind file for our Ch2WebForm.aspx page is the file Ch2WebForm.aspx.cs.

In the remainder of the code in Ch2WebForm.aspx, most of the interesting stuff is happening inside the <body> element:

```
<html>
  ...
  <body>
    <form id="Ch2WebForm" method="post" runat="server">
      <p>This is my first ASP.NET web form!</p>
      <p>
        Select a color from the following list,
        and then click the button:
      </p>
      <p> 
        <asp:dropdownlist id="DropDownList1" runat="server">
        </asp:dropdownlist>
        <asp:button id="Button1" runat="server" text="Button">
        </asp:button>
      </p>
      <p>
        <asp:label id="Label1" runat="server">Label</asp:label>
      </p>
    </form>
  </body>
</html>
```

The code here consists of two types of content:

❑ Simple HTML tags (the <html> and <body> tags – and the <p> tags, which delimit paragraphs in the page)

❑ The three server controls (the asp:dropdownlist, asp:button, and asp:label controls) that we added to the page via the toolbox

Each of the three server controls also has the `runat="server"` attribute, which means that when the page is requested, each element is processed at the server, in order to generate HTML to be sent to the client. Each server control also has an automatically-generated `id`, which we'll use later to attach functionality to these controls. The `asp:label` control has some default text (the string `Label`), that displayed when the page is viewed – again, we'll add functionality to control that text later.

The HTML `<form>` tag is special here, because it also has a `runat="server"` attribute. This tag is also processed on the server at the time the page is requested, in order to generate HTML for the browser.

It's interesting to note that each of the elements here consists of an opening tag and a closing tag (for example, `<asp:label>` and `</asp:label>`) and that they're all properly nested. In fact, this is more important for the server controls than for the HTML tags, for the following reason:

❑ The server controls are processed on the server by the ASP.NET processor, which is very strict about how each ASP.NET element is arranged.

❑ The HTML elements (with the exception of the `<form runat="server">` element) are not processed at the server, but are passed to the browser as they are. Most browsers tend to be much more forgiving about missing end-tags and poor nesting, and can often compensate for such errors.

Visual Studio .NET applies good technique to all the tags, by ensuring that they are **well-formed**. Well-formedness is a set of rules about syntax of tags, which includes the rules about nesting and matching start/end-tags, and about which we'll learn more in Chapter 7. For now, VS.NET will take care of it for you, but it's worth being aware of it.

You've probably also noticed that all the HTML tags have been created using lower-case characters. You can control this using a setting in Visual Studio .NET. Click Tools | Options *from the main Visual Studio .NET menu; in the resulting dialog, select the* Text Editor | HTML/XML | Format *node on the left and look for the two drop-down boxes that specify how to format HTML tags and attributes. To make them all lowercase, select* Lowercase *and click* OK.

Again, most browsers are forgiving about use of case in HTML elements: you can use upper case, or lower case, or a mixture. We think that lower case is the most visually pleasant, which is why we've used that setting in this book.

We've seen the code that is processed on the server; what about the code that actually gets sent to the browser? You can look at this code by looking at the source code in the browser (the exact menu option depends on the browser; in Internet Explorer, right-click on the page and select View Source).

You'll see that the HTML code that we saw in the `.aspx` file is still there when the page reaches the browser. However, the ASP.NET `Page` directive has gone. Also, the `<asp:...>` tags have gone, and have been replaced by more HTML tags. In addition, the `<form runat="server">` element has been processed at the server, to generate more new HTML:

```
<html>
  ...
  <body>
    <form name="Ch2WebForm" method="post" action="Ch2WebForm.aspx"
        id="Ch2WebForm">
```

```
            <input type="hidden" name="__VIEWSTATE"
                    value="dDwtMTU2OTI3MDUzMzs7Pm+kNH6SXyOMuSvHGi4CeaaWdS8k" />
        <p>This is my first ASP.NET web form!</p>
        <p>
            Select a color from the following list,
            and then click the button:
        </p>
        <p> 
            <select name="DropDownList1" id="DropDownList1">
            </select>
            <input type="submit" name="Button1" value="Button"
                    id="Button1" />
        </p>
        <p>
            <span id="Label1">Label</span>
        </p>
    </form>
  </body>
</html>
```

The newly generated HTML is shown in the highlighted sections. Essentially, the ASP.NET processor has converted our server-side controls into elements that the browser can understand: for example, the `<asp:dropdownlist>` server control has been converted into an HTML `<select>` element. The ASP.NET processor has also added some information about something called *viewstate*, which we'll mention again later in this chapter and study in Chapter 6.

Now, let's do some work on our web form to make it do some interesting things.

Using the Properties Browser

The Properties browser in VS.NET will be an extremely useful tool for us in this book. The Properties browser shows the values of the properties of whatever element, control, or other item is currently "in focus", and allows us to change those property values. We used it earlier to change the pageLayout property of our Ch2WebForm.aspx page from GridLayout to FlowLayout.

The Properties browser is incredibly versatile. In this little example we'll use it to change the ids of our controls and to add some basic styling to the text, but we'll be using it throughout the book for changing all sorts of properties.

Try It Out – Setting Properties on our Page

We'll just use the Properties browser to make some adjustments to the property values of elements in the page, ready for the next stage of the example.

1. Return to the design view of Ch2WebForm.aspx (click the Design tab at the bottom of the main window). Check that the Properties browser is visible (if not, press *F4* to display it).

Now place the cursor within the first line of text. The Properties pane will display a <P> tag in the drop-down box at the top, which means that the properties we are about to assign apply to the paragraph element at just that point in the page:

2. Set the align property to Center, as shown above.

3. Next, select the style property. There is a lot we can add to the style property, and so VS.NET provides a Style Builder dialog to help. To start this off, click the ... button next to the style entry in the Properties browser:

4. In the Style Builder dialog, select the Font tab on the left. Click the ... button next to the Family field textbox to bring up the Font Picker dialog; use it to add the two installed fonts Verdana and Arial, and the generic Sans-Serif, in that order. (They'll be used in that order of priority; the final one will result in the default sans-serif font being used, if neither of the others is available.) Click OK on the Font Picker dialog when you're done.

5. Still in the **Style Builder** dialog, set the **Color** to **Maroon**; set the **Specific** size to be 12pt (which is an absolute value); set the **Effects** to **None**; and set the **Bold** property to **Bold**. The dialog should look like this:

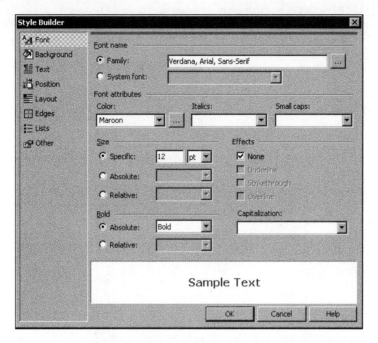

Click **OK** to close the dialog and apply the styling. You will see the changes reflected immediately in the design window.

6. Now place the cursor onto the second line of text. We'll leave this line as left-aligned (which is the default), but set the font for this paragraph as before (Verdana, Arial, generic Sans-Serif).

7. Now click the **DropDownList** control once to select it, then look in the **Properties** pane. Change the **ID** of this control to `ddlColorList`:

8. Next, click the Button control once only to select it. Set its ID property to be `btnSelectColor`, and change its Text property to `Apply Color`.

9. Finally, click the Label control once to select it. Set its ID property to `lblSelectedColor`, and remove any text from its Text property. In its Font property, set its Names sub-property to be Verdana and Arial, by separating the names as indicated in the dialog with a line return:

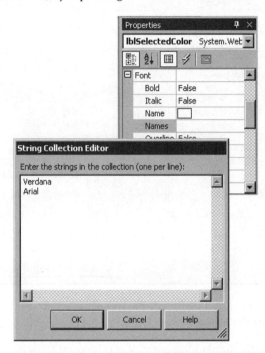

10. OK, now run the project again, by pressing *F5*. You should see the following results in your browser:

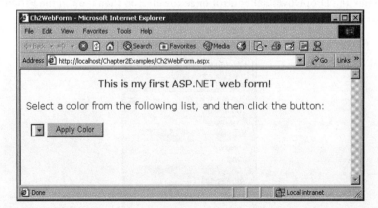

How It Works

There's still no functionality in our page yet, but it does look a little more styled. The style properties we changed have the visual appearance of our page, affecting the positioning an font of the text. Also note that the Text property of the button is being reflected in the wording that you see on the button now.

Let's look at the changes that have occurred to the HTML source code behind the scenes. Go back to the HTML view for the page in VS.NET, and look at the changes to the code there:

```
<body>
    <form id="Ch2WebForm" method="post" runat="server">
        <p style="FONT-WEIGHT: bold; FONT-SIZE: 12pt; COLOR: maroon;
                  FONT-FAMILY: Verdana, Arial, Sans-Serif;
                  TEXT-DECORATION: none" align="center">
        This is my first ASP.NET web form!
        </p>
        <p style="FONT-FAMILY: Verdana, Arial, Sans-Serif">
            Select a color from the following list,
            and then click the button:
        </p>
        <p> 
            <asp:dropdownlist id="ddlColorList" runat="server">
            </asp:dropdownlist>
            <asp:button id="btnSelectColor" runat="server"
                        text="Apply Color">
            </asp:button>
        </p>
        <p>
            <asp:label id="lblSelectedColor" runat="server"
                       font-names="Verdana,Arial">
            </asp:label>
        </p>
    </form>
</body>
</html>
```

Note the new style attributes in the first two <p> elements:

❑   In the first, the style attribute specifies the font-weight, font-size, color, and font-family of the text in this paragraph

❑   In the second, the style attribute just specifies the font-family

The third <p> element doesn't have a style attribute, because we didn't set one there. However, we did set the font-names attribute of the <asp:label> control, and that change is reflected in the code here.

*Setting style properties like this gets a bit tiresome when there are lots of elements on the page, and when you're trying to get many elements across many pages to look the same. The solution is to place style definitions into **classes** in a **cascading style sheet (CSS)** file, link that file into all your pages, and then use the classes to style the elements. We'll be using a cascading style sheet in the Friends Reunion application, so we'll take a look at CSS in Chapter 3.*

Finally, you can see that the changes we made to the ID properties of the three server controls are reflected in the text. These new IDs are chosen to reflect the purpose of the controls, as you'll see in the next section.

Using Code-Behind

So far we've just been working on the Ch2WebForm.aspx file, which contains the presentation elements of our page. We also have the code-behind file, Ch2WebForm.aspx.cs, into which we can place code that adds functionality to the elements of the page, making for a more interactive experience. It is in the code-behind file that we can place the event-handlers that handle events raised during the life of the page.

Earlier in the chapter, we pointed out the <%@ Page %> directive that appears in the first line of the Ch2WebForm.aspx file. As we noted, this line of code contains a reference to the code-behind file, and its purpose is to act as the link between the two files:

```
<%@ Page language="c#"
        Codebehind="MyPage.aspx.cs"
        AutoEventWireup="false"
        Inherits="Chapter2Examples.MyPage" %>
```

The Codebehind attribute points to the file name of our code-behind file, as we noted earlier. The Inherits attribute points to the namespace and class name defined in our code-behind file – we'll see these in the next example. The language attribute specifies that we're going to use C# whenever we write server-side code, hence our code-behind file must be written in C#.

Finally, the AutoEventWireup attribute tells ASP.NET how to associate an event with an event handler method. If it is set to true, then the specially-named event handlers Page_Load() and Page_Init() are called automatically by ASP.NET when the page runs. If it is set to false, then wiring code is required to wire these event handlers to their corresponding events (and this code is generated in the InitializeComponent() method by VS.NET). At the end of this example, we'll return to this and take a look at what has been generated for us.

Try It Out – Adding Functionality using Code-Behind

Let's create some interactivity in our example, by adding some functional code to the code-behind file. We'll create an array of three colors, and list them in the drop-down box. We'll invite the user to select a color and click the button – and we'll arrange that the button-click causes some text to appear in the label control, reflecting the user's choice of color.

1. In Solution Explorer, right-click on Ch2WebForm.aspx and select **View Code**: this will cause the code-behind file Ch2WebForm.aspx.cs to open in the IDE.

2. In Ch2WebForm.aspx.cs, look for the event-handler method called Page_Load(), and add this code to it:

```
public class Ch2WebForm : System.Web.UI.Page
{
  ...
  private void Page_Load(object sender, System.EventArgs e)
  {
    if (!(Page.IsPostBack))
    {
      ArrayList Colors = new ArrayList(3);
      Colors.Add("Red");
      Colors.Add("Green");
      Colors.Add("Blue");
      ddlColorList.DataSource = Colors;
      ddlColorList.DataBind();
    }
  }
  ...
}
```

3. Now return to Ch2WebForm.aspx, and select the **Design** view. Double-click on the **Button** control. VS.NET interprets this double-click as a signal that you want to write an event-handler for the "button-click" event on this **Button** control.

Thus, it creates an empty method called btnSelectColor_Click() in MyPage.aspx.cs, and wires this method up to the click event. Then it changes the display to show the code-behind file, MyPage.aspx.cs, with the cursor placed inside the btnSelectColor_Click() method ready for you to begin typing.

4. Type the following code into the btnSelectColor_Click() event handler method:

```
public class Ch2WebForm : System.Web.UI.Page
{
  ...
  private void btnSelectColor_Click(object sender, System.EventArgs e)
  {
    lblSelectedColor.Text = "You selected " +
                            ddlColorList.SelectedItem.Text;
    lblSelectedColor.ForeColor =
      System.Drawing.Color.FromName(ddlColorList.SelectedItem.Text);
  }
}
```

5. That's it! Now run the project by pressing *F5*. When the page loads, select a color from the drop-down box and click the **Apply Color** button:

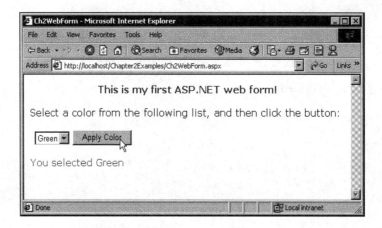

How It Works

All we've done here is add a few lines of functional code to the code-behind page. It didn't take much effort to add an interactive feature to the page (albeit a very simple one).

The first thing we needed to do was to create an array of colors and use them to make the three options in the drop-down list. We need this array to be created at the time the page first loads, so that it's already set up and ready for the first time the user clicks the **Apply Color** button.

For this reason, we add the code for this to the `Page_Load()` event handler method. This method is a private method of the `Ch2WebForm` class, which is the class of this page, and it runs when the page is loaded by the user. (We'll talk more about page-related events before the end of the chapter.)

Now, the `Page_Load()` event-handler runs *every* time the page is loaded. So, as expected, it runs when the page is first called. However, the **Apply Color** button is a server control, so when the user clicks on this button, the browser sends a request to the server for processing, and the page is reloaded. Therefore, the `Page_Load()` event-handler *also* runs each time the user clicks the **Apply Color** button.

So what we do is this. Each time the page is loaded, our `Page_Load()` code uses the `Page.IsPostBack` property to find out whether the request is a first-time request or a postback:

❑ If `Page.IsPostBack` is `false`, then it's a first-time request. In this case, we need the array to be created and used to add the three options to the drop-down list.

❑ If `Page.IsPostBack` is `true`, then it's a **postback** – that is, the page is being re-requested by the user so that the web server can process an event and regenerate the page. In this case, the data in the `Colors` array has already been generated once and used to create the options in the drop-down list; and those options are stored within the HTML that's sent to the browser, in coded format, in a hidden HTML `<input>` tag called **viewstate**:

```
<form ...>
  <input type="hidden" name="__VIEWSTATE"
         value="dDw0NDY2MjMzMjt0PDtsPGk8MT47 ... ... QFJWeORw=" />
  ...
</form>
```

54

So, we don't need to generate those options again: the viewstate will be sent up to the server with the request, and then used by the ASP.NET processor to regenerate the three items in the drop-down list.

We achieve all that in just the following few lines of code:

```
private void Page_Load(object sender, System.EventArgs e)
{
  if (!(Page.IsPostBack))
  {
    ArrayList Colors = new ArrayList(3);
    Colors.Add("Red");
    Colors.Add("Green");
    Colors.Add("Blue");
    ddlColorList.DataSource = Colors;
    ddlColorList.DataBind();
  }
}
```

The `Page.IsPostBack` property is described above; the three `Add()` method calls each add an item to the array; and the last two lines bind the array to the drop-down list, so that the list has three items in it.

*Displaying dynamic data is such a common task in web development, that **data binding** has been greatly enhanced in ASP.NET. We'll study this subject in more detail in Chapter 5.*

The button-click event-handler is much easier. When we double-click on the Button control, the IDE does two things:

❑ First, it creates an event-handler method in the code-behind file. Note that the IDE chose to name this event-handler method `btnSelectColor_Click()`, after the ID property of the button control (which we set to `btnSelectColor` earlier in the chapter) and the event it's intended to handle.

❑ Second, it "wires" the method to the `Click` event of that Button control – so that the application knows that it should run this method whenever that button is clicked. There are two places where we can easily see evidence of this wiring. One is in the auto-generated code in `Ch2WebForm.aspx.cs`, where the following highlighted line of code has been inserted into the `Initialize_Component()` method (which is hidden inside a region marked `Web Form Designer generated code`):

```
private void InitializeComponent()
{
  this.btnSelectColor.Click += new
                     System.EventHandler(this.btnSelectColor_Click);
  this.Load += new System.EventHandler(this.Page_Load);
}
```

The other is in the Properties browser. If you go back to the Design view for `Ch2WebForm.aspx`, click on the button, then click the Events button in its properties you'll see the name of the event-handler has been inserted next to the entry for the Click event:

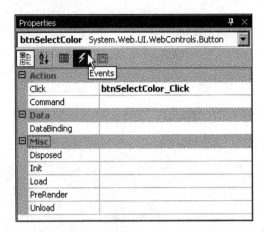

In the event-handler itself, there are just two lines of code. The first assigns some text to the Text property of the Label control, and the second changes the its foreground color. Both use the expression ddlColorList.SelectedItem.Text, which returns the value of the option that the user selected in the drop-down list before pressing the **Apply Color** button:

```
private void btnSelectColor_Click(object sender, System.EventArgs e)
{
    lblSelectedColor.Text = "You selected " +
                              ddlColorList.SelectedItem.Text;
    lblSelectedColor.ForeColor =
      System.Drawing.Color.FromName(ddlColorList.SelectedItem.Text);
}
```

There is one extra bit of work to do in the second line: notice that the selected color value is a String, but the ForeColor attribute expects an object of type System.Drawing.Color. Therefore, we use the FromName() method of the System.Drawing.Color class to create a Color object based on the string name of the color.

We'll revisit many of these concepts in later chapters. In particular, in the next chapter we'll concentrate on server controls, the different types of controls, and how they're used.

Other Aspects of ASP.NET

ASP.NET is an order of magnitude more structured than any other web development environment Microsoft has ever produced. We've already seen that it is object-oriented, event-driven, and control-based; it's design also heavily promotes the benefits of code reuse and code compilation.

In the remaining pages in this chapter, we'll have brief tour of some of these aspects of ASP.NET, and understand them a little better.

A Brief Tour of an ASP.NET Application

We've already seen some of the files in an ASP.NET application: specifically, each web form consists of an `.aspx` file and its associated `.aspx.cs` code-behind file. A quick look at the **Solution Explorer** (or, indeed, through Windows Explorer at the folder that contains the application) indicates that there are a number of other files created by default when VS.NET creates a new C# ASP.NET web application.

Let's look at some of them here. If you return to the **Solution Explorer** and click the **Show All Files** button (as shown), and expand the resulting nodes, you'll see a number of files that were previously hidden from view:

One of these files is the `Ch2WebForm.aspx.cs` code-behind file that was created automatically when we created our web form. Note that there's another file associated with the web form: it's a `.resx` file. This is known as a **resource file**, and its purpose is to support the VS.NET drag-and-drop visual designer.

What other files can we see here? Here's a brief résumé of the more important files, from the point of view of this book:

❑ Under the **References** node, we have a number of child nodes. Each one looks as if it relates to a namespace. In fact, these are the names of the assemblies that are linked to the application. Each assembly contains compiled code – these five contain the compiled classes contained in five namespaces (for convenience, many of .NET's namespace classes are compiled into assemblies of the same name as the namespace – for example, the `System.Data` namespace classes are compiled into `System.Data.dll`). The five shown in the screenshot are the five assemblies linked to an ASP.NET application by default when it's created in VS.NET, so the classes in these namespaces are available to us immediately.

❑ Further down the list, the next important files are `Global.asax` and `Global.asax.cs`. This is the place where we put the methods that handle application-level and session-level events (for example, the `Application_Start()` method that runs when the application starts up, and the `Session_Start()` method that runs whenever a new session starts). It's also a place to create application-scope and session-scope variables. We'll find some uses for `Global.asax` during the development of the *Friends Reunion* application, in subsequent chapters.

❑ At the bottom of the list, the `Web.config` file is used to customize the configuration of our web application. It can contain all sorts of information about application settings, security settings, session-state timeout settings, compilation settings, error-handling options, and so on. You'll see this file appear in quite a number of the following chapters, whenever we need to apply application-specific settings.

Finally, there are two files to mention more briefly:

❑ The `AssemblyInfo.cs` file contains assembly attributes relating to the compiled page. It controls versioning, signing of the assembly, culture information, and so on.

❑ The `Chapter2Examples.vsdisco` file is used by VS.NET to discover all of the files that make up the web application.

These two files are both created automatically by VS.NET when it creates the web application project. It is possible to change them by hand, but we will not be doing that in this book.

The Class View

The **class view** window is another tool that often comes in handy when working with ASP.NET applications. You can display this window by pressing *Ctrl+Shift+C*. This window offers us a slightly different view of our application – it displays the **class hierarchy** of the web application. If you look at the Class View tab of the `Chapter2Examples` project and expand a couple of nodes, you'll see the following:

In this screenshot, we can see a few event-handler methods:

❑ The `btnSelectColor_Click()` method that runs in response to the `Click` event of the `btnSelectColor` **Button** control

❑ The `Page_Load()` method that runs when the page loads

❑ The `InitializeComponent()` event-handler, which (as we saw a little earlier) is involved in the initialization of the page object

❑ The `OnInit()` event-handler, which we'll meet before the end of the chapter.

Under that, we can see the implementations of the button, drop-down list, and label controls that we created.

If you double-click any of these nodes, VS.NET takes you immediately to the point in the code at which that item is defined. As your applications grow more complex, you may find this to be a useful tool for finding your way round the code.

Object Orientation in ASP.NET

The .NET programming environment is an object-oriented programming environment, and that holds in .NET *web* application programming too. Take a look at our simple `Chapter2Examples` project. It contains a namespace called `Chapter2Examples`. This namespace contains a class called `Ch2WebForm` that is the page class for our `Ch2WebForm.aspx` web form (you can see this in the code in `Ch2WebForm.aspx.cs`):

```
namespace Chapter2Examples
{
  ...
  public class Ch2WebForm : System.Web.UI.Page
  {
    protected System.Web.UI.WebControls.DropDownList ddlColorList;
    protected System.Web.UI.WebControls.Button btnSelectColor;
    protected System.Web.UI.WebControls.Label lblSelectedColor;

    private void Page_Load(object sender, System.EventArgs e)
    {
      ...
    }
    ...

    private void btnSelectColor_Click(object sender, System.EventArgs e)
    {
      ...
    }
  }
}
```

From this code fragment, we can see that:

❑ The `Ch2WebForm` page class is inherited from a base class called `Page`, which belongs to the `System.Web.UI` namespace

❑ The `Ch2WebForm` page class contains member declarations and can contain public and private properties, and so on

❑ Each of the controls in the page (the drop-down list, the button, and the label) is declared as a protected member of the `Ch2WebForm` page class – each is an instance of a class that lives in the `System.Web.UI.WebControls` namespace

All this comes from the fact that ASP.NET gives us a truly object-oriented approach to web application development.

Reusability and Encapsulation

The object-oriented nature of ASP.NET also manifests itself in the level of **code reusability** that is possible. The Ch2WebForm page provides a very simple example of this: each of the three controls in the Ch2WebForm.aspx page is a reuse of an existing class. Each class is developed and tested by Microsoft, compiled, ready-to-use, and easy to deploy. When we're developing web forms, we don't need to think about the internal complexities of these controls' classes – we just drag-and-drop to create instances of the classes in our code.

The three controls we used in that example are just a small sample of the vast library of classes made available in the .NET Framework. As we mentioned earlier, there are some 17 namespaces, which contain the classes that make up ASP.NET's core functionality. These namespaces organize the classes into logical groups; each of them is prefixed with the name System.Web.

Much of the structure of ASP.NET applications is built up from theses classes, so we spend some of our time creating instances of ASP.NET classes or writing our own classes that inherit from them (as we saw in the Ch2WebForm example). There isn't space to list them all here, but it's worth noting a few of the most commonly-used namespaces:

❑ The System.Web namespace contains classes for processing ASP.NET pages at their lowest level, and defining how ASP.NET relates to the web server. This namespace contains classes for handling information passed via HTTP, as we discussed in Chapter 1.

❑ The System.Web.UI namespace contains a lot of functionality that we use when constructing our pages. It's one level of abstraction higher than the classes contained in the System.Web namespace. When we construct an ASP.NET page, it's the classes in this namespace that are used to ensure the page has the correct structure. (The Page class is one of the classes in this namespace.) These classes define the functionality available to all ASP.NET pages. We'll get to understand this better when we see how pages are loaded and processed, later in this chapter.

❑ The System.Web.UI.WebControls and System.Web.UI.HtmlControls namespaces contain the control elements that we add to the page. (For example, the DropDownList, Button, and Label controls we added to the Ch2WebForm page are all instances of classes contained in the System.Web.UI.WebControls namespace.) Each of these controls inherits some basic functionality from the System.Web.UI.Control class, but they also add their own functionality on top of this to provide us with a rich user interface element. We'll learn a lot more about the classes in these namespaces in Chapter 3.

❑ The System.Web.Services namespace and its child namespaces are somewhat different from all the rest; they are specifically designed for the development of web service applications. We'll defer discussion of this until Chapter 9.

Finally, note that our ASP.NET applications are not restricted to using the classes of the System.Web.* namespaces! Elsewhere in the .NET Framework, there are many other (non-ASP.NET-specific) namespaces, whose classes can be used in ASP.NET applications to connect to data sources, build complex graphical interfaces, manage file systems and configuration, and perform many other tasks. In fact, we'll be making good use of some of them during the course of the book.

Compilation

Many readers of this book will already be aware that a program created in C# must be compiled before it can be run. The same is true in C# ASP.NET applications, where there is a two-stage compilation process:

❑ In the first stage, the code is compiled into **Microsoft Intermediate Language** (**MSIL**).

❑ In the second stage, the **Just-In-Time** (**JIT**) **compiler** compiles the MSIL into machine code. This stage occurs when the page is first called.

Thus, the first call to a web page demands slightly more work (the JIT compilation from MSIL to machine code); second and subsequent calls to the page will receive a slightly faster response because the page class is already fully compiled by then.

When we prepare a VS.NET web application for execution, all of the code files within the application (including the code-behind files) are compiled into an MSIL **assembly** – the web application depends on this assembly to run.

When we run an application in debug mode (as we did earlier in the chapter by using the *F5* shortcut), VS.NET first creates the assembly – then it uses the assembly file to run the application. The assembly file for the example in this chapter is called `Chapter2Examples.dll`.

The Lifecycle of a Page

Finally in this section, it's helpful to take a look at the sequence of events that occurs beginning when a user requests an ASP.NET page, and ending with that page being rendered in the user's browser.

This sequence of events depends on whether the request is the *first* request of that page, or a *subsequent* request for the same page that is initiated via a postback. We saw this in the Ch2WebForm example, in which the task of getting the options in the drop-down list was achieved by data-binding an array (when the user first loaded the page) or by using the encoded data in the viewstate (when the user pressed the Apply Color button and generated a postback).

The following diagram shows what happens each time the client requests a page, via either an original request or a postback:

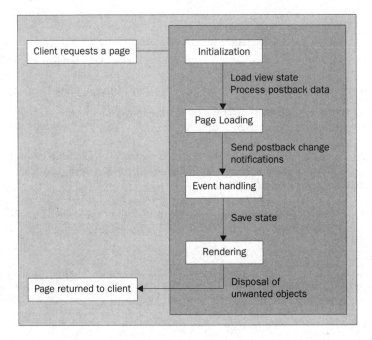

In this diagram, there are five main events – Initialize, Load, Pre-render, Render, and Dispose – and we are able to add code that is processed at each of these stages. Other actions also occur between these main events, filling the picture of how a page is processed.

- ❑ **Initialization**: When the page request is first received by the ASP.NET processor, the Init event is the first to be raised. This event is used to set up the framework of the page, and to prepare the controls on the page for rendering. The default method for handling this event is the OnInit() method. We can add code to this event handler in certain situations, but in general this event is used internally by ASP.NET.

  Following the Init event, there are a couple of smaller processes. First, if there is any **viewstate** then it is loaded. In other words, the ASP.NET processor looks for data that was contained in the page in a hidden <input name="_ _VIEWSTATE"> tag, and has been included in the page request. If it finds any such data, it reads and decodes it, ready for use in the (re)generation of the page. In the Ch2WebForm example, this equates to collecting encoded data contained in the <input name="_ _VIEWSTATE"> tag that relates to the options in the drop-down list.

  Second, the **postback** data is processed. In the Ch2WebForm example, when the user clicks the Apply Color button, the web form fires a postback containing information for the server to process (specifically, the color selected by the user in the drop-down box).

- ❑ **Page loading**: When a page is loaded, the the main event raised is the Load event. The default method for handling the Load event is an OnLoad event-handler; however, VS.NET always adds a line of code to the InitializeComponent() method that we met earlier, to specify that the Load event is handled by the Page_Load() method instead:

```
private void InitializeComponent()
{
    this.Load += new System.EventHandler(this.Page_Load);
}
```

We can add code to the Page_Load() method to control what happens when our page is loaded. (In the Ch2WebForm example we used this technique to check whether the request was a postback, and if not, to generate an array and use it to populate the options in the drop-down list.)

❑ **Event handling**: In this generically-named stage, the ASP.NET processor deals with a series of events that are raised and handled. If the page is being posted back then this includes events raised by the user. For example, the Click event of the btnApplyColor button control would be handled here.

The PreRender event is also handled at this stage. The default method for handling the PreRender event is called OnPreRender(), and we write code here to perform last-minute changes to the way the page is rendered. (The changes we make here can be preserved across postbacks, unlike changes affected in the Render() event-handler that we'll meet at the next stage). We can then save the state of our page into the viewstate that will be returned to the page.

❑ **Rendering**: In this stage, we have code that renders the page that will be sent back to the browser, by generating the HTML that our browser will have to display. We can make more last-minute changes that affect how our page is rendered, by adding code to the Render() event-handler, which handles the Render event. (Note the change in naming convention here: peculiarly, the even-handler is not called OnRender().)

❑ **Disposal of unwanted objects**: In this final stage, we have code that cleans up by disposing of unused objects, such as data connections that we've finished with.

Summary

We started this chapter with a definition of ASP.NET. We said that it is

> *"... an event-driven, control-based architecture that generates content and dynamic client-side code from server-side code using functionality described in the* System.Web *classes of the .NET Framework."*

The intention of this chapter was to explore this definition, expanding and clarifying the assertions it makes, and demonstrating the concepts and techniques that derive from it. We've seen that:

❑ A web form is a special kind of ASP.NET page, that contains an HTML <form> element.

❑ A web form developed in VS.NET with C# consists of an .aspx file and an associated .aspx.cs code-behind file. These two files represent the separation of presentation code and functional code.

❑ The VS.NET IDE makes it easy to rapidly create web forms using drag-and-drop in the visual designer.

❑ Events and event-handling are core to ASP.NET, since events occur at many stages in an ASP.NET page. The lifecycle of a page runs through initialization, loading, event-handling and pre-rendering, rendering, and disposal.

❑ Adding a control to a web form page is very simple, and setting properties on a control is equally simple using the VS.NET tools. It's also very easy to write event-handlers, which contain the code that reacts to events raised by our controls.

❑ The functionality available to ASP.NET comes from a series of classes built into the .NET Framework. The classes contained in the `System.Web` namespace, and the 16 `System.Web.*` namespaces, contain a huge number of classes that provide much of the functionality we need to write web forms. This functionality includes class definitions for our controls, for handling the rendering process, and much more. The non-ASP.NET Framework namespaces are also available for us to work with.

❑ ASP.NET is a part of the object-oriented world of .NET, and its object-oriented nature brings flexibility and extensibility.

In the next chapter, we'll begin the task of the building a web application called *Friends Reunion*. By the end of that chapter we will have a simple working application, with a few different pages in it; and in each subsequent chapter we'll continue to add functionality and features to the application.

Along the way, we will build on the foundation of Chapters 1 and 2, and we will explore a number of concepts and technologies that help us to enhance the application. We'll look at controls, data access and data binding, state, XML and Schemas, web services, and security. We'll also consider some important development-related issues: debugging and exception-handling, performance, and deployment.

We'll start at the beginning, with a deeper exploration of user interfaces and server controls.

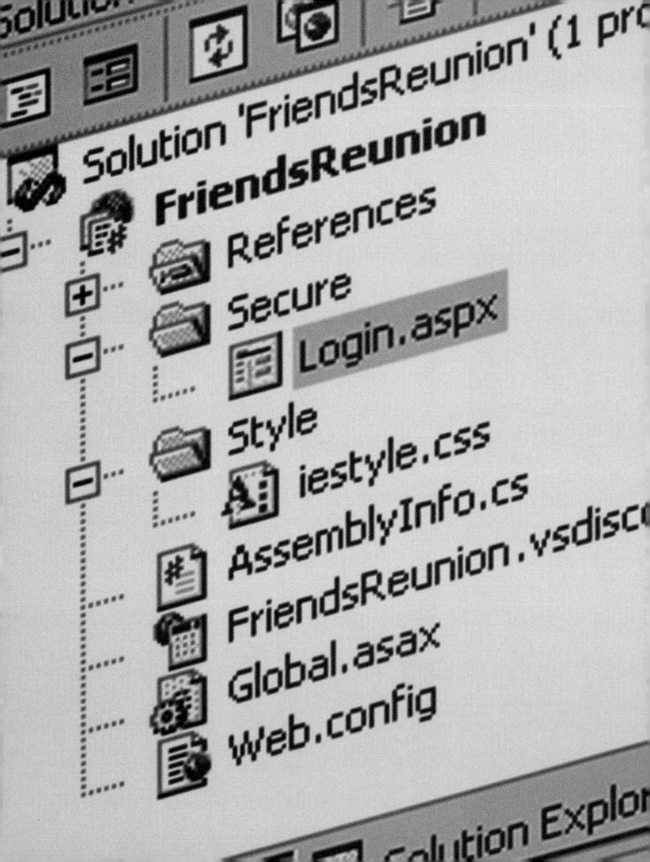

Solution 'FriendsReunion' (1 pro

FriendsReunion

References

Secure

Login.aspx

Style

iestyle.css

AssemblyInfo.cs

FriendsReunion.vsdisc

Global.asax

Web.config

Solution Explor

User Interfaces and Server Controls

In Chapter 2, we examined the architecture and purpose of web forms, and discussed how they improve the concept of a 'web page'. We also began to see how, in combination with the IDE provided by Visual Studio .NET, ASP.NET's **server** (or **server-side**) **controls** can transform web page design into the drag-and-drop ballet that our colleagues in the Windows desktop programming department have enjoyed for so long. The way that server controls work is ingenious: while you're designing your web application, they behave like any other control, allowing you to position them and set their properties through the familiar C# interface. At runtime, they generate the HTML code necessary to render themselves identically in web browsers, using nothing but standard HTML elements.

Mastering ASP.NET server controls will make you a highly productive web developer, with an intuitive feel for which controls should be used when. This chapter aims to teach this proficiency by describing:

❑ How Visual Studio .NET's 'HTML controls' compare with HTML elements

❑ How to react to events that take place in controls, on both the server side and the client side

❑ Different ways to change the appearance of controls, using attributes and stylesheets

❑ The advantages of web server controls, especially their design-time benefits

❑ How to make web-based data capture more reliable by using the validation controls

❑ The creation of user controls and custom controls that expand on built-in functionality

❑ Using the idea of dynamic content to generate user-aware web applications

Also in this chapter, we'll have our first look at a sample application that we'll be returning to in each chapter during the rest of the book. *Friends Reunion* is a simplified take on a class of web sites that is currently quite popular. The idea is to allow registered users to enter details of schools and colleges they've attended, or places they've worked. Then, people who were at the same place at the same time are given the opportunity to contact one another. As we progress, our application will become ever more complex, but we'll start here with some basics:

❑   A login form

❑   A registration form

❑   A page for general news items

We will also work on some common header and footer components.

Server Controls

Thanks to the examples in Chapter 2, you've already had a first experience of server controls: we created some examples that used the `Button` and `DropDownList` controls. In this chapter, you'll soon discover that most of the server controls at our disposal in Visual Studio .NET are every bit as easy to place and use. While a page is being designed, they appear as controls that we can configure through the **Properties** window, changing their appearance, default values, and so on. At runtime, ASP.NET transforms them into plain old HTML code that it sends to the browser.

Server controls offer real productivity gains over other methods of web page design, not only because of their ease of use, but also because they conform to the .NET programming model. They make the process of building a page as easy as designing a Windows Forms application. We drag controls on to our pages, tinker with their properties, and there's our user interface. There's simply no need to grapple with HTML – unless, of course, you really want to. Once you get used to the new model, you may never want to mess with HTML source code again!

> *If you've done some ActiveX controls programming before, perhaps used with ASP, it's worth pointing out that server controls are a very different thing. They don't need any client-side installation, and they're not Windows-specific.*

When you open a web form for editing in Visual Studio .NET, there are two areas of the **Toolbox** that contain user interface elements that we can place on our web pages:

The HTML area contains the HTML controls:

The Web Forms area contains the web controls:

We'll look at the HTML controls in this section, and leave the web controls until a little later on.

The namespace hierarchy looks like this:

*The terminology we have already seen so far, for different types of controls, may be a little confusing if you've never seen it before. Just remember that **all** controls are server controls, in the sense that they are dropped and configured in the Visual Studio .NET IDE, that their properties are set using the Properties window, and so on. The first division of these is between HTML controls and web server controls; HTML controls represent the HTML tag's equivalent of the server control. An **HTML server control** is a special type of HTML control, that runs on the server side. A **web server control** always runs on the server side.*

HTML Controls

The HTML controls in Visual Studio .NET correspond exactly with standard HTML elements: they have all the same properties, and they render precisely as you'd expect them to. For example, the ASP.NET Table control is equivalent to the HTML `<table>` element. If we were to drag one from the Toolbox onto an empty web form, this is how it would appear in the designer (don't worry about following along with this; we'll have a go at using some HTML controls in the next *Try It Out*):

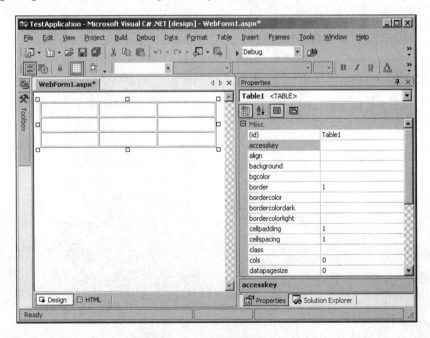

In the Properties window, we can change many aspects of the table, and you may recognize the names in the window (such as border, cellpadding, and cellspacing) as being the attributes of a traditional HTML table.

When we add a control to a web form in the Visual Studio .NET designer, HTML code for the control is generated, and we can see it (and modify it) by clicking the HTML button at the bottom of the designer. For the table shown in the screenshot above, Visual Studio .NET would generate the following HTML:

```
...
<body>
  <form id="Form1" method="post" runat="server">
    <table id="Table1" cellSpacing="1" cellPadding="1"
           width="300" border="1">
      <tr>
        <td></td>
        <td></td>
        <td></td>
      </tr>
      <tr>
        <td></td>
        <td></td>
        <td></td>
      </tr>
      <tr>
        <td></td>
        <td></td>
        <td></td>
      </tr>
    </table>
  </form>
</body>
</html>
```

There's nothing strange or magical here – just plain old HTML elements. By default, Visual Studio .NET is rather slap-dash about its use of capitalization! If you wish, you can change things so that Visual Studio .NET always uses all uppercase or all lowercase characters in its elements. To do this, use the Options... item in the Tools menu; the capitalization option is under Text Editor | HTML/XML | Format.

As the HTML controls are represented by regular HTML code, there's no processing required, and ASP.NET simply passes the markup to the client browser as-is. Also, we can use all of the traditional techniques for manipulating HTML controls, such setting attributes or executing client-side script. Let's now start the ball rolling with a demonstration of some HTML controls.

Try It Out – Building a Login Form

For this first example, we're going to create a simple login form that provides minimal authentication for users of our *Friends Reunion* site. As you'll see, it's amazing what you can do with little more than a table and a couple of text controls!

71

1. Create a new ASP.NET web application in Visual Studio .NET. Give it the name FriendsReunion:

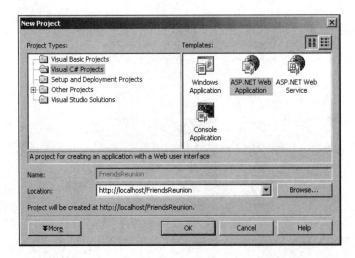

When the project is created, go to the **Solution Explorer** (use *Ctrl+Alt+L* to bring it up if it is not already visible), right-click on the **FriendsReunion** project and select **Properties**. Then select **Designer Defaults**, set the **Page Layout** item to **Flow**, and then select **OK**.

Back in the **Solution Explorer**, delete the **WebForm1.aspx** web form that is created by default.

2. Later in the book, we will endow the *Friends Reunion* application with secure login functionality. As a signal of that intent, we're going to place the login page in a sub-folder of its own, called **Secure**. So, in the **Solution Explorer**, right-click on the **FriendsReunion** project and choose **Add | New Folder** to add a new folder. Name it **Secure**.

3. Right-click the newly created folder and select **Add | Add Web Form...** to add a new web form. Name it **Login.aspx**.

4. Double-click on the **Table** control in the **HTML** tab of the toolbox to add one to the form.

5. Next, place the cursor on one of the empty cells in the third column, right-click on the same cell, and select **Delete | Columns**, so that our table now has just two columns.

6. Click the top-left cell, and type **User Name:**. In the cell below it, type **Password:**.

7. Now drag and drop a **Text Field** and a **Password Field** control respectively into the next cells along.

8. The last control to add is a **Button**; it should be placed in the first cell in the last row of the table. Using the **Properties** window, set its `value` property to `Login`, so that the page now looks like this:

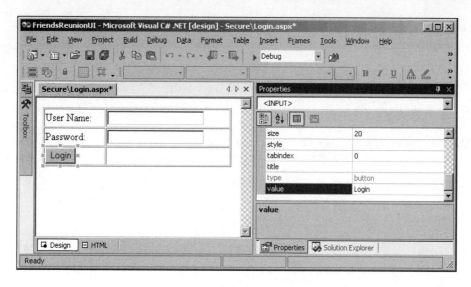

9. Finally, we can get rid of the unused cell to the right of the button. Right-click on it, and choose Delete | Cells from the context menu. Select the cell containing the button, and in the Properties window set its `colspan` property to 2. If you now switch to the HTML view using the HTML button at the bottom of the web form, you should see something like this:

```
<%@ Page language="c#" Codebehind="Login.aspx.cs"
        AutoEventWireup="false" Inherits="FriendsReunion.Secure.Login" %>
<!DOCTYPE HTML PUBLIC "-//W3C//DTD HTML 4.0 Transitional//EN" >
<html>
  <head>
    <title>Login</title>
    <meta name="GENERATOR" Content="Microsoft Visual Studio 7.0">
    <meta name="CODE_LANGUAGE" Content="C#">
    <meta name="vs_defaultClientScript" content="JavaScript">
    <meta name="vs_targetSchema"
        content="http://schemas.microsoft.com/intellisense/ie5">
  </head>
  <body>
    <form id="Login" method="post" runat="server">
      <table id="Table1" cellSpacing="1" cellPadding="1" width="300"
          border="1">
        <tr>
          <td>User Name:</td>
          <td>
            <input type="text"></td>
        </tr>
        <tr>
          <td>Password:</td>
          <td>
            <input type="password"></td>
        </tr>
        <tr>
```

```
            <td colSpan="2">
                <input type="button" value="Login"></td>
        </tr>
    </table>
  </form>
 </body>
</html>
```

10. Let's add a client-side handler for the Login button being pressed. Position the cursor next to the last <input> tag, and press the space bar to view the IntelliSense options available:

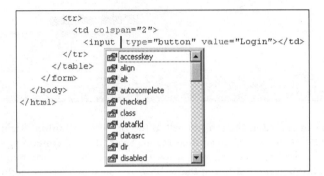

Scroll down to the onclick event (or just type its first few letters), and insert it (either by double-clicking, or by pressing the *Tab* key). Now add the small amount of code shown below, which will bring up a simple message box:

```
<td colSpan="2">
    <input onclick="alert('About to log in!');"
            type="button" value="Login"></td>
```

11. Right-click the Login.aspx page in the Solution Explorer and select Set As Start Page. Compile and run the solution by pressing *F5*, which also saves all files.

How It Works

The first thing we do is set the project's Page Layout property from Grid to Flow. This is because we will build all the pages in this application using FlowLayout, as we did in Chapter 2. Setting the property at the *project* level like this saves us the trouble of setting the pageLayout property each time we create a new page.

As we drop and set the controls' properties, the IDE automatically generates the corresponding HTML source code, as we saw when we switched to the HTML view. In this view, we also get the benefit of IntelliSense, which (among other things) lists all of the valid attributes for any HTML element.

When we view the page in a browser, the HTML code that we see in Visual Studio .NET is sent straight to the browser, which interprets it to render the controls that we placed in the designer. (In Internet Explorer, you can check this by right-clicking on the page and choosing View Source.) When you click the Login button, you should see this:

This demonstrates that we can perform client-side event handling as usual, by attaching script to the element's corresponding onXXX attribute, as we did here with onclick. If we want more sophisticated functionality, this script can call further client-side methods. Right now, however, we have a more pressing concern: our login form looks quite ugly, doesn't it? We need to add some *style* to our page.

Client-side script code can perform some complex tasks, and it's a subject to which whole books are dedicated. For more information about script code, try Beginning JavaScript *(Wrox, ISBN 1-86100-406-0) or* Professional JavaScript, 2nd Edition *(Wrox, ISBN 1-86100-553-9).*

Visual Styles

As we saw briefly in Chapter 2, we can use **cascading stylesheets** (**CSS**) to define visual characteristics that we can then apply uniformly to a range of items on one page, or a range of pages. Visual Studio .NET comes with an editor that makes creating CSS stylesheets easy, and we can start it up by clicking on the ellipsis (**...**) button next to the style property of an HTML control in the **Properties** window.

The editor is called the **Style Builder,** and it allows us to change every aspect of a particular control's appearance:

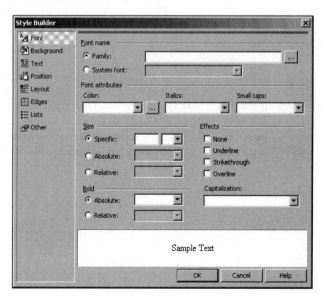

Unfortunately, adding the style for each control on the page can be tedious, and is certainly error-prone. Furthermore, if we decided at a later date to (say) change the font of all the `<input>` textboxes in our application, we would have some serious work to do, and it would be all too easy to miss one or two, spoiling the consistent feel. There's a better approach though. Still using the **Style Builder**, we can create a single stylesheet defining *all* the styles that we use, throughout our site. Let's see how that might work.

Try It Out – Creating a CSS Stylesheet

To create a CSS stylesheet that works across more than one web form, we can create it as a separate item that we then 'attach' to all web forms in which we want to use the definitions it contains. In this example, we'll start the process of building a stylesheet for our *Friends Reunion* application that we'll return to several times over the course of this chapter.

1. Continuing our desire for neatness, we'll place our stylesheet in its own sub-folder. Right-click on the project name in the **Solution Explorer** and create a new folder called `Style`.

2. Right-click the new folder, and select **Add | Add New Item...** From the right-hand window, select **Style Sheet**, and name it `iestyle.css`. To begin with, the new file will contain just an empty `body` element:

```
body
{
}
```

At this point, right-clicking the `body` element and selecting **Build Style** from the context menu will result in the appearance of the **Style Builder** we saw a moment ago. This time, however, we can use it to specify appearance characteristics that will apply to our whole application.

3. Select the **Background** category from the list on the left of the **Style Builder**, and choose a color from the **Color** drop-down, such as sensible **Silver**; but feel free to be as garish as you like! Select **OK** when you're done.

4. Next, we're going to ensure that all the tables in our application have the same basic appearance. Right-click anywhere on the stylesheet, select **Add Style Rule...** and from the **Element** dropdown on the dialog that appears, select **TABLE** and click **OK**.

5. Now right-click the new **TABLE** element, and select **Build Style...** again. Choose the **Tahoma** font as the **Family** value, and enter **8 pt** for the **Specific** field in the **Size** section:

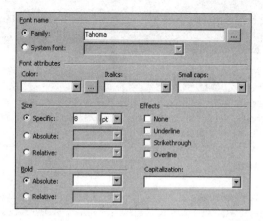

6. Click OK, and save the stylesheet. We can now associate the new stylesheet with the login form we built earlier by adding the following line at the top of the file's HTML code as follows:

```
<html>
  <head>
    <title>Login</title>
    <link href="../Style/iestyle.css" rel="stylesheet" type="text/css">
    <meta name="GENERATOR" Content="Microsoft Visual Studio 7.0">
      ...
```

Unfortunately, there's no drag-and-drop mechanism for adding this link so we have to do it manually.

7. Finally, we can save, compile, and run our application so far, again by using *F5*.

How It Works

As described above, the CSS stylesheet groups together the layout attributes that should be applied to all instances of a particular HTML element. By linking the stylesheet with a page through the `<link>` element, the styles it contains are applied to items on the page. The path to the stylesheet is relative, based on the location of the current web form – hence the need for the `..` syntax to 'step back' to the application's root directory.

Once we've saved the stylesheet and linked it to our page, we can see the effect of our handiwork when we reopen the page:

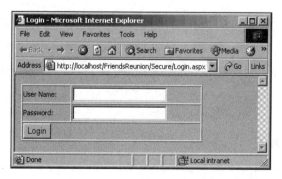

Without any further work on our part, the color we set for the `<body>` element is shown, and the text inside the table has taken on its new font. If we were to make changes to any of the values in the stylesheet, they would be automatically reflected on the page.

Creating a More Flexible Stylesheet

However, associating one style with all instances of a particular element isn't very flexible: what if we want to display some textboxes with one style, and some others with a different one? (Consider the HTML `<input>` element, which represents textboxes, buttons, password fields, checkboxes, and more!) There's another way to group styles together and associate them with elements: we have to use a CSS **class**.

Try It Out – Grouping Styles by Class Name

In this example, we'll use CSS classes to provide different styles to the textboxes and buttons in our application. Both of these are facets of the `<input>` element, so it would be impossible to do this by associating style rules with the element name.

1. If necessary, reopen the `iestyle.css` stylesheet in Visual Studio .NET, right-click anywhere on it, and select **Add Style Rule...**.

2. This time, instead of selecting an item in the **Element** drop-down, check the **Class name** radio button, and type **TextBox** (this will also appear in the preview box in the lower right corner, preceded by a period). Click **OK**.

3. Add the following code inside the new rule's braces:

```
.TextBox
{
    border-right: #c7ccdc 1px solid;
    border-top: #c7ccdc 1px solid;
    border-left: #c7ccdc 1px solid;
    border-bottom: #c7ccdc 1px solid;
    font-size: 8pt;
    font-family: Tahoma, Verdana, 'Times New Roman';
}
```

These additions should all be quite self-explanatory, but you'll notice that we've specified three fonts for the `font-family` value. These are in order of preference, so that if Tahoma is not available on the client machine then Verdana will be used (and failing that, Times New Roman).

4. Repeat Steps 2 and 3, this time entering **Button** in the **Class name** textbox. Use the code shown below:

```
.Button
{
    background-color: gainsboro;
    border-right: darkgray 1px solid;
```

```
      border-top: darkgray 1px solid;
      border-left: darkgray 1px solid;
      border-bottom: darkgray 1px solid;
      font-size: 8pt;
      font-family: Tahoma, Verdana, 'Times New Roman';
   }
```

5. Open the login page in **Design** view, select each of the two input boxes in turn, and set the `class` property of both to `TextBox`. Also, set the **Button**'s `class` property to `Button`. When you compile and run the page again, you'll see the controls change, reflecting the styles defined by each class.

6. Finally, select the table and set its `border` property to 0, and then save and run the page.

How It Works

On this occasion, we added new style rules to our stylesheet manually, but if you now open the **Build Style** dialog for any of them, it will be populated with the values we typed. Furthermore, IntelliSense is there to help us whenever we add a new line inside a rule, showing the styles currently available:

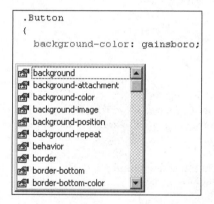

When we instruct a control to use a CSS class that we've defined in a stylesheet, Visual Studio .NET makes the association by using the HTML `class` attribute on the tag in the code that's sent to the browser. The `class` attribute is available to all HTML elements, and it's equally possible to associate controls with the styles in a stylesheet by adding it manually. When you open the page in the browser, you'll see this:

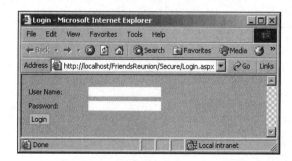

Well, that looks better! Better yet, we can now reliably and quickly apply the same style to any textbox we create, just by setting its **class** property to **TextBox**. Should we then make any further changes to the style rule, the associated controls would reflect them automatically.

For comprehensive information about CSS, we recommend Cascading Style Sheets *(published by glasshaus, ISBN 1-904151-04-3). Also useful are* HTML 4.01 Programmer's Reference *(Wrox, ISBN 1-86100-533-4) and* Professional Style Sheets for HTML and XML *(Wrox, ISBN 1-86100-165-7).*

HTML Server Controls

So far, we've seen some useful features of the Visual Studio .NET IDE, but what we've ultimately produced has been good old-fashioned HTML, with a little bit of JavaScript thrown in for good measure. One of the characteristics of web 'applications' like this is that the browser does most of the work, and the principles of client-side event handling haven't changed much since the technique first began to appear several years ago. ASP.NET, by contrast, is founded on the basis of server-side programming: events are trapped and handled on the server.

In ASP.NET, the events associated with web forms are classified into two categories:

❑   **Global events**

❑   **Page-specific events**

The first of these apply to the whole application or current user session, and are not specific to any particular page. Handlers for these events are placed in the Global.asax file, and we'll see more about how they work in Chapter 6. As we saw in the previous chapter, the page-specific events of a particular page are handled in that page's code-behind file, and it's this that we'll examine in more detail in the remainder of this chapter.

We can start by taking a look at the code-behind page for Login.aspx, by right-clicking on the page (in the **Solution Explorer** or the designer) and choosing **View Code**:

```
using System;
using System.Collections;
using System.ComponentModel;
using System.Data;
using System.Drawing;
using System.Web;
using System.Web.SessionState;
using System.Web.UI;
using System.Web.UI.WebControls;
using System.Web.UI.HtmlControls;

namespace FriendsReunion.Secure
{
  /// <summary>
  /// Summary description for Login.
  /// </summary>
```

```
public class Login : System.Web.UI.Page
{
  private void Page_Load(object sender, System.EventArgs e)
  {
    // Put user code to initialize the page here
  }

  [ Web Form Designer generated code ]
}
}
```

Since we've only used plain HTML controls so far, there's no information relating to them in the code-behind page – not even in the designer-generated code region:

```
#region Web Form Designer generated code
override protected void OnInit(EventArgs e)
{
  //
  // CODEGEN: This call is required by the ASP.NET Web Form Designer.
  //
  InitializeComponent();
  base.OnInit(e);
}

/// <summary>
/// Required method for Designer support - do not modify
/// the contents of this method with the code editor.
/// </summary>
private void InitializeComponent()
{
  this.Load += new System.EventHandler(this.Page_Load);

}
#endregion
```

Placing HTML *server* controls on the page, on the other hand, *does* result in code being placed in the code-behind file, as we'll see in the following example.

Try It Out – Converting to HTML Server Controls

Converting an HTML control to an HTML server control is simply a matter of right-clicking the control in the designer and choosing Run As Server Control from the drop-down menu. In this example, we'll do precisely that for the three <input> elements already on the login page, and we'll add a new element that provides the user with some feedback that their actions have had an effect.

1. Right-click on the two textboxes and the button in turn, and select Run As Server Control. As you do this, a small green arrow will appear in the top-left corner of each control, to indicate that it is indeed now a server control.

2. To make the ensuing C# code a little clearer, use the **Properties** window to change the IDs of the controls to `txtLogin`, `txtPwd`, and `btnLogin`. Save the file.

3. Underneath the login table, add a new HTML **Label** control, and convert it to a server control as before. Then set its ID to `lblMessage`, delete its text content, and clear its `style` property.

4. Double-click on the `btnLogin` control, and add the following line of code to the event handler:

```
private void btnLogin_ServerClick(object sender, System.EventArgs e)
{
    this.lblMessage.InnerText = "Authenticated on the server!";
}
```

5. Save and test the page by pressing *F5* as usual.

How It Works

Whenever we select **Run As Server Control** for an HTML element, a `runat="server"` attribute is added to that element's HTML declaration, and a protected class member representing that element is added to the class in the code-behind page. In the case of `Login.aspx`, the following member variables were added at the start of the code:

```
public class Login : System.Web.UI.Page
{
    protected System.Web.UI.HtmlControls.HtmlInputText txtLogin;
    protected System.Web.UI.HtmlControls.HtmlInputText txtPwd;
    protected System.Web.UI.HtmlControls.HtmlGenericControl lblMessage;
    protected System.Web.UI.HtmlControls.HtmlInputButton btnLogin;
    ...
```

Visual Studio .NET takes care of a lot of the necessary-but-tiresome details of writing pages, such as the skeleton code for event handlers. When we double-clicked the `btnLogin` control, the empty event handler was generated and attached to the default event of the button control, `ServerClick`, inside the `InitializeComponent()` method in the web form generated code. This is done by adding the following line:

```
this.btnLogin.ServerClick +=
    new System.EventHandler(this.btnLogin_ServerClick);
```

Additional handlers can also be attached in this way in other places in the code-behind page, such as the `Page_Load` handler.

Inside the click handler, our code simply tells the label to display a message: we can dynamically access and modify the properties of any of the server controls in the code-behind page. (We can't access the `<table>` itself, because that *isn't* a server control.) When we test the page now, we first get the alert message from the client-side script that we added before, and then, when the form is posted to the server, the following message is returned:

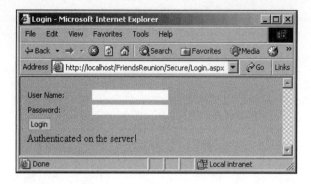

A Side Note: The Postback Mechanism

At this point, it would be reasonable to ask how the server-side code knows which control was clicked. In general, our form could contain any number of buttons, so how does ASP.NET determine which handler to call? To discover the answer to this, we have to look afresh at the HTML code that's generated at run time by ASP.NET, which we can see by going to View | Source in our browser. When the application is first launched, this is the code sent to the browser:

```
<body>
    <form name="Login" method="post" action="Login.aspx" id="Login">
        <input type="hidden" name="__EVENTTARGET" value="" />
        <input type="hidden" name="__EVENTARGUMENT" value="" />
        <input type="hidden" name="__VIEWSTATE"
         value="dDwtMTgxNjQwMjYyNDt0PDtsPGk8MT47PjtsPHQ8O2w8aTw3Pjs+O2w8dDxwP
                Gw8aW5uZXJodGdG1sOz47bDxBdXRoZW50aWNhdGVkIG9uIHRoZSBzZXJ2ZXIhOz4
                +Ozs+Oz4+Oz4gRx8VcLBdzVL3sMGF+RBsTFrWvw==" />
```

```
        <script language="javascript">
        <!--
          function __doPostBack(eventTarget, eventArgument) {
            var theform = document.Login;
            theform.__EVENTTARGET.value = eventTarget;
            theform.__EVENTARGUMENT.value = eventArgument;
            theform.submit();
          }
        // -->
        </script>
```

```
        <table id="Table1" cellSpacing="1" cellPadding="1"
               width="300" border="0">
          <tr>
            <td>User Name:</td>
            <td>
              <input name="txtLogin" id="txtLogin" type="text"
                     class="TextBox" /></TD>
          </tr>
          <tr>
            <td>Password:</td>
            <td>
```

```
                        <input name="txtPwd" id="txtPwd" type="password"
                               class="TextBox" /></td>
            </tr>
            <tr>
              <td colSpan="2">
                <input language="javascript"
                onclick="alert('About to log in!'); __doPostBack('btnLogin','')"
                       name="btnLogin" id="btnLogin" type="button" value="Login"
                       class="Button" /></td>
            </tr>
          </table>
          <div id="lblMessage"
               ms_positioning="FlowLayout">Authenticated on the server!</div>
      </form>
    </body>
  </html>
```

Notice the three hidden input fields that have been added, and the new script block containing a JavaScript function called _ _doPostBack(). This function receives two parameters, saves them in the first two hidden fields, and then submits the form to the server.

Further down the listing, we come to the onclick handler for btnLogin. In addition to the call to alert() that we added to this attribute earlier, there is now a call to the _ _doPostBack() function, to which is passed the button's id attribute.

The result is that when we click the button, the function saves the id of the control that caused the postback in a hidden field, and submits the form to the server. ASP.NET receives the form and uses the hidden _ _EVENTTARGET value to determine the appropriate handler for the event, which in this case would be our btnLogin_ServerClick() subroutine.

> *The other hidden field, _ _VIEWSTATE, is used to retain any values that we have entered on the form. For example, if we enter a user name before clicking the button, the user name is still shown after the postback. We'll be looking at this mechanism in more detail in Chapter 6.*

Web Server Controls

As well as all of the HTML controls (and their server-side variants), ASP.NET offers another set of controls for the use of web form programmers. These are the **web server controls** (or just **web controls**, since they're *always* server controls), and they're located in the Web Forms tab of the Toolbox. Many of these controls have direct HTML equivalents, but there are several new ones too. There are many reasons for choosing web server controls over HTML controls; here are the most important:

❑   Web server controls offer a layer of abstraction on top of HTML controls. At run time, some of them comprise a number of HTML elements, and therefore offer greater functionality with less design-time code. In a moment, we'll look at an example featuring the Calendar control, which demonstrates this idea quite nicely.

❑   Since web controls are independent of the markup that will render them at run time, some of them will render different HTML depending on the browser they're being viewed with, to improve compatibility. An example is the Panel control, which renders as a <div> on Internet Explorer, but as a <table> on Netscape browsers.

❑ Web server controls have a more consistent and logical object model than HTML elements, with some properties common to all web controls (including style-related properties such as BackColor, BorderColor, Font, and so on).

❑ Web server controls have a richer event model, making it easier to write server-side code for them.

❑ Design-time support for web server controls is greatly enhanced and more flexible. Some of these controls, for example, have their own Wizards, custom property pages, and the like.

❑ Web server controls provide typed values; in HTML controls, all values are strings.

❑ Since web server controls always run at the server, they are always available from within our server-side code (in the code-behind page).

Try It Out – Creating the News Page

In this example, we'll add a 'news' page to the *Friends Reunion* application, which will eventually fulfill the role of notifying the user of potential new contacts. For the time being, though, we'll just use it to display a calendar that allows the user to select a date. You've got to start somewhere!

1. We'll be using some images on our page, so create a new folder in the project, and call it Images. Select all the files from the Images directory in the code download, and drag and drop them onto the new folder in Solution Explorer.

2. Add a new web form to the root directory of the project, and call it News.aspx. Its pageLayout property should already be set to FlowLayout (because we changed this property at the project level earlier in the chapter).

3. From the Web Forms tab of the toolbox, drop a Panel control onto the new page. Set the following properties for it:

Property	Value
BackColor	#336699
Font | Bold	True
Font | Name	Tahoma
Font | Size	8pt
ForeColor	White
HorizontalAlign	Right

4. Set the panel's inner text to Friends Reunion. Then, drop a new Image control inside the panel, to the right of the text. Your form should look something like the following:

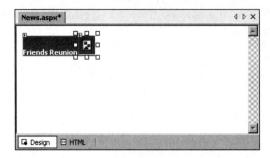

5. Set the properties of this `Image` control as follows:

Property	Value
ImageUrl	Images/friends.gif
ImageAlign	Middle

6. Enter the following text below the panel, after inserting an HTML paragraph tag (<p>) by pressing the *Enter* key: Welcome to the news for today! Here is the current calendar:.

7. Press *Enter* again after the text, and double-click on a `Calendar` control in the **Web Forms** tab of the toolbox. When it arrives in your application, set its ID to `calDates`.

8. Below the calendar, drop a `Label` control, and set its `Text` property to `Selected Date: `. The ` ` is an HTML character entity that inserts a space (strictly, a non-breaking space) after the colon.

9. For a little extra complexity, we'll add a drop-down list that allows the user to go straight to yesterday, today, or tomorrow. Next to the label, place a `DropDownList` control, and change its ID to `cbDay`. Click the ellipsis next to its `Items` property to bring up the **ListItem Collection Editor**. Click the **Add** button three times to add three items to the **Members** pane on the left, and set their properties as in the following table:

ListItem	Properties
0	Selected = True Text = Today Value = 0
1	Selected = False Text = Tomorrow Value = 1
2	Selected = False Text = Yesterday Value = -1

10. Click OK, and the page will now appear in the designer as shown below:

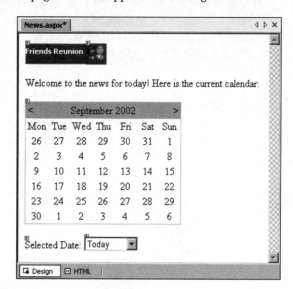

11. Set this page as the start page, and hit *F5* to run the project.

How It Works

The first thing to observe here is that, having set the Font property for the panel control, the Calendar, the Label, and the DropDownList all use the same font. This consistency derives from the fact that the controls inherit from more general controls that provide the common properties. For the controls we used on this page, the hierarchy is as follows:

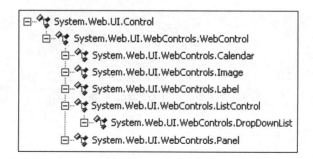

Except for the Control class at the top, all of these classes are to be found in the System.Web.UI.WebControls namespace. (The root Control class is also the base class for the HTML controls.) The Font property belongs to the WebControl class – and all of the derived controls inherit it, providing a very consistent model. Now let's take a look at the generated output:

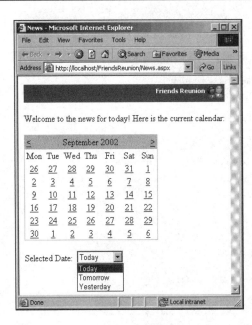

In fact, the `Calendar` control is by far the most sophisticated of the web server controls. We didn't have to write a single line of code, and yet we have a full-featured calendar that automatically allows the user to select other months by using the links displayed at the top of the control, to the left and right of the month name.

That's not all. ASP.NET tailors the control to work optimally in different browsers. Furthermore, it can be automatically localized for the culture of the user currently accessing the page (such as for Spanish users). This 'intelligent' rendering can be seen at work in the following screenshot:

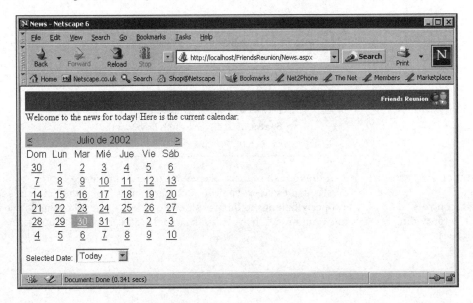

At run time, the calendar is rendered as an HTML table, with all the formatting in place. There is strong design-time support, including the Auto Format dialog, which we can use to apply a range of predefined designs. Just right-click on the calendar, and select the Auto Format... option from the context menu:

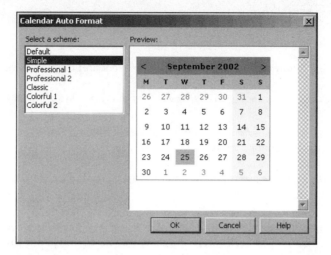

We'll set the auto format of the `Calendar` control to Simple for now, but feel free to experiment with the different built-in formats.

All of the more complex web controls, such as the `DataGrid` that we'll see in Chapter 5, offer easy formatting in a similar way – and we can also set these properties manually, of course. Also, just as for HTML controls, we can define CSS styles that apply to the web server controls throughout our application. To assign a style rule to a web server control, we specify its name in the control's `CssClass` property, and link the stylesheet to the page using the `<link>` element inside the `<head>` section, just as before.

Try It Out – Using CSS Styles with Web Controls

In this section, we'll do more to standardize the appearance of the controls in our application by creating some more style rules and applying them to our `News.aspx` web form.

1. First, we'll define a style that will apply fundamental formatting to any element that doesn't require something more specialized. Re-open the `iestyle.css` file and add the following `Normal` style rule:

```
.Normal
{
  font-size: 8pt;
  font-family: Tahoma, Verdana, 'Times New Roman';
}
```

2. Also, we'll change our color scheme. Change the `body` style rule to match the following:

```
body
{
  background-color: #f0f1f6;
  font-size: 8pt;
  font-family: Tahoma, Verdana, 'Times New Roman';
}
```

3. Then, add the following element to the `<head>` section of the `News.aspx` page:

```
<link href="Style/iestyle.css" rel="stylesheet" type="text/css">
```

4. Set the `CssClass` property of the label that reads **Selected Date:** to `Normal`. Set the `class` property of the **Welcome...** message to `Normal`, too.

5. Set the `CssClass` property of the drop-down list control to `TextBox`, and run the project.

How It Works

Just as HTML controls have the `class` attribute, web server controls have a `CssClass` attribute, and it has exactly the same effect – CSS styles work the same way for both types of control. Once the styles have been applied, our application looks like this:

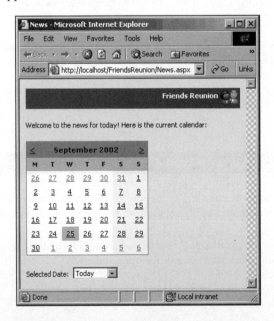

Handling Events

Handling events for web server controls is, in some ways, similar to the process for HTML controls but is *very different* from Visual Basic .NET's method. For web server controls, the property browser adds an Events icon at the top of the window, allowing us to see the events associated with a control, and to assign new ones:

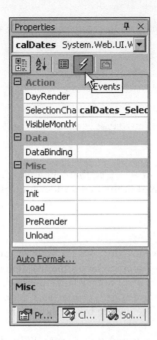

To associate a new handler, we just have to double-click the event. To associate it with an existing handler, we code it manually in the code-behind file, which we can select from the drop-down list. Note that the methods shown in the list are those that match the signature of the selected event.

Try It Out – Handling Events for Web Server Controls

To extend our example, we'll use some server-side event handling to make the link between the calendar and the dropdown control, and to report the currently selected date to the user. We'll arrange for selections in the dropdown to change the selected date in the calendar, and for any selection change to result in the 'current' date being displayed in a label control:

1. Add a new Label control at the bottom of the News.aspx file. Set its ID to lblMessage, and its CssClass to Normal. Clear its Text property.

2. Set the cbDay drop-down control's AutoPostBack property to True; then double-click on the control and add the following code to the handler:

```
private void cbDay_SelectedIndexChanged(
    object sender, System.EventArgs e)
{
    calDates.SelectedDate =
        DateTime.Now.AddDays(Convert.ToDouble(cbDay.SelectedItem.Value));
    lblMessage.Text =
        "Current Date: " + calDates.SelectedDate.ToLongDateString();
}
```

3. Double-click the calendar control to create the `SelectionChanged` handler, and add the following code:

```
private void calDates_SelectionChanged(
   object sender, System.EventArgs e)
{
   lblMessage.Text =
      "Current Date: " + calDates.SelectedDate.ToLongDateString();
}
```

4. The `News.aspx` page is now set up so that when we select an option from the drop-down list, the relevant day is highlighted in the `Calendar` control. Let's run the project in the usual way to see this in action.

How It Works

In the handler for the drop-down, we use the `SelectedItem` property to retrieve the drop-down box value (either 0, 1, or -1, as defined when we set up the list items earlier). We convert the value it contains to a double using the `Convert.ToDouble()` method, and then add this value to the current date before setting that as the `SelectedDate` property of the calendar. This will fire the calendar's `SelectionChanged` event, which we handle by displaying the new date in the `lblMessage` label.

To ensure that the event fires as soon as a change occurs in the drop-down list, we have to set the `AutoPostBack` property to `True`. This is an important step, because unlike the button and the calendar, drop-down lists don't cause a postback by default. Here is the typical output of our page as it now stands:

What stage have we reached? We now know that web server controls offer several features above and beyond those of the HTML controls that can make our time more productive. Their consistent object model is also beneficial, since once we've learned the set of properties that are available for one control, the chances are that we will see them again in others.

The events available for web controls are different from the HTML events that we can use in the attribute list of an HTML tag – there's no `onclick`, `onmouseover`, `onkeydown`, and the like. This is because web control events are exposed on the server, and so comprise only those appropriate for server-side processing. Imagine what would happen if our page caused a postback for every single mouse move operation! Even the `Click` event, which roughly corresponds to HTML's `onclick` event, is only available for those controls (such as buttons) where it makes sense.

For a complete description of all of the web server controls, and the events that each can fire, check out the information on MSDN.

Validation Controls

When you're creating a web form, especially one in which you hope to collect some data from your users, you'll often come across situations in which you need to place constraints on exactly what data they can submit. For example, you might want to mandate that a particular field must always be completed (say, a user name), or must adhere to a particular format (say, a social security number). In the past, this validation process had to be done manually, but ASP.NET comes with a set of **validation controls** that perform this task automatically.

Technically speaking, the validation controls are a subset of the web server controls, but there are enough new things to say about them that they deserve a section of their own here. Usually, they take the form of fields that are invisible most of the time, but become visible when a validation error occurs.

There are a number of validation controls available, and their names are almost self-explanatory:

- ❑ `RequiredFieldValidator`
- ❑ `CompareValidator`
- ❑ `RegularExpressionValidator`
- ❑ `RangeValidator`
- ❑ `CustomValidator`

In the examples to come, you'll see the first three of these in use; `RangeValidator` doesn't apply to our example (but it's not complicated to understand), while `CustomValidator` is only used to create our own validation controls.

The ASP.NET validation controls are capable of performing validation on the server and (for IE5+ browsers) on the client as well, via JavaScript. To force validation to take place, we can either call the `Page.Validate()` method, or call the `Validate()` method of every validation control on the page, which has the same effect. Each validation control has an `IsValid` property that indicates whether the data of its control is currently valid. There is a similar property at the page level that indicates whether all the validation controls on the page are in a valid state.

Try It Out – Building a New User Form

In this example, we'll build a form for capturing the details of a new user, and employ the validation controls to ensure that we receive valid information in certain fields.

1. Create a new web form in the `Secure` folder, named `NewUser.aspx`.

2. In the HTML view, add the `<link>` element to the `<head>` section, which associates the `iestyle.css` stylesheet with this page:

```
<link href="../Style/iestyle.css" type="text/css" rel="stylesheet">
```

3. Back in the Design view, place the cursor at the top left of the page, type Fill in the fields below to register as a Friends Reunion member:, and hit *Return* when you're done.

4. Drop an HTML Table control onto the page, and give it ten rows with two columns each. Set the table's ID to `tbLogin`, its `cellspacing` and `cellpadding` properties to 2, and the `colspan` property of the last row to 2. Delete the right-most cell in this row, and finally set the `border` property for the table to 0.

5. Enter text into the cells to mimic the screenshot below and add nine textbox web server controls to the right-hand column, setting their `CssClass` property to `TextBox`:

The simplest way of doing this is to place the first textbox, set its `CssClass` property, and then copy-and-paste it into the other locations.

6. At this stage, we will also modify our `iestyle.css` style sheet slightly, more specifically, the `TextBox` element. Add an extra line as follows to make the width of the textboxes larger:

```
.TextBox
{
  border-right: #c7ccdc 1px solid;
  border-top: #c7ccdc 1px solid;
  border-left: #c7ccdc 1px solid;
  border-bottom: #c7ccdc 1px solid;
  font-size: 8pt;
  font-family: Tahoma, Verdana, 'Times New Roman';
  width: 200px;
}
```

7. The last row contains a centered button control with an ID of btnAccept, a Text property of Accept, and a CssClass of Button.

8. Give the textboxes the following IDs, in the order they are displayed: txtLogin, txtPwd, txtFName, txtLName, txtAddress, txtPhone, txtMobile, txtEmail, and txtBirth. Set the TextMode property of the txtPwd textbox to Password.

9. To narrow the **Birth Date** field, which doesn't need to be as wide as in the screenshot above, add the following style rule to the stylesheet, and set txtBirth's CssClass property to SmallTextBox:

```
.SmallTextBox
{
  border-right: #c7ccdc 1px solid;
  border-top: #c7ccdc 1px solid;
  font-size: 8pt;
  border-left: #c7ccdc 1px solid;
  border-bottom: #c7ccdc 1px solid;
  font-family: Tahoma, Verdana, 'Times New Roman';
  width: 70px;
}
```

10. Drop a RequiredFieldValidator control next to the txtLogin textbox, and set its properties as in the following table. In the **Properties** window, the ControlToValidate property is set by means of a drop-down list that contains the names of all the web server controls on the form.

Property	Value
ID	reqLogin
ControlToValidate	txtLogin
Display	None
ErrorMessage	A user name is required!

11. Copy this `RequiredFieldValidator`, and paste it next to the `txtPwd` textbox. Set its properties as shown:

Property	Value
ID	reqPwd
ControlToValidate	txtPwd
ErrorMessage	A password is required!

12. Carry on and paste one of these validation controls next to the `txtFName`, `txtLName`, `txtPhone`, and `txtEmail` textboxes. For each, change the ID, `ErrorMessage`, and `ControlToValidate` properties as appropriate, making particularly sure that the latter refers to the correct textbox.

13. Drop a `CompareValidator` control next to the `txtBirth` textbox, and give it these properties:

Property	Value
ID	compBirth
ControlToValidate	txtBirth
Display	Dynamic
ErrorMessage	Enter a valid birth date!
Operator	DataTypeCheck
Type	Date

14. Drop a `RegularExpressionValidator` next to the `RequiredFieldValidator` for `txtPhone` (there is no problem with using these controls in tandem), and set these properties:

Property	Value
ID	regPhone
ControlToValidate	txtPhone
Display	None
ErrorMessage	Enter a valid US phone number!
ValidationExpression	U. S. Phone Number (Click the ellipsis!)

15. Drop another `RegularExpressionValidator` next to the `RequiredFieldValidator` for `txtEmail`, and set these properties:

Property	Value
ID	regEmail
ControlToValidate	txtEmail
Display	None
ErrorMessage	Enter a valid e-mail address!
ValidationExpression	Internet E-mail Address (Click the ellipsis!)

16. Drop a Label below the table, set its ID to lblMessage and clear its Text property. Set its CssClass property to Normal.

17. Drop a ValidationSummary control below this label, set its ID to valErrors and its CssClass to Normal. The form should now look something like this:

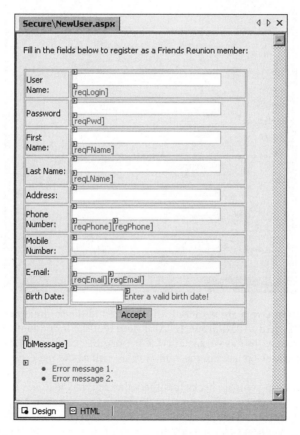

The validation controls on our NewUser.aspx form are now set up and ready to go.

How It Works

By setting the `Display` properties of the `RequiredFieldValidator` controls to `None`, we suppress any errors they produce from appearing in the control. Instead, we'll use the `ValidationSummary` control to display errors on the page. (Had we set `Display` to `Dynamic` or `Static`, any error messages would have appeared next to the field in question.) Since the **Address** and **Mobile Number** fields are optional, we didn't use any validation controls for those.

If you now compile and run the application with `NewUser.aspx` set as the start page, and submit the page after entering an invalid birth date *and nothing more*, you'll see this screen in your browser:

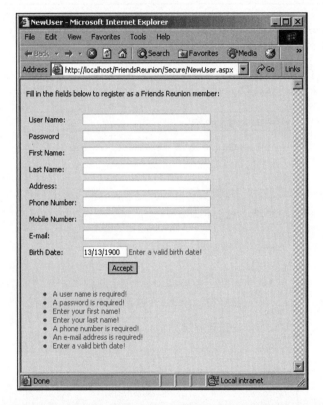

Notice how the validation errors are automatically collated in the summary control, whose format we can alter through its `DisplayMode` property. Also note that the individual validation controls don't display their error messages, just as we specified. For `compBirth`, whose `Display` property we set to `Dynamic`, the error message appears in the summary as well as the page.

The `compBirth` validation control checks that the value entered matches a `Date` data type (as a result of setting `Operator` to `DataTypeCheck` and `Type` to `Date`). When a `CompareValidator` is configured to perform this sort of check, the `ControlToCompare` and `ValueToCompare` properties are ignored. In other circumstances, we might use these properties to validate the field against another control's value, or against a constant value.

The `RegularExpressionValidator` controls for `txtEmail` and `txtPhone` contain a somewhat complicated string in the `ValidationExpression` property that we were able to set with the aid of the Visual Studio .NET IDE. As usual, it's quite possible to enter your own strings here, should you need to do so.

> *Regular expression syntax is a fairly advanced topic in its own right. You can find out more about it in* Professional JavaScript 2nd Edition *(Wrox, ISBN 1-86100-553-9), as regular expressions have been available in JavaScript since its early days. If you're a subscriber to ASPToday, there a number of articles related to it:*
>
> *Regular Expressions in Microsoft .NET*
> *http://www.asptoday.com/content/articles/20010309.asp*
>
> *Validating user input with the .NET RegularExpressionValidator*
> *http://www.asptoday.com/content/articles/20020528.asp*
>
> *String Manipulation and Pattern Testing with Regular Expressions*
> *http://www.asptoday.com/content/articles/19990505.asp*

To finish off this form for the time being, let's now handle the **Accept** button's `Click` event, and populate the message label with a string indicating the current status of the page. Double-click the button in the designer, and add the following code:

```
private void btnAccept_Click(object sender, System.EventArgs e)
{
   if (Page.IsValid)
     lblMessage.Text = "Validation succeeded!";
   else
     lblMessage.Text = "Fix the following errors and retry:";
}
```

This most recent addition demonstrates a subtle difference between handling validation with client-side JavaScript code, and causing a postback when the **Accept** button is clicked. Even if there are errors, the second message will never appear in IE4+ browsers, since validation occurs on the client side, thus preventing the user from submitting invalid values. The postback will not occur until all fields contain valid data. Under Netscape/Mozilla, however, you will see the second message while invalid data remains.

User Controls

In our *Friends Reunion* application, it would be good to have a common header and footer for every page, a common navigation bar, and so on. ASP.NET provides a straightforward reusability model for the page features that we create, in the form of the **user controls**. We create these controls in pretty much the same way as we create web forms, but they're saved with the special `.ascx` extension.

A user control doesn't contain the tags that usually start off a page, such as `<html>`, `<head>`, `<body>`, and so on. Also, instead of ASP.NET `<%@ Page %>` directives, it uses `<%@ Control %>` directives to customize certain features of the control. Without further ado, let's build ourselves an example, so that we can see what's going on.

Try It Out – Building a Header Control

To begin our experiments, let's build a header control that we can put to use on every single page in the *Friends Reunion* site. We'll make it look a little like the blue banner that currently sits at the top of the news page.

1. Create a new folder called `Controls`, right-click on it, and choose **Add | Add Web User Control** from the context menu. Call the new file `FriendsHeader.ascx`.

2. Drop a `Panel` web server control onto the page, and give it the following properties:

Property	Value
ID	pnlHeaderGlobal
CssClass	HeaderFriends

3. Set the text inside the panel to **Friends Reunion**.

4. Drop an image web server control inside the panel, to the right of the text, and set the following properties:

Property	Value
ID	imgFriends
CssClass	HeaderImage
ImageUrl	../Images/friends.gif

5. Drop another `Panel` web control next to the previous one. Clear the text inside it, and set the following properties:

Property	Value
ID	pnlHeaderLocal
CssClass	HeaderTitle

6. Drop an `Image` web server control inside this panel, and set the following properties:

Property	Value
ID	imgIcon
CssClass	HeaderImage
ImageUrl	../Images/homeconnected.gif

7. Drop a `Label` web control inside the same panel, to the right of the image, and set these properties:

Property	Value
ID	lblWelcome
Text	Welcome!

8. Save the control, which should now look like the following:

Just out of interest, switch to the **HTML** view to see how our control has been created. Notice the absence of any 'normal' HTML elements around the ASP.NET elements:

```
<%@ Control language="c#" AutoEventWireup="false"
          Codebehind="FriendsHeader.ascx.cs"
          Inherits="FriendsReunion.Controls.FriendsHeader"
          TargetSchema="http://schemas.microsoft.com/intellisense/ie5" %>
<asp:panel id="pnlHeaderGlobal" runat="server" CssClass="HeaderFriends">
   Friends Reunion
   <asp:image id="imgFriends" runat="server" CssClass="HeaderImage"
          ImageUrl="../Images/friends.gif"></asp:image>
</asp:Panel>
<asp:panel id="pnlHeaderLocal" runat="server" CssClass="HeaderTitle">
   <asp:image id="imgIcon" CssClass="HeaderImage" runat="server"
          ImageUrl="../Images/homeconnected.gif"></asp:image>
   <asp:label id="lblWelcome" runat="server">Welcome!</asp:label>
</asp:panel>
```

9. As you will have noticed, we've used some CSS styles that haven't yet been defined: `HeaderFriends`, `HeaderImage`, and `HeaderTitle`. Let's add those to the `iestyle.css` stylesheet now:

```
.HeaderFriends
{
   padding-right: 5px;
   padding-left: 5px;
   font-weight: bold;
   font-size: 8pt;
```

```
    font-family: Tahoma, Verdana, 'Times New Roman';
    width: 100%;
    color: white;
    background-color: #336699;
    text-align: right;
}
.HeaderImage
{
    vertical-align: middle;
}
.HeaderTitle
{
    padding-right: 5px;
    padding-left: 5px;
    padding-right: 10px;
    font-weight: bold;
    font-size: 8pt;
    font-family: Tahoma, Verdana, 'Times New Roman';
    width: 100%;
    color: white;
    background-color: #336699;
}
```

10. Open the `NewUser.aspx` form, and drag the `FriendsHeader.ascx` file from the Solution Explorer onto it, placing it just before the first line of text on the page. Add a new paragraph after the newly added control by pressing *Return*:

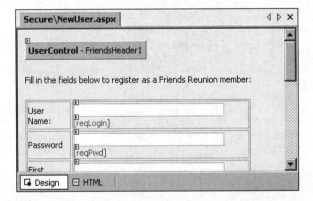

11. Save, compile, and run the application, and see what you get.

How It Works

The process of designing a new user control is just like creating a complete page – we drop controls and set their properties exactly as we have before. Apart from the lack of page-level elements, the HTML looks just like the code for a regular web form. Once created, we can place the control just as if it was a control from the toolbox. At that moment, the control is registered with the page with the `Register` directive, and the following lines are added to the page's HTML code:

```
<%@ Register TagPrefix="uc1" TagName="FriendsHeader"
             Src="../Controls/FriendsHeader.ascx" %>
    ...
<body>
   <form id="NewUser" method="post" runat="server">
     <P><uc1:FriendsHeader id="FriendsHeader1" runat="server">
       </uc1:FriendsHeader></P>
     ...
```

The `Register` directive at the top of the page tells ASP.NET where to locate and load the appropriate user control, from the URL specified in the `Src` attribute. It also associates the control with a prefix that's used when we define control instances, which we can change if we want to. When we open the `NewUser.aspx` page, we now get something like this:

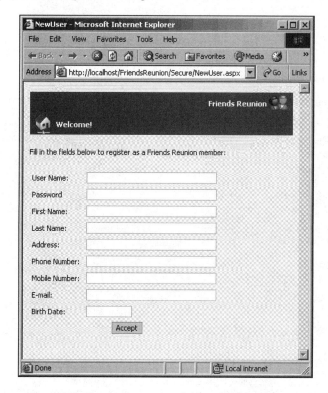

As long as you use server controls for the images in the header (in other words, don't use an HTML `Image` element without the `runat="server"` attribute), the relative paths will be properly resolved, no matter what the location of the page using the control.

Just dropping this control onto every page of our site will help to provide it with a consistent look and feel, building on the work we've already done with our stylesheets. However, always having the same icon and message on the left isn't ideal, so in a moment we'll see how to customize it for the current page. First, though, we'll deal with a problem that you may have noticed a couple of pages ago.

103

Side Note: Don't Believe Everything that IntelliSense Tells You

Be wary of getting too used to IntelliSense – if you do, you may find that you're missing out on something: there are some situations where IntelliSense is incomplete! If that sounds intriguing, read on; if not, wait for us at the start of the next *Try It Out* section – we'll be with you in just a moment.

Put simply, IntelliSense fails to offer some of the options that should be open to you when you're creating a CSS stylesheet. However, if you choose a legal value for a style that isn't recognized by IntelliSense, Internet Explorer *will* still render it as expected. The clearest example of this is the `vertical-align` property, which prompts the following response from IntelliSense:

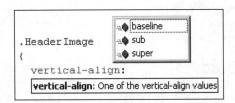

Exactly the same set of options (albeit with different names) appears in the Build Style wizard:

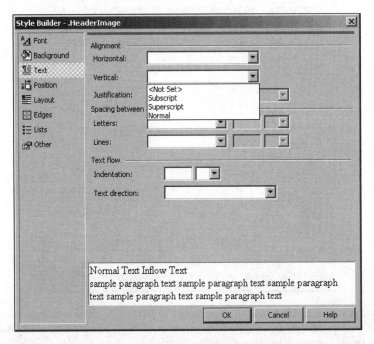

When we defined the `HeaderImage` CSS style rule, we used a `vertical-align` value of `middle`, and Visual Studio .NET complained about it. However, if we look at W3C's CSS1 Recommendation, the legal values are given as `baseline | sub | super | top | text-top | middle | bottom | text-bottom | `*`<percentage>`*. CSS2, a W3C Recommendation since May 12, 1998, adds "*`<length>`*` | inherit`" to the values defined by CSS1. (You can find these documents at http://www.w3.org/Style/CSS.)

Let's see what happens when we change this value in the `HeaderImage` style rule, and how it affects the alignment of the icon with the text next to it. As the value is set in a stylesheet, we can change it there, save the stylesheet, and see the effect by refreshing the page in Internet Explorer, without having to recompile:

Value	Effect
`vertical-align="baseline"`	
`vertical-align="sub"`	
`vertical-align="super"`	
`vertical-align="middle"`	
`vertical-align="text-top"`	

As you can see, even when we use values that IntelliSense doesn't recognize, and which are marked in the editor as being invalid for that CSS property, Internet Explorer renders affected items correctly. In this author's opinion, the last two are far better than the first three! So, we'll use `middle` from now onwards.

If the values are indeed legitimate, and Internet Explorer is happy to deal with them, surely there must be a way to convince IntelliSense that they're OK? In fact there is and the answer lies in an XML file called `cssmetadata.xml`, which (for default installations) you'll find in the folder at C:\Program Files\Microsoft Visual Studio .NET\Common7\Packages\1033.

The element we are concerned with can be found in the `Text Properties` section of this XML file and, by default, looks like this:

```
<cssmd:property-def id="vertical-align" type="enum"
        description="The vertical alignment of an element's text"
        syntax="One of the vertical-align values"
        enum="baseline sub super"/>
```

This element contains what we're looking for: you can see the values that Visual Studio .NET will 'accept' for the `vertical-align` property listed in the `enum` attribute. To 'fix' IntelliSense, we just have to add the other valid values as follows:

```
<cssmd:property-def id="vertical-align" type="enum-length"
        description="The vertical alignment of an element's text"
        syntax="One of the vertical-align values or a custom unit"
        enum="baseline sub super top text-top
                middle bottom text-bottom inherit"/>
```

We've also changed the `type` attribute in order to allow lengths to be assigned, and the `syntax` attribute to update the tool-tip help. Here's the 'new' IntelliSense:

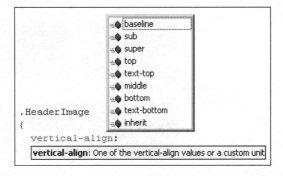

Unfortunately, the **Build Style** wizard won't reflect these new values, but at least we've stopped the IDE complaining about them!

Try It Out – Adding Properties to User Controls

Returning to our *Friends Reunion* sample application, we were talking (before our little diversion) about providing the ability for our user control to be customized for different pages. The technique for doing this is to define some properties for it that we can set when the control is instantiated. In this example, we'll make it possible to set the image and the message on the left-hand side of our user control banner.

1. Open the code-behind for the user control (right-click it and select **View Code**), and add the following code to it:

```
public abstract class FriendsHeader : System.Web.UI.UserControl
{
    protected System.Web.UI.WebControls.Panel pnlHeaderGlobal;
    protected System.Web.UI.WebControls.Image imgFriends;
```

```
protected System.Web.UI.WebControls.Panel pnlHeaderLocal;
protected System.Web.UI.WebControls.Image imgIcon;
protected System.Web.UI.WebControls.Label lblWelcome;

private void Page_Load(object sender, System.EventArgs e)
{
  // Put user code to initialize the page here
}

[ Web Designer generated code ]
```

```
private String _message = String.Empty;
private String _imageurl = String.Empty;

// Accessor method for the Message property
public string Message
{
  get { return _message; }
  set { _message = value; }
}

// Accessor method for the IconImageUrl property
public string IconImageUrl
{
  get { return _imageurl; }
  set {_imageurl = value; }
}

// Populate the controls with the property values
protected override void Render(System.Web.UI.HtmlTextWriter writer)
{
  if (Message != String.Empty)
    this.lblWelcome.Text = _message;
  if (IconImageUrl != String.Empty)
    this.imgIcon.ImageUrl = _imageurl;
  base.Render(writer);
}
```
```
}
```

2. Open the `News.aspx` page, and delete the panel and image we added previously as a header. Drop the new user control in its place, inserting a new paragraph after it as before.

3. Switch to the HTML view and find the line containing the control's declaration:

```
<uc1:friendsheader id="FriendsHeader1" runat="server"></uc1:friendsheader>
```

Add a `Message` attribute to it, like so:

```
<uc1:friendsheader id="FriendsHeader1" runat="server"
          Message="Welcome to the news page!"></uc1:friendsheader>
```

4. Open the `NewUser.aspx` page in HTML mode, and change the control's declaration to include both a `Message` attribute and an `IconImageUrl` attribute:

```
<uc1:friendsheader id="FriendsHeader1" runat="server"
        Message="Registration form"
        IconImageUrl="../Images/securekeys.gif"></uc1:friendsheader>
```

5. Save, compile, and run the page to see how our changes have affected the output displayed in your browser.

How It Works

We can add properties to a user control, just as we can add them to any other custom class. In this example, we've implemented two properties that control the message and the icon of the second panel through a couple of private member variables:

```
private String _message = String.Empty;
private String _imageurl = String.Empty;
```

We initialize the variables to empty strings in order to allow us to determine whether values have been supplied. In the `Render()` override, we only change the default image and message if we have non-empty values for the properties. (This handler is called just before the HTML code is sent to the client.) When we now open the `NewUser.aspx` page, we see something like this:

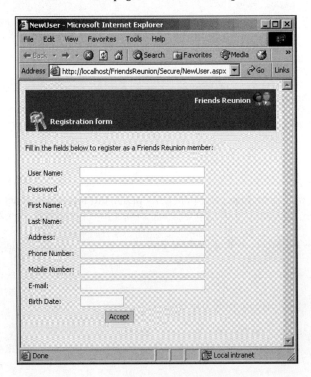

To complement the header we just created, we can build a footer called `FriendsFooter.ascx` by creating another user control with the following code:

```
<%@ Control Language="c#" AutoEventWireup="false"
           Codebehind="FriendsFooter.ascx.cs"
           Inherits="FriendsReunion.Controls.FriendsFooter"
           TargetSchema="http://schemas.microsoft.com/intellisense/ie5" %>
<asp:panel id="pnlFooterGlobal" CssClass="FooterFriends" runat="server">
  Friends Reunion Application -  Courtesy of Wrox Press <br>
  <b>Beginning C# Web Applications with Visual Studio .NET</b>
</asp:panel>
```

The style it uses is defined in our CSS stylesheet like this:

```
.FooterFriends
{
  font-size: 8pt;
  font-family: Tahoma, Verdana, 'Times New Roman';
  width: 100%;
  color: white;
  background-color: #336699;
  text-align: center;
}
```

Whenever we make changes to the user controls, the whole site will be instantly updated. Couple this with our extensive use of stylesheets, and we can completely renew the web application's appearance in a snap!

Now you can go back to each of the pages we have created so far in our *Friends Reunion* application and add the new header and foot controls to each one. Here's what the `Login.aspx` page will look like after we have added our user controls for the header and footer:

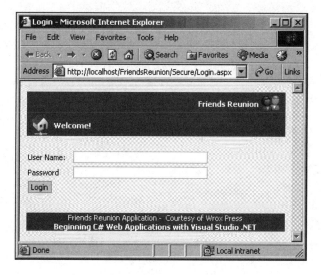

Custom Controls

Most of the built-in ASP.NET server controls offer great features, but the ASP.NET object model also allows us – and even encourages us – to extend them through **inheritance**. A control such as this that extends base functionality is called a **custom control**.

When creating a custom control, the particular base class we choose to inherit from will depend on the situation we face. We could inherit from the `TextBox` control if we wish to incorporate some custom processing into its behavior, or we might inherit from the top-level `WebControl` base class to provide customized UI rendering.

In this section, we'll start by looking at some simple custom controls, and increase their complexity by incorporating more advanced features. Our aim here is really just to raise your awareness of custom controls, which can be an invaluable addition to the ASP.NET web designer's toolbox. For a comprehensive study of this important feature, take a look at *Professional ASP.NET Server Controls – Building Custom Controls with C#* (Wrox, ISBN 1-86100-564-4).

Try It Out – Building the SubHeader Custom Control

In this example, we're going to create a simple custom control that displays a sub-header beneath our page header control, containing today's date and a link to the registration page.

1. Right-click the project name, and select Add | Add Class.... Give the new class the name `SubHeader.cs`.

2. Add the following code to the code-behind file:

```
using System;
using System.IO;
using System.Web.UI;
using System.Web.UI.WebControls;

namespace FriendsReunion
{
  public class SubHeader : WebControl
  {
    // The URL to navigate to if the user is not registered
    private string _register = string.Empty;

    public SubHeader()
    {
      // Initialize default values
      this.Width = new Unit(100, UnitType.Percentage);
      this.CssClass = "SubHeader";
    }

    // Property to allow the user to define the URL for the
    // registration page
    public string RegisterUrl
```

```
  {
    get { return _register; }
    set { _register = value; }
  }

  // This method is called when the control is being built
  protected override void CreateChildControls()
  {
    // Clear any previously loaded controls
    this.Controls.Clear();
    Label lbl;

    // If the user is authenticated, we will render their name
    if (Context.User.Identity.IsAuthenticated)
    {
      lbl = new Label();
      lbl.Text = Context.User.Identity.Name;

      // Add the newly created label to our collection of child controls
      this.Controls.Add(lbl);
    }
    else
    {
      // Otherwise, we will render a link to the registration page
      HyperLink reg = new HyperLink();
      reg.Text = "Register";

      // If a URL isn't provided, use a default URL to the
      // registration page
      if (_register == string.Empty)
      {
        reg.NavigateUrl = Context.Request.ApplicationPath +
          Path.AltDirectorySeparatorChar + "Secure" +
          Path.AltDirectorySeparatorChar + "NewUser.aspx";
      }
      else
      {
        reg.NavigateUrl = _register;
      }

      // Add the newly created link to our collection of child controls
      this.Controls.Add(reg);
    }

    // Add a couple of blank spaces and a separator character
    this.Controls.Add(new LiteralControl(" - "));

    // Add a label with the current data
    lbl = new Label();
    lbl.Text = DateTime.Now.ToLongDateString();
    this.Controls.Add(lbl);
  }
}
}
```

3. Add the following style to the `iestyle.css` stylesheet:

```
.SubHeader
{
  border-top: 3px groove;
  font-size: 8pt;
  color: white;
  font-family: Tahoma, Verdana, 'Times New Roman';
  background-color: #4f82b5;
  text-align: right;
}
```

4. Open the `News.aspx` page in HTML view, and add the following directive at the top of the page, which will allow us to use our new custom control:

```
<%@ Register TagPrefix="wx"
            Namespace="FriendsReunion" Assembly="FriendsReunion" %>
```

5. Right below the user control we used, add the following line:

```
<wx:subheader id="SubHeader1" runat="server" />
```

6. Set `News.aspx` as the start page, run the project, and sit back and admire your handiwork!

How It Works

Our new custom control derives from the `WebControl` base class, just like the intrinsic ASP.NET web controls. The base class provides properties for setting the control's layout, such as its `Width`, its `CssClass`, and so on, which we set at construction time. We've added a property to hold a URL, in rather similar fashion to what we did for our user control:

```
// The URL to navigate to in case if is not registered
private string _register = string.Empty;

public SubHeader()
{
  // Initialize default values
  this.Width = new Unit(100, UnitType.Percentage);
  this.CssClass = "SubHeader";
}

// Property to allow the user to define the URL for the
// registration page
public string RegisterUrl
{
  get { return _register; }
  set { _register = value; }
}
```

The main difference is the way that the control's interface is built. For our user control, we just dropped controls onto the design surface, as we would have done for a web form. For the custom control, a special method named `CreateChildControls()` is called whenever ASP.NET needs to rebuild our control ready for display. Inside this method, we create the control hierarchy – that is, we specify the controls that make up our custom control by using the special `this.Controls` collection. (This property comes from the `Control` base class, so any server control can be a container for any other control(s) in this model.) We have to create and configure the new controls programmatically before they are appended to that collection:

```
    // If the user is authenticated, we will render their name
    if (Context.User.Identity.IsAuthenticated)
    {
      lbl = new Label();
      lbl.Text = Context.User.Identity.Name;

      // Add the newly created label to our collection of child controls
      this.Controls.Add(lbl);
    }
    else
    {
      // Otherwise, we will render a link to the registration page
      HyperLink reg = new HyperLink();
      reg.Text = "Register";

      // If a URL isn't provided, use a default URL to the
      // registration page
      if (_register == string.Empty)
      {
        reg.NavigateUrl = Context.Request.ApplicationPath +
          Path.AltDirectorySeparatorChar + "Secure" +
          Path.AltDirectorySeparatorChar + "NewUser.aspx";
      }
      else
      {
        reg.NavigateUrl = _register;
      }

      // Add the newly created link to our collection of child controls
      this.Controls.Add(reg);
    }

    // Add a couple of blank spaces and a separator character
    this.Controls.Add(new LiteralControl(" - "));

    // Add a label with the current data
    lbl = new Label();
    lbl.Text = DateTime.Now.ToLongDateString();
    this.Controls.Add(lbl);
  }
```

Also of note here is that we have used the `Context.User.Identity.IsAuthenticated` property to display the **Register** link selectively. As you'll see in Chapter 10, this property identifies an authenticated user, according to the authentication method selected. If the user is authenticated, the `Identity.Name` property will contain their user name.

When you open the `News.aspx` page, you should see something like the following:

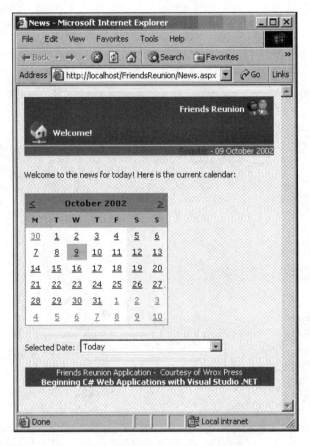

We'll learn more about security settings in Chapter 10, but for now, follow these simple steps to simulate an authenticated user:

❑   Open the IIS administration console (Start | Settings | Control Panel | Administrative Tools | Internet Services Manager). In the Default Web Site node under your server name, right-click the FriendsReunion application, and select Properties. Select the Directory Security tab, and click the Edit button in the Anonymous access and authentication control section.

❑   Uncheck Anonymous Access, and check Integrated Windows authentication and Basic authentication:

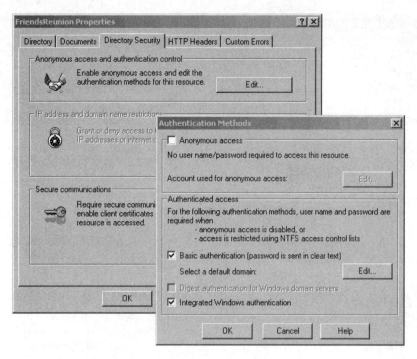

Now, we can switch from an 'authenticated' user to an 'unauthenticated' user just by changing the following setting in the application's `Web.config` file:

```
<authentication mode="Windows" />
```

or:

```
<authentication mode="None" />
```

The first, which is the default, will make the currently logged-in Windows user's name visible:

The second of these will result in the usual **Register** link being shown in the sub-header.

At run time, there's not much difference between this control and the user control we created for the header, but the custom control stands out at design time. With the `News.aspx` page in design view, we can immediately see the difference:

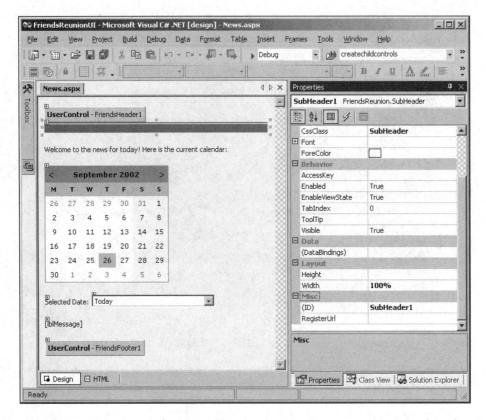

Unlike the user control, which isn't even rendered at design time, our custom control renders itself on screen, and provides the complete set of visual properties available for all web server controls through the Properties window. Toward the bottom of that window, we can see the RegisterUrl property that we added. This is far more intuitive than the user control approach, at the cost of just a little extra effort on the part of the control's developer.

Dynamic Content

For our next trick, we'll take a look at a subject that will become increasingly important when we look at database access in the next two chapters, dynamic content. Simply put, a dynamic application is one that's capable of altering its content or appearance at run time, depending on the identity of the user viewing the page, or the nature of some information from a database, or some other indeterminate condition. In fact, we've already seen one form of dynamic content on our news page, where we displayed either the user name or a link to the registration page, depending on whether the current user was already authenticated.

The way we achieved our dynamism was to use the custom control's Controls property to add new controls to the hierarchy. We know that this property comes from the base Control class, and as such is available to all web server controls. Perhaps surprisingly, the Page itself *also* derives from this class, and handles the controls it contains in precisely the same manner. The hierarchy is as follows:

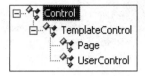

Another way to achieve dynamic content is by manipulating the Visible properties of the controls on the page – if we set a web server control's Visible property to False, it won't even be sent to the client browser, so it certainly won't be displayed! It's then easy to flip the property to True from code, with the result that controls can be displayed selectively according to certain conditions.

Try It Out – Dynamically Building Navigation Controls

As a further example of dynamic content, we will now create the Default.aspx entry page for our site. This will be the page that all users visit after they've logged in, and the links it offers will vary according to who they are. In it, we'll use a PlaceHolder control to define the location of the controls we add to the page programmatically.

1. Add a new web form to the project's root directory, and call it Default.aspx.

2. Drop the FriendsHeader.ascx and FriendsFooter.ascx controls onto it. Set their IDs to ucHeader and ucFooter.

3. Add the SubHeader custom control by switching to HTML view, and adding a Register directive and a <wx:subheader> element, just as we did for the News.aspx page. This time, set its ID to ccSubHeader.

```
<%@ Register TagPrefix="wx"
            Namespace="FriendsReunion" Assembly="FriendsReunion" %>
    . . .
        <wx:subheader id="ccSubHeader" runat="server" /></P>
```

4. While in HTML view, add a <link> element for the iestyles.css stylesheet.

5. Below the headers, type a description for the page, such as, Welcome to the Friends Reunion web site – the meeting place for lost friends! Set its class property to Normal, and start a new paragraph after it.

6. Drop a PlaceHolder web control, and set its ID to phNav. This marks the location on the page where all of the controls we add will be placed.

7. Open the code-behind file, and delete the following line at the top of the code:

```
using System.Drawing;
```

We do this because both the System.Drawing and System.Web.UI.WebControl namespaces contain an Image class, so the compiler doesn't know which one to use. Hence, we delete the using line that we don't need. Alternatively, we could have used the fully qualified name for the Image class that we want to use.

8. Add the following code to the Page_Load() method:

```
private void Page_Load(object sender, System.EventArgs e)
{
    Table tb = new Table();
    TableRow row;
    TableCell cell;
    Image img;
    HyperLink lnk;

    if (Context.User.Identity.IsAuthenticated)
    {
        // Create a new blank table row
        row = new TableRow();

        // Set up the News image
        img = new Image();
        img.ImageUrl = "Images/winbook.gif";
        img.ImageAlign = ImageAlign.Middle;
        img.Width = new Unit(24, UnitType.Pixel);
        img.Height = new Unit(24, UnitType.Pixel);

        // Create a cell and add the image
        cell = new TableCell();
        cell.Controls.Add(img);

        // Add the new cell to the row
        row.Cells.Add(cell);

        // Set up the News link
        lnk = new HyperLink();
        lnk.Text = "News";
        lnk.NavigateUrl = "News.aspx";

        // Create the cell and add the link
        cell = new TableCell();
        cell.Controls.Add(lnk);

        // Add the new cell to the row
        row.Cells.Add(cell);

        // Add the row to the table
        tb.Rows.Add(row);
    }
    else
    {
        // Code for unauthenticated users here...
    }
```

```
        // Finally, add the table to the placeholder
        phNav.Controls.Add(tb);
    }
```

9. Set `Default.aspx` as the start page, and save and run the application. Turn **Anonymous access** in IIS on and off to see how the results differ, just as before:

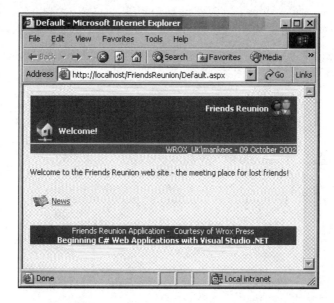

How It Works

The special `PlaceHolder` control has been designed with dynamic control loading in mind: it forms an invisible container for controls that we insert later, and positions them correctly in the hierarchy that's defined by the `Page.Controls` collection. The `PlaceHolder` doesn't render HTML to the client itself; it's only useful for this sort of scenario.

The `Page_Load()` event handler instantiates a new `Table` web control that will hold the links we add. When we finish the process of adding links, we add the table to the placeholder control. If we need to, we can add as many controls to the placeholder as we need – it's not limited to just one.

Avoiding Code Duplication

At this point, we've developed a set of controls that will help us to create a consistent look and feel for the application. At the moment though, we have to add the user controls and the custom control to every new page manually. We can avoid this tedious task with a custom base page that can load user and custom controls dynamically.

Try It Out – Building a Custom Base Page

Our technique for this final example will be to create a new class that inherits from and builds upon the `System.Web.UI.Page` class. Once we've set it up with the header and footer controls we want to use, we'll inherit from the new class in all of our web forms, providing them with that functionality by default.

1. Add a new class named `FriendsBase.cs` to the project, and add the following `using` statements at the top:

```
using System;
using System.IO;
using System.Web.UI;
using FriendsReunion.Controls;
```

2. Now add the following code to the rest of the class:

```
public class FriendsBase : System.Web.UI.Page
{
    protected string HeaderMessage = String.Empty;
    protected string HeaderIconImageUrl = String.Empty;

    protected override void Render(System.Web.UI.HtmlTextWriter writer)
    {
      // Get a reference to the form control
      Control form = Page.Controls[1];

      // Create and place the page header
      FriendsHeader header;
      header = (FriendsHeader) LoadControl
        (Request.ApplicationPath + Path.AltDirectorySeparatorChar +
          "Controls/FriendsHeader.ascx");

      header.Message = HeaderMessage;
      header.IconImageUrl = HeaderIconImageUrl;
      form.Controls.AddAt(0, header);

      // Add the SubHeader custom control
      form.Controls.AddAt(1, new SubHeader());

      // Finally, add the page footer
      FriendsFooter footer;
      footer = (FriendsFooter) LoadControl
        (Request.ApplicationPath + Path.AltDirectorySeparatorChar +
          "Controls/FriendsFooter.ascx");
      form.Controls.AddAt(Page.Controls[1].Controls.Count, footer);

      // Render as usual
      base.Render(writer);
    }
}
```

3. Add a new web form to the project called `Info.aspx`. Its `pageLayout` property should already be set to `FlowLayout`.

4. Type some place-holding text, say, **This is an information page.**, on the new form.

5. As usual, add the `<link>` element pointing to the `iestyles.css` stylesheet.

6. Open the code-behind page, and change the class declaration to:

```
public class Info : FriendsBase
```

7. Add the following lines to the `Page_Load()` subroutine:

```
private void Page_Load(object sender, System.EventArgs e)
{
    HeaderIconImageUrl = Request.ApplicationPath + "/Images/winbook.gif";
    HeaderMessage = "Informative Page";
}
```

8. Save and run the project with `Info.aspx` as the start page:

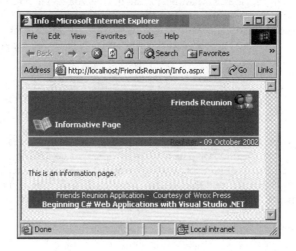

How It Works

By default, web forms inherit directly from the base `Page` class, but this is not a requirement. It's possible to inherit from any `Page`-derived class, creating a great opportunity for adding common behavior across pages. Our web application take advantage of this to insert header, sub-header, and footer controls to every page automatically, releasing the page developer from the need to drop and place these controls all the time. It's now just a case of inheriting from the new base page, as we did in Step 6, by changing the `System.Web.UI.Page` default base class to point to the `FriendsBase.cs` class.

The base page class loads controls onto the page by two methods. For user controls, we have to use the special `LoadControl()` method, provided by the `TemplateControl` class from which both `UserControl` and `Page` derive. Once it is loaded and assigned to a variable of the correct type, we can access the properties and methods of the `UserControl`. After initializing it, we add it to the form's `Controls` collection, specifying *where* we want to add it by using the `AddAt()` method. The form itself is the control with index 1, as we saw above.

In order for inheriting pages to set the message and the icon to use (these were previously set directly in every page), the base page defines two protected variables called `HeaderIconImageUrl` and `HeaderMessage`, and uses them to set the controls appropriately. The footer works in the same way as the header.

The `SubHeader` custom control, on the other hand, doesn't need any special handling, and is treated just like any other server control. We add a new instance directly, without declaring a variable.

The special processing to set up our pages has been created by overriding the `Render()` method in the base page, and before exiting the function, we call `base.Render()` to add the controls and let the base `Page` class perform the usual rendering of the modified control hierarchy. Any derived class that wants to override this method *must* also call `base.Render()`, passing in the `writer` object that's used to create the appropriate output.

Finally, note that in the `Page_Load()` handler of the derived page, we had to use the full application path to the image. For this purpose, we employed the `Request.ApplicationPath` property, which includes the virtual directory path (such as `/FriendsReunion`). The custom base page gives us exactly the same result as we achieved in the `Default.aspx` and `News.aspx` pages, but with almost no code required in `Info.aspx` at all!

Summary

During this exploratory journey into ASP.NET's brand-new web forms landscape, we have uncovered a lot of new features. We looked at the various categories of server controls – HTML controls, web controls, user controls, and custom controls – and performed some of the most common tasks with them. The consistent object model makes it easy to handle all of them in a standard manner, and server-side event-driven programming raises programmer productivity to a new level.

Almost every part of the architecture is extensible, so that once you've mastered the built-in functionality, you can move on and extend it to provide powerful and reusable user controls or custom controls. This is a big leap forward for web application developers, who are no longer constrained by the limitations of the default features.

Although we've touched upon the idea of creating dynamic web sites in this chapter, we haven't yet considered the most important tools for creating them: **databases**. In the next chapter, we'll learn how they can be used with web forms to make great applications with minimal code.

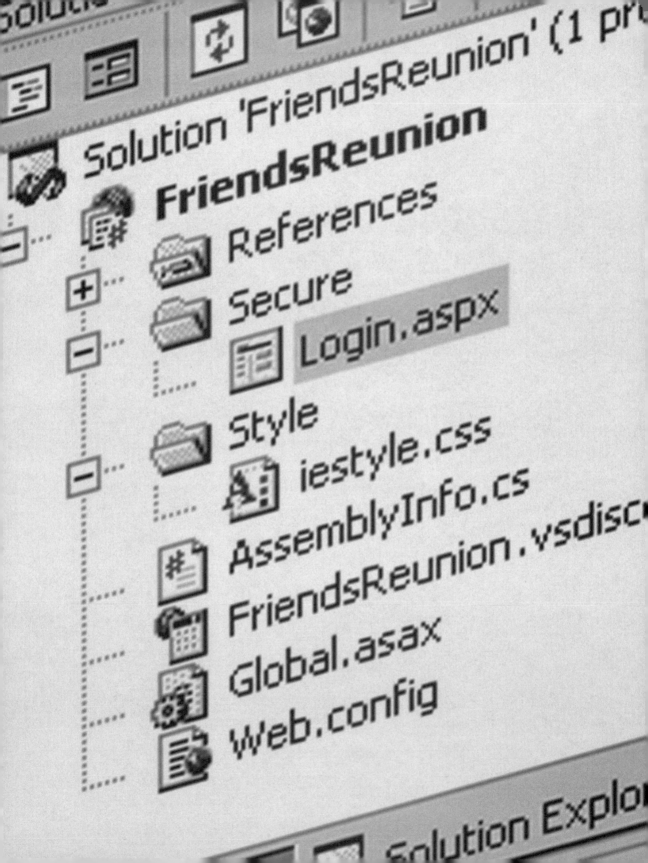

Solution 'FriendsReunion' (1 pr

FriendsReunion
References
Secure
Login.aspx
Style
iestyle.css
AssemblyInfo.cs
FriendsReunion.vsdisc
Global.asax
Web.config

Solution Explor

ADO.NET

In Chapter 3, while we were talking about HTML controls, web controls, user controls, and custom controls, we made a number of references to the myriad of additional functionality that becomes available when data access is brought into the mix. In our nascent *Friends Reunion* application, for example, we could keep a permanent store of all the people who have entered their details into the form, and allow the creation of links between those records, so that users returning to the site are immediately presented with a list of the people who want to contact them. We could also let them see complete details of each other, so that they can get in touch.

To manipulate the data stored in databases, ASP.NET uses **ADO.NET**, Microsoft's new data access strategy. ADO.NET contains many classes that ease the process of building dynamic web applications, the most interesting of which we will be discussing over the course of the next two chapters. As we do so, we will be considering the following topics:

- ❑ The overall architecture of ADO.NET
- ❑ An overview of how to use ADO.NET to access different data sources, using the so-called **data providers**
- ❑ Adding and reading data to and from a database, and displaying it on a web form in our *Friends Reunion* application
- ❑ Modifying data that is already stored in a database
- ❑ What **datasets** are, and how to use them

Before we start coding, we'll take a brief tour of the ADO.NET architecture. If, from experience, you're already familiar with the terms and concepts of ADO.NET, feel free to skip the next section, and instead move directly to the *Try It Out* sections that follow it.

The Architecture of ADO.NET

Before we go any further, let's get something out of the way; the name 'ADO.NET' doesn't actually stand for anything at all, and before you raise a hand to point out that ADO originally stood for **ActiveX Data O**bjects, just remember that Microsoft has decreed that ADO.NET is the name of a technology, and *not* an acronym! More significantly, ADO.NET is a significant technological leap forward from ADO, and has a substantially different architecture, so it's well worth taking a look at its overall design.

Whenever we want to access data in a database, the most common technique for doing so involves first connecting to the database, and then issuing a SQL statement. ADO.NET supports these two concepts, which together allow interaction between our code and a source of data. The diagram below shows a **command object**, which will usually contain a SQL statement, using a **connection object** to reach the database.

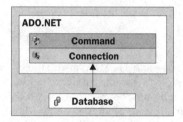

Besides direct SQL statements, a command object can also be used to execute a stored procedure that's already present in the database.

Now, depending on the query being executed, we may expect to retrieve a single value (from a SELECT COUNT(x) ... statement, for example), a result set (from a SELECT * FROM ... statement), or no result at all (from an INSERT or UPDATE statement). Even in the last case, however, it can be useful to know the number of table rows that were affected. For each of these options, there are different methods of the command object that we can use to execute the command:

Command method	Returns
ExecuteScalar()	An Object containing the value
ExecuteReader()	A **data reader object**, for accessing a result set
ExecuteNonQuery()	An Integer with the number of rows affected by the command

The first and last of these methods are really quite simple, and we'll see them in action shortly. The second, however, is more complex, and deserves a little more explanation here. A data reader object is a fast, read-only, forward-only, connected cursor to the data returned from the database. As such, it represents a very efficient way to display the results of an SQL statement.

Using a data reader is very similar to using the other 'reader' objects in the .NET Framework, such as StreamReader, XmlReader, and so on. We get a reference to it (by calling ExecuteReader() in this case), we call Read(), and if that returns True (meaning that more data is available to be read), we use its methods to access data in the current position. Typically, for result sets containing multiple rows of data, we'll have a code structure like this:

```
reader = command.ExecuteReader();
while (reader.Read())
{
  // Process current row
}
```

From this point, to access the values contained in the columns inside the current row, we can use using any of the following approaches:

❑   The data reader object has GetXXX() methods for retrieving typed values. Methods such as GetBoolean(), GetString(), GetInt32() receive the index of the column as an argument, and return a value of the appropriate type. Inside the code block shown above, we could write:

```
Response.Write(reader.GetString(0));
```

If we know the name of a column but not its index, we can use the data reader object's GetOrdinal() method, which receives the column name and returns its position:

```
int pos = reader.GetOrdinal("CategoryID");
```

❑   The data reader object has a default Item property that provides direct access to the column values. We can pass either an int representing the column's position or a String with the column's name. The value returned is of type object, so we will need to convert it to the target data type explicitly:

```
int id = (int) reader["UserId"];

// Or accessed by column order
int id = (int) reader[0]
```

❑   The data reader object has a method called GetValues() that fills an array with the values in the columns. This method receives an object array, and fills it with the values in the current row:

```
object[] values = new object[3];
reader.GetValues(values);
```

If you wish, you can use the data reader's FieldCount property to initialize the array. In the code shown above, the array will be filled with the values from the first three columns of the current record.

Before you head off and try to find classes called Connection, Command, and DataReader in the .NET Framework, we'd better tell you that they don't actually exist as such. In ADO.NET, each different type of database has to be accessed using its own version of these objects. A particular set of these objects for a particular database is called a **data provider**. The methods we've mentioned so far are common to all data providers, but a provider may provide additional features that are unique to the database it deals with.

Data Providers

Why do we need to use data providers? Wouldn't it be less complicated to have a single set of objects for accessing any kind of database? This is an approach that's been taken in the past, but there's a problem with it: in order to have a common set of objects across disparate databases, an abstraction layer has to be implemented on top of database-specific features. This adds overhead and causes a performance impact. Also, a lowest-common-denominator approach has to be taken in the design of the classes, which hinders the possibility of making database-specific features easily available.

In ADO.NET, each database can be accessed using classes that take best advantage of its specific features. At the time of writing, the following .NET data providers exist:

❑ **SQL Server** – This provider is located in the `System.Data.SqlClient` namespace, and provides classes for working with SQL Server 7.0 (or later) databases. It contains the `SqlConnection`, `SqlCommand`, `SqlDataReader`, and `SqlDataAdapter` classes, and it's an integral part of ADO.NET.

❑ **OLE DB** – This provider is located in the `System.Data.OleDb` namespace, and provides classes for working with any data source for which an OLE DB driver exists. It contains the `OleDbConnection`, `OleDbCommand`, `OleDbDataReader`, and `OleDbDataAdapter` classes. It too is an integral part of ADO.NET.

❑ **ODBC** – This provider is located in the `Microsoft.Data.Odbc` namespace, and it provides classes to work with any data source with an installed ODBC driver. It contains the `OdbcConnection`, `OdbcCommand`, `OdbcDataReader`, and `OdbcDataAdapter` classes. Installation has to be performed manually by downloading a package from http://msdn.microsoft.com/downloads/default.asp?url=/downloads/ sample.asp?url=/msdn-files/027/001/668/msdncompositedoc.xml.

❑ **Oracle** – Once installed, this provider's classes are located in the `System.Data.OracleClient` namespace, where you'll find the `OracleConnection`, `OracleCommand`, `OracleDataReader`, and `OracleDataAdapter` classes. It has to be downloaded and installed separately from the .NET Framework, from http://msdn.microsoft.com/downloads/default.asp?URL=/downloads/sample.asp? url=/msdn-files/027/001/940/msdncompositedoc.xml.

❑ **MySql** – Yes, there's even a data provider for this database engine, although this time it's not from Microsoft. Instead, you can purchase and download it from Core Lab's web site, at http://crlab.com/mysqlnet.

Clearly, the different data providers will all have very different implementations as a result of the variety of database technologies they have to deal with. As stated earlier, however, they're very similar as far as we're concerned; they have common methods and properties for us to use. This means that, generally speaking, choosing a provider is a matter of performance, not of features. The product-specific providers (SQL Server and Oracle) offer superior performance for the databases they are designed to work with, compared with the generic OLE DB or ODBC providers. The SQL Server provider, for example, communicates with the database using its own proprietary format, TDS (Tabular Data Stream), resulting in significant performance gains.

For the examples in this chapter, we'll use the SQL Server data provider to connect to MSDE. If you haven't already explored this aspect of databases in this book, the relevant information is located in Appendix B. As far as the SQL Server data provider is concerned, MSDE is indistinguishable from SQL Server, which means that the actual classes we'll be using to read data are:

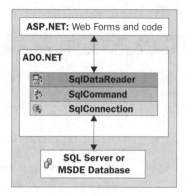

In fact, this picture is still incomplete, but we can fill in the rest of the details as we go. Specifically, there are two kinds of object left out: **data adapters**, which are components of the data providers (as mentioned in the discussion above) and the generic `DataSet` object. We will take a look at both of these in depth shortly, but first we can see some concrete uses of what you've already learned.

Programmatic Use of ADO.NET

We've started this chapter at a rapid pace, but if you're not absolutely sure that you understand how all of this works, don't worry: things will start to become clearer when we begin to look at the code. Now that you've at least begun to get a feel for how data access works in ADO.NET, let's make a start on improving our *Friends Reunion* application to take advantage of it.

Adding Data to a Database

In Chapter 3, we built a form called `NewUser.aspx` that accepted data from the user. Clearly though, such a form is pretty useless unless we're able save that data somewhere! That's precisely what we'll do now, and we will use a `SqlCommand` object to achieve it.

After the user has finished entering their details into the form, we will insert a new row into the `User` table of the `Friends` database. This table has the following structure:

User
UserID
Login
Password
FirstName
LastName
DateOfBirth
PhoneNumber
CellNumber
Address
Email
IsAdministrator

[handwritten notes:]

eg connection)

datasource — fright\vsdotnet

connectionstring =

workstation id= FRIGHT; packet size=4096; integrated security=SSPI;
data source = "fright\vsdotnet"; persist security info=false;
initial catalog = Northwind

129

The database that we're going to use for our data is called `FriendsData`. It is a detached SQL Server database, and can be found in the code download and is ready to use. If you haven't attached a database to MSDE before, take a look in Appendix B as it contains details such as how to install and set up MSDE, how to use the Server Explorer window, and how to connect to databases using the built-in features of the Visual Studio .NET IDE.

Try It Out – Adding a New User

For this first example, we will rewrite the handler for the `NewUser.aspx` form's **Accept** button to store the details in that form in the `FriendsData` database. We'll also add the improvement that we began to implement at the end of Chapter 3, that of inheriting the `FriendsBase` base class for all forms.

1. Open the `NewUser.aspx` page, and delete the user controls it contains.

2. Add the following imports at the top of the code-behind file, as we'll be using classes from these namespaces:

```
using System;
using System.Collections;
using System.ComponentModel;
using System.Data;
using System.Data.SqlClient;
using System.Drawing;
using System.Text;
using System.Web;
using System.Web.SessionState;
using System.Web.UI;
using System.Web.UI.WebControls;
using System.Web.UI.HtmlControls;
```

3. To take advantage of the common base page we created in Chapter 3, change the base class for our page:

```
public class NewUser : FriendsBase
```

4. Just as you learned in Chapter 3, change the page icon and the message text in the `Page_Load()` event handler:

```
private void Page_Load(object sender, System.EventArgs e)
{
    base.HeaderIconImageUrl =
        Request.ApplicationPath + "/Images/securekeys.gif";
    base.HeaderMessage = "Registration Form";
}
```

5. Now add the handler for the **Accept** button, which previously just tested the contents of the various textboxes for validity. In its new form, it will be responsible for building and executing the SQL `INSERT` statement that will add a new user to the database.

In this method, efficient string manipulation is achieved through the use of a `StringBuilder` object. We also take advantage of string formatting, which makes replacing placeholders in a string with (an array of) values a breeze.

```csharp
private void btnAccept_Click(object sender, System.EventArgs e)
{
  if (Page.IsValid)
  {
    // Save new user to the database
    SqlConnection con;
    string sql;
    SqlCommand cmd;
    StringBuilder sb = new StringBuilder();
    ArrayList values = new ArrayList();

    sb.Append("INSERT INTO [User] ");
    sb.Append("(UserID, Login, Password, FirstName, LastName,");
    sb.Append(" PhoneNumber, Email, IsAdministrator, Address,");
    sb.Append(" CellNumber, DateOfBirth) ");
    sb.Append(
    "VALUES ('{0}', '{1}', '{2}', '{3}', '{4}', '{5}', '{6}', '{7}', ");

    // Optional values without quotes as they can be the Null value.
    sb.Append("{8}, {9}, {10})");

    // Add required values to replace
    values.Add(Guid.NewGuid().ToString());
    values.Add(txtLogin.Text);
    values.Add(txtPwd.Text);
    values.Add(txtFName.Text);
    values.Add(txtLName.Text);
    values.Add(txtPhone.Text);
    values.Add(txtEmail.Text);
    values.Add(0);

    // Add the optional values or Null
    if (txtAddress.Text != string.Empty)
      values.Add("'" + txtAddress.Text + "'");
    else
      values.Add("Null");

    if (txtMobile.Text != string.Empty)
      values.Add("'" + txtMobile.Text + "'");
    else
      values.Add("Null");

    if (txtBirth.Text != string.Empty)
      values.Add("'" + txtBirth.Text + "'");
    else
      values.Add("Null");
```

```
        // Format the string with the array of values
        sql = String.Format(sb.ToString(), values.ToArray());

        // Connect and execute the query
        con = new SqlConnection(
            "data source=(local)\\NetSdk;initial catalog=FriendsData;user id=sa");
        cmd = new SqlCommand(sql, con);
        con.Open();

        bool doredirect = true;

        try
        {
          cmd.ExecuteNonQuery();
        }
        catch
        {
          doredirect = false;
          this.lblMessage.Visible = true;
          this.lblMessage.Text =
            "Insert couldn't be performed. User name may be already taken.";
        }
        finally
        {
          con.Close();
        }

        if (doredirect)
          Response.Redirect("Login.aspx");
    }
  else
  {
    lblMessage.Text = "Fix the following errors and retry:";
  }
}
```

6. To make the text of the `lblMessage` label stand out better in case of any errors, set its `ForeColor` property to `Red`.

7. Save and run the project with `NewUser.aspx` as the start page. If you now try to create a new entry for a user that already exists, you'll see something like the following:

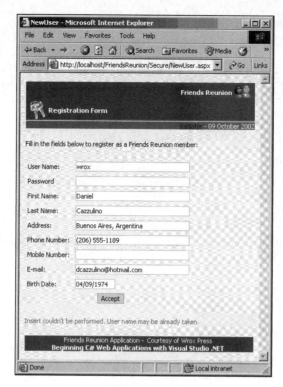

For the sake of simplicity, if the row is successfully inserted (that is, a new record is created in the database), the user will be redirected to the login page, where they will (eventually) be able to enter their user name and password for the account just created.

> *If you are having trouble connecting to your database using a user name of* sa *and a blank password, check in Appendix B for details on how to modify your registry to accept this authentication method.*

How It Works

As you saw in Chapter 3, the `Page.IsValid` property represents an accumulation of the validation state of all the validation controls on the page. If all of them are in a valid state, the property will return `True`.

The process of building the SQL `INSERT` statement itself isn't too complicated. We have used the `String.Format()` approach, employing a `StringBuilder` object to append the SQL statement and the list of fields. We used an `ArrayList` for the list of values to use, taking into account that optional values will be `Null` if no value is specified on the form. When we're done, we simply format the string with the values:

```
sql = String.Format(sb.ToString(), values.ToArray());
```

As far as our focus in this chapter is concerned, the database connectivity code comes next. As you know, our first order of business is to create connection and command objects, and the very next line of code achieves the first of these two tasks:

```
con = new SqlConnection(
    "data source=(local)\\NetSdk;initial catalog=FriendsData;user id=sa");
```

The constructor for a connection object requires you to specify a number of pieces of information, and the precise nature of this information will depend on the data store in question – consult the MSDN documentation for more information on this subject. Here, we're supplying the following arguments:

Parameter	Description
(local)\\NetSdk	The name of our MSDE instance
FriendsData	The name of the database to connect to
sa	The name of the user with rights to access that database

Next, we use the connection object and our SQL query string to create a new command object. With that done, we can open the connection to the database, ready for our command to be executed against it:

```
cmd = new SqlCommand(sql, con);
con.Open();
```

Any block of code that executes against an open database should (at the very least) always be placed inside a try...finally block, giving us a chance to close the connection before execution terminates unexpectedly.

For more on exception-handling, see Chapter 11.

Inside the block, we use the command object's ExecuteNonQuery() method, as the INSERT statement doesn't return results. (We *could* optionally check the number of rows affected, but we're simply ignoring it here.) Depending on the outcome of the command execution, either success or failure, which is tracked by the doredirect variable, we redirect the user to the login page:

```
bool doredirect = true;

try
{
  cmd.ExecuteNonQuery();
}
catch
{
  doredirect = false;
  this.lblMessage.Visible = true;
  this.lblMessage.Text =
    "Insert couldn't be performed. User name may be already taken.";
}
finally
{
  con.Close();
}
```

```
if (doredirect)
   Response.Redirect("Login.aspx");
```

As you can see, using `ExecuteNonQuery()` is pretty simple, but it's all you need in order to execute `INSERT`, `UPDATE`, and `DELETE` statements.

Retrieving Data from a Database

Now that we have a means by which to add new users to a database, the obvious next step is to learn how to retrieve that information at a later date. In our *Friends Reunion* application, there is nowhere more in need of this ability than the login page – when someone comes along and enters a user name and a password, we want to discover whether such a user exists, and whether the password they've supplied is correct. Once we have the ability to log a user on, we'll be able to offer them a way to view and edit their own information, but one thing at a time!

Before we look at the data access code, however, we need to make a few changes to our application's security settings. This topic will be explained in more detail in Chapter 10, but we'll run through the specifics of this particular case here.

Try It Out – Setting up Security

Simply put, we need to configure our application so that the login page is *always* the first one users see, regardless of how they try to access our application. Furthermore, we need to arrange things so that unregistered users can navigate from the login page to `NewUser.aspx`, but to no other pages. Here's how we do that:

1. Just as we did in Chapter 3, use the IIS administration console (Start | Programs | Administrative Tools | Internet Services Manager) to enable Anonymous access for our application:

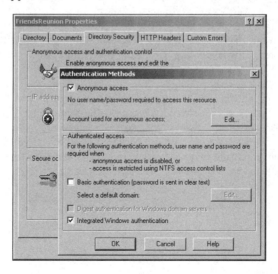

This setting means that IIS won't handle authentication, delegating that responsibility to ASP.NET and its settings. Integrated Windows authentication is enabled by default, and is needed to debug the application from Visual Studio .NET.

2. Open the `Web.config` file for the application, locate the `<authentication>` element and modify it so that it looks like the following, noting the inclusion of an `<authorization>` element:

```
<authentication mode="Forms" />
  <forms loginUrl="Secure/Login.aspx" />
</authentication>
<authorization>
  <deny users="?" />
</authorization>
```

Briefly, this tells ASP.NET that we will use a form to authenticate our users, and also specifies its location. Then, we specify that anonymous users can't access any page on this application (`deny users="?"`). With this setting in effect, clients will be automatically redirected to the `Login.aspx` page whenever they try to open *any* ASP.NET page in this application.

3. Finally, anonymous users will need to access the `NewUser.aspx` form in order to register, so we have to enable anonymous access to that. Add the following code to the `Web.config` file, just above the closing `</configuration>` tag:

```
<location path="Secure/NewUser.aspx">
  <system.web>
    <authorization>
      <allow users="*" />
    </authorization>
  </system.web>
</location>
```

With these settings in place, we can move on and finish the `Login.aspx` form. When the form is submitted, we will receive a user name and a password, and we will need to check that those values match an existing user in our database. What we need from the database is the user ID that corresponds to the credentials passed in. This ID will be used from then on to retrieve various pieces of information for the current user.

Once we have a valid user ID, we need to tell ASP.NET that the user is authenticated, and let them see the page they originally requested. This is achieved by calling the `System.Web.Security.FormsAuthentication.RedirectFromLoginPage()` method, passing in the user ID. After this method has been called successfully, the user will be able access any resource in the application. In addition, we'll be able to retrieve the ID at any time, from any page, by reading the `Context.User.Identity.Name` property. This makes it easy to customize the content of a page according to the current user.

Try It Out – Finishing the Login Form

In this example, we'll put the things we just talked about into code. In the handler for the Login button, we'll use the `ExecuteScalar()` method to retrieve the ID of a user with a given login name and password:

1. Open the `Login.aspx` form, and then delete the header and footer controls that we added previously, leaving only the table with the textboxes and the Login button. Add a line of explanatory text such as, Enter your user name and password to access the special features of this application.

2. Switching to the HTML view, add a panel containing an image and a label at the bottom of the page to hold any authentication error messages that may occur:

```
    <p>
      <asp:panel ID="pnlError" Runat="server" Visible="False">
        <img src="../Images/error.gif" align="absmiddle"> 
        <asp:label ID="lblError" Runat="server" ForeColor="Red">
        </asp:label>
      </asp:panel>
    </p>
  </form>
 </body>
</html>
```

3. Then, in the code-behind page, change things to match the following:

```
using System;
using System.Collections;
using System.ComponentModel;
using System.Data;
using System.Data.SqlClient;
using System.Drawing;
using System.Web;
using System.Web.Security;
using System.Web.SessionState;
using System.Web.UI;
using System.Web.UI.WebControls;
using System.Web.UI.HtmlControls;

namespace FriendsReunion.Secure
{
  public class Login : FriendsBase
  {
    protected System.Web.UI.HtmlControls.HtmlInputText txtLogin;
    protected System.Web.UI.HtmlControls.HtmlInputButton btnLogin;
    protected System.Web.UI.HtmlControls.HtmlGenericControl lblMessage;
    protected System.Web.UI.HtmlControls.HtmlInputText txtPwd;
    protected System.Web.UI.WebControls.Label lblError;
    protected System.Web.UI.WebControls.Panel pnlError;
```

```
private void Page_Load(object sender, System.EventArgs e)
{
  base.HeaderIconImageUrl =
    Request.ApplicationPath + "/Images/securekeys.gif";
  base.HeaderMessage = "Login Page";
}

[ Web Form Designer Generated Code]

private void btnLogin_ServerClick(object sender, System.EventArgs e)
{
  SqlConnection con;
  string sql;
  SqlCommand cmd;
  string id;

  con = new SqlConnection(
  "data source=(local)\\NetSdk;initial catalog=FriendsData;user id=sa");
  sql =
    "SELECT UserID FROM [User] WHERE Login='{0}' and Password='{1}'";

  // Format the string with the values provided
  sql = String.Format(sql, txtLogin.Value, txtPwd.Value);
  cmd = new SqlCommand(sql, con);
  con.Open();

  try
  {
    // Retrieve the UserID
    id = (string) cmd.ExecuteScalar();
  }
  finally
  {
    con.Close();
  }

  if (id != null)
  {
    // Set the user as authenticated and send him to the
    // page originally requested.
    FormsAuthentication.RedirectFromLoginPage(id, false);
  }
  else
  {
    this.pnlError.Visible = true;
    this.lblError.Text = "Invalid user name or password!";
  }
}
}
}
```

4. Save all your changes, and then run the application with Default.aspx as the start page. You should find that you're taken to the login page automatically:

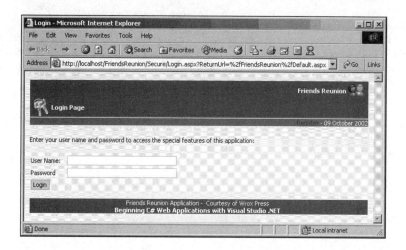

How It Works

From now on, all of the web forms that we add to this project will inherit from the `FriendsBase` class that we created in Chapter 3. We will also always use the two fields provided by the base class to set the text and the image for the current page. On this occasion, that was done in the `Page_Load()` handler:

```
private void Page_Load(object sender, System.EventArgs e)
{
  base.HeaderIconImageUrl =
    Request.ApplicationPath + "/Images/securekeys.gif";
  base.HeaderMessage = "Login Page";
}
```

The settings we've applied to the `Web.config` file will redirect the browser to the `Login.aspx` page when we start the project. After entering values for the user name and password and clicking the button, the code in `btnLogin_ServerClick()` is executed. The steps performed there are:

❑ Create a new `SqlConnection` object, using the same connection string as last time. After the object is created, it remains closed until we explicitly call the `Open()` method later on:

```
con = new SqlConnection(
"data source=(local)\\NetSdk;initial catalog=FriendsData;user id=sa");
```

❑ Specify the SQL statement to execute against the database:

```
sql =
  "SELECT UserID FROM [User] WHERE Login='{0}' and Password='{1}'";
sql = String.Format(sql, txtLogin.Value, txtPwd.Value);
```

❑ Create a new `SqlCommand` object, using the query string and connection we've created and open the connection:

```
cmd = new SqlCommand(sql, con);
con.Open();
```

❑ In the next line, we use the `ExecuteScalar()` method of the `SqlCommand` object to retrieve the single value we're selecting. (If the SQL expression returned more than one row and/or field, only the first field of the first row would be passed back to our code by this method.) As we built the SQL statement to return the user ID, that's what we'll get, after casting it to a string:

```
try
{
  // Retrieve the UserID
  id = (string) cmd.ExecuteScalar();
}
finally
{
  con.Close();
}
```

❑ Next, we check whether a valid user ID was returned. If it wasn't, then either the user name or the password must have been incorrect, so we show an error message. If everything is fine, we use the `RedirectFromLoginPage()` method to send the user to the page they requested in the first place. If you take a closer look at the URL in the screenshot on the previous page, you will notice that a **ReturnUrl** query string value has been appended to it. This is how `RedirectFromLoginPage()` knows where to redirect the user:

```
if (id != null)
{
  // Set the user as authenticated and send him to the
  // page originally requested.
  FormsAuthentication.RedirectFromLoginPage(id, false);
}
else
{
  this.pnlError.Visible = true;
  this.lblError.Text = "Invalid user name or password!";
}
```

As we said, once the user has been authenticated here, we can access their user ID from any code-behind page through the `Context.User.Identity.Name` property.

From now on, we will use the word `wrox` as both username and password in our examples – the database comes pre-loaded with some information for this user. After a successful logon, the user is presented with a welcome page, in which (if you remember our work in Chapter 3) the sub-header that displays the date also includes the following code:

```
protected override void CreateChildControls()
{
  // Clear any previously loaded controls
  this.Controls.Clear();
  Label lbl;
```

```
// If the user is authenticated, we will render their name
if (Context.User.Identity.IsAuthenticated)
{
  lbl = new Label();
  lbl.Text = Context.User.Identity.Name;

  // Add the newly created label to our collection of child controls
  this.Controls.Add(lbl);
}
else
{
  ...
```

As a result of the changes we've made, the label now displays the user's ID, rather than their name – but we'll be putting that right in Chapter 10. Finally for now, Context.User.Identity.IsAuthenticated is working just as it did before – it returns true if the user has entered valid credentials in the Login.aspx form. One difference, though, is that the code after the else statement will never be executed, because in that case (an unauthenticated user accessing the page) the browser will automatically be redirected to the login page.

Changing the Data in a Database

In general, details of the kind we've collected in our registration form do not remain the same forever, so it seems only reasonable that we should give our users the opportunity to change the data we hold about them. As the updated information is of exactly the same format as they used when they first registered, however, we can use the same form and just change some of its code. Specifically, we can discover if the user accessing NewUser.aspx is a new user seeking to register, or a registered user trying to modify their profile, by testing Context.User.Identity.IsAuthenticated.

Try It Out – Editing a User's Profile

In the case of a registered user, we will preload the form with the existing data by using the command object's ExecuteReader() method. When the time comes to save the data back to the database, that is, when the **Accept** button is clicked, we'll test the same property to determine whether an UPDATE or an INSERT is appropriate. The INSERT code is already in place, so we just need to add the UPDATE, again using the ExecuteNonQuery() method.

We'll also make a slight modification to the SubHeader.cs custom control that we built in Chapter 3, so that it shows a link to allow the user to change their profile. Since the 'register' link and the 'profile editing' link both point to the same page, NewUser.aspx, we only have to change its text.

1. Open the SubHeader.cs file, and modify the code in CreateChildControls() as follows:

```
protected override void CreateChildControls()
{
  // Clear any previously loaded controls
  this.Controls.Clear();
  Label lbl;
  HyperLink reg = new HyperLink();
```

```
    if (_register == string.Empty)
    {
      reg.NavigateUrl = Context.Request.ApplicationPath +
        Path.AltDirectorySeparatorChar + "Secure" +
        Path.AltDirectorySeparatorChar + "NewUser.aspx";
    }
    else
    {
      reg.NavigateUrl = _register;
    }

    if (Context.User.Identity.IsAuthenticated)
      reg.Text = "Edit my profile";
    else
      reg.Text = "Register";

    this.Controls.AddAt(0, reg);

    // Add a couple of blank spaces and a separator character
    this.Controls.Add(new LiteralControl(" - "));

    // Add a label with the current data
    lbl = new Label();
    lbl.Text = DateTime.Now.ToLongDateString();
    this.Controls.Add(lbl);
}
```

2. Next we will need to perform a couple of quick admin tasks. If you have not already done so, set the `Default.aspx` page to inherit the `FriendsBase` class and delete all the existing controls except the placeholder. Also, modify the introduction line for the page to something like, Welcome to the Friends Reunion application. Select the desired link to access the functionality on the site:.

3. If you recompile the project after making just these changes, and reopen the `Default.aspx` page (you may need to log in again), this is what you'll see:

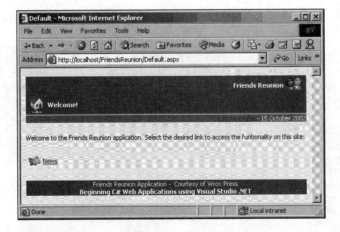

4. Let's now modify the `Page_Load()` handler in the `NewUser.aspx` page to preload the form with a registered user's data:

```
...
using System.Data.SqlTypes;
...

    private void Page_Load(object sender, System.EventArgs e)
    {
      base.HeaderIconImageUrl =
        Request.ApplicationPath + "/Images/securekeys.gif";
      base.HeaderMessage = "Registration Form";

      // Postbacks will typically be caused by the validator
      // controls in non-IE browsers
      if (Page.IsPostBack)
        return;

      // If this is an update, preload the values
      if (Context.User.Identity.IsAuthenticated)
      {
        // Change the header message
        base.HeaderMessage = "Update my profile";

        SqlConnection con;
        string sql;
        SqlCommand cmd;
        SqlDataReader reader;

        sql = "SELECT * FROM [User] WHERE UserID='" +
          Page.User.Identity.Name + "'";
        con = new SqlConnection(
            "data source=(local)\\NetSdk;initial catalog=FriendsData;user id=sa");
        cmd = new SqlCommand(sql, con);
        con.Open();
        reader = cmd.ExecuteReader(CommandBehavior.CloseConnection);

        if (reader.Read())
        {
          // Retrieve a typed value using the column's ordinal position
          int pos = reader.GetOrdinal("Address");
          this.txtAddress.Text = reader.GetString(pos).ToString();

          // Avoid using the pos variable altogether, but
          // get the typed value
          this.txtBirth.Text =
reader.GetDateTime(reader.GetOrdinal("DateOfBirth")).ToShortDateString();

          // Convert directly the untyped Object returned by the
          // indexer to a string
          this.txtEmail.Text = reader["Email"].ToString();
          this.txtFName.Text = reader["FirstName"].ToString();
```

```
      this.txtLName.Text = reader["LastName"].ToString();
      this.txtLogin.Text = reader["Login"].ToString();
      this.txtPhone.Text = reader["PhoneNumber"].ToString();
      this.txtPwd.Text = reader["Password"].ToString();

      // Use SQL Server type to have additional features
      pos = reader.GetOrdinal("CellNumber");
      SqlString cel;
      cel = reader.GetSqlString(pos);
      if (!cel.IsNull)
        this.txtMobile.Text = cel.Value;
    }
    reader.Close();
  }
}
```

5. We can test this code by compiling the project and refreshing the previous page. If you click on the Edit my profile link, you'll see that the values are preloaded on the form:

6. Next, to organize the code better, let's create a private routine called InsertUser(), and move the code from the btnAccept_Click() handler to it:

```
private void InsertUser()
{
    ...
}
```

7. With that in place, let's create another new routine that will handle the update scenario. Inevitably, it's rather similar to the code for inserting new entries; it's called `UpdateUser()`:

```
private void UpdateUser()
    if (Page.IsValid)
    {
        // Update the existing user
        SqlConnection con;
        string sql;
        SqlCommand cmd;
        StringBuilder sb = new StringBuilder();
        ArrayList values = new ArrayList();

        // Build the SQL string
        sb.Append("UPDATE [User] SET ");
        sb.Append("Login='{0}', Password='{1}', FirstName='{2}', ");
        sb.Append("LastName='{3}', PhoneNumber='{4}', Email='{5}'");

        // Add required values to replace
        values.Add(txtLogin.Text);
        values.Add(txtPwd.Text);
        values.Add(txtFName.Text);
        values.Add(txtLName.Text);
        values.Add(txtPhone.Text);
        values.Add(txtEmail.Text);

        // Add optional values directly
        if (txtAddress.Text != string.Empty)
            sb.Append(", Address='" + txtAddress.Text + "'");

        if (txtMobile.Text != string.Empty)
            sb.Append(", CellNumber='" + txtMobile.Text + "'");

        if (txtBirth.Text != string.Empty)
        {
            // Pass date in ISO format YYYYMMDD
            DateTime dt = DateTime.Parse(txtBirth.Text);
            sb.Append(", DateOfBirth='");
            sb.Append(dt.Year.ToString("d4"));
            sb.Append(dt.Month.ToString("d2"));
            sb.Append(dt.Day.ToString("d2"));
            sb.Append("'");
        }

        sb.Append(" WHERE UserID='{6}'");
```

```
      // Get the UserID from the context.
      values.Add(Context.User.Identity.Name);
      sql = String.Format(sb.ToString(), values.ToArray());

      // Connect and execute the query
      con = new SqlConnection(
          "data source=(local)\\NetSdk;initial catalog=FriendsData;user id=sa");
      cmd = new SqlCommand(sql, con);
      con.Open();

      bool doredirect = true;

      try
      {
        cmd.ExecuteNonQuery();
      }
      catch
      {
        doredirect = false;
        this.lblMessage.Visible = true;
        this.lblMessage.Text = "Couldn't update your profile!";
      }
      finally
      {
        con.Close();
      }

      if (doredirect)
        Response.Redirect("../Default.aspx");
    }
  }
```

8. Finally, add the following code to the now empty btnAccept_Click() handler:

```
private void btnAccept_Click(object sender, System.EventArgs e)
{
  if (Context.User.Identity.IsAuthenticated)
    UpdateUser();
  else
    InsertUser();
}
```

9. Save and compile the project. If you run the project again and log in to the application, you can click the new link in the subheader and not only see the form preloaded with values, but also change any of its values. It is even possible for the user to change their user name, because that's not being used as the primary key for the table – something that we can now appreciate!

How It Works

The change in the subheader control is very straightforward: we just change the text of the link according to the `IsAuthenticated` property for the current request. The interesting thing is happening in the `Page_Load()` routine, where we create the database connection and command objects as usual, but assign the result of executing the command to a variable of type `SqlDataReader`:

```
SqlDataReader reader;
...
reader = cmd.ExecuteReader(CommandBehavior.CloseConnection);
```

The parameter passed to `ExecuteReader()` indicates that we want the reader to close the connection when we close the reader later on. For all of the available values for this parameter, take a look at the MSDN help.

To read the values that form the result of our query, we start by checking that a row has actually been returned, by calling the `Read()` method:

```
if (reader.Read())
{
```

After that, and partly for show, we use of the various options that are available with the reader. First, we use the `GetOrdinal()` method to retrieve the position of a column in the reader, so that we can get a typed string using the `GetString()` method, which needs this value:

```
// Retrieve a typed value using the column's ordinal position
int pos;
pos = reader.GetOrdinal("Address");
this.txtAddress.Text = reader.GetString(pos).ToString();
```

The next line takes the same approach, but avoids the need for an extra variable by calling the `GetOrdinal()` method from inside the `GetDateTime()` method call:

```
// Avoid using the pos variable altogether, but
// get the typed value
this.txtBirth.Text =
reader.GetDateTime(reader.GetOrdinal("DateOfBirth")).ToShortDateString();
```

This reduces the amount of code we need to write, at the expense of a little added complexity – note that as the value returned is a typed `DateTime` object, we can use its methods to format the date. The following lines show the most common approach, where we simply use the data reader object's indexer that receives the column name and returns an `Object`. We can convert this object to a string very easily indeed:

```
// Convert directly the untyped Object returned by the
// indexer to a string
this.txtEmail.Text = reader["Email"].ToString();
this.txtFName.Text = reader["FirstName"].ToString();
this.txtLName.Text = reader["LastName"].ToString();
```

```
this.txtLogin.Text = reader["Login"].ToString();
this.txtPhone.Text = reader["PhoneNumber"].ToString();
this.txtPwd.Text = reader["Password"].ToString();
```

The last bit of code is a peek at the extra features we can get from a `SqlDataReader` object. Accessing the native data types of a SQL Server database can improve application performance, since by doing so we avoid the conversion between SQL Server data types and .NET's data types. However, this does make it harder to change the data provider if we decide to use a different database in the future. In this block, we use the `SqlString` type, which has (among other things) an `IsNull` property that can tell us whether a value is present:

```
// Use SQL Server type to have additional features
pos = reader.GetOrdinal("CellNumber");
SqlString cel;
cel = reader.GetSqlString(pos);
if (!cel.IsNull)
  this.txtMobile.Text = cel.Value;
```

Finally, we close the reader, which will also close the connection as a result of the `CommandBehavior.CloseConnection` value that we specified when we first executed the command:

```
reader.Close();
```

When the user clicks the **Accept** button, we check the `IsAuthenticated` property, and call the update or the insert routine accordingly:

```
if (Context.User.Identity.IsAuthenticated)
  UpdateUser();
else
  InsertUser();
```

If you compare the code for the `UpdateUser()` routine with that for the insert routine that we created earlier, you will find that the two are almost identical. The only difference lies in the SQL statement building process, so we don't need to go any deeper there.

Completing the Picture – The DataSet Object

Until now, we've been looking at a **connected** model for accessing a database – that is, our code retains a connection to the database for the duration of our interactions with it. Data reader objects are very useful if we only have to move forward through the results of a query and display some values quickly, but an open connection is a valuable resource. Also, if we need to pass the retrieved data between methods, perform some processing before displaying it, or move back and forth through the results, a data reader simply doesn't cut the mustard. What we need is some way to extract data from the database on a semi-permanent basis, so that we can close the database connection for a while, and manipulate the data as we see fit. In other words, we want a way to deal with data that's **disconnected** from the data source.

An ADO.NET object that we introduced earlier but haven't examined so far is the `DataSet`. Unlike the data reader, command, and connection objects that we've been using, `DataSet`s are not data provider-dependent. `DataSet` is a class in the `System.Data` namespace, and instances of it can be used with any data source. A `DataSet` object can be thought of as an in-memory relational database, as it contains a collection of `DataTable` objects, which in turn contain collections of `DataColumn` and `DataRow` objects:

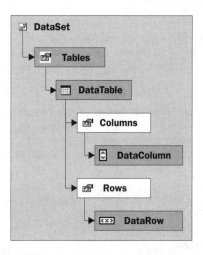

The data in a `DataSet` object can be inserted, updated, and deleted, and the object retains the details of any such modifications. However, being a generic, disconnected store for data, the dataset is completely 'unaware' of the data source, by which we mean that a dataset can be created from a database, a file, or programmatically, and it will remain always independent from the original source.

Data Adapters

Another object, which *is* data provider-specific, handles the process of filling the `DataSet` with data from a database, and posting changes back to that database. This object is a **data adapter**, and each data provider contains its own version: `SqlDataAdapter`, `OleDbDataAdapter`, `OdbcDataAdapter`, and so on. The data adapter uses command objects to retrieve data from a database, and later to post changes (inserts, updates, or deletes) back to it. In diagrammatic form, the interaction between these objects is:

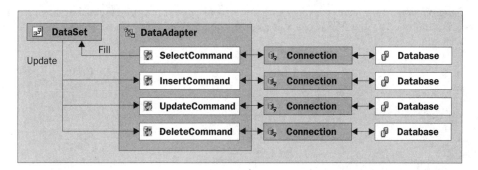

As shown in the figure, a data adapter object has two key methods, `Fill()` and `Update()`. Both of these take a `DataSet` as an argument, and use the command objects with which the data adapter is configured to interact with the database. During a `Fill()` call, the adapter executes its `SelectCommand`, and loads the data into the corresponding tables inside the `DataSet`. During an `Update()` call, the adapter inspects the data in the `DataSet`, and calls each command depending on what's happened to each row (it may have been inserted, updated, or deleted). As stated above, the `DataSet` itself keeps track of all such changes.

> *Note that the `DataAdapter` isn't in fact directly connected to the database(s), but through the commands as shown above. Each of the commands can be configured independently to point to **any** database, so it is actually possible to perform the `SELECT` from one database and do the `UPDATE` on another one.*

So, let's recap: connection and command objects are used *every* time there is a need to access a database. From there, we can choose to use a connected mode, and use a data reader that's retrieved as a result of executing a command, or we can take advantage of the disconnected `DataSet` object, and use a data adapter to provide the link between it and the database. The complete picture for ADO.NET would then be:

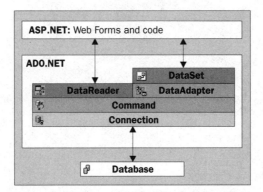

With the exception of the `DataSet`, the names of the other elements here are abstractions, since the actual class names are specific to each data provider.

Using a DataSet Object

In our *Friends Reunion* application, users can enter information about the places they have studied or worked at in the past, so that fellow users can contact them. This information is kept in the following tables in the database:

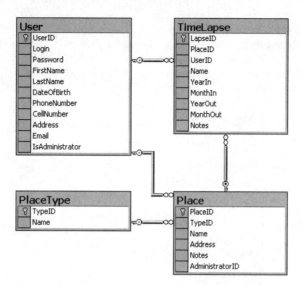

The `TimeLapse` table allows a `Name` to be specified, where the user can describe what it was they doing in that place. For example, if the place was "Columbia University", the name of the time lapse could be "Systems Engineer", meaning that the user was in that role at that place for the period of time in question.

Try It Out – Assigning Places

For the next addition to the application, we'll build a form to allow the user to enter all of this information. We'll need to load any existing places they've registered, and allow the editing of this list, as well as the creation of new records in the `TimeLapse` table. As you've probably guessed, we'll be filling a `DataSet` object with all of the relevant information.

1. Add a new web form to the application, calling it `AssignPlaces.aspx`.

2. Add a link to the stylesheet we've been using so far:

```
<link href="Style/iestyle.css" type="text/css" rel="stylesheet">
```

Also, change the code-behind page so that we inherit from the `FriendsBase` class, and also add a `using` statement for the namespace we'll be using:

```
...
using System.Data;
using System.Data.SqlClient;
...
public class AssignPlaces : FriendsBase
```

3. This form will contain a `Panel` called `pnlExisting`, containing a `PlaceHolder`, which will be filled dynamically with a control for each time lapse record found, in much the same way that you saw in Chapter 3. It will also contain an HTML table with its `border` property set to 0, with text boxes and a combo box for the creation of a new record. Finally, there's a button for performing the insert operation. This is what the page should look like:

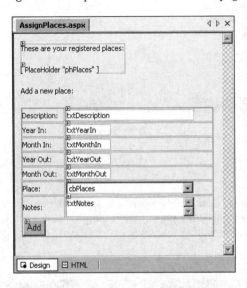

In the screenshot, the text inside each control is the ID to use for that control; the button's ID should be `btnAdd`. We've set `CssClass` to `TextBox` for `txtDescription`, `cbPlaces`, and `txtNotes`, while all of the other textboxes have the `SmallTextBox` value, and the button has `Button`.

If you wish, you could use `RequiredFieldValidator` controls on each of the required fields here, and you could use a `CompareValidator` control to ensure that period is sensible (so that `YearIn` is forced to be equal to or less than `YearOut`, for example). In this example though, we'll focus only on the data access aspects.

4. Add the following code to the `Page_Load()` routine; it really just sets the agenda for the work to come.

```
private void Page_Load(object sender, System.EventArgs e)
{
    base.HeaderMessage = "Assign Places";

    LoadDataSet();
    InitPlaces();
    InitForm();
}
```

5. The first method, `LoadDataSet()`, will load a `DataSet` with all of the information needed by this page, and will necessarily be available as a class-level variable. Once we finish loading the data, the other two methods will initialize the interface. Let's see the loading process:

```
    DataSet ds;

    private void LoadDataSet()
    {
      SqlConnection con;
      string sql;
      SqlDataAdapter adExisting;
      SqlDataAdapter adPlaces;
      SqlDataAdapter adPlaceTypes;

      con = new SqlConnection(
      "data source=(local)\\NetSdk;initial catalog=FriendsData;user id=sa");

      // Select the place's timelapse records, descriptions, and type
      sql = "SELECT TimeLapse.*, Place.Name AS Place, ";
      sql += "PlaceType.Name AS Type FROM TimeLapse, Place, PlaceType ";
      sql += "WHERE TimeLapse.PlaceID = Place.PlaceID AND ";
      sql += "Place.TypeID = PlaceType.TypeID ";
      sql += "AND TimeLapse.UserID = '" + Context.User.Identity.Name + "' ";

      // Initialize the adapters
      adExisting = new SqlDataAdapter(sql, con);
      adPlaces =
        new SqlDataAdapter("SELECT * FROM Place ORDER BY TypeID", con);
      adPlaceTypes = new SqlDataAdapter("SELECT * FROM PlaceType", con);

      con.Open();
      ds = new DataSet();

      try
      {
        // Proceed to fill the dataset
        adExisting.Fill(ds, "Existing");
        adPlaces.Fill(ds, "Places");
        adPlaceTypes.Fill(ds, "Types");
      }
      catch
      {
        // Just pass the exception up
        throw;
      }
      finally
      {
        con.Close();
      }
    }
```

6. The InitPlaces() method uses the DataSet we just filled to add items to the panel at the top of the page: a summary of each existing place, and a link to allow the user to delete it. We saw how to create dynamic content in Chapter 3, but now we use data from the DataSet to drive the process:

```
private void InitPlaces()
{
  LiteralControl lbl;
  string msg;
  LinkButton btn;

  phPlaces.Controls.Clear();
  msg =
    "Type: {0}, Place: {1}. From {2}/{3} to {4}/{5}. Description: {6}.";

  foreach (DataRow row in ds.Tables["Existing"].Rows)
  {
    lbl = new LiteralControl();

    // Format the msg variable with values in the row
    lbl.Text = string.Format(msg, row["Type"], row["Place"],
      row["MonthIn"], row["YearIn"],
      row["MonthOut"], row["YearOut"], row["Name"]);

    btn = new LinkButton();

    // Assign a unique ID to the control
    btn.ID = row["LapseID"].ToString().Replace("-", string.Empty);
    btn.Text = "Delete";

    // Pass the LapseID when the link is clicked
    btn.CommandArgument = row["LapseID"].ToString();

    // Attach the handler to the event
    btn.Command += new CommandEventHandler(OnDeletePlace);

    // Add the controls to the placeholder
    phPlaces.Controls.Add(lbl);
    phPlaces.Controls.Add(btn);
    phPlaces.Controls.Add(new LiteralControl("<br>"));
  }
  // Hide the panel if there are no rows
  if (ds.Tables["Existing"].Rows.Count > 0)
    pnlExisting.Visible = true;
  else
    pnlExisting.Visible = false;
}
```

7. In the previous method, we attached the same handler to all of the link buttons, but because each of them has a different CommandArgument, we can use that value to determine which row to delete. The code to perform the delete is little different from the database access code we've seen so far: it builds the SQL statement, creates the connection and command, and executes the command:

```
private void OnDeletePlace(Object sender, CommandEventArgs e)
{
  // e.CommandArgument receives the LapseID to delete
```

```
SqlConnection con;
SqlCommand cmd;

// Connect and execute the query
con = new SqlConnection(
"data source=(local)\\NetSdk;initial catalog=FriendsData;user id=sa");
cmd = new SqlCommand("DELETE FROM TimeLapse WHERE LapseID='" +
  e.CommandArgument.ToString() + "'", con);
con.Open();

try
{
  cmd.ExecuteNonQuery();
}
catch
{
  // Just pass the exception up
  throw;
}
finally
{
  con.Close();
}

LoadDataSet();
InitPlaces();
}
```

8. The `InitForm()` method initializes the form fields. It blanks any previous content, and it loads the combo box with the available places – but it only does these things if the page is being accessed for the first time:

```
private void InitForm()
{
  if (!(IsPostBack))
  {
    // Clear existing values
    txtDescription.Text = string.Empty;
    txtMonthIn.Text = string.Empty;
    txtMonthOut.Text = string.Empty;
    txtNotes.Text = string.Empty;
    txtYearIn.Text = string.Empty;
    txtYearOut.Text = string.Empty;
    cbPlaces.Items.Clear();

    // Initialize combo box
    ListItem item;
    DataRow[] types;

    // Access the table by index
    foreach (DataRow row in ds.Tables[1].Rows)
```

```
  {
        // Find the related row in Types data table
        types = ds.Tables["Types"].Select(
          "TypeID='" + row["TypeID"].ToString() + "'");

        item = new ListItem();

        // Explicitly use the Item default property
        item.Text = types[0]["Name"].ToString();
        item.Text += ": " + row["Name"].ToString();

        // We can access the row's column by index too
        item.Value = row[0].ToString();
        cbPlaces.Items.Add(item);
     }
  }
}
```

9. For brevity, we will omit the code for the `btnAdd`'s `Click` event handler, as that's just a simple `INSERT` statement that creates a new row for the `TimeLapse` table. We've already seen how those work, and you can download the full version of this code from the Wrox web site.

10. Compile and run the project with `AssignPlaces.aspx` as the start page. After logging on as the `wrox` user, you should see something like this:

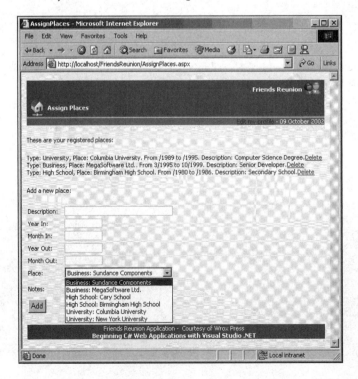

How It Works

Of the three methods that deal with what the user sees on the screen, the only one that interacts directly with the database is LoadDataSet(). Once the DataSet has been filled with data by this procedure, we don't need to refer to the database in InitPlaces() or InitForm(). This is a direct result of the disconnected nature of DataSet objects.

The data adapter class has a constructor that receives a SQL statement that's used to initialize its SelectCommand property. This has the same effect as setting this property to an existing command later on. To the same constructor, we also pass the SqlConnection that the command should use. In our code, you can see three adapters being created – one to retrieve full details, one that's just for places, and one that's just for type names.

```
// Initialize the adapters
adExisting = new SqlDataAdapter(sql, con);
adPlaces =
  new SqlDataAdapter("SELECT * FROM Place ORDER BY TypeID", con);
adPlaceTypes = new SqlDataAdapter("SELECT * FROM PlaceType", con);
```

As we're only retrieving data here (as opposed to editing or updating it), we don't need to configure anything else, so we can just proceed to connect to the database and create a new DataSet object:

```
con.Open();
ds = new DataSet();
```

Inside the try block, we just call each adapter's Fill() method, passing the dataset and name that you want to give to the DataTable that's created as a result. If we didn't specify a name here, we'd get tables called Table1, Table2, and so on:

```
try
{
  // Proceed to fill the dataset
  adExisting.Fill(ds, "Existing");
  adPlaces.Fill(ds, "Places");
  adPlaceTypes.Fill(ds, "Types");
}
```

Once we've filled the DataSet, we can access its data using various approaches. In InitPlaces(), which fills the placeholder at the top of the user's screen, we use a couple of different ones. First, we access the table from the DataSet's Tables property, using the table name we used when we filled it:

```
foreach (DataRow row in ds.Tables["Existing"].Rows)
{
```

Now, we can use the foreach construct to iterate through the rows of the table in the same way that we would iterate through any standard collection or array. The DataRow class contains a default Item property that can receive the column name (or its index), and retrieve the value in that column:

```
lbl.Text = string.Format(msg, row["Type"], row["Place"],
  row["MonthIn"], row["YearIn"],
  row["MonthOut"], row["YearOut"], row["Name"]);
```

The `InitPlaces()` method is just creating a literal control and a link button that's initialized with the values of each row. The link button will pass the row's `LapseID` column value, which is the primary key of the `TimeLapse` table, to the event handler for the **Delete** button. We also use this value to be the button control's ID, after removing the – character:

```
// Assign a unique ID to the control
btn.ID = row["LapseID"].ToString().Replace("-", string.Empty);
btn.Text = "Delete";

// Pass the LapseID when the link is clicked
btn.CommandArgument = row["LapseID"].ToString();

// Attach the handler to the event
btn.Command += new CommandEventHandler(OnDeletePlace);
```

This way, the handler we attached to all the buttons will know which record to delete, as this value is used to build the DELETE SQL statement:

```
private void OnDeletePlace(Object sender, CommandEventArgs e)
{
    // e.CommandArgument receives the LapseID to delete
    SqlConnection con;
    SqlCommand cmd;

    // Connect and execute the query
    con = new SqlConnection(
    "data source=(local)\\NetSdk;initial catalog=FriendsData;user id=sa");
    cmd = new SqlCommand("DELETE FROM TimeLapse WHERE LapseID='" +
      e.CommandArgument.ToString() + "'", con);
```

Finally, in `InitForm()`, which sets up the values in the combo box, we use some of the other choices offered by a `DataSet`. The most interesting one is that while we iterate through the records in the `Places` table, we perform a `Select` in the `Types` table to find the row corresponding to the current `TypeID`:

```
types = ds.Tables["Types"].Select(
    "TypeID='" + row["TypeID"].ToString() + "'");
```

The `Select()` method receives an expression that's equivalent to an SQL WHERE expression, and retrieves an array of `DataRow` objects matching the criteria. In our case, we know there will only be one row returned. Next, we explicitly use the row's `Item` property to add the place type to our list:

```
item.Text = types[0]["Name"].ToString();
```

Then, we finish building the item's text, and add it to the items available in the combo box:

```
item.Text += ": " + row["Name"].ToString();

// We can access the row's column by index too
item.Value = row[0].ToString();
cbPlaces.Items.Add(item);
```

For a more complete discussion of ADO.NET, you could read either Beginning Visual Basic
.NET Databases *(Wrox, ISBN 1-86100-555-5), or* Beginning ASP.NET Databases *using C#*
(ISBN 1-86100-741-8).

Updating Default.aspx

To round off our application for this chapter, we will need to update Default.aspx to reflect the
latest addition in functionality to our *Friends Reunion* case study. Previously, when we were transferred to
the Default.aspx page after logging into the application, there was only one link present, namely to
the News.aspx page. Now that we have another page that we can enable the user to access, we should
include this also.

In our Default.aspx.cs code-behind page, add the following code in the Page_Load method:

```
// Create a new blank table row, this time for Assign Places link
row = new TableRow();

// Assign Places link
img = new Image();
img.ImageUrl = "Images/flatscreenkeyb.gif";
img.ImageAlign = ImageAlign.Middle;
img.Width = new Unit(24, UnitType.Pixel);
img.Height = new Unit(24, UnitType.Pixel);

// Create the cell and add the image
cell = new TableCell();
cell.Controls.Add(img);

// Add the cell to the row
row.Cells.Add(cell);

// Set up the Assign Places link
lnk = new HyperLink();
lnk.Text = "Assign Places";
lnk.NavigateUrl = "AssignPlaces.aspx";

// Create the cell and add the link
cell = new TableCell();
cell.Controls.Add(lnk);

// Add the new cell to the row
row.Cells.Add(cell);

// Add the new row to the table
tb.Rows.Add(row);
```

It will come to no surprise to you that it looks very similar to the code required to render the News link.

This modification to the code will produce the following change in the `Default.aspx` page:

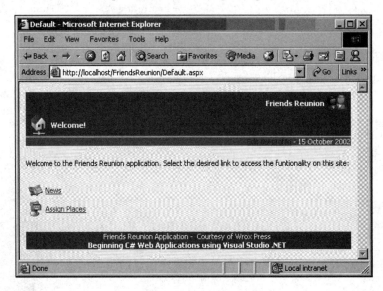

Summary

Data access is essential for all but the most trivial web application. We have learned the basis of ADO.NET, Microsoft's new strategy for data access, and we have seen how the various pieces fit in the whole picture of web application development.

We started to add some data-aware pages to our application, which allowed us to leverage the power of data-driven pages. We discussed how to programmatically access a database and handle its data. We were able to display that data in web forms, taking advantage of the knowledge we got from previous chapters, and we have started to use some of the features available in Visual Studio .NET, such as the Server Explorer.

Up to now, however, we have been typing a lot of code manually. Visual Studio .NET goes much further in programmer productivity, introducing the key concept of components. We got an introduction to what they are and how they work in conjunction with the IDE to perform some coding tasks for us. In the next chapter, we will dig into some exciting new features introduced by Visual Studio .NET to simplify web forms and data interaction through the concept of **data binding**. We will also learn how to use the more advanced wizards provided by components, and how to leverage web server controls to display and edit data in highly customizable ways though the use of another new concept, **templates**.

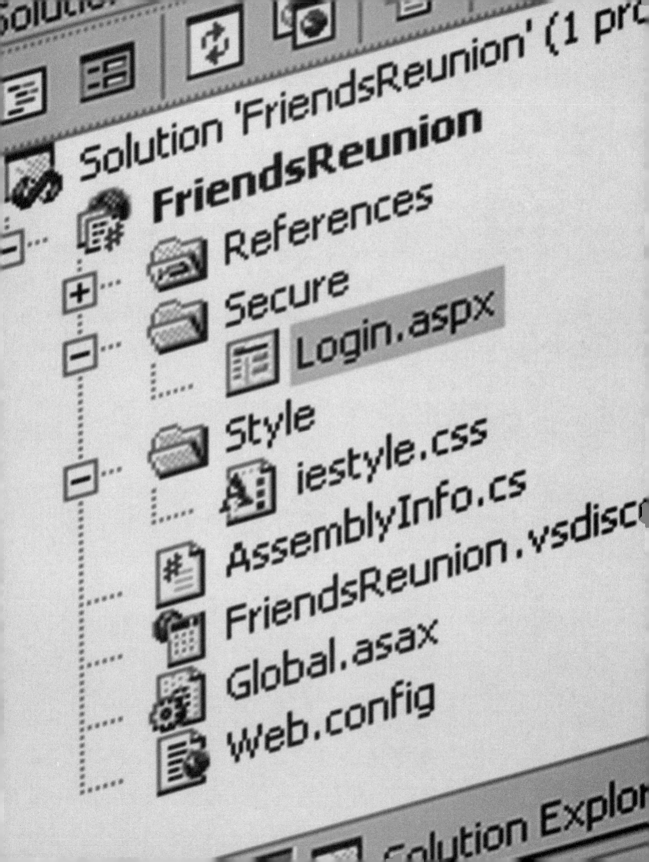

Solution 'FriendsReunion' (1 pro

FriendsReunion

References

Secure

    Login.aspx

Style

    iestyle.css

AssemblyInfo.cs

FriendsReunion.vsdisco

Global.asax

Web.config

Solution Explo

Data Binding

In Chapter 4, we learned how to interact with a database using the ADO.NET classes, and in this chapter we'll build on that. We'll first take a sneak peek at Visual Studio .NET's new **component architecture**. This opens the door to the automatic generation of data-access code, and we'll be discussing it in greater depth towards the latter part of this chapter. We'll also take a tour of the new **data binding capabilities** provided by ASP.NET, a feature that allows us to write less code and let the platform do the heavy work of transferring data from ADO.NET objects to our web forms. From this point, we'll be able to take full advantage of another technique that relates closely to data binding, called **templates**, which will allow us to customize the look and feel of the controls in which our data is displayed, all from the IDE and with full drag-and-drop support.

During this chapter, we will:

- ❏ Cover components in brief to get ourselves up and running
- ❏ Learn how to use simple data binding to show data on a form
- ❏ Make use of more complex binding that involves sets of data and presents it in tabular fashion, automatically
- ❏ Use the interaction between .NET components and the IDE to let Visual Studio .NET generate code on our behalf
- ❏ Take advantage of typed datasets, which improve the experience of data binding at design-time, and offer some other improvements to our code
- ❏ Take a look at templates, and apply them to customize the display and of complex sets of data
- ❏ Find out how to enable the editing of data through our web pages

Introduction to Components

Having come this far in the book, you may be starting to wonder what happened to the *Visual* part of Visual Studio .NET and Visual C# – we've been writing code as if we had nothing better than Notepad! Happily, Visual Studio .NET does come with some great productivity enhancements, including Wizards and designers that can make most data-related work a breeze. Now that you know the basics of ADO.NET, however, you'll have a better understanding of what's going on behind the scenes.

The fundamental concept that supports these features of the Visual Studio .NET IDE is the **component**. Putting out of your mind for a moment the various other meanings that have been ascribed to this word over the years, a *component* in Visual Studio .NET is a class that (directly or indirectly) implements the `System.ComponentModel.IComponent` interface. Most of the time, such a class will inherit from `System.ComponentModel.Component`.

A Visual Studio .NET component closely interacts with the IDE, and can be dropped onto a designer (like the web forms designer), appearing as an item in a section below the user interface elements. All of the ADO.NET classes we've seen are components, and as such, they also cooperate with and use services provided by the designer. For example, this is what a `SqlConnection` component that's been dropped from the Toolbox's Data tab onto an empty page looks like:

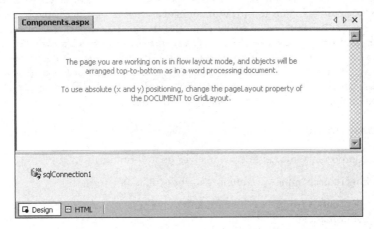

When a component is placed on a designer, it starts interacting with it, providing properties and Wizards that the developer can use to configure the component. Behind the scenes, the designer works together with the component to generate source code representing the actions we perform. As always, the best way to understand what's going on is to build an example.

Try It Out – Configuring a Connection Component

In this very short demonstration, we'll see what happens when we place a database component onto a form in a Visual Studio .NET design screen.

1. To our `FriendsReunion` project, add a (temporary) new web form called `Components.aspx`.

2. In the **Toolbox**, locate the **Data** tab, and drop a `SqlConnection` component onto the form. Use the **Properties** window to change its `Name` to `cnFriends`.

3. In the same window, from the drop-down list next to the `ConnectionString` property, you can either select **<New Connection...>** and use the **Data Link** dialog to configure a new connection, or you can use the `FriendsData` connection that we created before. This is another advantage of creating those connections with the **Server Explorer**!

4. Switch to the code view, and take a look at the code that has been generated for us.

How It Works

Components don't have a UI, so they appear in a separate section at the bottom of the page. In this example, we used the component to build the value for the `ConnectionString` property. After the steps we performed, the code-behind page contains the following:

```
using System;
using System.Collections;
using System.ComponentModel;
using System.Data;
using System.Drawing;
using System.Web;
using System.Web.SessionState;
using System.Web.UI;
using System.Web.UI.WebControls;
using System.Web.UI.HtmlControls;

namespace FriendsReunion
{
  /// <summary>
  /// Summary description for Component.
  /// </summary>
  public class Component : System.Web.UI.Page
  {
    protected System.Data.SqlClient.SqlConnection cnFriends;

    private void Page_Load(object sender, System.EventArgs e)
    {
      // Put user code to initialize the page here
    }

    #region Web Form Designer generated code
    override protected void OnInit(EventArgs e)
    {
      //
      // CODEGEN: This call is required by the ASP.NET Web Form Designer.
      //
      InitializeComponent();
      base.OnInit(e);
    }
```

```
/// <summary>
/// Required method for Designer support - do not modify
/// the contents of this method with the code editor.
/// </summary>
private void InitializeComponent()
{
  this.cnFriends = new System.Data.SqlClient.SqlConnection();
  //
  // cnFriends
  //
  this.sqlCon.ConnectionString = [YOUR_CONNECTION_STRING];
  this.Load += new System.EventHandler(this.Page_Load);


}
#endregion
  }
}
```

The web form designer generated the code in the #region section automatically. It also defined a protected variable, cnFriends, for the connection we added. The InitializeComponent() method creates the connection and sets the ConnectionString that we set through the **Properties** window. This method is called when the page is initialized, in the Page_Init() event handler. There is no magic here, just plain old variables and initialization code that we could have written by hand.

In truth, the component that we've chosen to add here offers only limited advantages over manual coding, but, later on in the chapter, we'll see how other components, such as the SqlDataAdapter, can perform some quite complex tasks on our behalf.

Dynamic Properties

Another advantage of components is the availability of **dynamic properties**, which can be configured to load their values from the application configuration file, Web.config. In Visual Studio .NET, dynamic properties live in a special section under the **Configurations** heading in the **Properties** window. Once again, the designer works together with the component to generate the appropriate code, this time for retrieving data from Web.config. Let's see how that happens.

Try It Out – Configuring a Dynamic ConnectionString

In this example, we will now modify the SqlConnection component we just added to use a dynamic property for the connection string. This is a significant improvement over the approach we've been using so far, which involved hard-coding the value everywhere we needed access to the database.

1. Open the Components.aspx web form in design view, and select the cnFriends component. In the **Properties** window, expand the (DynamicProperties) element. Click the ellipsis button next to ConnectionString, check the **Map...** box, and accept the dialog:

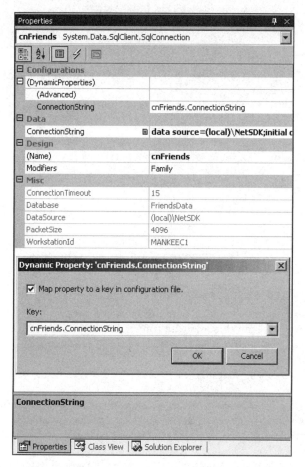

Note that a small icon has appeared next to the ConnectionString property under the **Data** category, indicating that this is now a dynamic property.

How It Works

The (DynamicProperties) section in the **Properties** window works in conjunction with components, showing only the properties that can be dynamically configured. If we now take a look at the Web.config file, we will see that something similar to the following element has been added:

```
<appSettings>
    <!--  User application and configured property settings go here.-->
    <!--  Example: <add key="settingName" value="settingValue"/> -->
    <add key="cnFriends.ConnectionString"
         value="data source=(local)\NetSDK;
         initial catalog=FriendsData;
         persist security info=False;
         user id=sa;workstation id=MANKEEC1;
         packet size=4096" />
</appSettings>
```

If you now look again at the code-behind page, you'll see that there have been some changes there too:

```
private void InitializeComponent()
{
  System.Configuration.AppSettingsReader configurationAppSettings =
    new System.Configuration.AppSettingsReader();
  this.cnFriends = new System.Data.SqlClient.SqlConnection();
  //
  // cnFriends
  //
  this.cnFriends.ConnectionString =
    ((string)(configurationAppSettings.GetValue(
      "cnFriends.ConnectionString", typeof(string))));
  this.Load += new System.EventHandler(this.Page_Load);
}
```

The new `configurationAppSettings` variable is an instance of the `AppSettingsReader` class, which allows access to the values in the `Web.config` file. The property's value is retrieved with this object, using the key that was built by the dynamic property, and cast explicitly to a string. Whenever we change the setting in the configuration file, this page will automatically use the new value.

There's actually another method of getting hold of the values that we store in `Web.config` file. We can modify the code that we've been using to create connection objects so far to use the following syntax:

```
con = new SqlConnection(
  ConfigurationSettings.AppSettings("cnFriends.ConnectionString")
```

In fact, we can use the `Web.config` file to store pretty much anything we want, and retrieve it with this syntax. This way, this central repository can be used both for the components we use through the IDE, and from our custom code, significantly improving maintenance.

The advantage of this shortcut over an `AppSettingsReader` object is that it requires less code, but the object can offer better performance if we have to retrieve several settings at once – it caches the `<appSettings>` section as we read it, and performs physical access to the file only once. If the `Web.config` file is fairly big, using `AppSettingsReader` can be more suitable.

> The `ConfigurationSettings` class is located in the `System.Configuration` namespace, so we can either add a `using` statement or use the fully-qualified class name.

With the database concepts you've learned so far, we're ready to build some useful data-aware applications, but the introduction to components we have looked at has been just a peek into the possibilities that are available in Visual Studio .NET. We'll be taking a much closer look at them, later in this chapter. We'll see how they reduce the amount of code we have to type, and how they can provide advanced functionality for our applications with hardly any effort. For now though, we'll move on to the main topic of this chapter, that of data binding.

Data Binding

You may recall our work with the `NewUser.aspx` page from Chapter 4. When we added the capability to pre-load the form with information from the database (for the current user, to allow them edit their profile), we used code in the code-behind page to set the values to be displayed in the various controls. The code looked like this:

```
// Convert directly the untyped Object returned by the
// indexer to a string
this.txtEmail.Text = reader["Email"].ToString();
this.txtFName.Text = reader["FirstName"].ToString();
this.txtLName.Text = reader["LastName"].ToString();
this.txtLogin.Text = reader["Login"].ToString();
this.txtPhone.Text = reader["PhoneNumber"].ToString();
this.txtPwd.Text = reader["Password"].ToString();
```

The need to display data from a data source – in this case, a `DataReader` object – is a situation that crops up time and time again. For this reason, ASP.NET supports the concept of **data binding**, which frees us from writing code like that shown above. The idea behind data binding is that the link between the data source and the controls that will display it is known at design time, and will rarely (if ever) change at run time.

To use data binding, we provide each control property that will display data at run time with a **binding expression** that represents that data at design time. At run time, we resolve the binding expression to its actual value, and assign that to the control property instead.

Before we discuss the precise format and run-time behavior of binding expressions, let's see where and how we can use them. A binding expression can be specified in HTML source code, in place of any web server control's property value, such as:

```
<asp:Label id="lblPending" runat="server" Text='<%# EXPRESSION %>' />
```

Here, we see a binding expression, `<%# EXPRESSION %>`, replacing the `Text` property value of a `Label` web server control. This is probably the most common use, but there's nothing to stop you from using data binding for the label's `BackColor` property, if that's what you want to do. This use of data binding is called **simple binding**, because resolution of the expression results in a single value.

To get the expression evaluated and have the results placed in the control's property, we have to call the control's `DataBind()` method. This method is inherited from the `Control` base class, and as such, it is available to all controls, even the page itself. Its effects propagate to all child controls too, so a call at the page level will cause all of the data binding expressions on a page to be evaluated, and the results placed in the corresponding properties.

Binding Expressions

A binding expression is evaluated in the context defined by the code-behind page – that is, all of the page-level variables, methods, and properties that are available in the code-behind page can be used as binding expressions. For example, we could have a method called `GetPending()` that performs a database query and then returns a string to be bound. We might use that as follows:

```
<asp:label id="lblPending" runat="server" Text='<%# GetPending() %>' />
```

Similarly, if we had a page-level variable called `userID`, we could bind that to any control we wanted with the following code (for a label in this case):

```
<asp:label id="lblPending" runat="server" Text='<%# userID %>' />
```

Just as easily, we could refer to a dataset variable defined in the code-behind page to show the count of the rows in a table, for example:

```
<asp:label id="lblPending" runat="server"
         Text='<%# dsUser.Tables[0].Rows.Count %>' />
```

As you can see, the mechanism is very flexible – it just leaves us to perform the appropriate variable initialization or method coding. If we're intending to use data binding, though, we have to do a little forward planning. Typically, we'll define a page-level variable to hold the data (say, a `DataSet`), fill it using a `DataAdapter` as you saw in Chapter 4, and finally call `DataBind()` in the page itself. This will cause all the controls that have binding expressions to be populated with the values from the just-filled `DataSet`.

> **The important thing to remember is that the code-behind members to be used in binding expressions must be either `Public` or `Protected` in order to be accessible at the moment binding occurs.**

The DataBinder Class

If we need to format a string prior to displaying it, we can use a helper class that's provided in the `System.Web.UI` namespace, called `DataBinder`. This class contains a static method called `Eval()`, which receives an object, an expression, and (optionally) a format string. The object is used as the context in which to evaluate the expression, and the result of the evaluation is formatted with the last parameter if specified.

If we wanted to apply special formatting to a user's birth date, for example, we could use this:

```
<asp:label id=lblBirth runat="server"
         text='<%# DataBinder.Eval(dsUser.Tables[0].Rows[0],
         "[DateOfBirth]", "{0:MMMM dd, yyyy}") %>'>
</asp:label>
```

Here, the first parameter to `Eval()` – the row we want to display the value from – is used as the context in which the second parameter is evaluated. Finally, the format string is applied.

It's worth taking a little more time to understand the inner workings of the `Eval()` method, as we'll be using it a lot from this point on – especially when we start to use the IDE to generate code for us. To illustrate the forthcoming discussion, we'll use the following expression, which displays the count of rows in a dataset's table, padded with zeros up to six digits:

```
<%# DataBinder.Eval(dsUser, "Tables[0].Rows.Count", "{0:D6}") %>
```

Here, we've passed the dataset as the first argument, which will be the context for the expression. Now, in order for the `Count` to be retrieved, each 'step' in the expression has to be evaluated separately and used as the starting point for the next. To evaluate this expression, `Eval()` first evaluates `dsUser.Tables(0)`, then uses the result of that to evaluate `Rows`, and uses this last result in turn to evaluate `Count`. When it encounters an indexer expression start symbol, which can be either `[` or `(` (for Visual Basic .NET users), it evaluates it as a whole, up to the closing symbol, again either `]` or `)`.

The important consequence of this way of working is that two consecutive indexer accesses won't be properly evaluated. For example, look at what happens if we rewrite the earlier expression for displaying the user's birth date:

```
<asp:label id=lblBirth runat="server"
           text='<%# DataBinder.Eval(dsUser,
           "Tables[0].Rows[0](""DateOfBirth"")", "{0:MMMM dd, yyyy}") %>'>
</asp:label>
```

This is perfectly valid C# code for accessing the `DateOfBirth` column in the first row of the table, but if you tried it here, you'd actually get the string `System.Data.DataRow` displayed! `Eval()` splits the expression into `Tables[0]` and `Rows[0](""DateOfBirth"")`, according to the dot separating them. It then looks for the starting parenthesis, and evaluates it up to the closing one. This means that first, it will retrieve the first table in the `Tables` collection, and then it will only evaluate `Rows[0]`, silently ignoring the second indexer accessor.

If we add a dot between the two accessors, as follows, both of them will be properly evaluated:

```
<asp:label id=lblBirth runat="server"
           text='<%# DataBinder.Eval(dsUser,
           "Tables[0].Rows[0].(""DateOfBirth"")", "{0:MMMM dd, yyyy}") %>'>
</asp:label>
```

Of course, this is not valid C# code, but in this context, it's the only way to have things work as they should.

Adding Data Binding to Friends Reunion

After all of that, let's start using these new ideas to get some new functionality for our application. The way that *Friends Reunion* is intended to work is that when users make requests for fellow users to get in touch with them, a record will be placed in the `Contact` table. This table has the following structure:

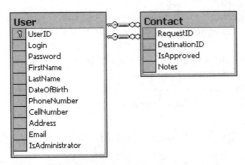

At first, a new record in the `Contact` table will have its `IsApproved` flag set to 0, indicating that this is a request waiting to be approved. In our application, a requesting user must be approved by the target user in order for the former to be able to see the latter's details. In this discussion, we will focus on the view of the target user – that is, the one specified in the `DestinationID`.

Before the target user approves a contact that has placed a request, they will surely want to see that user's details. We will now build a form that receives a `RequestID` as a query string parameter, and displays information about that user in a table. In it, we will take advantage of data binding. For the purposes of this demonstration, we will be using most of the binding expression variants you've seen; in your own applications, you'll probably use the one that best suits your needs and programming style.

In the form's code-behind page, we'll write a method that counts the number of pending requests the user has, and use data binding to display this value too. Finally, a button will allow the user to update the `IsApproved` flag whenever they want to approve the contact. Once the flag has been updated, the user will be redirected to the page they came from, which will be `News.aspx`.

Try It Out – Displaying Information about Fellow Users using Data Binding

Eventually, the page we're about to create will be arrived at as a result of navigation from `News.aspx`, in the course of which the `RequestID` will be passed as a query string. When we test this example, we'll have to simulate that by assembling the string ourselves, but don't let that put you off – we'll deal with `News.aspx` later.

1. Add a new web form called `ViewUser.aspx` to the project, adding the link to the usual stylesheet, and changing the code-behind page to inherit from the `FriendsBase` class.

2. Add a style rule called `TableLines` to the stylesheet. This will help us to make our HTML tables look consistent across our site:

```
.TableLines
{
  border-top: #c7ccdc 1px solid;
  border-bottom: #c7ccdc 1px solid;
  border-right: #c7ccdc 1px solid;
  border-left: #c7ccdc 1px solid;
  padding-top: 5px;
```

```
    padding-bottom: 5px;
    padding-right: 5px;
    padding-left: 5px;
}
```

3. Add an HTML table with six rows and two columns. Set its ID to `tbLogin`, its `class` property to `TableLines`, `border` to 0, and `cellpadding` and `cellspacing` to 2.

4. Add `Label` web server controls to the cells on the right, except for the last row, which will contain a `HyperLink` control, with ID `lnkEmail`. Below the table, add some text and a label to reflect the following form layout:

5. Add a web server `Button` control, and set its ID to `btnAuthorize`, its `CssClass` to `Button`, and its `Text` property to `Authorize Contact`.

6. Switch to the HTML view, and make the following changes to add data binding expressions to the controls:

```
...
<body>
  <form id="ViewUser" method="post" runat="server">
    <table class="TableLines" id="tbLogin"
           cellSpacing="2" cellPadding="2" border="0">
      <tr>
        <td>
          <p>Name:</p>
        </td>
        <td><asp:label id=lblName runat="server"
               Text='<%# dsUser.Tables[0].Rows[0]["FirstName"] + " " +
                         dsUser.Tables[0].Rows[0]["LastName"] %>'>
          lblName</asp:label></td>
      </tr>
      <tr>
        <td>Birth Date:</td>
        <td><asp:label id=lblBirth runat="server"
```

```
                     Text='<%# DataBinder.Eval(dsUser.Tables[0].Rows[0],
                           "(DateOfBirth)", "{0:MMMM dd, yyyy}") %>'>
              lblBirth</asp:label></td>
        </tr>
        <tr>
          <td>Phone Number:</td>
          <td><asp:label id=lblPhone runat="server"
                  Text='<%# dsUser.Tables["User"].Rows[0]["PhoneNumber"] %>'>
              lblPhone</asp:label></td>
        </tr>
        <tr>
          <td>Mobile Number:</td>
          <td><asp:label id=lblMobile runat="server"
                  Text='<%# DataBinder.Eval(dsUser,
                           "Tables[User].Rows[0].(CellNumber)") %>'>
              lblMobile</asp:label></td>
        </tr>
        <tr>
          <td>Address:</td>
          <td><asp:label id=lblAddress runat="server"
                  Text='<%# DataBinder.Eval(dsUser.Tables["User"].Rows[0],
                           "(Address)") %>'>
              lblAddress</asp:label></td>
        </tr>
        <tr>
          <td>E-mail:</td>
          <td><asp:hyperlink id=lnkEmail runat="server"
                  navigateurl='<%# DataBinder.Eval(dsUser.Tables,
                                "(User).Rows[0].(Email)", "mailto:{0}") %>'>
              Send mail</asp:hyperlink></td>
        </tr>
      </table>
      <p>The user has
        <asp:label id=lblPending runat="server"
            Text="<%# GetPending() %>">
            lblPending</asp:label> requests for contact pending.</p>
      <p><asp:button id="btnAuthorize" runat="server"
            Text="Authorize Contact" CssClass="Button"></asp:button></p>
    </form>
  </body>
```

7. Next, open the code-behind page and add the following `using` statements to the top of the page:

```
using System;
using System.Collections;
using System.ComponentModel;
using System.Configuration;
using System.Data;
using System.Data.SqlClient;
using System.Drawing;
using System.Web;
using System.Web.SessionState;
```

```
using System.Web.UI;
using System.Web.UI.WebControls;
using System.Web.UI.HtmlControls;
```

8. We will also need to add the `DataSet` as a public variable, and perform the database access in the `Page_Load()` event handler:

```
...
public DataSet dsUser;

private void Page_Load(object sender, System.EventArgs e)
{
    string userID = Request.QueryString["RequestID"];

    // Ensure we received an ID
    if (userID == null)
      throw new ArgumentException(
        "This page expects a RequestID parameter.");

    // Create the connection and data adapter
    SqlConnection cnFriends = new SqlConnection(
      ConfigurationSettings.AppSettings["cnFriends.ConnectionString"]);
    SqlDataAdapter adUser = new SqlDataAdapter(
      "SELECT * FROM [User] WHERE UserID='" + userID + "'", cnFriends);

    // Initialize the dataset and fill it with data
    dsUser = new DataSet();
    adUser.Fill(dsUser, "User");

    // Finally, bind all the controls on the page
    Page.DataBind();
}
```

9. The next method, `GetPending()`, will return the value that's used in the `lblPending` label to show the number of pending requests for this user:

```
public string GetPending()
{
  string userID = Request.QueryString["RequestID"];

    // Ensure we received an ID
    if (userID == null)
      throw new ArgumentException(
        "This page expects a RequestID or UserID parameter.");

    // Create the connection and command to execute
    SqlConnection cnFriends = new SqlConnection(
      ConfigurationSettings.AppSettings["cnFriends.ConnectionString"]);
    SqlCommand cmd = new SqlCommand("SELECT COUNT(*) FROM Contact " +
                     "WHERE IsApproved=0 AND DestinationID='" +
                     userID + "' ", cnFriends);
```

```
cnFriends.Open();

// Ensure the connection is closed after execution
try
{
  return cmd.ExecuteScalar().ToString();
}
catch
{
  // Just pass the exception up
  throw;
}
finally
{
  cnFriends.Close();
}
}
```

10. The last piece of code that we need to add here is the handler for the **Authorize** button. This
will just perform an update of the IsApproved flag:

```
private void btnAuthorize_Click(object sender, System.EventArgs e)
{
  string userID;
  string sql;
  SqlCommand cmd;

  userID = Request.QueryString["RequestID"];

  sql = "UPDATE Contact SET IsApproved=1 WHERE " +
        "RequestID='{0}' AND DestinationID='{1}'";
  sql = String.Format(sql, userID, Page.User.Identity.Name);

  // Create the connection and command to execute
  SqlConnection cnFriends = new SqlConnection(
   ConfigurationSettings.AppSettings["cnFriends.ConnectionString"]);
  cmd = new SqlCommand(sql, cnFriends);
  cnFriends.Open();

  // Ensure the connection is closed after execution
  try
  {
    cmd.ExecuteNonQuery();
  }
  catch
  {
    // Just pass the exception up
    throw;
  }
  finally
  {
    cnFriends.Close();
```

```
        }

        // Return to the news page
        Response.Redirect("News.aspx");
    }
```

11. Finally, save and compile the project. Open a browser window, and point it to the newly created page with the following parameter appended to the URL: ViewUser.aspx?RequestID=436EA455-BABD-4ca2-9D30-7B4F4608A068. After you log in to the application (again, with `wrox` as the user name and password), you should see the following page:

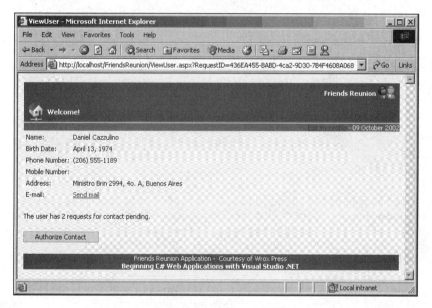

How It Works

The code in `Page_Load()` starts by checking for the existence of the `RequestID` parameter, and then creates a connection and a data adapter to perform the query. As we learned at the start of this chapter, we are no longer hard-coding the connection string. Instead, we are using the value stored in the configuration file:

```
SqlConnection cnFriends = new SqlConnection(
    ConfigurationSettings.AppSettings["cnFriends.ConnectionString"]);
SqlDataAdapter adUser = new SqlDataAdapter(
    "SELECT * FROM [User] WHERE UserID='" + userID + "'", cnFriends);
```

After we have the objects configured, we create and fill the dataset that we defined at the class-level as a public variable:

```
dsUser = new DataSet();
adUser.Fill(dsUser, "User");
```

Now, instead of manually assigning each property to the corresponding value in the dataset, we let the data-binding mechanism do its work and evaluate the expressions we used in the page's HTML source. We do this by explicitly calling `DataBind()` at the page level, so that every control on the page gets evaluated:

```
Page.DataBind();
```

To see exactly what's going on, though, we need to take a look at the different binding expressions we used, starting with the first one:

```
<td><asp:label id=lblName runat="server"
        Text='<%# dsUser.Tables[0].Rows[0]["FirstName"] + " " +
                  dsUser.Tables[0].Rows[0]["LastName"] %>'>
    lblName</asp:label></td>
```

Here, we directly specify the values from the dataset variable that we defined in the code-behind page, first accessing the value using the indexer, and then doing it explicitly using the `Item` property. Notice that we can also perform simple string concatenation inside the expression.

```
<td><asp:label id=lblBirth runat="server"
        Text='<%# DataBinder.Eval(dsUser.Tables[0].Rows[0],
                  "(DateOfBirth)", "{0:MMMM dd, yyyy}") %>'>
    lblBirth</asp:label></td>
```

This time, we use `DataBinder.Eval()`, because we want to give the date a special format. We split the expression just after the row to evaluate is selected (`dsUser.Tables[0].Rows[0]`), and let the method resolve the indexer property access with `"(DateOfBirth)"`. Note the relaxed syntax here – the default `Item` property actually receives a string, so the 'correct' value to pass to `Eval()` should be `"(""DateOfBirth"")"`. The version we've used is much neater, though!

```
<td><asp:label id=lblPhone runat="server"
        Text='<%# dsUser.Tables["User"].Rows[0]["PhoneNumber"] %>'>
    lblPhone</asp:label></td>
```

This is just to show that if we don't use `DataBinder.Eval()`, we have to code the expression as valid C# code. In this case, that means passing the proper string to access the column value.

```
<td><asp:label id=lblMobile runat="server"
        Text='<%# DataBinder.Eval(dsUser,
                  "Tables[User).Rows[0].(CellNumber)") %>'>
    lblMobile</asp:label></td>
```

Getting hold of the mobile number reprises a couple of the earlier themes, but you can see that in the last part of the expression – the actual column value retrieval – we had to add a dot between the two default property accessors. Without it, you'll get the string `System.Data.DataRow` in the form, because that's the string representation of the row object itself, rather than the column value.

```
<td><asp:hyperlink id=lnkEmail runat="server"
        navigateurl='<%# DataBinder.Eval(dsUser.Tables,
                          "(User).Rows[0].(Email)", "mailto:{0}") %>'>
    Send mail</asp:hyperlink></td>
```

Last, we provide a third argument to the Eval() function, as a result of which the formatting is applied just as if the following were called directly in our code:

```
String.Format("mailto:{0}", dsUser.Tables("User").Rows[0]("Email"))
```

At the bottom of the page, we have a rather simpler data binding expression, where we bind the lblPending label to the GetPending() method we created in the code-behind page:

```
<asp:label id=lblPending runat="server"
    Text="<%# GetPending() %>">
    lblPending</asp:label> requests for contact pending.</p>
```

The GetPending() method itself simply returns the count of pending requests for the current user in the Contact table:

```
SqlCommand cmd = new SqlCommand("SELECT COUNT(*) FROM Contact " +
                    "WHERE IsApproved=0 AND DestinationID='" +
                    userID + "' ", cnFriends);
```

The btnAuthorize handler just performs an update and redirects the user to the News.aspx page. To use the command, we call ExecuteNonQuery(), as we don't expect a result to be returned.

Binding to Sets of Data

Up to now, we have been binding to *single* items of data – each of our binding expressions has selected just one value from the database. In order to generate the table on the ViewUser.aspx page, we had to write a different expression for each cell. There is an easier way; to display *sets* of data, we can use some of the controls provided with ASP.NET that support binding to multiple items.

ASP.NET comes with several controls for displaying sets of data, such as DataGrid, DataList, and Repeater. These controls provide a DataSource property that can be set to point to the data we want to display. When this type of binding is used, the control itself is in charge of iterating through the data source and formatting the data for display, in a fashion that's configured using the control's properties.

The concept of a *data source* is fairly wide here, and is by no means a synonym for DataSet. These controls can be bound to *any* set of data, provided that the object containing the data implements the IEnumerable interface. This definition certainly includes the DataSet, but also encompasses the ArrayList, a collection, and so on.

In our application, we want to display the current user's list of pending requests for contact. This information can be easily displayed in tabular format, so we will use a DataGrid control.

Try It Out – Displaying Pending Contacts in a DataGrid

The process we'll follow here involves filling a `DataSet` with the data, setting it to be the data source for the grid, and calling the grid's `DataBind()` method. In addition, the control will be placed inside a panel, so we can later hide it if there turns out to be no pending requests.

1. As our starting point, we'll use the `News.aspx` page that we created in Chapter 3. However, its existing controls aren't of much use any more (it had a calendar, a combo box, the user controls, and so on). You'll recall that the header and footer controls were moved to the `FriendsBase` base class, so we should make this page inherit from that one. Once we've tidied up a little, the page source should look like the following:

```
<%@ Page language="c#" Codebehind="News.aspx.cs"
         AutoEventWireup="false" Inherits="FriendsReunion.News" %>
<!DOCTYPE HTML PUBLIC "-//W3C//DTD HTML 4.0 Transitional//EN" >
<html>
  <head>
    <title>News</title>
    <link href="Style/iestyle.css" type="text/css" rel="stylesheet">
    <meta content="Microsoft Visual Studio 7.0" name="GENERATOR">
    <meta content="C#" name="CODE_LANGUAGE">
    <meta content="JavaScript" name="vs_defaultClientScript">
    <meta content="http://schemas.microsoft.com/intellisense/ie5"
          name="vs_targetSchema">
  </head>
  <body>
    <form id="News" method="post" runat="server">
      <p> </p>
    </form>
  </body>
</html>
```

2. In the design view for the `News.aspx` file, drop a `Panel` web control onto the form and set its ID to `pnlPending`.

3. Change the text inside the panel to something meaningful, such as These users have requested to contact you:, and add a carriage return.

4. Drop a `DataGrid` web control inside the panel, and set its ID to `grdPending`.

5. Add the following namespace `using` statement:

```
using System;
using System.Collections;
using System.ComponentModel;
using System.Configuration;
using System.Data;
using System.Data.SqlClient;
using System.Drawing;
```

```
using System.Web;
using System.Web.SessionState;
using System.Web.UI;
using System.Web.UI.WebControls;
using System.Web.UI.HtmlControls;
```

6. Switch to the code-behind page, delete the `cbDay_SelectedIndexChanged()` and `calDates_SelectionChanged()` methods, and change the `Page_Load()` handler as follows:

```
private void Page_Load(object sender, System.EventArgs e)
{
    // Configure the icon and message
    base.HeaderIconImageUrl =
      Request.ApplicationPath + "/Images/winbook.gif";
    base.HeaderMessage = "News Page";

    string sql;
    sql = "SELECT [User].FirstName, [User].LastName, Contact.Notes, ";
    sql += " [User].UserID FROM [User], Contact WHERE ";
    sql += " DestinationID='" + Context.User.Identity.Name + "' AND";
    sql += " IsApproved=0 AND [User].UserID=Contact.RequestID";

    // Create the connection and data adapter
    SqlConnection cnFriends = new SqlConnection(
      ConfigurationSettings.AppSettings["cnFriends.ConnectionString"]);
    SqlDataAdapter adUser = new SqlDataAdapter(sql, cnFriends);
    DataSet dsPending = new DataSet();

    // Fill dataset and bind to the datagrid
    adUser.Fill(dsPending, "Pending");
    grdPending.DataSource = dsPending;
    grdPending.DataBind();
}
```

7. Set `News.aspx` as the start page and then do the usual save and run. After the usual `wrox` login, you'll see a list of users who have asked to contact you, as well as their user IDs on the far right of the table:

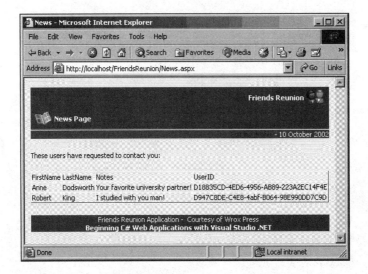

8. Once you're satisfied that everything works as described, go back to News.aspx, right-click on the data grid, and select **Auto Format...**. Play with the different styles, which will surely remind you of Excel's auto-format feature. Look at how the page source changes when you modify the look and feel of the grid, and how these settings are also available for modification in the **Style** section of the **Properties** window for the data grid. For now, we will set the format of the data grid to **Simple1**.

How It Works

Once again, we perform the data binding programmatically, at page loading time. To do so, we first query the database for records in the Contact table that have the IsApproved flag set to 0 and for which the DestinationID matches the current user:

```
sql = "SELECT [User].FirstName, [User].LastName, Contact.Notes, ";
sql += " [User].UserID FROM [User], Contact WHERE ";
sql += " DestinationID='" + Context.User.Identity.Name + "' AND";
sql += " IsApproved=0 AND [User].UserID=Contact.RequestID";
```

We then create the connection and the data adapter as usual, and fill a new DataSet. Finally, we set this DataSet to be the data source for the grid, and call the grid's DataBind() method:

```
grdPending.DataSource = dsPending;
grdPending.DataBind();
```

When this method is called, the DataGrid control will iterate through the DataSet and add a row to the table for each record it contains. If any of the available style properties are set, such as when we've used the **Auto Format...** option, the grid uses them to format the rows. By default, the DataGrid creates a column in the table for each column in the dataset.

We could also have chosen to declare the DataSet variable at the class level, and used the following binding expression on the grid:

```
<asp:dataGrid id="grdPending" runat="server"
              DataSource="<%# dsPending %>">
</asp:dataGrid>
```

Doing so would allow us to avoid assigning that property directly in our code, so we could safely delete the following line:

```
grdPending.DataSource = dsPending;
```

So far, so good, but we can't be happy with the way things stand: the column names at the top of the table are awful, and it certainly isn't good to display the UserID column at all. Let's see what we can do about that.

Try It Out – Customizing DataGrid Columns

To improve matters, we're going to change the headers, and use the UserID column to provide a link to the ViewUser.aspx page that we built earlier. This way, whenever the user sees a new request, they can ask for additional details – and, optionally, authorize that request using the button provided in the corresponding form. Operationally speaking, we need to override the automatic column generation feature, and provide our own definitions instead.

1. Click back to the design view of News.aspx, right-click on the data grid, and select **Property Builder**.... Notice how the user interface looks very similar to that of the **Style Builder** we saw in Chapter 3.

2. Select the **Columns** category, and uncheck the **Create columns automatically at run time** checkbox at the top of the form.

3. From the **Available columns** listbox, select **Bound Column** and click the > button three times, to add the first three columns. Select each of the new columns from the list and set the following property values for them:

Header Text	Data Field
First Name	FirstName
Last Name	LastName
Notes	Notes

4. Next, from the same listbox, select **HyperLink Column** and click the > button again. Set its properties as follows:

Form Field	Value
Header text	Details
Text	View

Table continued on following page

183

Form Field	Value
URL Field	UserID
URL format string	ViewUser.aspx?RequestID={0}

5. If you wish, feel free to play with the various formatting options that are available under the Format and Borders sections. When you've finished, you should be faced with something like this:

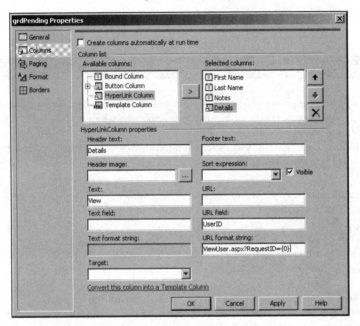

6. When you save the changes and run the application again, you should find that the appearance of the application has improved significantly:

How It Works

To make this discussion a little easier, we've taken all of the styling information out of the code being presented here. If you have applied some automatic formatting, you can remove it by selecting the **Remove Auto Format** scheme from the **Auto Format** dialog. The code generated for the grid should then look something like this:

```
<form id="News" method="post" runat="server">
  <p>
    <asp:panel id="pnlPending" runat="server">
      <p>These users have requested to contact you:</p>
      <p>
        <asp:datagrid id="grdPending" runat="server"
                      autogeneratecolumns="False">
          <columns>
            <asp:boundcolumn datafield="FirstName"
                             headertext="First Name"></asp:boundcolumn>
            <asp:boundcolumn datafield="LastName"
                             headertext="Last Name"></asp:boundcolumn>
            <asp:boundcolumn datafield="Notes"
                             headertext="Notes"></asp:boundcolumn>
            <asp:hyperlinkcolumn text="View"
               datanavigateurlfield="UserID"
               datanavigateurlformatstring="ViewUser.aspx?RequestID={0}"
               headertext="Details"></asp:hyperlinkcolumn>
          </columns>
        </asp:datagrid></p>
    </asp:panel>
  <p></p>
</form>
```

Our `DataGrid` control now has a child element called `<Columns>`, which contains four new controls that correspond to the four columns we set up above. The first three of these are `boundcolumn` controls, and you can see how their `datafield` and `headertext` attributes correspond with the columns in our `DataSet` and the labels in the `datagrid` respectively. The fourth column in the table is implemented with a `hyperlinkcolumn` control, in which the `datanavigateurlformatstring` attribute provides a skeleton within which to perform string formatting, using the `datanavigateurlfield` as the first argument.

This apparent complexity simply renders the appropriate link to the `ViewUser.aspx` file, with the expected `RequestID` parameter being added according to each row in turn. The data grid is performing most of the binding work itself, using the properties that we set, rather than us having to provide binding expressions directly.

Working Visually with Data

Leaving aside the help we just received from the DataGrid, we find ourselves in a situation that's not dissimilar from the one we faced in Chapter 4: so far, the Visual Studio .NET IDE hasn't provided us much help with our data-related tasks. We've done all of the data binding manually, and we've been accessing the database directly from our code, just as we did before. In fact, the IDE provides a number of facilities to make our coding easier, and we'll take a look at those features in this section, and indeed the rest of the chapter.

The Visual Studio .NET IDE can help us out by generating code automatically (both HTML source, and the code-behind page), based on settings we specify through the **Properties** window or in dedicated Wizards. To get the best out of it, however, we need to introduce some new concepts that are fundamental to these improved features.

Data Components

Earlier in this chapter, we saw how a SqlConnection component can be dropped from the **Toolbox** onto a web form, resulting in the automatic generation of some code on our behalf. However, we noted at the time that the benefits of using that particular component weren't exactly compelling. A better example of potential benefits is provided by the SqlDataAdapter component, which we've used frequently in our programs so far. In Visual Studio .NET, we can visually configure this component, including all its internal Command objects for SELECT, INSERT, UPDATE, and DELETE statements. In fact, provided that the SELECT is reasonably straightforward, Visual Studio .NET can even create the INSERT, UPDATE, and DELETE statements on our behalf!

When you drop a SqlDataAdapter component onto a web form, you're presented with a Wizard. (If you close the Wizard, you can reopen it by right-clicking on the component and choosing **Configure Data Adapter....**) The Wizard is very complete, allowing not only the creation of SQL statements, but also the creation of new stored procedures (or the reuse of existing ones). Here's a screenshot of the Query Builder that it makes available for this purpose:

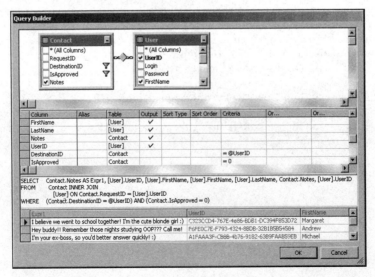

What you can see here is the result of building exactly the same query we used previously to fill the grid of pending requests for contact, except that we now use a parameter (@UserID) to filter the results. (A parameter is like a placeholder to be filled when the query is executed; we'll see how to set a parameter's value in a later example.)

To see how the data adapter is being 'magically' configured, you only have to look at the InitializeComponent() method in the code-behind page, which will contain the code that corresponds to the settings you've made through the wizard. The TableMappings property that appears in the **Properties** window and the initialization code tells the adapter which tables and fields in the SelectCommand to map to which tables and columns in the DataSet. This means that the names of neither the columns nor the tables in the DataSet have to match those in the source database.

It's also possible to use the **Properties** window to set the property of one data component to point to another one that's present on the same page. For example, we can set a SqlDataAdapter's SelectCommand property to point to an existing SqlCommand component in the page, and set the latter's Connection property to point to a SqlConnection component in turn. This makes it very easy to share a common connection object, for example, between multiple data adapters.

Typed DataSets

To complete the discussion of the help that Visual Studio .NET provides with data retrieval, we can use a special type of DataSet – a **typed dataset** – to gain some additional benefits, both for the visual design of our applications, and for our code. You'll recall that when we discussed how to access the tables, rows, and column values in a DataSet, you saw that we could do so using the string name of the element:

```
dsUser.Tables["User"].Rows[0]["FirstName"];
```

or using its index:

```
dsUser.Tables[0].Rows[0][0];
```

The code is simple in both cases, but it shows a drawback of the DataSet object: a typo in the name of a table or a field won't be trapped at compile time. Instead, it will produce a runtime exception. The alternative, which is to access the values with indexes, introduces a dependency on the SQL statement that's used to acquire the data – if we happen to change the fields returned (or even just their order), the code will not work as expected.

ADO.NET introduces the concept of a **typed dataset**, which is an automatically generated class that inherits from the generic DataSet class, but adds properties and classes to reflect the tables and rows in a type-safe manner. Once instantiated, a typed dataset is an object like any other, and we can use it to write code like this:

```
UserData() ds;
UserData.UserRow ur;
string value;

ur = (ds.User.Rows[0], UserData.UserRow)
value = ur.UserID;
```

We can now access the tables as direct properties of the dataset (as in ds.User.Rows[0]), and after a straightforward cast to the specific row type, we can access the fields as properties of the row itself (as in ur.UserID). This feature improves our productivity, as we don't have to worry about getting the names and indexes of tables and fields right – if we get them wrong, IntelliSense will tell us about it! Furthermore, the values in the columns of a typed dataset also have properly assigned types, making it impossible to (say) assign a string to a column that's expecting an integer.

A typed dataset can be generated from a data adapter component that's been placed on a web form. Provided that it has a valid SelectCommand assigned, we can right-click on it and choose the **Generate Dataset** option, and a typed dataset will be created based on the structure of the information that's retrieved by the command. We can give the new dataset a name and choose to add an instance of it to the current form, in order to use it right away.

Going through this process creates a **schema** for the dataset that contains a definition of its structure (such as tables, columns, and their types) in a file that has a .xsd extension. This file is a special type of XML document, which we will examine more closely in Chapter 7. It can be opened inside the IDE, where the designer will show the various pieces that make up the dataset's structure.

As is so often the case, a lot of these ideas will become clearer with an example. In the next section, we will improve the features of our News.aspx still further, to display a list of approved contacts as well as the 'pending' ones. The query will be very similar to the one we used last time, except that we'll be looking for the IsApproved flag to be set to 1. The new list will appear above the existing one, and since the users on the list have already been approved, we'll show the user more complete data about them, and provide a link to send them e-mail. We will also provide a link to another page showing their complete information – this will be the ViewUser.aspx form, with a slight change to hide the **Authorize Contact** button, as that won't be needed in this case.

Try It Out – Retrieving Contacts from the Database

In this example, as well as implementing the features described above, we'll see how using a typed dataset results in improvements to the support that's available through the IDE for configuring the way data is bound to the grid.

1. Open the News.aspx page, and add a carriage return before the panel where we show the pending requests. Add a new Panel web server control, set its ID to pnlApproved and change the text inside it to **These are your approved contacts:**.

2. Drop a DataGrid inside the panel, next to the text, and set its ID to grdApproved. Add a carriage return to separate it from the text.

3. Now let's configure the data components. First, drop a SqlConnection object onto the form, set its (Name) property to cnFriends, and use the ConnectionString property under the DynamicProperties category to map this value to the value in our Web.config file, cnFriends.ConnectionString. As the value will be already present in the Web.config file (we put it there earlier in this chapter), the value will be loaded and shown in the ConnectionString property under the **Data** category, with an icon to indicate that it's a dynamic value:

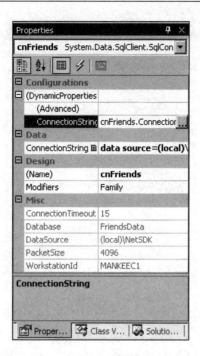

4. Drop a `SqlDataAdapter` component from the **Toolbox's Data** tab onto the web form designer, and a Wizard will appear. Choose **Next**, and select the **FriendsData** data connection from the drop-down list. (The list is populated from the connections in the Server Explorer that point to a SQL Server database.)

5. In the next step, the Wizard offers the option to use SQL statements or stored procedures to access the database. Select the first option, and move on. The next step allows you to set various advanced options, use the **Query Builder** or directly type the SQL statement to use. Whichever method you choose, the final SQL statement should be:

```
SELECT [User].FirstName, [User].LastName,
       [User].PhoneNumber, [User].Address,
       [User].Email, [User].UserID
FROM [User]
INNER JOIN Contact ON [User].UserID = Contact.RequestID
WHERE (Contact.DestinationID = @UserID) AND (Contact.IsApproved = 1)
```

You can also uncheck the **Generate Insert...** checkbox in **Advanced Options**, as we won't be making changes to the dataset's data, and those additional commands won't be needed.

6. Click next and then **Finish** to close this Wizard and change the data adapter's `(Name)` to `adApproved`. Optionally, expand the `SelectCommand` property and set its `(Name)` to `cmApproved`. Notice how the Wizard automatically detected that an existing `SqlConnection` on the page was already pointing to the same SQL Server connection, and used it for the command's `Connection` property:

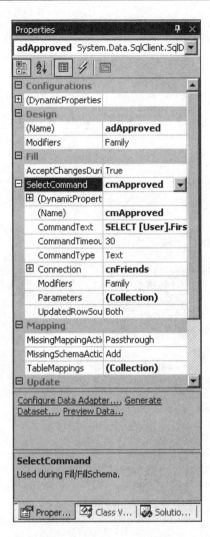

If you like, you can take a look at the SelectCommand's Parameters collection, and see that the @UserID parameter we used is already configured with the appropriate type. We will fill this parameter with the current user's ID before we fill the dataset, so that we only get the contacts for the current user.

7. Let us now generate a typed dataset to be filled by this data adapter. Click the **Generate Dataset...** link that appears in the **Properties** browser, or right-click the data adapter and select the similarly named menu option. In the dialog that appears, type ContactsData as the new dataset name – this will be the name of the generated DataSet-inheriting class. The checkbox near the bottom of this dialog specifies that we want to add an instance of this dataset to the current web form designer. Accept the dialog.

8. Change the newly added dataset component's (Name) to dsApproved.

9. Set the data grid's DataSource property to point to dsApproved. Now you should see the real column names displayed in the grid, instead of the dummy columns we saw before.

10. Open the Property Builder for the data grid. In the Columns pane, see how the list of fields is now shown in the Available columns listbox. This makes it much easier to choose which columns to display. Add all of them except for Email and UserID, and remember to uncheck the box at the top of the pane (Create automatic columns...).

11. Finally, we'll add two hyperlink columns, to allow the sending of mails and the viewing of user details. We've already seen how columns like this work, so we'll just list the values we have to use. This is the first hyperlink column:

Form Field	Value
Header text	Contact
Text	Send mail
URL Field	Email
URL format string	mailto:{0}

and this is the second one:

Form Field	Value
Header text	Details
Text	View
URL Field	UserID
URL format string	ViewUser.aspx?UserID={0}

Notice that URL Field is now a combo box that shows the list of columns in the typed dataset. We're passing a different query string parameter to ViewUser.aspx, so that it knows we're not asking for the details of a pending request for contact (it receives a RequestID in that case).

12. Now for the 'hard' part in the code-behind page. Below the existing code in Page_Load(), add the following to complete the command, fill the dataset, and bind to the data grid:

```
// Fill approved contacts
adApproved.SelectCommand.Parameters["@UserID"].Value =
                              Context.User.Identity.Name;
adApproved.Fill(dsApproved);
grdApproved.DataBind();
```

That is really *all* we need to code! To finish things off, though, let's add two lines at the end to hide the panels if there is no data to show:

```
if (dsPending.Tables[0].Rows.Count == 0)
    pnlPending.Visible = false;
if (dsApproved.User.Rows.Count == 0)
    pnlApproved.Visible = false;
```

13. Before we save and run the project, we'll apply a little bit of auto-formatting. Right-click on the data grid and set the Auto Format... dialog to Colorful 4 and accept this. With this page set as the start page, and after the usual login process, you will get something like this:

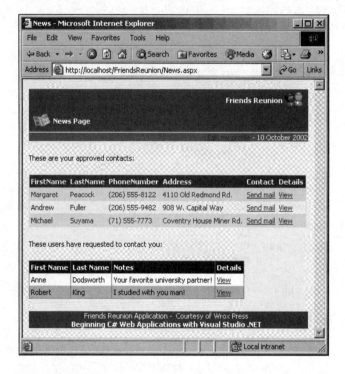

How It Works

The data components we dropped on the page, the Wizards, and the settings we specified are all reflected in the code-behind page by variable declarations at the class level:

```
public class News : FriendsBase
{
    // Web server controls here...
    protected System.Data.SqlClient.SqlConnection cnFriends;
    protected System.Data.SqlClient.SqlDataAdapter adApproved;
    protected System.Data.SqlClient.SqlCommand cmApproved;
    protected FriendsReunion.ContactsData dsApproved;
```

Each component has its own variable, and the last one – the dataset – is the most interesting. It's not defined as a generic `DataSet`, but rather as our custom `FriendsReunion.ContactsData` class. This is the class that was generated by the adapter when we asked it to do so. The variables for the components, just like their server controls counterparts, are initialized inside the `InitializeComponent()` method, which is placed inside the `Web Form Designer generated code` region.

The key point to bear in mind about this demonstration is that the code we wrote to load the list of pending requests in the last section, which performs exactly the same task as the code here, took 12 lines to achieve the same results as 3 lines here! That's four times less code – certainly *not* a minor detail. The code has been greatly simplified because all of the variable initialization code is generated automatically. We only have to pass the adapter the value for the current user ID, fill the dataset, and call `DataBind()` on the grid:

```
// Fill approved contacts
adApproved.SelectCommand.Parameters["@UserID"].Value =
                              Context.User.Identity.Name;
adApproved.Fill(dsApproved);
grdApproved.DataBind();
```

> *Just in case you're concerned with the database connection, it is opened by the data adapter, and closed as soon as it doesn't need it anymore.*

Finally, note that when we checked for the existence of rows in the two datasets, we could use the new property in our typed dataset that points to the right table:

```
if (dsApproved.User.Rows.Count == 0)
  pnlApproved.Visible = false;
```

instead of the following syntax, which we had to use for the generic dataset:

```
if (dsPending.Tables[0].Row.Count == 0)
  pnlPendingVisible = false;
```

Last of all, let's make a slight modification to the `ViewUser.aspx` page, to take account of the fact that it can now receive a user ID query string parameter. If that happens, it has to hide the **Authorize Contact** button. Change the `if` statement that checks for the ID in its `Page_Load()` event handler to match this:

```
// Ensure we received an ID
if (userID == null)
{
  userID = Request.QueryString["UserID"];
  if (userID == null)
  {
    throw new ArgumentException(
      "This page expects a RequestID or UserID parameter.");
  }
```

```
        else
        {
          btnAuthorize.Visible = false;
        }
    }
```

Here, we just hide the button if we receive a `UserID` parameter instead of a `RequestID`. Otherwise, we throw an exception. Remember that you'll need to make the same change in the `GetPending()` method.

Advanced Data Binding

Sometimes, there is a need for more flexibility over the rendering of data than a table with simple row and cell values. ASP.NET supports better customization of output through the use of **templates**. A template is a piece of ASP.NET/HTML code that can contain binding expressions, and is used inside a data grid column (for example) as a skeleton for each row/cell's representation. The web forms designer offers great integration with this concept, and makes their design a breeze.

Controls that support templates include `DataGrid`, `DataList`, and `Repeater`. Third-party controls may also support them.

Try It Out – Using a Templated Column in a DataGrid

In this example, we'll use templates to display four items in a cell: two small images, and the user's phone number and address. This will replace the columns that we previously used for this purpose. To do so, we'll need to create a template for that cell, and then take advantage of what you learned earlier about simple data binding to link values to the labels inside it.

1. Open the `News.aspx` page, right-click on the `grdApproved` data grid, and select Property Builder.

2. In the Columns pane, remove the PhoneNumber and Address columns. Next, select the Template Column element from the Available columns listbox, and add it to the list of Selected columns. Using the arrows at the right of the listbox, move the column up and position it above the Contact column.

3. Set the Header text form field to Info, and click OK.

4. To add controls inside the template column, we have to start editing it. Right-click on the data grid again, and a new menu option will be available: Edit Template. Inside it, select the only item available: Columns[2] - Info. You will see that the grid layout changes, and now shows four sections named HeaderTemplate, ItemTemplate, EditItemTemplate, and FooterTemplate.

5. Drop two `Image` and two `Label` web server controls inside the ItemTemplate section. Set the `ImageUrl` property of the images to `Images/phone.gif` and `Images/home.gif` respectively; the section should then look like this:

6. Next, select the first label, and open the DataBindings dialog for it.

7. In the Simple binding listbox, locate the Container | DataItem | PhoneNumber node. Note that once again, the complete list of fields available is shown, because we're using a typed dataset.

8. Do the same for the other label, this time binding it to Container | DataItem | Address.

9. Right-click on the template, and choose the End Template Editing menu option.

10. Save everything you've done so far, make this the start page, and then run the project. You will now see something like this:

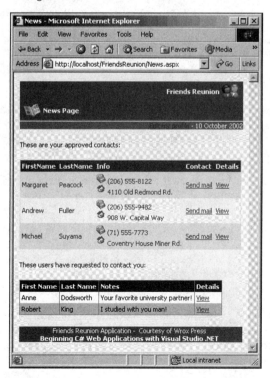

How It Works

When we add templated columns to a data grid, the **Edit Template** popup menu option is enabled. Inside this menu, the template design process is exactly the same as for the page itself: we drop controls on the sections we want, we set the controls' binding, and so on. As a result, the web form designer generates the following HTML code (again, we've removed the auto-formatting information to make the code more readable):

```
<asp:datagrid id=grdApproved runat="server"
      AutoGenerateColumns="False" DataSource="<%# dsApproved %>">
  <columns>
    <asp:boundcolumn datafield="FirstName"
                     headertext="FirstName"></asp:boundcolumn>
    <asp:boundcolumn datafield="LastName"
                     headertext="LastName"></asp:boundcolumn>
    <asp:templatecolumn headertext="Info">
      <itemtemplate>
        <p>
          <asp:image id="Image1" runat="server"
                     imageurl="Images/phone.gif"></asp:image>
          <asp:Label id=Label1 runat="server"
  Text='<%# DataBinder.Eval(Container, "DataItem.PhoneNumber") %>'>
          </asp:label><br>
          <asp:image id="Image2" runat="server"
                     imageurl="Images/home.gif"></asp:image>
          <asp:Label id=Label2 runat="server"
  Text='<%# DataBinder.Eval(Container, "DataItem.Address") %>'>
          </asp:label></p>
      </itemtemplate>
    </asp:templatecolumn>
    ...
```

The important element inside an `<asp:templatecolumn>` element is `<itemtemplate>`. As you can see, it just contains ordinary server controls with binding expressions just like the ones we've seen so far. New concepts, however, are the `Container` and the `DataItem`, both of which are used in the binding expression. The first part of the binding expression evaluation, `Container.DataItem`, resolves to the current item being bound – in our case, the current row in the data table.

At run time, when the grid finds a templated column, it creates the template, performs the bindings, and adds the controls to the cell, resulting in the rich output we saw.

Paging

We've arranged for the panels to disappear if there's nothing to display, but what happens if there are a very large number of things to display? We could end up with a very long page indeed, which wouldn't be a great way to treat our users. Happily, there's something we can do about that, too.

The technique known as **paging** consists of dividing the total count of items to be displayed by the maximum number of items we want to display simultaneously, and showing only that subset of data. By also providing a means to navigate back and forth among these 'logical' pages, we can allow our users to browse through the data a page at a time.

Paging is very common for applications such as the list of products for a big company, a list of expenses for the last two years, or a complete set of stock quotes. While we don't expect such a lengthy list (unless the user is really popular!), we will demonstrate its use anyway.

Try It Out – Adding Paging

The `DataGrid` control has intrinsic support for paging, and all that's required to take advantage of it is to set a couple of properties and handle a single event that's fired when the user changes the current page. We will add this functionality to our `grdApproved` grid, limiting the visible rows to only two, so that we can see paging take place.

1. Change the `grdApproved` properties as follows:

Property	Value
AllowPaging	True
PageSize	2

2. Locate the `PagerStyle` property, and set the following sub-properties:

Property	Value
Mode	NextPrev
NextPageText	Next >
PrevPageText	< Previous
HorizontalAlign	Left

3. To reconfigure the page when the user moves back and forth through the records, we have to wire up and handle the `PageIndexChanged` event that's fired by the data grid. To do this, first create an event handler for the `PageIndexedChanged` event for the `grdApproved` data grid by clicking on the **Events** button (the little lightning bolt as mentioned earlier) and double-clicking on the `PageIndexChanged` event. Now we can modify the handler that is created:

```
private void grdApproved_PageIndexChanged(object source,
    System.Web.UI.WebControls.DataGridPageChangedEventArgs e)
{
    // Set the new index
    grdApproved.CurrentPageIndex = e.NewPageIndex;

    // Fill approved contacts
    adApproved.SelectCommand.Parameters["@UserID"].Value =
        Context.User.Identity.Name;
    adApproved.Fill(dsApproved);
    grdApproved.DataBind();
}
```

4. Save and run the page, and voilà – we have paging:

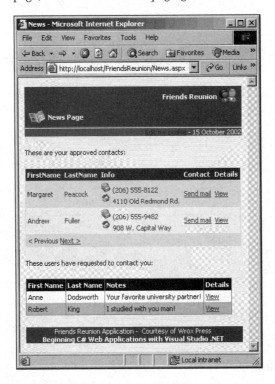

How It Works

We start the process by setting two properties that enable the paging mechanism in the grid: `AllowPaging` and `PageSize`. The pager mode and style is set next, where we set the text the links will have, as well as their placement in the footer. Once the pager links are in place, they raise the `PageIndexChanged` event when the user clicks on them, which we handle in the code-behind page:

```
private void grdApproved_PageIndexChanged(object source,
    System.Web.UI.WebControls.DataGridPageChangedEventArgs e)
{
  // Set the new index
  grdApproved.CurrentPageIndex = e.NewPageIndex;

  // Fill approved contacts
  adApproved.SelectCommand.Parameters["@UserID"].Value =
    Context.User.Identity.Name;
  adApproved.Fill(dsApproved);
  grdApproved.DataBind();
}
```

The code sets the new index it receives as the second argument to the event as the `CurrentPageIndex` property of the grid, and performs the binding again. As a result, the data grid will automatically skip the rows that don't fit in the current page, according to the page size we set.

Freestyle Data Binding and Editing – The Data List

With all of the features we've seen for the DataGrid, it is quite a challenge to find a control that's more suitable to our data displaying needs. Sometimes, though, we need even more control over presentation than the data grid will allow us. For example, if we want to display rows in some arbitrary, non-tabular format, a data grid doesn't seem like a good fit. Sure, we could use a complex template and a single cell, but ASP.NET comes with another control that is better suited to this task – the DataList. With regard to the data binding process and the design of templates, this control is very similar to the data grid, but it has no concept of columns.

As a template-only control, the data list is highly flexible, but crucially it also supports the concepts of selecting, editing, updating, or canceling the editing of an item. We can use different templates for each of those actions, and react to events fired by the control to perform the actual work against the database. The events fired by the data list are, not surprisingly, SelectedIndexChanged, EditCommand, UpdateCommand, and CancelCommand. But how does the control know when any of these actions has taken place?

To cause these events to be fired, we have to place a Button, LinkButton, or ImageButton control in a template, and set its CommandName property to one of the following values, according to the event we want to cause: Select, Edit, Update, or Cancel.

The data list decides which template to use for each item in the data source based on some properties that we can set. When SelectedIndex is set to a value different from -1, the corresponding item at the specified index will be rendered using the SelectedItemTemplate. Likewise, if EditItemIndex is set to a value other than -1, the EditItemTemplate will be used for that item. ItemTemplate and AlternatingItemTemplate are used to render the remaining items that are neither selected nor being edited.

In our handlers for the events mentioned, we will update the SelectedIndex or EditItemIndex to reflect the user's action, and to get the item rendered accordingly.

Adding a DataList to our Application

In our application, users create records in the TimeLapse table to reflect the places they have been to – we created a web form for that purpose in Chapter 4. The record reflects that a user has been in a certain place for a certain period of time – the place can be a high school, a college, or even a company they've worked for. The different categories of places are defined in the PlaceType table.

In the Place table, each place has an associated AdministratorID field, which is the ID of the user authorized to modify its data. A user should be able to look at the places our application works with, and in the case that they are also the administrator for a place, they should be able to modify its data, such as its address or notes.

We'll take advantage of the DataList's flexibility to allow this new functionality on our application. The process involves configuring data components (as we did before), designing templates for the data list, and then binding the data when necessary. We can edit the various templates available in the data list by right-clicking on it and selecting the appropriate menu option under Edit Template.

Try It Out – Showing Places in a DataList Control

In this example, we'll build a page that displays the list of places registered for the application, showing only their names and an icon to let the user select them. Once selected, complete data about the place will be displayed. The following screenshot shows what we will achieve, with one place selected after the user clicked the corresponding arrow next to it:

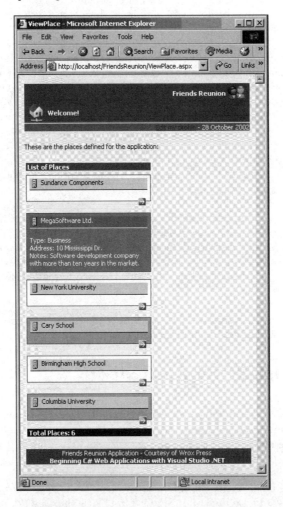

1. To our burgeoning project, add a new web form named `ViewPlace.aspx`. Add the usual stylesheet to it, and change the code-behind page to inherit from `FriendsBase`.

2. Drop a `SqlDataAdapter` component onto the form and configure it as we did before, setting the SQL statement to `SELECT * FROM Place`. Without leaving this Wizard step, click the **Advanced Options** button and leave only the first option checked. When the Wizard has finished, change the name of the adapter to `adPlaces`.

3. Change the added `SqlConnection`'s name to `cnFriends` and set its `ConnectionString` to use the dynamic property value, as we did before.

4. Set `InsertCommand` and `DeleteCommand` to None in the property browser, as we won't allow these operations for the data adapter. Leave `UpdateCommand` as it is, but change its name to `cmUpdate` – we'll be using updates later on.

5. As well as the details from the `Place` table, we also want to display the place type, which resides in the `PlaceType` table. Change the name of the select command to `cmSelect`. Click the ellipsis next to the `CommandText` property, add the `PlaceType` table, and add the `Name` field to the output, setting its alias to `TypeName`. Then click **OK**.

6. Select the **Generate Dataset** data adapter action, and enter `PlaceData` as the name for the new dataset. Set the new component's name to `dsPlaces`. Using a typed dataset will be useful when we come to customize the `DataList` control, as field names will be readily available.

7. At last, having set up the database access code, we can get on to displaying the data. Enter some introductory text such as **These are the places defined for the application:**, Drop a `DataList` control onto the page, and set the following properties:

Property	Value
ID	dlPlaces
DataSource	dsPlaces
DataMember	Place
DataKeyField	PlaceID
BorderStyle	Solid
BorderWidth	1px
Width	220px

8. Before we move on to the control layout, ensure the following styles are present in the stylesheet:

```
.Hidden
{
  visibility: hidden;
  display: none;
}
.PlaceHeader
{
  border-bottom: 1px solid;
}
.PlaceItem
{
  border-right: #336699 1px solid;
  border-left: #336699 1px solid;
```

```
  border-top: #336699 1px solid;
  border-bottom: #336699 1px solid;
  padding-right: 5px;
  padding-left: 5px;
  padding-top: 5px;
  padding-bottom: 5px;
  margin-top: 5px;
  margin-bottom: 5px;
}
.PlaceTitle
{
  font-weight: bold;
  width: 100%;
  color: white;
  background-color: #336699;
}
.PlaceSummary
{
  font-weight: bold;
  width: 100%;
  color: white;
  background-color: black;
}
```

9. In order to describe how to set up the templates, we'll use a combination of screenshots and tables for the different controls and their associated properties. Let's start with the **Header and Footer Templates** section of the data list:

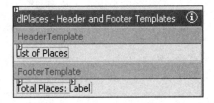

In the **Header Template** section, place a `Panel` control, set its `CssClass` to `PlaceTitle`, and enter text in it as above. In the **Footer Template** section, drop a `Panel` as well, with `CssClass` set as `PlaceSummary`, type the text shown above and finally, place a `Label` *within* it. Using the **DataBindings** dialog called up by clicking on the ellipsis next to (DataBindings) in the properties window, set the following custom binding expression:

```
DataBinder.Eval(dsPlaces, "Tables[Place].Rows.Count")
```

The dialog looks like this and we shall be using it quite often in this *Try It Out* and the next one:

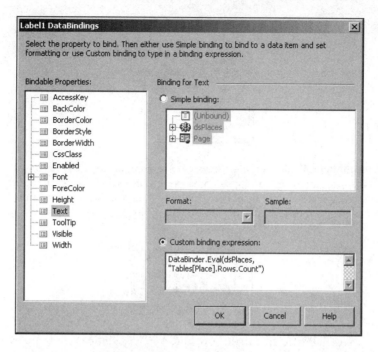

10. Next, we move on to the Item Templates group and to ItemTemplate. Drop an HTML `Flow Layout Panel` and set these properties for it:

Property	Value
style	BACKGROUND-COLOUR: white
class	PlaceItem

Inside it, drop a web forms `Panel` with `BackColor` set to `Gainsboro` and `CssClass` to `PlaceHeader`. Position the cursor inside it and drop an HTML `Image` control with `src` set to `Images/building.gif` and `align = middle`. Next to it, drop a web forms `Label`, and set the following custom data binding expression using the method detailed in the previous step:

```
DataBinder.Eval(Container, "DataItem.Name")
```

Finally, below the `Panel`, drop an `ImageButton` and set the following properties for it:

Property	Value
AlternateText	Select
ImageUrl	Images/bluearrow.gif
CommandName	Select
ImageAlign	Right

The layout of the template should look like the following by now:

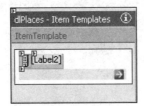

11. For the AlternatingItemTemplate section, we can simple copy the entire Flow Layout Panel, including its controls from the previous step into this section. This is because they are essentially displaying the same behavior so we can simply reuse code we have created previously. We only want to change its style property to define BACKGROUND-COLOR: lightskyblue:

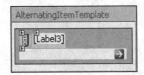

12. Finally we reach the SelectedItemTemplate, which is a little more complex than the previous templates. To start with, let's copy the panel we configured for the previous templates. First we will change the containing Flow Layout Panel's style property to be COLOR: white; BACKGROUND-COLOR: #5d90c3. Now change the existing web forms Panel BackColor to Gray.

Next to the existing Label, drop another one with CssClass set to Hidden, and ID to lblAdministratorID. Then, set the following custom data binding expression:

```
DataBinder.Eval(Container, "DataItem.AdministratorID")
```

This Label will be used to determine whether the current user can edit the selected row or not, and set the ImageButton's Visible property accordingly. The style ensures it won't appear in the display, yet it will be rendered (unlike setting Visible = False) so we can use it. Change the ImageButton properties to:

Property	Value
AlternateText	Edit
ImageUrl	ImageUrl = Images/edit.gif
CommandName	Edit
Visible	False
ID	cmdEdit

Right before this button, enter a carriage return, and type text and add labels to reflect the following arrangement:

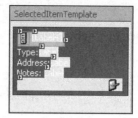

We'll run through the custom data binding expressions we need to set for the labels in the following table. Since the font is quite tricky to see, we'll go through them from top to bottom:

Control	Value
Label4	DataBinder.Eval(Container, "DataItem.Name")
Label5	DataBinder.Eval(Container, "DataItem.TypeName")
Label6	DataBinder.Eval(Container, "DataItem.Address")
Label7	DataBinder.Eval(Container, "DataItem.Notes")

13. Reopen the code-behind page, and add the following code that prevents the data list from being displayed if there are no places to display:

```
private void Page_Load(object sender, System.EventArgs e)
{
    if (!Page.IsPostBack)
      BindPlaces();
}
```

```
private void BindPlaces()
{
  adPlaces.Fill(dsPlaces);
  if (dsPlaces.Place.Rows.Count == 0)
  {
    dlPlaces.Visible = false;
  }
  else
  {
    dlPlaces.DataBind();
  }
}
```

Double-click on the data list in the **Design** view to create the handler for the SelectedIndexChanged event and add the following code:

```
private void dlPlaces_SelectedIndexChanged(
  object sender, System.EventArgs e)
```

```
    {
      this.BindPlaces();
    }
```

14. Save and run the page. Test the selection mechanism, and see how the template is applied to the selected item to show the complete details.

How It Works

The `DataList` has three template groups available to edit:

❑   Header and Footer Templates

❑   Item Templates

❑   Separator Templates

Data binding works just as we saw for the data grid – at run time, the template is instantiated, binding expressions are evaluated, and controls are added to the output for each element in the data source.

The important controls in these templates are the `ImageButtons` that we've placed at the bottom right of each. The values that we've assigned to the `CommandName` properties of these buttons – `Select` and `Edit` – have special meanings: the data list uses them to raise the events we discussed above. We'll take care of editing in a moment, but right now let's see what happens when the user clicks on the `cmdSelectItem` `ImageButton` of an item (or an alternating item).

In this case, the data list detects the `Select` command name, and raises the `SelectedIndexChanged` event. Inside this event handler, we just re-bind the data:

```
    private void dlPlaces_SelectedIndexChanged(
      object sender, System.EventArgs e)
    {
      this.BindPlaces();
    }
```

The data list automatically tracks the currently selected element, and as you can see, this rather simple procedure can have a powerful impact.

An interesting point to note here is that we didn't bother to set our own IDs for the controls. This would usually be considered to be bad practice, but the process that's in play results in several controls being created from the same template, making it impossible to predict the ID of a run-time control. (If this didn't happen, there would be naming collisions.) If you can't predict the ID of a control at run time, there is little point in setting it to anything special at design time.

The final step that we need to make in order to complete this discussion of data binding is to allow the user to edit an item. To enable this feature, we'll add a handler to the code-behind page to receive the `EditCommand` event, which will be fired when the `cmdEdit` button, defined earlier, is clicked. Just as we stated above though, we will need to hide this button if the current user doesn't match the place's administrator.

We will create an editing template that uses data binding to load the editable fields. If the user accepts the changes, we will post the changes back to the database, using the configured data adapter.

1. We will begin by copying the `Flow Layout Panel` of the **SelectedItemTemplate** and placing it in the **EditItemTemplate** section. Set its `style` property to `HEIGHT: 100px; BACKGROUND-COLOR: lemonchiffon`. Delete all the controls except for the web form's `Panel` and its contents at the top, and set its `BackColor` property to `Wheat`. Change the remaining image `src` to `Images/edit.gif`.

2. We will next build the following layout:

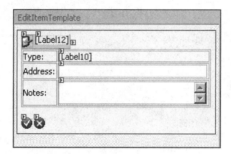

3. First of all, insert an HTML `Table` with two columns and three rows *outside* the `Panel` control, as in the above screenshot. You will need to switch to HTML view to remove the additional column. Set the `class` property to `TableLines` and its `border` to 0.

After entering the text in the left-most cells, drop controls and set their properties as follows:

Control	Property	Value
Label	Data binding expression	DataBinder.Eval(Container, "DataItem.TypeName")
TextBox1	ID	txtAddress
	CssClass	Textbox
	Data binding expression	DataBinder.Eval(Container, "DataItem.Address")
TextBox2	ID	txtNotes
	CssClass	TextBox
	TextMode	MultiLine
	Data binding expression	DataBinder.Eval(Container, "DataItem.Notes")

Below the table, enter a carriage return, and drop two `ImageButton` controls and set the following properties for them:

Control	Property	Value
ImageButton1	ID	cmdUpdate
	CommandName	Update
	AlternateText	Save
	ImageUrl	Images/ok.gif
ImageButton2	ID	cmdCancel
	CommandName	Cancel
	AlternateText	Cancel
	ImageUrl	Images/cancel.gif

Finally, next to top `Panel` we have an existing `Label` for which we should set the following properties:

Property	Value
ID	lblPlaceID
CssClass	Hidden
Data binding expression	DataBinder.Eval(Container, "DataItem.PlaceID")

We will use the value bound to it to determine the row that needs to be updated.

When you have finished adding the inner controls, you can safely remove the height and width styles and let the table adjust its size to its content.

4. Now we will add the appropriate event handlers to the code-behind page. First, we'll deal with the `ItemDataBound` event, which is fired when an item is being bound to the template. We receive the current item in the argument to the event, and we want to show the **Edit** button only for users whose ID matches the current place's `AdministratorID`. Switch to the **Events** view in the property browser, select the `DataList` and double-click the `ItemDataBound` event. In the new event handler, add the following code:

```
// Intercept the moment an item is being bound to data
// and set the visible property of the Edit button
private void dlPlaces_ItemDataBound(
   object sender, System.Web.UI.WebControls.DataListItemEventArgs e)
{
   // Is the item selected?
   if (e.Item.ItemType == ListItemType.SelectedItem)
   {
      // Locate the hidden Label containing the AdministratorID
      Label admin = (Label) e.Item.FindControl("lblAdministratorID");
```

```
        // If it matches the current user, show the Edit button
        if (admin.Text == Page.User.Identity.Name)
            e.Item.FindControl("cmdEdit").Visible = true;
    }
}
```

5. In all of the event handlers, we call `BindPlaces()` at the end, to recreate the controls in the data list according to the last changes made. Whenever the Edit button is clicked, we will also need to update the data list's `EditItemIndex`, and set it to the `ItemIndex` of the item passed with the arguments to the event. Double-click the `EditCommand` event in the property browser and add the following code to the method:

```
private void dlPlaces_EditCommand(
    object source, System.Web.UI.WebControls.DataListCommandEventArgs e)
{
    // Save the edit index
    dlPlaces.EditItemIndex = e.Item.ItemIndex;
    BindPlaces();
}
```

6. Of course, the user could (as users often do) just change their mind and directly select another item without either canceling or accepting the current's item edit session. In this case, we only have to reset the `EditItemIndex` by adding the following line to the existing handler:

```
private void dlPlaces_SelectedIndexChanged(
    object sender, System.EventArgs e)
{
    // Remove the edit index just in case we were editing
    dlPlaces.EditItemIndex = -1;
    this.BindPlaces();
}
```

7. Once editing is started, the user can cancel it, which resets the `EditItemIndex` property. We also set the `SelectedIndex` property to leave the user positioned on the item they were editing. Double-click on the `CancelCommand` event to create a handler for it and enter the following code:

```
private void dlPlaces_CancelCommand(object source,
    System.Web.UI.WebControls.DataListCommandEventArgs e)
{
    // Reset the edit index
    dlPlaces.EditItemIndex = -1;

    // Set the selected item to the currently editing item
    dlPlaces.SelectedIndex = e.Item.ItemIndex;
    BindPlaces();
}
```

8. Another option is for the user to click the OK button to perform an update. At this time, we reload the dataset, locate the row corresponding to the current `PlaceID`, and issue an `Update` through the data adapter. Finally, we reset the indexes as we did for `CancelCommand`:

```
private void dlPlaces_UpdateCommand(object source,
    System.Web.UI.WebControls.DataListCommandEventArgs e)
{
    // Find the updated controls
    TextBox addr = (TextBox) e.Item.FindControl("txtAddress");
    TextBox notes = (TextBox) e.Item.FindControl("txtNotes");
    Label place = (Label) e.Item.FindControl("lblPlaceID");

    // Reload the dataset and locate the relevant row
    adPlaces.Fill(dsPlaces);
    string sql = "PlaceID = '" + place.Text + "'";
    PlaceData.PlaceRow row = (PlaceData.PlaceRow)
    dsPlaces.Place.Select(sql)[0];

    // Set the values using the typed properties
    row.Address = addr.Text;
    row.Notes = notes.Text;

    // Update the row in the database
    adPlaces.Update(new DataRow[] {row});

    // Reset datalist state and bind
    dlPlaces.EditItemIndex = -1;
    dlPlaces.SelectedIndex = e.Item.ItemIndex;
    dlPlaces.DataBind();
}
```

9. Save and run the page, and edit the *MegaSoftware Ltd.* place, adding or changing its comment, for example.

How It Works

Let's start from the beginning. When `BindPlaces()` is first called, the first time the page is run, the `DataList` iterates through the data source and binds the corresponding template with each row. At this time, the `ItemDataBound` event is raised. In the handler for that event, we react only to items of type `ListItemType.SelectedItem`, as they are the only ones that have the Edit button we want to show, if it is appropriate to do so.

Note that even when we have given the control an ID, we have to use the `FindControl()` method (inherited from the base `Control` class) to access the label that contains the `AdministratorID` field value. To understand this, we have to recall that the controls in the corresponding template are created *once for each row*. The e argument passed to this event handler (and to the others too) has an `Item` property that contains the collection of controls created for the current item. We call `FindControl()` on this collection to retrieve the label.

If the current user ID matches the administrator ID, we set the `Visible` property of `cmdEdit` to `True`. With the button visible, the user can start editing the item by clicking it, which causes the `EditCommand` event to be fired. In this handler, similar to what we did for the `SelectedIndexChanged` event, we save the index received in the data list's `EditItemIndex` property, and re-bind the data. At this stage, the data list will render the following interface:

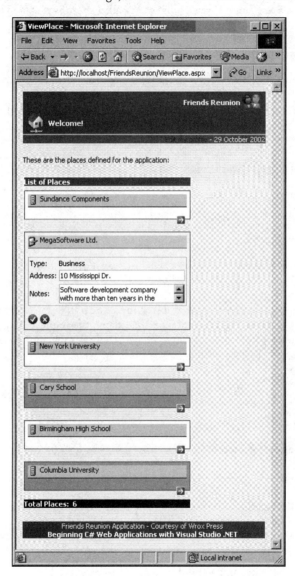

Now, the user can stop editing simply by navigating to another item. This is handled in the `SelectedIndexChanged` event handler, which resets any previous `EditItemIndex` value to -1, and calls `DataBind()` to refresh the display.

On the other hand, the user can click the **Save** or the **Cancel** button. If they choose the latter, the `CancelCommand` event is raised, in response to which we reset the `EditItemIndex`, and set the `SelectedIndex` to the current element. The user will then be positioned in the element they were just editing.

Finally, if they click the **Save** button, the `UpdateCommand` event is raised. The handler for this event performs the following steps:

❑ Locate the control with the data to be used for the update, as in:

```
TextBox addr = (TextBox) e.Item.FindControl("txtAddress");
```

❑ Get a reference to the original row. To achieve this, we first reload the dataset:

```
adPlaces.Fill(dsPlaces);
```

Then, we build a filtering expression with the `PlaceID` found in the corresponding (hidden) label:

```
string sql = "PlaceID = '" + place.Text + "'";
```

Then we define a `row` variable using the corresponding typed dataset class, `Places.PlaceRow`:

```
PlaceData.PlaceRow row = (PlaceData.PlaceRow)
dsPlaces.Place.Select(sql)[0];
```

Note that we use the `Select()` method of the `Place` table, which receives a SQL expression and returns an array of `DataRow` objects that match the request. We take the first element in the resulting array (`dsPlaces.Place.Select(sql)(0)`) and perform a type conversion to assign the value to the `row` variable.

❑ Set the new values on the row:

```
row.Address = addr.Text;
row.Notes = notes.Text;
```

❑ Submit changes to the adapter:

```
adPlaces.Update(new DataRow[] {row});
```

Here, we use the overload of the `Update()` method that receives an array of `DataRow` objects. We initialize the array in the same method call with the single row edited. As the adapter has a configured `UpdateCommand`, it will know how to submit changes in the row we passed to it to the database.

❑ Reset the data list state, and re-bind:

```
dlPlaces.EditItemIndex = -1;
dlPlaces.SelectedIndex = e.Item.ItemIndex;
dlPlaces.DataBind();
```

We don't call `BindPlaces()` here, because we've already loaded the dataset – and we know that we have at least one row, because we've just edited it!

Summary

Data access is essential for all but the most trivial web applications. However, the data-access code itself should not hinder a programmer's productivity. Easy and intuitive data facilities are crucial in a good development environment, and Visual Studio .NET together with ADO.NET fulfils both requirements. In this chapter, we have examined what ADO.NET is about, and looked at its components and how they interact. We also saw that Visual Studio .NET includes some powerful wizards and design-time advantages that have not previously been seen in a Microsoft product.

Components and data binding make the process of displaying and editing data a breeze. We learned how it works with simple controls, and with the more advanced DataGrid and DataList controls. We saw the incredibly versatile templates, and used them to achieve some real-world goals. Our *Friends Reunion* sample application became much more useful, and is a good example of the possibilities of the new platform.

In the next chapter, we will learn about the importance of state in web applications; and we'll find out how ASP.NET overcomes the stateless nature of the HTTP protocol through its impressive state management features.

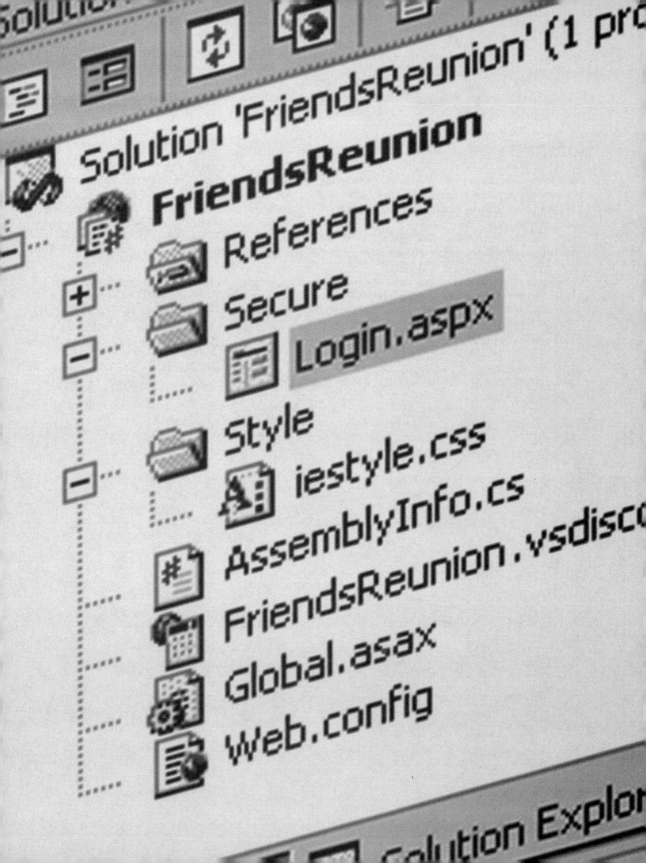

Solution 'FriendsReunion' (1 pro

Solution 'FriendsReunion'
FriendsReunion
    References
    Secure
        Login.aspx
    Style
        iestyle.css
    AssemblyInfo.cs
    FriendsReunion.vsdisco
    Global.asax
    Web.config

Solution Explor

ASP.NET State Management

Back in Chapter 1, we discussed the particularities of web applications and the **stateless nature** of the HTTP protocol. Every time a page is requested, the server processes it, returns it to the client, and complete forgets about it. The same happens on the client side; every page received is a completely new one, even if it comes from the same URL, after a postback for example. It's immediately evident that if we want to keep some information about the current user, such as their login information, selected items in a shopping basket, preferences about the site, filled form fields, selected values, and so on, generally called the application **state**, and keep it alive while they use the application, we need some sort of mechanism from ASP.NET or HTML itself, as HTTP (the protocol) doesn't provide one.

We will discuss the variety of state handling features ASP.NET brings, as well as the more traditional approaches provided by HTML and browsers, and where to use each one. We will build a search engine for the *Friends Reunion* case study application, and take advantage of all the state-related features to make it fast, resource-conservative, and user-friendly.

In this chapter we will learn about:

- ❑ Where the state can be stored
- ❑ Different scopes available
- ❑ When we should use each one
- ❑ How to preserve server resources
- ❑ Server state configurations and options

State Storage and Scope

Let's start by saying that **state** is any kind of information that needs to remain active for a period of time. This period can be the entire application life, the time a user spends using it, the page life before the user browses to another page, and so forth. Examples of each are a global visitor counter, items selected while shopping on a site, and values entered on a form field.

We already know the HTTP protocol that drives web applications is **stateless**. With that fact in mind, we have only two places in which to store the state:

❑   **Server** – The application on the server side, that is, ASP.NET, can keep this data in some place and provide the page developer with some way to retrieve and save values there. We will later analyze where this state can be stored.

❑   **Client** – We can keep data on the client machine, and rely on the browser to submit it to the server each time a new request is performed, so that the application on the server side can use it.

ASP.NET provides mechanisms to save data on both sides, but usually, their categorization takes into account the **scope** of the data. That is, where it can be accessed from, and by whom. Organized by the storage location used by each feature, available state utilities in ASP.NET are:

❑   **Server:**

  ❑   **Application** – This is the data that is accessible by all users during the entire life of the application

  ❑   **Session** – Keeps state associated with each user (for example, a shopping basket)

  ❑   **Transient state** – Data that only lives during the processing of a single request

❑   **Client:**

  ❑   **View state** – Retains data related to a page, such as filled form fields

  ❑   **Cookies** – Keeps arbitrary data on the client browser

  ❑   **Querystring** – Passes values between the client and the server in the URL itself

  ❑   **Hidden Form Fields** – Form fields containing data useful to the application but hidden from the user

We will start by discussing session state, which is easier to tackle first, and then move to application state and the rest of the utilities.

Session State

Some applications may need to keep user data while the user is surfing the site or performing some task that takes several steps, such as filling a shopping basket or proceeding to checkout. It would be impossible to get all the data required for those tasks in a single page, so we need a way to store such items in some place. Of course, this data must be **private** to each user; selected items or credit card information must not be accessible to other users performing the same tasks!

The first problem ASP.NET faces here is the HTTP protocol's statelessness; there's no way the server can identify a returning user (the same user requesting another page, for example) just by looking at the HTTP request itself. So, whenever session state is needed for a user, ASP.NET creates a random, unique ID called the **session ID**, and, by default, attaches it to the client in the form of a **cookie**, although we can have the session ID appended to the URL as well.

A cookie is a small piece of data (usually 4KB maximum) that is kept by the client browser and handed back to the server on each subsequent request. We will see more on cookies towards the end of this chapter.

This way, ASP.NET can identify a returning user based on their saved session ID. This sort of identity card given to the user is reclaimed when they leave the application, or the session times out. So the next time they return, a new identification will be created.

*Creating a session ID to identify a returning user **doesn't** imply they have been authenticated. Authentication is a different process, related to security, and discussed in Chapter 10.*

Recall that some users erroneously think that cookies can be harmful and disable them in their browsers, so we will later see a way to still gain the benefits of sessions without using cookies.

Based on the session ID, ASP.NET provides a separate store for each user. Once the user is identified, ASP.NET can provide access to it. The session data is held in an object of type `HttpSessionState` that is available through any of the following class properties:

- `Page.Session`
- `Page.Context.Session`
- `HttpContext.Current.Session`

They all point to the same object, which we can use to keep data. This code could be placed in a code-behind page to access the session data:

```
// Save a value to the session state
Session["creditcard"] = txtCard.Text;

// Retrieve the value later to proceed to checkout
string card = Session["creditcard"];
```

Since all our pages inherit from `Page`, we can use `base.Session`, `this.Session`, or just `Session` to access this object, as we did above.

The session object provides properties and methods that deal with the session, such as `Abandon()`, `Clear()`, `RemoveAll()` (which internally calls the previous one, so I wonder why is it even there), `Count`, `Keys`, and others. Look at the MSDN help for a list of members and what they are used for, although most of the members are almost self-explanatory.

We will now use session state in a new feature we will add to the *Friends Reunion* case study application. Up to now, users have been able to log in, see some news related to them such as requests for contact and approved contacts, and so on, but so far, there's no way for them to search for fellow users. We will add this search facility, and additionally allow the user to perform searches within previous results, in order to narrow the initial search. This is a good place to use session state, as the whole dataset can be kept there, to perform subsequent narrowing searches against it.

A very important consideration we must take into account is that session state is held on the *server*, thus consuming resources. If we allowed users to perform very wide searches, with potentially thousands of records being retrieved from the database (assuming our application is successful enough!) and saved to session state, the server would be brought to its knees very soon. So, we will use a configurable limit of maximum allowed results for the search engine, through the application configuration file, Web.config. This is very common practice in most search engines, even Microsoft's search engine.

Try It Out – Creating a Search Engine

1. Add a new web form to the application, called Search.aspx.

2. Just as we did in previous chapters, add the link to the stylesheet:

```
<link href="Style/iestyle.css" type="text/css" rel="stylesheet">
```

3. Import the following namespaces at the top of the code-behind page:

```
using System;
using System.Collections;
using System.ComponentModel;
using System.Configuration;
using System.Data;
using System.Data.SqlClient;
using System.Drawing;
using System.Text;
using System.Web;
using System.Web.SessionState;
using System.Web.UI;
using System.Web.UI.WebControls;
using System.Web.UI.HtmlControls;
```

Make the page inherit from FriendsBase and add the icon and page header message:

```
public class Search : FriendsBase
{
  private void Page_Load(object sender, System.EventArgs e)
  {
    // Configure the icon and message
    base.HeaderIconImageUrl =
      Request.ApplicationPath + "/Images/search.gif";
    base.HeaderMessage = "Search Users";
  }
  ...
```

4. Drop an HTML Table onto the page and set the following properties:

Property	Value
id	tbResults
border	0
width	100%

Ensure that the table contains only one row and two cells, and that both cells' `valign` attribute is set to `top`.

5. Switch to source HTML view and add the following code inside the first `<td>` element:

```
<td valign="top">
  <asp:panel id="pnlResults" cssclass="SearchResults" runat="server">
    Search results:
    <hr width="100%" size="1">
    <asp:label id="lblLimit" runat="server" /><br><br>
    <asp:datagrid id="grdResults" runat="server" />
  </asp:panel>
</td>
```

This is the panel that will hold the results from the search.

6. Switch to design view again. Inside the second cell element, drop a `Panel` named `pnlSearch`, set its `CssClass` to `Search`, and type **Search Friends Reunion:** for its text. Drop an HTML `Horizontal Rule` (`<hr>` element) below the text, and an HTML `Table` below it with `border` set to 0 and `width` to 100%. It should have two columns and seven rows, with the last one having only one cell with its `colspan` property set to 2. Finally, type the following text and drop four `TextBoxes`, two `DropDownLists` (a.k.a. combo boxes), and two `Buttons` so that the panel looks like the following:

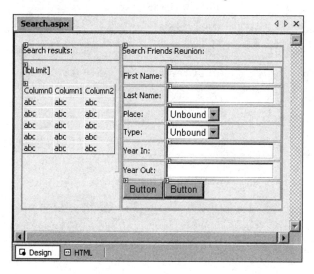

7. Set the following IDs for the controls, working down the page through them:

- ❏ `txtFirstName`
- ❏ `txtLastName`
- ❏ `cbPlace`
- ❏ `cbType`
- ❏ `txtYearIn`
- ❏ `txtYearOut`
- ❏ `btnSearch`
- ❏ `btnSearchResults`

8. Next, set the controls' properties as follows:

Control	Property	Value
`txtFirstName`	`CssClass`	`MediumTextBox`
`txtLastName`	`CssClass`	`MediumTextBox`
`cbPlace`	`CssClass`	`MediumTextBox`
	`DataTextField`	`Name`
	`DataValueField`	`PlaceId`
`cbType`	`CssClass`	`MediumTextBox`
	`DataTextField`	`Name`
	`DataValueField`	`TypeId`
`txtYearIn`	`CssClass`	`SmallTextBox`
`txtYearOut`	`CssClass`	`SmallTextBox`
`btnSearch`	`CssClass`	`Button`
	`Text`	`New Search`
`btnSearchResults`	`CssClass`	`Button`
	`Text`	`Within Results`

9. Finally, add the following new styles to the stylesheet:

```
.MediumTextBox
{
  border-right: #c7ccdc 1px solid;
  border-top: #c7ccdc 1px solid;
  font-size: 8pt;
```

```
     border-left: #c7ccdc 1px solid;
     width: 140px;
     border-bottom: #c7ccdc 1px solid;
     font-family: Tahoma, Verdana, 'Times New Roman';
}
.Search
{
     width: 217px;
     border-right: silver 1px solid;
     padding-right: 5px;
     border-top: silver 1px solid;
     padding-left: 5px;
     padding-bottom: 5px;
     border-left: silver 1px solid;
     padding-top: 5px;
     border-bottom: silver 1px solid;
     background-color: gainsboro;
}
.SearchResults
{
     padding-right: 5px;
     padding-left: 5px;
     padding-bottom: 5px;
     padding-top: 5px;
}
```

10. You may need to close and reopen the page in order for the styles to be reflected at design time. The form should look like the following by now:

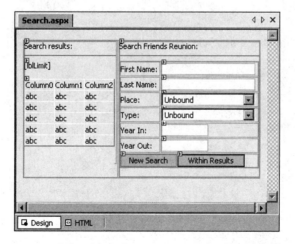

11. Note that we set the `DataTextField` and `DataValueField` properties for both combo boxes. That's because we will be binding them to a data source. Just as we did in Chapter 5, drop a `SqlConnection` and two `SqlCommand` components on the page, naming them `cnFriends`, `cmPlace`, and `cmType` respectively. Then, set the following properties for them:

Property	Value
cnFriends.ConnectionString (from DynamicProperties)	cnFriends.ConnectionString
cmPlace.Connection	cnFriends
cmPlace.CommandText	SELECT PlaceID, Name FROM Place ORDER BY Name
cmType.Connection	cnFriends
cmType.CommandText	SELECT TypeID, Name FROM PlaceType ORDER BY Name

12. Now we will load the results of both commands into the combo boxes in the Page_Load method:

```
private void Page_Load(object sender, System.EventArgs e)
{
  // Configure the icon and message
  base.HeaderIconImageUrl =
    Request.ApplicationPath + "/Images/search.gif";
  base.HeaderMessage = "Search Users";

  SqlDataReader r;
  cnFriends.Open();

  // Initialize comboboxes
  try
  {
    r = cmPlace.ExecuteReader();
    cbPlace.DataSource = r;
    cbPlace.DataBind();
    r.Close();
    cbPlace.Items.Add(new ListItem("-- Not selected --", "0"));
    cbPlace.SelectedIndex = cbPlace.Items.Count - 1;

    r = cmType.ExecuteReader();
    cbType.DataSource = r;
    cbType.DataBind();
    r.Close();
    cbType.Items.Add(new ListItem("-- Not selected --", "0"));
    cbType.SelectedIndex = cbType.Items.Count - 1;
  }
  finally
  {
    cnFriends.Close();  // Ensure connection is closed
  }
}
```

We have used data binding before, in Chapter 5, so we already know what's involved. The `DataTextField` and `DataValueField` properties on the combo boxes define what values to load from the data source, which is set to the reader. As we learned in previous chapters, we use a data reader because it's faster, read-only and forward-only, which is everything that's needed to load the controls.

The two lines after we close the reader add an item to allow the user to specify that no filter should be applied for that field.

13. Let's drop a `DataSet` on the page now and select **Untyped** option from the dialog. We will use it to load the results of the query. Set its name to **dsResults**. We are using a `DataSet` instead of a `DataReader` because we will need this object later to perform refining searches. A `DataReader`, being a connected and forward-only cursor, isn't suitable for this.

14. Now we need to prepare the data properties of the data grid we added in Step 5 to support databinding to this new dataset:

Property	Value
grdResults.DataMember	User
grdResults.DataSource	dsResults

15. Double-click the **New Search** button and add the following code to the handler, which will perform the initial search, and save the results to session state:

```
private void btnSearch_Click(object sender, System.EventArgs e)
{
    StringBuilder sql = new StringBuilder();

    // Limit maximum resultset size
    sql.Append(@"SELECT TOP ");
    sql.Append(ConfigurationSettings.AppSettings["searchLimit"]);
    sql.Append(@"
        [User].UserID, [User].FirstName, [User].LastName,
        Place.PlaceID, Place.Name AS PlaceName,
        PlaceType.Name AS PlaceType, PlaceType.TypeID,
        TimeLapse.Name AS LapseName, TimeLapse.YearIn,
        TimeLapse.MonthIn, TimeLapse.YearOut, TimeLapse.MonthOut
    FROM [User]
    LEFT OUTER JOIN TimeLapse ON
        TimeLapse.UserID = [User].UserID
    LEFT OUTER JOIN Place ON
        Place.PlaceID = TimeLapse.PlaceID
    LEFT OUTER JOIN PlaceType ON
        Place.TypeID = PlaceType.TypeID
    ");

    // Build the WHERE clause now
    StringBuilder qry = new StringBuilder();
```

```
if (txtFirstName.Text != String.Empty)
{
  qry.Append("[User].FirstName LIKE '%");
  qry.Append(txtFirstName.Text).Append("%' AND ");
}
if (txtLastName.Text != String.Empty)
{
  qry.Append("[User].LastName LIKE '%");
  qry.Append(txtLastName.Text).Append("%' AND ");
}
if (cbPlace.SelectedItem.Value != "0")
{
  qry.Append("[Place].PlaceID = '");
  qry.Append(cbPlace.SelectedItem.Value).Append("' AND ");
}
if (cbType.SelectedItem.Value != "0")
{
  qry.Append("[PlaceType].TypeID = '");
  qry.Append(cbType.SelectedItem.Value).Append("' AND ");
}
if (txtYearIn.Text != String.Empty)
{
  qry.Append("TimeLapse.YearIn = ");
  qry.Append(txtYearIn.Text).Append(" AND ");
}
if (txtYearOut.Text != String.Empty)
{
  qry.Append("TimeLapse.YearOut = ");
  qry.Append(txtYearOut.Text).Append(" AND ");
}

string filter = qry.ToString();
if (filter.Length != 0)
{
  sql.Append(" WHERE ");

  // Add the filter without the trailing AND
  sql.Append(filter.Remove(filter.Length - 4, 4));
}

SqlDataAdapter ad = new SqlDataAdapter(sql.ToString(), cnFriends);
dsResults = new DataSet();
ad.Fill(dsResults, "User");

// Adjust label for results
if (dsResults.Tables["User"].Rows.Count <
  Convert.ToInt32(ConfigurationSettings.AppSettings["searchLimit"]))
{
  lblLimit.Text = "Found " +
    dsResults.Tables["User"].Rows.Count.ToString() +
    " users matching your criteria on initial search.";
}
else
```

```
  {
    lblLimit.Text = "You're working with the first " +
      ConfigurationSettings.AppSettings["searchLimit"] +
      @" results.  If you're looking for someone who's not in this list,
    please search again with a more precise search criterion.";
  }

  // Place results in session state
  Session["search"] = dsResults;

  BindFromSession();
}
```

The method called at the end, `BindFromSession()`, performs the actual biding from the dataset found in the session:

```
private void BindFromSession()
{
  dsResults = (DataSet) Session["search"];
  grdResults.DataBind();
}
```

We created a separate method in order to call the same binding method from the code that narrows search results.

16. Double-click the **Within Results** button and add the following code to the handler. This handler will filter the previously retrieved dataset with further criteria, using the dataset's `Select()` method:

```
private void btnSearchResults_Click(object sender, System.EventArgs e)
{
  dsResults = Session["search"] as DataSet;

  // If we can't get the previous results then we lost session
  // information (failure), or no previous results were available.
  // Default to normal search.
  if (dsResults == null) btnSearch_Click(sender, e);

  StringBuilder qry = new StringBuilder();
  if (txtFirstName.Text != String.Empty)
  {
    qry.Append("FirstName LIKE '%");
    qry.Append(txtFirstName.Text).Append("%' AND ");
  }
  if (txtLastName.Text != String.Empty)
  {
    qry.Append("LastName LIKE '%");
    qry.Append(txtLastName.Text).Append("%' AND ");
  }
```

```
      if (cbPlace.SelectedItem.Value != "0")
      {
        qry.Append("PlaceID = '");
        qry.Append(cbPlace.SelectedItem.Value).Append("' AND ");
      }
      if (cbType.SelectedItem.Value != "0")
      {
        qry.Append("TypeID = '");
        qry.Append(cbType.SelectedItem.Value).Append("' AND ");
      }
      if (txtYearIn.Text != String.Empty)
      {
        qry.Append("YearIn = ");
        qry.Append(txtYearIn.Text).Append(" AND ");
      }
      if (txtYearOut.Text != String.Empty)
      {
        qry.Append("YearOut = ");
        qry.Append(txtYearOut.Text).Append(" AND ");
      }

      string filter = qry.ToString();

      // Remove trailing AND
      if (filter.Length != 0) filter = filter.Remove(filter.Length - 4, 4);

      DataRow[] rows = dsResults.Tables["User"].Select(filter);

      // Rebuild results with new filtered set of rows, maintaining
      // structure
      dsResults = dsResults.Clone();
      foreach (DataRow row in rows)
      {
        dsResults.Tables["User"].ImportRow(row);
      }

      // Place results in session state.
      Session["search"] = dsResults;

      BindFromSession();
    }
```

17. As the search results may now be saved to session state, we could check for that when the page is loaded, and automatically bind the datagrid if the data is there. Add the following line immediately before the end of the Page_Load method:

```
    if (Session["search"] != null) BindFromSession();
```

18. We're almost done. Recall that in the btn_Search handler we are using a setting from the Web.config file that specifies the limit of rows retrieved from a search. Add this setting to the configuration file:

```
<appSettings>
  ...
  <add key="searchLimit" value="15" />
</appSettings>
```

We have deliberately set it to a very low value in order to see it in action with the small set of test data included with the sample database.

19. Finally, add the link in the `Default.aspx` page to allow the users to access the search feature. We do this, as we saw in Chapter 4, by placing the following code in the `if` block of the `Page_Load` method:

```
// Create a new blank table row, this time for Search link
row = new TableRow();

// Search link
img = new Image();
img.ImageUrl = "Images/search.gif";
img.ImageAlign = ImageAlign.Middle;
img.Width = new Unit(24, UnitType.Pixel);
img.Height = new Unit(24, UnitType.Pixel);

// Create the cell and add the image
cell = new TableCell();
cell.Controls.Add(img);

// Add the cell to the row
row.Cells.Add(cell);

// Set up the Search link
lnk = new HyperLink();
lnk.Text = "Search";
lnk.NavigateUrl = "Search.aspx";

// Create the cell and add the link
cell = new TableCell();
cell.Controls.Add(lnk);

// Add the new cell to the row
row.Cells.Add(cell);

// Add the new row to the table
tb.Rows.Add(row);
```

20. We are now in a position to test the search engine by setting `Search.aspx` and compiling and running as usual.

How It Works

If you perform a search with all the fields empty, you should see something like the following:

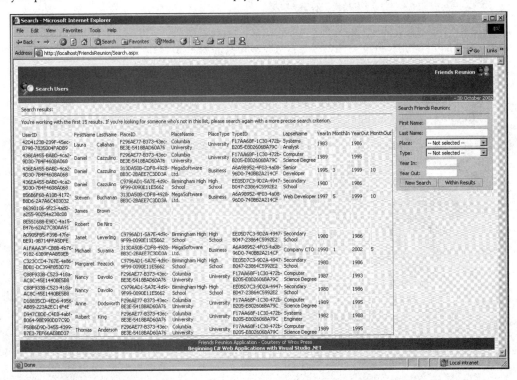

We will improve the datagrid as we go, because we surely don't want all those GUIDs being displayed, right? What's important to notice up front is the message being displayed. It states that we're working with the first 15 records, because the initial search exceeded that limit. If we set a lower value, the message will change accordingly.

Now try to narrow the search by specifying 1980 in the Year In field and clicking the Within Results button (filtering through the combo boxes won't work yet, but we will see what's wrong when we get to the view state section). This time, instead of hitting the database again, the search is performed in-memory on the server, a feature offered by the DataSet class. We're retrieving only the matching rows from the previously saved dataset:

```
DataRow[] rows = dsResults.Tables["User"].Select(filter);
```

Note that after we get the rows satisfying the new filter, we clone the structure of the saved dataset, and start importing the rows into its User table:

```
dsResults = dsResults.Clone();
foreach (DataRow row in rows)
{
  dsResults.Tables["User"].ImportRow(row);
}
```

The code that follows is just like the version that searches against the database. The dataset is saved to the session, and the helper method, `BindFromSession()`, is called:

```
Session["search"] = dsResults;

BindFromSession();
```

Note that directly assigning the value to the session with the same key as before replaces any previous value. On the other hand, if the key doesn't exist, it's added automatically.

The limit we placed on the maximum result rows allowed is a very important feature. This prevents the user from selecting a huge resultset and affecting our server resources. Note also that because the dataset is now placed in the session state, if the user navigates to other pages in the application and later comes back to the search page, the previous results will still be there, and therefore will be displayed. It is a good moment to ask how to get rid of it, how long a session lasts, and if there's a way to perform some actions when the session is started.

Controlling Session State

Removing items from the session state when we don't need them any more will preserve server resources. This can be done either by assigning a null value to an existing key:

```
Session[key] = null;
```

or by calling the `Remove()` method:

```
Session.Remove(key);
```

Even though both effectively remove the reference to the item, thus allowing the garbage collector to remove the object from memory, the latter is more appropriate, as it completely removes both the value and the associated key.

We can also use the `Clear()` method which removes all items.

Try It Out – Removing Session State Items

1. The user will be able to perform some actions related to their search results, such as clearing the items, and we will add others as we go. We will add a panel below `pnlSearch` we created above. Insert a new line (press *Enter*) right after the search panel on the right of the page, and drop a `Panel`, name it `pnlActions` and set its `CssClass` to `Search`.

2. Enter the text Actions: inside the panel, and drop an HTML horizontal rule below it, but still inside the panel.

3. Drop an HTML `Table` below the rule, with only one row (we will add more later) and two columns, and set the following properties for it:

Property	Value
border	0
cellpadding	4
style	WIDTH: 100%

4. Type the text **Clear Results** in the rightmost cell, and drop a web server `ImageButton` control on the leftmost cell, with the following properties:

Property	Value
ImageUrl	Images/results.gif
Tooltip	Clear all results from the search
(ID)	btnClearResults

5. The form should look like the following now:

6. Double-click the `ImageButton` to get to the event handler and enter the following code:

```
private void ClearResults_Click(
  object sender, System.Web.UI.ImageClickEventArgs e)
{
```

```
                 Session.Remove("search");
                 SetResultsState(false);
         }
```

7. Once the results have been cleared, we don't want the clear results panel being displayed any more. Also, we want to hide the results panel altogether, leaving just the search panel visible, and hide the button to perform refining searches too. When a new search is performed though, we want to restore the visibility of all those controls. Additionally, we are setting the `btnSearch` text to something more meaningful, depending on visibility. For that purpose, we create the helper `SetResultsState()` method:

```
private void SetResultsState(bool visible)
{
    pnlActions.Visible = visible;
    pnlResults.Visible = visible;
    btnSearchResults.Visible = visible;
    btnSearch.Text = visible ? "New search" : "Search";

    // If setting to visible, it's because there are results to bind to
    if (visible) BindFromSession();
}
```

Note that the method receives a Boolean indicating the visibility to set. The last line takes into account that if we are turning the visibility on, it's because there are new results to display, and thus calls the `BindFromSession()` method we used before.

8. We can now modify the following line in `Page_Load` to take into account the visibility of panels when the page is entered, from:

```
if (Session["search"] != null) BindFromSession();
```

to:

```
SetResultsState(Session["search"] != null);
```

Note that we pass the argument telling whether there are results in session state or not.

9. We will also need to restore this visibility in `btnSearch_Click`. We will replace the following line:

```
BindFromSession();
```

with:

```
SetResultsState(true);
```

10. Save and run the page.

231

How It Works

The most important bit of code here is when we remove the object from session state:

```
Session.Remove("search");
```

Toggling visibility of items depending on session state presence makes the following page appear the first time now:

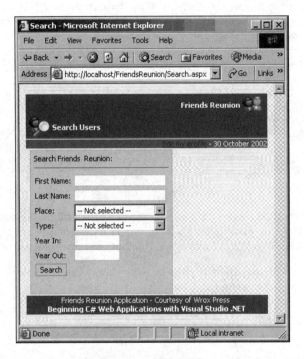

To gain more granular control over session state, ASP.NET provides two events that are fired at different points during the life of the user session; Start and End. We can attach event handlers for them through the special file Global.asax. This file allows us to add handlers to these kinds of events that are global in the sense that they don't happen inside a single page or control. There are other events that we will use as we go along through this chapter; we only have to use the following special syntax in the Global.asax code-behind file to handle the session Start and End events:

```
protected void Session_Start(Object sender, EventArgs e)
{
  // Fires when the session is started
}

protected void Session_End(Object sender, EventArgs e)
{
  // Fires when the session ends
}
```

The empty signatures are already placed there whenever you start a new web application. A good use of such methods would be, for example, to release expensive or locked resources, such as a file or a database connection, if you keep it in session state (a pretty unadvisable practice given the fact that ADO.NET already provides connection pooling), or to initialize some context related to the user as soon as the session starts, such as reloading a previously saved shopping cart.

However, you should use session state carefully because it can severely affect scalability if it's used without care. We have been careful to limit the amount of information placed there, for example.

Configuring Session State

We can tweak several settings related to this feature though the application configuration file, in a section called, guess what, `sessionState`:

```
<sessionState
    timeout="timeout in minutes"
    cookieless="[true|false]"
    mode="[Off|InProc|StateServer|SQLServer]"
    stateConnectionString="tcpip=server:port"
    stateNetworkTimeout=
      "for network operations with State Server, in seconds"
    sqlConnectionString="valid SqlConnection string, minus Initial Catalog"
/>
```

The first attribute is easy to grasp: it specifies the minutes to keep a session alive after activity has ceased. If the user remains inactive for the specified lapse of time, a new session will be created afterwards, thus losing all previous state.

The other settings require a closer look.

Session IDs and Cookies

When we introduced session state, we said the generated session ID is stored by default in a cookie, which is later read by ASP.NET on further requests to determine the session state to associate with the current user. We also said that some users may have disabled cookies in their browsers, so how do we enable session state for them?

The answer lies in the second setting for the `sessionState` configuration element:

```
    cookieless="[true|false]"
```

When we set the `cookieless` value to `true`, ASP.NET will append the Session ID to the URL itself, and append it to any relative URL existing on the requested page. If you simply change this setting in `Web.config`, and navigate to `News.aspx` (you can click the link in the home page), you will notice the change immediately:

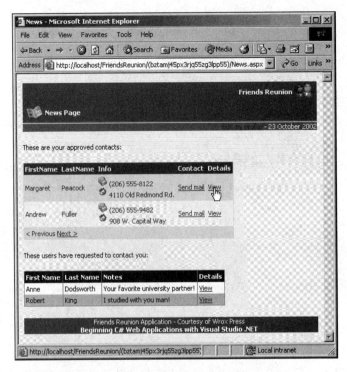

Notice the URL shown in the status bar, as well as the URL in the address bar. You should be aware that this mechanism adds a processing step as all the links in the page have to be rewritten to include the session ID, and further requested URLs have to be parsed to extract it and to get the actual resource URL (without the session ID).

> **ASP.NET dynamically adds the session ID to all *relative* links, but not to *fully-qualified* links.**

State Modes

Up to now, we never said where the objects we place in the session object are stored. ASP.NET provides three options when it comes to session state storage, configurable through the mode setting and related attributes:

```
mode="[Off|InProc|StateServer|SQLServer]"
```

We will see which attributes apply to each in turn. Here is what the different modes mean:

- ❏ InProc – This is the default setting. All the state is kept in-memory, in the same process that is running the application. This provides maximum performance, but if the application is restarted, or the process hangs for some reason, all the session data associated with your users is lost.

- StateServer – This setting allows us to separate the state storage from the process that is running our application. It is used in conjunction with the two following attributes:

```
stateConnectionString="tcpip=server:port"
stateNetworkTimeout=
  "for network operations with State Server, in seconds"
```

We can specify the address and port of the machine that will keep the state information in its own process and memory. This isolates the state from our application, protecting it from failures. In the state server machine, we have to start the ASP.NET State service, either from the Services console or from the command prompt with:

```
> net start aspnet_state
```

We can configure this service to be started automatically too. We can specify that the state server be the same machine holding our application by setting the IP to 127.0.0.1. This will protect state from application restarts, but not from machine restarts. You should also note that taking the state storage out of the application process imposes a performance impact, especially if the state server is located in another machine on the network. You should carefully determine if retaining your session information justifies this impact.

- SQLServer – If you absolutely *have* to preserve session state at all costs, this setting is for you. This mode saves all the session state in a SQL Server database, so it can survive any failure in your application, server, and even database server (provided the database itself survives!). Setting this mode involves configuring the following attribute of the sessionState element:

```
sqlConnectionString="valid SqlConnection string, minus Initial Catalog"
```

We also have to run a script to prepare the required database where the state is stored. It is usually located in the Windows directory at Microsoft.NET\Framework\ *[version]*\InstallSqlState.sql.

At the time of writing, the version is v1.0.3705.

Fortunately we don't need SQL Server 2000 Query Analyzer to run this script. MSDE comes with an (ugly) command-line utility called osql. The following command will run the script on the server and prepare the database and tables needed to hold state:

```
> osql -S [servername] -U [login] -P [pwd] < InstallSqlState.sql
```

We could even have clustered SQL Servers for maximum reliability. This mode is the most robust way to protect critical session state, but it is the most expensive in terms of performance. A round trip to the database will be needed for each request, which can severely affect the application responsiveness. Also, the network may become a bottleneck under high load.

Application State

Sometimes, there's a need to keep some data *globally* available to *all* users, who can share it. Of course, you can think of a database record as application-level state: all users can query it as needed. The performance impact would be unacceptable though, especially if it's used very often, and additionally, it involves several steps, such as opening the connection, issuing a query, and managing the results, just as we learned in Chapter 4. What's more, we would be limited to storing records, not arbitrary objects (unless we use serialization, but that's off topic. You can find more about object serialization in the MSDN documentation at ms-help://MS.VSCC/MS.MSDNVS/cpguide/html/cpovrserializingobjects.htm).

To make matters easy, ASP.NET supports the concept of an **application state**. Each web application has its own set of globally available state, which can be accessed and used as easily as session state. The data is held in an object of type `HttpApplicationState`, which is available through any of the following class properties:

- ❑ `Page.Application`
- ❑ `Page.Context.Application`
- ❑ `HttpContext.Current.Application`

This kind of state is obviously kept on the server side too. Notice that the storage options available for session state (state server and SQL Server) are not available for application state, which will be lost on application/machine restarts.

Usually, application state is loaded from some permanent store (a database for example) when the application is started, and saved for later use (if it's appropriate) when the application ends. These events, just like their session counterparts, can be handled in `Global.asax` file too:

```
protected void Application_Start(Object sender, EventArgs e)
{
}

protected void Application_End(Object sender, EventArgs e)
{
}
```

During the application's life, application state is used anywhere we need it, retrieving it, changing its value, and so on, but because it's available to all users simultaneously, we must take care of **concurrency**. For example, if we implement a global counter of visitors, and increment its value any time a new session is started, it's possible that between the retrieval of the current counter, and the saving of the new incremented value, another user increments the value too, so the second write will overwrite the previous value. What we need is to *synchronize* access to the application value when we are about to change it. The `HttpApplicationState` object provides two methods to do just that:

```
Application.Lock();
// Read and change values
Application.UnLock();
```

The code that accesses the application state between the Lock() and UnLock() method calls is protected from concurrency, that is, it's ensured to be executed by only one user at a time. Note that other users trying to access the application state during the lock will be blocked until the lock is released, so you should use locking for the minimum possible time.

Let's now implement all these features in a global counter of visitors to the *Friends Reunion* application. We will increment the counter when new sessions start, and display this value in the footer user control we created back in Chapter 3.

Try It Out – Implementing a global counter

1. Open the Global.asax code-behind page, and add the following code to the Session_Start skeleton code:

```
protected void Session_Start(Object sender, EventArgs e)
{
  Application.Lock();
  if (Application["counter"] == null)
  {
    Application["counter"] = 1;
  }
  else
  {
    Application["counter"] = ((int)Application["counter"]) + 1;
  }
  Application.UnLock();
}
```

2. Open FriendsFooter.ascx in **Design** view and add the following text and label control below the existing text:

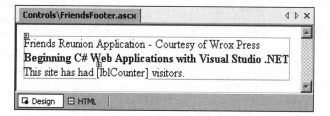

```
Controls\FriendsFooter.ascx                              ◁ ▷ ✕

Friends Reunion Application - Courtesy of Wrox Press
Beginning C# Web Applications with Visual Studio .NET
This site has had [lblCounter] visitors.

 ▣ Design    ▣ HTML
```

3. Open the code-behind page for this user control and add the following code:

```
private void Page_Load(object sender, System.EventArgs e)
{
  lblCounter.Text = Application["counter"].ToString();
}
```

4. Now we can save and run the pages of our application and see the results.

How It Works

When we start the application again, a new session is created. As the application has just been started, the 'counter' application state value will be null, so the value 1 is assigned directly. The footer then retrieves this value and displays accordingly:

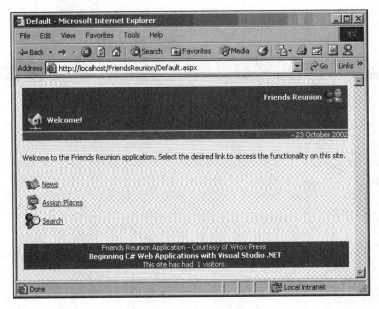

As you will remember, session IDs are saved by default as a browser cookie, so to simulate a new user session, you can just browse to the application using another browser, such as Mozilla or Netscape, or restart the current browser and navigate back to the application. ASP.NET will not find the session cookie and will thus believe it's a new user. This time, the handler in Session_Start will find the previous value in the application state, and will increment it.

Note that we have protected the code that performs the increment using Lock() and UnLock() methods.

Now add a blank line to the application Web.config file. Save it and refresh the page. Oops! The counter is again set to 1! What happened is that any change to the application configuration results in an application restart, so that the new settings take effect. The same would happen if the ASP.NET process is stopped and restarted for some reason, such as a failure. Of course, a global counter that resets automatically every time the application is restarted isn't of much use!

> Any change to Web.config (either the root one or anyone in subfolders) or Global.asax results in an application restart.

If we want to preserve and later restore application state from some permanent storage such as a file or a database, we can do so in the global events we saw above.

Try It Out – Preserving and Restoring Application State

1. There is a table in the *Friends Reunion* database; its purpose is to hold the global counter. It's called (guess what) Counter, and contains a single field, Visitors. Open the Global.asax code-behind page, and add the following imports:

```
using System;
using System.Collections;
using System.ComponentModel;
using System.Configuration;
using System.Data.SqlClient;
using System.Web;
using System.Web.SessionState;
```

2. Add the following code to retrieve the counter to Application_Start:

```
protected void Application_Start(Object sender, EventArgs e)
{
    SqlConnection con;
    SqlCommand cmd;

    // Get the connection string from the existing key in Web.config
    con = new SqlConnection(
        ConfigurationSettings.AppSettings["cnFriends.ConnectionString"]);
    cmd = new SqlCommand("SELECT Visitors FROM Counter", con);
    con.Open();

    try
    {
        // Retrieve the counter
        Application["counter"] = (int) cmd.ExecuteScalar();
    }
    finally
    {
        con.Close();
    }
}
```

3. Add the following code to save the counter to Application_End:

```
protected void Application_End(Object sender, EventArgs e)
{
    SqlConnection con;
    SqlCommand cmd;

    // Get the connection string from the existing key in Web.config
    con = new SqlConnection(
        ConfigurationSettings.AppSettings["cnFriends.ConnectionString"]);
```

```
          cmd = new SqlCommand("UPDATE Counter SET Visitors=" +
                               Application["counter"].ToString(), con);
     con.Open();

     try
     {
       cmd.ExecuteNonQuery();
     }
     finally
     {
       con.Close();
     }
   }
```

4. Finally, let's modify the `Session_Start` event, as the counter will always be there now, since it will be initialized by `Application_Start`:

```
protected void Session_Start(Object sender, EventArgs e)
{
  Application.Lock();
  Application["counter"] = ((int)Application["counter"]) + 1;
  Application.UnLock();
}
```

5. From the **Server Explorer**, set an initial value on the `Visitor` field of the `Counter` table.

6. Save and run the application and see what differences the changes in the code have made.

How It Works

The counter is now kept in the database, thus preserving it across application restarts:

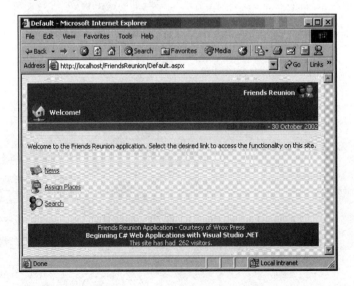

You can try this by making a small change to Web.config and refreshing the page. It won't change unless a new session is started. When we retrieve the counter, we use ExecuteScalar, which returns the value of the first column in the first row, which is just what we need. Note that both select SELECT and UPDATE queries work with the whole table, as we will always keep a single record, so we don't need to worry much.

Application Object and Events

You may have noticed that the Global class in the code-behind page of Global.asax inherits from HttpApplication. This means that this file actually *is the application*. An instance of this class is instantiated when the application is first started by the ASP.NET runtime. We can access this instance though the HttpContext.ApplicationInstance property.

So the various empty event handlers you see in Global.asax are actually the events exposed by the base HttpApplication class. You can learn more about them in the product MSDN. The special Application_EventName (or Session_EventName as we saw above) is an easy way to attach to the event, but it's equally possible to do so manually, for example in the class constructor:

```
public Global()
{
  InitializeComponent();
  base.BeginRequest += new EventHandler(MyRequestHandler);
}
```

There are many events and methods we can override from the base HttpApplication class. Some of them can be very useful depending on your application requirements, and we will actually use one of them, AuthenticateRequest in Chapter 10, to customize application security.

This global availability makes Global.asax a good place for common features used throughout the application. For example, a method to send mails from the application can be placed there, like this:

```
public SendMail(string to, string message)
{
  // Send the mail
}
```

and later used from any page by casting the application instance to the Global class type and calling the method:

```
Global app = (Global) Context.ApplicationInstance;
app.SendMail("user@target.com", "This is a mail from Friends Reunion");
```

We will let your imagination fly here, since *Friends Reunion* doesn't have any requirement for global functions.

Side Note – Modules and Global.asax Method Signatures

In ASP.NET, most of the functionality is implemented by so-called **modules**. These modules are classes that get instantiated when the application starts and participate in the processing of a request. Session state is one such module. You can see the predefined modules in the `%WINDIR%\Microsoft.NET\Framework\v1.0.3705\CONFIG\machine.config` file, in the `<httpModules>` section. Here are some of them:

```
<httpModules>
    <add name="OutputCache" type="System.Web.Caching.OutputCacheModule"/>
    <add name="Session" type="System.Web.SessionState.SessionStateModule"/>
    ...
</httpModules>
```

Other modules are included for authorization and security features that we will learn about in Chapter 10. What's important here is that modules are associated with a name, such as `Session`.

When the application object is created, it looks at all the methods placed in the `Global.asax` file and splits their name based on the underscore character. If the method name starts with `Application`, it attaches the method as an event handler of the event on the `HttpApplication` class with the name and signature that follows the underscore character.

If the method name doesn't start with `Application`, it looks at all configured modules, trying to match a module name with the part before the underscore and then tries to find an event in the module with the name and signature matching that part following the underscore. If it finds a match, it creates the corresponding delegate object and appends it to the event. In C# terms, this is what it's doing:

```
((System.Web.SessionState.SessionStateModule)
    this.Modules["Session"]).Start += new EventHandler(Session_Start);
```

Note that the method name can also be `Session_OnStart` and it will be attached properly too.

View State

ASP.NET introduces this new concept to solve one of the most common problems web developers have faced in the past: how to retain HTML form state across postbacks. By **form state** we mean selected values, filled fields, and so on. This had to be done manually in the past, retrieving the posted values and setting them back again on the fields when the page returned. **ASP.NET view state** handles this situation and more, such as remembering not only the selected value in a combo box but also all the values in the list!

Back in Chapter 3, when we analyzed the postback mechanism, we saw that a hidden form field is automatically added by ASP.NET:

```
<body ms_positioning="FlowLayout">
    <form name="Default" method="post" action="Default.aspx" id="Default">
        <input type="hidden" name="__VIEWSTATE"
               value="dDwtOTk4MjU3NjkzOzs+5LhhCG/25vTEDfp0bTJAhwkpYFQ=" />
    ...
```

You can see this code by selecting **View | Source** in your browser when the rendered `Default.aspx` page is displayed. We can see the more immediate advantage of view state in the `NewUser.aspx` form. If we fill all the fields, and select an existing login, we will get an error message, but the form fields will remain with the filled values:

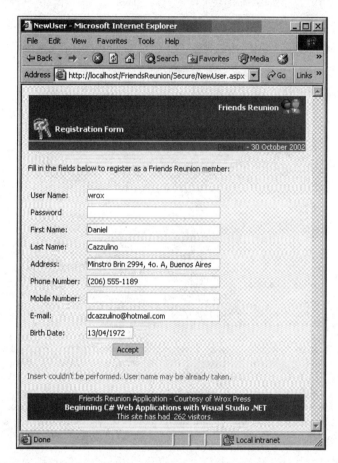

We didn't have to add any additional code in order to preserve the values, even when an error has occurred during insertion. What happened is that field values were pre-loaded automatically by ASP.NET, and later persisted to the `__VIEWSTATE` hidden field, so that later postbacks also retain these values. We have seen in Chapter 1 the overall page life cycle. Now we can take a closer look at the events happening right after the `Init` event, and right before the `Render` event:

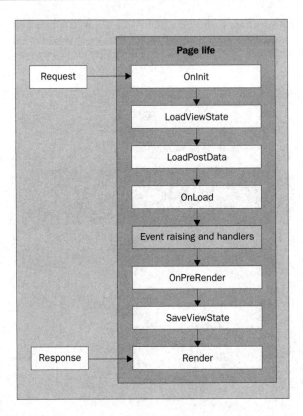

The content of the hidden field is parsed and placed again in the control's properties right after the OnInit() method call, that is, the LoadViewState box shown above. The new, posted values are then processed, the LoadPostData box above. The gray box in the middle is the moment where our event handlers are called. Now you can realize why we can simply ask for a textbox Text property in order to get the value entered in a form: the methods shown above have taken care of loading the values entered by the user on the appropriate server controls!. No more need to use Request.Form collection! As you can see, view state doesn't hold resources on the server side: it's a client-side state feature.

An interesting case where we can see all these concepts applied is that of a value selected in a combo box being changed. When the page is initially submitted to the browser, view state contains the items in the list with the first selected (for example). If the user changes the selected element, upon postback, LoadViewState will load the previously unselected items. Next, the LoadPostData will contain the newly selected item. Based on this information, the new item in the server control will be marked as selected, and ASP.NET will also know it has to raise the SelectedIndexChanged event at the appropriate time (after OnLoad). This is how the whole event-based structure works.

Inside our handlers, we can set controls' values as usual, and the SaveViewState() method will take care of persisting it to view state for later use. When the page is posted back again, that value will be automatically loaded by ASP.NET. Now we can understand the importance of the moment we use to perform processing: if we change values in the Render method, that won't get persisted to view state, and thus will be lost upon postback. OnPreRender, on the other hand, or in fact any event handler we attach to a control, is a good place to do so.

As view state is saved to a hidden input field in the rendered HTML, it increases the page size at run time and also adds processing on the server because it has to deal with it and perform the steps we saw above. Thus, we should enable it only when it's really needed. It can be configured at four levels:

❑ **Web server control** – All these controls have an `EnableViewState` property to enable/disable this feature.

❑ **User controls** – These controls also have an `enableViewState` property. It can also be configured through the @ `Control` directive:

```
<%@ Control enableViewState="True|False" %>
```

❑ **Page** – `enableViewState` page property, or through the @ `Page` directive:

```
<%@ Page enableViewState="True|False" %>
```

❑ **Web application** – Through the `<pages>` element in `Web.config`:

```
<pages enableViewState="true|false" />
```

Unfortunately, it's enabled by default for all pages and controls, so we have to manually disable it when we don't need it.

We will now take advantage of view state to avoid reloading the combo boxes on each page load.

Try It Out – Preserve Processing by Using View State

1. Change the code in `Page_Load` of the `Search.aspx` page to match the following:

```
private void Page_Load(object sender, System.EventArgs e)
{
  // Configure the icon and message
  base.HeaderIconImageUrl =
    Request.ApplicationPath + "/Images/search.gif";
  base.HeaderMessage = "Search Users";

  SetResultsState(Session["search"] != null);

  if (!IsPostBack)
  {
    // Previous code to load values here...
  }
}
```

2. Run the page and perform a search with all fields blank, and select View | Source. Note the *huge* value in the hidden _ _VIEWSTATE field.

3. Go back to the page design view, select the datagrid and set its `EnableViewState` property to `false`.

4. Repeat Step 2. Notice how the hidden field value has now been dramatically reduced. If you take the string inside the field and paste it in Notepad and save the file in both cases, you will see the size is reduced from approximately 19k to 6k!

How It Works

The `Page` class exposes an `IsPostBack` property that can be used to determine if the page is being accessed for the first time or not, so we only load the values from the database on the first hit. Note that on further postbacks, we don't load the values, but they are not lost, as view state keeps track of them and reloads them each time. You can see this every time a new search is performed, and the values on the combo boxes remain in place.

You will also notice that the filter by place or type now works as expected. If you take a second look at the figure showing the sequence of events during the page life, you will notice that `OnLoad()` method is called *before* our event handlers. As we were data binding the combo boxes at that moment, we were effectively removing the user selection before the handler for the search button could retrieve the selected value, and that's why it didn't work. Now that the binding is performed only once, selection is preserved, and the event handler can successfully retrieve the filter.

When we disabled view state for the datagrid, we prevented ASP.NET from persisting all the information in the grid (including rows, data, and even style!) to view state, thus preserving a lot of bandwidth our users will appreciate, and also relieved the server from processing all that state about the grid that wasn't used by our code.

You can try disabling view state at the page level, and see how the values in the combo boxes get lost thereafter. Of course if the values in the combo boxes change frequently, you will probably want to reload them each time, but this is not the case for us.

Using View State as a Data Store

View state can also be used much like session and application state to hold arbitrary data. This opens opportunities to avoid using session state whenever the data we need to track is only relevant to a single page. It can be accessed from our code using syntax identical to that of session and application state:

```
// Save a value to view state
ViewState["selected"] = true;

// Retrieve the value later
bool selected = (bool) ViewState["selected"];
```

Even if strictly speaking, almost anything can be saved to view state, even a whole `DataSet`, it is optimized for simple values such as strings, integers, Booleans, arrays, `ArrayList`, and `Hashtable` types. Saving objects to view state involves a process known as **serialization**, which converts an object to a string representation, which can later be deserialized back to its original form. The types we mentioned have optimized serializers that produce very compact representations and have almost no performance impact upon deserialization, unlike, for example, a dataset, which will be *very* slow to process!

Beware that, as view state increases the HTML payload (the size of the page sent to the browser, and therefore of the form posted back), it's not well suited for large amounts of data.

In our search engine, it would be useful to allow the user to select desired records in order to perform some action with them later, such as sending a request for contact to all of them in one step. We will add the selection feature now, using view state to keep this list.

Try It Out – Enabling Record Selection with View State

1. We will use an `ArrayList` object to keep a list of selected items. We will have to customize the datagrid to enable this functionality, so first ensure its `EnableViewState` property is set to `False`. Also, add the following import to the code:

```
using System;
using System.Collections;
using System.Collections.Specialized;
using System.ComponentModel;
using System.Configuration;
using System.Data;
using System.Data.SqlClient;
using System.Drawing;
using System.Text;
using System.Web;
using System.Web.SessionState;
using System.Web.UI;
using System.Web.UI.WebControls;
using System.Web.UI.HtmlControls;
```

2. Apply the Auto Format style Colorful 4 to the datagrid and set its `AutoGenerateColumns` property to `False`.

3. Next, switch to HTML view. Inside the datagrid control declaration, right below the `footerstyle` element, add the following column definitions:

```
<asp:datagrid id="grdResults" ...>
  ...
  <footerstyle forecolor="#4A3C8C" backcolor="#B5C7DE"></footerstyle>
  <columns>
    <asp:templatecolumn headertext="Sel">
      <itemtemplate>
        <asp:imagebutton id="imgSel" runat="server"
                         tooltip="Toggle user selection"
        commandargument='<%# DataBinder.Eval(Container, "DataItem.UserID") %>'
          commandname="SelectUser" imageurl="Images/unok.gif" />
      </itemtemplate>
    </asp:templatecolumn>
    <asp:boundcolumn datafield="FirstName" headertext="First Name" />
    <asp:boundcolumn datafield="LastName" headertext="Last Name" />
```

```
<asp:boundcolumn datafield="PlaceName" headertext="Place" />
<asp:boundcolumn datafield="PlaceType" headertext="Type" />
<asp:boundcolumn datafield="LapseName" headertext="Lapse" />
<asp:boundcolumn datafield="YearIn" headertext="Year In" />
<asp:boundcolumn datafield="MonthIn" headertext="Month In" />
<asp:boundcolumn datafield="YearOut" headertext="Year Out" />
<asp:boundcolumn datafield="MonthOut" headertext="Month Out" />
</columns>
...
```

We can't add these bound columns through the **Property Builder** as we did in Chapter 5 because the `DataSet` we are using is untyped.

4. Return to **Design** view, make sure the datagrid is in focus, and then select the **Events** button on the toolbar in the **Properties** window.

5. Double-click the **ItemDataBound** event and add the following code to the handler:

```
private void grdResults_ItemDataBound(object sender,
  System.Web.UI.WebControls.DataGridItemEventArgs e)
{
  if (ViewState["selected"] == null) return;

  StringCollection sel = (StringCollection)ViewState["selected"];
  ImageButton img = e.Item.FindControl("imgSel") as ImageButton;

  if (img == null) return;

  if (sel.Contains(img.CommandArgument))
  {
    img.ImageUrl = "Images/ok.gif";
    img.CommandName = "DeselectUser";
    e.Item.ForeColor = Color.Red;
  }
}
```

This event handler will be called every time a new item (data row) is created and bounded to the data source.

6. Return to the design view. This time double-click the **ItemCommand** event and add the following code to the handler:

```
private void grdResults_ItemCommand(object source,
  System.Web.UI.WebControls.DataGridCommandEventArgs e)
{
  if (e.CommandName == "SelectUser")
  {
    StringCollection sel = ViewState["selected"] as StringCollection;
    if (sel == null)
    {
      sel = new StringCollection();
```

```
      ViewState["selected"] = sel;
    }

    if (!sel.Contains((string)e.CommandArgument))
      sel.Add((string)e.CommandArgument);

    BindFromSession();
  }
  else if (e.CommandName == "DeselectUser")
  {
    StringCollection sel = ViewState["selected"] as StringCollection;
    sel.Remove((string)e.CommandArgument);

    BindFromSession();
  }
}
```

This handler will be called when the image button is clicked.

7. Finally, in order to show the count of selected items, let's drop a label below the whole table, named lblSelected, clear its Text property, and add the following method to the code-behind page:

```
protected override void Render(HtmlTextWriter output)
{
  if (ViewState["selected"] != null)
  {
    lblSelected.Text =
      ((StringCollection)ViewState["selected"]).Count.ToString() +
        " users selected.";
  }
  base.Render(output);
}
```

We're using the Render() method because we don't worry about storing this value in view state as it will probably change in every postback.

8. Finally, let's clear this view state value whenever the **Clear Results** image button is clicked:

```
private void btnClearResults_Click(
  object sender, System.Web.UI.ImageClickEventArgs e)
{
  Session.Remove("search");
  ViewSate.Remove("selected");
  SetResultsState(false);
}
```

9. Save and run the page.

How It Works

If we perform a search with a Place filter set to Columbia University, we will see results similar to this:

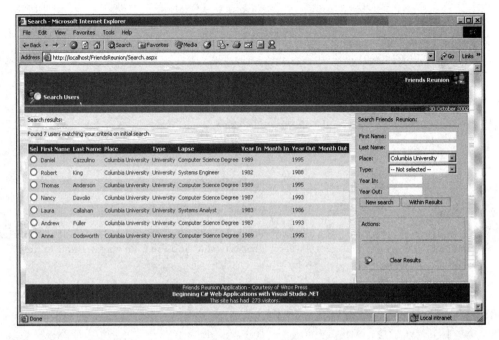

After we select a couple users from the grid, the page will look like this:

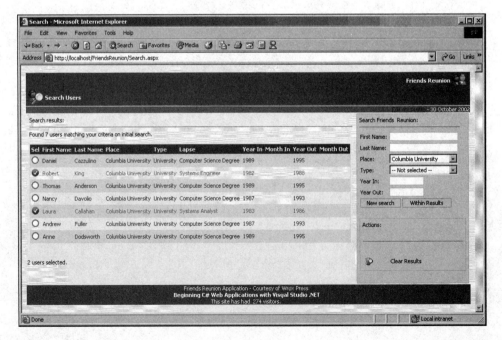

Note that because selection is performed on a per-user basis, if a user appears in more than one row (appears in more than one place), all of these 'copies' will be selected/deselected at once.

We used bound columns in the grid and a templated column, something we learned to do in Chapter 5. Whenever we click the selection button, the `ItemCommand` is fired. In order for this event handler to receive the user ID of the user in the row, we used a databinding expression:

```
<asp:imagebutton id="imgSel" runat="server" tooltip="Toggle user selection"
commandargument='<%# DataBinder.Eval(Container, "DataItem.UserID") %>'
commandname="SelectUser" imageurl="Images/unok.gif" />
```

The handler then saves the argument it receives to view state:

```
if (!sel.Contains((string)e.CommandArgument))
  sel.Add((string)e.CommandArgument);
```

It then binds the data again in order to let the next handler reflect the change in the selection. This change involves setting the forecolor of the row and changing the button's image. All this is performed in the `ItemDataBound` handler, which is fired for each row being bound after the `DataBind()` method is called inside the `BindFromSession()` method, and checks if the current item is selected or not. Note that it determines so from the collection saved to view state during the `ItemCommand` handler, and by comparing the `CommandArgument` of the image in the current row, which contains the user ID placed there by means of the binding expression we used:

```
if (sel.Contains(img.CommandArgument))
{
  img.ImageUrl = "Images/ok.gif";
  img.CommandName = "DeselectUser";
  e.Item.ForeColor = Color.Red;
}
```

Note that we are also changing the `CommandName` property to perform a deselection if the item is already selected. This information is used in the `ItemCommand` handler to determine if it should add an item to (or remove an item from) the `StringCollection`:

```
if (e.CommandName == "SelectUser")
{
// Add the e.CommandArgument value to the list
}
else if (e.CommandName == "DeselectUser")
{
// Add the e.CommandArgument value from the list
}
```

Finally, the override in the `Render()` method now shows the count of selected users, which is also taken from view state:

```
lblSelected.Text =
  ((StringCollection)ViewState["selected"]).Count.ToString() +
  " users selected.";
```

We could very easily add a new action to the **Actions** panel to clear the selection. Just adding a new row to the existing table inside the panel, dropping an `ImageButton` and setting its handler to the following would be enough:

```
private void btnClearSelection_Click(
   object sender, System.Web.UI.ImageClickEventArgs e)
{
   ViewState.Remove("selected");
   BindFromSession();
}
```

Not surprisingly, the syntax is just the same as we used to remove elements from session and application state, and to the line added to the `btnClearResults_Click` event handler. We just need to set the appropriate values for the `ImageButton`'s properties, that is, `ImageUrl` and, optionally, `TooTip`.

Transient State

There are many occasions where all you need is for the state to last for the duration of the request, and then be discarded completely automatically. One such scenario is whenever you need to pass data between pages, or even between controls at different stages of page processing, especially if such controls are contained in separate classes (like our header and footer user controls, or our `SubHeader.cs` custom control class). In those cases, we may need a way to pass data between them, but it only needs to last for the time it takes to process the current page request.

We could use session state, but that is clearly an overkill solution: we are wasting server resources for a state that doesn't need to last for the whole session duration. Even if we can preserve resources by manually removing the items once we're done, if session state is configured to be stored in a separate state server or even SQL Server as we have learned, we would suffer the corresponding performance impact.

ASP.NET provides a class that represents the context of the current request, the `HttpContext` class. We have already seen how we can access application or session state using properties provided by this class, through its `HttpContext.Current.Session` and `HttpContext.Current.Application` properties. What's more, an instance of this class is readily available as a property of the `Control` class, from which `Page` and all server controls derive: `Context`. We will call this instance the `Context` object from now on.

In addition to these properties, the `Context` object has an `Items` property that can hold any kind of data. Whatever we place there is automatically discarded as soon as the request finishes processing. That's why we call it **transient**, because it's never persisted, unlike session, application, and view state, and cookies, as we will see shortly.

We will see it in action in our application too. Now that the user has a list of the users they are interested in contacting, we have to provide them with a means to send a request to all of them in one step. For this purpose we will send them to another page where they will enter the desired message and post the request. We will use `Transient` state to pass the list of selected users we have been saving in view state (which obviously doesn't live across pages) to the target page.

Try It Out – Passing the List of Selected Users to Another Page

1. Add a new row to the table inside the **Actions** panel. As we did before, drop an `ImageButton` on the leftmost cell with ID `btnRequest`, set its `ImageUrl`, and type some meaningful text to the rightmost one. The form ought to look something like this:

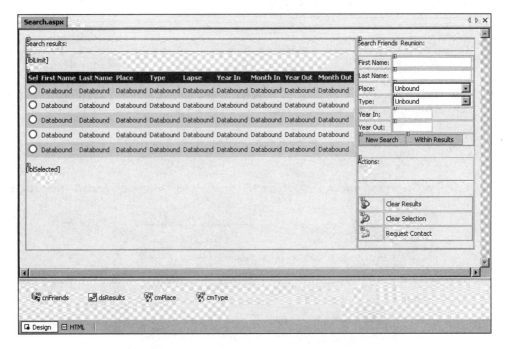

2. Double-click the new button, which should have the ID `btnRequest`, and add the following code to the event handler:

```
private void btnRequest_Click(
    object sender, System.Web.UI.ImageClickEventArgs e)
{
    Context.Items["selected"] = ViewState["selected"];
    Server.Transfer("RequestContact.aspx");
}
```

3. Add a new web form called `RequestContact.aspx`. As usual, add the link to the stylesheet and make the page inherit from `FriendsBase`.

4. Add the following imports at the top of the code:

```
using System;
using System.Collections;
using System.Collections.Specialized;
using System.ComponentModel;
using System.Data;
using System.Data.SqlClient;
using System.Drawing;
using System.Text;
using System.Web;
using System.Web.SessionState;
using System.Web.UI;
using System.Web.UI.WebControls;
using System.Web.UI.HtmlControls;
```

5. Drop a `SqlConnection` component on the page, name it `cnFriends` and configure its `ConnectionString` through `(DynamicProperties)` as we have done before.

6. Drop a `SqlCommand` component onto the form and set its `Connection` property to point to the connection component. Name it `cmUsers` and set its `CommandText` property to:

```
SELECT      FirstName + ', ' + LastName AS Expr1, UserID
FROM        [User]
```

7. Insert some text and drop a `TextBox`, a `Button`, a `ListBox`, and a `Label` to match the following UI:

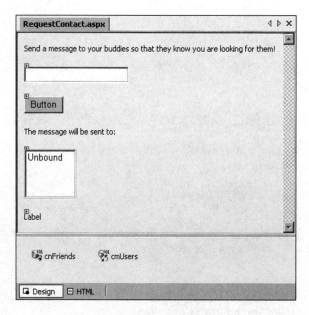

Set the controls IDs as in this list, from top to bottom:

- ❏ txtMessage
- ❏ btnSend
- ❏ lstUsers
- ❏ lblSuccess

Now set the following properties for them:

Control	Property	Value
txtMessage	CssClass	Normal
	MaxLength	300
	TextMode	Multiline
	Height	88px
	Width	424px
btnSend	CssClass	Button
	Text	Send
lstUsers	CssClass	Normal
	Rows	10
	Width	224px
lblSuccess	Font.Bold	True
	ForeColor	#0000C0
	Text	(none)

8. Add the following lines to the Page_Load method:

```
private void Page_Load(object sender, System.EventArgs e)
{
  base.HeaderMessage = "Contact your buddies!";
  base.HeaderIconImageUrl =
    Request.ApplicationPath + "/Images/contact.gif";

  // Initialize the list of users only once
  if (!IsPostBack)
  {
    // Retrieve selection from transient state
    StringCollection sel =
      Context.Items["selected"] as StringCollection;
```

```
      // If no selection was made, go back to seach...
      if (sel == null || sel.Count == 0) Server.Transfer("Search.aspx");

      StringBuilder sql = new StringBuilder();

      // Build the WHERE clause based on the list received
      sql.Append(cmUsers.CommandText).Append(" WHERE ");
      foreach (string id in sel)
      {
        sql.Append("UserID = '").Append(id).Append("' OR ");
      }

      sql.Remove(sql.Length - 3, 3);
      sql.Append("ORDER BY FirstName, LastName");
      cmUsers.CommandText = sql.ToString();

      SqlDataReader r;
      cnFriends.Open();
      r = cmUsers.ExecuteReader(CommandBehavior.CloseConnection);

      // Add the items with the corresponding ID
      while (r.Read())
      {
        lstUsers.Items.Add(new ListItem(
          r[0].ToString(), r[1].ToString()));
      }
      r.Close();
    }
  }
```

9. Double-click the `btnSend` button and add the following code:

```
private void btnSend_Click(object sender, System.EventArgs e)
{
  StringBuilder sql = new StringBuilder();
  sql.Append(@"INSERT INTO Contact
  (RequestID, IsApproved, Notes, DestinationID)
  VALUES ('");
  sql.Append(Context.User.Identity.Name);
  sql.Append("', 0, '").Append(txtMessage.Text);
  sql.Append("', '");
  string qry = sql.ToString();

  cnFriends.Open();
  try
  {
    foreach (ListItem it in lstUsers.Items)
    {
      cmUsers.CommandText = qry + it.Value + "')";
      cmUsers.ExecuteNonQuery();
    }
    lblSuccess.Text = "Message successfully sent!";
```

```
      }
      finally
      {
        cnFriends.Close();
      }
    }
```

10. Now we can save and run the page and see what the effects are.

How It Works

If we now perform a search, select some users, and click the button to request a contact, we will be taken to the `RequestContact.aspx` page, but just before we get to it, the code in the event handler saves the list we were saving in view state to transient state:

```
    Context.Items["selected"] = ViewState["selected"];
    Server.Transfer("RequestContact.aspx");
```

Note that we use `Server.Transfer()` instead of `Response.Redirect()`. By using this method, ASP.NET passes the processing responsibility to the specified page, but doesn't terminate the current execution context, nor the request, which is rather transferred to the target page. As the processing shift takes place on the server side, the client browser doesn't know that it happens, and that's why the URL stays the same after the transfer:

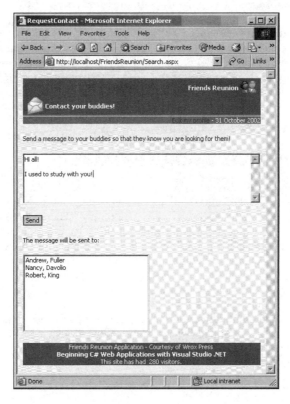

This page takes advantage of both transient state and view state. The first is used to populate the listbox when the page is first hit (it's not a postback):

```
if (!IsPostBack)
{
  // Retrieve selection from transient state
  StringCollection sel =
    Context.Items["selected"] as StringCollection;
```

Note that if a postback was performed, the `Context.Items` collection would be empty this time, and there would be no way of getting to the user selection again. Here is where the page takes advantage of view state to preserve the values loaded initially. This makes it possible to get the IDs of the selected users directly from the loaded listbox, as shown by the code in the `btnSend_Click` handler:

```
foreach (ListItem it in lstUsers.Items)
{
  cmUsers.CommandText = qry + it.Value + "')";
  cmUsers.ExecuteNonQuery();
}
```

As we learned in previous chapters, requests for contact are saved to the `Contact` table, together with the ID of the user requesting the contact (extracted, as usual, from `Context.User.Identity.Name`), so we perform an insert for each item in the list with those values.

We can appreciate the utility of transient state clearly here, but it's even more useful if the data being passed is more complex, such as a dataset or a complex object hierarchy. It doesn't suffer from the performance (both client and server side) problems of view state regarding complex sets of data, as it can pass any kind of data, nor does it impose a threat to server scalability as session state potentially does, as it's automatically discarded as soon as the request has finished processing. Due to this very fact, it's not suitable for scenarios when we need to preserve the values across requests; that's why we call it *transient*.

Storing Information using Cookies

Basically, a **cookie** is a key-value pair of strings stored on the client browser. We have already mentioned cookies when we talked about session state. We saw that they are used when they are enabled in the browser to keep the session ID, which is simply a string. Cookies are useful for that kind of storage, which doesn't take much space and where security isn't too important (don't save a credit card number in a cookie for example!). The available storage space for cookies is browser-specific, but the corresponding W3C specification states that a minimum of 4KB has to be available, and at least 20 cookies per site have to be allowed. So, even if some browsers may allow more than this, it's usually wise to stick to these limits if you want to avoid erratic behavior across browsers.

A cookie in ASP.NET is represented in an instance of the `HttpCookie` class. This object can have a name and a value on its own, or contain several name-value pairs inside it. It has `Name` and `Value` properties, but also contains a `Values` property to hold multiple values should we need to.

Also, there is a `Cookies` property in both `Page.Request` and `Page.Response`, representing the received cookies and the ongoing ones.

A very common use for cookies is to keep user preferences regarding site appearance. We will add a feature to allow our users to change their preferred background color for the site. We will add a control to the common footer user control to change it. Doing so, however, will imply some modifications to the `FriendsBase` class, which will also be the one in charge of applying the style change based on the cookie value. While we analyze the changes involved, you will get a deeper understanding of the page lifecycle, and how controls (both user and custom controls) need to be aware of it in order to behave properly.

The first thing to analyze is how are we going to trap the event fired when the control we will add to the footer (a combo box with a list of colors) changes. The answer may seem obvious: double-click the control and add the event handler. However, if we take a look our current `FriendsBase` class, we will realize that we are actually creating and loading these controls in the `Render()` method override. We did so before, since we didn't need to support postbacks, nor view state. If you look at the picture of the page lifecycle a few pages back though, you will realize that this method is the last one on the chain. All chances to get the event handlers called have already gone. Therefore, when the control causes a postback as a consequence of a change, the ASP.NET runtime won't be able to find the control to call its handler, because it won't exist yet. The only way to get the event handlers called, then, is not only to create the controls on a previous stage, but also append them to the page's `Controls` collection, which is the only way a page can access its children. The place to do so is `OnInit`.

Let's get to the code now.

Try It Out – Using Cookies to Keep User Preferences

1. Open `FriendsFooter.ascx` in HTML view and add the following code:

```
    </strong>This site has had 
  <asp:label id="lblCounter" runat="server"></asp:label> visitors. 
  <asp:image id="imgShow" runat="server" imageurl="../Images/down.gif"
      imagealign="AbsMiddle" tooltip="Change preferences"></asp:image><br>
    <div id="tbPrefs" style="DISPLAY: none; TEXT-ALIGN: center">BackColor:
      <asp:dropdownlist id="cbBackColor" runat="server" cssclass="Normal"
                      autopostback="True"></asp:dropdownlist></div>
  </asp:panel>
```

2. Modify `Page_Load` as follows:

```
    private void Page_Load(object sender, System.EventArgs e)
    {
        lblCounter.Text = Application["counter"].ToString();

        imgShow.Attributes.Add("onclick",
          "document.getElementById('tbPrefs').style.display='block';");
        imgShow.Style.Add("cursor", "pointer");
```

```
        if (!IsPostBack)
        {
          cbBackColor.Items.Clear();

          // Empty item to clear color preference
          cbBackColor.Items.Add(String.Empty);
          ColorConverter cv = new ColorConverter();

          // Retrieve current color preference to preselect the item
          Color selected = Color.Empty;
          if (Request.Cookies["backcolor"] != null &&
            Request.Cookies["backcolor"].Value != null &&
            Request.Cookies["backcolor"].Value != String.Empty)
          {
            selected =
              (Color)cv.ConvertFromString(Request.Cookies["backcolor"].Value);
          }

          TypeConverter.StandardValuesCollection col =
            cv.GetStandardValues(null);
          ListItem li;
          foreach (Color c in col)
          {
            li = new ListItem(c.Name, ColorTranslator.ToHtml(c));
            if (c.Equals(selected)) li.Selected = true;
            cbBackColor.Items.Add(li);
          }
        }
      }
    }
```

Since we are using the `TypeConverter` class, we will also need to add the following import:

```
namespace FriendsReunion.Controls
{
  using System;
  using System.ComponentModel;
  using System.Data;
  using System.Drawing;
  using System.Web;
  using System.Web.UI.WebControls;
  using System.Web.UI.HtmlControls;
```

3. Switch to design view, where the control should look like the following now:

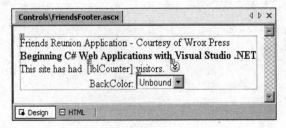

4. Double-click the combo box and add the following code:

```
private void cbBackColor_SelectedIndexChanged(
  object sender, System.EventArgs e)
{
  Response.Cookies.Add(new HttpCookie(
    "backcolor", ((DropDownList)sender).SelectedItem.Value));
}
```

5. Open `FriendsBase.cs` file. Just as we discussed before this section, we will need to add the controls to the hierarchy on the `OnInit()` method. We will do so and also keep a reference to the loaded controls. For that purpose, let's modify the class code as follows:

```
public class FriendsBase : System.Web.UI.Page
{
  protected string HeaderMessage = String.Empty;
  protected string HeaderIconImageUrl = String.Empty;

  FriendsFooter _footer;
  FriendsHeader _header;
  SubHeader _subheader;

  protected override void OnInit(EventArgs e)
  {
    _header = (FriendsHeader) LoadControl
      (Request.ApplicationPath + Path.AltDirectorySeparatorChar +
        "Controls/FriendsHeader.ascx");
    _footer = (FriendsFooter) LoadControl
      (Request.ApplicationPath + Path.AltDirectorySeparatorChar +
        "Controls/FriendsFooter.ascx");

    _subheader = new SubHeader();

    // Add to the Controls hierarchy to get proper
    // event handling, on rendering we position them
    Page.Controls.AddAt(0, _header);
    Page.Controls.AddAt(0, _subheader);
    Page.Controls.AddAt(0, _footer);
    base.OnInit(e);
  }
}
```

We will also need to import these namespaces:

```
using System;
using System.IO;
using System.Web.UI;
using System.Web.UI.HtmlControls;
using FriendsReunion.Controls;
```

6. The code for the `Render()` method will look different now:

```csharp
protected override void Render(System.Web.UI.HtmlTextWriter writer)
{
    // Remove the controls from their current place in the hierarchy
    Page.Controls.Remove(_header);
    Page.Controls.Remove(_subheader);
    Page.Controls.Remove(_footer);

    // Get a reference to the form control
    HtmlForm form = (HtmlForm)Page.Controls[1];

    // Reposition the controls on the page
    form.Controls.AddAt(0, _header );
    form.Controls.AddAt(1, _subheader );
    form.Controls.AddAt(form.Controls.Count, _footer );

    //Set current values
    _header.Message = HeaderMessage;
    _header.IconImageUrl = HeaderIconImageUrl;

#region UI customization
    // New cookies are set to Response by the color selector
    string bg = Response.Cookies["backcolor"].Value;

    // if not, check Request for a previously saved cookie
    if (bg == null &&
      Request.Cookies["backcolor"] != null &&
      Request.Cookies["backcolor"].Value != null &&
      Request.Cookies["backcolor"].Value != String.Empty)
    {
      bg = Request.Cookies["backcolor"].Value;

      // preserve cookie in the response
      Response.Cookies.Add(Request.Cookies["backcolor"]);
    }

    // Do we have a value to work with?
    if (bg != null && bg != String.Empty)
    {
      // Enclose form in a DIV to display the backcolor
      HtmlGenericControl div = new HtmlGenericControl("div");
      div.Style.Add("background-color", bg);

      // Relocate the form inside the DIV
      Page.Controls.Remove(form);
      Page.Controls.AddAt(1, div);
      div.Controls.Add(form);
    }
#endregion

    // Render as usual
    base.Render(writer);
}
```

7. That's it! Save and run the page. Try clicking on the new icon next to the visitor count and selecting a color from the combo box.

How It Works

To get the list of available colors and to convert to/from HTML representations, we use two classes in the `System.Drawing` namespace: `ColorConverter` and `ColorTranslator`. Those are exactly the same classes Visual Studio .NET uses to handle color properties in the property browser and style builder. We added a little piece of JavaScript to the image `onclick` attribute (actually an event on the client side) to show the hidden panel containing the color selector.

The first thing you will notice is that as soon as you select a color from the list, the change takes place. That is a consequence of the `autopostback` attribute we added to the combo box. The workaround to get the event handler called involves creating and adding the control at an arbitrary position in the hierarchy during initialization (`OnInit`):

```
Page.Controls.AddAt(0, _footer);
```

and later removing it and adding it to the desired position (last in the `Controls` collection) for rendering purposes:

```
Page.Controls.Remove(_footer);
HtmlForm form = (HtmlForm)Page.Controls[1];
form.Controls.AddAt(form.Controls.Count, _footer );
```

By keeping the controls' instances in class-level private variables, removing them and adding them to the `Controls` collection is very easy, as we don't have to find the controls in the hierarchy previously. This technique allows the event handler for the `SelectedIndexChanged` event to be called after initialization has completed. Inside this handler we just save the selected HTML value to a cookie in the `Response.Cookies` collection:

```
Response.Cookies.Add(new HttpCookie(
    "backcolor", ((DropDownList)sender).SelectedItem.Value));
```

Then, as the final step in the page life, comes the `FriendsBase.Render()` method, which besides repositioning controls as we have seen and setting the header message and icon, checks the status of the cookies, both from `Response` and `Request`, and based on that, creates an enclosing `<div>` element where it places the whole form, to get the background color displayed:

```
Page.Controls.Remove(form);
Page.Controls.AddAt(1, div);
div.Controls.Add(form);
```

The process for relocating the form is exactly the same we used to position the other controls. As all this code is placed in the base class for all our pages, they all gain this feature immediately. The home page (`Default.aspx`) would look like this now, after we changed the color preference and expanded the preferences panel at the bottom:

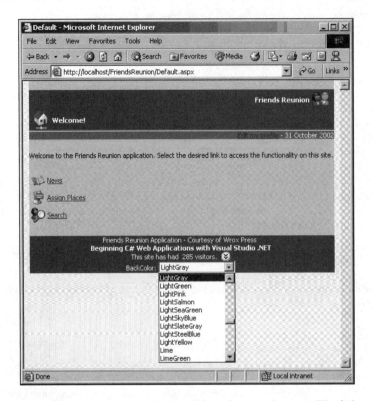

If the user restarts their browser right now, they will lose their preference. That's because the cookie expires with the browser session by default. In order to change this behavior, we can just add the following line to `FriendsBase.Render()`:

```
div.Controls.Add(form);
Response.Cookies["backcolor"].Expires = DateTime.MaxValue;
```

Passing Data with Query Strings

A query string is everything appended to a URL after the name of the page plus a question mark, such as in the following:

```
http://friendsreunion.com/ViewUser.aspx?UserID=99
```

Some would consider that passing data in the query string between pages is a way to keep state too. If you believe so, then we have been using this form of state before, for example, when we provided a link to view details about a user in `News.aspx`, which rendered very similarly to the example above to pass the user ID to the `ViewUser.aspx` page. It comes in especially handy when we use it in conjunction with databinding, as we did. We retrieved this value simply with:

```
userID = Request.QueryString["UserID"];
```

Note that the key used is the value before the = and the value we get is the string following it. The `QueryString` property is of type `NameValueCollection`, containing all the key-value pairs found in the URL. If multiple values are needed, they have to be separated by an & sign.

Except for this and similar cases where small sets of data need to be passed, this mechanism is not recommended. HTTP 1.0 web servers usually don't handle more than 255 characters in a query string, nor do older browsers. HTTP 1.1 solved this, but older browsers still won't work.

Passing Data with Hidden Form Fields

Finally, using hidden form fields to pass data between the client and the server, and between pages is also possible. We can simply add an HTML input field to the form, set its type to `hidden`, and then set values on it, either on the client side using script or on the server. This is an example hidden field:

```
<body ms_positioning="FlowLayout">
  <form name="Default" method="post" action="Default.aspx" id="Default">
    <input type="hidden" name="myField" value="myValue" />
```

We can get the values in a hidden form field using the `Request.Form` property:

```
string value = Request.Form["myField"];
```

You already know that view state uses this technique so you can easily imagine your own applications of it, and they don't necessarily have to be simple, as you can see!

This concludes our journey through the exciting ASP.NET state management features.

Summary

Equally important as dynamic features for web applications is the ability to retain state in its different forms. ASP.NET offers a wide range of possibilities, filling all the gaps of the past and creating new and improved state handling approaches such as view state and transient state. We have covered each of the features it offers and learned the differences between them. We also discussed the performance and scalability tradeoffs among them, and offered some hints on where to use each one.

We've taken advantage of session state to allow the user to perform refining searches for fellow users. We have taken into account scalability problems that may arise and placed a limit on maximum search results, and also discussed different storage locations for this state data. We then used view state to further increase our application's responsiveness by reducing the HTML payload as a result of enabling it only when needed, and also reduced server-side processing by avoiding reloading data and instead letting view state take care of reconstructing UI elements, such as combo boxes.

We then moved to more advanced uses of view state as a store for arbitrary data, and added the possibility to select users from the search results and stored those selections in view state. Next, we learned about a new feature available in ASP.NET, transient state, which allowed us to pass this selection data between pages without consuming server resources.

We discussed application state, and used it to provide a global count of visitors to our application, and finally used the most traditional client-state feature, cookies, to store user preferences for the site's background color.

Our application is becoming more mature, offering not only the possibility to register, add places, and search for fellow users, but also doing so in a user-friendly and responsive way. We have built this functionality by taking advantage of ASP.NET state management features, as well as all we learned in previous chapters about server controls, ADO.NET, and databinding.

It's now time to open up our application to partners and associates, and we will take advantage of XML, XML schemas, and web services to allow them to access our data and interact with our application. We will learn about these exciting new technologies and the great potential they offer in the upcoming chapters.

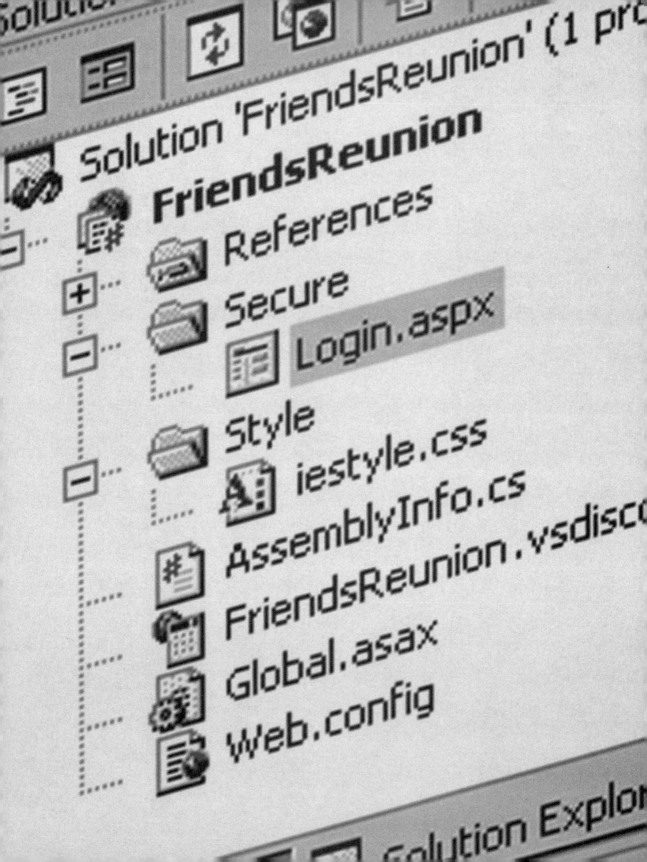

Solution 'FriendsReunion' (1 pro

Solution 'FriendsReunion' (1 pro
FriendsReunion
References
Secure
Login.aspx
Style
iestyle.css
AssemblyInfo.cs
FriendsReunion.vsdisc
Global.asax
Web.config

Solution Explor

Markup Languages and XML

In Chapters 4 and 5, we introduced the concept of working with data. We placed a relational database behind our web application, and used it predominantly for data storage. We also used ADO.NET techniques to manipulate and organize data as it passed between the user and the database. By the end of Chapter 5, the *Friends Reunion* web application was acting as a "middle man", allowing individuals (on one side) to interact with the data stored within the database (on the other).

Of course, there is more to data than just storage and manipulation. Internet connectivity is now widespread, and it is often desirable to have disparate applications working together across the Internet on related tasks. In this type of scenario, we need a way for such applications to *exchange* data. Exchanging data involves formatting the data in a way that is compatible with all of our applications, and is easy to transport between applications.

For example, suppose we wanted to extend the *Friends Reunion* application, to allow a subscribing college or other institution to upload or download information about its users and attendees. To achieve this, there would need to be some agreement about the format of the data, and how the data would be transferred. Ideally, we would build on a data format that is standardized and universally understood.

It sounds complex, but in fact **Extensible Markup Language** (**XML**) makes it all much easier. In fact, XML was devised largely in answer to the generic need for a ubiquitous, transportable data format – and as we'll begin to see in this chapter, it's very powerful.

As it happens, Microsoft has subscribed heavily to XML in its implementation of .NET – you have probably already noticed that. XML is becoming increasingly important in a number of ways, and over the course of the next two chapters we will touch on only a few of its applications.

In this chapter, we will:

- ❑ Take a look at the concept of markup that underpins XML

- ❑ Understand the basic principles of an XML document, and see some sample XML documents

- ❑ Learn about the two properties of XML documents – well-formedness and validity – that allow us to read and work with them

- ❑ See how we can use an XML Schema to describe the structure of an XML document, and how XML Schemas play a very important part in XML-based applications

In Chapter 8, we'll take this preparatory work and use it to extend the features of the *Friends Reunion* application – to create a feature that allows an individual to upload an XML document containing details of many registrants from a single college or institution.

XML is a markup language. To get a good understanding of XML, it helps if we first understand what we mean in the broader sense by the terms *markup* and *markup language*. Let's start our exploration there.

Markup Languages

Whenever you look at a document, you are looking at an organized set of data. Consider some everyday examples:

❑   Your salary slip contains data that relates to the amount of money you earned, and how much was deducted in tax

❑   A recipe for chocolate cake is an organized collection of data, telling you what ingredients you'll need (and how much of each), what method you should use to combine them all, and the cooking time and temperature

❑   This book is also an organized collection of data: specifically, it is an ordered set of headings, paragraphs, and illustrations

The data in documents such as these is generally arranged visually in such a way that the organization of the data is clear to the human eye, and is therefore easy for us humans to read. In a similar way, we often need our computerized applications to be able to read a document and deduce the structure and organization of the data contained within it. To do this, we use **markup**.

Markup consists of tags or markers that exist in the document along with the data, and describe the different elements of data within the document. Let's consider an example:

```
<recipe title="Classic Chocolate Cake">
  <ingredients>
    <ingredient>
      <description>Eggs<description>
      <quantity>2</quantity>
    </ingredient>
    <ingredient>
      <description>Butter<description>
      <quantity unit="oz">4</quantity>
    </ingredient>
    ...etc...
  </ingredients>
  <method>
      Cream the butter and sugar. Add the milk and beaten eggs.
      Sieve in the flour and cocoa, and fold into the mixture.
      Turn into a lined cake tin and place into the oven.
  </method>
  <cookingTime unit="min">25</cookingTime>
  <ovenSetting unit="C">180</ovenSetting>
</recipe>
```

This example clearly describes a recipe for chocolate cake. All the information (or data) relating to the recipe is contained between the opening `<recipe>` tag and the closing `</recipe>` tag. Within the recipe, there is an organized list of ingredients, a method, and information about the cooking time and temperature. This document may not look like the attractive glossy cookbooks you see in the bookshops these days, but all the necessary information is presented in a well-organized, well-structured, unambiguous way.

HyperText Markup Language

In fact, we've seen markup before – in the HTML that is generated by our web applications and sent to the browser for display. HTML is a **markup language** – it is a set of tags and attributes that allow us to describe (or mark-up) the structure of a particular type of document. (In fact, HTML is specifically designed to describe the structure of web page documents.)

The data in an HTML document is intended for *display* (in a browser window), so the markup in an HTML document is intended specifically to *describe* the way the browser should *display* the data. For example:

```html
<html>
  <body>
    <h1>Classic Chocolate Cake</h1>
    <p>
      <b>Ingredients</b><br/>
      2 eggs<br/>
      4oz butter<br/>
      4oz sugar<br/>
      4oz self-raising flour<br/>
      1oz cocoa<br/>
      2tbsp milk<br/>
    </p>
    <p>
      <b>Method</b><br/>
      Cream the butter and sugar. Add the milk and beaten eggs.
      Sieve in the flour and cocoa, and fold into the mixture.
      Turn into a lined cake tin and place into the oven.
    </p>
    <p>
      <b>Cooking Time:</b> 25 minutes<br/>
      <b>Oven Setting:</b> 180C<br/>
    </p>
  </body>
</html>
```

Like the earlier document, this HTML document contains all the data required for our chocolate cake recipe. However, the markup in this document structures the data very differently. The data in this document is *not* structured as a recipe (there is no `<ingredients>` section and no `<method>` section). Instead, it is structured as a web page (with a heading and a sequence of paragraphs).

We can send this HTML document to a browser. Because the browser is programmed to recognize HTML tags, it will be able to work out the structure of the HTML document (the sequence of headings and paragraphs, etc.) by reading the tags, and hence display all the elements of the document in the right places on the page:

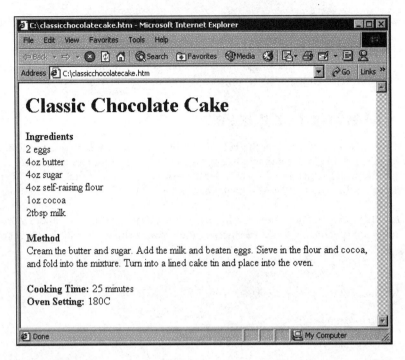

Unsurprisingly, browsers are not programmed to recognize the `<recipe>` tag or the `<ingredients>` tag, and so the recipe structure (in our first example) means nothing to a browser. There would not be much point sending the recipe markup to a browser. However, the recipe markup would be very useful, say, as part of a custom application that deals with archives of thousands of recipes.

Extensible Markup Language (XML)

So, markup is used to describe the structure and organization of data within a document. We describe the structure of a *web page* document using a markup language called HTML. But not every document is a web page; sometimes we need to describe data using a structure that does not resemble web page structure at all. In that case, HTML will not do the job: we need a different markup language. For example:

❑   We've already seen a recipe document, which describes the structure of a recipe using special "recipe markup" tags like `<ingredients>` and `<cookingTime>`:

```
<recipe title="Classic Chocolate Cake">
  <ingredients>
    ...etc...
  </ingredients>
  <method>
    ...etc...
  </method>
  <cookingTime unit="min">25</cookingTime>
  <ovenSetting unit="C">180</ovenSetting>
</recipe>
```

Here, everything between the `<recipe>` and `</recipe>` tags is recipe information, and we use other tags to describe the exact nature of each bit of configuration data.

❑ We've also seen other types of markup already in this book – for example, in the configuration files used by our *Friends Reunion* web application:

```
<configuration>
  <appSettings>
    <add key="sqlCon.ConnectionString" value="...etc..." />
  </appSettings>
  <system.web>
    <authentication mode="Forms">
      <forms loginUrl="Secure/Login.aspx" />
    </authentication>
    <customErrors mode="RemoteOnly" />
    ...etc...
  </system.web>
  <location path="Secure/NewUser.aspx">
    <system.web>
      <authorization>
        <allow users="*" />
      </authorization>
    </system.web>
  </location>
</configuration>
```

The principle here is similar: everything between the `<config>` and `</config>` tags is configuration data, and we use other tags to describe the exact nature of each bit of configuration data. As a result, the configuration data can be interpreted and its structure deduced programmatically, whenever it is required within the application.

These two examples have a common ancestor: they are both examples of **Extensible Markup Language** (**XML**). XML is a little like HTML, in that each is a tag-based and attribute-based text format for describing the structure of the data in a document. The main difference is that HTML is a language of tags and attributes for describing a *specific* structure (a web page), while XML is a more generic language that allows you to use almost *any* names for your tags and attributes.

The Significance of XML

As a data format, XML has a number of important characteristics that are its strengths. In particular, it is a **text-based** data format (this fact should be fairly obvious from the two samples above). In other words, any XML document is a plain-text document that contains both data and the markup that describes its structure. This means that:

❑ XML data is easy to store. We can store XML in text documents on hard disk

❑ XML data is easy to transfer. It's as easy as transferring a plain text file or an HTML file

❑ XML data is easy for machines to read. Hence, XML is highly compatible with many different types of system

❑   XML data is easy for humans to read. This makes it easy for a human to interpret the data in an XML document, and even makes it possible for humans to write XML documents using a keyboard. (This was one of the requirements that was considered when XML was being developed.)

Equally important is the fact that XML is a standard developed by the **World Wide Web Consortium (W3C)** – an independent organization responsible for developing web standards – and the W3C's XML 1.0 specification is a globally accepted specification. This means that:

❑   Any XML document can be expected to obey a standard set of rules, regardless of platform or software vendor.

❑   Any application that produces XML is expected to produce XML that adheres to the same standard (regardless of the operating system and programming language with which the application is developed or run).

❑   Any application that reads XML data is expected to be able to read XML that adheres to the same standard (again, regardless of operating system and programming language, or the origin of the XML document).

In other words, any two applications that need to exchange XML data can do so regardless of platform or programming language.

The home page for all W3C XML specs and work in progress can be found at http://www.w3.org/XML.

Some Applications of XML

Since the release of XML 1.0 in 1998, XML has found its way into plenty of diverse areas of computing. This section is not a comprehensive list of its uses, but rather is intended to illustrate the usefulness of XML, and how a good grounding in this important technology will help us in many areas.

For example (and as we mentioned at the beginning of the chapter), Microsoft has adopted XML as a cornerstone of the .NET web applications model. These are just a few places in which XML is directly relevant to us in this book:

❑   **In configuration files.** We have already seen how ASP.NET uses the `Web.config` XML file to contain configuration settings for web applications. In fact, XML-based configuration files are used throughout the .NET Framework. XML's hierarchical and readable format makes it easy to locate and change configuration details.

❑   **In web forms.** The data contained by web controls on a page is represented by XML fragments inside HTML, and can be seen when the page is opened in HTML view. This information is used by the controls to render themselves appropriately.

❑   **In web services.** As we'll see in Chapter 9, web services are generally invoked using an XML-based language called **SOAP**, which is also used for returning results.

In the area of data access, XML provides a convenient standard way of passing data between applications and databases. As we'll see, XML is inherently hierarchical in its nature; this hierarchical nature means that XML lends itself very well to representing the structure of the data, and relationships between elements of the data:

- ❏ **In interoperability.** XML is platform- and language-neutral, so it is ideal for moving data between disparate database products and operating systems.

- ❏ **In ADO.NET support.** The `DataSet` object, which we studied in Chapter 4, has extensive support for XML, including the ability to read and save files and streams in this format through its `ReadXml()` and `WriteXml()` methods.

- ❏ **In its support from major database vendors.** Most major database vendors now build some degree of XML support into their products. For example, many products can now return the results of queries in XML format. Some products can natively read and process XML files, and XML strings within stored procedures (using functions or types added to their respective languages). SQL Server, Oracle, and IBM's DB2 all offer native XML support.

XML has also found many applications in e-business:

- ❏ As a platform-neutral standard, XML is the perfect candidate for data representation in e-business, where business partners need their systems and applications to interact and communicate, and where systems range from the latest super-sleek setups to ancient monoliths.

- ❏ In the past, the standard for business communication was Electronic Data Interchange (EDI). Unfortunately, EDI was very difficult to understand and costly to implement. XML, in conjunction with the Internet, makes it much easier for smaller companies to implement e-commerce solutions.

The Nature of an XML Document

The nature of XML as a data format implies that that it imposes a set of formatting rules. If a document conforms to these rules, then we say that it is a **well-formed** XML document.

The key rules of XML are simple, and mostly very intuitive:

1. **Matching start and end tags.** Any block (or **element**) of data that begins with a start tag (for example, `<myElement>`) should end with a matching end tag (in this case `</myElement>`). For example, the following element is well-formed:

```
<quantity>2</quantity>
```

2. **Empty elements.** An element composed of a start-tag/end-tag pair, but with no data in between them, can be abbreviated by using a single **empty tag**. For example, we can replace the following element:

```
<description></description>
```

with this empty element (note the position of the / character):

```
<description/>
```

3. **Attributes.** If we want to add attributes to an element, we can write them within the element's start tag. The attribute is a name–value pair expressed using the format `att_name="att_value"` (where the value is expressed as a string and enclosed in single- or double-quotes). For example, the following element is well-formed:

```
<quantity unit="oz">4</quantity>
```

We can also add attributes to an empty tag:

```
<freezeable duration="3 months" />
```

4. **Case-sensitivity of tag- and attribute names.** Tag names and attribute names are case-sensitive. In particular, this means the case of an element's end tag must match the case of its start tag. For example, the following element is *not* well-formed:

```
<Quantity>2</quantity>
```

5. **Nesting.** Elements must be properly nested. In other words, if an element contains another opening tag the it should also contain its closing tag. For example, the following is well-formed:

```
<player><name>Joe DiMaggio</name></player>
```

By contrast, the following is *not* well-formed:

```
<player><name>Joe DiMaggio</player></name>
```

6. **Top-level element.** There must be one (and only one) top-level element that encloses all other elements in the document.

Any XML document that meets these requirements is said to be well-formed. In fact, the chocolate cake document we presented at the beginning of this chapter is a well-formed XML document.

Checking for Well-formedness

When an application opens an XML document, it uses an **XML parser** to check that the document is well-formed. The parser is part of the XML implementation that your application uses whenever it has to deal with XML documents. (For example, Microsoft's .NET Framework provides an implementation through the classes in the `System.Xml` namespace, and Sun does something similar for Java programmers.) The W3C's XML standard specifies that a 'conformant' XML implementation must reject an XML document if it is not well-formed.

If your application opens an XML document that *is* well-formed, then the parser will accept the document. This indicates to the application that it should be able to read the document.

An XML document that is *not* well-formed is useless. If your application opens an XML document that is *not* well-formed, then the parser will reject it – it will generate an exception that tells your application that the document is not well-formed.

XML Data Exchange

We've taken a good look at some examples of XML documents, and we've taken a look at what makes a well-formed XML document. We also noted that XML is particularly useful when it comes to data exchange. Specifically, XML is a *text*-based data formatting mechanism. This means that the XML data format is compatible with any application (regardless of operating systems and languages), and that it is easy to transfer XML documents from one system to another.

Over the remainder of this chapter and during the next two, we'll develop our *Friends Reunion* application a little further, by adding a couple of data exchange features that make use of different XML data exchange techniques. As we go, we'll learn a lot more about XML and how it is used in web applications. We'll begin by describing one of the features that we're going to add.

Suppose that a college or other institution wants to upload information about a number of its students to our *Friends Reunion* web application – or that a social group (such as an Old Classmates' Society) wants to add the details of *all* of its members to our site. In its current form, our application doesn't enable an individual to upload details about lots of people *at the same time* – instead, that individual would need to use the existing interface to insert the details of each member manually. If there are more than a few members in the group, then this will be a fairly laborious task!

It would be much easier on the individual concerned if we allowed them to upload the *complete* set of details of their members all at once, as an XML document. The XML document would pass from the individual's web browser to the *Friends Reunion* application server. Then the application would read and interpret the uploaded XML document, and display the information on-screen:

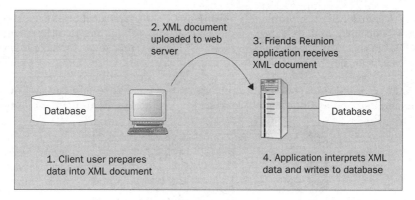

From there, we could extend the feature further and have the application place the uploaded data into our database (as shown in Step 4 above). We'll only go as far as Step 3 in the book, but you should learn enough in the book to be able to build Step 4 yourself if you wish.

XML Schemas and Validation

Before we rush in and build the upload tool, we have some preparatory work to do. In particular, it's quite easy to see that, unless we impose some careful checking mechanism, an individual will be able to upload *any* type of document to our web application. We need to develop a mechanism that checks the uploaded document, to confirm that it contains *exactly* the kind of information that the *Friends Reunion* application expects.

We can break this checking process into two parts:

❑ First, of course, our application needs to be able to **read** the XML document. In other words, we need to check that the uploaded document *is* an XML document, and that it is well-formed.

❑ Second, our application needs to be able to **interpret** our well-formed XML document. What does this mean? Well, the application's task is to understand the data in the document, extract it, and perform some task with it (in our case, display it on screen or place it into the database). If the document contains tags and attributes that the application doesn't understand, then the application will not be able to extract the data it's looking for – and it will be unable to complete the job.

We've already talked about the first of these: we will use the .NET Framework's XML parser to check for well-formedness. Right now, let's focus on the second part of the check – ensuring that the XML document contains the expected tags and attributes.

A Sample XML File

The best way to start solving this problem is to work out the tags and attributes that we expect an uploaded XML document to have. (Then, in the next section, we'll formalize this by writing something called an **XML schema**.) So, let's look at what we need a typical uploaded XML file to contain, for the purposes of this application.

When the XML file is uploaded, our application will extract the data from it and use it to populate the `TimeLapse` and `User` tables of our database. Here's a reminder of the structure of those tables:

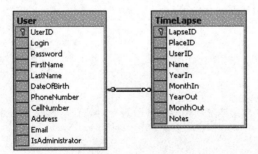

We will not dwell on the process of database updates here: the main point of showing this is that it tells us about the type of attendee-related information that individuals will want to include in their XML document. The `TimeLapse` table holds data that describes how long a particular individual (or user) spent at a particular institution (or place), while the `User` table holds more general information about users.

Our XML document will contain data about a collection of users that attended a particular place. For each user, the document will contain data about the individual, and it may also contain data about the attendance details of that user.

So, here's an example XML document that shows the kind of structure we're looking for. It has a single root element (called `<Friends>`), which specifies the identity of the institution submitting the document in an attribute called `PlaceID`. The `<Friends>` element is then allowed to contain `<User>` elements (one for each user) and `<Attendee>` elements (each element describes the period of attendance of a user):

```xml
<?xml version="1.0"?>
<Friends PlaceID="C9796AD1-5A7E-4d9c-9F99-0090E11E5662">
  <User>
    <UserID>E81A8BCD-47A3-4038-9F7B-2DF25C741833</UserID>
    <Login>jbrown</Login>
    <Password>nitsob</Password>
    <FirstName>John</FirstName>
    <LastName>Brown</LastName>
    <PhoneNumber>042-700-7007</PhoneNumber>
    <Address>23 Olton Boulevard, Stamford</Address>
    <Email>jbrown@wrox.com</Email>
  </User>
  <User>
    etc...
  </User>
  <User>
    etc...
  </User>

  <Attendee Name="High School Complete">
    <UserID>E81A8BCD-47A3-4038-9F7B-2DF25C741833</UserID>
    <YearIn>1972</YearIn>
    <MonthIn>9</MonthIn>
    <YearOut>1977</YearOut>
    <MonthOut>7</MonthOut>
    <Notes>I played cymbals in the school band!</Notes>
  </Attendee>
  <Attendee Name="...">
    etc...
  </Attendee>
  <Attendee Name="...">
    etc...
  </Attendee>
</Friends>
```

The `<?xml ... ?>` line at the beginning of this document is just a processing instruction. Processing instructions are common in XML documents; they're not part of the data itself but explain how the data has been prepared. In this case, it says that we're using W3C XML version 1.0.

We've deliberately chosen tags and attributes that match the field names used in the database (things like `User`, `UserID`, `YearIn`, and so on). We don't have to do this, but it would help us if we were to use this feature to extract data from the XML file and insert it into the database.

We've also decided not to use a one-to-one mapping between the elements of the document and the fields in the database tables. Instead, we've tried to give the XML document a more intuitive layout, allowing us to demonstrate the full functionality of .NET's XML objects, which you'll see later on.

For instance, the `PlaceID` and `YearIn` fields of the `TimeLapse` table are treated differently in our document. We're making the assumption that all of the attendance records contained in a given XML document will relate to the same institution, but they will contain data about people who attended the institution at different times. Thus:

❑   Since all the attendees in a given XML document attended the same organization, the document only needs to mention the organization once (in the `PlaceID` attribute of the `<Friends>` tag).

❑   By contrast, the `YearIn` data for users in a given XML document could be different for each individual user's attendance record, so for each attendance record we mark up that data as a sub-element of each `<Attendee>` element.

How is a document like this created? It could be typed into a text editor such as Notepad, or it could be created using a specialist XML editor like the one included with Visual Studio .NET. Alternatively, it could be generated by a program that extracts the information from the organization's database and places it into a file of this format. We will not worry about that: we will leave it to individual institutions and societies to decide how they want to create their XML documents. (However, we will be able to help them, by supplying them with the XML Schema definition that we will begin to build shortly.)

Markup Languages, Schemas, and Validation

When we come to write the application code that interprets the uploaded XML file, we will write code that assumes the XML document has a certain structure (the sample document above gives us an idea of that structure). But it's quite dangerous to make that assumption without some kind of explicit verification: if the XML document has the wrong structure, the application will fail in some unpredictable way.

What we should really do is perform a formal *check* that the XML document has the structure that the application expects. We need to perform this check immediately *after* the application has checked that the XML document is well-formed (so we know we can read it), but *before* the application starts interpreting it.

To perform this check, we can use an **XML Schema**. An XML Schema is a way of describing a markup language. More accurately, it describes the structure of the language formally and very precisely:

❑   It states precisely what element names are allowed, and what attribute names are allowed.

❑   It can also state the permitted relationships between elements (for example, that a `<User>` element can contain a `<UserID>` element, but not the other way round).

❑   It can impose restrictions on the values (or types of values) contained in elements or attributes.

When the application receives an XML document, we can check that it has the appropriate structure by **validating** it against the schema. If the XML document adheres to the rules described in the schema, then we say that the XML document is **valid** – it contains the expected structure:

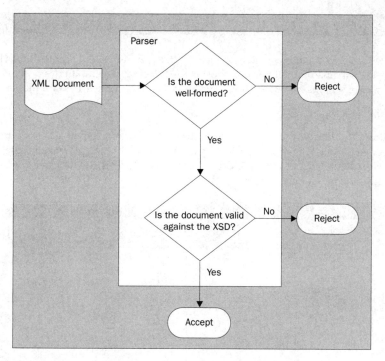

Thus, an XML document usually needs to pass *two* important tests before we can use it. First we check that it is *well-formed* (and thus that we can read it). Then we check that it's *valid* (and thus that we can interpret it).

XML Schemas

The way we write an XML Schema is in the form of an **XML Schema Definition** (**XSD**) file. We'll get to see an XSD file shortly. As you'll see, an XSD file is actually just an XML file that uses special tags and attributes designed to describe XML Schemas! (We'll say more about this shortly.)

Because the XML Schema can be completely described in a single XSD file, it's very transportable. This means that, not only is it a valuable part of our *Friends Reunion* application, but we can send it to the developers of client applications. These developers can use the XSD file to find out the exact structure of the XML documents that their custom applications should be generating, and to even validate the generated XML before it is uploaded – and thus ensure that their uploaded XML documents are not rejected by the *Friends Reunion* application.

Moreover, because an XSD file is written in XML, it's language-independent and platform-independent. Therefore, *any* client developer should be able to make use of our XSD, once we've written it.

So, we'd better get down to writing it! We'll devote the remainder of this chapter to building and understanding our XML Schema. Our schema will describe the precise tags and attributes that the *Friends Reunion* application expects from an uploaded XML document that contains details of attendees. In the next chapter, we'll write the part of the application that allows a user to upload an XML document, and the part that checks the XML document (for well-formedness and for validity against our schema), and the part that then interprets the uploaded XML and puts it onto the screen.

Try It Out – Creating a New XML Schema

Now that we've covered the basics, the best way to get a grip on what a schema looks like is to have a go at building the schema that defines our chosen XML format. Again, there's nothing stopping us using Notepad to create a schema manually, but Visual Studio .NET has a great tool that makes the job much less painful.

1. We'll use the *Friends Reunion* application from the end of Chapter 6 as a starting point. Open the project, right-click on the project name in the Solution Explorer, and select **Add |
Add New Item**. Choose the **XML Schema** template from the **Data** category, name the new file `Friends.xsd`, and click **Open**:

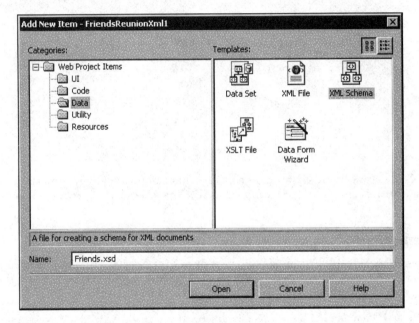

When the empty schema has been created, you'll be presented with a blank design surface onto which you can drag various items from the **Toolbox** in order to create our schema. This is the **XML Designer**.

2. Open the **Properties** window, which will be showing the options available for the root element of an XML schema, `<xs:schema>`. These options represent the attributes that may be set on this element, and will therefore apply to the schema as a whole.

Locate the `targetNamespace` property. You'll notice that it is set to a default value, `http://tempuri.org/Friends.xsd`. Change it to `urn:wrox-friends`.

There's not much to see yet, but let's find out more about what we've done in these steps, and how they contribute to the overall schema.

How It Works

Just like the Visual Studio .NET form designer, the XML designer is a visual tool that generates code behind the scenes that corresponds to the drag-and-drop actions we perform. You can see the code it produces by clicking the XML button at the bottom left corner of the designer:

If you do this now, you'll see that our schema currently consists of a single, empty `<xs:schema>` element, which looks like this (I've formatted it a little here to make it more legible):

```xml
<?xml version="1.0" encoding="utf-8" ?>
<xs:schema id="Friends"
           targetNamespace="urn:wrox-friends"
           elementFormDefault="qualified"
           xmlns="urn:wrox-friends"
           xmlns:mstns="urn:wrox-friends"
           xmlns:xs="http://www.w3.org/2001/XMLSchema">
</xs:schema>
```

You can see that it's just a regular XML file, right down to the `<?xml ?>` processing instruction at the start. In accordance with the rules of well-formedness, this file has a single root element – the `<xs:schema>` element. As we build the schema over the course of the next few pages, you'll see that we add "child" elements to this element, which all go between the opening `<xs:schema>` tag and the closing `</xs:schema>` tag.

Notice in particular how there are a number of `xmlns` attributes in the opening `<xs:schema>` tag. These relate to the namespaces that we will use in our example. Let's take a minute to understand namespaces, before we continue building the schema itself.

XML Namespaces

XML namespaces are similar in principle to .NET namespaces, in that an XML namespace provides a way to group together elements that belong to a particular context under an identifying name. In XML, the name of a namespace is just a string, but it must be a *unique* string.

Why is uniqueness important? Suppose we were working on an application that made use of two different XML Schemas. Suppose also that both schemas allowed a `User` tag. Necessarily, these two `User` tags have different meanings, because each one only makes sense within the context of its own schema. So in order for the application to tell them apart, it uses namespaces. Each namespace has a name, and in order to guarantee that the names of different namespaces are different, we use a uniqueness rule for naming them.

The recommendation is that we should identify namespaces using URIs (that is, URLs or URNs), because URIs must, by their nature, be unique. When an organization's developers create schemas for its data, they can place the schemas within namespaces that specify the organization's own URLs (for example, Wrox Press might choose namespace names that begin `http://www.wrox.com`, and Microsoft might choose namespace names that begin `http://www.microsoft.com`). This gives each organization control of the uniqueness of its own namespace names, by guaranteeing that they are unique from those of all other organizations.

Using XML Namespaces in the Application

So, how do we plan to use XML namespaces in this example? Well, namespace names are used both in the XSD document that contains the schema, and in the XML document that contains the data.

First, in the schema document, we use a (unique) URN to identify the target namespace of this XML Schema:

```
<xs:schema id="Friends"
           targetNamespace="urn:wrox-friends"
           elementFormDefault="qualified"
           xmlns="urn:wrox-friends"
           xmlns:mstns="urn:wrox-friends"
           xmlns:xs="http://www.w3.org/2001/XMLSchema">
```

Then, we use the `xmlns` attribute to specify the default namespace of the schema. Here, it is set to the same value that we just set for the `targetNamespace` attribute. The effect of this is that any element appearing inside the schema element without a prefix will be assumed to belong to that namespace.

Second, in the XML document itself, we specify that an element belongs to a schema within a particular namespace by using the `xmlns` attribute on that element. For example, to associate a whole XML document with one namespace, we would add the `xmlns` attribute (for that namespace) to the root element of the document:

```
<?xml version="1.0" encoding="utf-8"?>
<Friends xmlns="urn:wrox-friends"
         PlaceID="C9796AD1-5A7E-4d9c-9F99-0090E11E5662">
  <User>
  ...etc...
```

When we add a namespace to an element (in the way that we added the `urn:wrox-friends` namespace to the `<Friends>` element above), all of the children of that element children inherit that namespace too.

What if we have multiple namespaces in use within a single XML document? In that case, we can use a different prefix for each namespace. For example, the following (hypothetical) code states that the prefix `wf` is to be equated with the namespace `urn:wrox-friends`:

```
<?xml version="1.0" encoding="utf-8"?>
<wf:Friends xmlns:wf="urn:wrox-friends"
            xmlns:ms="http://www.microsoft.com/Friends"
            wf:PlaceID="C9796AD1-5A7E-4d9c-9F99-0090E11E5662">
  <wf:User>
  ...etc...
  </wf:User>
  <ms:User>
  ...etc...
  </ms:User>
```

Then, the `wf:User` element is from the `urn:wrox-friends` namespace, while the `ms:User` element is from the `http://www.microsoft.com/Friends` namespace.

Note that the value of the `<xs:schema>` element's `elementFormDefault` attribute comes into play here:

```
<xs:schema id="Friends"
           targetNamespace="urn:wrox-friends"
           elementFormDefault="qualified"
           ... >
```

This attribute is set to `qualified`, which means that each element must be qualified by a namespace label set using `xmlns` (as we did in both of the document fragments above).

Building the XML Schema

Returning to our schema, we have just an empty schema at the moment – it contains no rules about tags or attributes at all. Now we will start adding these rules, so that the XSD begins to take shape.

Try It Out – Adding an Element

Every XML document must have exactly one root element, and our XML documents will be no different. We will start by adding the definition for the root `<Friends>` element to our XSD.

1. Switch back to the **Schema** view of the XSD file using the button at the corner of the designer.

2. Open the **Toolbox**. At the moment, it offers just one tab, called **XML Schema**, which contains all the items used when designing a schema:

Double-click on **element** to drop one onto the design surface.

3. Change the new element's name from the default `element1` to `Friends`, either through the **Properties** window or by clicking inside the element in the designer:

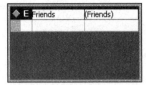

4. Drag an attribute from the **Toolbox**, and drop it onto the `Friends` element. Change its `name` to `PlaceID`, and check that `string` is selected in the right-hand column:

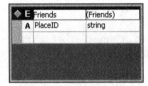

How It Works

The element we have added corresponds to the root `<Friends>` element of the XML format we are going to use for uploads:

```
<?xml version="1.0" encoding="utf-8"?>
<Friends xmlns="urn:wrox-friends"
         PlaceID="C9796AD1-5A7E-4d9c-9F99-0090E11E5662">
 ...etc...
</Friends>
```

Our schema now specifies that it must have the name `Friends`. It also says that the `Friends` element can have a string attribute called `PlaceID`. (The attribute is not compulsory, however. In fact, by default, attributes are optional. See the *Restricting Element Occurrence* section later in this chapter.) If we switch again to the XML view, we can check out the schema markup that Visual Studio .NET has generated, based on what we added in the designer:

```
<?xml version="1.0" encoding="utf-8" ?>
<xs:schema id="Friends"
           targetNamespace="urn:wrox-friends"
           elementFormDefault="qualified"
           xmlns="urn:wrox-friends"
           xmlns:mstns="urn:wrox-friends"
           xmlns:xs="http://www.w3.org/2001/XMLSchema">
  <xs:element name="Friends">
    <xs:complexType>
      <xs:sequence />
      <xs:attribute name="PlaceID" type="xs:string" />
    </xs:complexType>
  </xs:element>
</xs:schema>
```

Note that all of the new elements use the xs prefix. The xs prefix is associated with the XML schema namespace:

```
<xs:schema id="Friends"
           ...
             xmlns:xs="http://www.w3.org/2001/XMLSchema">
```

This marks these elements as XML Schema elements, and they must therefore obey the rules of validity for XML Schemas. That is, elements must follow the required order, and have valid values and attributes, such as the type attribute on the <xs:attribute> element.

According to the validity rules for an XSD (which aren't shown here – see the W3C's XML Schema specification at http://www.w3.org/XML/Schema for details), an <xs:element> which is a direct child of the <xs:schema> describes the *root* element of any document that conforms to this schema. The name attribute of our <xs:element> element here defines the name that the root element must have, so here it is <Friends>.

Any <xs:element> element in an XSD can contain further xs elements that describe the content allowed for that element in XML documents matching the schema. The first child element of a <xs:element> element must always be one of the two described below:

❑ <xs:simpleType> – this is either a custom type, or an XSD type such as xs:string, xs:boolean, or xs:integer (the complete list is displayed in the drop-down combo box we saw above, when we made PlaceID a string type). Custom simpleTypes are modifications of the basic XSD types that will (for example) restrict numbers to a given range of values, or specify maximum and minimum lengths for string-based types. simpleType elements cannot contain attributes or child elements – they can only represent a simple value.

❑ <xs:complexType> – this is for elements that may contain attributes, other elements, or other content. Defining a complex type is a bit like defining a new class in a project, in that we define its structure in the abstract, and then all 'instances' of it will have that same structure. The schema that has been produced so far specifies that the <Friends> element may have an attribute called PlaceID, and this attribute value is of type xs:string.

Definition of a Complex Type

The most useful elements that can appear in an <xs:complexType> element are <xs:sequence>, <xs:choice>, and <xs:attribute>. We've already seen <xs:attribute> in action, and the only thing to add is that its type *must* be one of the XSD simple types (or a custom simple type), because an XML attribute can't contain other elements.

The <xs:sequence> element defines the elements that can appear in instances of the type, and the order in which they must appear. Each element is defined by an <xs:element> element. By default, each element in the sequence is compulsory and only one of each element can be present. (This sounds inflexible, but in fact we can use the minOccurs and maxOccurs attributes to permit multiple occurrences and optional elements, as we'll see later.) If a document contains elements in the wrong order, it is said to be an **invalid** instance of the schema.

The <xs:choice> element, by contrast, defines a set of interchangeable elements. By default, only one member of the set can be present in an XML instance document. There's a third xs element for describing groups of allowed elements in an instance document: <xs:all>. This describes a set of elements that can appear in any order.

The plan that we've devised has <User> and <Attendee> elements inside the root <Friends> element. This arrangement would best be represented by <xs:sequence>, as we expect the elements to appear in a specific order, and there can be multiple instances of each element.

Try It Out – Defining the <User> Element

Let's build on the schema that we've created so far, and start to define the <User> element. This will involve two steps: first, we have to specify that we want it to be a child of the <Friends> element; second, we have to say what we want it to contain.

1. If necessary, switch to the visual designer, by pressing the **Schema** button. You may find it helpful to switch to **XML** view after each of the following steps, and see the code that is being generated – we'll explain what it all means after Step 5.

2. Drag an element from the **Toolbox**, and drop it onto the **Friends** element that we added earlier, to indicate that the new element is a child of <Friends>. This relationship is shown in the designer by a solid line from the **Friends** element to the new element:

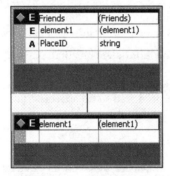

Note that the new element is represented not only by the new graphic below **Friends**, but also by a new row within the **Friends** element, currently with the default name of **element1**.

3. Change the name of this element from **element1** to **User**, by typing either in the new element, or in the new row of the **Friends** element.

4. Drag another element from the **Toolbox**, this time placing it on the new empty element that we have just added. Set its name to **UserID**.

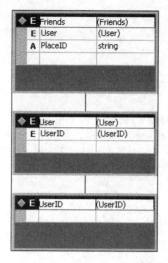

5. Using the dropdown in the right-hand column, set the type of the UserID element to string. As simple types, string elements can't contain any attributes or child content, and so the third box, representing the UserID element, disappears from the designer:

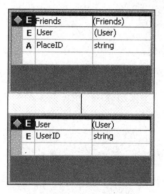

How It Works

When we add the `<User>` element in Steps 2 and 3, the code generated consists of a complex type element with an empty `<xs:sequence>` inside it, pretty much like the code created for the `<Friends>` element:

```
<?xml version="1.0" encoding="utf-8" ?>
<xs:schema id="Friends" ...etc... >
  <xs:element name="Friends">
    <xs:complexType>
      <xs:sequence>
        <xs:element name="User">
          <xs:complexType>
            <xs:sequence />
          </xs:complexType>
```

```
            </xs:element>
          </xs:sequence>
          <xs:attribute name="PlaceID" type="xs:string" />
        </xs:complexType>
      </xs:element>
    </xs:schema>
```

The new code has been placed inside what was the empty `<xs:sequence>` child element of `<Friends>`, as the new `<User>` element will be a direct child of the root element in instance documents. A similar process takes place when we first add the `<UserID>` element in Step 4. Visual Studio .NET represents it by default as a complex type, with an empty `<xs:sequence>` element:

```
<?xml version="1.0" encoding="utf-8" ?>
<xs:schema id="Friends" ...etc... >
  <xs:element name="Friends">
    <xs:complexType>
      <xs:sequence>
        <xs:element name="User">
          <xs:complexType>
            <xs:sequence>
              <xs:element name="UserID">
                ...
            </xs:sequence>
          <xs:complexType>
        ...etc...
</xs:schema>
```

Once we set the type to string in the designer in Step 5, the code is reduced to:

```
<?xml version="1.0" encoding="utf-8" ?>
<xs:schema id="Friends" ...etc... >
  <xs:element name="Friends">
    <xs:complexType>
      <xs:sequence>
        <xs:element name="User">
          <xs:complexType>
            <xs:sequence>
              <xs:element name="UserID" type="xs:string"></xs:element>
            </xs:sequence>
          </xs:complexType>
        </xs:element>
      </xs:sequence>
      <xs:attribute name="PlaceID" type="xs:string" />
    </xs:complexType>
  </xs:element>
</xs:schema>
```

This occurs because the string type is a simple type. Such elements can't contain child elements, so they don't require the extra information that the `<xs:complexType>` element specifies. Nor, therefore, is there any need to draw it as a separate element on the design surface.

Try It Out – Completing the <User> Element Definition

Now go ahead and repeat Steps 4 and 5 to define the nine remaining child elements of `<User>`. Add one for each field in the corresponding database table, in the order and of the type given below:

◆	E	User	(User)
	E	UserID	string
	E	Login	string
	E	Password	string
	E	FirstName	string
	E	LastName	string
	E	DateOfBirth	date
	E	PhoneNumber	string
	E	CellNumber	string
	E	Address	string
	E	Email	string

If you've ever used graphical database design tools such as those included with Visual Studio .NET, you may recognize the layout of schema elements on the designer, as they appear pretty much like a database table, with a row for each child element.

We will not discuss XML data types in detail in this book. If you're curious about the different data types, what they mean, the range of valid values, and so on, take a look at the *XML Schema Part 2: Datatypes* document (http://www.w3.org/TR/2001/REC-xmlschema-2-20010502).

Try It Out – Adding an Element Directly

As well as adding new child elements by dragging and dropping from the Toolbox, we can do it by typing directly into the table. Let's see this in action as we create the definition of the `<Attendee>` element.

1. Click on the empty row at the bottom of the graphic representing the Friends element, and type in Attendee. When you hit *Enter*, it will place an Attendee element like so:

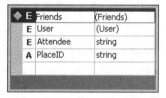

◆	E	Friends	(Friends)
	E	User	(User)
	E	Attendee	string
	A	PlaceID	string

2. Change the type of Attendee from the default (string) to Unnamed complexType, which appears right at the top of the list. This step creates a new empty element below the Friends element, alongside the existing User element. This is where content of the Attendee element can be described.

3. Type a new element name of UserID into the **Attendee** element, and leave the type as **string**.

4. Add another row, with the name YearIn, and set its type to **integer**.

5. Add three more rows of type **integer**, with the names MonthIn, YearOut, and MonthOut.

6. Now add a final element, called Notes, which is a **string**.

7. We also want to specify that the `<Attendee>` element will have a `Name` attribute. Add a new row called Name, and then click the capital E that appears in the left-most column to open a drop-down list. Select **attribute**:

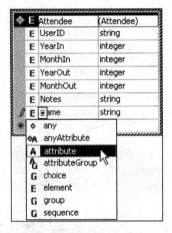

8. This is how the **Attendee** element should now appear in the designer:

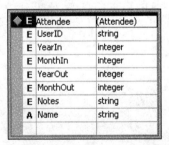

How It Works

When we use the drag-and-drop approach to create a new element, it creates a complex type by default. Now, we see that when we create a new element by typing directly into the designer, the behavior is opposite – it creates simple types by default. More precisely, this technique creates a **string** type each time.

This behavior means we have to change the type of the <Attendee> element to Unnamed complexType. When we do this (in Step 2), Visual Studio .NET produces exactly the same <complexType> definition as it generated when we were dragging and dropping from the Toolbox:

```xml
<?xml version="1.0" encoding="utf-8" ?>
<xs:schema id="Friends" ...etc... >
  <xs:element name="Friends">
    <xs:complexType>
      <xs:sequence>
        <xs:element name="User">
          ...etc...
        </xs:element>
        <xs:element name="Attendee">
          <xs:complexType>
            <xs:sequence />
          </xs:complexType>
        </xs:element>
      </xs:sequence>
      <xs:attribute name="PlaceID" type="xs:string" />
    </xs:complexType>
  </xs:element>
</xs:schema>
```

For the *child* elements of <Attendee>, the default behavior is more-or-less what we want – these elements are all simple types and most of them are the default string type too. The other default when adding new rows to an element is that the new item is itself an element. In the final step, we had to change the Name row, specifying Name as an attribute using the drop-down list.

Defining a Custom Simple Type

Usually, databases place restrictions on the permitted values for given fields. For example, the SQL Server type called varchar is a string, with a certain maximum length set by the database designer. XSD schemas also allow us to define such restrictions, by defining **custom simple types** that modify intrinsic XSD types according to our specific needs. In fact, they derive a new type from a base type – once we've selected the base type, we specify the limitations we require.

Try It Out – Defining a Custom Simple Type

A suitable use of a custom simple type in our case is to restrict valid IDs to strings of exactly 36 characters. Let's see how to go about arranging that.

1. From the Toolbox, drop a new simpleType element onto a blank area of the design surface, and give it the name KeyDef. Note that by default, the new type derives from the string type, as shown in the right-hand column on the top line.

2. On the blank row below the name and type, click on the first column of the row and turn it into a facet, indicated by the capital F. You can now open the drop-down list for the second column and select length. Tab to the next column, and enter 36:

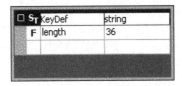

3. Then, set all of the "ID" items in our schema to the newly created simple type. There are three to change: the two `<UserID>` elements (one inside the `<User>` element, and the other inside `<Attendee>`), and the `PlaceID` attribute of the `<Friends>` element.

How It Works

Visual Studio .NET offers a variety of restrictions, which it calls **facets**, on XSD base types. The available facets depend on the base type in question, and most are self-explanatory. For the KeyDef type, which is derived from the string simple type, you may have noticed that there were options for length and maxLength.

> *For a complete list of base types and available facets, see the* W3C XML Schema Part 0: Primer *document at* http://www.w3.org/TR/xmlschema-0.

If you look at the XSD code (by clicking the XML button on the bottom-left of the pane), you'll see that the new type is defined as a child of the root `<xs:schema>` element. This means that this type definition is available to all other elements in the document, and we refer to it as a **global type**. A global type must have a name so that other elements can reference it; it is therefore also a **named type**.

It's also possible to define global *complex* types, which we can reuse in several places in a schema (just as we have done here, by using the `KeyDef` type definition in the `UserID` and `PlaceID` items).

Incidentally, this probably helps to explain why an element such as `<Attendee>`, which is local to the `<Friends>` element, is described as an *unnamed* complex type.

Restricting Element Occurrence

By default, each element defined by a schema must appear once (and only once) in the instance document. Clearly, this is not appropriate for all cases. In particular, in our example, we want to allow multiple `<Attendee>` and `<User>` elements in a single XML document.

By contrast, some of the fields in our database are optional, and they won't always have values. For instance, the `MonthIn` and `MonthOut` fields of the `TimeLapse` table can be null.

We can cater for requirements like these through the `minOccurs` and `maxOccurs` attributes of XSD elements, and we'll do that now.

Try It Out – Setting Minimum and Maximum Occurrences

We'll use this example to set up the rules we just described: we'll allow multiple instances of the `<User>` and `<Attendee>` elements, force the presence of the `PlaceID` attribute, and change the settings of a few other attributes too.

1. Select the User element of the Friends element in the designer, and open its Properties window. Set the maxOccurs property to unbounded, and the minOccurs property to 0.

2. Now select the Attendee element of the Friends element in the designer, and open its Properties window. Set the maxOccurs property to unbounded, and the minOccurs property to 0.

3. Now select the PlaceID attribute of the Friends element, and set its use property to required (which means that this attribute *must* be set on the <Friends> element of instance documents).

4. Now select the DateOfBirth element of the User element. Set its minOccurs property to 0. We can leave maxOccurs at the default setting.

5. Repeat Step 4 for the CellNumber element of the User element.

6. Repeat Step 4 for three elements of the Attendee element: MonthIn, MonthOut, and Notes.

7. Save the file using *Ctrl-S*.

How It Works

The minOccurs and maxOccurs properties determine the lower and upper limits for the number of occurrences of that element allowed in an instance document. Setting minOccurs to zero makes an element optional (it means we can have zero of that element, or any number up-to-and-including the upper limit). Setting maxOccurs to unbounded means that there is no upper limit. This is we want for the <User> element, because this could be the case should an institution not have any new users to add, but just be adding existing users as attendees of new courses.

Notice that the <Friends> element itself doesn't have minOccurs and maxOccurs properties available. This is because, as the root element, there must be *exactly one* occurrence present in any instance document, by definition.

In XML, *attributes* can either appear once (within a given element) or not at all. Accordingly, Visual Studio .NET gives us the choice of setting them as optional, prohibited, or required, where the first of these is the default. We want to set this property to required for the PlaceID attribute, as that must be present for us to be able to make sense of, and process, an XML file that we receive.

Viewing the Entire Schema

We have finished our schema! Maybe this seems like a lot of work before we get to write a single line of code, but we'll soon see the great benefits that this preparatory endeavor can bring. This is how our finished schema looks to the designer:

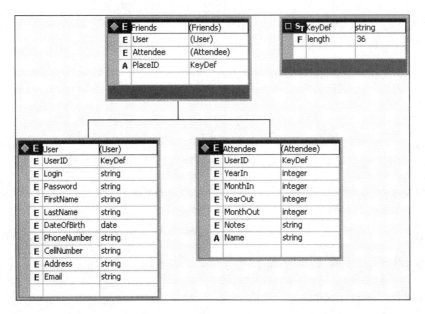

If we now switch to XML view, Visual Studio .NET allows us to validate the schema, and hence double-check that we haven't made a mistake (such as setting a invalid type for an element or attribute, or introducing an error when modifying the file manually). Select Validate Schema from the Schema menu, and any invalid content in the schema will be underlined and added to the Task List (and if there are no errors, you'll see a No validation errors were found message at the bottom left of the development window).

Summary

Markup plays an important role in web applications, because one of the key tasks of such applications is to deliver web pages to client browsers. We use HTML to mark up the information in a web page, and the HTML describes the structure of that page in terms of headings, paragraphs, tables, images, and so on.

HTML is a markup language specifically designed for describing the structure of web pages. XML is also a form of markup, but it is much more generic – we can use XML to describe the structure of any type of data. XML, like HTML, is text-based markup – it uses tags and attributes to describe the different elements of data. Because XML is text-based, it's ubiquitous – we can use XML techniques in any environment or language, and to allow any combination of platforms to communicate with one another. In particular, in .NET, Microsoft has invested heavily in XML.

In our application, we plan to allow a client application (such as an "Old Classmates Society") to be able to upload a single XML document, containing attendance details of any number of attendees, to our *Friends Reunion* application. When the file has been successfully uploaded, we plan to have our *Friends Reunion* application read XML data, interpret it, and channel it into the correct tables and fields of the database.

The application will only be able to do that if the uploaded XML adheres to a very specific structure. Therefore, in this chapter, we've written the XML Schema that precisely *describes* the structure to which these XML documents must adhere. When we receive such a document, we will validate it against the XML Schema to ensure it has the correct structure, and thus is useable.

As we've seen, the XML Schema definition document (an XSD file) is itself written in XML. Perhaps this sounds a little confusing, but it really makes a lot of sense: a schema document is a structured block of data, so it makes sense to describe it using special XML tags (like `<element>` and `<attribute>`) that describe the allowed elements and attributes in an XML data document. The exact description of all the permitted elements and attributes in an XSD is contained in a schema within the namespace `http://www.w3.org/2001/XMLSchema`.

XML in general, and XML Schemas in particular, are quite advanced topics, and there are many aspects that we have left untouched. For more in-depth information, try the following books published by Wrox Press:

❑   *Beginning XML, 2nd Edition* (ISBN 1-86100-559-8)

❑   *Beginning C# XML* (ISBN 1-86100-628-4)

❑   *Professional XML for .NET Developers* (ISBN 1-86100-531-8)

❑   *Professional XML Schemas* (ISBN 1-86100-547-4)

We've covered all the *preparatory* material for the upload feature of our *Friends Reunion* application, and in the next chapter we'll take advantage of it by building an XML document that adheres to our XML Schema, and writing the feature that uses the XML Schema to interpret and understand the uploaded XML.

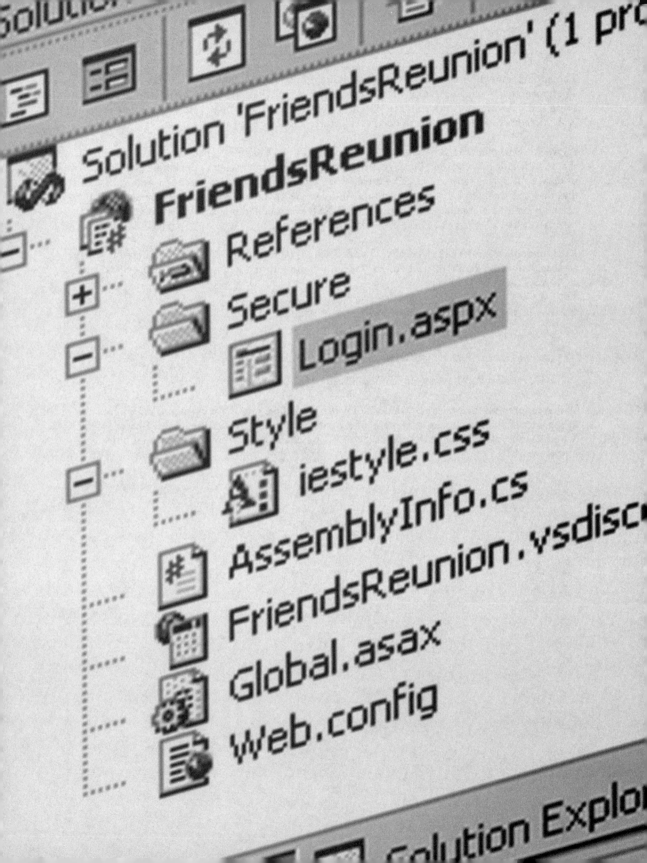

Solution 'FriendsReunion' (1 pro

Solution 'FriendsReunion' (1 pro
FriendsReunion
References
Secure
Login.aspx
Style
iestyle.css
AssemblyInfo.cs
FriendsReunion.vsdisc
Global.asax
Web.config

Solution Explor

XML and Web Development

The XML Schema that we created in Chapter 7 is a document that describes a certain data structure. Specifically, it describes the XML data structure that a third party must use when it uploads an XML document (containing details of multiple attendees of a college or other institution) to the *Friends Reunion* web site.

The best way to think of an XML Schema is as a set of rules for the data structure. We (as developers of the *Friends Reunion* application) will use our schema, or "set of rules", in this chapter, when we write the code that interprets an uploaded XML document and saves its data to the database. (As you'll see, we'll write code that assumes that any uploaded document contains *only* the tags and attributes that are allowed by the schema.) When a user compiles a data document containing attendee details, they should use the same set of rules. Provided we all work to the same rules, as defined in the schema, each uploaded document will be compatible with the application; so the application should be able to process the uploaded document without any problems.

The preparatory work that we did in Chapter 7, to create the schema document Friends.xsd, puts us in a good position to complete the XML upload feature. In this chapter, we'll make use of it as we build the feature, and we'll continue our studies of XML in the process. We will:

❑ Use the Visual Studio .NET IDE to create a sample XML document that validates against our XSD

❑ Build a feature that allows a user to upload an XML file onto the web server, via a browser interface

❑ Build the back-end functionality that reads and interprets the uploaded XML document, extracts the relevant data and displays it on screen.

The last of these three items requires a number of steps. In that part, we'll need to perform a number of XML-related tasks:

❑ Validate an XML document against a specified XSD, to ensure it has the expected structure

❑ Read the XML data, to see what information is there

❑ Query the XML data, to search for a particular piece of data

Using XML, XML Schemas, and XPath, all of these tasks are easy – and that is part of what makes XML and its satellite technologies such a powerful set of tools. By the end of this chapter we will have employed some of the most fundamental XML-related capabilities.

Creating XML Documents in Visual Studio .NET

With our XSD document complete, we can start to build some valid XML documents. There are many different tools and techniques available for writing and generating XML documents. Because XML is text-based, we can (for example) use a simple text editor such as NotePad to type data and markup into a document by hand.

It's occasionally convenient to do that, but there are some more powerful tools around that are specifically designed for XML-based development – XMLSpy is one, and (as we'll see in this chapter) the Visual Studio .NET IDE also contains some nifty features for creating XML documents.

There's also the question of how a third party user would generate an XML document ready for upload. It's possible that they might use a development tool such as XMLSpy or VS.NET; however, if they were planning to upload XML documents on a regular basis, taking data from their own database, then it would be appropriate for them to spend some effort building an application that used our XML Schema to generate XML documents programmatically.

*We're not going to build such an application in this book. However, the Friends Reunion application will use programmatic techniques (not to build an XML document, but to **extract** data from an XML document), later in this chapter; so you'll get an idea of the kind of thing we mean when we talk about programmatic techniques.*

Let's spend the next few pages generating some sample XML documents using the VS.NET IDE.

Creating XML Documents Visually

As we said, the Visual Studio .NET IDE has some very useful features for generating XML documents. These features are useful not only for creating small test files, but also for working with XML configuration files in custom applications, for example.

Try It Out – Creating a Valid XML Document

First off, we need a sample instance document that conforms to the schema (Friends.xsd) that we built in Chapter 7. Once we've got that XML document, we'll be able to use it to test the XML upload functionality of our web application that we're going to build before the end of this chapter.

1. Right-click on the project to add a new item; select the XML File template from the Data category, and name the file upload.xml.

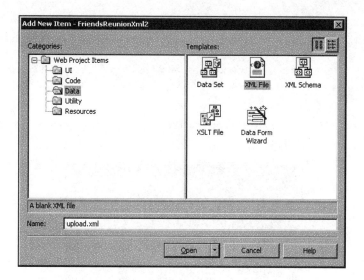

2. The IDE will show you an XML window with a single line of code – an XML processing instruction. Below that, start typing in a new `<Friends>` element. Give it an `xmlns` attribute, to set the `urn:wrox-friends` namespace as the default:

```
<?xml version="1.0" encoding="utf-8" ?>
<Friends xmlns=
```

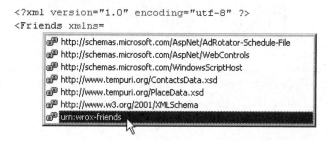

Here's a neat trick. When you've selected the appropriate attribute value in an IntelliSense menu (as shown above), type a double-quote character to have Visual Studio .NET insert the selected value, and wrap it inside quotes.

3. Type a right-hand angled bracket (>) to mark the end of the tag; the closing `</Friends>` tag will automatically appear after the cursor.

4. Now we'll add the `<Friends>` element's required `PlaceID` attribute. To do this, place the cursor just before the > character of the opening `<Friends>` tag, and insert a space. IntelliSense will recognize that you want to insert an attribute, and will offer a list of the names of all the valid attributes that you're allowed to put there:

```
<?xml version="1.0" encoding="utf-8" ?>
<Friends xmlns="urn:wrox-friends"
```

As it happens, there's only one – **PlaceID**. Choose that, and type an equals sign; this will insert `PlaceID=""`.

5. The value of the `PlaceID` attribute must be a GUID (a Globally Unique Identifier). Don't try to make up a value here – we can use the GUID generator that is built into Visual Studio .NET.

To do this, select **Create GUID** from the **Tools** menu. Check option **4. Registry Format...** from the dialog that appears:

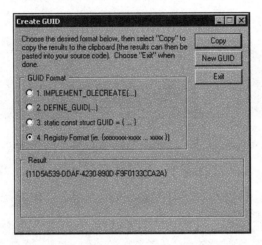

Click the **Copy** button, and paste the result into the XML document (between the two double-quotes). The GUID is enclosed in surrounding braces – you will need to delete those.

There is no need to exit the **Create GUID** dialog, and it can be left open in the background until it's needed again. Just remember to click **New GUID** each time you need a new ID.

6. Now we'll add a `<User>` element. Place the cursor between the `<Friends>` and `</Friends>` tags, hit *Enter*, and type a left-hand angled bracket. Select **User** from the drop-down list that appears, and type the end bracket.

7. Inside the `<User>` element, add the desired child elements. Start by adding an empty `<UserID>` element.

8. The value of the `<UserID>` element must also be a GUID. Return to the **Create GUID** dialog; click the **New GUID** button to create a new GUID, then click the **Copy** button to copy it to the clipboard.

Now paste the result into the XML document (between the `<UserID>` and `</UserID>` tags). Again, the GUID is enclosed in surrounding braces, and you'll need to delete them.

9. Now go ahead and add the remaining child elements for `<User>`. Recall that `DateOfBirth` and `CellNumber` are optional elements, because we defined them with `minOccurs=0`; for simplicity, we'll leave them out here. You should finish up with something that looks like this:

```
<?xml version="1.0" encoding="utf-8" ?>
<Friends xmlns="urn:wrox-friends"
         PlaceID="11D5A539-DDAF-4230-890D-F9F0133CCA2A">
  <User>
    <UserID>5E4706A4-756F-4b65-8FFA-A62B3E6A6EEA</UserID>
    <Login>brobson</Login>
    <Password>skipper</Password>
    <FirstName>Bryan</FirstName>
    <LastName>Robson</LastName>
    <PhoneNumber>0191-700-7007</PhoneNumber>
    <Address>16 The Mews, Borwich</Address>
    <Email>brobson@wrox.com</Email>
  </User>
</Friends>
```

10. Finally, we can validate the document against the schema, to check that it satisfies the rules of the schema. To do that in the VS.NET IDE, you just need to choose Validate XML Data from the XML menu. This document should validate successfully. If there *are* validation errors, they will be underlined with a green wavy line in the editor, and listed in the Task List window.

How It Works

As soon as we type the xmlns attribute, IntelliSense starts to do its magic. Firstly, we are offered a list of available namespaces for the project, including the urn:wrox-friends namespace used by our schema. The other namespaces in the list correspond to the ones used by the by the Visual Studio .NET IDE.

Once the namespace is specified, IntelliSense uses the associated XML Schema to make suggestions as we type. Visual Studio .NET provides a list of all elements that are valid according to the schema, and this list is context-sensitive – so we only see <Attendee> and <User> elements when we're in the process of inserting an element into the <Friends> element. Note, however, that the list is ordered alphabetically, so it doesn't necessarily reflect the actual schema constraints, particularly when the order of elements can be important. For instance, <Attendee> and <User> elements are suggested for children of <Friends>, but we know that if we are going to add any <User> elements, they must appear *before* any <Attendee> elements, as defined by an <xs:sequence> element in the schema.

The validation process that we use at the end is exactly the same as the one that we'll apply programmatically in a moment, and it demonstrates the value of namespaces. At design time, they enable the IDE to activate IntelliSense and validation; at run time, they allow the elements in a file to be matched unambiguously to their definition in the appropriate schema.

Creating XML Documents in Data View

There's another way to create an XML document visually when we have a schema for it: the **data view**. Click Data in the lower left corner of the designer (next to the XML button), to open a two-pane view. Here, the left pane is entitled Data Tables, while the right pane is entitled Data – and it's in the latter that we're going to add data to our XML file.

If an element is specified as a complex type in the schema, it will be represented in the Data view as a data table. The simple type attributes and elements within that complex type will appear as fields within the table. In our document, the <Friends>, <User>, and <Attendee> elements are the complex types; this is why they are listed as 'tables' in the left pane (as shown in the screenshot below).

When a complex type element is enclosed inside another complex type (such as the <User> and <Attendee> elements inside the <Friends> root element), we will be presented with a navigation link in the Data pane that lets us get inside the contained elements. Click the link, and it will expand to list the child elements:

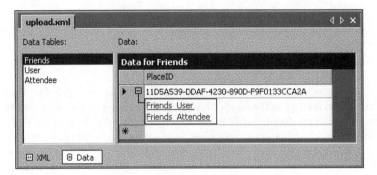

In order for elements to be put in the *right place* in the XML file, we must *follow the links* through the elements until we get to the level where the new element must be placed. This is important, because the tool doesn't prevent you from selecting the User or Attendee 'tables' directly (through the left-hand menu), and creating elements right there. If you do that, the resulting elements are placed under a *new* root <Friends> element (not under the existing <Friends> element). The result would contain two nested <Friends> elements, and that would be invalid according to our schema.

Try It Out – Adding an Element in Data View

Let's see how the data view works in practice, as we create a new <Attendee> element in our upload.xml XML file.

1. Click on the Friends User link in the Data pane for the Friends data table (as shown in the previous screenshot).

2. Try adding a new user directly in the grid. It will look something like this:

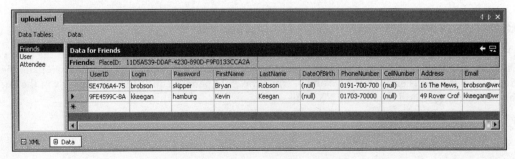

3. Switch back to the XML view, and have a look at the new data that you've generated:

```
<?xml version="1.0" encoding="utf-8" ?>
<Friends xmlns="urn:wrox-friends"
         PlaceID="11D5A539-DDAF-4230-890D-F9F0133CCA2A">
  <User>
    <UserID>5E4706A4-756F-4b65-8FFA-A62B3E6A6EEA</UserID>
    ...etc...
    <Email>brobson@wrox.com</Email>
  </User>
  <User>
    <UserID>9FE4599C-8A07-42f7-950E-B1452B74B5B7</UserID>
    <Login>kkeegan</Login>
    <Password>hamburg</Password>
    <FirstName>Kevin</FirstName>
    <LastName>Keegan</LastName>
    <PhoneNumber>01703-700007</PhoneNumber>
    <Address>49 Rover Croft, Hairsden</Address>
    <Email>kkeegan@wrox.com</Email>
  </User>
</Friends>
```

4. Note that because we navigated inside the `<Friends>` element to the desired child 'table', the elements have been added inside the appropriate parent element.

The data view (tables-and-rows) approach is suitable for most XML files, but the IDE does not allow you to use this feature for some schema designs. For example, if we have child elements with the same name but different parent elements – a perfectly valid schema definition – the data view won't be available.

Programmatic Manipulation of XML in .NET

Microsoft has made a substantial commitment to XML with the .NET platform. The Framework contains .NET namespaces that encompass classes implementing almost every XML-related standard:

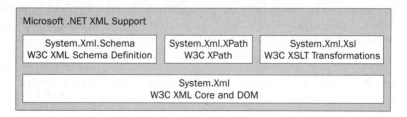

In the examples contained in the pages ahead, we will use classes contained in the `System.Xml` and `System.Xml.Schema` namespaces to load and validate an XML file, ready for use in our web application.

Reading and Validating XML

In .NET, the task of reading an XML document from a file is accomplished in pretty much the same way as any other file type is read. As for other types, the source of the XML need not be a file – rather, it can be any form of **stream**, such as an in-memory stream, a file stream, or a network stream.

Throughout the .NET Framework, the process of reading a stream follows the same pattern: a reader object systematically steps through the stream from start to end, through a succession of calls to the Read() method. Each method call reads a new portion of the stream, and returns a Boolean value; Read() returns True unless the stream has been reached, in which case Read() returns False. As we progress through the stream, the methods and properties (provided by the specific reader implementation) allow us to retrieve information and data for the current position in the stream.

The diagram below illustrates some of the readers offered by the framework classes that are relevant to XML handling:

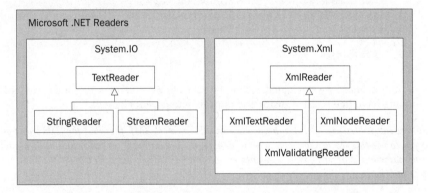

The readers in the System.IO namespace are relevant to us because we can pass them to overloaded constructors of many of the XmlReader-derived classes in order to read XML content from them. We'll see this very mechanism in action in our application later on.

Uploading an XML File

Our first step towards creating the 'upload' feature requires us to add a new web form to the application that will be used to receive a file from the client. To make the web form visually appealing, we will use an ASP.NET server control from Microsoft called TreeView. The TreeView control makes it very simple for us to display hierarchical information, and so it's perfect for showing XML content.

In order to make the TreeView control available in our application, you must download and install the **Internet Explorer WebControls** server control onto the web server. At the time of writing, this download is around 650Kb, and you can get it from Microsoft's web site by choosing the Automatic Install option from the drop-down list on the page at the URL http://msdn.microsoft.com/downloads/samples/internet/asp_dot_net_servercontrols/webcontrols/default.asp.

The `Treeview` *control works in all browsers, but it will be much smoother in IE because it takes advantages of IE 'behaviors', a feature that exploits DHTML. In order to view it in the* **Toolbox**, *right-click on the* **Toolbox**, *select the* **Customize Toolbox** *option, and add the* `TreeView` *control from the* **Microsoft.Web.UI.WebControls** *namespace under the .NET Framework Components tab in the list:*

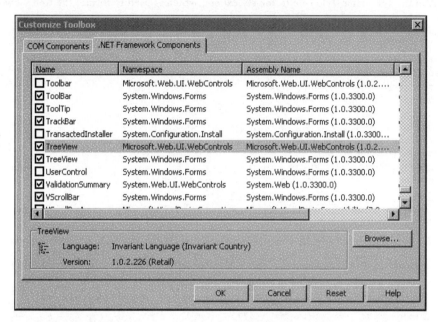

We're going to build a web form that can receive an XML file posted by the user, and perform further processing on it. First, it will show the contents of the uploaded file in the `TreeView` control, so the user can see if the information they're sending is correct. We will also add links to the schema file that's used to validate the incoming file, and to a sample XML file that users can either view or load in the page for testing purposes.

Try It Out – Creating the UploadList Form

In this first section, we will build the form and review key settings in it. The code for the specific features we intend to offer will be added in later sections.

1. Ensure that you have downloaded and installed the `TreeView` control, as described above.

2. Add a new web form to the *Friends Reunion* project, and name it `UploadList.aspx`. Make the page inherit the `FriendsBase` class we built in Chapter 3, to add the site header and footer. To do this, switch to the code view (`UploadList.aspx.cs`), and change the class declaration line to:

```
public class UploadList : FriendsBase
```

3. Add the link to the stylesheet that we've been using so far inside the `<head>` section:

```
<link href="Style/iestyle.css" type="text/css" rel="stylesheet">
```

4. Add the following style rule to the stylesheet, which is used to format the tree view control:

```
.TreeView
{
  border-right: #c7ccdc 1px solid;
  padding-right: 15px;
  border-top: #c7ccdc 1px solid;
  padding-left: 5px;
  font-size: 8pt;
  padding-bottom: 5px;
  border-left: #c7ccdc 1px solid;
  padding-top: 5px;
  border-bottom: #c7ccdc 1px solid;
  font-family: Tahoma, Verdana, 'Times New Roman';
  background-color: #f0f1f6;
}
```

5. Now, we're going to add the necessary text and controls on the form to give it the following layout:

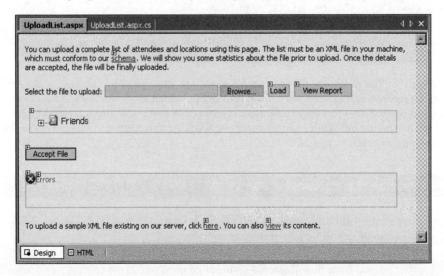

The following tables contain the properties of the controls, in order of their appearance on the page, from left to right and top to bottom. The control type is specified on the left, between square brackets, with a brief description of what the control does. The control's ID and other (non-default) property values are listed on the right. Take all these from the Web Forms tab in the Toolbox unless stated otherwise.

If you haven't built the application before, you will need to do so (or the Toolbox will make some of these controls unavailable):

[HyperLink] A link to the schema file we built, so that partners can check the validity of their files	ID	hySchema
	Text	schema
	NavigateUrl	friends.xsd
	Target	_blank

The name property is important in the next control. Although we never use it in the code, the mechanism is rather dependant on the existence of a value here:

[HTML File Field] (take this from HTML tab) Allows the user to upload a file from their machine.	id	fldUpload
	class	Button
	style	WIDTH: 238px
	name	fldUpload

[Button] Allows the user to upload a file from their machine.	ID	btnLoad
	CssClass	Button
	Text	Load

[Button] Redirects the user to a page showing statistics about the file they posted.	ID	btnReport
	CssClass	Button
	Text	View Report

[TreeView] Shows information in the XML file.	ID	tvXmlView
	CssClass	TreeView
	ExpandedImageUrl	images/opened.gif
	ImageUrl	images/findfolder.gif
	SelectedImageUrl	images/selected.gif
	Height	Clear this field.
	Visible	False
	Nodes	Add a root node and two children to it, with the text Friends, User, and Attendee respectively, using the editor that appears.

Table continued on following page

| [TreeView]
Shows information in the XML file. | TreeNodeTypes | This is a collection of node type definitions, which can be used to give new nodes a default formatting. Add a new type using the **TreeNodeType Collection Editor**. Set its **ID** and **Type** to **Normal**, and set the **DefaultStyle** to font-size:8pt; font-family:Tahoma,Verdana,'Times New Roman';. |
| | ChildType | This sets the default style for new nodes. Set it to Normal (this is the one we created in the previous property). |

[Button] Saves the posted file to the database.	ID	btnAccept
	CssClass	Button
	Text	Accept File

[Panel] Displays any errors found in the incoming file.	ID	pnlError
	Visible	False

Stretch the panel to make it quite wide, and then place the next two controls inside it:

[Image] (take this from **HTML** tab) The icon for errors. This is not a server control, so we don't need an ID.	align	absmiddle
	src	images/error.gif

[Label] Contains the error messages.	ID	lblError
	ForeColor	Red
	Text	Errors

[LinkButton] Allows the user to load a sample file, already existing in our server, for testing purposes and to grasp the format they need to adhere to.	ID	btnDefaultXml
	Text	here

[HyperLink] Provides a link to the sample XML file so the user can view it in the browser or download it for testing.	ID	hyXmlFile
	Text	view
	NavigateUrl	upload.xml
	Target	_blank

6. Add the following code to the `Page_Load()` event handler to configure the header image and text (as described in Chapter 3):

```
private void Page_Load(object sender, System.EventArgs e)
{
  HeaderIconImageUrl =
              Request.ApplicationPath + "/images/pctransfer.gif";
  HeaderMessage = "Upload Attendees";
}
```

7. Return to the HTML view, and find the `<form>` tag. Change its `id` attribute, and add a new attribute called `encType`, so that the tag looks like this:

```
<form id="frmUpload" method="post" encType="multipart/form-data"
      runat="server">
```

8. Our page is now complete, so set it as the start page, and compile and run with *F5*. After the usual login process (using `wrox` as user name and password), this screen should appear in your browser:

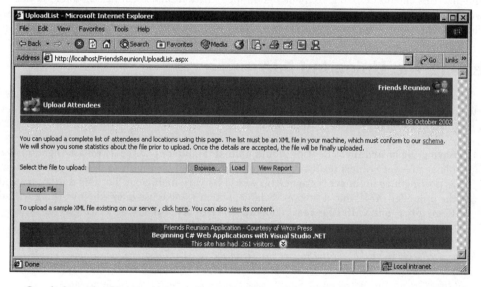

On clicking the **Browse** button, the user will be presented with the standard Windows dialog for locating files.

How It Works

As we said, the objective of this form is to allow a partner institution to submit an XML file containing all their users and attendees. In order to specify the file that to upload, the user has to click the **Browse** button. The control that makes this possible is an HTML `<input>` control, whose `type` attribute is set to `file`. However, when the file is selected, the form is not posted. We placed a **Load** button control on the form, but in fact any postback caused by any server control will cause the file to be uploaded.

For the file to be sent to the server, the form not only has to use a `post()` method but *also* has to specify the `encType` attribute:

```
<form id="frmUpload" method="post" encType="multipart/form-data"
      runat="server">
```

The link at the top of the form (pointing to the schema we created), and the link at the bottom of the form (pointing to the sample XML file), each have their Target property set to _blank. This causes the requested file to appear in a *new* browser window – so that the user can inspect those files without leaving the main Upload Attendees form.

When the file is uploaded, we will use the values contained in the file to fill the TreeView control. We'll do that in the next section, but there are a couple of things to say about this control right now. Note that the TreeView control is very similar to its Windows counterpart, and basically consists of a collection of `TreeNode` elements that can in turn contain other `TreeNode` elements, and so on. The server control provides several options to add style to it, such as defining the style to use to render child nodes, and so on. We used the `TreeNodeTypes` property to define a `Normal` node type, and then used it in the `ChildType`.

Finally, we provide the user with access to the schema file we have built, and to our sample XML document – this should help to give them a good idea of what their own files should look like. The first of two links at the foot of the page allows the user to load our sample document, so they can test the application features; the second link will open a new window with the sample file in it.

Receiving the Uploaded File

The feature we are building will allow the user to preview the file's contents, see some statistics about it, and later decide if they actually *want* to post the information in the file to the database. In order to allow this, there are three areas that need to be addressed:

❑ **Saving the posted file.** The user should upload the file only once. If we ask them to select the file again every time a postback is performed, it could become very frustrating for them, just as posting it again in every round-trip would be very inefficient. For this reason, we will save the uploaded XML into a session variable, which we will use later when working with the file. Remember that XML is just text content, so we're actually saving a string value here.

As this is a testing scenario, we don't pay much attention to size limits, scalability issues, and so on. Some would say it would be better to save the file in the server's file system, while others would complain that the I/O access and security permissions involved would actually turn out to be slower and less efficient. Such topics would have to be evaluated in a production environment.

❑ **Setting up the reader.** Configuring an `XmlValidatingReader` object requires several steps, so we will move all that code into a private function.

❑ **Using the reader.** We'll create another routine in which we use the reader to add nodes to the `TreeView` control, to show the XML contents on the web page. This will help the user to preview the file they are about to post, prior to confirmation.

We'll complete these three tasks over the course of the next three *Try It Out* sections.

Try It Out – Saving the Posted XML File

Let's analyze the code for reading and saving the incoming file to the session variable that we'll use later on.

1. Add the following `using` statements right at the top of the code-behind file, `UploadList.aspx.cs`:

```
using System.Xml;
using System.Xml.Schema;
using System.IO;
using Microsoft.Web.UI.WebControls;
```

The last of these points to the namespace where the `TreeView` control and its related classes are located. When you dropped that control onto the page, a reference to the `Microsoft.Web.UI.WebControls.dll` assembly was automatically added. It will come as no surprise that this is the assembly that contains the namespace we imported.

2. Add the following procedure to the `UploadList` class, in the same file:

```
// Save the input file if appropriate
private void SaveXml()
{
  if (Request.Files[0].ContentLength != 0)
  {
    //Save the uploaded stream to Session for further postbacks
    StreamReader stm = new StreamReader(Request.Files[0].InputStream);
    string xml = stm.ReadToEnd();
    Session["xml"] = xml;
    Session["file"] = Request.Files[0].FileName;
  }
}
```

3. Double-click the **Load** button, and add the following line:

```
private void btnLoad_Click(object sender, System.EventArgs e)
{
  SaveXml();
}
```

4. Grab a copy of the `upload.xml` file that we created earlier, and place it somewhere handy on your hard disk (say, `c:\upload.xml`).

5. Set a breakpoint in the line of code above, that contains the `SaveXML()` method call, so that we can test the new method. Compile and run with *F5*, and after the usual login process, use the **Browse** button to select the sample XML file (at `c:\upload.xml` or wherever you put it), and click the **Load** button.

How It Works

When you click the Load button (after selecting the XML file), the corresponding handler will be called. Press *F11* to step into `SaveXml()`. Inside the routine, we first check whether we received any content from the client:

```
if (Request.Files[0].ContentLength != 0)
{
    ...
```

The `Request.Files` property contains the list of uploaded files. We can't just use its `Count` property because of the way the HTML File Field control works: there will always be an item in this collection for each of these controls on a page, and we can only know if an actual file was submitted by checking for the `ContentLength` property of each element in this collection. As we know there will be only one element, we directly check for its length.

The `Files` collection itself contains a single `HttpPostedFile` object (`Request.Files[0]`) that represents the uploaded file, and it contains a number of useful sub-properties that describe the file being uploaded (`ContentLength`, `ContentType`, and `FileName`, for example).

Next, we see one of the reader implementations of the `System.IO` namespace in action – namely, the `StreamReader`:

```
StreamReader stm = new StreamReader(Request.Files[0].InputStream);
```

Its constructor requires an object of type `Stream`, which we get from the `InputStream` property of the posted file. This `Stream` contains the uploaded content. We put of all the file content returned by the reader into a variable called `xml`, and then we place the content of the variable into a `Session` item called `xml`. We also hold the original filename in a second `Session` variable, called `file`:

```
string xml = stm.ReadToEnd();
Session["xml"] = xml;
Session["file"] = Request.Files[0].FileName;
```

The `ReadToEnd()` method returns the whole file – that is, the XML document – as a single string. While you're running the code in debug mode, you can check that the contents of the file are there by placing the cursor above the variable for a while.

Validating XML from a Web Application

The `XmlValidatingReader` class that we will use derives from `XmlReader`, so it shares many properties and methods with that class. It also adds a set of new properties (that is, it **extends** the class) to set options required for validation. In this text, we'll use the term **validator** to refer to an instance of this class.

Once the validator is configured, we can start reading an XML file and taking values from it, just as we would with a regular `XmlReader` object. Behind the scenes, though, the object ensures that the file is valid as it is read, according to the settings we have made. There are two ways that we can configure our validator to react when validation errors are found in the XML source. It can:

❑   Throw exceptions. This is the default mode. When an error is found, processing is aborted and an `XmlSchemaException` is thrown.

❑   Fire the event handler attached to the `ValidationEventHandler` event of the `XmlValidatingReader` class. When a handler is specified for this event, the validator won't throw an exception when an error appears; instead it will call the handler. It is up to the developer to collect information inside the handler and respond accordingly.

Clearly, the second of these allows more complete reporting of any failures found in an XML file, and at the same time it allows us to continue through the document and process all elements.

Try It Out – Setting up Validation

We can now move on to the second part of our three-bullet list. In this example, we'll write the code to set up the `XmlValidatingReader` object.

1.   Declare the following private member at class level (before the `Page_Load()` event handler). As a naming convention, we prefix class-level variables with an underscore so that we can easily differentiate them from local variables inside a method:

```
private string _errors = String.Empty;
```

2.   Add the handler for the validation event. It needs to have exactly the signature specified here, and we'll be using it later on when we configure validation:

```
private void OnValidation(object sender, ValidationEventArgs e)
{
    _errors += "<b>" + e.Severity.ToString() + "</b>: "
                    + e.Message + "<br>";
}
```

3.   The procedure responsible for reading and displaying the XML content doesn't need to know that it's using an `XmlValidatingReader` instance – it only cares about the reading methods. We'll isolate it from our initialization code for the validator in a function that returns a generic `XmlReader` object type:

```
private XmlReader GetReader()
{
    if (Session["xml"] == null)
        throw new
        InvalidOperationException("No XML file has been uploaded yet.");

    // Build the XmlTextReader from the in-memory string saved above
    StringReader xmlinput = new StringReader((string)Session["xml"]);
    XmlTextReader reader = new XmlTextReader(xmlinput);

    // Configure the validating reader
    XmlValidatingReader validator = new XmlValidatingReader(reader);
```

```
    validator.ValidationEventHandler +=
                        new ValidationEventHandler(OnValidation);

    // Read the schema from a URL to avoid file access security checks
    XmlSchema schema = XmlSchema.Read(
        new XmlTextReader("http://localhost/"
            + Request.ApplicationPath
            + "/friends.xsd"),
        null);

    validator.Schemas.Add(schema);
    validator.ValidationType = ValidationType.Schema;
    return validator;
}
```

How It Works

The XML processing code (which we will build in the next *Try It Out*) will call the `GetReader()` method to get the object it will use to process the XML file. Notice that we return a generic `XmlReader` object from the method:

```
private XmlReader GetReader()
{
    ...
```

In this way, the act of getting hold of an object for reading the file is independent of the actual `XmlReader` implementation being used to work through it. This makes it easy for us to turn validation off just by returning an `XmlTextReader` instead of an `XmlValidatingReader`.

We first check to see if there is actual content in the `Session` variable we saved before. The first time the page loads, or if an error on the server causes session information to be lost, we raise an exception. We use an `InvalidOperationException`, already defined in the .NET Framework, since it seems to be an appropriate exception to throw in such conditions. That is, we are trying to read an XML file when none has been uploaded before:

```
if (Session["xml"] == null)
  throw new
    InvalidOperationException("No XML file has been uploaded yet.");
```

Next, we set up a `StringReader` from the `System.IO` namespace, which we will use as the source when we create our XML reader. In effect, the `StringReader` class applies a `TextReader` implementation to a simple string, which we can then pass to an `XmlTextReader` constructor:

```
// Build the XmlTextReader from the in-memory string saved above
StringReader xmlinput = new StringReader((string)Session["xml"]);
XmlTextReader reader = new XmlTextReader(xmlinput);
```

We could have avoided declaring the `xmlinput` variable altogether (and constructed it directly inside the `XmlTextReader` constructor), but this way the code is clearer. At this point, if wished to disable validation, we could just add the following line:

```
    return reader;
```

But instead, as we *do* want to validate, we use the `XmlTextReader` to create an instance of the `XmlValidatingReader` class. We also set the validator's `ValidationEventHandler` property, to tell it what method it should use to handle events (such as encountering errors) that occur during the validation process. In this case, it will be the `OnValidation()` method:

```
    // Configure the validating reader
    validator = new XmlValidatingReader(reader);
    validator.ValidationEventHandler +=
                        new ValidationEventHandler(OnValidation);
```

We'll look at the `OnValidation()` method in a moment, to see how that works.

The validator needs a reference to the schema that it should validate against, through its property called `Schemas`, which is a collection of `XmlSchema` objects. We add our schema using the shared `Read()` method of the `XmlSchema` class, which loads and returns the specified schema. We initialize the reader used by this method with a URL to side-step the checking of file access permissions:

```
    // Read the schema from a URL to avoid file access security checks
    XmlSchema schema = XmlSchema.Read(
        new XmlTextReader("http://localhost/"
            + Request.ApplicationPath
            + "/friends.xsd"),
        null);
```

The second parameter to the `Read()` method is a validation handler to deal with any errors that are found in the schema itself. In this case, we will assume the schema is valid. Once we've loaded the schema, adding it to the collection of schemas for the validator is simple:

```
    validator.Schemas.Add(schema);
```

Finally, we return the initialized `XmlValidatingReader` object:

```
    validator.ValidationType = ValidationType.Schema;
    return validator;
}
```

Now, let's return to look at how errors are handled during the validation process. We have created a class-level variable, `_errors`, that will help to handle the errors that can occur during the reading phase. It is initialized to an empty string, and will accumulate error messages:

```
    private string _errors = String.Empty;
```

If an error is found during the reading phase, this is considered as an event, so it is handled by our nominated event handler – the `OnValidation()` method.

```
private void OnValidation(object sender, ValidationEventArgs e)
{
    ...
```

If the validator finds an error, it calls this procedure, passing in information about the event in the e parameter, which is of type ValidationEventArgs. This parameter supplies details about the error that we append to the string variable _errors for later use. We want to know the severity of the validation failure (which will be either an Error or a Warning) and the error message itself, with some formatting to display nicely in the page:

```
_errors += "<b>" + e.Severity.ToString() + "</b>: "
            + e.Message + "<br>";
}
```

Should we need it, the Exception property of the ValidationEventArgs class holds the actual exception that was caught. This property is of type XmlSchemaException, and it can be queried to obtain comprehensive information about the error, including the line number and position where the error occurred, the schema object causing the exception, and so on. For short files though, the Message property contains just about everything we need to locate the problem. For example, a UserID with a length other than the 36 characters required by the schema will generate a message string something like this:

```
The 'urn:wrox-friends:UserID' element has an invalid value according to its data
type. An error occurred at (4, 50).
```

Processing the Uploaded XML Data

The XmlSchema class is Microsoft's implementation of the W3C standard, and it performs validation while the XML stream is read. There is no need for a special validation method. Remember that these readers are read-only and forward-only, which makes them fast and light, but also means that we need to process the XML while we are still validating it. We will not know that the *entire* XML file meets the requirements of our schema until we have finished processing it.

As you examine the following example, notice that the code for retrieving data from the validator (that is, the XmlValidatingReader object) always refers to **nodes** in the first instance, rather than to elements, or attributes, or text. This is due to the way that the reader perceives the XML: as it moves through the document, one by one it comes across the entities that document contains. The next 'thing' that it comes across could be an element, or an attribute of an element, or the content of an element. We use the generic term, node, to refer to all of these things. When each entity arrives in our code, we have to find out what it is.

Try It Out – Displaying XML Data

With that said, it's time for us to implement the steps that process the XML file. We're going to read the elements, and display them in the tree view.

1. We will place the reading and processing code in a method called BuildTreeView():

```
private void BuildTreeView()
{
  TreeNode node = null;
  TreeNode topnode;
  TreeNode parentnode = null;
  XmlReader reader;
  String parent = String.Empty;

  this.pnlError.Visible = false;

  // Save the incoming file if appropriate
  SaveXml();

  try
  {
    reader = GetReader();

    // Clear the tree view
    this.tvXmlView.Nodes.Clear();
    topnode = new TreeNode();

    // Add nodes to hold new users and attendees
    topnode.Text = "File: " + Session["file"].ToString();
    topnode.Nodes.Add(new TreeNode());
    topnode.Nodes.Add(new TreeNode());
    this.tvXmlView.Nodes.Add(topnode);

    while (reader.Read())
    {
      if ((reader.NodeType == XmlNodeType.Element) &&
          (reader.LocalName == "User" || reader.LocalName == "Attendee"))
      {
        // Add the parent User or Attendee node
        parentnode = new TreeNode();
        parentnode.Text = reader.LocalName;

        // Place the node inside the right parent node
        if (reader.LocalName == "User")
          topnode.Nodes[0].Nodes.Add(parentnode);
        else
          topnode.Nodes[1].Nodes.Add(parentnode);

        AddAttributes(reader, parentnode);
        parent = reader.LocalName;
      }
      else if ((reader.NodeType == XmlNodeType.Element) &&
               (parent == "User" || parent == "Attendee"))
      {
        // If it's an element node we need to add it and its attributes
        node = new TreeNode();
        node.Text = reader.Name;
        AddAttributes(reader, node);
        parentnode.Nodes.Add(node);
```

```
          }
        else if (reader.NodeType == XmlNodeType.Text && node != null)
        {
            // If it's a text node, set the text value of the previous node
            node.Text += ": " + reader.Value;
        }
      }

      // Finally, add the count of elements to the top node values
      topnode.Nodes[0].Text =
            "New Users (" + topnode.Nodes[0].Nodes.Count.ToString() + ")";
      topnode.Nodes[1].Text =
            "Attendees (" + topnode.Nodes[1].Nodes.Count.ToString() + ")";
      this.tvXmlView.Visible = true;

      // Check for errors accumulated during validation
      if (_errors.Length != 0)
        throw new InvalidOperationException(_errors);
    }
    catch (Exception ex)
    {
      this.lblError.Text = ex.Message;
      this.pnlError.Visible = true;
    }
}
```

2. Add the AddAttributes() helper method next:

```
// Helper method of BuildTreeView that adds the attributes found as
// child nodes of the passed node, using a different icon
private void AddAttributes(XmlReader reader, TreeNode node)
{
  if (!(reader.HasAttributes))
    return;

  TreeNode child;
  TreeNode attrs = new TreeNode();

  attrs.Text = "Attributes (" + reader.AttributeCount.ToString() + ")";
  attrs.ImageUrl = "images/attributes.gif";
  attrs.ExpandedImageUrl = "images/attributes.gif";

  for (int i = 0; i < reader.AttributeCount; i++)
  {
    child = new TreeNode();
    reader.MoveToAttribute(i);
    child.Text = reader.Name + ": " + reader.Value;
    child.ImageUrl = "images/emptyfile.gif";
    attrs.Nodes.Add(child);
  }

  node.Nodes.Add(attrs);
```

```
    // Reposition the reader
    reader.MoveToElement();
}
```

3. Now we have to remove the call to `SaveXml()` in the **Load** button handler, and put in its place a call to `BuildTreeView()`. This is because we actually want to reload the contents of this control. As you see from the code above, the call to `SaveXml()` is performed inside that method already:

```
private void btnLoad_Click(object sender, System.EventArgs e)
{
    BuildTreeView();
}
```

4. Save the solution and run the page. After the usual login process, load the `upload.xml` file we created, just as we did before. This time, the XML file will be represented in a tree view:

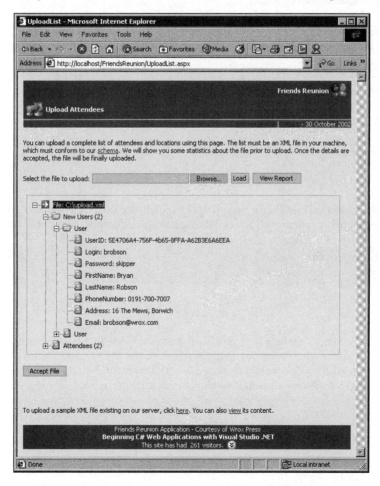

How It Works

When the user clicks the **Load** button, a postback is caused. The code in the button handler calls the `BuildTreeView()` method, where we save the incoming XML file and then use an `XmlTextReader` to create nodes and add them to the tree view. We also append any attributes that my be found, by calling the helper `AddAttributes()` method. The nodes are created programmatically by initializing new variables, assigning their properties, and finally adding them to the parent node. For example, take a look at the following code, which initializes and adds the top-level nodes:

```
// Clear the tree view
this.tvXmlView.Nodes.Clear();
topnode = new TreeNode();

// Add nodes to hold new users and attendees
topnode.Text = "File: " + Session["file"].ToString();
topnode.Nodes.Add(new TreeNode());
topnode.Nodes.Add(new TreeNode());
this.tvXmlView.Nodes.Add(topnode);
```

We add different nodes to these two top-level nodes depending on the current element name – that is, either a `<User>` or an `<Attendee>` element.

If a validation error occurs while the tree view is being built, the handler we created in the previous section will be called, and the error will be appended to the `_errors` variable. The code will continue processing and adding nodes, until finally we check whether this variable contains any error messages, and throw an exception if appropriate:

```
// Check for errors accumulated during validation
if (_errors.Length != 0)
  throw new InvalidOperationException(_errors);
```

Note that this exception that we throw ourselves is handled in exactly the same as other exceptions that may happen, through a common `catch` section (we'll discuss exceptions in detail in Chapter 11):

```
catch (Exception ex)
{
  this.lblError.Text = ex.Message;
  this.pnlError.Visible = true;
}
```

To finish off this section, let's take a look at what happens to a file that contains some validation errors. This time, add the `uploadBad.xml` file that's available in the code download for this chapter, which contains an error in an ID (shorter than it should be), and an invalid `<Institution>` element (not expected according to the schema). After we click the **Load** button, the following screen should appear:

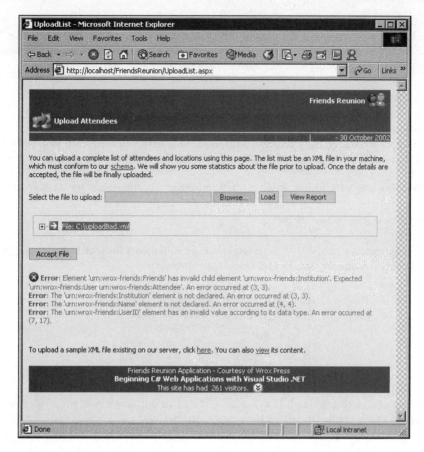

XML schema validation provides our system with a watertight seal against invalid data. As it's an external text file, we can modify our schema should our business requirements change, without necessarily recompiling or even stopping the web application.

Querying XML Documents: XPath

XML represents a powerful and increasingly popular way of storing data, so it would be a huge shortcoming if there were no way to perform queries against that data. Now, we know that the de facto standard for querying relational data stores is SQL, so why can't we just use that to extract data from our XML documents?

The answer lies in the differences between the relational model of tables and rows, and the hierarchical structure of XML documents, where elements can be arbitrarily nested to any depth. This is why the W3C came to the rescue again with **XPath**, which is, as the specification says, "a language for addressing parts of an XML document."

More information on XPath can be found at http://www.w3c.org/TR/xpath.

XPath will be immediately familiar if you have an understanding of the file structure of a modern PC, and particularly if you remember the days of the DOS command prompt. This is because XPath is based on the same slash-separated notation to locate items. The following XPath expression, for example, would locate all of the <User> elements in our sample XML document:

```
/Friends/User
```

The first slash indicates that the search should start from the root node of the document. The following elements compose a path, called a **location path**, that leads to the elements we want to be included in the result. When an XPath expression like this is executed, the result is a collection of nodes (a **node set**).

We can refine this query by adding some further constraints on the results we want returned:

```
/Friends/User[LastName="Brown"]
```

This revised expression would only return those <User> elements for which the <LastName> child element has the text value Brown. Let's dissect this expression:

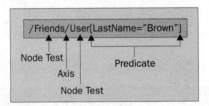

A set consisting of an axis (optional) plus a node test and an optional predicate is referred to as a **location step**. In the example above, we have two location steps: /Friends, and /User[LastName="Brown"].

The **axis** determines the direction in which we move down the location path. We can move to child nodes, as we did above, with the forward slash, which means that the next step is evaluated against the children of the previously evaluated step. Other possibilities include moving to the parent node (../), and staying in the current node (.).

Another important feature of XPath is its numeric, string, and Boolean functions, which include count(), sum(), string-length(), starts-width(), contains(), and some others. You can find the complete list of functions, axes, and other features of XPath in the specification itself at http://www.w3.org/TR/1999/REC-xpath-19991116.html, or you might choose one of the following books:

- ❑   *Beginning XML, 2nd Edition* (Wrox, ISBN 1-86100-559-8)

- ❑   *Professional XML for .NET Developers* (Wrox, ISBN 1-86100-531-8)

Try It Out – Building the Reports Form

In our application, we want to provide some statistical information about the uploaded file, such as a report of new users and a count of attendees. We will achieve this using the features of XPath, without having to traverse the file laboriously.

1. Add a new web form to the application, and name it `UploadListReport.aspx`. As usual, make the class defined in the code-behind page inherit the `FriendsBase` class:

```
public class UploadListReport : FriendsBase
```

2. Link this form to our application stylesheet with the following element within the `<head>` element of the page:

```
<link href="Style/iestyle.css" type="text/css" rel="stylesheet">
```

3. Add two tables, two textboxes, two link buttons, two image controls, and three labels (all from the **Web Forms** tab in the **Toolbox** unless stated otherwise) and configure them as detailed in the following tables, until your form looks something like this:

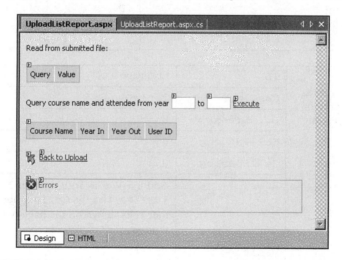

[Table] This table will contain the statistics values we retrieve using XPath queries against the file.	ID	tbReport
	CssClass	TableLines
	GridLines	Both
	CellPadding	0
	CellSpacing	0

Table continued on following page

[Table] This table will contain the statistics values we retrieve using XPath queries against the file.	Rows	Add a new row, with its BackColor set to #D3E5FA. Use the Cells property to add the two cells shown on the page (you'll just need to insert the Text property of each cell).

[TextBox] The starting year for the XPath query to filter attendees.	ID	txtYearFrom
	CssClass	SmallTextBox
	MaxLength	4
	Width	36px

[TextBox] The ending year for the XPath query to filter attendees.	ID	txtYearTo
	CssClass	SmallTextBox
	MaxLength	4
	Width	36px

[LinkButton] Performs the query with the range of years specified.	ID	btnExecute
	Text	Execute

[Table] Holds the results from the previous query execution.	ID	tbDates
	CssClass	TableLines
	GridLines	Both
	CellPadding	0
	CellSpacing	0
	Rows	Add a new row, with its BackColor set to #D3E5FA. Use the Cells property to add the four cells shown on the page (you'll just need to insert the Text property of each cell).
	Visible	False

[ImageButton] Will redirect the user back to the upload page.	ID	btnBackImg
	AlternateText	Back to Upload
	ImageUrl	images/back.gif
	ImageAlign	Middle

[LinkButton] Redirects the user back to the upload page.	ID	btnBackLink
	Text	Back to Upload

[Panel] Displays any errors found in the incoming file.	ID	pnlError
	Visible	False

Stretch the panel to make it quite wide, and then place the final two controls inside it:

[Image] (take this from HTML tab) The icon for errors. This is not a server control, so we don't need an ID.	align	absmiddle
	src	images/error.gif

[Label] Contains the error messages.	ID	lblError
	ForeColor	Red
	Text	Errors

How It Works

This form will show the statistics that we'll add in the code-behind page. The table at the top of the page will be populated with the results of some predefined queries, while the second table will execute a custom XPath query built from the value in the textboxes above it. It will allow the user to select the <Attendee> elements whose child elements' <YearIn> and <YearOut> text values match the desired range.

Before moving on to perform the queries, however, we need to introduce one last XML-related standard: the Document Object Model.

The Document Object Model (DOM)

TextReader-based objects provide forward-only access to the underlying XML data, which means that as soon as we move forward, we lose all information pertaining to the previous element. Clearly, such an approach is unsuited to querying a document, because we would end up reading the entire file for every query we perform. Even if the element we were looking for was the first one in the document, there would be no way to know that for sure, and we would have to read it in its entirety to be certain.

To perform queries effectively, we really need the complete document in memory, so that we can perform all the queries we want without the need to re-parse the file. The W3C again has the answer: the **Document Object Model** (or **DOM**).

The DOM defines the way an XML document is stored in memory, and how its nodes are loaded, accessed and changed using a 'collection' approach: each node contains other nodes as children, and these in turn can contain other nodes, and so on. The DOM allows us to navigate back and forth between child and parent elements too, tinkering with them as we go – it is neither forward-only nor read-only.

DOM is built on several key building blocks. The fundamental one is the concept of the Document, which is to DOM what the Schema element is for XSD. This important object is implemented by the .NET Framework in the System.Xml.XmlDocument class.

Try It Out – Querying a DOM Document

With that information in mind, we're ready to build the code for performing XPath queries, as we outlined above.

1. Open the code-behind page for the UploadListReport.aspx web form, and add the following imports at the top of the file:

```
using System.IO;
using System.Xml;
using System.Xml.XPath;
using System.Text;
```

2. Add the GetReader() helper method to the UploadListReport class. This method will serve the same purpose as the function by the same name in the UploadList.aspx page:

```
private XmlReader GetReader()
{
  XmlTextReader reader;
  StringReader xmlinput;

  if (Session["xml"] == null)
    throw new InvalidOperationException("No Xml file has been uploaded.");

  // Build the XmlReader from the in-memory string saved above
  xmlinput = new StringReader((string)Session["xml"]);
  reader = new XmlTextReader(xmlinput);
  return reader;
}
```

3. Locate the Page_Load() method, and place the following code inside it:

```
private void Page_Load(object sender, System.EventArgs e)
{
  // Configure header
  base.HeaderIconImageUrl =
                    Request.ApplicationPath + "/images/print.gif";
  base.HeaderMessage = "Upload Attendees - Report";

  XmlDocument doc;
  XmlReader reader;

  XmlNodeList nodes;
  XmlNamespaceManager mgr;
```

```
TableRow row;
TableCell cell;
StringBuilder sb;

try
{
  // Retrieve the reader object and initialize the DOM document
  reader = GetReader();
  doc = new XmlDocument();
  doc.Load(reader);

  // Initialize the namespace manager for the document
  mgr = new XmlNamespaceManager(doc.NameTable);
  mgr.AddNamespace("wx", "urn:wrox-friends");

  // List of new users
  nodes = doc.SelectNodes("/wx:Friends/wx:User", mgr);
  row = new TableRow();
  cell = new TableCell();
  cell.Text = "New Users: " + nodes.Count.ToString();
  row.Cells.Add(cell);

  sb = new StringBuilder();
  foreach (XmlNode node in nodes)
  {
    sb.Append(node["LastName", "urn:wrox-friends"].InnerText);
    sb.Append(", ");
    sb.Append(node["FirstName", "urn:wrox-friends"].InnerText);
    sb.Append(" (");
    sb.Append(node["Email", "urn:wrox-friends"].InnerText);
    sb.Append(")");
    sb.Append("<br>");
  }

  cell = new TableCell();
  cell.Text = sb.ToString();
  row.Cells.Add(cell);
  this.tbReport.Rows.Add(row);

  // Queries returning XPath intrinsic types
  XPathNavigator nav = doc.CreateNavigator();
  XPathExpression expr;

  // Total number of attendees anywhere in the document
  row = new TableRow();
  cell = new TableCell();
  expr = nav.Compile("count(//wx:Attendee)");

  expr.SetContext(mgr);
  cell.Text = "Global count of new attendees: " +
                            nav.Evaluate(expr).ToString();
  cell.ColumnSpan = 2;
  row.Cells.Add(cell);
```

```
        this.tbReport.Rows.Add(row);

        // The last attendee in the file, in document order
        row = new TableRow();
        cell = new TableCell();
        expr = nav.Compile(
                "string(//wx:Attendee[position() = last()]/wx:UserID)");
        expr.SetContext(mgr);
        cell.Text = "Last attendee ID in file: " +
                                    nav.Evaluate(expr).ToString();
        cell.ColumnSpan = 2;
        row.Cells.Add(cell);
        this.tbReport.Rows.Add(row);
    }
    catch (Exception ex)
    {
        this.lblError.Text = ex.Message;
        this.pnlError.Visible = true;
    }

    if (this.tbReport.Rows.Count == 1)
        this.tbReport.Visible = false;
}
```

4. Double-click on the `btnBackImg` and `btnBackLink` controls in the designer to create `Click` event handlers for each of these. Add the line of code below to each handler to allow the user to navigate back to the `UploadList` form:

```
private void btnBackImg_Click(object sender,
                            System.Web.UI.ImageClickEventArgs e)
{
    Response.Redirect("UploadList.aspx");
}

private void btnBackLink_Click(object sender, System.EventArgs e)
{
    Response.Redirect("UploadList.aspx");
}
```

5. Leave this page now, and open the `UploadList.aspx` web form in the designer. Double-click the **View Report** button, and add the following code to the event handler that is created:

```
private void btnReport_Click(object sender, System.EventArgs e)
{
    SaveXml();
    Response.Redirect("UploadListReport.aspx");
}
```

6. With the `UploadList.aspx` page set as the startup page, run the project with *F5*.

7. Select the sample XML file to upload, click **View Report**, and you should see a summary that looks something like this:

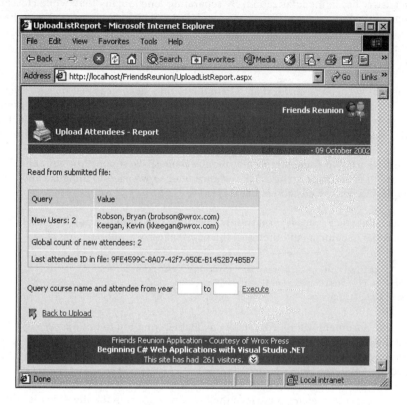

How It Works

When we click the **View Report** button in the previous page, this page takes up the XML we saved in the session variable and produces the report we see in the table at the top of the page. In order to achieve this, we load an XmlDocument from it, and perform the queries we need.

Loading the document involves retrieving an XmlReader that points to the XML string in the session variable, just as we did in the previous section, and passing it to the Load() method of the XmlDocument class:

```
// Retrieve the reader object and initialize the DOM document
reader = GetReader();
doc = new XmlDocument();
doc.Load(reader);
```

We use a class called XmlNamespaceManager when we perform the queries. To understand better why this class even exists, we need to understand the great effort Microsoft made to separate out functionality and make individual objects more manageable, lighter, and faster.

We saw how `XmlValidatingReader` builds upon the `XmlTextReader`. We also learned how to pass XSD schemas to it. Why was the schema a separate object and not an intrinsic part of the validating reader? The answer lies in modularization. By separating functionality that, while closely related, doesn't belong to the same classes, we achieve modularity, which allows each class to be simpler, easier to use, and more easily upgraded with new features. That effectively makes it all more manageable. As an example, the validating reader not only works with the new XSD schemas, but it also validates against older DTD and XDR formats.

Now, imagine that we need to perform an XPath query on a document that doesn't use namespaces (this is a perfectly legal task). If namespace management – that is, the resolution of XML prefixes and related operations – were built-in to the XPath classes, we would be wasting memory and making the classes more complex than required for this particular scenario. Hence, .NET separates namespace-related operations into their own class (the `XmlNamespaceManager` class), and we only need to instantiate that class when we need to issue queries that require namespace support. In our case, the schema design enforces the use of namespace in the XML instance files, so we need to initialize and use this class whenever a query is performed against these files.

Initializing the namespace manager is a simple operation: we simply create it and tell it to use the names found in the document, and then add the namespaces we will be using in our queries:

```
// Initialize the namespace manager for the document
mgr = new XmlNamespaceManager(doc.NameTable);
mgr.AddNamespace("wx", "urn:wrox-friends");
```

Once loaded, the document will be completely available, from top to bottom. We will focus here on the methods that the `XmlDocument` class provides to perform queries against data – it contains many more methods and properties to work with, and they can be found in the MSDN documentation simply by typing XmlDocument in the Help's Index window.

For now, we will execute a query to retrieve the list of new users in the file – that is, all `<User>` elements that are present in the document, and children of the `<Friends>` element:

```
nodes = doc.SelectNodes("/wx:Friends/wx:User", mgr);
```

It really is that easy to get the results! Note that we need to include the namespace prefixes on both element names in the XPath expression, because our document uses a namespace. Prefixes allow us to locate elements that belong to different namespaces, and it's the namespace manager that's responsible for resolving them. Of course, we can still use documents without a namespace, and execute queries without using this class at all, but we could hardly validate a document like that.

Once we get the results, displaying them in the table is just a question of creating the appropriate `TableRow` and `TableCell` objects to contain the information about it. To build the result string containing all the users in the file, we use the `StringBuilder` class:

```
sb = new StringBuilder();
foreach (XmlNode node in nodes)
{
    sb.Append(node["LastName", "urn:wrox-friends"].InnerText);
```

```
            sb.Append(", ");
            sb.Append(node["FirstName", "urn:wrox-friends"].InnerText);
            sb.Append(" (");
            sb.Append(node["Email", "urn:wrox-friends"].InnerText);
            sb.Append(")");
            sb.Append("<br>");
        }
```

As we iterate through the nodes found, the `StringBuilder` accumulates a sort of summary about new users, containing their full name and e-mail address (between parentheses). Note that each node offers some accessors to get at its content – here, we've used the `InnerText` property to extract that content as a string value.

So far, we've loaded the first row with data about the users. The next query uses a different approach. The XPath specification defines four basic types that can result from executing expressions: node set, Boolean, number (floating-point), or string. When we use the `XmlDocument`'s `SelectNodes()` method (or for that matter, the `SelectNode()` method, which returns the first node in the results), the XPath expression issued *must* evaluate to a node set (although this might contain only one node). For example, the following query is a valid XPath expression that returns a number, representing the count of `<Attendee>` elements found in the entire document. It would fail if we used it for the `SelectNodes()` method. Note that the double slash (`//`) at the beginning of the expression means that we're looking for *all* `<Attendee>` elements *anywhere* in the document, starting from the root:

```
        expr = nav.Compile("count(//wx:Attendee)");
```

If we wish to execute expressions that return simple types, instead of node sets, we need to use XPath-specific classes like these:

```
        // Queries returning XPath intrinsic types
        XPathNavigator nav = doc.CreateNavigator();
        XPathExpression expr;
```

The `XPathNavigator` is an object returned by the `XmlDocument.CreateNavigator()` method, and is optimized for XPath execution and navigation. The `XPathExpression` object is used to pre-compile commonly used queries, in a similar way to stored procedures in database systems. This can speed up execution, because it allows us to reuse the expression and avoid repetition of the string-parsing step that interprets the query. We can also find the return type of the expression dynamically, through its `ReturnType` property.

In order for the expression to resolve the namespace used, it needs an associated `XmlNamespaceManager`, which is performed by calling the `SetContext()` method:

```
        expr.SetContext(mgr);
```

Finally, we evaluate the expression and convert the result to a string:

```
        cell.Text = "Last attendee ID in file: " +
                                    nav.Evaluate(expr).ToString();
```

333

After adding the corresponding row and cells to the results table, the rest of the method is almost identical to what we have already seen, except for the following lines of code:

```
// The last attendee in the file, in document order
row = new TableRow();
cell = new TableCell();
expr = nav.Compile(
           "string(//wx:Attendee[position() = last()]/wx:UserID)");
```

As the comment indicates, this query returns the UserID of the last <Attendee> element found in the document, for the user's verification purposes. More importantly though, this expression illustrates a number of useful XPath functions:

❑   string() – in this case, it converts the UserID node to its string value

❑   position() – returns the position of the context element (in our case, <Attendee>)

❑   last() – returns the position of the last element in the context node

Note that a predicate (the part of an XPath expression appearing in square brackets) can appear in any or all location steps. Here, a predicate selects the last <Attendee> element so that we can access its child <UserID> element. This element is converted to a string and shown in the results table. This query isn't particularly useful in the context of our application, but it does show the power behind XPath expressions, and the flexibility available for performing complex queries.

Building XPath Expressions Dynamically

As a final feature for our site, we are going to let the user enter a range of years, and query the uploaded file for matching nodes.

Try It Out – Querying Based On User Input

To do this, our code will build an XPath expression based on what's contained in the textboxes on the UploadListReport page when the Execute button is pressed. It will use the values to filter the matching nodes, and show them in the second (currently invisible) table on the page.

1. Open the UploadListReport page in the designer, double-click the Execute button (btnExecute), and add the following code:

```
private void btnExecute_Click(object sender, System.EventArgs e)
{
    XmlDocument doc;
    XmlReader reader;

    XmlNodeList nodes;
    XmlNamespaceManager mgr;

    TableRow row;
    TableCell cell;
```

```
    try
    {
      // Clear any previous state
      row = this.tbDates.Rows[0];
      this.tbDates.Rows.Clear();
      this.tbDates.Rows.Add(row);

      // Set up the document and namespace manager for it
      doc = new XmlDocument();
      reader = GetReader();

      doc.Load(reader);
      mgr = new XmlNamespaceManager(doc.NameTable);
      mgr.AddNamespace("wx", "urn:wrox-friends");

      nodes = doc.SelectNodes(
               "/wx:Friends/wx:Attendee[wx:YearIn >= " +
                               this.txtYearFrom.Text +
                               " and wx:YearOut <= " +
                               this.txtYearTo.Text + "]", mgr);

      foreach (XmlNode node in nodes)
      {
        row = new TableRow();
        row.Cells.Add(new TableCell());
        row.Cells.Add(new TableCell());
        row.Cells.Add(new TableCell());
        row.Cells.Add(new TableCell());

        // Set values
        row.Cells[0].Text = node.Attributes["Name"].Value;
        row.Cells[1].Text = node["YearIn", "urn:wrox-friends"].InnerText;
        row.Cells[2].Text = node["YearOut", "urn:wrox-friends"].InnerText;
        row.Cells[3].Text = node["UserID", "urn:wrox-friends"].InnerText;
        this.tbDates.Rows.Add(row);
      }

      this.tbDates.Visible = true;
    }
    catch (Exception ex)
    {
      this.lblError.Text = ex.Message;
      this.pnlError.Visible = true;
    }
  }
}
```

2. Hit *F5*, leaving `UploadList.aspx` as the start page. Select the sample XML document, and click **View Report**.

3. Insert a range of years in the boxes on the `UploadListReport` page, and click **Execute** to view the results. Here is an example of the output when the years 1970 and 1990 are inserted into the textboxes:

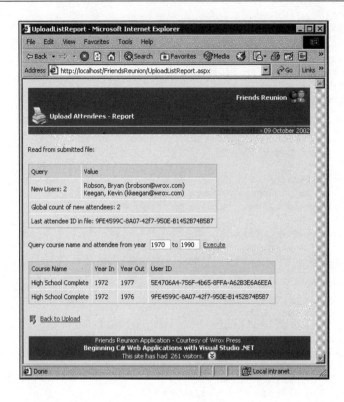

How It Works

When we click the Execute button, an XPath expression is built using the values in the textboxes. We use this dynamically-created expression to retrieve the results in a very similar way to before, adding rows and cells to the table.

The query can be executed multiple times, so we must clear the existing rows before each new query. We have to be careful not to delete the header row, though, which we accomplish by saving it to a variable before we clear the rows, and adding it back as the new header row afterwards. The execution of the expression is straightforward:

```
nodes = doc.SelectNodes(
        "/wx:Friends/wx:Attendee[wx:YearIn >= " +
                      this.txtYearFrom.Text +
                      " and wx:YearOut <= " +
                      this.txtYearTo.Text + "]", mgr);
```

In other words, our queries will typically be represented by strings such as this:

```
/wx:Friends/wx:Attendee[wx:YearIn >= 1970 and wx:YearOut <= 1990]
```

Once we have the results loaded in the table, we can change the values and click the Execute button again, to reload the table with the new values.

XmlDocument versus XmlReader

So there are two basic approaches available when accessing an XML file; the `XmlReader` and the DOM through `XmlDocument`. In this section, I'd like to sum up what differentiates one from the other, to help make the correct decision when deciding between them.

The primary difference is that the DOM caches an entire document in memory, while `XmlReader` and derived classes provide forward-only, read-only access to documents, with no caching.

This difference gives rise to a range of pros and cons for both. The following table analyzes key features of both techniques, and compares implementations. I have added **CON** or **PRO** as a conclusion for each case:

XmlReader	XmlDocument
Context	
The reader doesn't persist any information about the file. Once the cursor has moved on, there is no access at all to the previous element. To preserve information, we have to set up our own mechanisms and variables. **CON**	The document is completely loaded in memory when opened, and it stays there until we are done with it. This means we can move freely from the current element to its parent, siblings, and children. The complete document is available to provide any context information we may require. **PRO**
Resources consumed	
Stemming from the previous CON, the reader gets its most important PRO: it consumes minimal resources because of the fact that only the current element is held in memory. As soon as the position is changed, the previous element is discarded, and its resources freed up. **PRO**	Loading a complete document in memory can become a serious hindrance, especially for applications that work with large files. For smaller files, the impact is less noticeable, although even then, several concurrent users of a web application can quickly gobble up significant resources. **CON**
Random Access	
These readers only provide sequential access – to find a particular element, we must start at the beginning and work our way through. This can be a real problem if we need to access elements scattered through the XML 'tree'. **CON**	Nodes can be accessed using indexes or names, even queried using XPath, as we learned. This complete random access support makes the DOM ideal for storing configuration files, or offline data files. **PRO**

Table continued on following page

Read-write access	
As the name implies, `XMLReader` and family can only read. **CON**	The `XmlDocument` class provides complete control over elements in a file – we can add, remove, and change them. This makes it very suitable for data storage (from a form, for example) and for offline client-side functionality (where we send intermittent batch updates to the server). **PRO**
Speed	
The reader can be considerably faster, because it is so lightweight. If read-only access is suitable for a scenario, these classes are well worth consideration. **PRO**	Due to the comprehensive features it offers, DOM can take much longer to load and read a document from top to bottom than a reader. Improvements can be made through caching, but this will only increase the already high level of resources consumed. **CON**
Ease of use	
The reader has several methods, and the fact that it simultaneously represents the reader object and the current element makes the interface somewhat clumsy. For example, some methods will be useful when the current element is of some specific type, but not when it is positioned over another type. We have to work harder with readers – for instance, if we wish to retrieve the value of an element (with the `Value` property), we must first check the `HasValue` property to determine whether the current element can have a value or not! **CON**	The DOM has a more structured specification. There is an inheritance tree of classes, which starts from a general node type, and adds specialization for other node types. The base `XmlNode` class is very easy to master, and it is inherited by all the other disparate node types, greatly helping our learning curve. **PRO**

This list is by no means a definitive comparison, but aims to provide some guidance. However, like almost everything in programming, there is no guaranteed formula for successfully choosing one technique over another, and we must weigh up the particular needs of each application.

A loaded `XmlDocument` object can also be used for validation. We can use its `OuterXml` property to get a string with the whole XML file, and handle it exactly the same way we did for the string session variable. The code would look like the following:

```
// The doc variable has been loaded elsewhere
xmlinput = new StringReader(doc.OuterXml);
reader = new XmlTextReader(xmlinput);

// Configure the validating reader
validator = new XmlValidatingReader(reader);
```

Clearly, the advantages of an `XmlDocument` aren't so clear with regards to validation, as we are only using its string representation. It turns out to be that it is actually much more suitable for the querying scenario we have seen above.

Summary

In Chapters 7 and 8, we have learned some important concepts about the usage of XML in web applications. We saw several standards that are regulated by the W3C and have a crucial role to play in the evolution of the web.

When we use XML files, we need to understand the difference between well-formed XML and valid XML. Looking at valid XML led us to the W3C's XML Schema Definition specification. We looked at some of the most important elements for defining the structure of XML instance documents, such as simple types, complex types, sequences, and attributes. We added occurrence constraints and learned how to restrict a base type to meet our needs. We added validation to our application using the schema we built, and it proved to be simple yet highly flexible and powerful. Storing validation logic for incoming data separate from business logic by the use of schemas helps maintenance and minimizes the coding required should our validation requirements change.

We exploited the full power of the XML support built into Visual Studio .NET, to visually create both schemas and instance documents. We saw how a schema enables IntelliSense during the creation of an XML document, and also played with the visual designers provided for drag and drop authoring.

A closer look at .NET's XML classes shed some light on the close relation between disparate namespaces, such as `System.IO` and `System.Xml`, as we used them in conjunction when building a useful upload feature for our application. On the way, we had a go with an add-in custom control, in this case the `TreeView` from Microsoft.

While reading XML may suffice for some applications, we usually need to perform queries against XML data. XPath is designed to fulfill this goal, and we applied it to generate statistical information about the file being uploaded to our web page.

Finally, we examined the W3C's DOM standard, and its implementation in the .NET Framework: the `XmlDocument` class. We contrasted it with the `XmlReader` alternative, to determine which situations each is most suited to.

These chapters should provide a foundation that I hope will be useful as you work through the next chapter – which is about the very important emerging XML technology of web services.

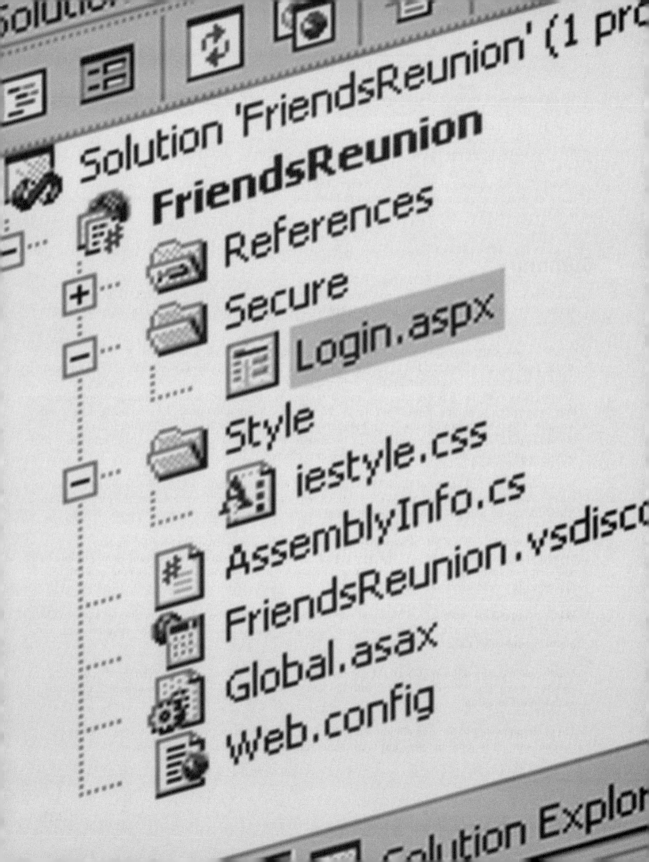

Web Services in Web Applications

We've looked at the creation of web applications, connecting these applications to data sources, and then adding XML functionality to them, all using the *Friends Reunion* application. In this chapter, we'll make use of what we've learned from these topics, applying it to a different aspect of web development, one that opens up a wealth of new functionality to us – **web services**.

Web services are seen by many as critical to the future of Internet-connected applications. Such a bold claim can be made for two main reasons. First, they allow remote applications to be connected together regardless of the distance between them, and second, they allow systems developed on other platforms and in different languages, such as Linux and Java, to integrate with functionality developed in .NET. They do this by giving us the ability to provide functionality in a manner similar to publishing web pages – accepting a request for a URL and providing a response – making them available to any compatible client connected to the Internet.

In this chapter, we'll explain what is unique about web services that causes them to be lauded so much, and cover everything you need to know in order to create and use your own. This will achieved by doing the following:

- ❑ First, we'll build up a definition of what a web service is
- ❑ Next, we'll create a web service for the *Friends Reunion* application
- ❑ Then we'll create a further application that makes use of this web service
- ❑ Finally, we'll cover advanced topics such as error handling and performance

Overview of Web Services

Following the brief description of a web service above, it's a good idea to define it in more detail before we roll up our sleeves and start writing one. We'll do this by first covering what a web service is, how they came to be, and how they compare to the server/browser model that we learned about in Chapter 1.

Web services are parts of a system that are externally exposed (like web pages) via a new, open standard. This allows disparate applications to talk to one other and share information. The web services standard itself is built upon further standards such as HTTP and XML. By making use of such widely accepted technologies, web services aren't reliant on any proprietary system or vendor. This allows support for them to be freely developed for any platform and language; .NET, Java, Perl, and so forth.

A web service itself is a collection of methods (functions and subroutines) that can be called from a remote location. These methods accept and return parameters, just as normal methods can, allowing for the vast majority of (appropriate) functionality that is used internally in an application to be exposed to the wider public.

Although web services themselves are fairly new, the concept behind them isn't. There has long been the need for disparate applications to communicate with each other in order to share information and functionality; this is called **distributed services**. Historically, tying these applications together was done on an ad hoc basis, with only the parties involved in the integration deciding on the structure and format of the data. As it became clear that a standardized specification would lower costs and shorten development timescales, several options were put forwards – DCOM and CORBA for instance. These options were based on proprietary formats, however, slowing their uptake by developers, and creating barriers to their use. They also imposed further technical issues, such as requiring the use of TCP/IP ports that are regularly blocked by firewalls. An alternative approach was needed that wasn't vendor- or platform-specific – enter web services.

Having such a flexible mechanism available gives us two main features that can be demonstrated if we take the creation of a corporate web site as an example. First, we have the opportunity to draw on all of the specialist functionality and information of a separate application, just as easily as we'd make use of functionality provided to us by the .NET Framework. This would allow us to retrieve data such as the company's current stock price, or news in the relevant industry sector for display on the site – providing more information to the end user (and hopefully making the site more popular in the process). Second, we can publish information, allowing other applications to consume it. In this example, the company's product catalogue could be published in a format that allows other sites to make use of the information, potentially increasing sales. In the case of our *Friends Reunion* application, web services can be used to cater for the creation of affiliate sites, allowing people to sign up to the system from the web site of their old high school, for instance.

Relationship to the Server/Browser Model

A simple way of visualizing a web service would be to think of it as a web page, which, rather than returning information that is useful to an end user, returns information that can be consumed by another application. In its simplest form, requests for information are made in a similar manner – calling a URL and passing any required information either on the URL (a GET), or as the body of the request (a POST). Further, more complex mechanisms such as **SOAP** are also available, which we'll look at in due course later in this chapter. Requests for these URLs are then handled by IIS and the .NET runtime, just as they would be for a web request; any processing necessary is performed by code written by the developer, and the results are returned as the body of the HTTP response. However, rather than the response being an HTML document containing markup for display, it is made up of an XML document that contains data.

The diagram below shows the process of making a request for a web-service – from this logical point of view, it is the same as that of a web browser requesting a page:

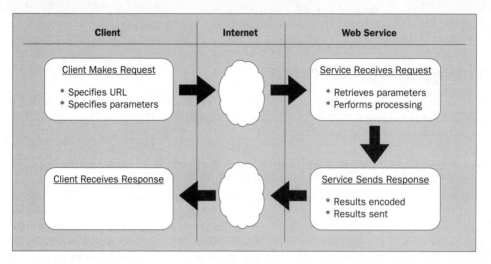

Although web services and web pages are very similar in nature, the fundamental purpose of them is different – web services are intended as a standard way of transmitting information between two computers. This leads to several key differences:

Web Page	Web Service
Has a user interface	Does not have a user interface (although it's not part of the standard, Microsoft does provide us with a simple way of testing our web services using an auto-generated interface, in a similar manner to the way error pages are automatically generated for us)
Designed to interact with users	Designed to interact with other applications
Designed to work with web browser clients	Designed to work with any type of client or device

To cater for these, and other technical differences, web services are created distinctly in Visual Studio .NET, and have a different file extension from web pages; .asmx rather than .aspx. This allows the .NET runtime to process them differently, and provide extra functionality that we'll take a look at later in the chapter.

Visual Studio .NET Support for Web Services

Prior to the release of .NET, Microsoft's main offering for the creation of web services was in the form of a simple command-line tool, the **SOAP Toolkit**. Although this did a lot of the hard work for us, it certainly wasn't the easiest way of getting an introduction to the topic. Like many other new areas such as XML, which we've already looked at earlier in this book, Visual Studio .NET has tightly integrated the creation of web services into the IDE.

To the developer, creating a web service is now almost identical to writing a user control or the code-behind page for a web form. Other features that we'll look at later in the chapter allow for the automatic creation of a UI for testing web services, and treating them just like normal methods when they're called from within our code.

Providing a Web Service

To get a real understanding of what constitutes a web service, and how one is developed, we're going to expose some of the functionality of our *Friends Reunion* application through such a service. The areas of functionality that we're going to focus on are:

❑ The creation of a method similar to the login action on the web site, allowing a user ID to be retrieved when supplied with a user name and password

❑ The retrieval of contact-requests for a given user of the system

In order to provide that functionality, it's important that we first understand *how* methods are exposed. As mentioned earlier, a web service is simply an ASMX file, much like an ASPX web form. This is called on a URL, just as a web page would be. For instance, if we had a web service named `MyWebService.asmx`, we could potentially host it at http://localhost/MyWebService.asmx.

Within each web service, we add **web methods**. If a web service is thought of as a class (which it technically is), then a web method is akin to marking a function as `public` on a class, making it available externally. In the case of `MyWebService.asmx`, we could add web methods called `GetMyName` and `GetMyAge` which actually implement the functionality that we're trying to expose. Although the way in which these methods are called depends on the format used – HTTP-GET, HTTP-POST, and so on, the methods are always called from the containing URL.

To add such functionality to our solution, and to ensure that it works correctly, there are several steps involved:

❑ Create a new **ASP.NET Web Service** project to contain the service functionality

❑ Create an ASMX file that will provide the web methods that can be called

❑ Add all of the methods that are needed for the service to the code-behind class for the ASMX file

❑ Build the project

❑ Test the project

To start with, we'll just implement the simpler of the two functions we mentioned briefly earlier – retrieving a user ID. This will allow us to focus on the service, rather than getting too involved in the logic of the application.

'Try it Out – Creating a Web Service

In order to create our web service, we'll add a new project to the solution. This allows us to separate the functionality of the web site from that of our web services, and manage permissions, and so on, separately.

It is possible to create a completely fresh solution separate to our solution containing the Friends Reunion application, but it means having to run two instances of Visual Studio .NET at once when debugging. It is much more convenient to have the application project and the application in the same solution.

1. To create this web service project, right-click on the FriendsReunion solution line at the top of the Solution Explorer tree and then select Add | New Project... to bring up the Add New Project dialog. Now we can choose to add a C# ASP.NET Web Service project to our solution. Make sure that the location of the project is http://localhost/FriendsService in the textbox at the bottom of the dialog and then hit OK to create the project:

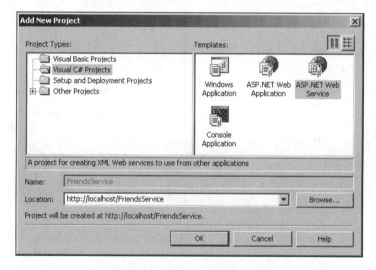

2. A new set of items will now appear in the Solution Explorer tree to represent this project:

One of these files, Service1.asmx, can have any web methods we wish to define added to it. Rather than go through the process of amending this file, we'll remove this and add our own with a more appropriate name. (If we left the name as it was, then people would have to access our web methods via a URL containing the unhelpfully named Service1.asmx.) So, right-click on the Service1.asmx file in the Solution Explorer, and select the Delete option to remove it.

Now add a new web service: right-click on the FriendsService project node, and choose the Add | Add Web Service... option. In the dialog that this brings up, enter FriendsInfo.asmx into the Name field and click Open:

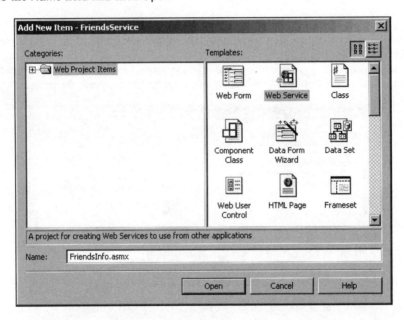

3. Before we start building the functionalityof the web service, we'll need to add a key for the database connection string. To do this, open the Web.config file and insert an <add> element within the <appSettings> element, that looks like this:

```
<appSettings>
  <add key="cnFriends.ConnectionString"
       value="data source=(local)\NetSDK;
       initial catalog=FriendsData;
       persist security info=False;
       user id=sa;workstation id=MANKEEC1;
       packet size=4096" />
</appSettings>
```

This is just like the one we used in the Web.config file for the main *Friends Reunion* web site project, that we created in Chapter 5. Your connection string is likely to need a different workstation ID, and different username/password attributes if you've configured your database differently.

4. Next, we need to create a `SqlConnection` and a `SqlCommand` to interact with the database. To do this, return to the new `FriendsInfo.asmx` file, in design view. In this view, we'll be able to drag and drop the database components that we need onto the design surface – just as we have done in earlier chapters.

From the **Data** tab of the **Toolbox**, drag and drop a `SqlConnection` onto the design surface. Set the `Name` property of this to `cnFriends` and select the `ConnectionString` property from the `DynamicProperties` section, mapping it to the suggested default key of `cnFriends.ConnectionString` that we have been using since Chapter 4.

Once the connection has been created, drag and drop a `SqlCommand` onto the design surface, and rename it to `cmUser`. Next, set the `Connection` property to the **Existing** connection of `cnFriends`. We can now add the `CommandText` required to retrieve the login information, as we did earlier in the book. To do this, click on the ellipsis within the `CommandText` field in the Solution Explorer, and enter the following SQL query:

```
SELECT     UserID
FROM       [User]
WHERE      (Login = @Login) AND (Password = @Password)
```

Your screen should match the following:

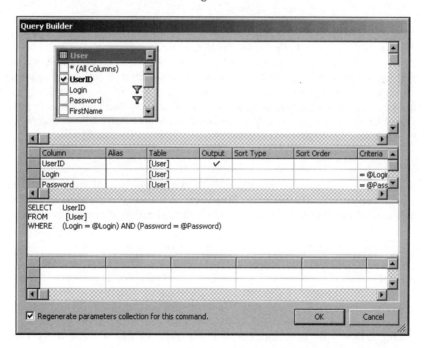

5. Now we can switch to the code-behind view to start developing our web methods. The code-behind view should present you with a fairly standard looking class; we'll look at the differences between this and other classes shortly, but for now we can just get on with adding a web method of our own.

The first method we'll create is called `GetUserID()`. This will take a user's user name and password, and return their user ID. This value can then be made use of to authenticate requests before retrieving information for that specific user. To create this method, all that needs to be done is have the following code entered into the class:

```
[WebMethod]
public string GetUserID(string login, string password)
{
  cmUser.Parameters[0].Value = login;
  cmUser.Parameters[1].Value = password;
  string id;

  try
  {
    cnFriends.Open();
    id = (string)cmUser.ExecuteScalar();
  }
  finally
  {
    cnFriends.Close();
  }

  return id;
}
```

When the web service was originally created, the IDE would have placed a short HelloWorld() web method example in it for you to see how the functionality works. This is a sample web service that simply returns the string, Hello World to anyone who calls it. It is provided as a template for the creation of our own web services, and as a means for testing. We won't be showing you how to get it running here as all you need to know is explained in the method's comments, so you can delete it without causing any concerns. If you leave it there, it can always be uncommented and run to help you diagnose the any problems you run into.

How It Works

Creating a web method within a web service really is that simple; Visual Studio .NET takes care of all of the pain for us. It knows to do this because of the slight differences in the class and function we've defined from standard ones. The first thing to note is the definition of the class itself:

```
public class FriendsInfo : System.Web.Services.WebService
```

As you can see, this class inherits from the `WebService` base class. This means that it automatically takes on all of the characteristics of a `WebService`, leaving us with little to do in order to implement the functionality that we need.

The second thing to note is the attribute that we place at the top of our method declaration:

```
[WebMethod]
```

It is this attribute that informs the C# compiler to perform all of the actions necessary to expose our functions as part of the web service. In order to make a method available as part of our service, the method must be prefixed with the [WebMethod] attribute. If we wanted, we could also write methods in this class that are made public, and can be consumed from within our application. Unless they are marked with this attribute, however, they would not form part of the publicly visible web service.

Testing the Web Service

Now that we've implemented a web method, we'll want to test it out. Testing this is similar to testing a web application; it can all be done using a web browser. In some ways, it is far simpler, however, due to the fact that the functionality is contained within discrete methods that take and return specific parameters, rather than the verbose, UI-driven nature of web pages.

Try it Out – Testing a Web Service

In order to test any methods that we create, we must do the following:

❑   Set the web service project and .asmx file that we're going to test

❑   Build and run the project

❑   Select the web method to test

❑   Enter the parameters and execute the method

1.   To test web service functionality, we must first specify the default item that we're interested in. To do this, right-click on the FriendsService project within the Solution Explorer, and set it as the startup project (this ensures that when we run the solution, it is this project that begins).

Next, right-click on the FriendsInfo.asmx file within this project, and set this as the start page. This has the same effect as in a web application – informing the environment that when the solution is built and run, it should navigate to this location by default.

2.   The next step is to compile and run the solution using *F5*, and then we can see the results:

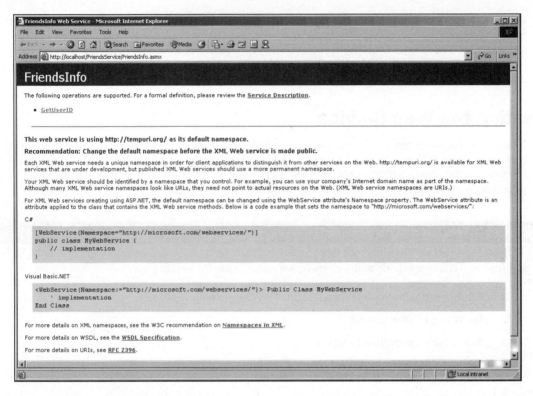

Keep in mind that this page is only meant for testing purposes, and isn't intended as a public interface to the web service. Having said that, whenever we create a web service using Visual Studio .NET, this is always available to us and other users as a method of discovering what the web service offers, and a way of testing it. The main point of interest to us on the page is the list of hyperlinked methods that are displayed near the top of the screen. This list takes us to a definition of every function or subroutine that was marked as a web method in our code.

3. The pages that are displayed when we select the hyperlinked method names presented to us provide the means to test our web service. Click on the one entry in the list, GetUserID – this will take you to a second page that is again generated by .NET:

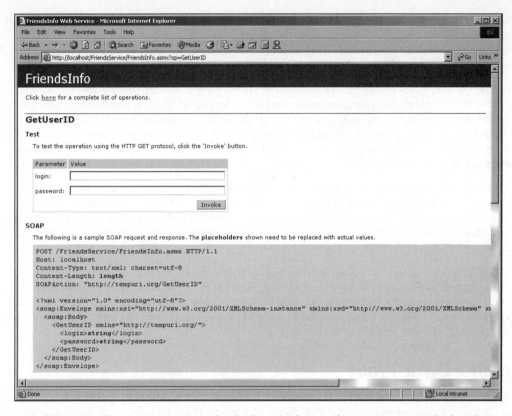

This page allows us to test the individual method using the HTTP-GET method, and provides us with other details such as the SOAP requests and responses that are used beneath the hood to make the necessary calls. (You can ignore this information for now; we'll discuss it shortly.) Enter the usual user name and password combination of wrox and wrox and then click the Invoke button. This will create a new window in which the method is called. The method should return the following XML, containing the user ID for the wrox user:

```
<?xml version="1.0" encoding="utf-8" ?>
<string xmlns="http://tempuri.org/">
  436EA455-BABD-4ca2-9D30-7B4F4608A068
</string>
```

How It Works

If we take a look at the URL once we'd clicked the Invoke button, we can see how the method was selected and called:

http://localhost/Friendsservice/FriendsInfo.asmx/GetUserID?Login=wrox&Password=wrox.

The web method itself is called by appending its name after the URL to the ASMX file, and passing the parameters to the method on the query string in the same way we pass parameters to a web page. If we want to, we can edit these parameters directly.

Obviously, passing a username and password over an unencrypted URL should not be carried out in production systems; in addition to using unencrypted HTTP, web services can also use HTTPS. This could then be combined with methods of calling web services other than an HTTP-GET, ensuring that parameters aren't placed on the URL, and that all of the data is encrypted.

While these web pages provide us, as developers, with a great means of viewing and testing web services, the textual descriptions, textboxes, and so on, are not of the structured nature used by other applications when interfacing with web services. If the Service Description link is selected from the FriendsInfo.asmx page, we are taken to a page with the query string parameter of ?WSDL. This parameter can be added to any ASMX URL, and provides us with the WSDL (**Web Service Description Language**) definition of the service.

This WSDL definition is an XML document that specifies all of the methods and data types that compose our web service. It is used by other systems to retrieve all of the information necessary to call a service. If you view this document, you'll see that it defines the parameters that are expected when the () method is called, and the response that this returns. It then goes on to detail the way that the method can be called – either through an HTTP-GET, and HTTP-POST, or through a SOAP call.

The HTTP-POST method of calling web services performs exactly the same function for web services as it does for web applications – rather than passing parameters on the URL as in the case of an HTTP-GET, it sends them in the body of the request. SOAP calls are an alternative to either of these methods; they make use of XML documents for the sending of parameters and the retrieval of return-values. We'll look at SOAP in more detail later in the chapter.

Complex Data Types

The web method that we've created above returns a string. As we mentioned, applications making use of the functionality that we expose determine this by examining the WSDL definition of our services. While returning such simple data as strings and integers will work fine this way, what happens when we want to return something more complicated, such as an object containing all of the requests for contact for a person?

When retrieving this information from the database, and passing it around internally using normal methods, we could use a DataSet. If we implement a web method that does just the same, then we can test it in our browser and see how it is dealt with.

Try It Out – Returning Complex Data Types

To implement this functionality we'll need to create a new method, within our service, that takes in a user ID as a parameter and returns a DataSet. Within this method, we can have a simple piece of SQL code that returns all of the contact requests for that individual.

1. Add the following new web method to the FriendsInfo class in FriendsInfo.asmx.cs:

```
[WebMethod]
public DataSet ContactRequests(string userId)
{
  string sql = @"
    SELECT [Notes], [FirstName], [LastName], [Email]
```

```
        FROM [Contact] INNER JOIN [User] ON
        [UserID] = [RequestID] WHERE [DestinationID] = '" + userId + "'";

    DataSet requests = new DataSet();
    new SqlDataAdapter(sql, cnFriends).Fill(requests);
    return requests;
}
```

2. Add the following `using` statement to the top of the code:

```
using System;
using System.Collections;
using System.ComponentModel;
using System.Data;
using System.Data.SqlClient;
using System.Diagnostics;
using System.Web;
using System.Web.Services;
```

3. Save, recompile, and restart the application. You'll see that there are now two methods listed on the page that is displayed, since we now have two web methods in the code-behind page.

Click on the **ContactRequests** link; this brings up the test page for this method. Paste the user ID that was generated from the `GetUserID()` method into this textbox and click the **Invoke** button. This will generate a new browser window, containing the XML that the .NET Framework generates from the `DataSet`.

The output should be similar to the screenshot below. It's a rather large XML document:

How It Works

To retrieve all of the contact requests, we need both the entries from the Contact table in our database, and the user's information from the User table. We write the SQL to do this using a JOIN, linking the RequestID field in the Contact table to the corresponding user:

```
SELECT
  [Notes], [FirstName], [LastName], [Email]
FROM
  [Contact]
INNER JOIN
  [User] ON [UserID] = [RequestID]
```

This is the SQL that we've specified in the sql variable in the ContactRequests() web method. This method takes in the user ID that we'd previously given out as a parameter, and inserts its value into the SQL string using concatenation:

```
public DataSet ContactRequests(string userId)
{
   string sql = @"
     SELECT [Notes], [FirstName], [LastName], [Email]
     FROM [Contact] INNER JOIN [User] ON
     [UserID] = [RequestID] WHERE [DestinationID] = '" + userId + "'";
```

When we return a complex data-type, such as a DataSet from a web method, it undergoes a process known as **XML serialization**, whereby an object gets converted to an XML string that represents it. XML is a good technology for doing this as it allows for arbitrarily large and complex data structures, making it possible to store almost any type of data in a convenient format. DataSets have better support than most objects for converting to this string-based representation, but almost all data types can be serialized automatically, whether they are structs, arrays, or some other type.

Serialization is only half of the story, though. Once another application has retrieved the data in this format, it can de-serialize it back into an object. De-serialization is the reverse process to that performed above; it takes the XML string that was built during serialization, and creates an object of the correct type, ready-populated with the data contained within the XML document (and hence representing the original object).

Thankfully, rather than having to implement the serialization and de-serialization process ourselves, when we create a web service, .NET creates a wrapper for us, allowing all of this processing to happen behind the scenes, leaving us to just get on with writing our applications. We'll see this de-serialization in action shortly, when we make use of the services that we've created. Before doing this, it's important to note that, in allowing Visual Studio .NET to take care of all of this for us, we can no longer return this data to a non-.NET application without writing a lot of wrapper code ourselves.

Consuming a Web Service

Now that we've created a web service, the logical next step is to **consume** (or make use of) it from another program, just as a third-party would do. As a demonstration of this, we'll create a test application that, rather than displaying the XML that is produced when we test a method using an Internet browser, makes use of the services as though they were functionality local to the application.

To implement our consumer, we'll need to create a new project. In this case we'll create a standard Windows application to show that web services aren't only useful in the creation of web applications. To start with, we'll just test out our `Login()` method. In order to do this, we'll need to create textboxes for the username and password, and add a reference within our project to the web service to allow us to make use of its functionality.

1. Add a new C# Windows Application project to the solution and call it WebServiceConsumer. This application can be located anywhere on your local machine. Once the IDE has finished creating all the associated files, it will present you with a blank form.

2. Onto this form, drag two `TextBox` controls, two `Label` controls, and one `Button` control. These controls should have their `Name` and `Text` properties set as detailed below:

Control	Name	Text
Label1	lblLogin	User name:
Label2	lblPassword	Password:
TextBox1	txtLogin	(none)
TextBox2	txtPassword	(none)
Button	btnTest	Test Service

The controls should be arranged on the form so that they appear like this:

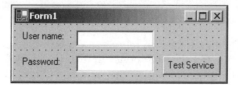

3. The next step is to **reference** the web service so that the functionality we're going to develop can make use of it. Adding a **web reference** performs a similar function to adding a reference to a .NET assembly – it allows the IDE to know the location of the external objects we're using and methods we're calling.

To add a web reference, locate the References folder for the current project in the solution tree, right-click on it, and select the Add Web Reference... option from the context menu.

355

This will bring up the Add Web Reference dialog (shown in a moment), which allows you to locate web services being hosted, either locally or at any publicly visible URL. It also allows you to view details about them and test them (where supported) before they're added to the project.

To add the reference, enter the location of our web service into the Address bar at the top of the dialog. The URL for this should be http://localhost/FriendsService/FriendsInfo.asmx.

Hit the Go button (the little green arrow next to the Address bar). The IDE will retrieve the URL specified, and display details about the service in the two panes. The left-hand pane will contain the same web page that we saw when we browsed to the web service in our browser. The right-hand pane displays details of the actual web services that are available at that URL. If there is an error retrieving web service information from the specified URL then it will be displayed in this right-hand pane.

Once the URL has been located, and the pages have loaded, the dialog should look like this:

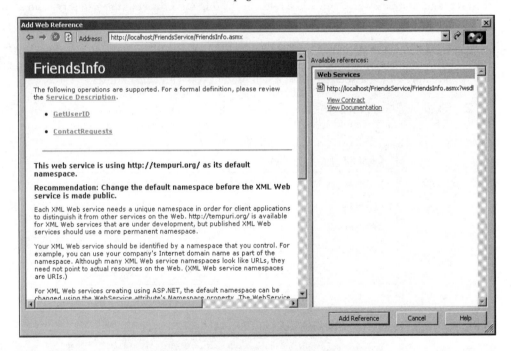

4. To complete the addition of the web reference, click on the Add Reference button. It's worth noting that we can also test the web service in this window before clicking the button; if we are making use of a third-party web service, it is a good idea to ensure it's functioning as expected before trying to make use of it.

   To make the name of the web reference more memorable and meaningful, right-click on the localhost entry in the tree (in the Solution Explorer) and rename it to FriendsService. It will then allow us to use that as the part of the fully-qualified name for the service.

The project tree for **WebServiceConsumer** will now look like the following:

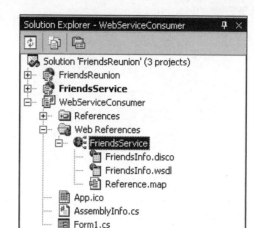

5. Now we can start adding code that makes use of the web methods just as though they were in a built-in class, such as a `DataSet` – the runtime will take care of calling the remote service and handling the data marshaling. This code will be called when the **Test Service** button is clicked, so to create a procedure to contain the functionality, simply double-click the button, and let the environment create the procedure, called `btnTest_Click`. In this procedure, enter the following code fragment to retrieve the user ID for the user name and password specified:

```
private void btnTest_Click(object sender, System.EventArgs e)
{
    FriendsService.FriendsInfo fi = new FriendsService.FriendsInfo();
    string userId;

    userId = fi.GetUserID(txtLogin.Text, txtPassword.Text);

    MessageBox.Show(userId);
}
```

6. That completes the implementation of the simple consumer application, so we can save, compile, and run it. In order to run this project, you'll need to set it as the startup project for the solution (by right-clicking on the project and selecting **Set as Startup Project**, as we have done in previous examples). Once the application is running, enter `wrox` as both the user name and password in the appropriate textboxes, and click the **Test Service** button. Note that for this test application, the **Password** field has been left as a standard textbox; we could easily have masked the input (by setting the `PasswordChar` property of the textbox to * or any other character), but this application is just for testing the web service, so we want to make it as easy-to-use as possible.

The application should bring up a message box containing the user ID for the wrox user of the *Friends Reunion* application:

If you enter details of a user that does not exit, then an empty string will be returned to the application, causing a blank message box to be displayed.

How It Works

The code with the btnTest_Click method first creates two variables – one to contain an instance of the FriendsInfo web service, and a string to store the returned UserID. The subsequent lines of code call the method GetUserID() (passing in the user name and password entered), and display the user ID in a message box. Note how the call to the GetUserID() method looks identical to calls to any other regular class method.

As mentioned above, the .NET runtime takes care of determining that the method we're calling is actually part of a web service. This is done at compile time, meaning that all of the wrappers required are created there and then, rather than on the fly when the web method is being called.

Try It Out – Retrieving Contact Requests

Now that we've seen how our GetUserID() method can be called from within an application, we can extend our consumer application to retrieve the contact-requests for users. To do this, we'll need to call the ContactRequests() method, passing in the user ID that we've retrieved, and add a DataGrid to the form in order to present the DataSet of results that are returned.

1. To add a DataGrid to the test application, expand the form to make some space, then drag one from the **Toolbox** onto the space created. Change its Name property to grdResults:

2. Switch back to the code view for the form, and replace the MessageBox.Show() method call with the following code, which will call the ContactRequests() method and bind the results to the DataGrid:

```
private void btnTest_Click(object sender, System.EventArgs e)
{
    FriendsService.FriendsInfo fi = new FriendsService.FriendsInfo();
    string userId;
```

```
userId= fi.GetUserID(txtLogin.Text, txtPassword.Text);
```

```
DataSet requests;
requests = fi.ContactRequests(userId);
grdResults.DataSource = requests.Tables[0];
}
```

The only point to note here is that the DataSource is being specified as requests.Tables[0]. This ensures that, when the data grid is drawn, the results will automatically be displayed, rather than requiring the user to expand the tables within the data set to find them.

The IDE normally adds the System.Data reference to the top of your code automatically, but if it hasn't then you should add the following using statement yourself:

```
using System.Data;
```

3. Start the application again and we'll see the effects of our coding. Enter the same user name and password, and click the Test Service button. This will now present the user with a full listing of all their outstanding contact requests, which will look like the following:

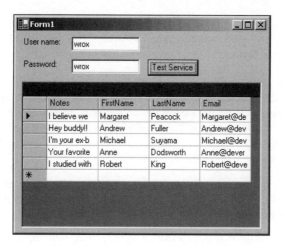

How It Works

When we make a call to a web method within our code, we're not talking directly to the remote web method. What actually happens is that .NET creates a **proxy** around the web service. This is a class that appears outwardly as though it is the method that we want to call itself. When we make a call to the imported functionality, it is this proxy that our code talks to; it deals with the nuts and bolts of passing requests to the service. It also deals with serializing parameters being passed in to the method, and de-serializing return values.

This class is generated as soon as we add the reference to the web service in our project. If we select the Show All Files option in the Solution Explorer, we can find this class as a child of the Reference Map item that is now shown in the project.

SOAP

Although there's no need for us to go deep down into the gory details (as .NET takes care of it all for us) it's useful to know where the buzz-word **SOAP** (which originally stood for **Simple Object Access Protocol**) comes in to all of this, as it plays a fundamental behind-the-scenes role in web services.

SOAP is an alternative means of making remote method calls to the HTTP-GET (and HTTP-POST) options that we've already discussed. It is used in .NET as the default method for accessing web services. This is due to the richer functionality that it offers, namely a more structured way of alerting the calling application to errors (which we'll cover shortly), support for return parameters (reference parameters), and other such features.

SOAP is a specification that defines the XML format for messages to be sent in. The specification consists of three items:

❑ An **envelope** that defines a framework for describing what is in a message and how to process it

❑ A set of encoding rules for expressing instances of **application-defined data types**

❑ A convention for representing **remote procedure calls and responses** (in the case of .NET, this is HTTP); all of this encoding is in XML

The latter two of these items should just be taken as is – there's not much that we can do with them simply, they just define how operations are to be performed and data is to be defined. The first, the *envelope*, is worth looking at further.

As mentioned above, SOAP uses XML to send information between applications as messages. This usage of XML supports the sending of the data in a well-structured format; this allows us to provide more robust systems than would be the case if the only way of accessing web services was by passing parameters on a URL – imagine trying to pass an entire dataset around using only a query string!

Within the SOAP envelope, two main types of message exist, both of which are based on XML:

❑ **SOAP Request** – This is sent to a SOAP-compliant application (such as IIS) to invoke a method exposed by a web service. The request includes such information as the arguments required by the method.

❑ **SOAP Response** – This is returned from a SOAP-compliant application and contains the results of processing a SOAP request, if it completed successfully.

There is a direct comparison between the SOAP request and response, and the standard HTTP request and response. In the case of our web services, each of the SOAP messages maps directly to the underlying HTTP messages.

If an error occurs during processing that is not handled, or the developer throws an exception, then a special type of message, a **SOAP Fault**, is sent in place of the SOAP response. This message contains details of the exception that was thrown, and allows us to provide information about errors in a standardized format that can be interpreted by a system easily, as opposed to the error pages that get displayed to alert users to errors in web-applications.

As mentioned above, a SOAP message is transmitted within an **envelope**, just like sending a letter. This allows extra information to be transmitted along with the message. The diagram below shows the basic structure of a SOAP message, whether it's a request or a response:

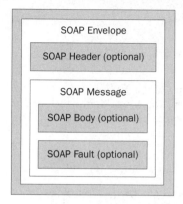

❑   The SOAP Envelope contains the entire SOAP message.

❑   The SOAP Header contains information about transactions, security, logon information, the source of a request, and so on. These are similar in functionality to HTTP headers

❑   The SOAP Message contains either a SOAP fault or a SOAP body item.

❑   The SOAP Body contains the bulk of the request/response message, including the name of the method to call and the parameters that are to be passed to it, or the response generated after the call.

❑   The SOAP Fault contains details of errors that occurred. This is only available if an un-trapped error was raised, and can only ever be part of a SOAP response message.

Other than when we're testing our methods through a browser, or when we implement a lot of the nuts and bolts work of creating web services ourselves rather than relying on Visual Studio .NET, we never really get exposed to the underlying SOAP messages. If an application being developed has to integrate with a platform other than .NET, then such messages become far more important, as they may not be directly compatible with the output generated by the IDE.

We can see an example of a SOAP request and response if we browse to the URL http://localhost/FriendsReunion/FriendsInfo.asmx?op=GetUserID.

Beneath the input boxes that allow us to enter the user name and password information, we are presented with a sample SOAP request and response for the method, GetUserID(), that we are examining. The first block of code details the request. This can be split into two parts; the XML document that is the data we're interested in sending, and all of the information that is required to send this document via HTTP. The headers merely ensure that the HTTP request being sent is well-formed and complies with standards. Beneath this is the SOAP message that we're interested in:

```
<?xml version="1.0" encoding="utf-8"?>
<soap:Envelope xmlns:xsi="http://www.w3.org/2001/XMLSchema-instance"
               xmlns:xsd="http://www.w3.org/2001/XMLSchema"
```

```
                         xmlns:soap="http://schemas.xmlsoap.org/soap/envelope/">
    <soap:Body>
      <GetUserID xmlns="http://tempuri.org/">
        <login>string</login>
        <password>string</password>
      </GetUserID>
    </soap:Body>
  </soap:Envelope>
```

We can see in this that the structure of the XML follows the diagram we saw earlier very closely. The root node in the document is the `soap:Envelope`, which in turn contains a `soap:Body`. This body then details the name of the method to be called, along with the parameters to pass to it. The occurrences of *string* within the `login` and `password` tags are where we'd insert the values for these parameters – `wrox` for instance.

Error Handling in Web Services

As with any piece of code, there is the potential for an error to occur during the processing of a web service. This may either be through a mistake in the original implementation, or because an external error has occurred, such as losing a database connection. In the .NET projects we've looked at so far, this is handled through the throwing of **exceptions**. Such exceptions aren't only used when an unhandled error occurs; they can also be **thrown** within code whenever we want to abort processing, and signify to the caller that a special (usually undesired) state has been reached.

This method is also available to us when we're developing web services. The main caveat here is with the details that are returned to us when we allow Visual Studio .NET to create the proxies around services for us; every exception that is thrown is wrapped up within another `SOAPException` error, which doesn't store all of the details of our original .NET exceptions, making handling them a little more difficult. This does not stop us from handling errors in a manageable fashion, however, as we see below.

Try It Out – Handling Errors

To show how we can handle errors, we'll have to update both our web service, and our consumer application; the service needs to throw exceptions when an error occurs, and the consumer needs to trap and make use of them.

1. Looking at the `GetUserID()` function that we wrote in our web service, it should be clear that if an invalid user name and password are passed into the system, it will simply return an empty string. Rather than have the calling application determine that this empty string means that no match was found, we can throw an exception that informs the application of the result if no match was found.

To add such a mechanism to the service, first switch to the code view of the `GetUserID()` method in `FriendsInfo.asmx` and modify the code in the function as follows:

```
public string GetUserID(string login, string password)
{
  cmUser.Parameters[0].Value = login;
  cmUser.Parameters[1].Value = password;
  string sql = "SELECT [UserID] FROM [User] " +
    "WHERE [Login] = '{0}' AND [Password] = '{1}'";
  cmUser.CommandText = string.Format(sql, login, password);
  string id;

  try
  {
    cnFriends.Open();
    id = (string)this.cmUser.ExecuteScalar();
  }
  finally
  {
    cnFriends.Close();
  }
  if(id==null || id.Length==0)
  {
    throw new SoapException("No user ID found!",
      SoapException.ClientFaultCode, Context.Request.Url.AbsoluteUri);
  }
  return id;
}
```

Now, whenever the user passes in a user name and password that don't correspond to a user ID, the application will throw a SoapException, derived (inherited) from a standard Exception. Since the application throws a SoapException, we also need to add the following using statement to the top of the code-behind page:

```
using System.Web.Services.Protocols;
```

2. Now that we've altered this method so that it specifically throws exceptions, we must update our consumer application to ensure that it doesn't fall over when no matching user ID is found. In other words, we need to make use of this exception, by catching it whenever it is thrown.

To do this, switch back to the code view of the Form1.cs file in the **WebServiceConsumer** application, and locate the btnTest_Click method, and add a try...catch block like this:

```
private void btnTest_Click(object sender, System.EventArgs e)
{
  FriendsService.FriendsInfo fi = new FriendsService.FriendsInfo();
  string userId;

  try
  {
    userId= fi.GetUserID(txtLogin.Text, txtPassword.Text);
  }
```

```
    catch (SoapException ex)
    {
      grdResults.DataSource = null;
      MessageBox.Show("An error occurred:\r\n" + ex.Message);
      return;
    }

    DataSet requests;
    requests = fi.ContactRequests(userId);
    grdResults.DataSource = requests.Tables[0];
}
```

You'll need to add a `using` statement for the `System.Web.Services.Protocols` namespace to this file, too:

```
using System.Web.Services.Protocols;
```

In addition to alerting the user, the assignment of `null` to the data grid's data source ensures that old values aren't still displayed on the form, and the `return` call exits the routine. Note, that again, since we are catching a `SoapException`, we need to add an extra `using` statement to the top of the code.

3. Start the project, and click on **Test Service** without entering a user name or password. A dialog will pop up, almost as we expected. It doesn't simply contain the following text that we'd expect:

> An error occurred:
> No UserID found!

Rather, you'll be presented with something like this:

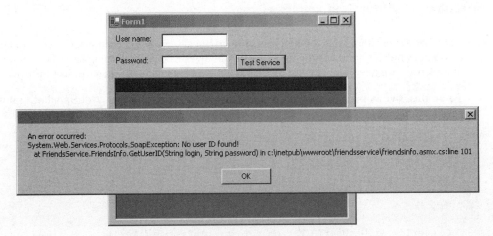

This is due to the wrapper that .NET has created around our web service for us, and unfortunately, there's little we can do to resolve the issue without writing our own wrapper.

4. We might not be able to stop the errors from being formatted in this manner when they're returned, but we can write a bit of code to retrieve solely our original message using string manipulation, as long as we only ever return a single line error message. To do this, amend the `catch` block as follows:

```
catch (SoapException ex)
{
    grdResults.DataSource = null;
    MessageBox.Show("An error occurred:\r\n" +
        ex.Message.Substring(45, ex.Message.IndexOf("\n") - 45));
    return;
}
```

After this modification, clicking on the **Test Service** button as before, we will be presented with a different, more aesthetically pleasing dialog box:

How It Works

Within our code, we can throw exceptions just like in any other code. These could technically be any exception supported by the CLR, such as an `ArgumentException`, an `ApplicationException`, and so on. Rather than use these, we are provided with a special type of exception, the `SoapException`. This provides us with a structure within which can store more appropriate and detailed information than with more generic exceptions. Such information includes the URL at which the error occurred, and details of what caused the error.

In our example above, these two items were determined by the respective values `SoapException.ClientFaultCode` and `Context.Request.Url.AbsoluteUri`. The `ClientFaultCode` value specifies that the error was due to the values that were passed into the function, and the `AbsoluteUri` property returns the location at which the code is running. When we passed these values to the constructor of the `SoapException`, we made use of one of the six overloaded methods. Alternatives exist that allow us to return more or less information.

No matter how we configure our `SoapException`, it will always be wrapped within a containing `Exception` whenever we throw it from a web method that Visual Studio .NET has generated the wrapper for. If we ever needed to make use of the full power of `SoapExceptions`, we'd be forced to do more of the work ourselves.

From the example just given, it should be clear that providing an error handling mechanism in your code not only allows for the simple detection of certain conditions, but also allows for richer interaction with the user, informing them of mistakes, prompting them to retry, and so on. In a real-world application, such error handling should also be added to the `ContactRequests()` method, in case an invalid user ID was passed through as a parameter.

Web Service Efficiency

Performance is a consideration with any application, and web services are no exception. With web services, there are two main approaches to efficiency and optimizing performance:

❑   Caching

❑   Asynchronous communication

This section covers each of these in relation to our *Friends Reunion* application, showing how they can be applied.

Caching

In many ways, caching in web services is very similar to caching with web-pages; a **duration** is specified to determine how long a response is cached for, and after the request has been processed for the first time (with a given set of input parameters), this version will be cached until the duration has expired. We will describe below how to add caching to web methods, and also cover when and when not to cache information.

Try It Out – Caching Information

Adding caching to web services is done on a per-method basis – each method can have its own caching settings applied. The data being returned by one of our methods – `ContactRequests()` – is fairly static in nature. Although a new contact-request may be made, it is more than likely not imperative that the recipient of this request sees it immediately, making it suitable for caching.

1.   To add this functionality, open the code view of the `FriendsInfo.asmx` file in our `FriendsService` project. In this file, locate the `ContactRequests()` web method. The function's definition is already prefixed with the attribute `[WebMethod]`. To implement caching, just amend this attribute so that it reads as follows:

```
[WebMethod(CacheDuration=600)]
```

This specifies, in seconds, how long the item should be cached for. In this case, we've chosen 600 seconds, or 10 minutes.

2.   We haven't changed the signature of any of the methods in the service, so there is no need to update the reference from within our consumer. You just need to recompile the application to ensure that this change is applied; then we're ready to test the application again to see that this caching is working. You can do all this by the *F5* (compile-and-debug) shortcut.

3.   With the test application running, enter the username **wrox** and password **wrox**, and click **Test Service** button. This will show all the requests for contact that this user has made so far.

Now switch to the web site, log in with the same username and password, and make a *new* request for contact using the `Search.aspx` facility created in Chapter 6.

When that's done, return to the test application and click the **Test Service** button again. If less than 10 minutes has passed since the *last* time you pressed the **Test Service** button, the test application's datagrid will show you the cached version of the data again – so you won't see the new request for contact you just added via the web site. But if you took *more* than 10 minutes to add the new request for contact, then the data in the cache will have expired and will be regenerated – so the datagrid *will* include the new request for contact.

Caching Wisely

Although caching can greatly improve performance (the speed boost with our `ContactRequests()` method should be noticeable when testing the application), we should always cache information judiciously.

For instance, if we added caching to the `GetUserID()` method, we could end up with some very unhappy users. This could happen if a user tried to access the system with an incorrect password, and a 'fail' response is returned. If their password was then changed to that (previously incorrect) one, then they would not be able to access the system until that cached response expired, and a new 'valid' one was generated. Caching should only be added to methods that don't need to guarantee returning information that is correct to the second. This makes them very useful for caching results of intensive processing, such as weather reports, but not for far more dynamic data, such as current stock market prices for trading systems.

Asynchronous Communication

In situations where the most up-to-date data must be used at all times and the amount of data involved is large, an alternative method of improving performance is often possible – **asynchronous communication**. This differs from the traditional model where, once the request is made, the program continues to wait until a response is received. With asynchronous communication, once a request has been made, the application is free to continue running. Once the response has been prepared and transmitted, the program will be notified that it can make use of the data that has been returned.

This notification takes place through a user-defined method (known as an **event sink**) which is associated with the service. This method is called when the web method has completed processing, and can retrieve the values returned from the web service from the parameters passed into it:

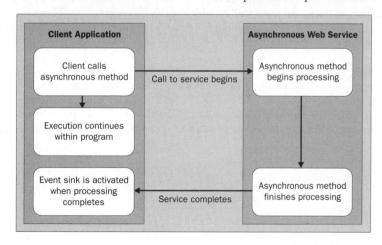

By making use of this paradigm, feedback can be given to the user much more quickly, even if all they are told is that they will be notified once their requested task has completed, and the processing goes on in the background. Such a mechanism can be implemented simply with .NET web services, as the framework takes care of all of the hard work for us, as well as providing us with simple wrappers for methods such as `ContactRequests()` (which we've already used above, and which is the synchronous version of the request), it also provides us with others versions of that request, `BeginContactRequests()` and `EndContactRequests()`. Although it's beyond the scope of this book, these methods can be used to start asynchronous calls, and deal with them when they terminate. Further details of this can be found in *Professional ASP.NET Web Services* (Wrox, ISBN 186100-545-8).

In our *Friends Reunion* application, we could make use of the features such a communications method gives us by uploading an XML document, like the one we created in Chapter 8. If this document became fairly large, then rather than waiting for the request to finish processing before continuing, we could provide a status bar showing the progress of the import, leaving the user free to continue working on other tasks.

Refining our Web Service

As well as these two main methods of increasing efficiency, other options are available to us, from simple options like reducing the amount of data being transferred, to more complex solutions, such as adding state to our web services.

Reducing the Amount of Data Involved

The constituents of servicing a request for a web method can be split into three parts:

- ❏ Requesting information
- ❏ Performing processing
- ❏ Returning results

We've just covered how to lower the processing overhead using caching, but this still leaves the time taken to request data and retrieve results. This part of the overall round trip time is governed by two factors – the amount of data, and the speed at which it can be transmitted. There is little that we can do to improve transmission speed without paying for faster Internet connections, leaving us with the option of lowering the amount of data transferred.

When we're making simple calls, such as to the `GetUserID()` method, there is little that can be done to decrease the amount of data; there is very little there to start with. In the case of retrieving a list of contact-requests, we could replace the dataset used with a simpler data type that is more portable across platforms, such as an array. The main drawback to doing this would be the reduction in flexibility; the structure of a dataset could be amended without altering the type, which is not necessarily the case with an array.

Try it Out – Returning Less Data

Given that datasets are a very heavyweight method of storing data, there are several options open to us when trying to optimize the `ContactRequests()` method. The first thing we'll do is return the dataset as an XML string, omitting the verbose schema that accompanies the serialization of datasets. We'll then update the consumer to make use of this amended data format. Once that's done, we'll take a look at ways of returning even less data in highly performance-critical situations.

1. In the `FriendsInfo.asmx.cs` file, locate the `ContactRequests()` method, and update it to match the code below, causing a `string` to be returned rather than a `DataSet`:

```
public string ContactRequests(string userId)
{
  string sql = @"
    SELECT [Notes], [FirstName], [LastName], [Email]
    FROM [Contact] INNER JOIN [User] ON
    [UserID] = [RequestID] WHERE [DestinationID] = '" + userId + "'";

  DataSet requests = new DataSet();
  new SqlDataAdapter(sql, cnFriends).Fill(requests);
  return requests.GetXml();
}
```

2. Because we've altered the *signature* of the web method, it no longer either accepts or returns the same number or type of parameters that it did previously.

As the web reference could technically be a link to functionality on the other side of the world that is unavailable for long periods of time, .NET doesn't automatically update the details of these references; as far as our test application is concerned, we've not changed our web service at all. To synchronize it with the latest version of the service, you must rebuild the project (by selecting the **Rebuild Solution** option from the **Build** menu).

3. Now switch to the `WebServiceConsumer` project. Right-click the **FriendsService** entry under **Web References** in the solution tree for the project, and then select the **Update Web Reference** option.

4. With the references updated, we can tweak the code to make use of our amended method. Within the `btnTest_Click` method in the `Form1.cs` file, modify the following code:

```
private void btnTest_Click(object sender, System.EventArgs e)
{
  FriendsService.FriendsInfo fi = new FriendsService.FriendsInfo();
  string userId;

  try
  {
    userId= fi.GetUserID(txtLogin.Text, txtPassword.Text);
  }
```

```
    catch (SoapException ex)
    {
      grdResults.DataSource = null;
      MessageBox.Show("An error occurred:\r\n" +
        ex.Message.Substring(45, ex.Message.IndexOf("\n") - 45));
      return;
    }

    DataSet requests = new DataSet();
    requests.ReadXml(new StringReader(fi.ContactRequests(userId)));
    grdResults.DataSource = requests.Tables[0];
  }
```

Also add the following `using` statement so that we can use the `StringReader` class:

```
using System.IO;
```

This will create a new `DataSet`, then read the information into it from the XML string that is now returned from our web service. Once the `DataSet` is populated, we can bind the data grid to one of its tables, just as before.

5. If you like, you can start the project, and prove that this functionality works. What is more interesting, though, is testing the `ContactRequests()` method in a browser. To do this, type http://localhost/FriendsService/FriendsInfo.asmx into the browser, click the ContactRequests link, and type in the User ID as before. The window showing the returned XML will look similar to the following:

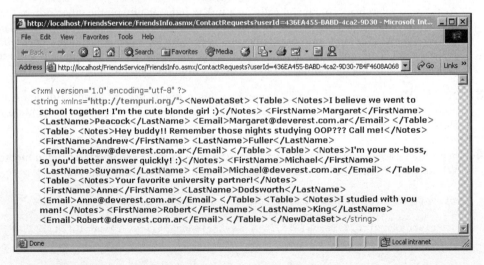

If you compare this with the screenshot earlier in the chapter, you'll can see that there is far less data present.

How It Works

Retrieving the contact requests from the database into a dataset isn't an expensive operation, as we can assume that our connection to the database server from the web server is of high bandwidth. It is returning the data from here to the client that can cause poor performing applications. To overcome this, we can take this dataset, and convert it into a more lightweight structure, in this case, simply a string, within the business logic of the service. We can then return this simpler data instead, making for a far lower data overhead.

If we look back at the screenshot above, we can see that the XML that defines the dataset is not indented or highlighted nicely, unlike the rest of the XML. This is because, as far as the web service is concerned, we are merely returning a string that needn't contain an XML document. As well as a point of interest, it is worth noting that this also means we have lost the ability to validate the data being returned against a rigid schema; *any* string would now be an acceptable output of the method, even though a dataset at the client couldn't be populated from it. For this reason, whenever we perform an optimization such as this, we should ensure that the data we've retrieved is of the correct format.

Further Optimizations

If datasets did not support the lightweight GetXml() method, we'd have to resort to alternative means of returning less data. The options we have available to us are the same as those we'd have with other types of object, and allow us a finer level of control over the amount, and format of the data returned.

Try It Out – Returning Custom Data Types

To demonstrate this, we can create a new method that returns the same data as our ContactRequests() method, but with a different name. By implementing it this way, we can compare the output of the methods side by side, and won't have to update our WebServiceConsumer application when we're finished.

1. Within the FriendsInfo.asmx code-behind file, we can see that, in the SQL statement, we are returning the following fields:

❑ FirstName

❑ LastName

❑ Email

❑ Notes

To represent this, we can add a struct called ContactItem to the FriendsInfo class, as follows:

```
public struct ContactItem
{
  public string FirstName;
  public string LastName;
  public string Email;
  public string Notes;
}
```

2. Next, add a new web method, called `ContactRequestsCustom()`, to the `FriendsInfo` class. This new class is exactly the same as the existing `ContactRequests()` method, except in the lines highlighted below:

```
[WebMethod(CacheDuration=600)]
public ContactItem[] ContactRequestsCustom(string userId)
{
    string sql = @"
      SELECT [Notes], [FirstName], [LastName], [Email]
      FROM [Contact] INNER JOIN [User] ON
      [UserID] = [RequestID] WHERE [DestinationID] = '" + userId + "'";

    DataSet requests = new DataSet();
    new SqlDataAdapter(sql, cnFriends).Fill(requests);

    ContactItem[] list = new ContactItem[requests.Tables[0].Rows.Count];
    for (int i = 0; i < requests.Tables[0].Rows.Count; i++)
    {
      list[i].FirstName = (string)requests.Tables[0].Rows[i]["FirstName"];
      list[i].LastName  = (string)requests.Tables[0].Rows[i]["LastName"];
      list[i].Email     = (string)requests.Tables[0].Rows[i]["Email"];
      list[i].Notes     = (string)requests.Tables[0].Rows[i]["Notes"];
    }
    return list;
}
```

As you can see, we've simply changed the return type, and replaced the `GetXml()` method call with a block of lines that move the data into an array containing `ContactItems`, and we return that array instead of the XML.

3. Rebuild the solution with these amendments, browse to the `FriendsInfo.asmx` file with a browser, and run the `ContactRequestsCustom()` web method. You'll be presented with an XML document similar to the following:

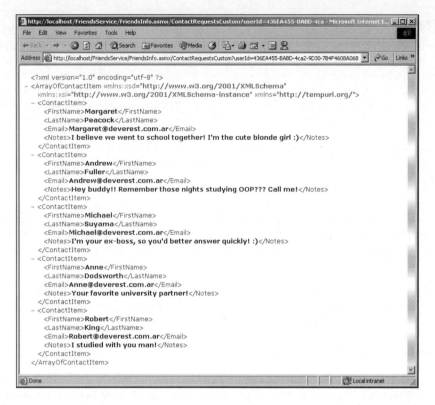

How It Works

As we saw earlier in the chapter, objects are converted into a string representation of themselves via a process of serialization. When we serialize an array of `ContactRequest` items, we obtain a structure consisting of:

❑   One tag to represent the array itself (`ArrayOfContactRequest`)

❑   One tag (`ContactRequest`) to denote the start/end of each `ContactRequest`

❑   One tag for each property of the `ContactRequest` (`FirstName`, `LastName`, and so on)

When we make use of this type of serialization, rather than the `GetXml()` method on a dataset, we not only return XML containing the data, but also have a definition of the structure of this XML provided in the WSDL for the service. This allows us to ensure that the data we're retrieving is of the right type, and in the right format, before we try to process it. There are performance considerations with this, also. When we return XML documents (as opposed to strings that merely happen to contain XML), validation that requires processing time has to take place to ensure that the document matches the schema.

The amount of information transmitted is a very important factor in overall performance as it can improve the performance across the board, even if we've already implemented asynchronous communication, caching, and other such techniques. Of course, once we have made such a change, applications that we had previously written (such as our WebServiceConsumer application) would need updating to make use of such changes in data types.

Adding State to Web Services

If we take a look at all of the web methods we have developed, we can see that they are all **stateless**. That is to say that the application doesn't remember the previous calls that have come in to it, or store any information based upon them. As a result of this, by default, we couldn't call one method that specified what place we are interested in, and then make subsequent calls related to this place, as we would be able to do with many other objects, such as a `SqlConnection`. An example of how this could be implemented in our *Friends Reunion* application is shown below:

```
localhost.Place MyPlace = new localhost.Place();
MyPlace.CurrentPlace = "Birmingham High School";
Debug.WriteLine(MyPlace.GetAddress());
MyPlace.UpdateNotes("There are no notes for this place");
```

This is the same issue that web developers came up against with traditional web application development, and the solution is also the same – the use of the `Session` object. This is exactly the same `Session` that is used for web sites, and functions in the same way – storing a cookie on the calling machine to identify it to .NET.

Adding such support for stateful web services is largely taken care of for us by the framework. From the point of view of the creation of a web service, all we need to do is update the attributes of the web service in a similar style to setting the `CacheDuration`:

```
[WebMethod(EnabledSession="true")]
```

The way this web service is consumed is slightly more interesting; since we're writing an application to use web services, rather than an internet browser, the cookie that is used to track our requests is only stored as long as we've got the same instance of an object. As an example of this, once `MyPlace` is set to `null`, or goes out of scope in the block of code above, the cookie is lost, and the session is ended. This can be seen as the web service equivalent of closing a browser window. There are ways of persisting these cookies, but these themselves must then be stored in some further location, such as another session.

Due to these limitations, and because of the added overhead that making use of session information and cookies has, we should be careful about when we use state with web services. It's also worth considering that stateful services may not be supported by other platforms.

As there is no real use for state in our web services, and the subject of session state was covered thoroughly in Chapter 6, there's no need for us do delve into an example here – it really is as simple as updating the attribute, though! For further information on this topic, you can refer to *Professional ASP.NET Web Services* (Wrox, ISBN 186100-545-8).

Third-party Web Services

Although it is very gratifying to create our own web services and publish them so that they can be used by other applications we create, and by those we tell about them, this barely scrapes the surface of the number of developers that may be interested in the information and functionality we have to share. Not to mention the web services that other people can provide to us to improve or speed up the development of our own applications.

We are helped out greatly in this area. This is one of the main reasons why web services are succeeding where previous technologies have failed. The solution to this is quite elegant – the creation of a web service to let developers know about other web services. This is known as **UDDI** (**U**niversal **D**escription, **D**iscovery, and **I**ntegration). Using these directories, you can look up the functionality that other developers have made available to the public, and inform others of your own services easily. These listings are maintained not only by Microsoft, but by several other companies including IBM. The simplest way to test these out is using Microsoft's own UDDI directory, though. To do this, you can simply select to add a new web reference in a project, and enter the URL http://uddi.microsoft.com/inquire.

Other than the services listed at this location, many of the more popular (and useful) web sites on the Internet are beginning to make their functionality available via web services. Two of the most interesting ones to try out with our *Friends Reunion* application are Google's search service, and Microsoft's MapPoint service. These can be found at the following web pages:

❑   www.google.com/apis

❑   www.microsoft.com/mappoint/net

These services can be utilized in your applications in an identical manner to those we create ourselves – by adding a web reference in the same way we did for our Windows forms client application. The only differences with commercial services are the requirements for information such as registration information to be passed in to method calls to allow usage statistics, billing data, and so on to be maintained by the provider. Using these services, you could click a link on the details of a person, and see all matches for them returned from a search engine, or you could display a map of a place next to its address.

Summary

In this chapter, we've had a brief introduction to web services, showing how they're not only an open standard in themselves, but are built up from other open standards such as HTTP and XML. We've seen that by making use of web services we have a method for allowing disparate applications to interact with one another very simply, whereas it would have taken a great deal of painstaking integration work in the past.

These features and ease of use were put into action in the development of web service functionality for our *Friends Reunion* application through the provision of such functionality as returning a user ID based upon user name and password information, and retrieving a list of contact requests for an individual. By creating a test application, we showed how this functionality can be used (consumed) as simply as any other object in .NET, once a reference has been added within the project.

After we'd created and used our own web services, we took a look at one of the key underlying technologies of web services, SOAP, which allows information to be passed around in a structured XML format. We then went on to look at exceptions, and saw how this tied in to SOAP with the `SoapException` object.

Following this we discussed the performance of services – how we can improve it by retrieving less data both using built-in mechanisms, and by writing our own. Other, more advanced topics were covered in this section too – the development of asynchronous and stateful web services.

Finally, we looked at how we can publish our web services so that others can use them, and how we can find third-party services to utilize in our own applications, and gave a few examples of services currently out there that can be used to add further functionality to our *Friends Reunion* application.

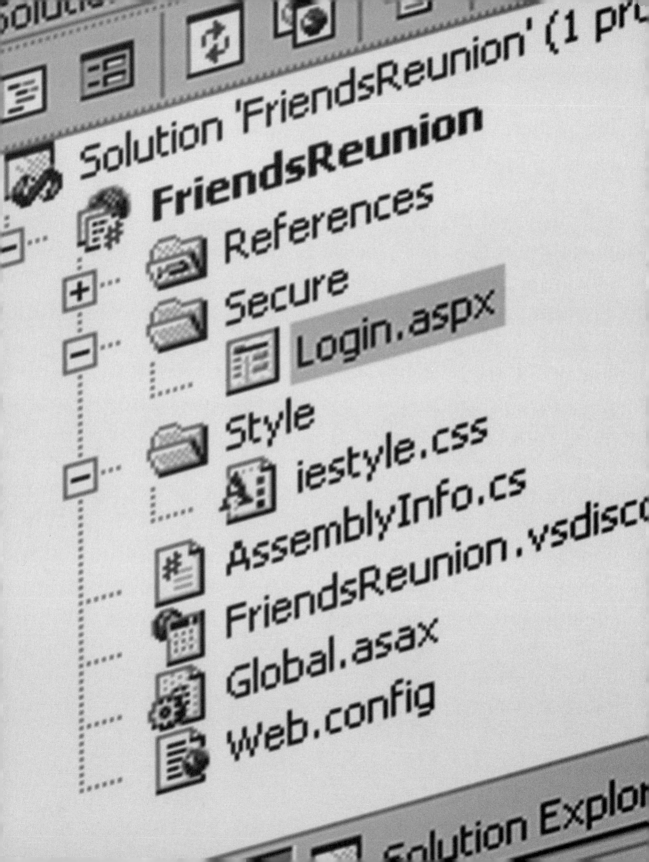

ASP.NET Authentication, Authorization, and Security

The role of **security** in an application is related to the need to restrict the ability of a user to access certain resources, or to perform certain actions. For example, a web application may offer administrative tools that should only be accessible to authorized users, or information that's restricted to registered users. (In fact, we've already seen this kind of thing in our *Friends Reunion* application.) It's also possible to apply different security-related settings at the web server level.

In this chapter, we will focus on ASP.NET, and see how to configure and take advantage of the security features it offers. ASP.NET works closely with IIS to provide the infrastructure available, so we will take a look at their interaction too.

During this chapter, we will discuss:

- ❑ The ASP.NET security infrastructure
- ❑ Interaction between ASP.NET, IIS, and the operating system
- ❑ Authentication and authorization – what are they and how they interact
- ❑ ASP.NET security settings
- ❑ Authentication options and how to use them

We've already seen some of these concepts in action, but we haven't said much about how they actually work. We will take a closer look at the mechanics during this chapter, and will gain a much better understanding of what is going on behind the scenes.

Overview

Security is a long-standing concept that pervades all kinds of software, including:

❑ Operating systems (think of the Windows NT/2000/XP login process)

❑ Web servers (think of the IIS manager's Application Settings and Directory Security settings)

❑ Database servers (remember the login process to add a connection to MSDE in Chapter 4)

❑ Desktop applications (you must know several)

❑ Web sites (such as e-commerce sites, or even Hotmail)

In each of these cases, the main purpose is to prohibit the unauthorized user from the ability to access sensitive information or perform sensitive tasks and actions. For example, we may want to prevent a user from posting comments on a site unless that user is logged in; or we may want to prohibit a developer from deleting records in a table, or creating a new database in a server, unless that user is sufficiently authorized.

With Internet connectivity available almost everywhere, this becomes increasingly important, because the information in your application has the potential to be exposed to the entire world. If an application isn't 'secure' (that is, if unauthorized access is possible), then you run the risk that users will be unwilling to trust it to keep critical information.

Whether you configure it carefully or not, your ASP.NET web applications will always have some kind of security in place. This is a consequence of the security architecture itself, which can be divided into three layers:

❑ **The operating system.** Unless you are using DOS or Windows 9x, there will always be some security in place. Windows NT/2000/XP use domains to keep users' information, and to ensure that they have permission to access resources such as files and folders, printers, network shares, and so on. Users must always log in before using the system, and every request made by a user is checked for the necessary permission before it is actioned.

❑ **The web server.** A web server runs in the operating system, and as such, also uses the security infrastructure built into it. Even when 'anonymous' access is enabled for an application, it will actually be bound to the account specified for the anonymous user – by default, the `IUSR_MACHINENAME` account.

❑ **The web application.** In order to run, an ASP.NET application needs IIS (of course), so it may come as no surprise that the security available in the previous two levels is always in effect, whether we explicitly decide to use it or not. At this level, we have some additional configuration options and features that ASP.NET offers over plain IIS settings.

Security Infrastructure

Before we dig into the implementation of the various security options available for our ASP.NET web applications, we will discuss some more generic concepts that are related to security in general, and to ASP.NET – IIS interaction in particular.

Essential Terminology

Because they crop up so frequently in discussions about security, we can start by making absolutely sure that we know what's meant by two key terms: authentication and authorization. If we get this right now, much of what follows will become a great deal easier.

Authentication and Authorization

In order for a user to get access to a resource with restricted access, they must first by **identified** and **authenticated**. This means that they have to provide some sort of identifier (such as a login name) and credentials (such as a password). (Here, the login name allows them to say who they are, and the password allow them to *prove* that they are who they say they are.) The way these credentials are validated depends on the authentication schema we choose. ASP.NET offers several, and we will discuss them during this chapter.

Once the user has been identified, and their identification has been authenticated, another step known as **authorization** takes place. Here, the process consists of checking whether the authenticated user has permission to access the resource they asked for. For example, an ordinary user may not be allowed to access certain administrative features of a web application.

As a side effect of authentication, an application may also provide customized content that's tailored at the current user accessing the resource. In fact, some applications will use security concepts with the sole aim of offering the user an improved experience through **personalization** – that is, by supplying content filtered according to their needs.

Credential Stores and Security Tokens

So: authentication is the process of positive identification of a user based on the credentials they supply. In order to perform this process, the credentials supplied by the user are compared to those existing in a **credential store**. Once again, the nature of the credential store depends on the type of authentication. For example, Windows authentication compares the credentials against a Windows domain. Passport sites such as Hotmail, MSN, eBay, and McAfee use the Microsoft-owned Passport credential store, which is in charge of the authentication. The credential store could also be a database, an XML file, or any other media that we decide to use for this purpose. We will later discuss the types of authentication we can choose for our ASP.NET applications.

In order to allow a security-aware application to detect that the current user has already been authenticated, a **security token** is attached to that user. The security token is used to keep information about the user; again, its format and manner of use depend on the application. In a Windows environment, for example, this token is directly associated with the user while their session remains open. It is later used as a sort of key when the user performs an action such as opening a folder or printing a document – security settings on any of these objects may bar them from accessing the resource. (In a web environment, things are somewhat different, because of the disconnected and stateless nature of the HTTP protocol. We will see later how ASP.NET solves this problem.)

Once the user has been authenticated, and their security token is in place, authorization happens. Once more, the association between a resource and the list of users allowed to access it depends on the specific application type or environment. For example, restrictions in access to files and folders in Windows are kept in so-called **ACLs**, or **access control lists**. These are set though the Security tab of the Properties window corresponding to the file or folder. This picture shows the security settings of a folder called MyArchive:

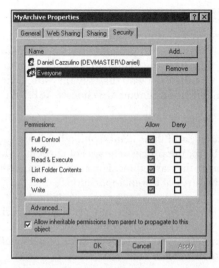

If you have used COM+ before, you may have used the Component Services MMC snap-in to assign permissions to COM+ applications. In this case, it also uses the Windows domain credentials store, just like the folder's properties window we saw above, but assigns access permissions to components based on them. The following picture, for example, shows a component that can only be accessed by managers:

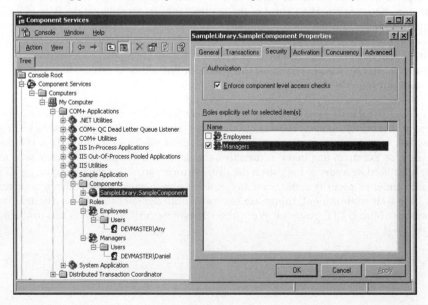

In ASP.NET applications, there are other options for assigning permissions to resources, which we will see soon.

Role-Based Security

If you take a closer look at the first of the two pictures opposite, you'll see that Everyone isn't a user at all – rather, it is a Windows **group**. The second picture shows a similar idea: that of **roles**, such as Employees and Managers. This leads us to the next key concepts.

If we focus on the process of assigning permissions to resources, we can easily imagine the administrative nightmare it would be to assign them to one user at a time, especially if we have a large number of users. What's more, each new user created would have to be manually added to all of the resources they are supposed to be able to access. To avoid this, a higher-level construct is created, in which users are assigned to groups or roles according to application requirements. For example, a project administration and tracking system may define groups such as 'administrators', 'developers', 'testers', and 'users'.

This generalization allows us to apply permissions according to roles, as well as (or even instead of) according to individual users. New users can then be included in certain roles. The most obvious advantage to this is that once a particular permission has been assigned to a role, new users with that role will automatically gain that permission. For example, if there is a resource that allows a developer to upload the code they have developed, and which is obviously restricted to users who are included in the 'developers' role, a new programmer hired by the company will be able to access it automatically, provided they are included in the 'developers' role when the system administrator creates their account.

A user can be included in more than one role simultaneously. For example, a user may be added to the 'developers' and 'testers' roles, if that user performs tasks related to both roles simultaneously. (Some would say, with good reason, that this is not a good idea!)

Principal and Identity

In order for an application to use these security concepts, it needs a way to access them – for example, it must be able to check that the current user is included in a certain role, and to act accordingly. The .NET Framework supports and exposes this scheme through the concepts of **principal** and **identity**.

A principal is an object that contains the roles associated with a user. It also contains an identity object that encloses information about that user. Together, they map onto the functionality we have shown above for Windows and COM+ security. In fact, though you may not have noticed it at the time, we have already used these objects in our *Friends Reunion* application, to pass around the current user's ID, and to check if they were authenticated. In Chapter 4, we had the following:

```
if (Context.User.Identity.IsAuthenticated)
{
   ...
```

and:

```
id = Context.User.Identity.Name;
```

383

`Context.User` contains the `Principal` object associated with the current user for ASP.NET applications. `Context` is a property of the base `Control` class (from which `Page` and all server controls derive), and as such is available to all of the code in our code-behind page. (It's actually a shortcut to the static `HttpContext.Current` property. We discussed this object with regards to state management in Chapter 6.)

If you look at the type of this property (place the cursor above `User`, and IntelliSense will do the rest), you'll find that it's actually an interface, `IPrincipal`. Likewise, the `Identity` property is of type `IIdentity`. This abstraction allows us to use the methods and properties defined in those interfaces irrespective of the concrete types of principal and identity, which depend on the type of authentication used, as we will see shortly. These two interfaces belong to the `System.Security.Principal` namespace, and provide the most common properties and methods we may need when working with role-based security:

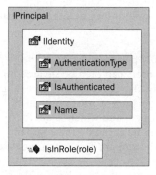

The `Page` object provides access to the principal through a `User` property too, which actually points to the same value in `Context.User`.

Processing and Initialization

In Chapter 1, we saw that when a request for an ASP.NET resource (such as an `.aspx` page) is received by IIS, it is handed to the ASP.NET processor (an ISAPI module), which continues processing the request. In order to understand how the security context is initialized, we need to take a closer look at what happens beyond that point:

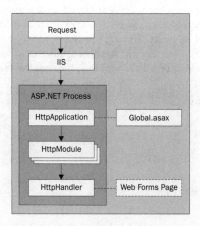

When the ASP.NET processor (`aspnet_wp.exe`) receives the request from IIS, it hands it to the application corresponding to the page requested. As we saw in Chapter 6, the `HttpApplication` object is defined in the `Global.asax` file of your web application, hence the line in the drawing showing that relationship:

```
public class Global : System.Web.HttpApplication
{
  ...
```

In turn the `HttpApplication` passes the request through any `HttpModule` that's configured for the application. These modules have the chance to process the request at various points, attaching to the corresponding events fired by the application, such as `AuthenticateRequest`, `BeginRequest`, and `EndRequest`. Of course, these events, being fired by the class defined in `Global.asax`, can also be handled in that class. You can see empty skeletons for those event handlers in the code-behind file:

```
public class Global : System.Web.HttpApplication
{
  ...
  protected void Application_BeginRequest(Object sender, EventArgs e)
  {
    // Fires at the beginning of each request
  }

  protected void Application_EndRequest(Object sender, EventArgs e)
  {
    // Fires at the end of each request
  }

  protected void Application_AuthenticateRequest(Object sender,
                                                 EventArgs e)
  {
    // Fires upon attempting to authenticate the user
  }
  ...
}
```

The key event for security initialization is `AuthenticateRequest`, which is fired whenever a client requests a resource for which some kind of authorization is set. We will shortly see how we can configure this for our application.

If you want to know about other events available for the `HttpApplication` class, check the MSDN documentation.

Security-related modules subscribe to this event, and initialize the security context *before* the request is handled by the particular page the user asked for. Several modules are configured by default for all our web applications, and you can find them in the `%WinDir%\Microsoft.NET\Framework\ v1.0.3705\CONFIG\machine.config` file, in the `<httpModules>` section (something we saw back in Chapter 6). Here are the ones we're interested in right now:

```
<httpModules>
    ...
    <add name="WindowsAuthentication"
         type="System.Web.Security.WindowsAuthenticationModule"/>
    <add name="FormsAuthentication"
         type="System.Web.Security.FormsAuthenticationModule"/>
    <add name="PassportAuthentication"
         type="System.Web.Security.PassportAuthenticationModule"/>
    ...
</httpModules>
```

Depending on the authentication scheme we choose for our application (which we'll discuss in the next section), the appropriate module loads and sets the current principal and identity objects:

❑ If we choose Windows authentication, the module will use the information passed by IIS (which must be configured to use the same type of authentication) to create a `WindowsIdentity` object with the user's Windows account name, such as `MYCOMPANY\Daniel`. It will then use this object, together with the list of Windows groups to which the user belongs, to initialize a `WindowsPrincipal` object. The new principal object is set then to the `Context.User` property.

❑ If Passport authentication is used, the user will be redirected to the Microsoft Passport login page (more on this later). When the user is redirected back to our application from this page, the module will use the information passed back to create a `PassportIdentity` object. As roles can't be configured in Passport (because it is only intended to authenticate users) a `GenericPrincipal` object has to be initialized with the newly created identity. Finally, the object must be set to the `Context.User` property. All this has to be done manually for Passport, as the `PassportIdentity` object itself contains the methods to perform the checks.

❑ Finally, if we choose Forms authentication, the module will rely on a cookie-based mechanism. (We described how cookies work back in Chapter 6.) As we will see in a moment, Forms authentication settings include a `loginUrl` setting that points to a web forms page to be used for authentication purposes.

The Forms authentication module will check for the presence of an **authentication cookie** in the current request. If it finds one, it will use the information in it to create a `FormsIdentity` object. This module doesn't support roles either, so this identity object is used to create a `GenericPrincipal`, which is set to the `Context.User` property. If the cookie is *not* present, the user is redirected to the login page. A utility method that we've been using already, `FormsAuthentication.RedirectFromLoginPage()`, is used to allow the module to create the authentication cookie and save it to the client browser's cookie collection. Once this process finishes, the user is redirected to the page they asked for originally, this time with the cookie in place.

With all of this new information, we can complete the previous picture:

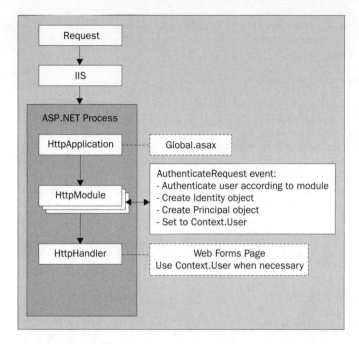

If this infrastructure is not enough for our particular security requirements, we can extend it by creating a handler for the AuthenticateRequest event in the Global.asax file. The .NET Framework provides us with another generic object that we can use for custom security, GenericIdentity, which we can use or even extend to suit our needs. Towards the end of this chapter, we will see how to do this, and discover why might we need to.

Application Security Configuration

A repeated refrain in this chapter is that the security behavior will largely depend on application configuration. As you already know, all application-wide settings are configured in a file called Web.config under the application root folder. We have already used some of the security settings here, but let's now take a look at all the options available.

In the configuration file, security-related settings are divided into three elements:

❑   <authentication>

❑   <authorization>

❑   <location>

In the following sections, we'll examine the purpose of each of these three elements.

Authentication Configuration

The <authentication> element defines the type of authentication that will be in force, and can contain child elements like <forms> and <passport> for those two types of authentication options. The element's syntax can be found in the MSDN help:

```
<authentication mode="Windows|Forms|Passport|None">
  <forms name="name"
         loginUrl="url"
         protection="All|None|Encryption|Validation"
         timeout="30" path="/" >
    <credentials passwordFormat="Clear|SHA1|MD5">
      <user name="username" password="password" />
    </credentials>
  </forms>
  <passport redirectUrl="internal"/>
</authentication>
```

When the authentication mode is set to Windows, all other tags will be ignored. For Forms authentication, all of the `<forms>` element's attributes have pre-configured default values, which are also found in the Machine.config file we saw above:

```
<forms name=".ASPXAUTH"
       loginUrl="login.aspx"
       protection="All"
       timeout="30" path="/">
```

So, if we configure Forms authentication only with the following syntax:

```
<authentication mode="Forms" />
```

then we will have to provide a login.aspx page under the application root. The other attributes and their meanings are explained in depth in the MSDN help.

So now we can fully understand the meaning of the configuration settings (in Web.Config) that we have been using so far:

```
<authentication mode="Forms">
  <forms loginUrl="Secure/Login.aspx"/>
</authentication>
```

We let the default values take effect, and only override the loginUrl attribute to point to the location of our login form.

Authorization Configuration

The `<authorization>` element is the one used in ASP.NET to assign permissions to resources. The process of creating this element and its sub-elements and attributes is therefore comparable to the process of assigning file or folder security in Windows, or to that of defining the application roles allowed in COM+, as we saw earlier. Again, the complete syntax of this element is found in the MSDN help:

```
<authorization>
  <allow users="comma-separated list of users|?|*"
         roles="comma-separated list of roles"
         verbs="comma-separated list of verbs" />
```

```
    <deny users="comma-separated list of users|?|*"
        roles="comma-separated list of roles"
        verbs="comma-separated list of verbs" />
</authorization>
```

The ? and * (which don't actually appear in the documentation) represent the anonymous user (that is, an unauthenticated user) and all users, respectively. The default setting for this element in Machine.config is:

```
<authorization>
  <allow users="*" />
</authorization>
```

In other words, all users are allowed to access the resources, unless otherwise specified in our application configuration file. The authorization setting we've been using for our application (in Web.Config) so far is:

```
<authorization>
  <deny users="?"/>
</authorization>
```

This means that we don't allow unauthenticated users to access any resource in the application.

Location Configuration

Finally, the <location> element can be used to specify <authorization> elements with regard to a certain path in the application. This is useful for setting exceptions to the rules defined for the whole application. We have used it before to explicitly allow anonymous access to the NewUser.aspx form, which wouldn't be available according to the authorization setting used above:

```
<location path="Secure/NewUser.aspx">
  <system.web>
    <authorization>
      <allow users="*"/>
    </authorization>
  </system.web>
</location>
```

If we didn't set this rule, unregistered users wouldn't be able to register themselves, since the NewUser.aspx page won't be available unless they were previously authenticated! The path can also be a folder instead of a specific file, so the following setting would work equally well:

```
<location path="Secure">
  <system.web>
    <authorization>
      <allow users="*"/>
    </authorization>
  </system.web>
</location>
```

389

In fact, using a <location> element with a path to a folder instead of a file (like the one we have just seen) is exactly equivalent to adding a Web.config file in that folder with the same authorization settings. So, we could achieve exactly the same as the <location> setting in the code we have just seen by adding a Web.config file to the Secure folder and adding the following elements to it:

```
<configuration>
  <system.web>
    <authorization>
      <allow users="*" />
    </authorization>
  </system.web>
</configuration>
```

It's worth noting how the process of authorization takes place here. There is another module, called UrlAuthorizationModule, that is registered by default to *all* web applications, and performs the checks. It is called *after* the other modules have processed the request, so it uses the Principal that was associated to the current user by the appropriate authentication module. This way, these checks are independent of the authentication mode selected. This means that we can use authorization elements to deny or allow access to certain roles, for example, and leave the settings intact even if we later decide to change the authentication mode, as long as the role names remain the same.

The settings in a configuration file apply to the current folder and all its child folders, except for the <location> element, which applies only to the element specified in its path attribute. Application configuration files are hierarchical, which means that we can place multiple configuration files in different folders under the root application path, overriding the appropriate elements whenever we need to.

These overrides can either broaden or tighten the settings in the parent folders. This may seem strange at first, but a second thought will reveal its usefulness: we can deny anonymous access to an application in general, just as we did for our *Friends Reunion* application, but make available a subfolder that contains such things as registration information or help pages.

Let's now move on and see how we can implement the three authentication modes (Windows, Passport, and Forms), and examine their advantages and drawbacks.

Windows Authentication

As stated above, Windows authentication works closely with IIS and Windows. In fact, ASP.NET doesn't do much more than receive what IIS passes it, and map it to .NET principal and identity objects. All of the business of exchanging credentials and authentication is handled at the IIS side, where Integrated Windows authentication (and optionally Basic authentication) should be used, with anonymous access disabled. This is most suitable for intranet and extranet scenarios, where the users are a part of your organization, and already have a Windows account in the company domain.

If you use Integrated Windows authentication, this will be the most secure method, as everything will be handled inside the Windows domain. In addition, access to pages can be set directly using file access permissions (like the one we saw at the beginning of the chapter), which makes for the lowest impact on your pages' design with regards to security. The user experience will also be improved, because users will not even need to log in to the application – the security token will automatically be passed to ASP.NET whenever the user opens the browser and points to a page.

> *In Chapter 4, we alternated between Integrated Windows authentication and Anonymous access settings. Now we can fully understand what was going on. The* Web.config *file was left with the default authentication mode of* Windows, *so when Integrated Windows authentication was turned on, the user automatically became authenticated – the token was received by ASP.NET behind the scenes. When we turned on Anonymous access, ASP.NET no longer received the Windows user's security token, so the user became unauthenticated.*

If you select this authentication mode in ASP.NET, and set the IIS security settings to use any method other than Anonymous access, you won't see the Windows login form unless you try to access the application through the Internet from another machine. Machines on your LAN will get the effect we achieved in Chapter 4: the credentials will be passed automatically, and you become authenticated to the application without entering a single word. On the other hand, trying to access the application through the Internet will open up the following window:

This window replaces the Forms authentication redirect to the login page that we've been using so far. The information entered in this window is encoded/encrypted according to the specific setting used in IIS. This pop-up window is exactly the same as the one that appears when you try to access a network share for which you haven't been authenticated, such as a share from a computer outside your domain.

Passport Authentication

Passport is an authentication service provided by Microsoft. It is the authentication service backing up Hotmail, MSN, and .NET Messenger, so you could say that it's a well-tested, streamlined, production quality, high volume service. However, setting it up for use in your web application is not such an easy task as with Windows or Forms authentication. It involves several steps:

1. Download and install the Microsoft .NET Passport SDK (at the time of writing, you can find this at http://msdn.microsoft.com/downloads/sample.asp?url=/msdn-files/ 027/001/885/msdncompositedoc.xml&frame=true).

2. Create a personal .NET Passport account for yourself (if you don't have one already).

3. Register an application with the .NET Services Manager site at http://www.netservicesmanager.com. You will need to provide additional information about yourself, and fill in several settings, for the new application to be created.

4. Then you get a key that must be installed in your server. After that, there are a couple more steps that are better described at http://msdn.microsoft.com/library/en-us/dncold/ html/ssf2psprtauth.asp?frame=true.

Finally, the actual authentication process is not as 'automatic' as it is for the other modules. Here, we have to create a `PassportIdentity` object manually, and use its methods and properties to interact with the service. Perhaps the worst part is that for production systems, you will have to pay a fee.

Forms Authentication

This has been the authentication mode of choice for our web application, for two reasons. First, it is easily implemented; second, it is the most likely to be used for web applications, as it allows for administration of users outside of Windows accounts, which is paramount for the Internet. However, we have already said that for intranet/extranet scenarios, Windows authentication is better suited.

The processing sequence that has been taking place in our *Friends Reunion* application is a typical Forms authentication interaction, and can be represented in the following diagram (numbers reflect the request's order of execution):

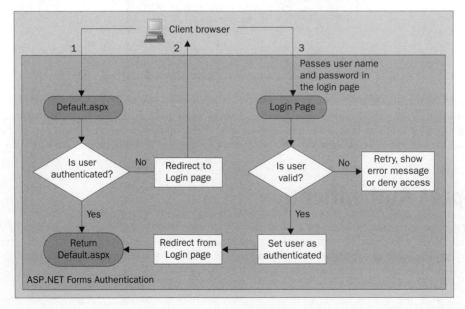

Here we see a user requesting a page that requires authentication (`Default.aspx`). If the user hasn't been authenticated previously with the application, they are redirected to the login page. After the user has entered a user name and password, and these credentials have been successfully validated, they are set as being authenticated. As we said, this involves the creation of an authentication cookie that is saved with the request and later passed back to the server on every subsequent request. Using the built-in infrastructure will suffice for most types of applications, such as our own *Friends Reunion*.

In the next example, we'll take a look at the login form we've been using so far, and elaborate on its functionality. We will then improve it by giving the user the ability to 'persist' their login information – that is, to save the cookie in order to survive browser restarts. This will allow the user to avoid the inconvenience of having to enter the same information again when they come back to the site. Most sites that offer this feature also allow the user to sign out of the application explicitly, so that any authentication cookies are removed from their machine. This is very important for users who access our application from public machines.

Try It Out – Improving the Authentication Process

Let's add the 'permanent' login and 'total' logout functionality to our application by way of some extra elements in the user interface.

1. Open the `Login.aspx` form and add a new row to the table that is already present (the easiest way to do this is to position the cursor in the cell with the **Login** button, and press *Ctrl+Alt+Up*). Drop in a **CheckBox** web server control named `chkPersist`, and set its `Text` property to match that of the screenshot:

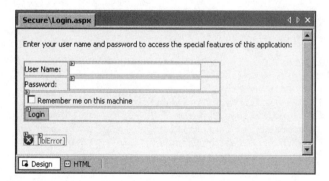

2. Now we can add the code to persist the cookie according to the user's selection in the new checkbox – a change to just one line!

```
private void btnLogin_ServerClick(object sender, System.EventArgs e)
{
  ...
  if (id != null)
  {
    // Set the user as authenticated
    // and send him to the page originally requested.
```

393

```
            FormsAuthentication.RedirectFromLoginPage(id, chkPersist.Checked);
    }
    else
    {
      this.pnlError.Visible = true;
      this.lblError.Text = "Invalid user name or password!";
    }
  }
}
```

3. Now let's add the logout feature. The natural place to put this is as a link next to Edit my profile, in the subhead control we created in Chapter 3. Open SubHeader.cs and add the code to create and add the new link next to the old one:

```
protected override void CreateChildControls()
{
  // Clear any previously loaded controls
  this.Controls.Clear();
  Label lbl;
  HyperLink reg = new HyperLink();

  if (_register == string.Empty)
  {
    reg.NavigateUrl = Context.Request.ApplicationPath +
        Path.AltDirectorySeparatorChar + "Secure" +
        Path.AltDirectorySeparatorChar + "NewUser.aspx";
  }
  else
  {
    reg.NavigateUrl = _register;
  }

  if (Context.User.Identity.IsAuthenticated)
  {
    reg.Text = "Edit my profile";
    reg.ToolTip = "Modify your personal information";
    HyperLink signout = new HyperLink();
    signout.NavigateUrl = Context.Request.ApplicationPath +
            Path.AltDirectorySeparatorChar + "Logout.aspx";
    signout.Text = "Logout";
    signout.ToolTip = "Leave the application";
    this.Controls.Add(new LiteralControl(" | "));
    this.Controls.Add(signout);
  }
  else
  {
    reg.Text = "Register";
  }

  // Add it (before the logout control, if it exists)
  this.Controls.AddAt(0, reg);
  this.Controls.Add(new LiteralControl(" - "));
```

```
    // Add a label with the current data
    lbl = new Label();
    lbl.Text = DateTime.Now.ToLongDateString();
    this.Controls.Add(lbl);
}
```

Note that we will actually redirect the users to a confirmation page, just like Passport does.

4. Let's now create the logout confirmation page. Add a new web form called `Logout.aspx`. Add the link to the usual stylesheet:

```
<link href="Style/iestyle.css" rel="stylesheet" type="text/css">
```

Also change the code-behind page to inherit the class from our `FriendsBase` class. Add a table with an image (`images/question.gif`) and some text (asking for confirmation, as shown in the screenshot). Also add a button (`ID="btnLogout"`, `CssClass="Button"`, `Text="Logout"`) to perform the actual logout operation:

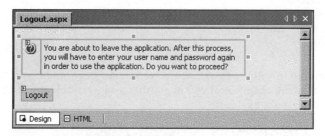

5. Add the following event handler to the **Logout** button:

```
private void btnLogout_Click(object sender, System.EventArgs e)
{
    // Remove the authentication ticket
    System.Web.Security.FormsAuthentication.SignOut();

    // Redirect the user to the root application path
    Response.Redirect(Request.ApplicationPath);
}
```

6. Add the following code to `Page_Load()` to set up the message and icon for the page:

```
private void Page_Load(object sender, System.EventArgs e)
{
    base.HeaderMessage = "Leave the Application";
    base.HeaderIconImageUrl =
                    Request.ApplicationPath + "/images/back.gif";
}
```

7. Finally, let's recap the security-related settings the application is using (in `Web.Config`):

```xml
<?xml version="1.0" encoding="utf-8" ?>
<configuration>
  ...
  <system.web>
    ...
    <authentication mode="Forms">
      <forms loginUrl="Secure/Login.aspx" />
    </authentication>
    <authorization>
      <deny users="?" />
    </authorization>
    ...
  </system.web>
  <location path="Secure/NewUser.aspx">
    <system.web>
      <authorization>
        <allow users="*"/>
      </authorization>
    </system.web>
  </location>
  ...
</configuration>
```

8. Run the application with `Default.aspx` as the start page, and log in (select the **Remember me on this machine** checkbox if you like). After a successful login, the default page with the new **Logout** link looks like this:

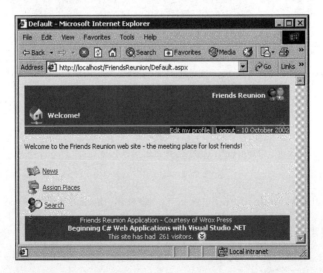

9. Close the browser window directly (don't log out). Now run the application again. What you see will depends on whether you checked the **Remember me on this machine** checkbox. If you did, then the cookie (which identifies and authenticates your identity) will be sent along with the request, so you won't need to log in – you'll see the **Welcome!** page directly. If you didn't, then you'll need to log in again.

10. Whichever way you get to the Welcome! page, you can formally log out (and destroy the cookie) by clicking the Logout link. This will take you to the confirmation page:

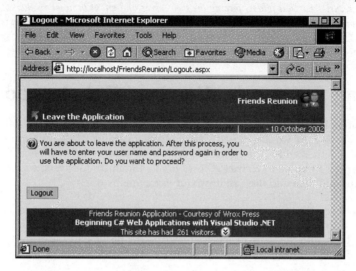

If you now confirm the logout, you will be sent back to the application's login page. The next time you start the application, you'll need to log in again.

How It Works

The login form uses the following method to set authentication:

```
FormsAuthentication.RedirectFromLoginPage(id, chkPersist.Checked);
```

As we stated above, this method takes care of creating the authentication cookie (also called a **ticket**), and saving it for subsequent requests. We pass the UserID, just as we did before, which is used to perform queries across the application. The new parameter we pass now, the Checked state of the checkbox, tells the method to create a persistent cookie that will be preserved in the client machine even across browser and machine restarts.

The other new feature is the logout link in the subhead control. The process for creating this is very similar to what we already had: we just add the link, and then add the previous link at the first position, to appear at the left of the new link:

```
this.Controls.AddAt(0, reg);
```

As you can see, the best advantage of Forms authentication is its flexibility. We have been able to authenticate against a database store of credentials, using the infrastructure absolutely as-is, and achieve some very acceptable results! We were able to query the database, customize content tailored to the current user, secure the whole application to require authentication, and we could even have used authorization on a per-user basis, although it wasn't needed for our application. Not bad for a sample project!

Putting the `Login` and `NewUser` forms in a separate folder from the rest of the application makes it easier to increase security for these two especially sensitive forms. One way to do this would be to set SSL security for that folder, forcing the web server and client browser to encrypt the entire conversation between them, making it impossible for hackers to get in the middle. This is an advanced topic that's treated in greater depth in Professional ASP.NET Security *(Wrox, ISBN 1-86100-620-9).*

Customizing Authentication and Role-based Security

Forms authentication is great, but it doesn't make use of the role-based features we talked about at the beginning of the chapter. As we saw, it will simply create an empty `GenericPrincipal` object, containing only the initialized `FormsIdentity` object. If we were to build an administration section in our application, and we wanted to restrict access only to administrator users, we would have to deny access to everyone, and then add the administrator users one by one.

To take advantage of role-based authentication, we have to customize the process. When we looked at the role-based security infrastructure and its overall architecture, we saw that the various authentication modules actually hook into the same events that we can use, particularly `AuthenticateRequest`, an event to which we can attach a handler in our `Global.asax` file.

We also learned that the infrastructure is prepared to work with any role-based scheme, as long as it works around the concepts of `IPrincipal` and `IIdentity`. So far, however, we've let the default modules take charge. Our only intervention in Forms authentication was to check a user name and password in the login form – we didn't have to bother about the cookies, encryption/decryption (yes, the cookie *is* encrypted), creation of the principal and identity objects, or anything else. Some things are going to have to change.

For our implementation of custom authentication, we will start by using the `GenericPrincipal` and `GenericIdentity` objects, which provide a reasonable and simple implementation for us to use. In case they are not enough, we can always inherit and extend them, or even implement `IPrincipal` and `IIdentity` directly in a custom class.

We already know the processing that takes place in order to make the default modules work. We can now apply that knowledge to build our custom authentication. As we stated, the key event to handle in the process is `AuthenticateRequest`. During the handler for this event, we can perform some actions, and then set the `Context.User` property to our custom principal and identity objects. As with any other authentication scheme, this security context will follow the user though pages, user controls, code-behind pages, and so on. We will be able to access these objects from any point in running code.

To customize authentication, we need to intercept the process at some point. In this instance, we'll leave the code as it is in the `Login.aspx` page, and let the Forms authentication module perform all the work it has been doing so far, until a certain point. Let's look again at the steps for a typical request in our application, and see where to override the default behavior:

1. User requests `Default.aspx` (this is the initial request to enter the application).

2. The `Application_AuthenticateRequest` event is fired; `IsAuthenticated = false`, so Forms module redirects to `Login.aspx?ReturnUrl=...`.

3. The redirect causes a new request to another page (namely `Login.aspx`).

4. The `Application_AuthenticateRequest` event is fired again – this time by the access to `Login.aspx`. The module realizes that this is the page for handling authentication, so it doesn't redirect to itself again.

5. The user enters credentials and submits. Posting the form to itself is actually another new request.

6. The `Application_AuthenticateRequest` event is fired again. `IsAuthenticated = false` again, so the module doesn't redirect.

7. Our code checks against database, and returns OK. The module saves `UserID` with the authentication cookie, and performs a redirect to `ReturnUrl` (`Default.aspx`).

8. As a result of the redirect, a new request is made for `Default.aspx`. This time, the authentication cookie is set.

9. The `Application_AuthenticateRequest` event fires; this is the first time we get `IsAuthenticated = true`. The application picks up processing from here, and rebuilds customized versions of `GenericPrincipal` and `GenericIdentity`, based on the information retrieved from the database using the `UserID` attached to the authentication cookie. It replaces the `Context.User` with the new complete `Principal`.

Note from the sequence above that the last `AuthenticateRequest` is the first one for which the `IsAuthenticated` property returns `true`. From now on, this is the only response that will be issued to an authenticate request, as the authorization cookie will be present, and the Forms authentication module will take care of recovering the `UserID` from it. We are actually customizing the authentication mechanism *after* the Forms authentication module has handled it.

We can refer to `Default.aspx` more generally as a "restricted page", which can be any protected resource in the application. Graphically, the interaction is as follows:

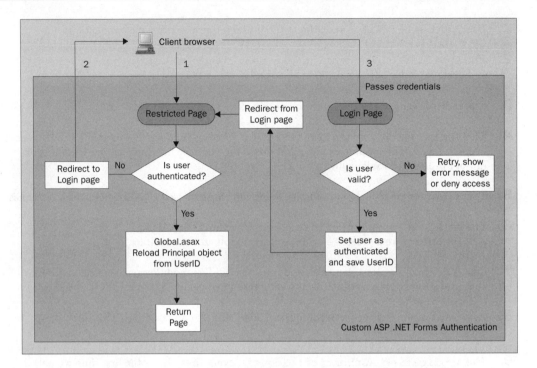

After we use the `FormsAuthentication.RedirectFromLoginPage()` method, the restricted page is actually requested again – but this time, with the security token set. At this time, we have a chance to override the default behavior implemented by Forms authentication, and we can set the `Context.User` property to an object that better represents our needs. This will be a `GenericPrincipal` that contains the roles associated with the current user.

Try It Out – Using and Replacing the Principal Object

In our database, there are only two roles: 'users' and 'administrators'. These roles aren't actually defined anywhere, but administrators are distinguished by the `IsAdministrator` flag in each record in the `User` table. This is the information we will use to create a `GenericPrincipal` containing the 'user' role, or both the 'user' and 'administrator' roles (an administrator will always be a user too).

1. Open the `Global.asax` code-behind file, and add the following import:

```
using System.Data;
using System.Data.SqlClient;
using System.Security.Principal;
using System.Configuration;
```

2. Find the `Application_AuthenticateRequest()` event handler, and add the following code to it:

```csharp
protected void Application_AuthenticateRequest(Object sender, EventArgs e)
{
  // Cast the sender to the application
  HttpApplication app = (HttpApplication)sender;

  // Only replace the context if it has already been handled
  // by forms authentication module (user is authenticated)
  if (app.Request.IsAuthenticated)
  {
    SqlConnection con;
    string sql;
    SqlCommand cmd;

    string id = Context.User.Identity.Name;

    con = new SqlConnection(
      ConfigurationSettings.AppSettings["cnFriends.ConnectionString"]);
    sql = "SELECT IsAdministrator FROM [User] WHERE UserId='{0}'";
    sql = String.Format(sql, id);
    cmd = new SqlCommand(sql, con);
    con.Open();

    // Ensure closing the connection
    try
    {
      object admin = cmd.ExecuteScalar();

      // Was it a valid UserID?
      if (admin != null)
      {
        GenericPrincipal ppal;
        string[] roles;

        // If IsAdministrator field is true, add both roles
        if (((bool)admin) == true)
        {
          roles = new string[] {"User", "Admin"};
        }
        else
        {
          roles = new string[] {"User"};
        }

        ppal = new GenericPrincipal(Context.User.Identity, roles);
        Context.User = ppal;
      }
      else
      {
        // If UserID was invalid, clear the context so they log on again
        Context.User = null;
      }
    }
    catch
```

```
          {
            throw;
          }
          finally
          {
            con.Close();
          }
        }
      }
```

3. Create a new folder named `Admin`, and add a new web form called `Users.aspx` to it. As always, add the stylesheet reference to it, and change the code-behind page so that it inherits from the `FriendsBase` class. Drop a `DataGrid`, give it the name `grdUsers`, and set its width to 100%. Right-click on the `DataGrid`, select **Auto Format**, and select **Colorful 4**. Add the text shown in the screenshot just before the `DataGrid`, so that the `Users.aspx` page looks something like this:

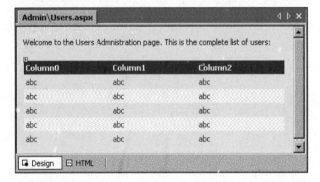

4. Drop a `SqlDataAdapter` object onto the form, and follow the Wizard as we did in Chapter 5 – first select the appropriate connection string, then select that you want to use **SQL statements**; then set the SQL statement to `SELECT * FROM [User]`. Then you can select **Finish** to complete the Wizard.

    Change the name of the `SqlDataAdapter` object to `adUsers`. Change the name of the connection to `cnFriends`.

    Now check the properties of the `SqlDataAdapter` object (`adUsers`). Its `SelectCommand` property should be `cmUsers` (change the `Name` property of `SelectCommand` if necessary). Also, if you haven't unchecked the **Generate insert...** advanced option, remember to set the `UpdateCommand`, `InsertCommand`, and `DeleteCommand` properties to `(none)`.

    Finally, set the `cnFriends` connection string property to use the dynamic configuration we used before. (Select the `(Dynamic Configuration)` property called `ConnectionString`, and use the button there to map the property to the key `cnFriends.ConnectionString` in the configuration file.)

5. Right-click the data adapter component (adUsers), and select Generate Dataset.... Select the New option button, and give it the name UserData. Accept the dialog, and rename the new dataset component to dsData.

6. Bind the data grid to this new dataset (by setting its DataSource property to dsData). The form will look something like this by now:

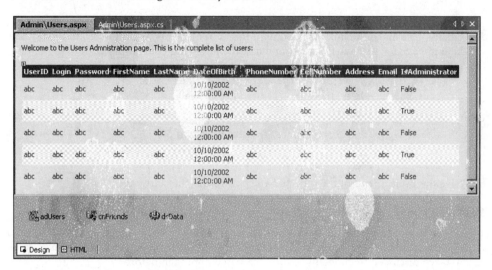

7. Let's add the code to load the dataset and bind the grid to display the data. Add the following code to the Page_Load() method of this page:

```
private void Page_Load(object sender, System.EventArgs e)
{
    base.HeaderIconImageUrl = Request.ApplicationPath +
                                            "/images/padlock.gif";
    base.HeaderMessage = "Administer Users";

    if (!IsPostBack)
    {
        this.adUsers.Fill(this.dsData);
        this.grdUsers.DataBind();
    }
}
```

8. Now we will add a link to this new page in the Default.aspx page, so that administrators have easy access to it. Open the Default.aspx page, and add the following code to the bottom:

```
<form id="Default" method="post" runat="server">
    ...
    <p class="Normal">
      <asp:placeholder id="phNav" runat="server"></asp:placeholder>
    </p>
```

```
    <p>
      <asp:hyperlink id="lnkUsers" runat="server"
                                navigateurl="Admin/Users.aspx">
        Users Administration Page
      </asp:hyperlink>
    </p>
  </form>
```

9. Finally, let's make the link visible only if the current user is an administrator. Open the code-behind page for `Default.aspx`, and add the following code at the bottom of the method:

```
private void Page_Load(object sender, System.EventArgs e)
{
    ...
    // Show the Admin link only to administrators
    this.lnkUsers.Visible = User.IsInRole("Admin");
}
```

10. Save the project, and run it with `Default.aspx` as the start page.

How It Works

As you can see from Step 9, the purpose of the code we added is to be able to control application behavior (in this case showing a link) based on the current user's role, instead of their particular user name or ID. We discussed the benefits of this role-based approach before.

So, just as we explained before we began to build this example, we're handling the `AuthenticateRequest` event in the `Global.asax` file in order to replace the default principal that's associated by Forms authentication with a custom one. This will allow us to add roles to the current user, based on the information in the database. Note that we used the application request's `IsAuthenticated` property, instead of the `Context.User.Identity.IsAuthenticated` property we've used before:

```
if (app.Request.IsAuthenticated)
{
    ...
```

We had to do this because the first time the page is accessed, the `Context.User` property isn't initialized yet, and we would have caused an exception. To take this into account, we could have replaced the code above with the following:

```
if ((Context.User != null) && (Context.User.Identity.IsAuthenticated))
{
```

If we pass the `IsAuthenticated` check, it will mean that Forms authentication has already done its work, and the `UserID` is placed where we're used to finding it: in the `Context.User.Identity.Name` property. This is the work that's already achieved in the `Login.aspx` page, and it's what we've been doing since Chapter 4.

In the remainder of the handler, we replace the empty `GenericPrincipal` object that's created by the Forms authentication module with one containing the actual roles the user belongs to. So, in the `Application_AuthenticateRequest()` handler, we retrieve the `UserID` and use it to issue a database query to discover whether it corresponds to an administrator or not. We use `ExecuteScalar()` as we expect a single Boolean value to be returned. As usual, we placed the code in a `try...catch` block and ensure the connection is closed in the `finally` section.

The `GenericPrincipal` constructor receives an identity and a string array containing the roles it belongs to. We reuse the identity created by Forms authentication, which is attached to the `Context.User.Identity` property we have been using, as we don't need to change anything about it:

```
ppal = new GenericPrincipal(Context.User.Identity, roles);
```

Finally, we attach the newly created principal to the `Context.User` property:

```
Context.User = ppal;
```

If you go back to the picture showing the flow for these actions, you'll notice that the next page to be processed is the page that was originally requested. So, when execution reaches our code for the page, it will have access to the new role-aware principal we attached. We use this in the `Page_Load()` method of the `Default.aspx` page to display a link to the user's administration page:

```
this.lnkUsers.Visible = User.IsInRole("Admin");
```

`User` is a property of the `Page` object that provides a shortcut to `Context.User`, and its `IsInRole()` method allows us to check whether it pertains to a specific role. Here, we see an administrator user logged in:

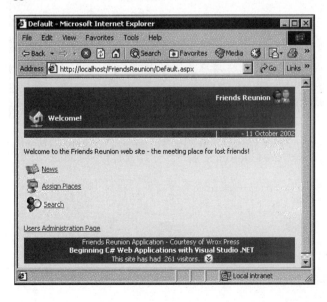

We have used our new, custom, roles-aware principal to display information on the page selectively. However, merely hiding or showing a link is not enough security: if a non-administrator user knows the administration page's location and name, they could type the address into the browser's address bar and gain access to a resource that is supposed to be restricted! To solve this, we will add a configuration file inside the `Admin` folder, to secure all the items in that folder.

If we add more administration tools later, the configuration file will automatically protect them too. Organizing an application into separate folders according to resource features makes it extremely easy to administer its security settings, and ensures that future growth won't become a maintenance nightmare.

Try It Out – Taking Advantage of Roles for Authorization

To secure the items in our new `Admin` folder, we just have to provide it with a new web configuration file, as we're about to see.

1. Right-click on the `Admin` folder, select **Add | Add New Item**, and choose **Web Configuration File** from the **Utility** folder:

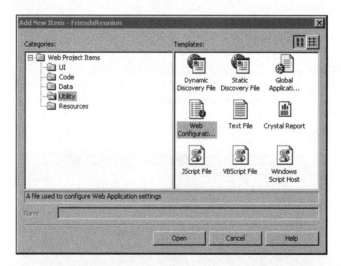

2. Open the `Admin/Web.Config` file that you've just created. Remove all of this file's content, and replace it with the following:

```xml
<?xml version="1.0" encoding="utf-8" ?>
<configuration>
  <system.web>
    <authorization>
      <allow roles="Admin" />
      <deny roles="User" />
    </authorization>
  </system.web>
</configuration>
```

How It Works

If a user who is not an administrator is logged in, they won't see the link to the administration page because the page's code hides it, according to the code we added in the previous example. But now, if the user tries to type the page's address directly into the browser's address bar, they *still* won't be allowed to access it, thanks to the configuration file we just placed in the folder. Instead, they will be redirected to the login page again, to provide appropriate credentials.

Up to now, we have been using user-related information to restrict access to resources, such as denying anonymous users, or granting all users. Now, we are taking advantage of role-based security to set permissions. This means that new administrator users registered with the application later on will automatically gain access to these resources, without any further changes to the application's configuration. If we'd used user-related information, we could have granted the wrox user access to this folder, but we would then have to add any new administrators manually.

Having logged on as a *non*-administrator user, try typing the URL directly into the browser's address bar, and see what happens – you should be redirected to the login page. All of these checks are performed automatically, and the redirection to the login page makes sense, since a user without the required role might even be an unauthenticated user. Only a user belonging to the administrator role will be able to see the administration page we built, regardless of how they try to access it.

Now, our *Friends Reunion* application has become much more secure, through the use of the concepts you've learned in this chapter. However, we certainly haven't covered every possible security-related feature available in .NET, as that is a subject for a whole book. The book in question is *Professional ASP.NET Security* (Wrox, ISBN 1-86100-620-9).

Summary

Security in web applications is very important, much more so than in traditional desktop applications. During this chapter, we have looked at some general security concepts, as well as modern role-based security.

We have examined the various authentication options available in ASP.NET, and provided some guidance that should allow you to choose among them. We discussed application configuration files in the context of security settings, and we used authentication and authorization to secure an application, and custom authentication to meet application requirements, showing the level of extensibility available in the general security infrastructure.

In order to understand the close relationship between IIS and ASP.NET, we saw an overview of the modular and extensible architecture that exists to process web requests, and how the various authentication options are implemented internally, as well as their interaction with the main web application.

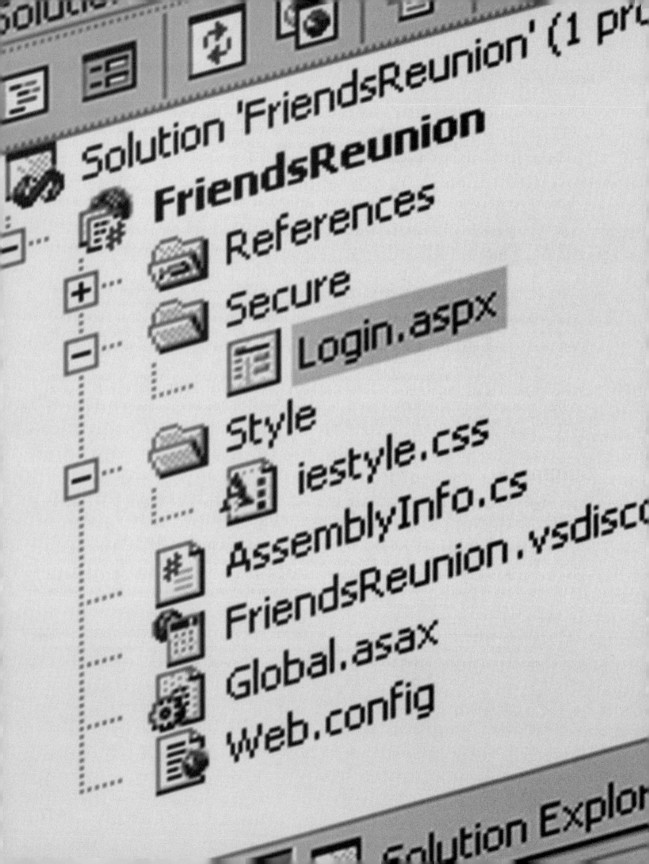

Debugging and Exception Handling

In the previous eight chapters, we've written and generated lots of code in our *Friends Reunion* application. In this chapter, we have two aims:

❑ To learn about techniques that will help us to ensure the code we've written is free of bugs

❑ To look at how to build in some exception-handling code that is designed to deal with unexpected runtime errors.

These two topics are often bundled together and confused with one another. That's because, although they are different, there is a sense in which they are related. If we can get ourselves a good understanding of exception handling, then it will help us to write robust code that is capable of dealing with unexpected occurrences. Then, if our application does have a bug, that bug is less likely to cause a horrible failure at run time because the exception-handling code will be designed to deal with it gracefully.

We'll devote the first part of the chapter to the subject of debugging. We will:

❑ Classify the different types of errors that may exist in our application, and look at which tools are most suitable for finding and fixing them

❑ Look at some alternative techniques that we can use for debugging applications without the aid of a debugger (this is going to be useful when you move your application from the test environment into a live environment)

❑ Demonstrate how to use the VS.NET Debugger to debug an application

This should give us a good understanding of what is offered by the .NET Framework in general, and ASP.NET in particular, in the battle against bugs.

In the second part of the chapter, we will introduce you to the subject of error-handling using exceptions. We'll show you:

❑ How to catch, throw, and rethrow exceptions

❑ How to define your own custom exceptions

❑ How to recover gracefully from an unhandled exception

❑ How to log *Friends Reunion* exceptions to the System Event Log

By the end of all this, you should have a good understanding of how the exception-handling mechanism works, and how to integrate it with some specific ASP.NET features.

Different Types of Errors

If you have any experience developing applications, then you already know that it's very difficult to rid an application entirely of errors. It doesn't matter how much effort you put into writing error-free code; programmers are human, and humans make mistakes. Therefore, we have to accept that we will not write perfect code first time, it's as simple as that.

After accepting we are not all as infallible as we'd like to think we are, the next thing to do is realize that we should at least try to *minimize* the number of errors in our code, and the effect that errors can have on our application's behavior. To do this, we need to understand a little about the different *types* of error that we may encounter.

We can classify errors into three distinct types: **syntax** errors, **semantic** errors, and **input** errors. As we will see, these three different types are all rather different in nature, and thus we need different tools and techniques in order to find and fix them.

Syntax Errors

A **syntax error** occurs when you write code that violates the rules of grammar of the programming language. A debugger will not be of any help in detecting and correcting syntax errors! The compiler is the main tool here. If the compiler detects a syntax error, it will refuse to complete compilation of the code, and so there will be no program to debug.

Syntax errors are said to be caught at **compile time** (because it is the compiler that catches and reports them). When you're building your C# web application in VS.NET, the C# compiler will check the C# code for syntax errors and output its results to the **Output** window. (To view the **Output** window, select View | Other Windows | Output from the menu bar or use *Ctrl+Alt+O*.) The **Output** window will contain a short description of each error, along with the file and line number in which it was found.

Locating Syntax Errors

Generally, the compiler will be able to tell you the location of a syntax error with reasonable accuracy. If there isn't a syntax error at the exact line reported by the compiler, then the error is usually located somewhere above the specified line (and probably within just a few lines). For example, consider this code fragment from `SubHeader.cs`:

```
 8      public class SubHeader : WebControl
 9      {
10          // The URL to navigate to in case the user
11          // is not registered
12          private string _register = string.Empty;
13
14          public SubHeader()
15          {
16              // Initialize default values
17              this.Width = new Unit(100, UnitType.Percentage);
18              this.CssClass = "SubHeader";
19          }
20      }
21
22          // Property to allow the user to define the URL
23          // for the registration page
24          public string RegisterUrl
25          {
26              get { return _register; }
27              set { _register = value; }
28          }
29
```

The code in this screenshot contains a simple syntax error – there's an extra closing brace at line 20 (the cursor is pointing at it). If we try to compile this code, the compiler will detect this syntax error and report it to the **Output** window. However, it doesn't detect the error at line 20, but it does detect that there's something at line 24 that isn't as it should be:

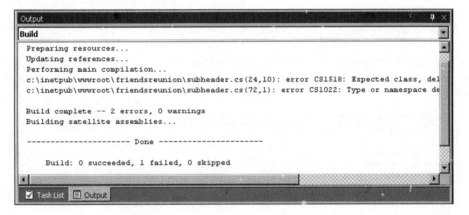

The compiler works from the top down, so in this case it assumes that the extra closing brace is a legal closing brace marking the end of the SubHeader class definition. Then, it comes across the RegisterUrl property definition and highlights the error there, complaining that it expected a class definition but got a property definition instead. Although the exact location of the error is not quite right, the information is enough for us to work out what's wrong in the code.

In fact, we didn't even need to compile the code to discover this syntax error. Look carefully at line 24 and you'll see that the IDE has underlined the string keyword (in red). That's because the IDE is automatically parses the file as we type, and highlights any syntax error it finds with a red underline. What Microsoft Word did for years for spelling mistakes is now done by VS.NET for syntax errors!

It's particularly worth watching out for typos, because they're probably the most common cause of syntax errors. But don't worry too much about them: with all the help from the IDE and the compiler, you should find it quick and easy to locate and fix syntax errors.

Semantic Errors

A semantic error occurs when the syntax of your code is correct but:

❑ some other rule is broken

❑ or the meaning of the code is not what you intended

❑ or the code does what you intended, but your intent is not a correct interpretation of the specification of the program

In some cases the compiler will be able to detect semantic errors (though of course, it can't possibly know what was written in the program's specification!).

Semantic Errors that get Caught by the Compiler

Here's an example of the type of semantic error that *can* be caught by the compiler – this example consists of some code that tries to use a non-existent property of the Button class:

```
Button btn = new Button();
btn.Age = 32;
```

If we try to compile such code, the compiler will complain and refuse to compile it. We can find out what is wrong by looking at the Output window again, where the compiler correctly yells at us that the Button class doesn't have a definition for Age:

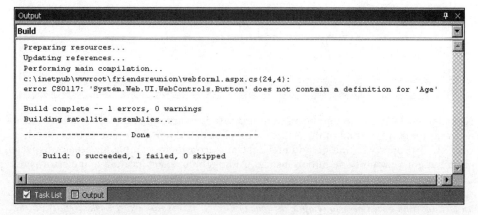

This kind of semantic error easy to fix: you just have to browse the Output window and satisfy the compiler's complaints.

Semantic Errors that don't get Caught by the Compiler

The other kind of semantic error is what we usually call a **bug**. Bugs get through the compilation stage and become part of a compiled application.

A bug can't be caught by the compiler because, as we mentioned at the top of this section, it is not a problem that can be identified by rigorous systematic application of a set of rules. Rather, a bug is a problem with the meaning of the code or the developer's interpretation of the requirements. The only way to find bugs is by testing the application – many bugs are found by the programmer or tester during the test cycle, or by the end user when the application is actually being used.

Semantic Errors that Cause an Exception

The following code contains an example of such an error:

```
Button btn = null;
btn.Text = "OK";
```

The developer who wrote these lines of code forgot to instantiate btn before using it. Therefore, the expression btn.Text (in the second line) evaluates to null.Text, which is nonsensical. But the compiler will not find this error, because the compiler doesn't run all the code – this error will only be found at run time. When these two lines of code are executed, an exception will be thrown and the application will terminate.

Semantic Errors that don't Cause a Exception

Not all semantic errors manifest themselves in such an obvious way as to raise an exception and cause a termination. Sometimes a program will continue to run after a semantic error has occurred, even though the logic it executes is in error (for example, if the flow of execution takes an inappropriate path or a variable contains an invalid value). Consider the following code excerpt from the InsertUser() method of the file NewUser.aspx.cs (in the Secure folder):

```
145
146        // Add required values to replace
147        values.Add(Guid.NewGuid().ToString());
148        values.Add(txtLogin.Text);
149        values.Add(txtPwd.Text);
150        values.Add(txtFName.Text);
151        values.Add(txtLName.Text);
152        values.Add(txtPhone.Text);
153        values.Add(txtEmail.Text);
154        values.Add(0);
155
```

If we swap the order of lines 150 and 151, the application will still appear to run smoothly; but it will contain a logic error that causes the first- and last-names of the newly registered user to be added at the wrong fields in the database.

Input Errors

An **input error** occurs when input into our application (from an external entity) is not of the expected form. For example, suppose the application is required to open a file that it expects to be in `.jpg` format, but it finds the file to be in a different format. Alternatively, consider when the application has a web form that invites the user to enter their date of birth, but they type a garbage value instead. These are input errors.

Input errors can and do happen. Moreover, input errors occur at *run time*, so no compiler will be able to help us to find them. We can only deal with input errors by anticipating the type of input errors that might happen, and preparing our code to be able to handle them.

As we will see in this chapter, the .NET Framework provides us with an **exception**-based mechanism that allows us to code our applications to handle input errors properly and recover from them gracefully.

An effective way to detect potential input errors – and many of the semantic errors that can't be detected by a compiler – is to test the application. Stages of testing (by programmers and testers) are common in application development of course, and at each stage the application is being tested (either manually or automatically, as we will discuss in Chapter 12) and its output examined for anything unexpected.

However, the fact is that the testing process is only half the story. We can test an application to confirm that it is not working as we expected. But testing, in itself, doesn't tell us much about where the error is and or how to fix it. That's why we also need **debugging**.

Debugging Web Applications

Debugging is the process of finding and fixing errors that can't be caught by the compiler. It's very common to associate the debugging process with the use of a **debugger** – a piece of software designed to help us find and fix bugs – but there are other ways to debug applications too.

In this chapter, we will take a look at some alternatives that .NET provides us through the classes found in the `System.Diagnostics` namespace, and through the more specific ASP.NET tracing features. We will also perform a useful debugging demonstration that doesn't use any debugger software at all. Finally, we will introduce the powerful Visual Studio .NET Debugger, and we will do some debugging of the *Friends Reunion* application.

ASP.NET Tracing

When developing an application, a useful technique is to include lines of code that print messages, which are specifically intended to help the developer determine the path of execution that the application takes, and the values of key variables at any given point in the application. This is what we call **tracing** the execution of our application.

If you have done much development work then it's very likely that you're used to using tracing code. In development of traditional Windows applications, tracing messages are often output to the screen or logged to a file; in ASP web application (written before ASP.NET) the most common tracing method was to use `Response.Write` to output the tracing messages to the browser, along with the output of the rendered page.

Implications of Tracing Techniques

When you're developing your ASP.NET web applications, there is nothing wrong in including your own tracing code (using `Response.Write` or your favorite technique) to help you fix bugs without resorting to a debugger. However, there are significant drawbacks that you should be aware of:

❑ Most importantly, it's likely that while you're looking for the error, your tracing output will be mixed in with the "actual" content of your page, and that makes it harder to read the original format of the page (this is a particular weakness of the `Response.Write` technique).

❑ After you've fixed the bug, you need to go back over your code and remove all the tracing code that helped you to trace the error in the first place!

❑ There is also a chance is some cases that the added tracing code has its own effect on the behavior of the application, and actually makes it harder to locate the problem.

Until now, every developer developing a web application had to re-invent the wheel, creating their own tracing mechanism and facing the problems described above. But now ASP.NET introduces a new tracing facility, intended to free the developer from such chores.

This new functionality – designed from the ground up to avoid all the drawbacks mentioned above – is implemented by the `TraceContext` class that is exposed via the public `Trace` property of the `Page` class. This makes the tracing feature easily available in every place where you deal with a page.

If we use the methods of the `TraceContext` class to output our tracing messages to the browser, ASP.NET arranges for these messages to be rendered at the bottom of the page – after the "proper" content of the page – so that the two different types of information being rendered don't get mixed. Apart from printing our custom messages, ASP.NET will also output key data for our page and application, like the items of the `Form` collection, the items of the `QueryString` collection, the `Application` state, the `Session` state, etc. We will cover this in detail in the following sections.

Enabling Tracing in ASP.NET

We can easily enable tracing for a page by setting the `Trace` attribute to `true` in the `Page` directive for our page:

```
<%@ Page Trace="true"
         Language="c#" AutoEventWireup="false"
         Codebehind="NewUser.aspx.cs"
         Inherits="FriendsReunionSec.NewUser" %>
```

Try It Out – Enabling Trace Information for the News Page

So, enabling trace information for a single page in our application is simple: we just specify the `Trace` attribute in the `Page` directive and set it to `true`. Let's do this for the news page of our *Friends Reunion* application, and take a look at the type of information it gives us.

1. Using Visual Studio .NET, browse the *Friends Reunion* files and open `News.aspx`. Switch to HTML mode and add the `Trace` attribute to the `Page` directive like this:

```
<%@ Page Trace="true"
        language="c#" Codebehind="News.aspx.cs"
        AutoEventWireup="false" Inherits="FriendsReunion.News" %>
```

If you prefer a "visual" approach, you can do this from the **Design** view. Click anywhere on the form (but not over a control!) so that the **Properties** window shows the properties of the page. Then find the **trace** property and set it to **True**.

2. In the Solution Explorer, right-click on `News.aspx` and choose **Set As Start Page**. Now press *Ctrl+F5* (this is the **start without debugging** shortcut) and login into *Friends Reunion*. After that you will be redirected to `News.aspx`. Notice that the tracing information has been appended after the regular output of the page:

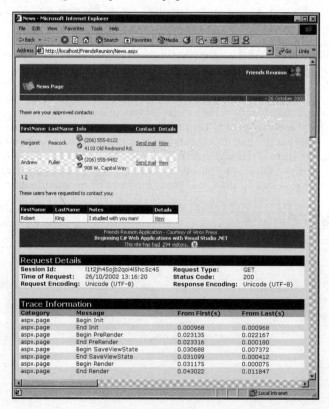

3. Scroll down through the tracing information. You'll see that it's divided into several different sections.

How It Works

As part of its normal processing, the Page class checks to see if tracing is enabled for the page before and after performing any major task (loading viewstate, processing events, rendering its content, etc.). If tracing *is* enabled, the Page class will output corresponding tracing messages by using the TraceContext class's Write method.

The trace is broken down into 10 sections:

❑ **Request details**: this is summary information with the details of the request we just made; it includes:

Field	Description
Session ID	This is the session ID for the specified request
Request Type	The HTTP method used (POST or GET)
Time of Request	The date and time the request was made
Status Code	The status code of the response (see http://www.w3c.org, RFC 2616, Section 6.1.1, for a list of these status codes)
Request Encoding	The character encoding for the request (for example, UTF-8, ASCII, etc.)
Response Encoding	The character encoding for the response (for example UTF-8, ASCII, etc.)

❑ **Trace information**: this includes all the trace messages that are generated automatically by ASP.NET and our application. The following information will be shown for each message:

Field	Description
Category	The category to which the message belongs
Message	The text of the message itself
From First (s)	The time (in seconds) since the first trace message was generated
From Last (s)	The time (in seconds) since the most recent previous trace message was generated

In the next example, we'll see how to add our own custom trace messages to this output.

❑ **Control tree**: this lists all the controls available in the page in an indented hierarchical fashion, which allows us to differentiate between parent and child controls. This is very useful, for example, when adding controls dynamically – to check that they are being added to the correct parent. Also, it shows the render size and viewstate size of each control, so we can check that neither of these values goes too high.

❑   **Session State**: this is a list of the name, type and value of all objects stored in the current `Session` collection.

❑   **Application State**: this is a list of the name, type and value of all objects stored in the `Application` collection.

❑   **Cookies collection**: this lists the name and value of each cookie that was sent with our request.

❑   **Headers collection**: this lists the names and values of the HTTP headers that the client sent to the server.

❑   **Form collection**: this displays the names and values of all form elements, along with the built-in _ _VIEWSTATE form field. These values should give us a brief representation of the state of each one of the controls contained in the page. Note that data for this section will not be displayed if our page doesn't contain a form (obviously!) or if it is our first request for the page – it will only be displayed on postbacks.

❑   **Querystring collection**: this comes handy when we need to check whether the page is really receiving a specific parameter via the querystring, and to find out what value has been set. We will get no output for this section if no parameters are specified.

❑   **Server variables**: this section provides a dump of all predetermined server environment variables.

Adding Custom Tracing Statements to Friends Reunion

The information we get by default by enabling tracing in a page (as demonstrated above) is very useful, and in many cases it provides us with enough information to allow us to isolate and solve a particular problem. However, tracing is more powerful than that: we can also add our *own* **tracing statements** that tell the application to output specific information that we need about the state of the application at any particular point.

The TraceContext class provides two methods that provide this capability: the Write() method and the Warn() method. Each of these writes a message to the **trace log** (the log of all trace information generated by the application).

Each of these methods has three overloads. In the example that follows, we'll use the one that takes two string arguments. The first argument corresponds to the **category** of the message we want to output, and the second argument is the **text** of the message itself. The ability to specify a category is useful as we'll see later, because we can define our own categories and have the trace output sorted alphabetically by category.

The only difference between the two methods is that the Warn() method marks its messages as warnings. Any message you output using this method will get rendered using a suggestive red color. This is useful when you're scanning the trace information, because it makes it easy to differentiate between regular trace messages and warning messages.

In order to exploit these capabilities of the ASP.NET tracing feature, let's output some trace messages of our own during the process where we insert new users. This will allow us to examine the path the code takes, and to check that everything is running as we expect it to.

1. Using VS.NET, open the `NewUser.aspx` file (in the `Secure` folder). Add a `Trace` attribute to the `Page` directive like we did in the previous example:

```
<%@ Page Trace="true"
        language="c#" Codebehind="NewUser.aspx.cs"
        AutoEventWireup="false"
        Inherits="FriendsReunion.Secure.NewUser" %>
```

2. Now switch to the Code view (`NewUser.aspx.cs`), and make the following changes to the `InsertUser()` method:

```
private void InsertUser()
{
    Trace.Write("FriendsReunion", "We're entering the InsertUser() method");

    if (Page.IsValid)
    {
        Trace.Write("FriendsReunion", "Data was validated ok");

        // Save new user to the database
        ...etc...

        // Format the string with the array of values
        sql = String.Format(sb.ToString(), values.ToArray());

        Trace.Write("FriendsReunion",
                    "Connection String used: " +
            ConfigurationSettings.AppSettings["cnFriends.ConnectionString"]);

        // Connect and execute the query
        ...etc...
        try
        {
            cmd.ExecuteNonQuery();
        }
        catch(Exception e)
        {
            Trace.Warn("FriendsReunion",
                       "An exception was thrown: " + e.Message.ToString());
            doredirect = false;
            this.lblMessage.Visible = true;
            this.lblMessage.Text = "Couldn't update your profile!";
        }
        ...etc...
```

```
      //if (doredirect)
      //    Response.Redirect("../Default.aspx");
    }
    Trace.Write("FriendsReunion", "We're leaving the InsertUser() method");
}
```

As well as adding five trace statements here, we've done two other things. First, we've added an Exception declaration to the catch block, so that the Trace.Warn() method there can report its Message property to the trace log. Second, we have commented out the Response.Redirect() call. This prevents the page from being redirected to Login.aspx, and gives us a chance to look at the trace information for the NewUser.aspx page.

The ConfigurationSettings class is from the System.Configuration namespace, so you'll need to make sure there's a using statement for this namespace at the top of the NewUser.aspx.cs file:

```
using System.Configuration;
```

Make sure you save this work before the next step.

3. Use *Ctrl+F5* to start the application without debugging. Click on the Register link; then fill in the registration form and click on the Accept button. After the page postback, scroll down a bit and have a look at the Trace Information section. It should read something like this:

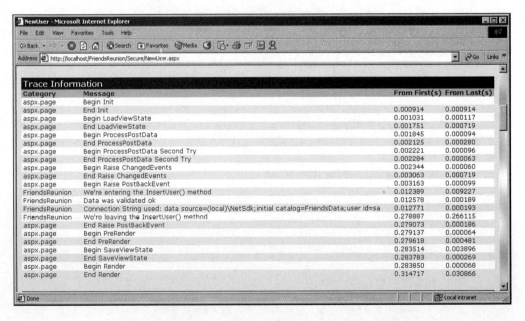

4. Now fill the registration form again, this time using the same username that you provided before. Click the Accept button and get a look at the Trace Information one more time:

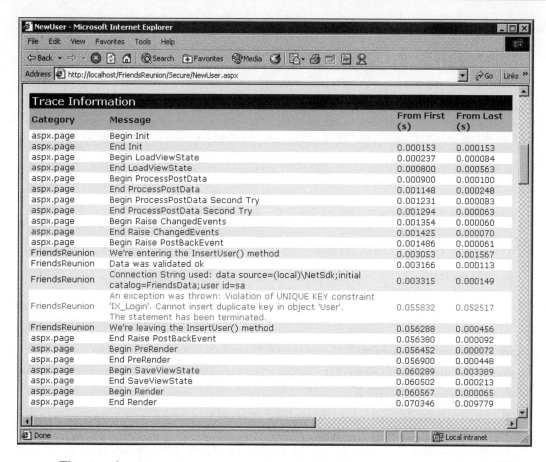

This time there is one extra trace message in the FriendsReunion category. The extra one is actually displayed in red, because it's a warning (generated by the Warn() method), which tells us that the user is trying to take a username that already exists on the database.

How It Works

Our new custom tracing code outputs messages to the Trace Information section in the same way as the Page class does. In this simple example, we've used the trace to check the execution path that the application takes. We expect the InsertUser() method to run, and we expect to see the four regular trace messages that we've placed in that method.

We don't expect any of those messages to be missing from the trace output, and we don't expect any of the messages to appear more than once. If they did, we could deduce that there is a problem with the application's flow, and then we would take further steps to pinpoint the exact problem and fix it.

We deliberately used the Trace.Warn() method in the catch block, because it helps us to see when the execution path leads to an exception being thrown. Finally, the From First (s) and From Last (s) columns tell us how much time has passed since the first message and since the previous message.

Enabling and Disabling Trace at the Application Level

We've seen how to enable tracing for a particular page. But if we're developing an application that contains lots of pages, it is potentially more convenient to enable tracing across the whole application in one go.

You can control this in the application's Web.config file, through the <trace> element, which belongs under the <system.web> element. If there is no <trace> element, you need to add one like the one shown below; if there's one there already, just change its enabled attribute to true:

```
<configuration>
   ...
   <system.web>
     <trace enabled="true" requestLimit="10" pageOutput="true"
            traceMode="SortByTime" localOnly="false" />
     ...
   </system.web>
   ...
</configuration>
```

With this set, all your pages will contain trace information. It's then possible to *disable* tracing on an individual page, if you wish, by setting Trace="false" in the Page directive of that page.

Attributes of the <trace> Element

As you can see, the <trace> element in Web.config has quite a number of other attributes, and it's worth a quick look over them to see what they're for:

❑   The enabled attribute allows us to enable or disable tracing for the application (its default is false).

❑   The requestLimit attribute is the maximum number of trace requests to be stored on the server (the default is 10). We'll see this in action in the next example, which looks at something called the trace viewer.

❑   The pageOutput attribute allows us to force the tracing information to be appended to the application's pages, in the way we've seen in the screenshots above.

❑   The traceMode attribute sets the mode used to display trace information. It can be SortByTime (which sorts them in the order they were processed) or SortByCategory (which sorts them by category). The default is SortByTime.

❑   The localOnly attribute allows us to specify where the tracing information is available. If it's set to true (the default), tracing information will only be available on the host server. For viewing trace information from a browser running on a PC *other* than the host machine, you have to set this to false.

Be sure to specify the exact casing we used above as attributes are case-sensitive; if you specify any with the wrong casing you will get an error.

The Trace Viewer

We have seen how to enable tracing for a single page or an entire application, and how to add our own tracing statements. Although all that may seem to be sufficient ASP.NET tracing capability, we are still missing an important feature that needs to be covered: namely `trace.axd`, or the **trace viewer**.

The purpose of the trace viewer is based on the fact that the server stores the tracing information for a specified number of the most recent requested pages. (By default, this number is 10 – we can use the `requestLimit` attribute of the `<trace>` element in `Web.config` to change this value.) You can use the trace viewer to access all that trace information.

This means that you can step through a number of different pages in the course of testing the application, and then review the trace for all those pages at your leisure when you've finished.

Try It Out – Using the Trace Viewer

In this example we are going to use the trace viewer to access the tracing information recorded by the server for the last 10 pages requested. We'll see summary and detailed views of the tracing information – all this with just a browser and a few clicks!

1. Make sure you have enabled tracing at the application level. As a reminder: you can do this by locating the `<trace>` element in the `<system.web>` section of the `web.config` file, and changing its `enabled` attribute to `true`.

2. Point your browser to *Friends Reunion*, log in and start surfing to different pages (News, User Administration, Assign Places, and so on).

3. Now browse to the `trace.axd` file in the application directory of *Friends Reunion* (`http://localhost/FriendsReunion/trace.axd`). Your output should look like this:

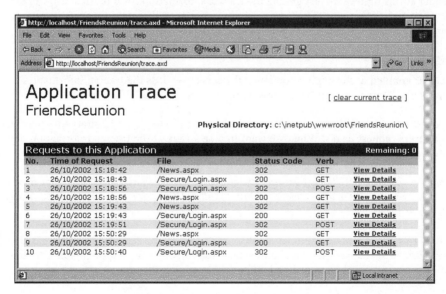

As you can see, `trace.axd` presents you with a summary list of the last 10 pages for which we have tracing information recorded. On each entry we have a link named View Details, which will get us to a details page.

4. Clicking on any of the View Details links will get you to the details page for that particular page:

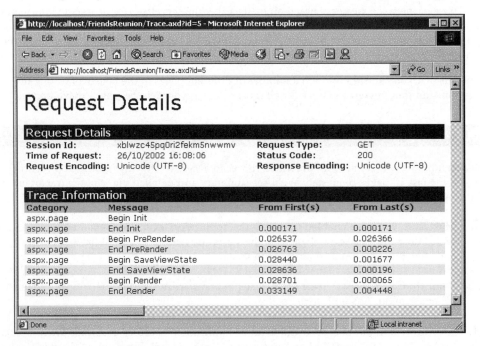

Note that at this time we're just getting the tracing information for a particular page, but we're not getting regular content now. That's because we're not actually requesting the pages now – we're just looking at the trace information that was generated at the time the page was requested.

How It Works

When trace is enabled at the application level, the server records the tracing information for pages most recently visited; the trace viewer makes this trace information available to us after the event.

This trace recording is totally transparent and doesn't require any special intervention by the user; it just happens as users request pages. When we want to take a look at the tracing information captured by the server, we just open a browser and navigate to `trace.axd`.

> *In fact, we can use any URL that begins with the application directory and ends with the filename* `trace.axd`, *so something as random as http://localhost/FriendsReunion/f1/f2/trace.axd will also do the job.*

Note that there's no such file as `trace.axd` in your application. What happens here is that the request is intercepted by a specialized HTTP Handler that responds by showing the recorded tracing information – instead of going to disk to look for the specified filename.

An HTTP Handler is a piece of code that gets a chance to work with HTTP requests at a basic level. Detailed discussion is out of scope of this book; if you want to learn more about the topic, try Chapter 13 of Professional ASP.NET (Wrox, ISBN 1-86100-488-5).

Tracing and Assertions in .NET

In a chapter about debugging, we really ought to take a look at some of the other features (aside from the ASP.NET-specific ones) in the .NET Framework that can help us to debug our applications. In this section, we're going to concentrate on **assertions** and how can we benefit from using them in our code.

An assertion is a statement in the programming code that enables you to test your assumptions about your application. Each assertion contains a **Boolean expression** that you believe to be true when the assertion executes:

❑   If the expression evaluates to `true`, your assumption about the behavior of your application is confirmed, increasing your confidence that the application is free from errors.

❑   If the expression evaluates to `false`, an error will be thrown and you will need to check what went wrong and made your assumption fail.

For example, if you write a method that calculates the age of a person you might assert that the result is greater than 0 and less than, say, 120.

If we include additional code to use assertions, will that added code have an impact on the performance and code size of our application? The answer is "no", because all assertion code is only compiled when we create a debug build; for release builds, it is automatically discarded. This means we can use assertions to write robust code without affecting the performance and code size of our final application.

Using Assertions in .NET Code

The.NET Framework provides an entire namespace, called `System.Diagnostics`, which is dedicated to diagnosing applications. This namespace contains very powerful classes that will allow you to manage system processes, performance counters, and event logs. For reasons of space, we can't cover all these here, but we recommend that you browse the documentation at http://msdn.microsoft.com/library for these classes – they'll come handy very often.

The tracing and assertion mechanisms are implemented by the `Trace` and `Debug` classes respectively. The two classes are almost identical, providing the same properties, methods, and method overloads. The only difference is that any code that uses the `Debug` class is only compiled for debug builds, while code written using the `Trace` class is compiled for both debug *and* release builds.

There isn't much to say about the `Trace` class as, for our purposes, it works in a similar way to the `TraceContext` class we saw in the previous example. One significant difference is that the `Trace` class by default will send its output to the Output window, instead of directing it to the rendered page.

There is one important (and slightly inconvenient) difference between the `Trace.Write()` and `Debug.Write()` methods and the `TraceContext.Write()` method: the order of arguments is inverted! The former expect the message text to be provided before the category name, while the latter expects the category to come first.

Using Assertions in Friends Reunion

Where we could use assertions in *Friends Reunion*? Let's take a look at the first lines for the `Render()` method of `FriendsBase.cs` file:

```
protected override void Render(System.Web.UI.HtmlTextWriter writer)
{
    ...
    // Get a reference to the form control
    HtmlForm form = (HtmlForm)Page.Controls[1];
```

Note that this code grabs a reference to the control at index `[1]` in the `Page.Controls` collection, and assigns it to the `form` variable, but it does so without checking that it really is a reference to the type of control we need there. The rest of the code in that method depends on the assumption that the variable `form` really *does* refer to a control of type `HtmlForm`.

> *How could the form fail to be there? It should be there for a page newly-created in VS.NET, but a developer might delete it in the course of editing the `.aspx` page (perhaps because the developer didn't need an `HtmlForm` control at all), or include some other controls before it (which would cause the desired `HtmlForm` control to be at an index higher than 1 in the collection).*

One way to solve this would be to modify the code so it doesn't depend on the `Form` control being positioned at an exact index. However, if we do that, it will affect the rest of our logic. So, we'll preserve the current code and instead use an assertion to ensure that the expression `Page.Controls[1]` really does refer to a control of type `HtmlForm`.

Try It Out – Adding an Assertion

Let's make use of an assertion in our *Friends Reunion* application for making sure we always have a `Form` control exactly at index `[1]` in the `Page.Controls` collection so the rest of our logic will work as expected. We will be adding a new page to display legal information about the use of our application.

1. Using VS.NET, add a new web form and name it `LegalStuff.aspx`. Then edit its code-behind file to make it inherit from our custom `FriendsBase` class instead of `System.Web.UI.Page`:

```
public class LegalStuff : FriendsBase
```

2. Now we need to alter the default HTML created by VS.NET for our page. Open `LegalStuff.aspx` in **HTML** view, and delete the entire `<form>` element (we won't need it in this page). Now add the following code:

```html
<html>
  <head>
    <title>LegalStuff</title>
    <meta name="GENERATOR" content="Microsoft Visual Studio 7.0">
    <meta name="CODE_LANGUAGE" content="C#">
    <meta name="vs_defaultClientScript" content="JavaScript">
    <meta name="vs_targetSchema"
          content="http://schemas.microsoft.com/intellisense/ie5">
    <link href="Style/iestyle.css" type="text/css" rel="stylesheet">
  </head>
  <body ms_positioning="FlowLayout">
    <asp:label runat="server" id="Label1">Legal Stuff</asp:label>
    <br/><br/>
    <asp:label runat="server" id="Label2">
      If you notice this notice you will notice
      that the notice is not worth noticing.
    </asp:label>
  </body>
</html>
```

3. Now open `FriendsBase.cs` and add the following line at the top of the file:

```csharp
using System.Diagnostics;
```

4. Still in `FriendsBase.cs`, edit the `Render()` method of the `FriendsBase` class to add our assertion code:

```csharp
protected override void Render(System.Web.UI.HtmlTextWriter writer)
{
  // Remove the controls from their current place in the hierarchy
  Page.Controls.Remove(_header);
  Page.Controls.Remove(_subheader);
  Page.Controls.Remove(_footer);

  Debug.Assert(
    Page.Controls[1].ToString()=="System.Web.UI.HtmlControls.HtmlForm",
    "Form control not found",
    "Any FriendsReunion page requires that a Form control be " +
    "located at index 1 of the Page.Controls collection");

  // Get a reference to the form control
  HtmlForm form = (HtmlForm)Page.Controls[1];
  ...
```

5. Select Project | Properties and make sure that your project's Configuration is set to Debug:

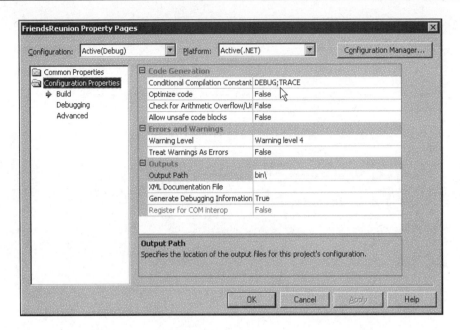

6. Set `LegalStuff.aspx` as the start page and press *F5* to start the application in the debugger; a new instance of Internet Explorer will open, showing the login page for *Friends Reunion*. Log in to the application and you will be automatically redirected to the `LegalStuff.aspx` page. However, the page will fail, and you'll see an unpleasant error message:

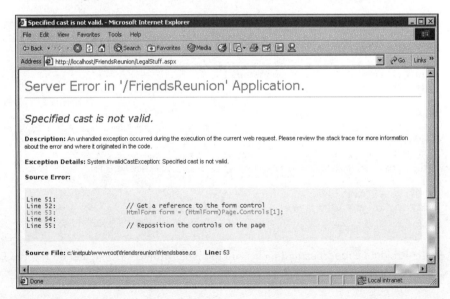

7. Go now to the VS.NET and take a look at the Output window (type *Ctrl+Alt+O* to make it visible). It should look like this:

```
Output                                                                              X
Debug                                                                               ▼
 ---- DEBUG ASSERTION FAILED ----
 ---- Assert Short Message ----
 Form control not found
 ---- Assert Long Message ----
 Any FriendsReunion page requires that a Form control be located at index 1 of the Page.Controls collection

       at FriendsBase.Render(HtmlTextWriter writer)   c:\inetpub\wwwroot\friendsreunion\friendsbase.cs(53)
       at Control.RenderControl(HtmlTextWriter writer)
       at Page.ProcessRequestMain()
       at Page.ProcessRequest()
       at Page.ProcessRequest(HttpContext context)
```

How It Works

Using the `Debug.Assert()` method we have asserted that the control at index `[1]` of the `Page.Controls` collection should always be of type `HtmlForm`:

```
Debug.Assert(
     Page.Controls[1].ToString()=="System.Web.UI.HtmlControls.HtmlForm",
     "Form control not found",
     "Any FriendsReunion page requires that a Form control be " +
     "located at index 1 of the Page.Controls collection");
```

In the first argument, we specify the Boolean condition we expect to evaluate to `true` at run time if everything is working as expected.

This assumption we're making should be true in order for our application to continue to run, because subsequent code expects it to be that way. If this assertion we've coded is not true then we can't guarantee how our application will perform – at best we might get some strange rendering, at worst there's the rude possibility of exceptions being thrown and our application terminating abruptly (as in this case).

When we started debugging *Friends Reunion* and requested the `LegalStuff.aspx` page (which doesn't include a `<form>` element) our assertion code eventually got executed and the Boolean expression evaluated to `false`. This caused the message text to be outputted to the debugger's Output Window.

The Visual Studio .NET Debugger

We've looked at a number of different methods for debugging our application, but we haven't yet looked at any debugging software. Let's round off this section with a look at the **Visual Studio .NET debugger**.

The VS.NET debugger takes many web developers into new territory – it's the first tool that enables us to debug a web application using techniques similar to those we'd use when debugging a traditional (Windows) application. In VS.NET, all you need to do in order to start the debugger is hit *F5*.

One of the most tedious problems found with previous versions of the debugger was its inability to detach from a running process without killing it. For a web application, if the debugger kills the process used to run the application then any state information will be lost. Now, thanks to the Common Language Runtime (CLR), the debugger can **detach** from a process without killing it – by selecting Debug | Stop Debugging from the menu bar.

The VS.NET debugger allows us to debug across different languages, and to debug multiple processes across machines. Besides these new features, there is more good news – many of the features that have been previously available only when debugging traditional applications can be used now for debugging web applications!

Let's start touring along the most useful debugger windows.

Breakpoints

In the VS.NET debugger, we can mark any line of code with a **breakpoint**. When the application runs in the debugger, and reaches a line that has a breakpoint, it causes the execution to pause. When the application has paused like this, it is said to be in **break mode**. With the application in break mode, we can perform a number of activities. We can examine the values of variables and object properties, and we can even change these values.

We can also ask the debugger to continue execution one line at a time, stepping through or over subroutines as we desire. Stepping through the code like this is a particularly useful technique, because it allows us to watch the code, observe the values contained in variables' object properties, in "slow motion" – and use this analysis to spot semantic coding errors.

To set a breakpoint in the code, you can click on the gray left margin on the line where you want execution to pause, or position the cursor over the line you're interested in and press *F9*. You will notice that a red filled circle appears, giving a clear indication that a breakpoint has been set and is enabled at that point:

```
// If IsAdministrator field is true, add both roles
if (reader.GetBoolean(0))
{
    roles = new string[] {"User", "Admin"};
}
else
```

Managing Breakpoints

It's often useful to have a few breakpoints in different places in your code. To allow us to manage our breakpoints, the VS.NET debugger provides us with a Breakpoints window. To view the Breakpoints window, select Debug | Windows | Breakpoints from the menu bar or press *Ctrl+Alt+B*:

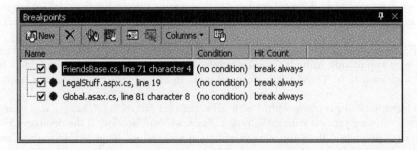

This window allows us to add and remove breakpoints. It also allows us to enable and disable breakpoints. (A disabled breakpoint will keep its place in the code, but won't pause execution when execution reaches that line of code.) We can also use this window to set the properties of a breakpoint.

To remove all your breakpoints in a single step, press Ctrl+Shift+F9.

In the next few examples we will get some hands-on experience of the VS.NET debugger, by applying it to our *Friends Reunion* application.

Try It Out – Setting a Breakpoint in the VS.NET Debugger

We'll start by creating a breakpoint that causes the application to pause whenever a request for an already authenticated user is about to be processed.

1. Double-click on `global.asax` to open `global.asax.cs`, and find the following line in the `Application_AuthenticateRequest()` method:

```
String id = Context.User.Identity.Name;
```

Set a breakpoint at this line, by clicking on the gray margin to the left of the code (adjacent to that line), or by placing your cursor on the line and hitting *F9*:

```
        protected void Application_AuthenticateRequest(Object sender, EventArgs e)
        {
            // Cast the sender to the application
            HttpApplication app = (HttpApplication)sender;

            // Only replace the context if it has already been handled
            // by forms authentication module (user is authenticated)
            if (app.Request.IsAuthenticated)
            {
                SqlConnection con;
                string sql;
                SqlCommand cmd;

                string id = Context.User.Identity.Name;

                con = new SqlConnection(
                    ConfigurationSettings.AppSettings["cnFriends.ConnectionString"]);
                sql = "SELECT IsAdministrator FROM [User] WHERE UserId='{0}'";
                sql = String.Format(sql, id);
                cmd = new SqlCommand(sql, con);
                con.Open();
```

If you like, you can view the detail about this breakpoint by looking in the **Breakpoints** window. To so this, type *Ctrl+Alt+B*:

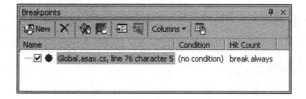

2. In the Solution Explorer, right-click on `Default.aspx` and select **Set as Start Page**.

3. Now we're ready to run the application in the debugger. Press *F5*. A new browser instance will open, pointing to the *Friends Reunion* login page. Enter the usual credentials (username wrox, password wrox).

Click the Login button: this submits the login request to the application. This will cause focus to switch to the Visual Studio .NET debugger, and you will see that yellow highlighting is used to pick out the line with the breakpoint on it.

Don't stop the application yet; we'll continue from here in the next *Try It Out*. First, let's see what we've done so far.

How It Works

Because we chose to run the application in the debugger, execution will pause whenever it reaches any line that has an (enabled) breakpoint. That's exactly what happens here: when the application receives the login credentials, it begins to process them. As part of that process, the application needs to execute the line on which we placed the breakpoint. When the application reaches that line, it does not execute it; instead, it pauses:

The debugger highlights the progress it has made by using yellow highlighting (in the code) and a yellow arrow (in the gray left-hand margin). At this point, the application is in break mode and the debugger is awaiting further instructions from us.

Breakpoint Properties

Note that we can do a lot with a breakpoint by changing its behavior. To view the properties of a breakpoint, select it in the Breakpoints window and then click on the Properties icon. This brings up the Breakpoint Properties window:

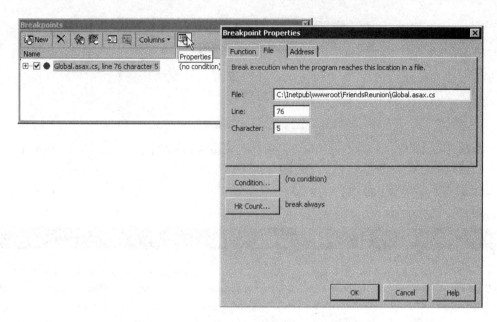

In particular, note the Condition... and Hit Count... buttons at the bottom at the bottom of this dialog:

❑   The first allows us to specify a **condition** that will be evaluated when the breakpoint is hit, and whose result will determine whether or not the execution is paused at that breakpoint. For example, we may want our *Friends Reunion* application to halt only when a user belonging to the 'Admin' group is logged in.

❑   The second allows us to specify the number of times a breakpoint must be hit before it pauses the application.

The Watch Window

One of the most important features a debugger has to offer is the ability to examine the internals of the application being debugged. In the VS.NET debugger, we use the Watch window to perform that task.

We can use the Watch window while debugging to check the current value and output type of any variable or expression. More importantly, the Watch window also allows us to *modify* a variable's value. This is a very powerful technique to use when debugging – it allows us to try different values for a variable, and watch the execution path to see how the application responds, without repeatedly restarting the application.

You will notice that there are actually *four* Watch windows available – named Watch 1, Watch 2, etc. These are provided to make easier to debug large applications – it allows us to group related variables into different windows and focus on the variables we need at a given time. In this chapter we'll just use the Watch 1 window (and we'll refer to it as the Watch window).

To open the Watch window, select Debug | Windows | Watch | Watch 1 from the menu bar. This window will be empty when you first view it, but you'll be able to see its three columns:

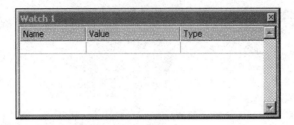

The Name column is where we type the expression we want to evaluate. When you do that, its value and output type appear in the Value and Type columns.

Let's make use of the Watch window now.

Try It Out – Step-by-step Execution and the Watch Window

Remember we left the *Friends Reunion* application in break mode at the end of the last *Try It Out*? Well, we'll pick it up from there, and use the Watch window to check the current values of some variables in the application.

1. Open a Watch window (select Debug | Windows | Watch | Watch 1 from the menu bar or press *Ctrl+Alt+W, 1*). We'll use it to watch the sql variable. To do this, type the name of the variable in the Name column:

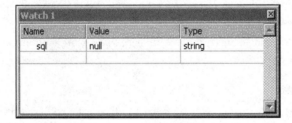

The Watch window will confirm the value and type of the sql variable. The application has not yet reached the point in its processing where it assigns a value to sql, so the Watch window correctly tells us that its value is still null. It also reports that sql is a **string** type.

2. Now return to the code window; the VS.NET debugger should still be using yellow highlighting and the yellow arrow to indicate the next line to be executed:

```
SqlCommand cmd;

string id = Context.User.Identity.Name;

con = new SqlConnection(ConfigurationSetting
```

Let's run the next few lines of code step by step. You can select **Debug | Step Over** for each step, but it's easier to use the shortcut, *F10*. So, press *F10* just once. This causes the highlighted line to be executed; VS.NET now pauses the execution before the next line (and the yellow highlighting and yellow arrow have moved to reflect that).

3. Press *F10* two more times, so that the application creates the new `SQLConnection` object and sets the value of the `sql` string variable:

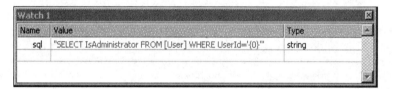

Immediately after the second click, go back to the **Watch** window. It is updated automatically to reflect the fact that the value of the `sql` variable has changed. It is now showing the value of the string we just assigned to it (and it's displayed in red, to show that the value has just changed):

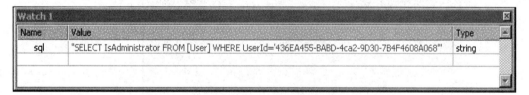

4. Pressing *F10* one more time will execute another assignment of the `sql` variable thus causing its **Value** column to change again. The **Watch** window will now look something like this:

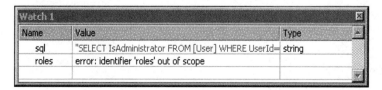

Hence, we get to peek at the SQL statement that will be sent to SQL Server.

5. Now let's add a watch for the `roles` variable. This time, find a place where the `roles` variable is used in the code (look within the `try` block of the `Application_AuthenticateRequest()` method), right-click on the variable and select **Add Watch**. This will place a new entry in the **Watch** window:

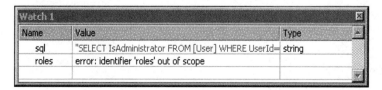

435

In the Value column you can see an error telling us that roles is currently out of scope. That's OK; in fact, it's what we'd expect, because we are watching a variable that hasn't been defined yet! We'll be using it in the next example.

6. Press *F10* a few more times, but stop before the following if clause is executed:

```
// Ensure closing the connection
try
{
    object admin = cmd.ExecuteScalar();

    // Was it a valid UserID?
    if (admin != null)
    {
        GenericPrincipal ppal;
        string[] roles;

        // If IsAdministrator field is true, add bot
        if (((bool)admin) == true)
        {
```

It would be really handy if we can tell whether the expression (bool)admin is going to evaluate to true or false *before* we execute the line. We can do this really quickly, using the QuickWatch window. Select the full expression for the condition (*just* the expression and *not* the brackets that enclose it), then right-click and select QuickWatch…. This will cause the QuickWatch window to open. This window works in a similar way to the Watch window, showing the expression you've selected and what the expression evaluates to:

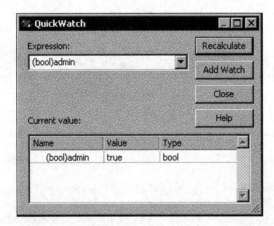

7. Now close the QuickWatch dialog, and hit *F10* one more time. You'll see that the expression really does evaluate to true, because the execution enters the if statement.

Again, don't stop the debugger just yet; we'll continue this exercise in the next *Try It Out.*

How It Works

You can see how the Watch window can help us to get information about what's happening inside the application. It can stay open all the time, so we can watch variables and expressions to see how their values change as the execution progresses. A value that is shown in red is one that was changed as a result of the last executed step.

The QuickWatch dialog works in roughly the same way as the Watch window, though you should note that it's modal. (So, you can step through the application with the Watch window open, but not the QuickWatch dialog.)

The `roles` variable is not a simple object – in fact, it's an array of objects. How does the Watch window cope with things like complex objects and arrays? We'll find out in the next example, in which we'll also see how to use the Watch window to *change* the value of a variable during the debugging process.

Try It Out – More on the Watch Window

We left the *Friends Reunion* application in break mode at the end of the last *Try It Out*, so we'll pick it up from there again, and do some more tasks with the Watch window.

1. Find the following line in the `Application_AuthenticateRequest()` method, a few lines on from the `if` block we discussed in the previous example:

```
Context.User = ppal;
```

Right-click on this line and select Run To Cursor. This will cause the application to execute a few steps further, as far as this line.

2. Check the value of `roles` in the Watch window. We have just stepped over the line that assigns the `roles` variable, so you should now be able to see that `roles` is of type string[ ] (an array of strings) with two strings. There's a + icon at the left of the variable name, which tells us that the type being watched is not a simple type. We can watch the types contained within roles by clicking on the + icon:

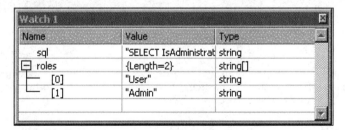

What does this show? Well, we logged in as the user called `wrox`, and this user is an administrator user. Thus, it belongs to both the `User` and `Admin` groups, and hence has two roles. These are the two roles are shown here.

3. Now, let's edit the value of the `roles` variable. In the Watch window, change the value of `roles[1]` (the string at index `[1]` in the array) from Admin to Guest, then hit *Enter*. The Watch window will look like this, and "Guest" will be highlighted in red to show that you've just changed it:

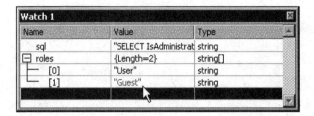

4. Finally, hit *F5* – this will cause the application to continue its execution from the point where we just left off, using any new values we inserted in the Watch window in the previous step:

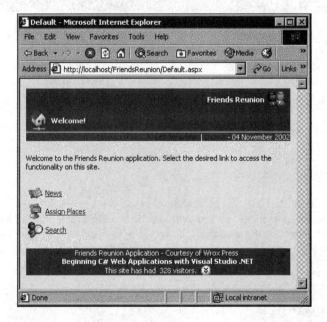

How It Works

In break mode, the Run to Cursor option in the context menu is a handy way of getting the application to execute as far as a certain point – it's particularly useful when the only other way of reaching the desired point is by hitting *F10* repeatedly.

One particularly interesting thing here is the way in which values changed in the Watch window can change the way the application behaves halfway through its execution. We can see evidence of this by looking at the way the application uses the value of `roles[1]`. First, the process above will log you in as an *administrator* user. That's because when the application is stepped through the lines of code that oversee the *login*, the value of `roles[1]` is Admin.

However, in the page that is shown at the end of Step 4 above doesn't display the **Users Administration Page** link (which is usually displayed to any administrator member). Why is that? Well, you may recall from Chapter 10 that this line of code (in `Default.aspx.cs`) is the line in which the application decides whether to show that link:

```
// Show the Admin link only to administrators
this.lnkUsers.Visible = User.IsInRole("Admin");
```

However, we changed the value of `roles[1]` (in Step 3 above) *before* the application executed that line. When this line is executed, the expression `User.IsInRole("Admin")` returns `false` (because we changed the `Admin` entry in the `roles` array in Step 3), and so the link remains invisible.

The Call Stack Window

When you call a method that calls another method, which in turns calls another method (and so on), a **call stack** is created. It's very useful to be able to see the call stack, and to do that we can use the **Call Stack** window.

The **Call Stack** window is only available while the application being debugged is in *break* mode – to see it, select **Debug | Windows | Call Stack** from the menu bar or press *Ctrl+Alt+C*.

This window has information about each method: its name, its parameters types, and its parameters values. As well as giving you a good idea of the path your code has taken, it also allows you to navigate forward and backward into the stack to debug at any place.

Try It Out – Using the Call Stack Window

So let's see the **Call Stack** window in action while debugging *Friends Reunion*.

1. Open the file `NewUser.aspx.cs` (in the `Secure` folder). Add a breakpoint at the first line of the `InsertUser()` method, by clicking on the gray margin to the left of the code (adjacent to that line), or by placing your cursor on the line and hitting *F9*:

```
private void InsertUser()
{
    Trace.Write("FriendsReunion", "We're entering the

    if (Page.IsValid)
    {
        Trace.Write("FriendsReunion", "Data was valid
        // Save new user to the database
        SqlConnection con;
```

Notice a red dot is added to that line indicating the active breakpoint. There's no need to remove the trace statements we added in previous examples – they will not affect this example.

2. Set `Secure/NewUser.aspx` as the starting page and press *F5* to launch the application. A new browser will open with the `Secure/NewUser.aspx` page showing; fill in the registration form and press the **Accept** button. Focus should turn to the VS.NET debugger and the **Call Stack** window (*Ctrl+Alt+C*) should look like this:

Notice that the first line shows that execution is stopped at the `InsertUser()` method, as expected. If you examine the remaining lines in the **Call Stack** window, you'll see what path the code took to finally get at this method.

How It Works

The breakpoint that we placed at the start of the `InsertUser()` causes the application to pause at that point, when we're running it using a debugger. After requesting the registration form, filling in the required data and clicking the **Accept** button, the application's path of execution eventually leads to the `InsertUser()` method, hits the breakpoint, and pauses.

At this point, the application is in break mode and we can access the **Call Stack** window. The **Call Stack** window tells us how the application got to the `InsertUser()` method; the second line in the **Call Stack** window shows that the `btnAccept_Click()` method was executed just previously, and is the method that called the `InsertUser()` method.

Further, the `btnAccept_Click()` method itself must have been called by some other method. In fact, the method responsible is a method named `Button:OnClick()`, which is the dispatcher for click events of the **Accept** button we clicked after filling the form. You can see this method named on the third line of the **Call Stack** window, after `btnAccept_Click()`.

Even further, you can check that `Button:OnClick()` was in turn called by `RaisePostBackEvent()`, which is the method called by .NET on noticing that this button control has an event to process.

Armed with these few pieces of debugging functionality, we're in a good position to go hunting for **bugs**, and that's what we'll talk about next.

Hunting for Bugs

Suppose the support team for the *Friends Reunion* application has received a number of e-mails lately from different people, reporting that they can't register successfully on the site.

Typically, these users didn't tell us much about what they experienced when the site failed on them. The only information they provided when contacting support was that they accessed our site, clicked on the **Register** link, filled in the registration form, and clicked the **Accept** button – and the next thing they saw on the browser was a custom error page.

Armed with the experience we just had using the Visual Studio .NET debugger, we can perform a debug session and try to reproduce the error and locate the problem.

Try It Out – Hunting for Bugs in Friends Reunion

We need to know what is happening in *Friends Reunion* to be able to respond to the e-mail enquiries of people who can't register successfully. Our strategy will be to reproduce (as closely as possible) the actions taken by one of the users who couldn't register.

1. Open the file `NewUser.aspx.cs` (from the `Secure` folder). Use the tip we provided in the *Breakpoints* section to clear all breakpoints at a single shot (*Ctrl+Shift+F9*). Then, in the `InsertUser()` method, which is the method that controls addition of new users, set a breakpoint on the line just before the `con.Open()` method call:

```
// Connect and execute the query
con = new SqlConnection(ConfigurationSettings.AppSettings["cnFrie
cmd = new SqlCommand(sql, con);
con.Open();
```

This breakpoint will allow us to pause execution of the application just before the database code executes – and hence step through that code and see whether it's causing a problem. This should help us to determine what may be wrong, or at least eliminate it from our enquiries.

2. Set `Default.aspx` as the starting page. Press *F5* to start debugging our application. A new browser instance should open pointing to the *Friends Reunion* home page. Click the **Register** link to navigate to the **Registration Form** page. Now start filling the form, using *exactly* the same data used by one of the users who contacted us:

Field	Value
User Name	pjenkins
Password	tucker
First Name	Peter
Last Name	Jenkins
Address	3768 Georgetown's Way
Phone Number	345-449-9481
Mobile Number	459-498-2031
E-Mail	peterjenkins@wrox.com
Birth Date	1/5/64

After completing all the fields, click on the **Accept** button to submit the information. Execution of our application will pause at the line where we placed the breakpoint – the focus will turn automatically to the VS.NET debugger.

3. We'll start by looking at what our variables are holding just to check that everything is as we expect. Place the cursor over the `values` variable, right-click and select **QuickWatch...** The **QuickWatch** dialog should open and expanding the _items property should give you this view:

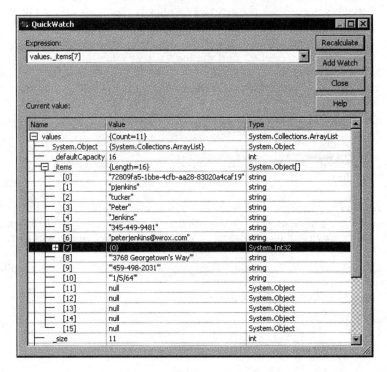

Here we can check that the data we entered back in the registration form is the same data that our application is handling now. This is as expected.

4. Don't close the **QuickWatch** window just yet; we'll use it to take a quick look at the value of the `sql` variable. In the **Expression** field, just type `sql` and then click the **Recalculate** button. The **QuickWatch** window will now show the value for the `sql` variable. You can check it quickly, but you shouldn't find anything wrong. Everything continues to be as expected.

5. We're running out of guesses. Use the **QuickWatch** window one more time to examine the `ConnectionString` property of the `con` variable (that is, the connection string we'll use for connection to the database). Type `con.ConnectionString` directly into the **Expressions** field and click the **Recalculate** button. One more time results are as expected.

It was worth examining all these things, because even though they didn't reveal a problem, each one eliminates another possibility. Close the **QuickWatch** window for now.

6. Press *F10* a few times to get to the cmd.ExecuteNonQuery() method call. In this line, we are calling the code that accesses the database:

```
// Connect and execute the query
con = new SqlConnection(ConfigurationSettings.AppSettin
cmd = new SqlCommand(sql, con);
con.Open();

bool doredirect = true;

try
{
    cmd.ExecuteNonQuery();
}
catch(Exception e)
{
```

This line is in a try block, so if anything goes wrong within this method, our code will jump to the catch block just below it. (We'll look at try and catch blocks and exceptions in the next section of this chapter.) So, press *F10* one more time. This causes the cmd.ExecuteNonQuery() call to be executed, and... the execution pointer *does* move to the catch block! So, something *does* go wrong during the ExecuteNonQuery() method call.

7. Press *F10* one more time so we enter the catch block, and examine the e variable that holds exception that has been raised. We'll use the **QuickWatch** window again, this time to examine the exception object, e. Move the cursor next to the e variable, right-click and select **QuickWatch**...; your output should look like this:

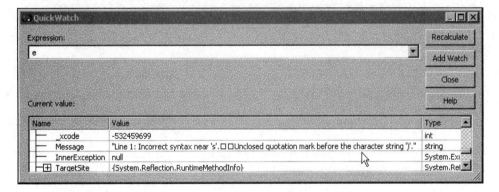

A quick look at the Exception object's Message property will reveal a clue: SQL Server is not happy with the SQL text near to the character s, and it says that we haven't provided a closing quotation mark.

So let's check the value of sql again – type sql into the **Expression** field and press *Enter*, and examine it more closely.

In fact, there *is* a syntax error in the SQL here! The problem arises because the value of the Address field contains a single-quote, and we don't escape it correctly:

443

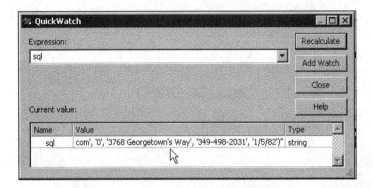

Thus, the string has an odd number of quotations marks. The syntax of this SQL is incorrect, and so SQL Server is unable to parse it.

8. You can check this theory, if you like, by restarting the application by selection Debug | Restart from the menu bar. Our application will be restarted and the previously opened browser will navigate to *Friends Reunion's* homepage. Click the Register link to navigate to the Registration Form page. Fill the form with the same data we've been working on and press the Accept button. Execution will stop at our previously set breakpoint.

9. Open the Watch window by selecting Debug | Windows | Watch | Watch 1 from the menu bar, type sql in the Name column and press enter. The value for the sql variable will appear in the Value column. Now edit this value by clicking over it and delete the quotation mark embedded in the address field:

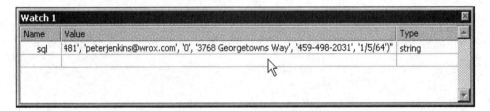

After getting rid of the suspicious quotation mark press enter to save the new edited value.

10. Press *F10* a couple of times to continue the execution of our application and see what happens now after executing the cmd.ExecuteNonQuery();. This time the catch block is not executed and we get directly to the finally block – which is normal – to close the connection. This means we have caught the bug! Now we need to code a fix for it.

11. Stop the debugging of our application by selecting Debug | Stop Debugging from the menu bar. Edit the NewUser.aspx.cs file by making use of the Replace() method to escape any quotation mark that may be entered by the user filling the form:

```
        // Optional values without quotes as they can be the Null value.
        sb.Append("{8}, {9}, {10})");

        // Escape any quotation mark entered by the user
        txtLogin.Text = txtLogin.Text.Replace("'","''");
        txtPwd.Text = txtPwd.Text.Replace("'","''");
        txtFName.Text = txtFName.Text.Replace("'","''");
        txtLName.Text = txtLName.Text.Replace("'","''");
        txtPhone.Text = txtPhone.Text.Replace("'","''");
        txtMobile.Text = txtMobile.Text.Replace("'","''");
        txtEmail.Text = txtEmail.Text.Replace("'","''");
        txtAddress.Text = txtAddress.Text.Replace("'","''");
        txtBirth.Text = txtBirth.Text.Replace("'","''");

        // Add required values to replace
        values.Add(Guid.NewGuid().ToString());
```

You can save this code and run the application again, and you should find that single-quotes in any of the fields should no longer cause a problem.

How It Works

By having the chance to run our suspect code one step at the time while checking the status of key variables, we were able to determine exactly what was going on. The QuickWatch window proved very useful in allowing us to examine the value of any variable. Meanwhile, the Watch window allowed us to make a change to one of our variables, and see how the application continued to run with the changed value.

Once we had identified the bug, it was easy to write a few lines of code to fix it.

Exceptions

An **exception** is a violation of an implicit assumption made by your code. For example, suppose that your application contains code to open a file that it depends upon, but that it doesn't first check that it *can* open the file. Here, your application is making an implicit assumption that the file will always be accessible. What happens if, when the code executes, it *can't* access that file (for example, because its missing or because the application doesn't have enough privileges to access it)? The underlying .NET framework class responsible for opening the file recognizes the reason why it *can't* open the file, and it **throws** an exception.

When an exception is thrown, the exception dictates the application's subsequent execution path:

❑ If the application is able to **catch** the exception, then it will. For this to happen, the application must contain special **exception-handling code**. This kind of code is generally designed both to catch the exception and to handle it in a controlled way.

❑ If the application is unable to catch the exception, then it will bubble up and eventually be caught by the CLR. This will result in an unfriendly exception message appearing on the browser. This is the most undesirable result, and the one we most want to avoid.

Of course, in the example described above, we could code the application to check that the file is accessible before it tries to open it, and to take an alternative execution path if the file is inaccessible. Then, a missing file would no longer be an unexpected occurrence, and no exception would be thrown. But realistically, it's impossible to code for all of the many things that can go wrong – so our code should also be ready to catch general exceptions thrown as a result of other unexpected situations.

In the remainder of this chapter we'll talk about exceptions: throwing them, catching them, and handling them.

Different Uses for Exceptions

So in fact, the example above tells us two things:

❑ First, when it's possible, we should avoid implicit assumptions in our applications, by writing code in our applications to anticipate places where things can go wrong and check for them.

❑ Second, we should also include exception-handling code in our applications, in order to deal with those exceptions that we can't anticipate.

It's clear from the discussion so far that exceptions are a good way to deal with unexpected situations and errors (in particular, input errors) such as missing files, unexpected user input, and network failures. However, it's also worth noting that not all exceptions are thrown in this way. In fact, .NET also allows us to throw exceptions deliberately, so we can also force the application to throw an exception in reaction to an expected problem. We'll see how this can be useful later in the chapter.

Exceptions and Result Codes: a Comparison

To appreciate the power of exceptions, it's useful to look at them in the light of older error-handling techniques. A common technique used in the absence of exceptions is that of the result code.

The concept of a **result code** is quite simple. Method A calls Method B, and when Method B finishes executing, its return value (the result code) is a coded value (usually an integer) that indicates what happened during its execution. Then, Method A must interpret the coded return value and act accordingly.

For years, developers have used this technique for their error-handling. If you have some experience in programming in the Windows environment, then you're probably familiar with the idea of watching for functions that return FALSE, calling the GetLastError function, and dealing with HRESULT codes.

Limitations of Result Codes

The result code technique suffers from two major limitations:

❑ **A result code is not descriptive**. A result code is commonly expressed using a simple type (such as an integer). So, for example, a result code that represents an error generally doesn't provide any detailed information on the error. If a client method receives an *invalid argument* error result code, all we can say for sure is that an argument is invalid; but there's no way to tell *which* of the arguments was invalid or *at what point* the error happened.

❏ **It's easy to ignore a result code.** If Method A calls Method B, it's Method A's responsibility to check the return code returned by Method B, and to act on it. So, it's the responsibility of the developer who writes Method A to ensure that it tests the result code of every method it calls. This is really tedious; moreover, it produces code that is hard to read (because it becomes bloated with condition-checking statements all over the place). It's very easy for developers to become undisciplined, and that undermines the purpose of result codes.

In short, it's well-established that a result code methodology produces code that is hard to maintain, and limited in capability.

How Exceptions Eliminate these Limitations

By embracing exceptions and exception-handling, Microsoft's .NET Framework tackles the limitations of result codes head-on. The following are the key characteristics that make exceptions a far superior methodology for handling errors for our applications:

❏ **Exceptions contain detailed information.** An exception contains lots of useful information that can be used at run time to judge how best to handle situation that caused it. This information is also helpful at development/testing time: it includes information about the source of the exception, a stack trace, and the exact source line at which the exception was thrown. With all this information we should be able to easily identify and fix bugs.

❏ **Exceptions can't be ignored**. If our application throws an exception and doesn't handle it, then the exception will ultimately caught by the CLR. There's no room for undisciplined coding: the exception methodology is far less forgiving and consequently your code will be more robust.

❏ **Exception-handling code is more manageable.** With result codes, you have to deal with the result of each method immediately after the method call, which means you have result-handling code all over your code files. By contrast, we can collect *all* exception-handling code for a page in one place in the file. If something goes wrong, then the CLR will catch up and direct execution to the handling code. That makes the code faster and easier to maintain.

❏ **Cleanup code is more manageable**: Just like the exception-handling code, we can put all the cleanup code in a single place in the file. Moreover, we can rely on it always being executed.

If you're used to using result codes, it means a change of habit. However, exceptions are such a powerful technique that the effort required to learn a little about exceptions and exception-handling will be effort well spent. The benefits you will see in your code are quite significant.

Exceptions and Exception-handling

We've talked a little about throwing and catching errors, and in this section we'll start to see some examples in code. The idea of throwing and catching is really a very simple one:

❏ When the application throws an exception, it's saying "Hey! Something's up. Maybe some rule was violated here. Someone needs to deal with this right away!!"

❏ When the application catches the exception, it's saying "OK, I'm ready to handle this violation right now. Let me deal with it."

In C# four keywords are used when dealing with exception handling: `try`, `catch`, `finally`, and `throw`.

447

Throwing Exceptions

From the point of view of our application code, there are two ways an exception can be thrown. The first is illustrated by the example described earlier, in which our application charges a framework class object with a task (such as opening a file), but the object can't complete the task; so it tries to inform the calling application of the problem by throwing an exception.

Alternatively, the application itself can throw an exception. To do this, we can use the `throw` keyword. For example, suppose we have a method called `CalculateDiscount()` that expects a parameter of type `double`, which must be a non-negative value. We can write code in this method to check the value passed, and throw an exception if the value is negative:

```
public void CalculateDiscount(double money)
{
   if(money<0)
     throw new ArgumentNullException("money",
                      "The money parameter can't be less than zero");
   ...
}
```

Catching Exceptions

How do we catch an exception once it's been thrown? Well for a start, the exception must be thrown from within a `try` block (like the one below), or it won't get caught at all. If the exception *is* thrown from within a `try` block, then it will be caught if there is an associated `catch` block that recognizes the type of exception thrown.

For example, we can call the `CalculateDiscount()` discount method from within a `try` block like this, and include a `catch` block that is ready to catch exceptions of type `ArgumentNullException`:

```
try
{
  CalculateDiscount(a);
  CalculateTax(a);
}
catch(ArgumentNullException e)
{
   // here we handle the exception...
}
```

The `try` block is used to enclose all the code that may throw exceptions. Note that there are just two lines in the `try` block above, but we can add as many lines of code as we want.

The `try` block is used to enclose all the code that may throw exceptions. In this example, there are two method calls in the `try` block. If either method call results in an exception of type `ArgumentNullException`, then the execution will immediately switch to the associated `catch` block, which will catch and handle the exception. This is the way in which we collect exception-handling code into a single location in the file, and hence improve the maintainability of our code.

Cleaning Up

The `finally` keyword allows us to specify a block of code that will always execute, whether an exception is thrown or not. The `finally` block, if we include one, goes just after the `catch` blocks.

Usually we will place our clean-up code in this block, so we can be sure that the proper cleaning up is done, and the state of our application continues to be consistent, even when an exception is thrown.

Try It Out – Improving a Simple Exception-handling Block

Let's take a look at an exception-handling block already coded into *Friends Reunion*. Armed with our new knowledge about exceptions, we will try to improve it.

1. Open the file `NewUser.aspx.cs`, and have a look at the `try` and `catch` blocks in the `InsertUser()` method:

```
try
{
  cmd.ExecuteNonQuery();
}
catch(Exception e)
{
  doredirect = false;
  this.lblMessage.Visible = true;
  this.lblMessage.Text = "Couldn't update your profile!";
}
finally
{
  con.Close();
}
```

2. Add two more `catch` blocks *before* the existing one, as shown below:

```
catch(SqlException e)
{
  doredirect = false;
  this.lblMessage.Visible = true;
  this.lblMessage.Text = "Insert couldn't be performed. " +
                         "User name may be already taken.";
}
catch(OutOfMemoryException e)
{
  doredirect = false;
  this.lblMessage.Visible = true;
  this.lblMessage.Text = "We just run of out memory, " +
                         "please restart the application!";
}
catch(Exception e)
{
```

```
            doredirect = false;
            this.lblMessage.Visible = true;
            this.lblMessage.Text = "Couldn't update your profile!";
        }
```

How It Works

Before we understand the change we made in Step 2, let's take a look at how it worked *before* we made the change. The `try` block shown contains any lines of code that may throw an exception – in this case, there's just one line of code and it contains a call to the `ExecuteNonQuery()` method:

```
    try
    {
        cmd.ExecuteNonQuery();
    }
```

When the application is executing and reaches the `try` block, it just steps into the `try` block and executes whatever code it finds within.

If an exception is thrown at any point, execution immediately jumps out of the `try` block, and the CLR starts to look for a way for the exception to be handled. In this case, there is a `catch` block that accepts an exception of type `Exception`. This is the generic exception type – all .NET exception types inherit from this one – so this `catch` block will be used to handle any type of exception:

```
    catch(Exception e)
    {
        ...
    }
```

Regardless of whether or not an exception is thrown, the database connection that was opened earlier in the page must be closed. This is our clean-up:

```
    finally
    {
        con.Close();
    }
```

In this code, we have just a single `catch` block, that will catch *any* type of exception (because all exception types inherit from the `Exception` class). The problem is that different types of exception require different handling. What we really need is to be able to identify the *type* of exception that is thrown, and have different `catch` blocks to handle these different types of exception in different ways.

So that's what we've started to do here. Instead of one `catch` block, we now have three:

```
    catch(SqlException e)
    {
        ...
        this.lblMessage.Text = "Insert couldn't be performed. " +
                            "User name may be already taken.";
    }
```

```
catch(OutOfMemoryException e)
{
  ...
  this.lblMessage.Text = "We just ran of out memory, " +
                         "please restart the application!";
}
catch(Exception e)
{
  ...
  this.lblMessage.Text = "Couldn't update your profile!";
}
```

The first catch block handles *only* exceptions of type SqlException. The SqlException class inherits from the Exception class: SqlException is a special type of Exception that is created when a SQL Server .NET data provider comes across an error generated by the database. Within this catch block, we can write special exception-handling code for this type of exception. (In this case, to keep it simple, we just customize the error message to reflect what we've detected.)

The next catch block handles *only* exceptions of type OutOfMemoryException. This type of exception occurs when the application server doesn't have enough memory left to continue executing the application. Again, we have special code within this catch block to handle this type of exception – this code is different from the code in the first catch block.

We've written exception-handling code in anticipation of a database error or out-of-memory error, but what if the try block code throws a different type of error? We've retained the final generic catch block to catch it. This catch block needs to contain more generic exception-handling code, because we can't be sure exactly what the problem is.

We could omit the final catch block. In that case, then exceptions of types other than SqlException and OutOfMemoryException would not be caught here, but would be passed up the call stack to the method that called InsertUser(). If that method couldn't handle the exception, then it would be passed to the next level of the call stack, and so on. If it is not caught when it reaches the top of the call stack, it is passed to the CLR – the user gets an unfriendly message on their browser and our application ends!

When an exception is thrown, at most one of these catch blocks will be used to handle it. The order of these three catch blocks is important – it acts as a filter. An exception of type SqlException will be caught by the top catch block, not the bottom one.

There are more improvements we could make here. In the first catch block, we could examine the properties of the SQLException object, e, to find out more about what error occurred within the database, and we could handle different types of database error in different ways within that catch block. However, we're going to move on to different things.

Defining Custom Exceptions

The exception types you've seen so far are classes provided by the .NET Framework. When you're writing a complex application like *Friends Reunion*, it can be useful to devise your own system of **custom exceptions** that contain detailed information about the kinds of errors that are specific to the domain of your application.

Try It Out – Creating Custom Exceptions

We'll create a couple of custom exception classes here, to see how its done, and then in subsequent examples in this chapter we'll use them to good effect.

1. Create a new class file to the project (using **Add | Add Class**), and call it
`FriendsReunionException.cs`.

2. Change the code so that the class inherits from `ApplicationException`, and so that it has two constructors like this:

```
public class FriendsReunionException : ApplicationException
{
  public FriendsReunionException()
  {
  }

  public FriendsReunionException(string message, Exception inner) :
                                          base(message, inner)

  {
  }
}
```

3. Now create another new class file to the project, and call this one
`DuplicateUsernameFRException.cs`.

4. Change the code in this class so that it inherits from `FriendsReunionException`, and so that it has two constructors like this:

```
public class DuplicateUsernameFRException : FriendsReunionException
{
  public DuplicateUsernameFRException()
  {
  }

  public DuplicateUsernameFRException(string message, Exception inner) :
                                          base(message,inner)

  {
  }
}
```

How It Works

The `FriendsReunionException` class will serve as the base class for any custom exception we define for our application. Having such a class will allow us to write a generic `catch` block able to catch *any* custom exception type defined by our application (and thus differentiate them from exceptions thrown by the framework). It inherits from the .NET Framework class called `ApplicationException`: this is a generic exception thrown when a non-fatal application error occurs, and it inherits from the more generic `Exception` class.

The `DuplicateUsernameFRException` class is an application-specific exception class that we'll use to handle errors caused when a user tries to register using a username that already exists in the database. It inherits from the `FriendsReunionException` class we just created.

Each of these classes contains two constructors. The more interesting one in each case is the one that contains two arguments: its purpose will become clear in the next example.

We've used Microsoft's recommendation by appending the word `Exception` to each of our exception classes, and by deriving them from the `ApplicationException` class.

Now it's time to see these classes in action.

Rethrowing Exceptions

When handling an exception within a `catch` block, it is sometimes useful to be able to perform a few important handling tasks within *that* `catch` block and then **rethrow** the exception so that it may be caught and handled by a different `catch` block (which then performs its own exception-handling tasks).

It can even be advantageous to catch one type of exception, perform our handling tasks and then rethrow it as a *different* type of exception – usually a more specific one that will provide more information on the type of exception being thrown.

Try It Out – Rethrowing Exceptions

Custom (application-specific) exception types can have a big part to play in this. We may catch a generic exception, identify how it relates to the application, and then rethrow it as an application-specific exception so that it can be handled appropriately.

1. Modify the exception-handling code of the `InsertUser()` method in `NewUser.aspx.cs`, as follows:

```
try
{
  cmd.ExecuteNonQuery();
}
catch(SqlException e)
{
    if (e.Number==2627)
      throw new DuplicateUsernameFRException("Can't insert record", e);
```

```
      else
      {
        doredirect = false;
        this.lblMessage.Visible = true;
        this.lblMessage.Text = "Insert couldn't be performed. ";
      }
    }
    ...
```

2. Now add the following code to the btnAccept_Click() method, in the same file:

```
private void btnAccept_Click(object sender, System.EventArgs e)
{
  if (Context.User.Identity.IsAuthenticated)
  {
    UpdateUser();
  }
  else
  {
    try
    {
      InsertUser();
    }
    catch(DuplicateUsernameFRException ex)
    {
      this.lblMessage.Visible = true;
      this.lblMessage.Text =
        "You are trying to register using a username that has " +
        "already been taken by someone else. " +
        "Please choose a different username. ";
    }
  }
}
```

How It Works

In the btnAccept_Click() method, we've placed the InsertUser() method call into a try block – so if the InsertUser() method throws an error then the associated catch block stands a chance of catching it. We're looking in particular for exceptions of type DuplicateUsernameFRException here:

```
    try
    {
      InsertUser();
    }
    catch(DuplicateUsernameFRException ex)
    {
      ...
    }
```

Within the InsertUser() method, we've changed the first catch block so that it examines the properties of the SqlException exception before deciding what to do next:

```
catch(SqlException e)
{
  if (e.Number==2627)
  {
    throw new DuplicateUsernameFRException(
                      "Unique index restriction violated", e);
  }
  else
  {
    doredirect = false;
    this.lblMessage.Visible = true;
    this.lblMessage.Text = "Insert couldn't be performed. ";
  }
}
```

Here, we're checking the type of error generated in the database:

❑   If the error number is 2627, it means that the "unique index" constraint in the database has been violated – which in this case means that the user is trying to register with an existing username. We have a custom, application-specific exception class for this situation: the DuplicateUsernameFRException class. So, we rethrow the exception as this new type, so that up the call stack the btnAccept_Click() method can catch it and handle it accordingly.

❑   If not, then some other database-related error has taken place, and we report a more generic error.

Note that we use the DuplicateUsernameFRException constructor with two arguments. The first argument is a string that contains a message relating to the exception, and the second is the exception object that was caught by this catch block. This allows information from the original exception to be available in the place where the rethrown exception is handled.

Back in the btnAccept_Click() method, the DuplicateUsernameFRException is caught and handled using exception-handling code designed specifically for that type of exception:

```
catch(DuplicateUsernameFRException ex)
{
  this.lblMessage.Visible = true;
  this.lblMessage.Text =
      "You are trying to register using a username that has " +
      "already been taken by someone else. " +
      "Please choose a different username. ";
}
```

Unhandled Exceptions

What happens when an exception is not handled in the hierarchy of calling methods or by some framework code? In this case, the exception is said to go **unhandled** and will be caught by ASP.NET, which will deal with the unhandled error by rendering a page that displays details of the unhandled exception.

Ideally, we should try to write exception-handling code such that every exception is handled within the application. But just in case an exception does bubble all the way up the call stack to the CLR, it would be better to show a friendly error page to your users than the default one provided by ASP.NET.

For this purpose, we have two events that will be called by ASP.NET when an exception is unhandled:

❑ The **Page_Error event**, which provides a way to trap errors occurring at the `Page` level.

❑ The **Application_Error event**, which provides a way to trap errors occurring at any place within our code. The application-wide scope of this event also makes it an ideal place for adding logging code.

If you provide handlers for both events, then they will both be executed – first `Page_Error` and then `Application_Error`. But in some circumstances (depending on how your application is coded), it may be appropriate that errors handled in `Page_Error` don't get to the `Application_Event`. In such cases you can use the `Server.ClearError` method after handling the error in `Page_Error`, thus causing the last error to be cleared and averting the `Application_Event` call.

Try It Out – Creating a Custom Error Page

In this example we will use an ASP.NET error-handling feature to redirect to our own friendly page in the situation when an exception goes unhandled.

1. Create a new web form and name it `CustomError.aspx`. Edit its code-behind file (`CustomError.aspx.cs`) to make the `CustomError` class inherit from `FriendsBase` instead of `Page`:

```
public class CustomerError : FriendsBase
```

2. While you're still at `CustomError.aspx.cs`, add the following lines to the `Page_Load()` method:

```
private void Page_Load(object sender, System.EventArgs e)
{
    base.HeaderMessage = "An error has been found!";
    base.HeaderIconImageUrl = "~\\images\\error.gif";
}
```

3. Now, edit `CustomError.aspx` in HTML view to add a link to the style sheet used in our application:

```
<head>
    ...
    <link href="Style/iestyle.css" type="text/css" rel="stylesheet">
</head>
```

4. While still in the HTML view of `CustomError.aspx` add some friendly error message within the `<form>` element:

```
<form id="CustomError" method="post" runat="server">
  <p>
    <font size="5" color="red">
      <img src="images/sad.gif"> 
      <b>An error has been found...</b>
    </font>
  </p>
  <p>
    We have detected an error in the Friends Reunion website. <br/>
    If this error persists, please contact our support team...
  </p>
</form>
```

5. After creating the custom error page, we need a way to tell ASP.NET that we want to show that error page instead of the default error page. To do this, edit the `<customErrors>` element of the `Web.config` file for our application like this:

```
<configuration>
  <system.web>
    ...
    <customErrors defaultRedirect="CustomError.aspx" mode="On" />
    ...
  </system.web>
</configuration>
```

6. Now all we need to test this is some code that explicitly throws an exception, so we can test that it works properly. To do this, we'll just edit `LegalStuff.aspx.cs` by adding this code to the `Page_Load()` method:

```
public void Page_Load(object sender, EventArgs e)
{
  throw new NullReferenceException();
}
```

Set `LegalStuff.aspx` as the start page and press *Ctrl+F5*. A new browser instance will open with the login page for *Friends Reunion*. Log in, and you will be automatically redirected to `LegalStuff.aspx`. You should get this output:

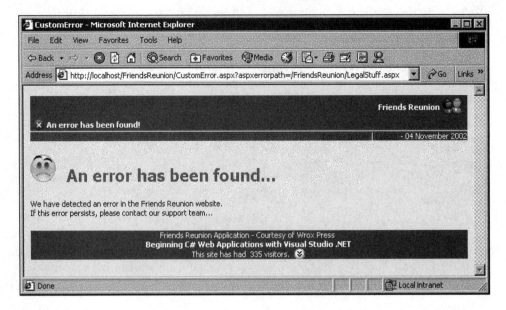

How It Works

When an exception is neither handled by the exception-handling code in the application, nor cleared in the `Page_Error()` or `Application_Error()` event handlers, ASP.NET will check the `<customErrors>` element of the `Web.config` file to see whether a default error page has been specified for our application. If its find one, it will transfer execution to it; if not, it will transfer execution to the default error page displaying all the information about the unhandled exception.

Try It Out – Logging Exceptions to the System Event Log

We mentioned earlier that the `Application_Error()` event-handler is an ideal place for adding application-wide logging of errors. It's ideal because it receives unhandled exceptions raised anywhere in our code, and not just on a specific page. Let's see how we can code this.

1. Open the `global.asax.cs` file, and edit it by adding the following using statement to the top of the file, and editing the `Application_Error()` method as follows:

```
using System.Diagnostics;
...
namespace FriendsReunion
{
  ...
  public class Global : System.Web.HttpApplication
  {
    ...
    protected void Application_Error(Object sender, EventArgs e)
    {
```

```
        EventLog.WriteEntry("FriendsReunion",
                        Server.GetLastError().InnerException.Message,
                        EventLogEntryType.Error);
    }
    ...
    }
}
```

2. That's all the code required! Press *F5* to run *Friends Reunion*; login into the application and then navigate to `LegalStuff.aspx` (which still has the funny code to throw a `NullReferenceException` in its `Page_Load()` method).

3. Now open the **Event Viewer** (Control Panel I Administrative Tools I Event Viewer), click on the Application Log. A list of the last Application events recorded should be displayed; locate the one whose Source column reads FriendsReunion and double-click on it:

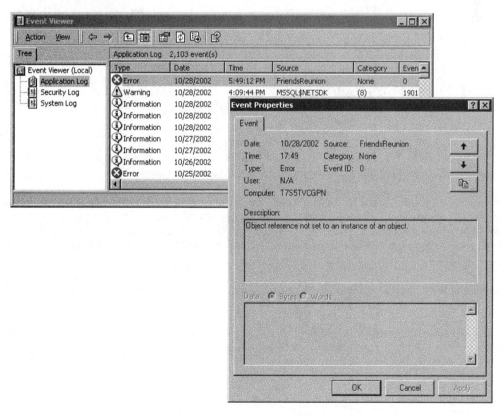

Be sure that the user which ASP.NET is running as has enough privileges to write to the System Event Log.

459

How It Works

We are handling the `Application_Error` event, which is called by ASP.NET when an exception goes unhandled. Thanks to the great `EventLog` class provided in the `System.Diagnostics` namespace, we need just one line of code to write to the System Event Log. Note that we're not clearing the exception (there's no call to `Server.ClearError`), so ASP.NET will then check `Web.config` for information on a default error page, if it finds one, will transfer execution to it.

Summary

We need to deal with different types of errors in different ways, and the .NET Framework has a fine array of features that help us to deal with these different types of errors. Syntax errors get caught by the compiler, as do some semantic errors. Input errors and other semantic errors get through the compiler, or don't occur until run time.

We can use a number of different diagnostic techniques to try to find and fix as many of these run time types of errors as possible at design time:

❑   ASP.NET provides a tracing mechanism that allows us to trace specific aspects of the application, as well as providing lots of basic data by default.

❑   The VS.NET IDE provides a powerful debugger, with many windows that allow us to pause execution, watch and change the values of variables, and step through the application in slow motion.

❑   The .NET Framework provides a network of generic and specific exception classes, and the opportunity to build our own custom exception classes. The C# language provides the functionality that allows us to catch and throw exceptions.

Some of these techniques are also useful for checking out problems when the application goes live. The exception-handling techniques continue to be useful because they can help the application to deal with most unforseen situations gracefully. We can also run the tracing mechanism quietly in the background of a live application if necessary, to find out more information about specific problems – which is very handy because the debugger can't help us in a live situation.

I've tried to provide you with enough examples to get you started, and plenty of ideas to prompt you to explore these concepts further in *Friends Reunion* or in your own applications.

We are armed with a good understanding of the different types of errors, and how to deal with them at design time and run time, and able to write a bug-free application. When it's written, we'll need to put it under heavy testing in order to measure how it is performing and what areas can be improved – and that's exactly what we're going to do in the next chapter.

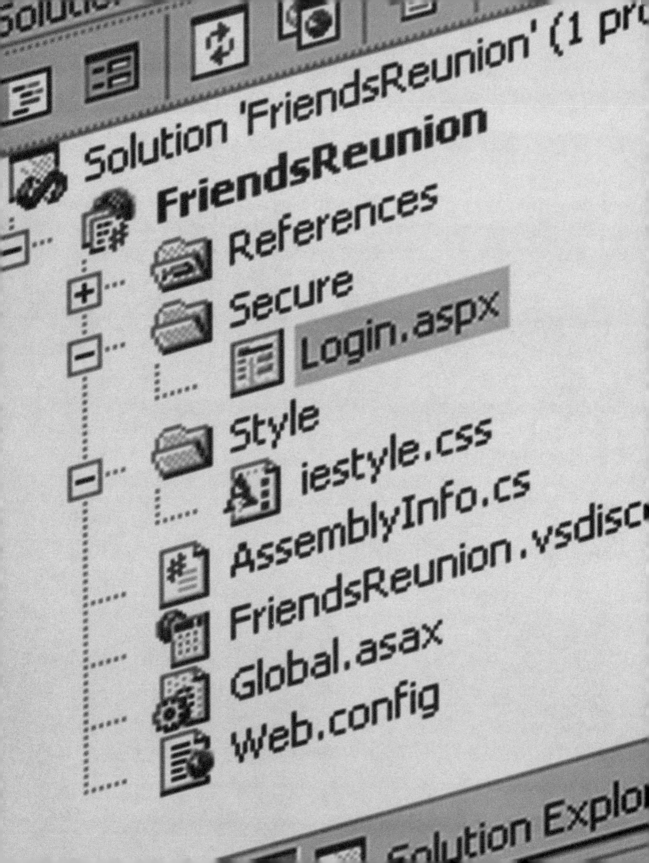

Caching and Performance Tuning

In the pages since the start of Chapter 3 we've been building up a realistic web application from scratch. In the course of developing the *Friends Reunion* application, you will have already grasped important concepts such as web forms, user controls, database access, XML and schemas, state, authentication, and so on. With all that you should have now a nice web application working on your desktop PC, and you can test it over and over again and it will work as expected.

In this chapter we will prepare to take our *Friends Reunion* application out of the relatively safe confines of your desktop PC, and put it under some real-world scenarios. We'll put it under some stress to see how well it is likely to perform in a live environment, with many users, and we'll look for areas that we can enhance, in order to make it perform even better. If you're thinking that we've already tested this application and wondering what needs improvement, read on: there is always room for improvement!

In order to accomplish our objective, we will:

- ❑ Discuss what we mean when we talk about 'performance'

- ❑ Present some performance monitoring tools, and demonstrate some useful load-testing techniques

- ❑ Explain what caching is, and how different types of cache (in different locations) can be used to get different effects

- ❑ Demonstrate how to use ASP.NET output caching and data caching to get some performance improvements

- ❑ Pinpoint other tips that we can use to improve resource usage

The Meaning of Performance

What do we mean when we say that an application "has good performance"? Ultimately, it comes down to the experience of the user. If our application is capable of supporting the requisite number of concurrent users, and that each user experiences acceptable response times, then our application is performing adequately.

So, any definition of "good performance" is *relative* – it's dependent on the requirements of the system (in terms of number of concurrent users, the activities they perform, and expected response times). An application that performs well under a regular load of 20 concurrent users may not perform well when the load increases to 100 users, and the application's resources are rather more stretched.

Since this chapter is about performance tuning (or essentially, improving the performance of an application), we should also try to understand what it means to 'improve' an application's performance. Given what we've already said, it follows that any performance improvement is about changing the application so that it can support greater numbers of concurrent users, and/or so that each of those users experiences improved response times.

So *how* do we improve an application's performance? Well, performance is only restricted by the available resources and the way the application uses them, so there are two obvious ways to improve performance:

❑ Increase the resources available to the application (more memory, broader network connections, etc.)

❑ Find the places in the application that make inefficient use of existing resources (or **bottlenecks**) and improve resource usage in those places.

Obviously, the second of these options is the most interesting one from our perspective. As we said, we know that *Friends Reunion* performs fine on a local machine with a single user, but to find out its weaknesses, we need to examine how our system's resources cope when the application runs under more stressful conditions. So, much of this chapter will be about monitoring aspects of our application's performance, locating bottlenecks, and doing something about them.

Of course, we can't examine the whole application in one chapter; we'll focus on a few places, find some places that can be optimized, and demonstrate some important techniques along the way.

It's useful to think of performance as a *characteristic* of your application. A good understanding of performance optimization techniques in ASP.NET is useful knowledge to apply right from the time you start designing your application. It's often easier and more effective to apply such techniques to the design, than to try to fit them retrospectively. But there are usually improvements that can be made, even when you've finished the build – and with a little judicious stress testing you'll be able to find out just how well the application really does perform under stress.

Some Performance-Monitoring Tools

In order to make judgements about the performance levels of our application, we'll need to do some monitoring; and for that we'll need some tools. Windows 2000 and Windows XP provide two tools that help us to monitor the resource usage of the system.

The Task Manager

The first is the **Task Manager**, which you can view by typing *Ctrl+Alt+Del* and clicking the Task Manager button. The Task Manager is most commonly used to provide a list of the applications running on your machine, the processes and memory used by those applications; it also provides readings on CPU and Page File usage, and other characteristics of resource usage.

Most readers will already be familiar with the Task Manager – it's what we turn to whenever we need to kill a non-responding application. Although it provides some useful statistics on how different areas of the system are performing, it is designed more for managing the applications on your system – it's not really intended to be used for serious performance measurement purposes.

The Performance Console (or PerfMon)

So let's turn our attention to the second of these tools. The **Performance Console**, usually referred as **PerfMon**, is actually composed of two tools, the **System Monitor** and the **Performance Logs and Alerts**. Together, they provide detailed data about the resources used by specific components of the operating system, and by programs that were developed with the collection of performance data in mind.

The System Monitor is of particular interest to us here. It allows us to monitor many different aspects of the system, providing different real-time views (graph, histogram and report) that help us to see how our system is performing.

Using the System Monitor in PerfMon

Let's have a look at the System Monitor, and start to familiarize ourselves with it. To start it up, go to the Control Panel and select Administrative Tools | Performance (or just select Start | Run and type perfmon). The Performance console should appear immediately:

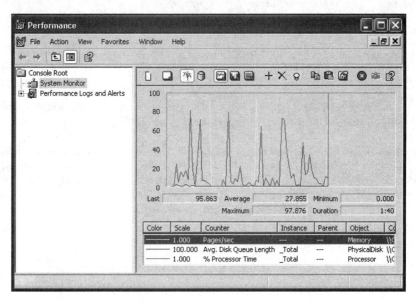

If you're running Windows XP, then the Performance console will look like this. If you're running Windows 2000, then it will look similar except that the Windows 2000 version doesn't automatically set up the three different-colored graphs into the area on the right of the window.

As we said, the System Monitor monitors use of resources as they change over time. The display above shows the System Monitor taking readings of three metrics (called **performance counters**) and plotting those readings against time on the graph.

In a moment, we'll start to configure the System Monitor to start monitoring some of the performance counters that will be particularly useful to us. But before that, we'll look a little more closely at what a performance counter *is*.

Performance Objects, Counters, and Instances

Performance data is defined in terms of **objects**, **counters**, and **instances**. A **performance object** is any resource, service or application that can be measured in some way. The processor and paging file on your system are two examples of such a resource – there are various aspects of the processor's activity and the paging file's activity that we can monitor over time.

Any given performance object has a number of different aspects that could be of interest to us. Each of these aspects is called a **performance counter**; every performance object has its own collection of performance counters. For example, the processor object includes 10 different counters that represent different aspects of its activity – for example, there's one for measuring the proportion of time the processor spends working (% Processor Time), and another for measuring the proportion of time it spends dealing with deferred procedure calls (% DPC Time).

We can relate this back to the screenshot we saw a moment ago. The three performance counters that you get by default if you're using Windows XP are these:

❑ The Memory object's Pages/sec counter

❑ The PhysicalDisk object's Avg. Disk Queue Length counter

❑ The Processor object's % Processor Time counter

If you're working in Windows 2000, and you can't see any counters yet, be patient: we're going to configure the System Monitor for our own purposes in a moment.

In some cases, the notion of a performance counter can be further dissected. If your system has more than one application, resource, or service of the same type, then we can represent each of these by its own **performance instance**. For example, if your system has two hard disks, the System Monitor still provides only one PhysicalDisk performance object; but each of the counters has three instances: one for each drive, and one (called _Total) to represent the sum total drive usage over both the drives.

Configuring the System Monitor

How do we set up System Monitor to show these performance instances? Right-click anywhere in the System Monitor and select Add Counters…:

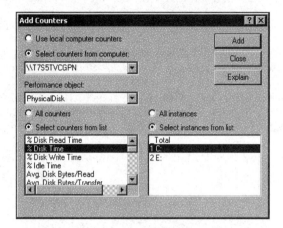

In the resulting dialog, select an object from the Performance object list. Then select one of the counters from the counters list, and (if there is an option) select one (or all) of the instances in the instances list. In the screenshot above, we've already chosen the % Disk Time counter of the PhysicalDisk object, and selected to watch the C: drive instance.

ASP.NET Performance Objects

There are many performance objects, which come from many different sources. Aside from the performance objects built into the operating systems, some other programs install their own performance objects. For example, Microsoft SQL Server installs its own set of performance objects, each of which comprises a collection of performance counters that we can use to monitor the internals of the database engine.

So, it may come as no surprise that when we install the .NET Framework, we *also* install performance objects for the CLR and for ASP.NET. These will allow us to monitor various aspects of the activity of the CLR and ASP.NET, to see what's going on while our ASP.NET application is running.

Try It Out – Configuring the System Monitor for Key Performance Counters

In this chapter, we'll focus on using seven performance counters (five of these relate to ASP.NET, one relates to CLR, and one relates to the processor). Let's configure PerfMon so that it shows all seven performance counters – then we'll be able to use it to monitor the *Friends Reunion* application as it executes.

1. If you haven't done so already, open PerfMon (select Start | Run and type perfmon) on the machine that's running the *Friends Reunion* application.

Make sure the System Monitor details pane is shown in the right-hand pane; if not, click on the System Monitor item under Console Root in the left-hand pane.

2. If there are any counters already showing, you can remove them (if you like), and start with a clean slate. To do this, select one of the items in the table under the graph, and click the ![X] button to delete it. Repeat this for each of the items in the table.

3. OK, now we're ready to add the counters that are of interest to us. In the right-hand pane, click the ![+] button (or right-click and select Add Counters) – this brings up the Add Counters dialog. Select the Use local computer counters radio button.

4. In the Performance object drop-down list, select ASP.NET. When you do this, the contents of the Select counters from list listbox (immediately below) will change accordingly, so that it shows all the counters that are made available by the ASP.NET performance object.

5. In the Select counters from list listbox, choose the Applications Restarts counter. Now click the Add button:

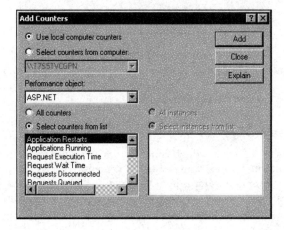

6. Repeat Steps 4 and 5 to add six more counters, one at a time, so that you have the seven counters detailed in the following table (we've done the first one already):

Performance Object	Performance Counter	Instance
ASP.NET	Application Restarts	
	Worker Process Restarts	
	Requests Queued	
ASP.NET Applications	Errors Total	_LM_W3SVC_Root_FriendsReunion
	Requests/sec	_LM_W3SVC_Root_FriendsReunion
Processor	% Processor Time	_Total
.NET CLR Exceptions	# of Exceps Thrown	aspnet_wp

7. Now you can close the Add Counter dialog. You should be able to see all the selected counters in a display at the bottom of the right-hand pane – each counter is represented by a different colored line.

8. Start up a browser and start surfing *Friends Reunion*. As you browse the pages and generate load on the server, and perform different activities within the application (registering a new user, logging in, accessing different pages, logging out, and so on), you can use the System Monitor to see how our seven monitored counters perform:

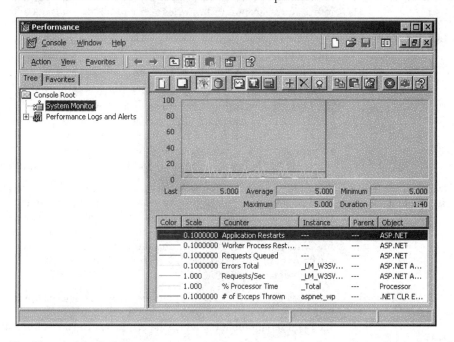

You'll probably find that your counters don't give exactly the same results as those shown in this screenshot. In fact, the results shown at the moment are of limited interest – it will get more interesting when we start to generate a heavier load on the server (that is, more than just one user!). Let's look at what we've done so far.

How It Works

There are so many counters available that we cannot possibly cover them all in this chapter. For example, the two performance objects provided by ASP.NET alone provide more than 60 counters:

❑ The **ASP.NET** performance object contains global-only counters that are not related to applications but to the ASP.NET engine itself.

❑ The **ASP.NET Applications** performance object includes per-application counters. When you select one of these counters, you can monitor the entire server, or select which instance of the counter you're interested in (there is one instance for each application). It was not possible to get this level of granularity in pre-.NET versions of ASP, because the counters available related to the activity of the entire server.

Here are the seven counters we've chosen to monitor. Although the last two counters are not ASP.NET-specific, they are still very important in helping us measuring our application performance:

Performance Object\ Performance Counter	Notes
ASP.NET\ Application Restarts	Shows the number of application restarts. An application could restart for a number of reasons; for example, as we saw in Chapter 6, ASP.NET forces an application restart whenever a modification is made to a configuration file or dependent file. Ideally this counter should be zero; if it's not then you may need to start hunting for the code that is causing your application to restart (for example, if the Web.config file is configurable via an admin page in your application).
ASP.NET\ Worker Process Restarts	Shows the number of worker process restarts. ASP.NET may periodically restart the worker process as a proactive measurement against memory leaks and other bugs that may affect performance. This is normal behavior, and is commonly referred as **scheduled recycling**. You need to keep an eye on those process restarts that are not caused by scheduled recycling but by errors in your application.
ASP.NET\ Requests Queued	Shows the number of requests that are waiting to be processed. If this counter starts to climb in proportion to the number of concurrent requests, then it means your application is receiving more concurrent requests than it is able to handle. Note that you can adjust the maximum queue length by setting the requestQueueLimit attribute of the processModel element in the machine.config file; the default setting is 5000.
ASP.NET Applications\ Errors Total	Indicates the total (cumulative) number of errors that the application has generated. The output value for this counter should be zero; if it isn't then you should identify and fix the errors before you continue testing.
ASP.NET Applications\ Requests/sec	Shows how many requests the application is serving per second. This counter should remain fairly constant, and at any rate within a "safe" range in relation to a constant load. If this counter shows regular troughs then it may be because the server is also required to perform other tasks (such as garbage collection), or because some other software running on the server is affecting performance. To correct this behavior, you will need to investigate what tasks your server is performing, and try to minimize them.
Processor\ % Processor Time	Shows how much processor time is being consumed by the application. You can expect this counter to increase with load. If it doesn't, your application is probably using multithreading features of some kind, and suffering from a problem called **contention**. (Multithreading is beyond the scope of this book, but there is plenty of online material about both multithreading in general and contention in particular.)

Performance Object\ Performance Counter	Notes
.NET CLR Exceptions\ # of Exceps Thrown	Shows the number of exceptions that are being thrown by the application. In terms of resources, exceptions are expensive. It's helpful to know where (and why) your application throws exceptions, and this counter helps us to be aware of them. Although the output for this counter is not *necessarily* supposed to be zero, you need to keep an eye on it just to make sure it doesn't go too high.

Using Other Counters

As we've said, the seven counters listed here constitute some of the key counters that can help us to measure a web application's performance, but they are just a small subset of the many counters available. The CLR alone already provides 10 performance objects (with a total of more than 80 counters!).

It's well worth spending some time with PerfMon, to familiarize yourself with some of the other counters. PerfMon provides a handy explanation of each counter (you can view the explanation by clicking on the Explain button of the Add Counters dialog). Of course, the more counters you learn about, the better armed you will be when it comes to the performance-testing process.

Version-specific ASP.NET Performance Objects

In the Add Counters dialog, you may have noticed at least two extra performance objects whose names contain the .NET version number:

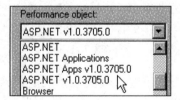

These are intended to support the side-by-side execution features of the CLR and ASP.NET. These objects contain counters that will apply only to that particular .NET version. The unique set that *doesn't* contain any version information in its name will apply to the highest version installed.

Custom Performance Objects

In fact, just as other programs provide their own custom performance objects and counters, it's also possible to write custom performance objects for your own applications. This is a potentially powerful way to create tools to measure details that are specific to your application. For example, if you're particularly interested in monitoring the number of users registered per minute, then you can do it using a custom performance counter.

We will not build any custom performance objects in this book; but if you want to learn more on developing and monitoring your own custom performance objects and counters, I recommend you take a look at *Professional Application Center 2000* (Wrox, ISBN 1-86100-447-8).

Avoiding External Overhead

Although it may be nice to have a real-time graph that shows how aspects of your system are performing, we need to be aware that the process of collecting and displaying this information is *itself* a process that consumes server resources! Of course, we should try to keep monitoring overhead to a minimum – the whole idea is to not overload your system with external tools like monitoring, screensavers, etc., which affect the accuracy of the readings. Here are a couple of ways to control this:

❑ One way is to control the frequency with which the System Monitor takes sample ratings. To do this, you need to bring up the System Monitor Properties dialog box (you can get it by clicking the 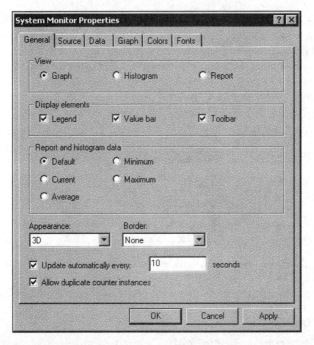 button), and select the General tab. Near the bottom, the Sample (or Update) automatically every *x* seconds option is the one we're interested in here. The higher this value, longer the System Monitor will wait between samples. Of course, this will reduce the amount of processing work that the System Monitor has to do, which may be necessary if your current hardware can't cope with the required processor power.

❑ Another slimmer approach, that will consume even fewer resources, is to avoid using the System Monitor at all – and to use the **counter logs** instead. You'll find the counter logs under the Performance Logs and Alerts node of the Performance console. Here, we can still specify all the counters we want to measure, and their performance data will be recorded silently (no fancy graphics this time!) to a log file from which we can later generate various reports (for example, to MS Excel, using the CSV output format).

So, now we know how to monitor the resources our application is using. To get some realistic results, we need to use these monitoring tools in a realistic testing scenario. This is the subject of the next section.

Performance-Testing the Application

It's important to think of our ASP.NET application as a real piece of software, just like any other software you've ever written, and to test it in all the same ways. Of course, there are lots of different types of testing processes we can (and should) apply to a piece of software during the course of its development, and it's important to appreciate that these different testing processes have different purposes. For example:

❑ **Functional testing** is about checking that the application conforms to the design specifications (that each module performs its tasks correctly, that there are no broken or missing links, that client-side scripts run smoothly, that web pages look fine on every different browser you intend to support, and so on).

❑ **Load testing** is about simulating the amount of load that the application needs to be able to support, and checking that the server can handle that load correctly (and without implications such as memory leaks). As we'll see, there are special tools that we can use to simulate large amounts of user activity, and hence reproduce the necessary load. Load testing falls fairly naturally into two areas:

   ❑ **Performance testing**, which is about *incrementally* increasing the load on the server while it can properly handle it, with the objective of finding out the maximum number of requests per second our server can handle without degradation.

   ❑ **Stress testing**, which is about subjecting the server to a *greater* amount of load than it is capable of handling. The objective here is to make the server break, so that we can find out how it behaves in such a situation. Although we are not expecting the server to *handle* the overload, we do want the server to *behave in a decent manner* (no data loss or corruption, etc.).

In this chapter, we're particularly interested in an aspect of *performance* testing; we'll place reasonable levels of load of the server to see how well it copes with that load, and – in particular – to identify bottlenecks with a view to improving the overall resource usage of our application.

To do this, we'll use the performance objects we've already met. We'll also need a way to simulate a number of end users browsing the *Friends Reunion* application simultaneously.

Applying a Load to our Application

In order to generate amounts of load on our server that we could not generate by other means, we will use a tool that is specifically designed for that job. In this chapter, we will use Microsoft's **Web Application Stress (WAS) tool**.

There are two reasons for choosing WAS here: it is simple to use, and it is freely available. We can use this tool to simulate a specified number of users, to specify the pages these simulated users will be surfing, and so on.

473

Installing the Web Application Stress Tool

At the time of writing, WAS is freely available from http://webtool.rte.microsoft.com/ – it's about 9.5MB in size. Before you install it, it's worth considering what machine you're going to install it onto.

If you don't have to a couple of networked PCs, then you *can* run through the exercise in this chapter by running WAS, and the *Friends Reunion* web application, and the database server all on the same machine. However, when you run WAS, it will take up most of the resources of the machine that it runs on – so you should be aware that your results will be skewed by the fact that WAS is using resources that would usually be available to the web application.

If you *do* have access to a couple of machines, and you can take advantage of this, then you'll get much more realistic results. Keep one machine for the *Friends Reunion* web application and database server, and install WAS onto the other one. (In this case, it makes sense to think of the former as the 'server' machine and the latter as the 'client' machine.)

The installation process is straightforward. The download consists of a single file, called **setup.exe**; just run this file and follow the on-screen instructions of the installer.

Getting Support for the Web Application Stress Tool

Although WAS is not officially supported by Microsoft, you are not on your own. There are other ways to get support for it:

❑ **WAS knowledge base**: in the WAS web site (http://webtool.rte.microsoft.com/) you'll find an option to search the online knowledge base for basic and advanced topics.

❑ **Peer support**: there is an e-mail discussion alias, webtool@microsoft.com, for providing peer support only.

❑ **Help files**: WAS comes with very complete online help that should help you in getting started using it.

> *We should mention that Microsoft also has a more recent tool, called Application Center Test (ACT), which supercedes WAS. ACT is supported by Microsoft, but it's not free. It does come bundled with Visual Studio .NET (but only the Enterprise Architect and Enterprise Developer editions). It provides enhanced features over WAS, like a new complete reporting capability and integration with the Visual Studio .NET IDE. You can learn more about Application Center at http://www.microsoft.com/applicationcenter/.*

Generating a Realistic Set of Data

To get an even greater approximation of reality, we should really expand the amount of data in our database. It currently holds just a few users, but once it gets established we would expect it to hold information about hundreds of people.

To do this, we'll run a little script to insert some extra data into the database.

We'll run a little SQL script that performs 1,000 loop iterations, adding one new user into the User table each time. You will find this script in the downloadable code for this book.

1. Grab the file `sp_User_Fill.sql`, and place it in a folder somewhere handy on your hard disk (say, `C:\temp`).

2. Start up a command window, and navigate to the folder where you placed `sp_User_Fill.sql`. Now run the following command:

```
C:\temp>osql -S server -d FriendsData -E -i sp_User_Fill.sql
```

So, if your database server is called DEVMASTER, then you should type:

```
C:\temp>osql -S DEVMASTER -d FriendsData -E -i sp_User_Fill.sql
```

3. In Visual Studio .NET, open the Server Explorer, browse to your FriendsData database and check the content of the User database table. You should find 1,000 new rows.

How It Works

The `.sql` file contains a simple SQL script that runs through a loop 1,000 times, adding a new user to the database table with each iteration:

```
WHILE @cnt<10 BEGIN
   SELECT @cnt = @cnt + 1
   SELECT @u = 'user' + CAST(@cnt as varchar)

   INSERT INTO [User]
      VALUES(NEWID(), @u, 'mypassword', 'Carlos', 'Garcia Saccone', GETDATE(),
             '(999) 999-9999', '(999) 999-9999', '7th. Avenue 1234, NY, USA',
             'sample@obies.com', 0)
END
```

Admittedly, each user will have the same personal details, but each user does have a unique ID; so this data should suffice for our purposes.

Preparing a Performance Test with a Simulated Load

Over the next few pages, we'll set up and perform a performance test. Specifically, we'll simulate a situation in which a number of *Friends Reunion* administrator users perform a couple of simple tasks:

❑ Logging into the application

❑ Then browsing to the Users Administration page to manage the list of current users

First, we'll need to write the **test script** – this is a document that describes the requests that each simulated user will perform. Then we'll set up the monitoring criterion in WAS; and finally, we'll run the test.

Try It Out – Creating the Administrator Users Script

So, to begin, we'll write the test script, using the WAS script-writing tool.

1. Open WAS (on your "client" machine) by going to Start | Programs | Microsoft Web Application Stress Tool.

2. You'll see a dialog that asks you what you want to do. Select Record (this option allows us to navigate to the site while WAS records our actions and generates a script to reproduce them):

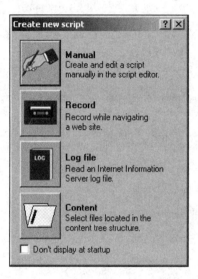

3. Now you will be prompted with a dialog that allows us to customize the creation of the script. We're not going to customize this script at all (though we'll examine these options in the section below). For now, just click the Next button to continue.

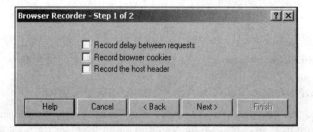

4. Next, you'll see a preparation dialog box. If you are ready to start recording the test script, press Finish.

5. Immediately, a new browser instance will open. We have started recording! Go to the browser and enter the URL for your *Friends Reunion* application. Log in as usual (using the username wrox and password wrox), so that you get to the Home page.

Now click on the **Users Administration Page** link – it should present you with a datagrid of current users.

6. Now click on the WAS window (but don't close the browser window just yet). In the WAS window, you should see something like this:

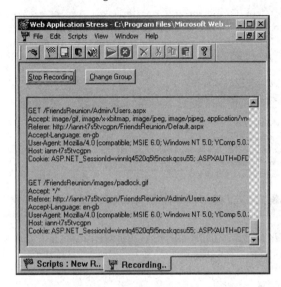

7. Click on the **Stop Recording** button. The **Recording** window will close (although it won't cause the opened browser instance to close automatically).

The WAS tool will display the **Scripts** window – you will be able to see a new item named **New Recorded Script**. It's a good idea to change its name to something more meaningful: FRSimpleAdminScript, for example:

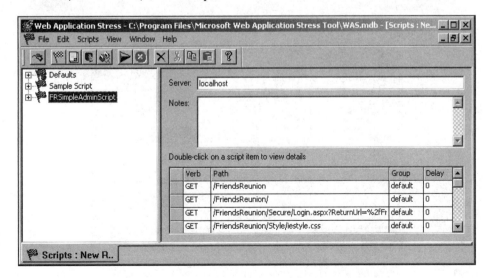

8. Now set the **Server** field to the one hosting our *Friends Reunion* application. If you are hosting *Friends Reunion* on the same machine that is running WAS then you don't need to make a change here (localhost is the default); if you've got different machines for the application and for WAS, then you'll need to type the application server name in the **Server** field.

9. Now we want to clean up the script generated by WAS, so that it does not include any static content. We can do this by clicking on the leftmost column of the desired row and then pressing **Delete** on our keyboard. For this test you should delete all .gif and .css files, so that your screen will end looking similar to this (with just six items on it):

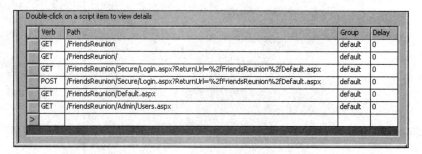

*It may seem a little odd to do this – after all, our testing might seem less realistic without all those essential static image and stylesheet files – but there is a reason behind it. Our objective here is to find out specifically how our **dynamic** pages are performing (how long they take to execute, etc.), with a view to finding and fixing bottlenecks in dynamic processing. If, by contrast, our objective was capacity planning (that is, finding out how many concurrent users the site can support, with a view to buying more hardware if necessary) then we would test both dynamic **and** static content now.*

10. While we are still at the **Scripts** window, we will adjust some settings of our newly created script. Click on the **Settings** node of the script and change the default **Warmup** time from 0 to 10 seconds:

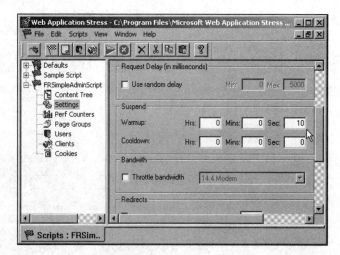

This will cause WAS to load-test our server 10 seconds before considering the test started, which will give our server some time to initialize itself in preparation for the test. So, for example, if the server needs to pre-compile any .aspx files, then this one-off pre-compilation will not skew the test results.

How It Works

By following the process above, we have just created our first WAS test script. It will play a crucial part in the *Friends Reunion* performance test we're going to describe in a few pages from here.

The script itself follows the steps that an administrator user of our application would usually perform at the beginning of a session – browsing to the home page, logging in, and then browsing to the Users Administrators page.

To create the script, we simply follow the steps that an administrator would follow – but we do it using a browser window that is being spied by our WAS session. The WAS tool watches what we do on the browser, and records each request and the server's responses into the test script. This cool feature saves us from writing the script by hand.

We've also specified a number of different settings that will affect the execution of the script, when we come to use it in the test. In particular, there were three checkbox options right at the beginning of the process. In this case, we opted not to use any of them, but it's worth knowing what they're for:

❑ The Record time delay between requests checkbox controls whether the script records the *pauses* you make while surfing the different pages of the application (this is known as **think time**, because it reflects the time that a user reads the content of a page and thinks about it before making the next request)

❑ The Record browser cookies checkbox controls whether the cookies sent to the browser will be recorded into the script or not.

❑ The Record the host header checkbox allows the recording of host header information.

There's another think time control in the Settings dialog: the Use random delay checkbox adds further variety to the amount of time between requests, by introducing a random interval of time.

We also adjusted the Warmup time, and removed the requests for static pages (as we explained at the time). WAS will save these settings along with the recorded script and will apply them when the script is executed.

Monitoring a Test in WAS

We've already seen how to monitor performance counters on a single machine, using the System Monitor. When we run a test through WAS, we need to tell WAS which performance counters we're interested in. So we'll do that next.

Try It Out – Setting up Monitoring in WAS

We've recorded our script and tweaked some defaults settings, and now we need to add the performance counters that run on the *server* machine (the machine we named in Step 8 of the previous *Try It Out*) and monitor the application's activity. This process is very similar the one we saw when adding counters to the System Monitor, earlier in this chapter.

1. While in the Scripts window select the Perf Counters node of our script.

2. The right pane will allow us to manage the counters for our script. By clicking on the Add Counter button an Add counter to report dialog will pop up allowing us to pick the counters we want to monitor (if you're using two machines, we've assumed you have them configured so the client machine user has privileges to access the performance counters on the server machine):

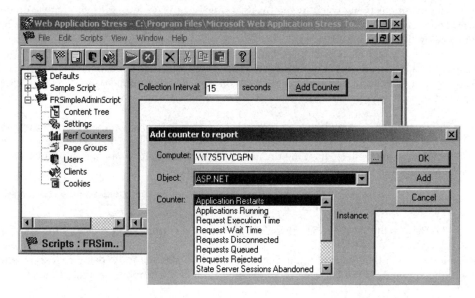

As you can see, this dialog box is similar to the one used by System Monitor that we saw earlier.

3. We want to monitor the counters on our server, so set the Computer field to point to the machine that's running the *Friends Reunion* application. If you're hosting *Friends Reunion* on the same computer as WAS, you shouldn't need to change this field.

4. Now add the performance counters using this dialog. Use the same seven counters we used in the System Monitor example earlier in the chapter (you may want to flick back a few pages to remind yourself of which ones we used). When you've done that, your screen should look like this:

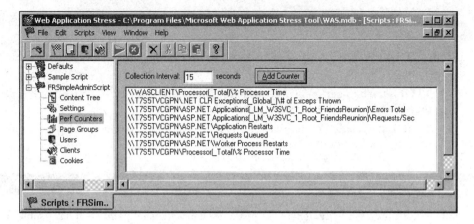

If you're using a separate machine for WAS, you may also choose to monitor the % Processor Time counter (in the Processor performance object) of the workstation running WAS, as shown above. You can add this counter to the seven counters listed above (just choose the correct machine name, object, and counter in the Add Counters dialog).

When you come to run the test, you can use this counter to check that the WAS machine is managing to keep up with the generation of the load. If you find this counter going over 80%, then it may be a signal that WAS is failing to generate all the specified load; if that's the case, it will invalidate your testing results.

How It Works

These are the performance counters that we want WAS to monitor while it performs the load-testing against the server. It's worth noting again that if you're using different machines to host the *Friends Reunion* web application and the WAS tool, then the counters to be added are counters on the *web server* machine. (When I took the screenshot above, I had *Friends Reunion* hosted on a server called T7S5TVCGPN, and WAS running on a separate machine called WASCLIENT.)

When we come to execute the test (in a moment), the WAS client will periodically poll these counters to gather the required counter data. In some aspects, it works in the same way as when we used the System Monitor. The main difference is that WAS can *simulate* many users performing various actions simultaneously, using the test script we've just written (while System Monitor simply observes and reports whatever the server is doing at any given time).

Thanks to WAS's integration of monitoring, we can handle all of this from a single user interface (on a remote client machine) that makes for much easier and much more effective testing – as we'll see when we run the test now.

Running the Performance Test

Now we've created our test script and specified what things we want to keep an eye on while performing the test, we are ready to run the performance test on our web server, and collect the results on the WAS client. In addition to the results from the performance counters we've just set up, we'll also be able to make use of a number of **performance metrics** that WAS collects. The following metrics will be of particular interest:

❑ **Machine Throughput**: this is the maximum number of requests per second that an application is able to serve.

❑ **Time to First Byte** (**TTFB**) and **Time To Last Byte** (**TTLB**). These metrics are usually measured in milliseconds:

❑ **TTFB** is the number of milliseconds that pass between the time the request is sent and the time the *first* byte of the response is received

❑ **TTLB** is the number of milliseconds that pass between the time the request is sent and the time the *last* byte of the response is received

Try It Out – Performing the Test

We've done most of the hard work. There are just a few short steps left, and we'll have some results to analyze.

1. Make sure the FRSimpleAdminScript node is selected in the left pane, then run the script by selecting Script | Run from the menu bar. (Alternatively, click the Run Script icon.) The test will begin and you will be presented with the following dialog:

When the test completes, the WAS tool should automatically display the Scripts window again.

2. To view the results, select View | Reports from the menu bar, or just click on the Reports icon:

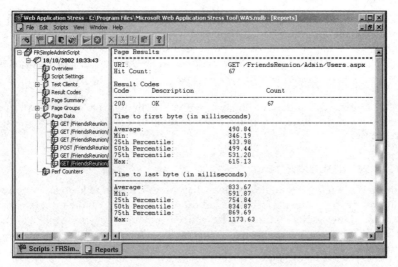

3. On the left pane of the Reports window you will see a list of all the scripts that have been run (there's just one here). Expand the node; you will find more nodes beneath, one for each occasion the script was run (these nodes are labeled with the date and time of execution – again, there's just one in this screenshot).

Beneath each dated node is the result data for that test. Click on the Page Summary node: this will show a short description of how each page involved in the test has performed (in terms of numbers of hits, TTFB Average, TTLB Average, etc.). WAS calculates these performance metrics automatically, based on the load it generates and the response it receives from the server. We'll examine and interpret these results in a moment.

4. Now click on the Perf Counters node, in the left pane. In the right pane, you'll see the results of the server's seven performance counters, as they were recorded by WAS during the test.

How It Works

We have just run our first load test against our server! After recording the scripts, eliminating unwanted requests for static content, modifying some default values to fit our needs, and setting up key performance counters, we now have our first test results.

When I checked the Perf Counters node after my test, I found that my server handled 6.50 requests/sec (which is sufficiently low to cause concern) while utilizing an average of 76% of processor time (which is a rather high average). The question is: Why?

You can have a closer look at how each individual page performed, by examining the Page Data node of our report. By briefly examining the data for each page, you may find that the results for Users.aspx differ significantly from the rest. Here are the figures that I got in my test:

Page	Average TTFB (milliseconds)	Average TTLB (milliseconds)	Downloaded Content Length (bytes)
Default.aspx	7.03	7.27	2360
Login.aspx	7.22	8.19	3040
Users.aspx	490.84	833.67	1054113

For some reason our server is taking almost 0.5 seconds in serving the first byte of that page, and then almost another 0.35 seconds (TTLB minus TTFB) to finish serving it up! Moreover, the output of Users.aspx is 1MB long! These two results probably help to explain why the server handling so few requests per second (6.50 requests/sec) on average.

Why is Users.aspx causing that much work to our server? It's probably because the page contains a full-fledged DataGrid control, loaded with the details of 1,000 users, just for display purposes. In the next section, we will make use of **caching** techniques to save our server the immense work of having to process this DataGrid on every request, and see how we can tweak it to produce smaller-sized pages.

Caching

A **cache** is an area of memory that stores recently-accessed data and resources, so that subsequent requests can reuse them without having them regenerated. When a web page is requested for the very first time, the page must be completely generated from scratch by the server, and sent back to that user in the HTTP response. But at the same time, the server can also arrange for the freshly-generated material in that page to be put aside into areas of cache, so that it can be user to serve subsequent requests from the same user or other users.

If we understand the implications of caching correctly, we can use it in our web applications to gain significant performance improvements. In particular, we need to think about *what sort* of content we can cache, *where* we can cache it, and for *how long*. We'll consider all these questions in the following pages.

Caching in a Web Architecture

In the web architecture, there a number of different places where a cache can reside, and it makes sense to cache different types of content in different places. To be more specific, consider that in general, a request/response is generally made either directly between the web client (the browser) and the web server, or indirectly via a proxy server:

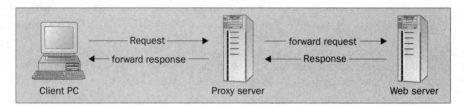

This, in fact, gives us three different places where we can cache content – the **client** (browser), the **proxy server**, and the **web server**. The implications of storing content in a cache is dependent on which cache location is used, as we'll discuss later in this section.

So, how does a web application benefit from caching? There are two main benefits that come from caching:

❑   First, we can eliminate the need to regenerate the same content many times (because we can generate it once and then cache it in the appropriate location.

❑   Second, depending on the nature of the content, we can try to cache it as close to the client as possible.

These two benefits manifest themselves in three immediately obvious ways:

❑   If content is cached close to the client, then we achieve a **reduction in latency** (that is, apparent inactivity) and hence improve the user experience.

❑   If content is cached close to the client, then we also achieve a **saving in bandwidth** (because the route from the client to the cache is shorter than the route from the client to the web server). In particular, if a resource is cached on the browser itself then network resources are eliminated altogether for that resource!

- By reusing generated content many times, we can vastly **reduce the workload** on our server, which can now just generate the material once and cache it (instead of regenerating it for each page request). The reduced demand on the server's resources will give an improvement in the server's overall performance.

Cache Expiration

Most items of content have a natural lifetime. In other words, at the time the content is generated it's usually possible to specify a date and time at which that freshly-generated content will become out-of-date. For example:

- On a site that publishes stock market shares, much of the data changes every few minutes, so we would not want cached data to last for more than a few minutes (otherwise users will almost always be looking at out-dated stock prices).

- By contrast, we can safely cache the pages of a web site that shows the results of sports fixtures, because those results don't change once they've happened.

We don't want cached data to hang around in the cache after it has become out-of-date. Therefore, any cached item has a **expiry date** that determines its life span – that is, for how long it will stay cached before it is considered invalidated and taken out of the cache.

There are essentially two ways to set the expiry date:

- **Absolute expiration**: this allows us to set the exact date and time when the cached content will expire.

- **Sliding expiration**: this is a time interval, and dictates for how long the cached item is permitted to live in the cache *after* the time it was last accessed.

Cache Management

There is another way that items are removed from a cache. Because a cache is just a block of memory (and therefore not infinite in size), there is a **cache management** mechanism that prevents the cache from filling up with non-expired items.

The way it does this, as we'll see later, is to examine the priority of all the items in the cache and remove those with the lowest priority – to make way for new items.

An item's priority is set at the same time as its expiration, at the time the item is generated and cached. The expiration setting and priority chosen depend very much on the type of data and the context – we'll see an example later.

Cache Locations

We mentioned earlier that there are a number of different places we can cache content, and that we can use different cache locations for subtly different purposes.

In particular, we mentioned that there are cache locations at the browser, the proxy server, and the web server. What is special about each of these locations? Let's examine each one in turn.

Caching at the Browser

Any browser has a **local cache**, which it can use for temporary storage of any received resources that are marked as cacheable by the content author. When a user requests the same resource a second time, the browser will check the local cache. If the resource is still there (that is, it has not expired or been removed), the browser will fetch the resource from the local cache rather than fetching it from the server.

The obvious advantage of this situation is that it provides zero latency – because the cached resource can be displayed immediately by the browser without the need to establish a connection and wait for a response. This is as fast as it gets! It also reduces the overall number of necessary transmissions of requests and responses over the network, and hence saves bandwidth. Finally, if the original resource required server resources to generate it, then it saves the server the trouble of repeating that work – so there's an overall reduction in demand on the server.

These are compelling benefits, and it's easy to conclude that browser caching seems like an ideal option. But it's not ideal in all situations. In particular:

❑   Some browsers choose not to honor the caching attributes specified by the page's author.

❑   If the user has specified any different settings on their browser, then these settings will override the default behavior. (For example, users of Internet Explorer can control the browser's internal cache by selecting Tools | Internet Options... and then clicking on the Settings button.)

It's important to realize that "caching a page at the browser" means that there's a copy of the cached item stored on the user's local machine. There are potential security and privacy implications here, because it's possible for other users of the same machine to access these resources.

In particular, it would be irresponsible to code your application to cache sensitive information such as bank account information at the browser (or, indeed, at the proxy server, as we will see in the next section).

Caching at the Proxy Server

As we illustrated earlier, a **proxy server** is a machine that sits between the web application server and the client machines, acting as an intermediary. It receives requests from client machines and forwards these requests to the origin server. It also receives the responses from the origin server and passes them back to clients.

When a proxy server receives a resource from a server, it checks to see whether the page author has deemed the resource to be "cacheable at the proxy server" (later on in this chapter, we'll see how we can do this in our own *Friends Reunion*). If so, the proxy server can store it in its own local cache.

The benefits of caching at the proxy are similar to caching at the browser. In particular, if the same resource is requested again (either by the same user or by another user via the same proxy server) then the proxy server is able to deliver the resource from its own cache, rather than by passing the request on to the server.

This saves on the server's resources, and bandwidth, and reduces response time in much the same way. Note that the saving is less significant – for example, we get reduced latency but not zero latency. To reduce latency of the cached request to a minimum, the proxy server is usually located close to the client machine.

On the other hand, a resource cached on a proxy server can be used to serve the requests of the hundreds (or thousands) of users whose requests are handled by that proxy server, regardless of the identity of the user who requested it first.

Proxy servers are usually put in place by ISPs; some corporations with many users also maintain their own proxy servers. As a consequence, you (as an application developer) generally don't have any control over the existence (or otherwise) of a proxy server. Therefore, while it's useful to take advantage of the possibility of proxy server caching, it is not something you can depend upon.

Caching at the Origin Server

Of course, caching content on the server doesn't get the content any near to the client. If the web server chooses to use its own cache to serve a request, then the content still needs to be transmitted back across the network – just as if it were freshly generated; so there are no savings in latency and bandwidth to be made from caching at the server.

However, caching at the server still allows us to reuse resources, avoiding unnecessary regeneration of those resources and hence reducing the server's workload.

While caching at the server doesn't look as attractive as caching at the client or proxy server, it is sometimes our only option – particularly when security and privacy issues are involved.

Ultimately, these three types of caching can help us save resources and get better performance. How much bandwidth and workload can we save? How much is latency reduced? The answers to these questions depend on where the content is cached, how often it is reused, and when it expires. But there's no doubt that, when used well, caching can help improve your site's performance significantly.

For this reason, ASP.NET has been designed with caching techniques in mind; so let's look at that now.

ASP.NET Caching

ASP.NET has its own **cache**. This cache is an area of memory (on the web server) that it uses to store the output of web pages; ASP.NET stores this output so that it can use it to serve subsequent requests from that memory, and hence avoid executing the page each time the page is requested. As we explained above, this reduces the overall amount of processing work required of the server, and the reduction in resources used results in improved performance.

The Microsoft ASP.NET Team has given us two APIs that allow us to access the cache:

❑   One is a high-level API, which uses a very simple declarative syntax that takes the form of a directive that can be applied to a page or user control.

❑   The second is a low-level API consisting of a single class (the Cache class, which belongs to the System.Web.Caching namespace) that can be used in code, allowing us to manage the cache programmatically.

The high-level API will save you some typing, while the low-level API requires some coding and a greater understanding of what's going on under the surface the details. Naturally, the latter is the one that gives us more control.

In ASP.NET's implementation of caching, there are two different types of caching that relate to the different types of content that can be cached. The first, **output caching**, is about caching the output generated by executing a page or a fragment of a page. We can use both the high-level and low-level APIs with this type of caching.

However, the ASP.NET cache is not limited to storing the output of pages: it's often effective to use **data caching** to cache data whose generation may be expensive in terms of resources (for example, a large DataSet is exactly the sort of thing we might cache using this technique). ASP.NET allows us to cache our own data by using the low-level cache API.

Let's look at both of these types of caching in more detail.

Output Caching

As we've said, **output caching** is about caching the output (or results) obtained when a page (or page fragment) is executed. It's clear from this definition that we're not obliged to cache whole pages – we can cache just a fragment of a page if that's an appropriate thing to do.

In a comparison between **page caching** and **fragment caching**, there are more similarities than differences. In principle, they work in the same way, but there are a few subtle differences that I'll explain in a moment.

Let's look at the principle first. When an .aspx page or .ascx page fragment is requested, the server checks to see whether the page has been marked as cacheable (using the OutputCache directive that we'll meet shortly), and that influences the process at two different stages (shown as shaded decision items in this flowchart):

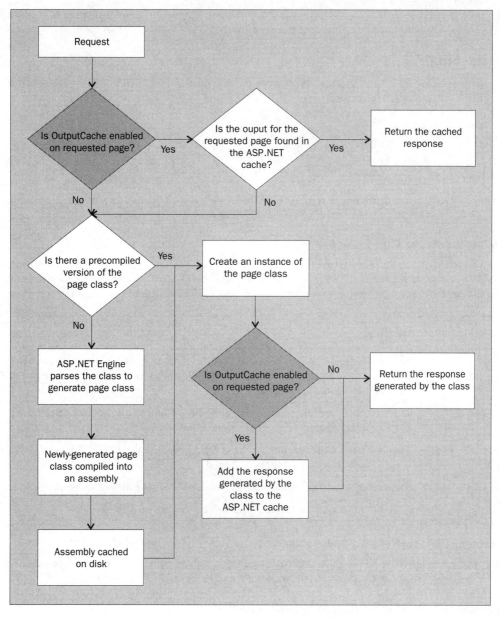

It first checks for the OutputCache directive right at the beginning of the process. If it finds that the page (or page fragment) is cacheable, then it checks for an existing cached instance of the page, and returns that – thus avoiding the subsequent parsing and compilation steps and saving server resources.

If the page is not cacheable, or if there is no cached instance, then the parsing and compilation steps occur as usual; and if the page is cacheable then the newly-generated page is placed in the ASP.NET cache so it can be used for subsequent page requests. .

The basic process described above applies to both page caching and fragment caching. Now let's look at the practicalities and note the differences between the two.

Page Caching

To enable caching for a specific page, we can use the OutputCache directive. Here's an example of what this directive might look like:

```
<%@ OutputCache Duration="3600"
                Location="Any"
                VaryByCustom="browser"
                VaryByParam="RequestID" %>
```

There are five possible attributes in total (the attribute not shown here is VaryByHeader). In fact, only the Duration and VaryByParam attributes are required.

Controlling Where the Page is Cached

The Location attribute refers to the three different places (browser, proxy server, and web server) at which we can cache resources. We can use this attribute when we write the page, to specify at which of these places we'll *allow* the output of our page to be cached. There are five possible settings here:

Location	Meaning
Any	This is the default value. It means that the output of the page *may* be cached at the client browser, at any "downstream" clients (such as a proxy server), or on the web server itself.
Client	This dictates that the output cache can only be stored on the local cache of the client who originated the request (that is, the browser).
Downstream	This dictates that the output cache can be stored in any HTTP 1.1 cache-capable device (such as a proxy server).
Server	This dictates that the output cache will be stored on the web server.
None	This dictates that the output cache will be disabled for this page.

Controlling the Lifetime of a Page in Cache

The Duration attribute allows us to control how long (in seconds) we want the page to exist in the cache. A page containing the directive shown above will be cached for one hour.

Using Parameters to Enable Different Versions of a Page

The VaryByParam attribute enables us to have different versions of our page cached. In the example above, VaryByParam is set to RequestID, so ASP.NET uses different values of the RequestID parameter sent either in the querystring of an HTTP GET or the parameters of an HTTP POST.

This is useful for pages like `ViewUser.aspx`, in our *Friends Reunion* application. The exact content of this page varies from user to user, and so there would be no value in caching a single version of the page for all users. So we can have the application differentiate between individual users by checking the value of the `RequestID` parameter; and by placing `VaryByParam="RequestID"` in the `OutputCache` directive of the page, we can have ASP.NET cache a different version of the page for each user.

If we don't want to cache different versions of the page based on the value of a parameter, then we just set `VaryByParam` to `none`:

```
<%@ OutputCache Duration="3600" VaryByParam="none" %>
```

We can also ask ASP.NET to cache a version of the page for *every* possible combination of parameters. To do this, we set `VaryByParam` to `*`; like this:

```
<%@ OutputCache Duration="3600" VaryByParam="*" %>
```

> *It's tempting to set `VaryByParam` to `*`, and hence to cache every possible version of the page. At first glance this seems like a good idea for improving overall performance. However, the cache is itself just a memory store of finite size – so the more output we choose to cache, the sooner the cache will fill up. Generally, a more selective approach is required; it's really only worth caching pages that are frequently accessed, or whose generation is expensive. There is little sense in caching pages that are almost never accessed, or simple pages that don't require any computation.*

Other Ways of Enabling Different Versions of a Page

The `VaryByHeader` and `VaryByCustom` attributes work like `VaryByParam`, in that they allow you to specify when new cached versions of our page should be created:

❑ The `VaryByHeader` attribute allows us to vary the cached versions of a page based on the semicolon-separated list of HTTP headers provided.

❑ The `VaryByCustom` attribute, when set to `browser`, allows us to vary the cached versions depending on the browser name and major version information. Alternatively, we can set it to the name of a *custom* method, in which we can implement our own logic that controls the versions to cache.

We can't demonstrate all of these attributes here, but we'll make use of the `VaryByParam` attribute in the example that follows later in the chapter.

Fragment Caching

Sometimes, we don't want to cache the entire page's output. For example, what if some fragment of the page is very dynamic in nature, while the remainder of the page changes very rarely? For example, what if we tried to cache a page that shows live stock quotes (which change every few minutes) along with daily news headlines (which change only every few hours). A high-valued `Duration` attribute would mean that the stock quotes are lasting far too long in the cache and becoming outdated; while a low-valued `Duration` attribute means that the less dynamic news headlines are being regenerated too often to be effective.

If we really want the stock values to be *live*, we should really generate them from scratch for each request, based on the current values at the moment the request is made. Page caching is not really suitable here; but we can use **fragment caching** instead.

Employing User Controls to Fragment the Page

Fragment caching is a new concept in ASP.NET. It is implemented in practice by using the user controls you've learned about in Chapter 3. The idea is that we employ user controls (like our `FriendsHeader.ascx` and `FriendsFooter.ascx` controls) to separate different kinds of content in the page. Then we apply an `OutputCache` directive in the same way as before, except that we add the directive to the appropriate `.ascx` files and not to the `.aspx` file. The result is that ASP.NET caches the output for *only* the fragments (that is, the user controls) whose `.ascx` file contains an `OutputCache` directive.

How would we use this solution to solve the problem of a page containing live stock quotes and news headlines? First, we would implement a user control to show the daily news, and have that user control cache for, say, two hours. So that `.ascx` file would contain a directive like this:

```
<%@ OutputCache Duration="7200" VaryByParam="none" %>
```

Then we could implement the stock quotes listing in a *separate* user control (which would also allow us to reuse it in a number of different pages), but *this* `.ascx` page would not contain any `OutputCache` directive and would therefore be regenerated at each request.

Other Differences between Page Caching and Fragment Caching

Fragment caching works in roughly the same way as page caching, though there are a couple of differences to be aware of:

❑ First, note that fragment caching does not support the `Location` attribute; the only valid place to cache a page fragment is the web server. This is because fragment caching is new in ASP.NET, and is consequently not supported by browsers and proxy servers.

❑ Second, fragment caching makes available an extra attribute – `VaryByControl` – that is not relevant in page caching. The `VaryByControl` attribute allows us to specify a semicolon-separated list of strings, representing the names of controls used inside the user control; ASP.NET will generate one cached version of our user control for each different combination of values.

Following the news/stocks example we've been using, suppose we added a `DropDownList` control to the news-headlines user control, with the intention of filtering by company name the displayed news:

```
<asp:dropdownlist id="Company" runat="server" Width="120px">
  <asp:ListItem Value="wrox">Wrox Press</asp:ListItem>
  <asp:ListItem Value="msft">Microsoft</asp:ListItem>
  <asp:ListItem Value="amex">American Express</asp:ListItem>
</asp:dropdownlist>
```

Then we can specify ASP.NET to cache different versions of our user control based on the value of the DropDownList control. For that we modify the OutputCache directive accordingly:

```
<%@ OutputCache Duration="7200" VaryByControl="Company" %>
```

Note that it's not possible to access a *cached* user control programmatically. This is because once the user control is cached, ASP.NET is not creating an instance of the control but just returns the cached output. This has an implication for us in the *Friends Reunion* application. Specifically, we can't use fragment caching for our FriendsHeader.ascx and FriendsFooter.ascx user controls, because they are manipulated programmatically each time we call them (for example, setting the message in the header and the user count in the footer) in a way that is not allowed for cached controls.

Applying Output Cache

However, we can use output caching to improve the performance results we got for Users.aspx earlier in the chapter, and we'll do that now.

Try It Out – Applying Output Cache

Generating the dataset of user information displayed in Users.aspx seems to be a real bottleneck, because it uses such a large amount of resource to generate the dataset and we're asking the application to regenerate the dataset each time the page is requested. One way round this is to cache the entire generated page in the ASP.NET cache, so that the page itself (and hence the dataset that contributes to it) is regenerated less often.

1. Open Users.aspx, and add an OutputCache directive just after the Page directive:

```
<%@ Page Language="c#" AutoEventWireup="false" Codebehind="Users.aspx.cs"
        Inherits="FriendsReunionSec.Admin.Users" %>
<%@ OutputCache Duration="300" VaryByParam="none" %>
<!DOCTYPE HTML PUBLIC "-//W3C//DTD HTML 4.0 Transitional//EN">
<html>
  <head>
    ...
```

2. Save the file. If you wish, use the WAS client machine to rerun the FRSimpleAdminScript we first tried earlier in the chapter, and examine the results to see whether there's a noticable improvement.

How It Works

The first time the page is requested, the application must generate the dataset in order to deliver the page, but subsequent requests for Users.aspx are served directly from the ASP.NET cache, and should be much faster because they require far less processing.

When I tested this using the FRSimpleAdminScript script on my WAS client machine, I recorded the following performance improvements:

Metric	Before	After (using OutputCache)
Requests/sec	6.5	22
Processor time	76%	60%

Thus, using the output cache in ASP.NET in this instance results in a quite significant improvement: we have more than tripled the number of requests our server can handle per second, while using 15% less processor power!

This isn't the only way to deal with the dataset-generation bottleneck in Users.aspx. *Instead of caching the entire page, we could have simply cached the dataset itself. The following section is all about this technique, and for comparison, demonstrates the technique in* AssignPlaces.aspx.

Data Caching

The lower-level API we mentioned earlier is the Cache class, which is contained in the System.Web.Caching namespace in ASP.NET – and we can use it for caching data that is costly to generate. The Cache class is as simple to use as the Session and Application objects we met back in Chapter 6.

There is just only one Cache object per application – which means that the data stored in cache using the Cache object is application-level data. To simplify things further, the Page class's Cache property makes the application's Cache object instance available in code.

The data cached through the Cache object is stored in-memory within the application. That does mean that this data will not survive an application restart. (In fact, this is the same as for the data stored in the Application and Session objects, unless you've arranged to store your Session data using the State Service or SQL State session modes, as we saw in Chapter 6.)

Adding Data to the ASP.NET Cache via the Cache Object

The easiest way to add an object to the Cache is by using the index syntax, and specifying a key-value pair like this:

```
Cache["CheckEffectOn"] = false;
```

```
Cache["MembersDataSet"] = dsMyDataSet;
```

The first of these assigns a Boolean value to the cached flag item called CheckEffectOn; the second assigns a dataset to the item called MembersDataSet. To use these cached values in code, we'd access them like this:

```
bool CheckEffectValue = (bool)Cache["CheckEffectOn"];
```

```
DataSet dsMembers = (DataSet)Cache["MembersDataSet"];
```

In each case, we have to cast the retrieved object explicitly. This is because the `Cache` object only handles references to the `System.Object` type (which allows it to store objects of any type).

This is not only way of adding items to the ASP.NET cache. There are two methods of the `Cache` object – the `Insert()` method and the `Add()` method – that are considerably more flexible. They're very similar in usage, but subtly different:

❑ The `Insert()` method should be used to overwrite existing items in the ASP.NET cache

❑ The `Add()` method should *only* be used to add new items to the ASP.NET cache (if you try to use `Add()` to overwrite an existing item, it will fail)

Each of these methods has the same seven arguments (though `Insert()` has some overloads that allow you to specify fewer than all seven). Using them is so similar that we'll only show you some examples of the `Add()` method now; though we will use the `Insert()` method when we apply some caching techniques to the *Friends Reunion* application in a few pages from now.

Dependencies and Priorities

To appreciate what we can to with `Insert()` and `Add()`, we need to know a little about dependencies and priorities. By specifying a **dependency** for an item when we insert it into the `Cache`, we're telling ASP.NET that the item should remain cached until a certain event occurs. The `Add()` and `Insert()` methods allow us to specify the dependency of a cached item at the time the item is cached, using these values:

Dependency Value	Meaning
CacheDependency	This allows us to specify a file or cache key. If the file changes our object is removed. If the cache key changes or becomes invalidated our object is also removed.
DateTime	This is a `DateTime` value that dictates the time at which the cached data expires (as we said earlier in the chapter, we use the term **absolute expiration** for this type of expiration).
TimeSpan	This is an interval of time that dictates how long the cached data can remain cached *after* the last time it was accessed (we use the term **sliding expiration** for this type of expiration).

We've mentioned **priorities** already. As we add more and more data to the cache, it becomes fuller and fuller. If the data expires at a reasonable rate, then there will always be room for more data to be added as the older cached data expires. But if not, then the cache will eventually fill up.

If the cache *does* fill up, then ASP.NET needs a way to start removing some of the less important items in the cache to allow new items to be cached. To decide which cached items it can delete, ASP.NET rates the importance of all the different items in the cache according to the **priority** of each item.

The priority of an item to be stored in the ASP.NET cache can be specified at the time the data is cached (using the `Add()` or `Insert()` method). These are the different priority levels, as classified in the `CacheItemPriority` enumeration:

Priority Value	Meaning
High	Items with this priority level set are the least likely to be removed when memory is low
AboveNormal	Items with this priority set will prevail over items with a priority of Normal or less
Normal	Items with this priority level will prevail over BelowNormal and Low priorities
BelowNormal	This is the second lowest priority available; items with this priority set will only prevail against items whose priority is set to Low
Low	Items with this priority levels will be the most likely to be removed when memory is low
Default	The default value for a cached item's priority is Normal
NotRemovable	When setting this priority level to an item we are telling ASP.NET to not remove it from the cache even if memory is low

When you're assigning the priority of an item, you should base the assignment on the resource cost needed to produce the item. The higher the cost, the higher the priority level.

Adding Objects to ASP.NET Cache using the Low-level API

So, if we wanted to use the Add() method to add a dataset object to the ASP.NET cache, we might write the method call like this:

```
DateTime dt = new DateTime(DateTime.Now.Year,12,31);
Cache.Add("MembersDataSet", dsMembers, null,
          dt, TimeSpan.Zero,
          Normal, null);
```

The first and second arguments are the key by which we reference the cached object, and the object to be cached. The third argument is null (signifying no dependency).

The fourth and fifth parameters are the absolute and sliding expirations. Here, we're saying that the cache should expire on the last day of the current year (dt). We want to specify that there is no sliding expiration, so we put TimeSpan.Zero into the fifth argument. The sixth parameter sets the priority to be Normal, using a value from the System.Web.Caching.CacheItemPriority enumeration.

This example is similar, but it specifies a sliding expiration of five minutes instead of an absolute expiration:

```
Cache.Add("MembersDataSet", dsMembers, null,
          DateTime.MaxValue, TimeSpan.FromMinutes(5),
          Normal, null);
```

Thus, if you want to set no absolute expiration, use `DateTime.MaxValue`; *if you want to specify no sliding expiration, use* `TimeSpan.Zero`. *It's not valid to provide values for both absolute expiration **and** sliding expiration at the same time; if you do, ASP.NET will throw an exception.*

We could add a dependency. In this example, the expiration is also dependent on the modification of a file, `friendsreunion.xml`:

```
CacheDependency dep = new CacheDependency("C:\\data\\friendsreunion.xml");
Cache.Add("MembersDataSet", dsMembers, dep,
        DateTime.MaxValue, TimeSpan.Zero,
        Normal, null);
```

and in this one, it's dependent on the modification of another item in the cache:

```
String[] dependencyKeys = new String[1];
dependencyKeys[0] = "MembersChanged";
CacheDependency dependency = new CacheDependency(null, dependencyKeys);
Cache.Add("MembersDataSet", dsMembers, dep,
        DateTime.MaxValue, TimeSpan.Zero,
        CacheItemPriority.Normal, null);
```

If you don't want to specify a `CacheDependency` object for your item you can pass `null` to that argument as we did in the first example.

In case you're wondering, the final argument is of type `CacheItemRemovedCallback`, and allows us to ask for notification whenever the cached item is evicted from the cache. We can write a custom method (like the `ItemRemovedCallback()` method here), and then specify that method in the seventh argument as follows:

```
public void ItemRemovedCallback(String key, Object value,
                                CacheItemRemovedReason reason)
{
  // this method will be called when the our item expires
}

Cache.Add("MembersDataSet", dsMembers, null,
        DateTime.MaxValue, TimeSpan.FromMinutes(5),
        Normal,
        new CacheItemRemovedCallback(this.ItemRemovedCallback));
```

Note that the `ItemRemovedCallback()` method (which is called whenever the cached item expires) has three arguments. The first is the key we used when we stored the item in the cache, the second is the stored object itself, and the third is the reason the item was evicted. There are four possible reasons listed in the `CacheItemRemovedReason` enumeration – check the documentation for more on that.

Data Caching in Friends Reunion

There are at least a couple of places in the *Friends Reunion* application that would benefit from some careful application of data caching. In particular, every time we perform an expensive query to the database and then hold the results in a DataSet, we can take the opportunity to cache the DataSet and avoid regenerating it unnecessarily for each request.

Try It Out – Caching Places-related Data

In this example, we'll use data caching in the pages that deal with all the places available to the application. We use this data in different pages, and we hit the database to get the data each time. If we could cache the data, and then use the *cached* data in any page that needs it, the resulting reduction in the demands on the server and network should give us an overall performance boost.

In particular, in AssignPlaces.aspx we have included a drop-down list that shows a list of available places. Let's use our newfound data caching skills there.

1. Open AssignPlaces.aspx.cs. Change the LoadDataSet() method by removing all the code used to get the Places data from the database. To do this, you just need to remove (or comment out) three lines:

```
private void LoadDataSet()
    {
        SqlConnection con;
        string sql;
        SqlDataAdapter adExisting;
        // SqlDataAdapter adPlaces;
        SqlDataAdapter adPlaceTypes;

        con = new SqlConnection(
            ConfigurationSettings.AppSettings["cnFriends.ConnectionString"]);

        // Select the place's timelapse records, descriptions, and type
        sql = "SELECT TimeLapse.*, Place.Name as Place, ";
        sql += "PlaceType.Name as Type FROM TimeLapse, Place, PlaceType ";
        sql += " WHERE TimeLapse.PlaceID = Place.PlaceID ";
        sql += " AND Place.TypeID = PlaceType.TypeID ";
        sql += " AND TimeLapse.UserID = '" + Context.User.Identity.Name + "'";

        // Initialize the adapters
        adExisting = new SqlDataAdapter(sql, con);
        // adPlaces = new SqlDataAdapter(
        //              "SELECT * FROM Place ORDER BY TypeID", con);
        adPlaceTypes = new SqlDataAdapter("SELECT * FROM PlaceType", con);

        con.Open();
        ds = new DataSet();
```

```
      try
      {
        // Proceed to fill the dataset
        adExisting.Fill(ds, "Existing");
        // adPlaces.Fill(ds, "Places");
        adPlaceTypes.Fill(ds, "Types");
      }
      catch
      {
        // Just pass the exception up
        throw;
      }
      finally
      {
        con.Close();
      }
    }
```

Note that we've only deleted the code that creates and initializes the `SqlDataApdater` for the `Places` data, and the code that fills the dataset with its contents.

We need to create a dataset for the `Places` data *somewhere*; we'll implement this functionally in a method called `CachePlacesDataSet()`. We'll create this method as a `protected` method of the `FriendsBase` class, so that it will be available to `AssignPlaces.aspx` and any other page that needs to use the cached data.

So, open `FriendsBase.cs` and add the following method to the `FriendsBase` class:

```
protected void CachePlacesDataSet()
{
  // generate the dataset
  SqlConnection con = new SqlConnection(
      ConfigurationSettings.AppSettings["cnFriends.ConnectionString"]);

  DataSet ds = new DataSet();
  SqlDataAdapter adPlaces;
  adPlaces = new
          SqlDataAdapter("SELECT * FROM Place ORDER BY TypeID", con);
  adPlaces.Fill(ds, "Places");

  // reset the flag
  Cache["PlacesChanged"] = false;

  // create a dependency based on the "PlacesChanged" cache key
  String[] dependencyKeys = new String[1];
  dependencyKeys[0] = "PlacesChanged";
  CacheDependency dependency = new CacheDependency(null, dependencyKeys);

  // insert the dataset into the cache,
  // with a dependency to the "PlacesChanged" key
  Cache.Insert("places", ds, dependency);
}
```

Add the following using clauses to FriendsBase.cs:

```
using System.Data;
using System.Data.SqlClient;
using System.Configuration;
using System.Web.Caching;
```

2. Now return to AssignPlaces.aspx.cs, and modify the InitForm() method so that it uses the *cached* dataset when populating the drop-down list:

```
private void InitForm()
{
  if (!(IsPostBack))
  {
    // Clear existing values
    ...

    // Initialize combo box
    ListItem item;
    DataRow[] types;

    // Declare dataset
    DataSet cachedDs;

    // If there is no cached dataset,
    // we need to generate it and cache it
    if(Cache["places"]==null)
      base.CachePlacesDataSet();
    cachedDs = (DataSet)Cache["places"];

    // Access the table by index
    foreach (DataRow row in cachedDs.Tables[0].Rows)
    {
      ...
    }
  }
}
```

3. Finally, we need to invalidate the cached dataset when someone uses ViewPlace.aspx to edit the places-related information in the database. We must do this to ensure that no part of our application (such as AssignPlaces.aspx) uses outdated data.

So, open ViewPlace.aspx.cs and add the following lines to the end of the dlPlaces_UpdateCommand method:

```
private void dlPlaces_SelectedIndexChanged(object sender,
                                     System.EventArgs e)
{
  // Remove the edit index just in case we were editing
  dlPlaces.EditItemIndex = -1;
  this.BindPlaces();
```

```
        // Invalidate the cached data set
        Cache["PlacesChanged"] = true;
    }
```

This will ensure that, whenever the list of places is modified, the cached dataset will expire.

How It Works

The three lines that we removed from the `LoadDataSet()` method are the lines that created, initialized, and filled the old dataset with its contents. After these changes, those three lines of code re-emerge in the `CachePlacesDataSet()` method, which is the place that now has responsibility for setting up the new cached dataset:

```
protected void CachePlacesDataSet()
{
    . . .
    SqlDataAdapter adPlaces;
    adPlaces = new
            SqlDataAdapter("SELECT * FROM Place ORDER BY TypeID", con);
    adPlaces.Fill(ds, "Places");
    . . .
```

In the same method, we then create a dummy cache entry called `PlacesChanged`, which we will use for dependency purposes (essentially it acts like a flag: we change its value to `true` whenever the data in the database gets changed, as we'll see in a moment):

```
    Cache["PlacesChanged"] = false;
```

Then we create a dependency to tie the life of our dataset to the modification of the dummy key:

```
    String[] dependencyKeys = new String[1];
    dependencyKeys[0] = "PlacesChanged";
    CacheDependency dependency = new CacheDependency(null, dependencyKeys);
```

Finally we use the `Insert()` method to insert the dataset in the cache (remember that the `Insert()` method works in a similar way to the `Add()` method we discussed earlier, but also allows us to overwrite existing cache entries):

```
    Cache.Insert("places", ds, dependency);
```

There are just two changes to the `InitForm()` method, which is the one that populates the drop-down list. First, we've *added* code to get it to check that the ASP.NET cache contains the `places` dataset, and create the dataset (using the `CachePlacesDataSet()` method) if necessary:

```
    if(Cache["places"]==null)
      base.CachePlacesDataSet();
```

Second, we've *changed* the next bit of code so that it uses the cached dataset, rather than a freshly-generated one:

```
        cachedDs = (DataSet)Cache["places"];
        foreach (DataRow row in cachedDs.Tables[0].Rows)
        {
            ...
```

Finally, the cached dataset should be regenerated when the database is updated (rendering the existing cached dataset out-dated). So, we've added a line of code to ViewPlace.aspx, to flag up changes to the database. This line of code changes the value of the dummy 'flag' cache item, Cache["PlacesChanged"], which is the subject of the cached dataset's dependency:

```
        Cache["PlacesChanged"] = true;
```

The result of all this is that, whenever a user requests AssignPlaces.aspx, the application will check for a cached version of the dataset first. If one exists, it will build the page using the cached dataset. If not (either because no dataset has been generated yet, or because the dataset has expired), then the application generates the dataset from scratch, places that dataset in the cache, and then uses that newly cached dataset to generate the page.

A Further Improvement

Notice that there is no cached dataset when the application first starts. The dataset will not be generated and cached until the first time someone requests AssignPlaces.aspx. This means that the first ever visitor to AssignPlaces.aspx will not be served as fast as subsequent visitors to the page – they'll have to wait slightly longer while the application generates and caches the dataset.

There is a way to eliminate this delay for AssignPlaces.aspx's first visitor. Namely, we can arrange for the dataset to be generated and cached at the time the application *starts*, by adding code to the Application_Start() event handler (in global.asax). This process requires identical code to that contained in the CachePlacesDataSet() method. Therefore, the best way to do this would be as follows. First, create a public **utility class**, which is accessible from anywhere in our code. Second, move the CachePlacesDataSet() method code to a public static method of this utility class:

```
public class FRUtility
{
  public static void CachePlacesDataSet()
  {
     ... code as before ...
  }
}
```

Third, replace the CachePlacesDataSet() call in AssignPlaces.aspx.cs so it calls the new FRUtility.CachePlacesDataSet() instead:

```
if(Cache["places"]==null)
  FRUtility.CachePlacesDataSet();
```

Finally, add a call to FRUtility.CachePlacesDataSet() in Application_Start().

Other ASP.NET Performance Tips

We have already learned plenty in this chapter about how to examine and improve the performance of specific pages, and we've seen a couple of demonstrations in which carefully-chosen caching techniques enhance the overall performance of the page and the application.

In the remainder of the chapter we'll take a look at some other ASP.NET performance tips. Not all of them are immediately applicable to the *Friends Reunion* application, but you will surely find them useful when developing your own applications.

Controlling ViewState

In the WAS tests that we performed earlier in the chapter, we noticed a couple of things about the Users.aspx page. First, it was taking a long time to generate the page. We identified that this was due to the fact that the server was required to generate a huge dataset (containing data about 1,000 users), and we dealt with that problem by arranging for a *cached* version of the page (from the ASP.NET cache) to be used if possible.

But there was another issue. Specifically, the size of the response itself (the number of bytes passed from server to client in the page response) is also very large. These were the results I generated in my test, and you probably got something similar:

```
Downloaded Content Length (in bytes)
-------------------------------------------------
Min:                          1054113
25th Percentile:              1054113
50th Percentile:              1054113
75th Percentile:              1054113
Max:                          1054113
```

Why is the response so large? Admittedly, we need to pass all the data (about the 1000 users) in the dataset to the client, otherwise the browser will be unable to display the data in the page. But in addition to that, these bytes *also* contain a hidden __VIEWSTATE form-field – which will at least double the size of the page.

We must ask ourselves the question: Is there any reason why viewstate should enabled for this DataGrid control? The page has no facility for the user to post back the user data to the server for handling; it contains no code for events on the DataGrid; and in fact there is nothing in the page that requires viewstate to be enabled.

Therefore, we are free to reduce the response size for this page by **disabling viewstate** for the DataGrid.

Try It Out – Disabling Viewstate on Users.aspx

Since viewstate is unnecessary on the DataGrid in Users.aspx, we'll disable viewstate on that DataGrid. Then we'll find out whether it has a noticeable effect on the overall response size of the page.

1. Open Users.aspx , select the DataGrid control, and view its **Properties** by pressing *F4*. Find its EnableViewState property, and set it to False. Save the file.

2. You can check in the HTML view that VS.NET has correctly changed EnabledViewState attribute for us in the code:

```
<asp:datagrid ...other attributes...
                enableviewstate="false">
   ...
</asp:datagrid>
```

3. Now go back to the WAS client, and run the FRSimpleAdminScript test one more time. When you've done it, check the Downloaded Content Length readings for Users.aspx again, to check that the download size of the page really has reduced. (You'll find this reading in the **Page Data** node on the results.)

How It Works

Well, first let's check that it does work! Here are the results that I got for Users.aspx after disabling viewstate on the DataGrid control:

```
Downloaded Content Length (in bytes)
-------------------------------------------
Min:                           337317
25th Percentile:               337317
50th Percentile:               337317
75th Percentile:               337317
Max:                           337317
```

The simple act of disabling viewstate has reduced the download size by two-thirds. It's also worth checking how much impact this has on the server's performance overall: in my results I found that my server is now able to handle 42 requests/sec – that's almost twice what I had before.

So, what's happening? When the DataGrid's viewstate was enabled, it simply allowed the state to be persisted across postbacks. For this, the state was being included in the page in encoded form, within the _ _VIEWSTATE field of the page. It is this that blew the page size up from a relatively acceptable 0.337 MB (in my case) to a massive 1.05 MB.

We simply identified that the page doesn't use the DataGrid's _ _VIEWSTATE data for anything useful on the server, and was therefore an unnecessary burden. By explicitly setting the DataGrid's enableViewState property to false, we tell the DataGrid not to persist any value into viewstate (the default for this property here is true). As a result, the _ _VIEWSTATE is much shorter, which improves things in two ways;

❑ First (and most obviously), the significant reduction in page size that we've seen in the results above

❑ Second, there's a saving on the server's resources because the server now has far less viewstate to encode or decode and process

Keeping an Eye on Viewstate

We've seen how enabled viewstate brings the potential danger of very big files that are slow to download, and thus affect the performance of our server. Viewstate is enabled by default; it's worth considering each of the controls used in each page to check whether it really depends on having viewstate enabled. If a particular control does *not* use its viewstate, then simply disable it by setting the control's `enableViewState` property to `false`.

In *Friends Reunion*, you could start by looking at the `Label` controls used in the `ViewUser.aspx` page. None of these label controls make use of its viewstate, so they can all be disabled.

Disabling Viewstate at Page Level and Application Level

In fact, in `ViewUser.aspx`, we can go one step better. If you consider the controls in that page, you'll notice that *none* of them need to keep their state between postbacks! So, we can deal with them all in one go by disabling viewstate for the whole page. To do that, we just set the `EnableViewState` attribute to `false` within the `Page` directive:

```
<%@ Page language="c#" Codebehind="ViewUser.aspx.cs"
        AutoEventWireup="false" Inherits="FriendsReunion.ViewUser"
        EnableViewState="false" %>
```

If you're writing an application that doesn't use viewstate at all, then you can disable viewstate at the application level by making a simple change to the application's `Web.config` file. Simply find the `<pages>` element, and set its `EnableViewState` attribute to `false`:

```
<configuration>
  ...
  <system.web>
    <pages ...
      EnableViewState="false"
    />
    ...
  </system.web>
  ...
</configuration>
```

Don't do this in the *Friends Reunion* application, because there are some parts of that application that do rely on viewstate!

Encryption Features of Viewstate

It is also important to check that the tamper-proofing and encryption features of viewstate are not enabled in your application if you don't really need the extra security that these features provide. This level of security will certainly impact on the performance of your application, so disable it if you don't need it.

The tamper-proofing mechanism can be specified by setting the `EnableViewStateMAC` attribute in the `Page` directive:

```
<%@Page ... other attributes ...
        EnableViewStateMAC="false" %>
```

There is no need to explicitly disable encryption, because it depends on `EnableViewStateMAC` being set to `true`.

Note that the value of the `EnableViewStateMAC` attribute *doesn't* affect your ability to use viewstate for individual controls. By contrast, if the value of the `EnableViewState` attribute is `false` then it disables viewstate-related security settings.

What to Put in Viewstate

Finally, we recommend that you are selective about what data types you store in viewstate. Integers, Booleans, hashtables, strings, and `ArrayLists` are OK, because the viewstate serializer is optimized to work with these types. Other types should be avoided if possible; saving other serializable types into viewstate is a slower process.

Response.Redirect and Server.Transfer

When the user is redirected between pages of an application using `Response.Redirect()`, the server sends an `HTTP/1.1 302 Redirect` response to the client passing the target URL; the `302 Redirect` response tells the browser to issue a new request with the new URL. Effectively, the redirection is handled by this extra round-trip between client and server, to finally get the user to the desired page:

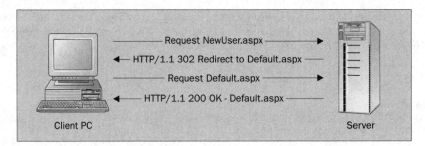

We can avoid this extra round-trip by employing `Server.Transfer()` instead of `Response.Redirect()`. `Server.Transfer()` transfers the execution to a different page within our application – it's a sort of "server-side redirect", in which the client doesn't notice that a redirect occurs.

Try It Out – Server-side Redirection using Server.Transfer

We can apply this improvement to our *Friends Reunion* application. It won't take a minute.

1. Perform a search (*Ctrl+Shift+F*) on the files in the *Friends Reunion* application, to find occurrences of the `Response.Redirect()` method call in the application. There are quite a few: for example, in `Logout.aspx.cs`, `NewUser.aspx.cs`, and `ViewUser.aspx.cs`.

2. Go to each one in turn, and replace the `Response.Redirect()` with a `Server.Transfer()` method call. The new method will take the same single parameter as the old one. Here's what we do in the `UpdateUser()` method in `NewUser.aspx.cs`:

```
if (doredirect) Server.Transfer("../Default.aspx");
```

How It Works

Replacing the `Response.Redirect()` method call with a `Server.Transfer()` method call simply means that the redirection is managed on the server, without a round trip to the client:

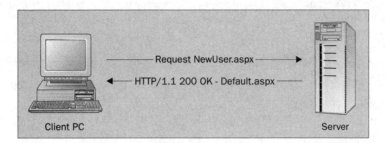

The performance improvement from this change manifests itself in two ways. First, the server now needs to handle just one request, instead of two. Second, there are only two messages sent (one request and one response) instead of four, and that reduces the delay perceived by the end user as they wait for a response to appear on the browser.

When you run the code to test this, you may also notice that the URL shown in the **Address** bar of the browser is the address of the original request (NewUser.aspx), even though the page returned to the browser is clearly Login.aspx. That's because the server transferred execution to Default.aspx without telling the browser about the transfer.

Conservative Use of Web Controls

We learned about the power of web controls back in Chapter 3. When you're using web controls, you need to be aware that they can involve a lot of processing work for the server, because these controls must be initialized, their properties set, their events handled, and so on. So, we should take a look at each web control in our application and ask ourselves, "Do we really need to use a web control for this?"

For example, take a look at the code in the `ViewPlace.aspx`. In particular, note the following `<asp:panel>` control there:

```
<headertemplate>
  <asp:panel id="Panel1" runat="server" cssclass="PlaceTitle">
    List of Places
  </asp:panel>
</headertemplate>
```

The `<asp:panel>` control here is not manipulated anywhere in `ViewPlace.aspx.cs` or in any other code. It's just used to hold three words of text, styled using the `PlaceTitle` CSS class. However, it's still a web control and consequently demands server processing time; but we don't want to waste this processing time on this control if it is not manipulated at all.

Try It Out – Avoiding Unnecessary Web Controls

We are looking for performance improvements, so we will rewrite `ViewPlace.aspx` to get a slight performance gain.

1. Open up `ViewPlace.aspx`, and replace the `<asp:panel>` control with an HTML `<div>` tag as follows:

```
<headertemplate>
  <div class="PlaceTitle">
    List of Places
  </div>
</headertemplate>
```

How It Works

The `<div>` element provides the same rendering effect as the `<asp:panel>` control, but doesn't require server-side processing. Note that we use the `<div>` element's `class` attribute to attach the same CSS class as we used before.

As an exercise you may want to go hunting for other controls in *Friends Reunion* that may be converted to plain HTML. `Label` controls are great candidates for this!

Using Session State

It's very convenient that we can just throw objects into session state and use them later, but this convenience comes at a cost. By default, session state is enabled, which means that ASP.NET does all the work involved in making the session-state feature available, even if you don't use it. Therefore, it's worth overriding the default value for those pages that do not perform any session handling.

We disable session state by setting the `EnableSessionState` attribute to `false` in the `Page` directive:

```
<%@ Page Language="c#" ...
        EnableSessionState="false" %>
```

If we have a page that *reads* values from session state (but does not *write* new values or *modify* existing ones), then it uses session state in a sort of **read-only** mode. In these cases, we can set the `EnableSessionState` attribute to `ReadOnly`, which will provide the page with access to session state but with less overhead (because it omits the writing capabilities).

If we don't use session state anywhere in our application, we can simply turn it off at the application level by setting the `<sessionState>` element's `mode` attribute to **O**ff in web.config:

```
<sessionState mode="Off"
        stateConnectionString="tcpip=127.0.0.1:42424"
        sqlConnectionString="data source=127.0.0.1;user id=sa;password="
        cookieless="false" timeout="20" />
```

Be careful to use an upper-case O when setting the value, because it is case-sensitive!

Finally, be aware that in **State Service** and **SQL State** session modes, session data must be serialized and deserialized to get it in and out of storage, and the cost of this processing will directly depend on the complexity of your objects.

Monitoring the Cache API

We have already mentioned the dangers of caching too many items, back when we first started to look at the caching capabilities of ASP.NET. The dilemma is simple:

- ❑ It's tempting to cache everything we generate, because it seems sensible to avoid the resource cost of regenerating items if we possibly can.

- ❑ However, the main cost of caching is memory utilization (the items must be stored somewhere!).

Ultimately, we need to avoid wasting our server's cache memory on an item if caching the item offers no benefit. If an item is not expensive to generate, or is rarely accessed, it's generally better to regenerate it each time it is needed.

With this in mind, it's helpful to have some way of monitoring the activities of the cache. There are a number of performance counters designed specifically for this purpose. In particular, it's worth taking a look in PerfMon, among the counters made available by the ASP.NET Applications performance object.

A key counter to keep in mind here is the Cache Total Turnover Rate counter. If this counter gives high-valued readings, it means that there are many items entering and leaving the cache per second. This could have a bad impact on performance, because of the resources involved in expiring items from the cache (particularly in terms of cleanup, etc.). If there is a consistently high volume of material being added to and deleted from the cache, any benefits of the caching process are likely to be outweighed by the additional processing power required to handle the high cache turnover rate.

If you use a lot of short expiry times, then your application will be particularly vulnerable to a high cache turnover rate. Of course, some items require short expiry by their very nature; if you need to use short expiry times, be aware that this could have an effect and use them carefully.

Improving Database Access

There are a number of factors that affect the efficiency of database access. The first (and perhaps most obvious) thing to consider is the way we write our queries. In the *Friends Reunion* application, we have used SQL text queries throughout. We've done this for one reason only – to simplify the code. We can give our application an instant performance boost by converting that code into **stored procedures**. Stored procedures are precompiled and highly optimized, and live within the database; that means we don't need to transmit and compile the entire query each time we use it. As a result, we benefit from reduced traffic between our web server and the database server and a significant reduction in the database server workload (especially for complex queries).

It's important to note also that the automatically generated commands that a `DataAdapter` component can produce are not optimized, and not as powerful as coding your own commands.

You should choose carefully when using a managed provider. Use one that is specifically written for the database engine you're targeting, instead of a generic one. If you're targeting Microsoft SQL Server, you should use the classes found in the System.Data.SqlClient namespace, rather than the more generic classes found in the System.Data.Odbc namespace. This will avoid an extra level of indirection and – better yet – your code will be speaking MS SQL native language (TDS), and thus dramatically improve performance.

What about the relative costs of DataReader and DataSet objects? We should use a DataReader in preference to a DataSet wherever possible. Remember that the disconnected nature of a DataSet is achieved by storing all the data in memory, so if you don't really need to cache the data you should be using a DataReader instead.

Finally, remember that the useful **connection pooling** offered by ASP.NET (which manages open connections and allows them to be reused, thus avoiding some connection-opening and -closing overhead) will only work if you use identical connection strings for identical datastores. If you have two connection strings that differ by even a single character, the connection pooling mechanism will consider them as different.

There's lots more information on these subjects in *Professional ASP.NET Performance* (Wrox, ISBN 1-861007-558).

Summary

Performance is a feature of our application, to be considered even before starting to write our very first line of code. As it happens, in this chapter we've made a number of retrospective changes to the *Friends Reunion* application:

- ❏ Caching expensive pages, page fragments, or data objects
- ❏ Disabling viewstate where appropriate
- ❏ Replacing Response.Redirect() with Server.Transfer()
- ❏ Replacing web controls with HTML elements where possible
- ❏ Disabling session state where possible

We managed to apply all these changes without too much effort, but it would have been a lot easier if we'd applied some of the practices here at the time we wrote the application. Certainly, at the time we design an application, it's often possible to pick out places where we have things like large, frequently-generated datasets. In those cases we should plan our cache usage as part of the application design, and establish the expiration of the cached object and convince ourselves that there will be enough cache memory to contain it.

The main cache area we've examined in this chapter is the ASP.NET cache – this is an area of memory on the web server that is provided by ASP.NET for output caching and for data caching. We've also seen that some items can also be cached further downstream, in areas of cache at the proxy server or in the browser itself.

Caching is undoubtedly one of the most powerful techniques available for improving web application performance. New ASP.NET caching features, such as the ability to cache the whole or a fragment of a page, are very well suited to their task. It's clear than we don't need to resort to tricky code to improve performance; we can write clean and maintainable code that uses the different features we have learned in this chapter and is very effective.

Our intention has been to demonstrate how to test your application and to suggest some of the options ASP.NET has on offer. There is much to explore, and I hope we've given you some ideas!

In the next chapter, we'll turn our attention to the task of preparing our application for deployment on production servers.

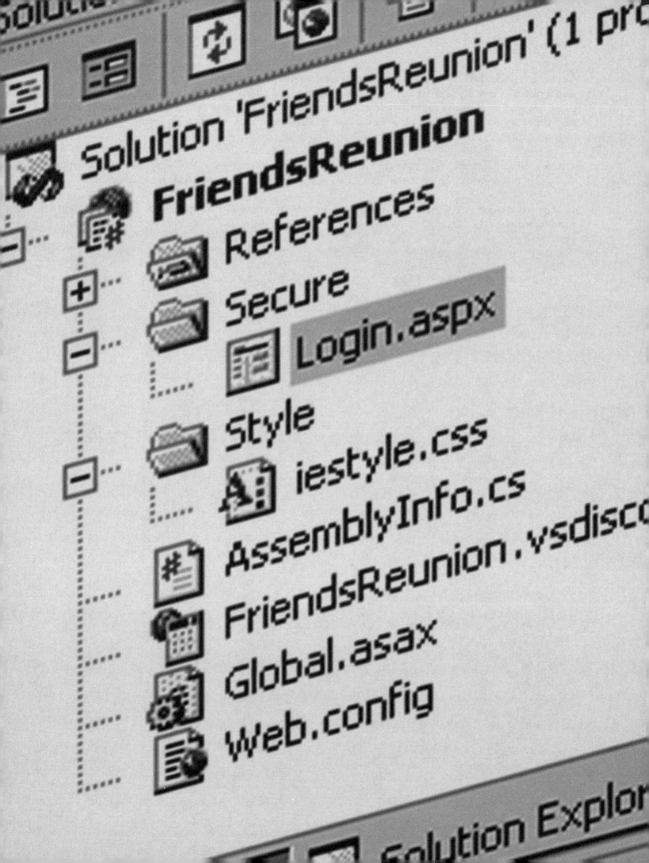

Publishing Web Applications in .NET

Throughout this book, we've examined how we can make best use of Visual Studio .NET for developing applications. Once we've finished developing the application, there are just a few final hurdles to overcome before it can be used by the world at large. These hurdles all relate to **publishing** and **maintaining** this application. In particular, we need to:

- ❑ Select and grouping the files required for an installation into a **deployment package**
- ❑ **Install** the deployment package on production servers
- ❑ Find a way to **configure** an application for the target system
- ❑ Find a way to **update** the application to fix bugs or add new functionality

The time and complexities involved in the deployment of a project are often overlooked. Once an application has been proved to function, to be reliable, and to fulfill the requirements set out for it, it is all too easy to assume that there is nothing more to do. But we still need to organize all the elements that make up the application – web pages, compiled components, databases, and so – and move them from the place where they were developed (usually one or more local workstations) to the hosting environment in a controlled way.

This chapter examines the functionality (provided by .NET) that comes into play when development of an application finishes, and deployment is required. First, we'll take a look at the historic solutions that have been available to us for producing installation packages, and then we'll move on to look at how this has changed with the introduction of .NET. Following that, we try out creating deployment packages in the following order:

- ❑ Installing an application by hand
- ❑ Creating a simple **deployment project** to do the same task, automating a lot of the effort involved

❑ Adding more complex functionality, such as user interaction to the deployment project, and allowing changes to the configuration to be made during deployment

❑ Adding custom actions to the installation of applications (including installation of 'external' parts of a system, such as databases)

Deployment Before .NET

Historically, the manner of deploying an application has been largely dependent on how the application was composed (that is, what was in it). For example:

❑ Traditional ASP files could simply be copied to a folder on the target machine, and as long as a **site** or **virtual directory** was configured in IIS, the application would run.

❑ If the application made use of **COM components** (the forerunner of .NET assemblies), things became much more complicated. We could register COM components by writing a batch file (a script with a .bat extension); we could even create a proper installation package that either registers the DLLs, or places them in COM+. Such installation packages could be created either using third-party applications, or using Microsoft's **Packaging and Deployment Wizard**, included with Visual Studio 6.0. Other methods were available for different platforms, such as Java.

The existence and popularity of such third-party applications for the creation of installation packages demonstrates the commonly-held opinion that Microsoft's offering didn't provide the functionality required, and left much to the developer.

Deployment in .NET

When Microsoft announced that it was planning to incorporate a fully-featured deployment manager into Visual Studio .NET, many were skeptical due to its track record. When you think how much simpler it is to deploy an application by hand than it used to be, it's easier to understand how a powerful installation builder can be added. In the end, an installation package just goes through the motions that are required when installing by hand – the simpler this process, the more easily such functionality can be implemented.

XCOPY Deployment

Possibly the most talked about aspect of installing .NET applications in general, and web applications in particular, is **XCOPY deployment**. This refers to the old MS-DOS tool XCOPY, which allows files and folders to be copied between locations with a wealth of options.

XCOPY can be used on its own, and we can make use of its ability to copy subfolders, validate the actions it's performed, ignore errors, select the files to copy based upon attributes (such as "Last Modified Date"), and so on. This is a huge leap forwards in comparison to the deployment of projects developed in older technologies such as ASP with COM DLLs – where, once all of the files had been copied, DLLs had to be registered and unregistered, entered into COM+, and so on.

Such a simple method of deployment is possible due to the self-describing nature of assemblies in .NET. Each assembly contains within itself all of the information required for other applications to make use of it (which means that we don't need to store metadata about the assembly in the registry). This feature, when combined with fact that .NET applications check specific folders (such as the current one) for libraries to be used with applications, means that the deployment of applications really can be as simple as copying files to the target machine.

Deployment Projects

With the solution to installation as simple as copying files, it may seem that there is little need for the inclusion of deployment-packagers with Visual Studio .NET. However, there are many secondary questions that need answering for each application. For example:

❑   Where do the files need to be installed?

❑   How do we provide the files in a manageable format (such as a compressed archive) to those installing the application?

❑   How do we create an entry in IIS that guarantees that the entry's settings are the same as on the development machines?

❑   What if the individuals installing the application aren't experienced with file manipulation? (We have to keep in mind that it's sometimes novice clients, not experienced developers, that have the responsibility of installing the application.)

❑   What if the user makes a mistake while performing a manual installation?

❑   How much time will be spent copying the files by hand (particularly if the system must be deployed to many machines, or is being updated on a regular basis)?

❑   What if certain parts of the application can be installed and updated separately from others?

❑   What if we need to provide further functionality, such as the installation of a database, or notification of a successful install for auditing purposes?

❑   Is our application going to be presented to end users as a commercial product (that they'll expect to install in a similar manner to all of their other software)?

❑   How do we provide late-breaking information and tips to users installing our applications?

By using **deployment projects** in .NET, we can deal with all of these issues, by providing a Wizard-style interface that guides users through the installation process, and allows them to make choices at the appropriate times.

Deploying a Web Application by Hand

Before we look at how we go about creating a deployment project using Visual Studio .NET, we'll run through the process of installing our ASP.NET application by hand. This way, we'll gain a better understanding of the underlying architecture involved and make the installation process easier to understand.

If we take a look at any web application in the **Solution Explorer** pane, we can see that it consists of a large number of files and folders. Here's an example from our *Friends Reunion* application:

However, this is only half of the story. If you click on the **Show All Files** button on the toolbar of the **Solution Explorer**, you'll see that several more files and folders are shown with a 'ghosted' appearance, along with + symbols next to many of the files:

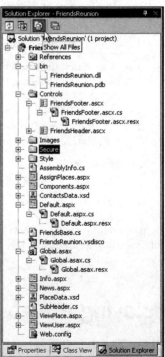

Many of these files are not required when deploying the project to another machine. For instance, all of the files with a .cs or .resx extension are merely source code for the application – this source code will not be required at run time, because it will have been compiled.

In order for the *Friends Reunion* the application to run, the following files are required:

- ❑   bin\FriendsReunion.dll – This is the project's DLL file, which contains the functionality representing the project's classes, methods, declarations, and so on. There is a class for each of the web pages that was created as part of the project.

- ❑   *.aspx and *.ascx – These files represent the individual web pages and user controls in the application. They contain any HTML required to render the page, along with references to controls that are used (such as <asp:textbox> tags), and a reference to the code-behind functionality that has been compiled into the FriendsReunion.dll assembly. As we just mentioned, the .aspx.cs and .aspx.resx files are not required for deployment because the code contained in those files is compiled into the FriendsReunion.dll assembly. The same is true for the source code contained in .ascx.cs and .ascx.resx files.

- ❑   Global.asax – This file links to the Global.asax.cs code-behind script, which is compiled into FriendsReunion.dll, and ensures that the code that we specified to execute when the application initializes actually runs. It here that we added the Application_AuthenticateRequest() functionality, back in Chapter 10 – this is the code that checks to see if a user has logged in or not. Again, source files that get compiled (those with a .cs and .resx extension) can be ignored.

- ❑   Web.config – This is the XML file that contains ASP.NET configuration information for the web application. We can change the values in this file without the need to recompile the entire project (this is also true for .aspx files – but not for code-behind files, which require compilation). This means that after installation, we can alter the Web.config file without affecting the other files mentioned above.

- ❑   Obviously, for our site to appear to users as we intend, the files contained in the Images and Style folders will also need to be included for deployment.

In addition to the .cs source files, there are several other files that aren't required for deployment. These include some files shown in the Solution Explorer, such as .pdb (Program DataBase) files that are created for each project, and other files that aren't shown, such as .csproj files that contain information about the project. If the installation process were for a web services project instead of a web forms application, the only noticeable difference would be the .asmx files that we'd need to include instead of .aspx files.

Now that we know exactly what files are actually required by an ASP.NET web application, let's try out the process of manual installation.

Try It Out – Deploying By Hand

We'll assume here that the destination server already has IIS installed, but does not yet have the .NET Framework installed. After all, it could be that this application is the first one in .NET to be deployed to your servers.

1. The first step is to install the .NET Framework runtime files so that IIS can recognize and process ASP.NET file types such as `.asmx`, `.aspx`, and so on. The Microsoft **.NET Framework Redistributable** installs the files required to run *any* .NET application, including web applications. This file is called `dotnetfx.exe`, and it can be found on the Microsoft Windows Component Update CD that came with Visual Studio .NET. It is located in a subdirectory named `dotNetFramework`.

Alternatively, we can use the .NET runtime, which is contained in an executable file called `dotnetredist.exe`. At the time of writing, you can download this file from Microsoft's web site, at http://msdn.microsoft.com/downloads/sample.asp?url=/ msdn-files/027/001/829/msdncompositedoc.xml.

By executing either of these files, you install all of the essential runtime libraries for all of the .NET languages (files such as `Sytem.dll`, `System.Data.dll`, and so on), as well as the runtime itself, which interprets the intermediate language (IL) that forms the compiled application. If it weren't for this runtime, then the applications created by .NET projects could not be run at all, as they don't contain **native code**. That is to say, the code must first be processed by the runtime, converting it to the physical instructions that execute on the machine.

> **To ensure correct execution, the version of .NET Framework Redistributable run on the target machine *must* be the same as the version of the .NET Framework installed on the machine that compiled the original project.**
>
> **If a different version is present, then although the application may execute, it may cause errors or strange behavior. This is one of the most common causes of installation failure (and something we'll return to later on).**

2. Next, copy the files that we listed above into a new folder somewhere on the target server's hard disk. The convention is to make this a subfolder of `C:\Inetpub\wwwroot`, although you're free to put it anywhere that seems appropriate, depending on the server's configuration. Throughout this example, it will be assumed that the folder chosen is `C:\Inetpub\wwwroot\FriendsReunion`. Here are the files to copy in full:

```
Admin\Users.aspx
Admin\Web.config
bin\FriendsReunion.dll
Controls\*.ascx
Images\*
Secure\*.aspx
Style\*
*.aspx
Global.asax
Web.config
```

Note that an asterisk (*) has been used to denote either all files in a given folder, or all files with a specific extension.

When copying the files across, you should ensure that the exact folder structure is recreated on the target server (in other words, the `FriendsReunion.dll` file is located in the `bin` folder, and so on). There is no need to register the DLL file itself.

3. Depending on the location of these files, you may need to create a virtual directory for them in IIS, set an alias for the folder, and set the physical folder directory as an application; or, if you have placed the files under `C:\Inetpub\wwwroot`, simply need to tell IIS that the directory is an application folder, by clicking the **Create** button on the **Directory** tab of the **Properties** dialog for it.

If you have not yet already done so, refer to Chapter 1 to see how to create and set up virtual directories in IIS.

4. Before we verify that the web site is installed properly, we're going to digress a little and see a good way to check the version number of the .NET Framework on the server (to ensure that it matches with that of our development machine). In the Internet Services Manager MMC snap-in (**Start | Settings | Control Panel | Administrative Tools | Internet Services Manager**), right-click on the **FriendsReunion** (virtual) directory, and select **Properties**. Then, press the **Configuration** button that appears in the lower right of the resulting dialog. This brings up another dialog that shows the file type associations for the .NET Framework runtime components.

Scroll down a little to the `.asmx` and `.aspx` extensions. Files of this type are run using the `aspnet_isapi.dll`, which will be located in a folder named after the version of the Framework to which it belongs. Below, we can see that the Framework version is 1.0.3705:

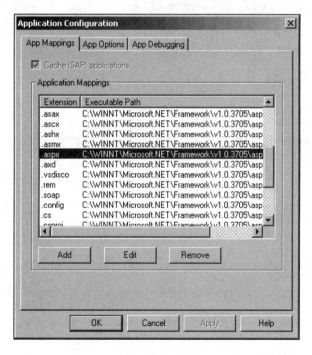

If you're getting problems when you run an application on the server, but it runs fine on the development machine, it's worth checking that both machines have the same version number installed. If not, you'll need to upgrade either the target server or the development machine. If you upgrade the development machine, then you'll also have to rebuild the project.

Problems with .NET Framework versioning will become more common as additional releases of the framework are made available by Microsoft. At the time of writing, version 1.0.3705 is the latest available.

5. Diversions aside, we're ready to test the installation. Open a web browser; the site should be displayed when you navigate to the URL http://<*servername*>/FriendsReunion, where <*servername*> is the name of the server to which the application has been deployed, or its IP address.

The web application's default page should now appear, allowing us to log in or register, as appropriate.

How It Works

Looking back at this process, we have taken the minimum number of files produced by Visual Studio .NET for an ASP.NET web application project, and copied them to a folder on our server. We then created a virtual folder that acts as an alias for this location, and allows users to view the site through a web browser.

Each of the `.aspx` files and `.ascx` files (and `Global.asax` etc) contains a line of code that specifies which class in our project contains the code-behind functionality for that page. When a page is requested, the .NET runtime looks within the DLL file for the necessary class, which will be compiled into `FriendsReunion.dll`. The runtime automatically looks for this DLL file in the `bin` subfolder of our application; this means that we had to do no more than copy each of the files to the correct location.

The only complication we had to deal with is ensuring that the version of the .NET Framework that we developed the application using is the same as the one on the target server.

Setup Projects in Visual Studio .NET

Having looked at the steps required to install the *Friends Reunion* web application onto a different machine manually, you should now have a good understanding of what any automated installer will have to do. With that in mind, let's move on to take a look at the project type Visual Studio .NET provides for installing web applications. This is the **Setup Project**, and it is found under the **Setup and Deployment Projects** node of the **New Project** dialog box.

A VS.NET setup project creates a single Windows installer file (with the `.msi` file extension). This installer file offers the user an easy-to-understand GUI for directing installation, which includes copying files, configuring the environment, and installing components into COM+. In addition to the manageability of a single file, such MSI installers also offer the benefit of remote deployment over earlier installer technologies (such as cabinet (`.cab`) file-based installers, as discussed below). This allows them to be installed on remote machines by system administrators, making their management far quicker and easier.

A **setup project** combines the output files from other Visual Studio .NET projects, along with any other necessary files, to create an installation file that can be copied and run on the system that is to host the application. Just for reference, the following table contains descriptions of the setup project types available in Visual Studio .NET:

Project Type	Description
Setup Project	Used to create installers for Windows Forms applications, as opposed to web applications. This is the only one of the options available with the *Standard Edition* of Visual Studio .NET. In order to make use of the other project types, an installation of either the *Professional Edition* or one of the *Enterprise Editions* is required.
Web Setup Project	Very similar to a standard Setup Project, but it is aimed to the deployment of web applications. It does this by tailoring the installation process to include the creation of a virtual directory in IIS automatically.
Merge Module Project	Can be reused in several installations. If certain groups of components or files are common to many applications, then instead of copying such files one-by-one into each setup project, we can create a merge module containing a group of files. We can then use the merge module in our setup project to include the common files that it contains automatically. Microsoft itself makes such merge modules available, for the .NET runtime, for example. One difference between merge modules and other setup projects is that they cannot be run on their own – they must be added to other setup projects in order to deploy the application(s) that they contain. Creating merge modules for common tasks follows a very similar procedure to regular setup projects.
Setup Wizard	Not really a setup type in its own right; it simply asks a series of questions in order to determine the setup project type to use. It also sets certain options within the setup configuration.
Cab Project	This option creates cabinet files that can be downloaded to a legacy web browser or platform. This project type lets us package ActiveX components so that they can be downloaded and installed onto a client's machine from a web site with a single click.

In Visual Studio .NET, setting up web setup projects (or any of the other setup project types) is very simple. VS.NET provides a series of editors to alter each stage of the installation – these editors allow us to specify amendments that should be made to the registry, any extra files that are required, the look of the installation interface, and so on. When you select a setup project in the Solution Explorer, the mini-toolbar at the top changes to display an icon for each of the editors available for the project. These icons are shown overleaf, along with a brief description of each:

Icon	Editor Type	Description
	File System Editor	Allows creating, updating, and property setting for all physical files, assemblies, and folders of the project to be installed.
	Registry Editor	For creating or modifying values in the registry of the machine where the application is being installed.
	File Types Editor	Can create specialist file type commands that assign processes to specific file extensions. Particularly useful if the installed project uses a unique file suffix.
	User Interface Editor	The install process comprises a series of dialogs that are displayed to the user. This editor allows us to amend or delete any of the default dialogs, or to create new custom dialogs of our own.
	Custom Actions Editor	Allows us to specify additional processes that should be performed on a target computer during installation. The process can take the form of a DLL, an executable, a script file, or an `Installer` class file within the solution. For instance, we could create a Visual Basic script that creates a new administrator, or an SQL script that creates a database.
	Launch Conditions Editor	The installer uses conditions specified in this editor to determine whether the installation can proceed, or dependent components need to be installed first.

Web Setup Projects

As mentioned above, the only project type we have available to us with the *Standard Edition* of VS.NET is the **Setup Project**. In order to try out the creation of a **Web Setup Project**, you'll require at least the *Professional Edition* of VS.NET. Whichever is available to you, it's still pertinent to read the steps involved below. You can recreate the main difference between the two – the creation of a virtual directory in IIS to host the application – by using custom actions, described later in this chapter.

Let's now see how this kind of project is created for our *Friends Reunion* application.

Try It Out – Creating a Web Setup Project

We'll now create a Visual Studio .NET web setup project that installs the *Friends Reunion* application, as demonstrated manually earlier:

1. Within the *Friends Reunion* solution, add a **Web Setup Project** from the **Setup and Deployment Projects** node of the **Add New Project** dialog. Call this project **FriendsReunionDeployment** (this project can be created in any convenient location) and click **OK**:

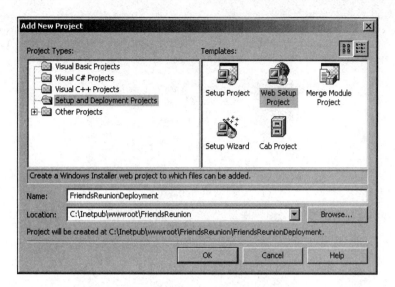

Once the FriendsReunionDeployment project has been created by the IDE, it will show up in the Solution Explorer, along with the other projects that have been created so far.

2. We now need to add the files that constitute our web site to the deployment package. To do this, click the **File System Editor** button on the toolbar at the top of the **Solution Explorer** pane, and you will see something like this:

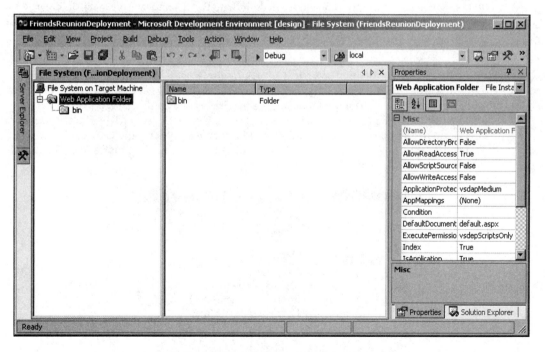

3. Using the File System Editor, we can add all of the files that are required by our web application in order to function. To do this, right-click **Web Application Folder** in the tree view on the left, and select the **Add | Project Output...** option. This brings up the following dialog:

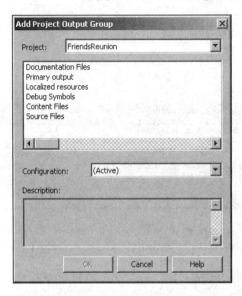

The **Project** drop-down list at the top of this dialog selects the project whose output we want to use from those currently attached to this solution. The list underneath the drop-down shows the different types of project output that we can choose, documentation for the project, primary output (such as DLLs), content files (.aspx files, etc.), and so on.

We want to add the primary output of the `FriendsReunion` project, which will include the .dll files in the installation, and we also want to do the same for the content files of the project. This will include the .aspx files, along with the associated `Web.config` file, and all of the images, styles, and so on that compose the project. To do this, select the `FriendsReunion` option from the **Project:** drop-down list, select both the **Primary output** and **Content Files** options (hold down *Ctrl* while clicking on each), and click **OK**. Leave the **Configuration** drop down at (**Active**). Once you've done this, the **FriendsReunionDeployment** project should look something like the following:

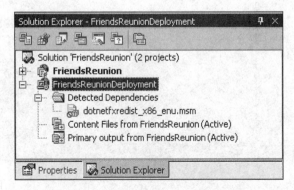

That's all we have to do to create a simple installer for our projects in Visual Studio .NET. To build the setup package, right-click the FriendsReunionDeployment project in the Solution Explorer, and choose the Build option from the menu.

As we'll see shortly, the deployment package won't work as things stand, so don't attempt to compile it just yet. We'll have a look at how this deployment package works first, before building it and trying it out.

How It Works

To add the files that we want to include for installation, we use the File System Editor. This editor uses a layout similar to Windows Explorer, with a tree view on the left, and a detail pane on the right, showing the contents of the folder selected. To include a file in the installation process, we just need to place it into the appropriate folder in this editor. By default, the bin folder is already created, ready for us to place our executables and DLLs.

When VS.NET builds a setup project after we've added such files, it creates all of the installation packages that we might need to distribute in order for our users to install our .NET application. We can see what these are by browsing to the folder that we specified when the FriendsReunionDeployment project was created. This folder will contain two subfolders, called Debug and Release, respectively. The compiled code for the installation will be found in one of these folders, depending on your project configuration – Debug by default. The files created are as follows:

❑ InstMSiA.exe – Installs the Windows Installer for Windows 9x (in other words, 95, 98), and Windows ME. This needs to be included only if we intend the application to be installed onto a machine that does not already have at least v2.0 of the Windows Installer present.

❑ InstMSiW.exe – Installs the Windows Installer for Windows NT, Windows 2000, Windows XP, and .NET Server. This needs to be included only if we intend the application to be installed onto a machine that runs one of these operating systems, and does not have the latest version of the Windows Installer present.

❑ Setup.exe and Setup.ini – This program, and its configuration file, will examine the system to determine whether the Windows Installer itself needs to be installed. If so, it will run whichever of InstMSiA.exe and InstMSiW.exe is appropriate. It will then install our application, using the file that we describe next. All of the other installation files must be in the same folder as these for this to work correctly, unless the Setup.ini file is edited by hand.

❑ FriendsReunionDeployment.msi – This is the package that contains all files for installing our application with the Windows Installer. If we are certain that the required version of the Windows Installer is already installed on the target machine, then this is the only file that we need to distribute.

Using the Windows Installer software is the default method of installing any Windows application, and Microsoft and other third-party software vendors throughout the industry use it.

Adding Outputs to Installers

After our investigation in the first part of this chapter, we know that the minimum files needed to run our web site are:

```
Admin\Users.aspx
Admin\Web.config
bin\FriendsReunion.dll
Controls\*.ascx
Images\*
Secure\*.aspx
Style\*
*.aspx
Global.asax
Web.config
```

When we selected the Primary output option from the Add Project Output Group dialog, the FriendsReunion.dll file in the bin folder was added to the deployment package. This file contains all of the compiled code-behinds for the project. By selecting the Content Files option too, we ensured that all of the other files listed above were also included. The entire list of options available to us is as follows:

Output Type	Description
Documentation Files	The documentation that has been produced for a project.
Primary output	The compiled executables and libraries (that is, files with a .exe or .dll extension). This does not include any DLL or EXE files that have simply been copied into the selected project – merely those that are created by the project. Libraries that are referenced by the primary output are, however, automatically added to the bin folder of the file system editor.
Localized resources	The locale- or culture-specific resources for a project.
Debug Symbols	The debugging files produced for the project, with either a .dbg or .pdb extension. These files are required for debugging the project remotely; they are not required if you are deploying a live commercial system.
Content Files	HTML and other client-facing files, such as .asmx, .aspx, .ascx, .htm, .css, and images. This also includes all files with an .asax extension
Source Files	These comprise the code-behind files for .aspx and .asmx pages, as well as other code files such as modules and classes. Similarly to the Debug Symbols, if the project is to be deployed to a live environment, rather than further development areas, these are not required.

Each of the entries for the content files and primary output is really just a shortcut to the project output files themselves – its sort of list of what files are to be included, rather than a copy of each individual file. This means that the setup package adjusts itself to use the latest version of the included files at the time the installation project is built, and hence reduces the danger of producing a setup package that installs an out-of-date application.

In addition to selecting project outputs, the file system editor also allows us to drag any files and folders located on our system directly into the desired output folder, either from Windows Explorer or from VS.NET's Solution Explorer pane.

Project Configurations

One final thing worth noting before we continue with the creation of our installer is the Configuration drop-down list that was present in the Add Project Output Group dialog. This specifies whether the setup project should use (Active), Debug .NET, or Release .NET output for the selected project:

❑ (Active) – Uses whichever one of the following two configurations has been set as the default configuration for the project you're attaching to this installation.

❑ Debug.NET – Includes debug information, making it possible to remotely step through code, trace errors, and so on. This provides a slight performance hit over Release .NET builds.

❑ Release .NET – Strips out all code that uses the debug command (see below), and also omits all debug information from compiled code.

It is also possible to select different code for different configurations at compile time, on a conditional basis. Look at this simple example as an illustration:

```
#if (DEBUG)
   Response.Write("Test code...");
#else
   Response.Write("Live code...");
#endif
```

This preprocessor directive (as denoted by a leading hash character, #) is similar to a regular `if` statement, except that it controls the behavior of the compiler itself, rather than the compiled code. So in this simple example, if we were to select Debug.NET as the active configuration for a project, then in this example, the command would write out the text `Test code...`; otherwise the text `Live code...` would be displayed.

The value DEBUG that is used for testing can be found in the Property Pages of our web application, which are displayed when we select the Properties option from its context-menu in the Solution Explorer. If you switch to the Build option of Configuration Properties in the pane to the left of the window, you can see the value shown to the right, under Conditional Compilation Constants. If you change the Configuration drop-down list to Release, you'll see that this value is no longer present:

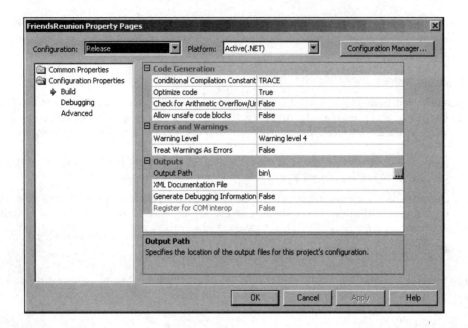

Dependencies and Outputs

When the `FriendsReunionDeployment` build process has finished examine the content of the VS.NET **Output** pane. In it, you'll find that the build process has generated a warning. It relates to the `dotnetfx.exe` file that we mentioned earlier, and it is there because the target machine must have the .NET Framework installed:

```
WARNING: This setup does not contain the .NET Framework which must be installed on
the target machine by running dotnetfx.exe before this setup will install. You can
find dotnetfx.exe on the Visual Studio .NET 'Windows Components Update' media.
Dotnetfx.exe can be redistributed with your setup.
```

When we installed the application manually, we dealt with this issue by manually copying the `dotnetfx.exe` file to the target machine and running it to install the .NET Framework. Now that we're having Microsoft's Installer do the work for us, we can (if we wish) include the `dotnetfx.exe` file in the installation package. But this comes at a cost – `dotnetfx.exe` is 40MB in size. It only needs to be installed once, so it's probably better to install it *manually* on the target machine, rather than as part of our application's installation. Also, it's worth noting again the importance of being careful about versioning – we must ensure that the correct Framework version is installed to deployment machines.

That said, however, it is extremely easy to include the `dotnetfx.exe` file with your installation. If you were watching closely earlier, you may have seen a file with a similar name, `dotnetfxredest_x86_enu.msm`, under the detected dependencies of our setup project in the **Solution Explorer**. To include this file in all subsequent installation packages generated from our project, we just right-click this entry, and uncheck **Exclude**.

The explanation behind this file's name and .msm extension is the fact that it is a merge module. This means that it contains one or more files required for a specific and common installation process. If you want to, you can view the files it contains by choosing Properties from the context menu, and clicking the ellipsis button for the Files property:

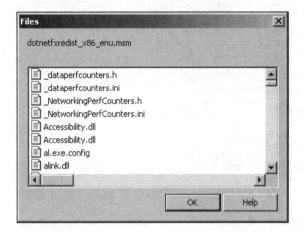

This list contains all files within the merge module. We'll return to look at merge modules in more detail later in the chapter.

At this point, you may be wondering how Visual Studio .NET knows that components like dotnetfx.exe should be included in the first place. Some files need other files to be installed already if they are to work correctly, and these other files are called **dependencies** of the files requiring them. To view the dependencies for the files in our install list, right-click either the appropriate item in the right-hand pane of the File System Editor or the Primary output option in the Solution Explorer, and choose Dependencies. The following is the list for the primary output of FriendsReunion:

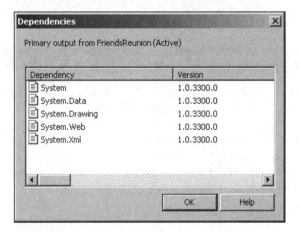

This dialog shows the components (and the component's versions) that this file or package is dependent on, and which must, therefore, be included in the installation for it to operate correctly. All of the above dependencies are installed with the .NET Framework (by running dotnetfx.exe).

Often, its also useful to know exactly *what* files are being included with the installation – especially in the case of these shortcuts to project outputs. To see a list of the files being installed, right-click on an item listed in the right-hand pane of the file system editor, and this time choose **Outputs**. Here's what we get with this option for the content files of the `FriendsReunion` project:

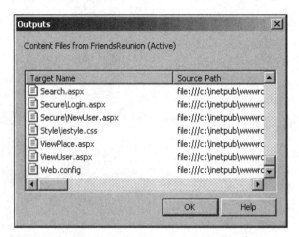

Being able to see the outputs and dependencies for files is invaluable when creating an installation project for a web application – preventing needless hours of hunting for missing files that were assumed to be present.

Using the Setup Project

Having touched the surface of a Visual Studio .NET Web Setup Project, we'd better find out what actually happens when we use the files it creates. Once we've seen that, we'll have a clearer idea of the aspects that we might want to change.

Try It Out – Running the Installation Package

This example does exactly what the title suggests. We're going to deploy the installation files to another folder, ideally on a remote machine, to see how they behave.

1. First, navigate to the folder on our local machine that contain the `.msi` file, and so on – this is the folder that was created when we build the deployment project. Its location is specified in the **Output** window, just as the project build begins. Copy the following files from this location to a single folder on the machine that is to be used for testing the installation:

```
FriendsReunionDeployment.msi
InstMsiA.Exe
InstMsiW.Exe
Setup.Exe
Setup.Ini
```

If you can, use another machine – the demonstration will be more effective. If you don't have one available, you can use a folder on the development machine for testing purposes. The folder you use for these files can be be any folder at all; it doesn't have to be the folder in which the web application will finally reside, and it ideally *shouldn't* be, because that brings the risk of leaving the installation files downloadable by end users. During the manual setup process, we had to set up IIS ourselves, but that won't be necessary this time.

2. Once the files are on the target machine, just double-click Setup.exe to start the install process. If the target machine doesn't already have the correct version of the Windows Installer, it will automatically be updated when this program is run. This process isn't particularly relevant to us, as there's nothing we can do to change it – it's an intrinsic part of Windows Installer-based applications. Instead, we'll concentrate on the installation of our web application.

3. The installation process now follows the standard Wizard format that almost all modern applications make use of; that of a sequence of dialogs that ask a series of questions, guiding the user through the installation process. In our case, all we need to do is confirm the details of the virtual directory for IIS, including the port to use:

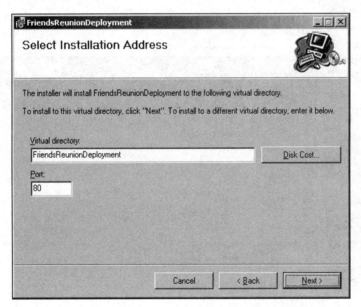

4. The values of these settings shouldn't be changed unless it is necessary, ensuring that the port to access the web site is left at the global standard of 80, and that the virtual directory name is relevant to the application we're installing (the global standard for web). Click the Next button twice, to complete this page and skip over the Confirm Installation page that informs the user that all the required information has been gathered.

When you reach the page with the Finish button, the installation is complete, and you can test the application. To do this, run Internet Explorer on the machine, and enter the URL http://localhost/FriendsReunionDeployment. This should show the home page of our site, just as when we installed the application manually.

How It Works

The installation process simply creates a folder with the same name as the setup project in the `Inetpub\wwwroot` folder, and specifies it as an application in IIS. If you browse to this directory, you'll see that all of the files here are those that we selected using the **File System Editor**; the `Primary output` and `Content files` from our project. The installer knows to place the DLLs into the `bin` subfolder ensuring, for security reasons, that they're not externally visible to site visitors.

Uninstalling a Project

Although the deployment packages that we create within Visual Studio .NET can automatically remove previous versions of software we've installed before proceeding, there are also times that we may wish to remove the projects manually ourselves. This can be done similarly to any other application – from within the **Add or Remove Programs** dialog in the **Control Panel**:

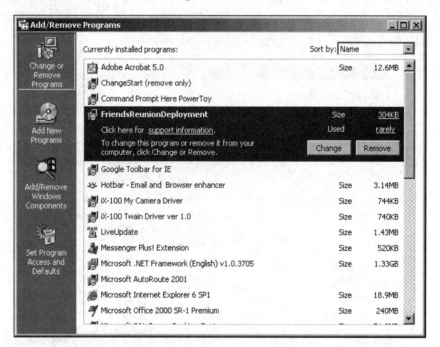

Advanced Functionality

We've managed to install the web application successfully; the next step is to add our other projects to the deployment package, producing an installer that's customized to our particular application, rather than a generic web site. As the web service can be handled in exactly the same manner as the web site and our consumer test application isn't needed for a live system, this just leaves us with the database.

If you have access to either of the *Enterprise* editions of Visual Studio .NET (*Enterprise Developer* or *Enterprise Architect*), you'll find a wealth of options for automating the relocation of the database from the development server to the live one. With less feature-rich versions – the *Standard Edition* most notably – there are far fewer options. The fundamental method of installing the database is the same, however – using a **custom action** in the setup project to perform the work, and the **user interface editor** to obtain any user input we need during the process.

Using the Server Explorer in the more advanced versions of Visual Studio .NET, we can automatically script the database (create a set of SQL statements that will recreate it), and add the output of this as the task to perform by the custom action. For this example, we'll demonstrate an alternative that works with the *Standard Edition*, to demonstrate that most issues can be worked around, regardless of VS.NET edition.

Adding a Custom File

Before we can make use of the more advanced features that will allow us to install our database, we need to add the database file itself to the installation project.

Try It Out – Adding a Custom File

We've already seen how we can place files in the Web Application Folder that is present in the File System Editor, adding them to the install package. We need to follow a similar process to add further files, namely the database:

1. Right-click on the File System on Target Machine node in the File System Editor, and select the Add Special Folder | Custom Folder option from the menu. Rename the folder that is created to Database.

Now switch to the Properties pane for this folder, and set the Property property to DBPATH. This will allow us to amend this installation folder by linking its name to the user interface we're going to create shortly:

533

2. Use Windows Explorer to navigate to the database file. This file is called
`Friends_Data.mdf`, and will be located wherever you decompressed it to after
downloading it from the Wrox web site. Drag and drop the file into the **Database** folder in
Visual Studio .NET.

*If warnings about not being able to find the source file are thrown up by Visual Studio .NET at this
point, you can probably ignore them – we'll cover correcting this shortly.*

That's it. Adding a custom file is as easy as that!

Editing the User Interface

With our database file added to the project, we can now set about allowing the user to enter the location of
the database server to which this file will be installed. We've seen the user interface that VS.NET creates
for the installation process by default, but we can change it to insert new dialogs or delete existing ones
that appear on the screen during the deployment process. To do this, we use the **User Interface Editor**. To
view this, use the appropriate toolbar button at the top of the Solution Explorer:

This editor is split into two sections. The upper section is for changing the main installation process, and
the lower section is for the "administrative install":

❑ The **Install** section details the user interface for installing from either the `.msi` file, or a
network-ready installation. (A network-ready installation is one that has been installed to a
network drive using the `msiexe.exe` Microsoft Installer command that we'll look at shortly.)
This section is used in almost all situations.

❑ The **Administrative Install** section pertains to the interface to use when a system administrator uses the `msiexe.exe` command to install the application to a network drive, ready for other users to install from via a standard install later. It can also be run by calling `setup.exe /a`. We can alter the user interface to suit the requirements of the administrator – for example, we may wish to allow the administrator to install to any network location, but to restrict the users' installation to a specific path. In such a case, we would disable the **Installation Address** dialog in the **Install** section, but leave it intact under **Administrative Install**. This section is only for installations onto a network or shared folders.

Each of these two sections is itself split into three:

❑ The **Start** subsection contains dialogs that will be displayed before installation takes place. It includes welcome screens, validation screens, folder browsing, custom actions, and so on.

❑ The **Progress** subsection contains dialogs that will appear during installation, such as a progress bar. Only the **Progress** dialog may be placed within this section, and it may only feature once.

❑ The **End** subsection contains dialogs that will be shown once the installation has completed – to display things such as a simple 'finished' message, details of documentation, or where to check for updates.

Before you get too enthusiastic about the possibility of adding dialogs to various stages of the installation process, you should know that, as with other third-party installers, the functionality they allow is very limited. In the case of Visual Studio .NET, such dialogs perform a specific task, and/or simply pass on user-entered values for use during the installation. These might be used to make crucial decisions related to the installation, or to provide values to place in the registry for retrieval by the application once it's been installed.

There are *fourteen* basic types of dialog that Visual Studio .NET will allow us to add to the installation sequence. Be aware that you may only have one of each type within a given installation. To reduce the effect that this restriction may have, the dialogs that are used most frequently (namely checkboxes and textboxes) have three dialogs each (A, B, and C), each of these being identical in design. So, if you have already added a **Checkboxes A** dialog and you want to add another checkbox dialog, you could use **Checkboxes B** instead.

Dialog Type	Description
Checkboxes (A, B, or C)	Presents up to four choices using checkboxes. Checkboxes can be used to set conditional values that are used throughout the installation process.
Confirm Installation	Allows the user to confirm settings such as installation location before the installation gets under way.
Customer Information	Prompts the user for information that may include name, company, and product serial number. Serial information can be checked immediately against a specified template. The customer information dialog, like many of the dialogs here, is built on a template and therefore offers little in the way of customization.

Table continued on following page

535

Dialog Type	Description
Finished	Notifies the user when installation is complete.
Installation Address	Allows the user to choose the IIS virtual directory where the application files will be placed.
Installation Folder	Allows the user to choose the folder where application files will be installed. This option is not available when we create a web setup project (it is intended for standard setup projects).
License Agreement	Presents a license agreement for the user to read and acknowledge. You, as the developer, can set the license.
Progress	Updates the user on the progress of the installation. This is the only dialog type that can be used in the Progress section of the installation.
RadioButtons (2, 3, or 4 buttons)	Presents a dialog containing a radio button that allows the user to choose between two, three, or four mutually exclusive options.
Read Me	Displays a file written in rich-text format.
Register User	Allows the user to submit registration details by running an executable that you supply. This executable can display a dialog of its own, capture the registration, and save it to disk, registry, or the Internet. This executable will most likely need the .NET runtime in order to work, and therefore it's better to place it at the end of the installation, once the runtime has been installed. Placing it at the end of the installation also lets us pass in values (using arguments) that have been collected from the user by the installer.
Splash	Presents a bitmap to the user, generally representing a logo for the company or product.
Textboxes (A, B, or C)	Prompts the user for custom information using one to three textboxes. The A, B, and C options work in the same way as the checkboxes we mentioned above.
Welcome	Presents introductory text and copyright information to the user.

The following items are included by default when we create a web setup project:

❑ Welcome

❑ Installation Address

❑ Confirm Installation

❑ Progress

❑ Finished

Try It Out – Modifying the Installation User Interface

Now we have a basic idea of the kind of functionality that can be added to an installer by adding dialogs, let's have a go at presenting the user with a textbox that allows them to specify a location to install the database to.

1. Select the `FriendsReunionDeployment` project in the Solution Explorer, and click the User Interface Editor icon on the toolbar.

2. On the dialog that is shown, right-click on the Start node of the Install section of the tree. From the menu that appears, select the Add Dialog option. The following pop-up window will appear. Select the Textboxes (A) option, and click OK.

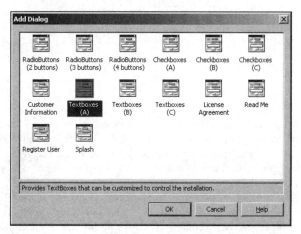

3. The dialog you've just added will appear at the bottom of the Start node, and the Start node itself will be highlighted with a blue wavy line. This is to indicate that the Textboxes (A) option has been places at an invalid location in the tree. In fact, it must appear *before* the Installation Address dialog. To move it, simply drag it up towards the Welcome node:

4. Next, we have to change the details that are displayed on this dialog when it is presented to the user. For one thing, we only require one textbox (rather than the three that are supported). To achieve this, and render the correct information, update the values of the following properties:

Property	Value
Banner Text	Database Location
Body Text	Choose a location to install the database
Edit1Label	Database Location:
Edit1Property	DBPATH
Edit1Value	[TARGETDIR]
Edit2Visible	False
Edit3Visible	False
Edit4Visible	False

How It Works

When the MSI installer created is run, it processes the forms in the order that they appear in the tree. Following the Welcome form, all of the custom forms that we define (such as our Textboxes (A) form) will be presented before the installation continues with the standard dialogs. These forms can capture data, display information, or both. Such data can then be used during the installation process by referencing the names of the items specified.

In the example above, we added a single textbox to the installation process, the value of which we linked to the DBPATH property that we created when we added the database file to the project. Creating this link means that changes in the textbox will update the location to which the file is deployed. By default, we're setting this location to [TARGETDIR]; this is an intrinsic property (denoted by the square brackets around it), which specifies the installation folder for the project as a whole.

Building the Project

Now that we've added the ability to deploy the database file to the target computer, we can rebuild our deployment project to make sure everything works fine. To do this, you can right-click on the deployment project, and selecting the Build option. If you do that right now, you will probably receive an error message similar to the following:

```
FriendsReunion Deployment.vdproj Unable to find source file '...\Friends_Data.MDF'
for file 'Friends_Data.MDF', located in '[DBPATH]', the file may be absent or locked.
```

If you get this error, it's because the database server keeps the file opened and locked whenever it's running. To remove this error, we'll need to stop the SQL Server Engine for a few seconds while we perform the build.

Try It Out – Managing the MSDE Service

The SQL Server Engine doesn't run as an application so to speak, so we can't simply "close it down". Instead, it runs as a **service**, or task, in the background. We need to stop this service in order to perform the build.

1. You can view all of the services running on your machine at any given time by going navigating to Start | Settings | Control Panel | Administrative Tools | Services. The screen that appears when this option is selected should look similar to the following:

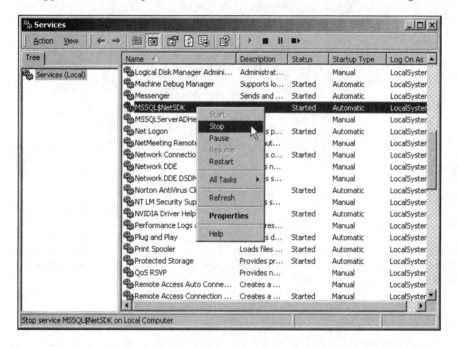

2. The entry we want begins with MSSQL, and is probably named MSSQL$NetSDK or MSSQLSERVER. Locate this item, right-click on it to bring up the context menu, and then select the Stop option (as shown in the screenshot above). This terminates the database server process.

3. With the SQL Server Engine service temporarily disabled, switch back to VS.NET, and try to build the project again. This time, it should complete successfully.

4. Once the build has finished, the SQL Server Engine can be started again. To do this, right-click on it once more, and select the Start option that should now be enabled.

5. When you run the resulting installation package to install the application, you'll find that it includes an extra screen, that prompts you for the desired database location:

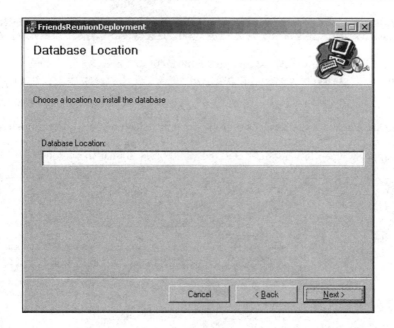

How It Works

While SQL Server is running, it maintains connections with all of the files it uses for storing database information, allowing it to have fast access and greater control over them. The cost of this is that it stops such files from being manipulated in the ways necessary to create installation packages. By stopping the SQL Server Engine service, we force SQL Server to be shut down, releasing all of its locks on these files in the process. With this done, any operations that need to be performed on these files, such as copying, can be carried out. Once the build has been completed, SQL Server can be restarted, at which point it will re-establish its locks on the files.

Custom Actions

Custom actions, as their name suggests, allow us to add bespoke operations to installers, catering for features that are unique to each project that are not supported by the out-of-the-box installer. These actions can be either an executable (.exe file) or .dll that can be attached to setup projects to perform such specific tasks. As the installation of a database is something that will have to be accomplished with most projects, it makes a great example of using these actions.

Try It Out – Registering the Database with a Custom Action

In this example, we'll create an executable program that can attach a backup of the SQL database file to our deployment server.

1. First, we need to create the executable that will perform the operations. To do this, add a new C# Console Application project to the solution, giving it the name of FriendsReunionDBInstaller.

2. Open up the `Class1.cs` file that appears in the Solution Explorer. Within the `Main` routine that is present in the class, we need to perform the following actions:

❑ Format the path we've passed through to the method, and append the database file name

❑ Create a connection to the database on our deployment server

❑ Remove any entry for the *Friends Reunion* database that's already present

❑ Attach the `.mdf` file we've copied to this machine to the database server

The code to do this first requires the following `using` statement added to the top of the class:

```
using System.Data.SqlClient;
```

Then, the code below performs all of those actions, in the order listed, and should be placed in the `Main` routine:

```
[STAThread]
static void Main(string[] args)
{
   try {
      SqlCommand sqlCmd = new SqlCommand();
      string DBPath = String.Join(" ", args);
      DBPath = System.IO.Path.Combine(DBPath, "Friends_Data.mdf");

      SqlConnection sqlConn = new SqlConnection(
        "data source=(local)\\NetSdk; initial catalog=master; user id=sa");
      sqlCmd.Connection = sqlConn;
      sqlConn.Open();

      Console.WriteLine("Checking for and removing existing database...");

      sqlCmd.CommandText =
        "SELECT TOP 1 * FROM [master].[dbo].[sysdatabases] " +
        "WHERE [name]='FriendsData' " +
        "IF (@@ROWCOUNT>0) DBCC DETACHDB([FriendsData])";

      sqlCmd.ExecuteNonQuery();

      Console.WriteLine("Installing database from: \"" + DBPath + "\"...");
      sqlCmd.CommandText = String.Format(
        "CREATE DATABASE [FriendsData] ON " +
        "(FILENAME='{0}') FOR ATTACH", DBPath);

      sqlCmd.ExecuteNonQuery();
      sqlConn.Close();
      Console.WriteLine("Installation Complete. Press [Return].");
   }
   catch (Exception ex)
```

```
    {
      Console.WriteLine("An error occurred during installation:\r\n"
        ex.ToString());
    }
    Console.ReadLine();
  }
```

You shouldn't worry too much about the SQL code that's contained in the `CommandText` properties – it's there specifically for dealing with the removal and creation of databases. Everything else should look fairly familiar, though, with the exception of the first couple of lines that manipulate the `DBPath` string. This manipulation is necessary due to the way that the `[DBPath]` property from our installer is passed through, and the need for it to be combined with the file name.

You should also ensure that the connection string entered is valid for the target server. In a real-world application, requesting details of the server (the server name, username, password, and so on) as part of the installation process would allow the application to be installed to alternative servers. For the sake of brevity of the example, we'll omit such functionality.

The calls to `Console.WriteLine()` and `Console.ReadLine()` are there just to let the user know what is going on during the installation.

3. With our code in place to attach the database, we now need to hook it up to the installer. The first step in accomplishing this is to add the primary output from project we just created to our deployment project. To achieve this, right-click on the **Database** folder, then select the **Add | Project Output...** option to bring up the **Add** dialog. In this dialog, select the FriendsReunionDBInstaller project, and highlight the **Primary output** option before clicking **OK**:

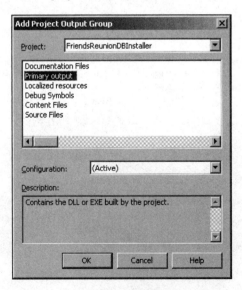

We now need to amend the settings for this output to ensure that it is not left on the system after installation. To do this, view its properties, and change the **Exclude** setting to **True**.

4. Now we need to arrange for the project to be called during the installation process. To do this, first select the Custom Actions Editor from the toolbar at the top of the Solution Explorer.

Next, on the Install node of the tree that appears to the left of the screen, right-click and select the Add Custom Action... option. This should bring up the Select Item in Project dialog. Select the Database option in the Look in: list, and the Primary output from FriendsReunionDBInstaller.

Click the OK button; this will add the item to the Install folder. Select this item, and view its properties. There are two things that we need to change here. First, the application we've created is a standard executable, rather than an InstallerClass (a special type of application that adheres to certain standards), so set that property to False. Second, we need to pass in the DBPath property to this program so that it can use it when attaching the database. To do this, set the Arguments parameter to [DBPath]. The completed properties pane should now appear similar to that shown below:

Property	Value
(Name)	Primary output from FriendsReunionDBInstaller
Arguments	[DBPath]
Condition	
CustomActionData	
InstallerClass	False

How It Works

Following the installation of all of the files specified in the File System Editor, the installer runs any tasks that have been specified in the Install folder of the Custom Actions view. These tasks can be executables such as command-line applications, Windows form-based applications, DLLs, and so on. Other useful files for custom actions are BAT, VBS, and WSH script files, all of which are simple and easy to create – they don't require separate projects. The values that have been captured through interaction with the user during the installation process can be passed as arguments to these custom actions, allowing them to perform tasks based upon the user's input.

Configuration Settings

One further complication with the deployment of an application is the **application configuration** – the values stored in appSettings section of the Web.config file. In our *Friends Reunion* application, we use this to store the connection string we use when making database calls. When deployed to a live environment, settings such as this need changing in order to make them relevant to the system in question.

In our solution, there is little need to make changes, as we've developed the system pointing to a database on our local machine (localhost), and are deploying it in this configuration too. If this weren't the case, then we'd have three options open to us. We could:

❑ Specify a different `Web.config` file in the deployment package

❑ Configure the installation package to edit `Web.config` based upon user input

❑ Have the user edit the `Web.config` file manually once the application has been installed

The first two options can be implemented using similar techniques to those described earlier in the chapter. In the first case, we can simply add the new `Web.config` file to the **Web Application Folder** in the **File System Explorer**. If we want to edit the `Web.config` file via the installation package, then we have a more complicated task on our hands – this would require a custom action and a dialog. This dialog could ask the user for the connection string that they wish to use. After the installation wizard has captured this information, we can pass it in as a parameter to the output of a project that we add as a custom action. This project could then read in the `Web.config` file as an XML document, update the correct setting, and write it back out to disk.

The final option listed above is not really desirable, because it removes the automated end-to-end installation of the application, exposing the user to the underlying nuts and bolts. It is, however, the simplest of the three options.

Launch Conditions

Launch conditions allow us to specify certain environmental conditions that must be satisfied before an installation can continue, or to locate a specific value that can subsequently be used within the installation process. For instance, we could vary the installation procedure according to the value of a particular registry key already set on the destination computer, or we could change the installation process (or stop it altogether) if a certain file is missing.

We can add or modify launch conditions using – unsurprisingly – the launch conditions editor:

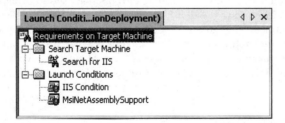

The launch conditions editor is divided into two sections, **Search Target Machine** and **Launch Conditions**, which work together to ensure that a given launch condition is met. The default conditions for web setup projects check for the presence of IIS version 4 or higher, and the .NET runtime.

Search Target Machine Node

In this section, we can set up a search for a registry entry, a file, or a Windows component. The result of the search can then be used in one of two ways:

❑ As a value to be used elsewhere in the installation

❑ In a test that must be satisfied in order for the installation to continue

The screenshot below shows the properties for the Search for IIS entry under Search Target Machine. Property denotes the name of the condition, which will be set to the value of the registry entry specified by the MajorVersion entry in the RegKey property. This gives excellent flexibility, but does require a certain amount of knowledge about the organization of the Windows registry:

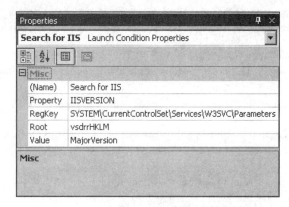

The Root (vsdrrHKLM) that is specified informs the installer to start looking under HKey_Local_Machine (HKLM) node within the root of the registry. Alternative values would have to be supplied to search within other root nodes, such as the current user's settings (HKey_Current_User).

Launch Conditions Node

Searches for items on the target machine are always performed before the processing of the launch conditions in this section, so any properties set by searches can be used here. If you again check the properties of the IIS Condition entry, you'll see the IISVERSION property mentioned above in use:

In the above screenshot, we also changed the Message to a more meaningful message –
Invalid IIS version found.

All launch conditions must evaluate to True if the installation is to take place, so the #4 above represents the minimum version number of IIS required in order to install the web application. The # is used to denote that the value stored in the registry is a hexadecimal value, and that a conversion is required when performing a comparison.

The Message property indicates the message to display if the condition is not met. In addition to being a literal string, as used here, it could also be a message stored in a resource and referenced by placing the name of it within square brackets, such as the standard IIS message [VSDIISMSG].

Try It Out – Setting a Launch Condition to Determine the ASP.NET Version

In this example, we'll check that the version of ASP.NET installed on the target machine is the same as that used for compiling the project. This is a perfect example of a launch condition for our deployment project.

1. To begin, open the launch conditions editor using the icon at the top of the Solution Explorer.

2. Right-click on Search Target Machine, and select Add Registry Search. Give it the name Search for ASP.NET:

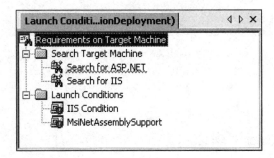

3. Don't worry about the blue wavy line that will appear underneath it – this indicates that the search is not yet set up properly, and it will disappear after the next step. Set the following properties for the condition:

Property	Value
Property	ASPNETVERSION
RegKey	SOFTWARE\Microsoft\ASP.Net
Value	RootVer

4. We now need to set up a launch condition that checks that the ASPNETVERSION property contains the version number of the .NET Framework on the development machine, which should be 1.0.3705.0. If you are in any doubt about the version number, simply use the test given earlier in this chapter for determining the version number to check this.

Right-click on Launch Conditions in the editor, choose Add Launch Condition, and give it the name ASP.NET Condition.

5. Set the Condition and Message properties of the new condition as shown, using the version number currently running on your development computer:

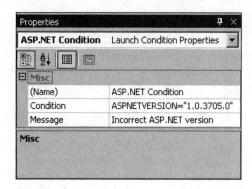

6. That's all that's required. When you now rebuild the setup project, the .msi file it creates will not proceed with the installation if a different version of ASP.NET is detected on the host machine.

Summary

We began this chapter by looking at why deployment projects were needed, and what options were available to us before the introduction of .NET. We saw that a web project can be published manually using XCOPY deployment, seeing how and where the files should be placed and we learned how this compared to the complexities involved with COM installations.

Next, we looked at setup and deployment projects; the .NET approach to distributing applications. Creating one of these allows us to transfer our application to a remote server in a professional manner, such as a single compressed archive.

We then learned about adding customizations to a deployment project. First, we saw how to add the database from our *Friends Reunion* application as a custom file, demonstrating in the process how our entire application, including all of the external resources that it required, can be installed as part of the same process. We then added an extra dialog to the installation project, to see how we can extend the interface provided by the installer, and customize it to the application we're releasing. The value we captured in this dialog was also used in the next area that we looked at – adding a custom action to the project to attach the database on the deployment server. Here we learned that we can make calls out to external programs during the installation process, allowing complex tasks to be performed.

We briefly examined how we could extend the functionality that we've examined to update the configuration files associated with applications. Finally in this chapter, we explored launch conditions, which allow us to check that the environment to which we are installing our application meets criteria that we can specify using the IDE.

Web Applications – An Overview

At the end of this chapter, and consequently the end of this book, it seems fitting to present an outline of the process of developing and then preparing a web application for deployment and installation, with an obvious focus on the areas we've been discussing most recently:

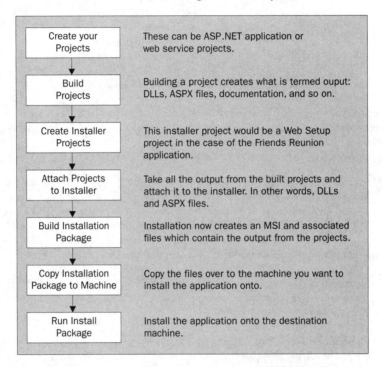

Over the course of the book, we've seen the end-to-end development of an application – from the creation of the solution in Chapter 3 to the deployment of the application on remote servers. The best way to take things forward is to experiment with what you've learned throughout the book. For further information and updates for the book, keep your eyes on the Wrox web site at http://www.wrox.com. You can also make use of the p2p lists at http://p2p.wrox.com, which are full of discussions between people in the same position as you — you never know what you might find. Good luck!

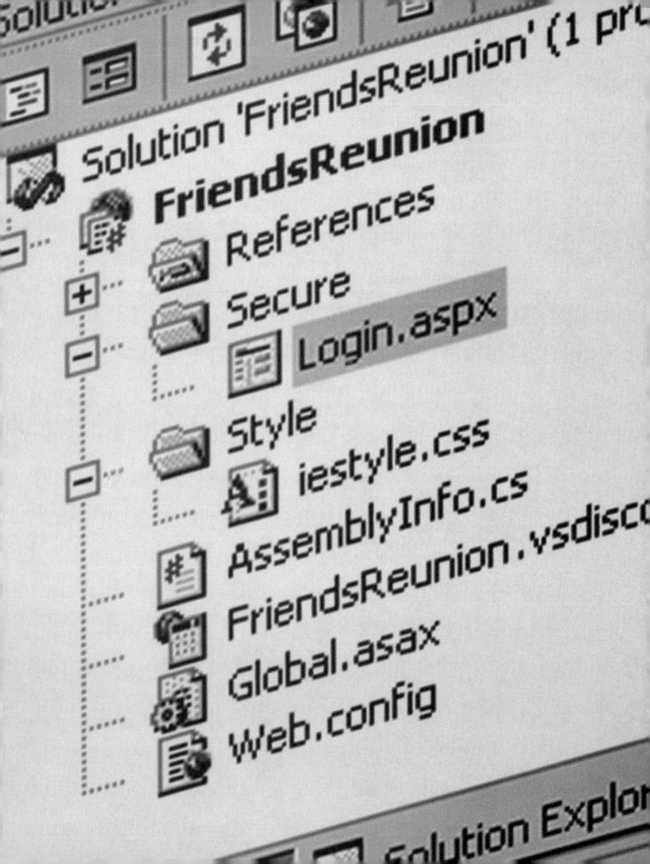

Friends Reunion

From Chapter 3 onwards in this book, we use the *Friends Reunion* application to apply the concepts we explore in each chapter. The application is intended to provide a web application where registered users can get in touch with other users who have attended the same schools or universities, or even worked in the same location.

We include many features such as utilizing databases, implementing counters and search engines, web services and so on. The tables involved in storing user information for the application look like this:

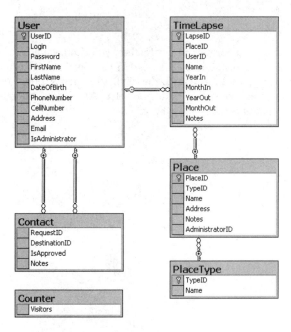

The institutions (schools, colleges, and other places that a user may have attended) are located in the Place table, which uses the PlaceType lookup table to specify the type of place (school, university, business, etc.). The user is able to register their attendance at different institutions into the TimeLapse table, in which they specify a friendly name for the lapse (such as "Systems Engineer Career"), the year/month in, and year/month out. There's also a free Notes field for any comments they wish to add.

When a user has matching or overlapping time lapse periods with another user, they can submit a request for contact with that user. This is represented as a row in the Contact table, whose IsApproved flag is initially set to 0, to indicate a pending request. The destination user (that is, the user receiving this request for contact) can optionally accept this request, and from there, the requester details are unveiled, allowing a direct contact.

Early on in the book we build a registration form, a login form, and a couple of report forms, which show the list of approved and pending contacts, as well as list of places and users for administrator users (those who have the IsAdministrator flag set to 1 in the User table). A Place has an Administrator, which usually is the user who registered the place. This user will be able to modify the place details later on.

We also build search functionality into the application with which a user can search for different matches, such as first and last name, place, type, and time lapse. The Counter table has a single field, Visitors, which is used to store a global counter for the number of visitors and preserve application state.

The code download package from the Wrox web site contains a FriendsDB folder, with a detached SQL Server database. In this folder, there are two files:

❑   Friends_Data.MDF

❑   Friends_Log.LDF

After extracting these files to your preferred destination, you can then attach them to your MSDE server instance, which is automatically installed by the *Samples and QuickStart* tutorials installer (more details on this can be found in Appendix B). To attach the database, open Visual Studio .NET and go to Server Explorer. Right-click the **Data Connection** node and select **Add New Connection**, or choose the **Connect to Database** icon, and set the following values:

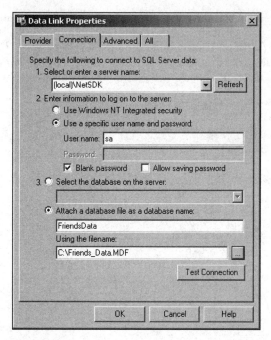

Change the server name to point to the desired target machine, as well as the user name and password. The last field must point to the MDF file you extracted previously. Accept the dialog and the connection will be added after attaching the database to the server. This connection can be used to administer the database, much like SQL Server Enterprise Manager does.

All the primary keys in our database use GUIDs, a fixed-length (char type) string of 36 characters.

Using GUIDs for Database Keys

A GUID is a unique value calculated using a complex algorithm that includes the network adapter ID and a timestamp. This ensures its uniqueness even across machines. The main benefit of this approach is that keys can be generated on the client machine, or in a middle-tier component, prior to posting data to the database. In the scenario analyzed in Chapters 7 and 8 about XML, this allows a partner institution to upload a file containing information about its attendees, with their IDs already assigned even before uploading the file, and it can save these values for future reference in its own system. If we use autonumeric fields, for example, we would have to send back the assigned IDs for every new row inserted.

The best news is that .NET has a class to generate these strings: the System.Guid class. Only one line of code is required to generate a new ID:

```
string id = Guid.NewGuid().ToString();
```

Other programming languages may provide their own means for generating GUIDs.

Once converted to a string, the GUID looks like a registry-key, which is a GUID itself by the way, for example 4e29f256-5ada-4344-baf7-20ae52dfa544.

If we want to add data to the tables manually, Visual Studio .NET has a built-in GUID generator to ease the process too. Select Create GUID from the Tools menu. Select option 4. Registry Format from the resulting form, and click the New GUID button each time you need a new GUID. Then, select the Copy button and paste the result in the destination place. The copy process automatically adds surrounding brackets, as shown in the Result section, which should be deleted manually:

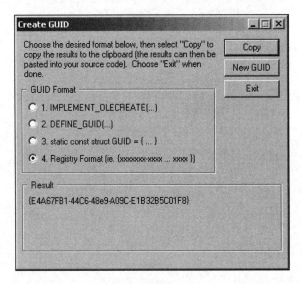

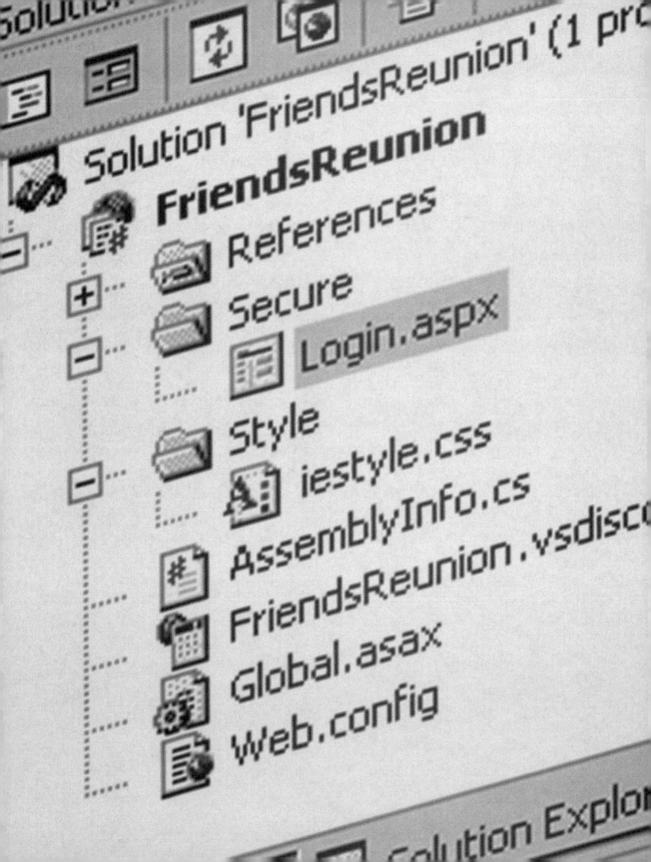

Configuration of IIS and MSDE

This appendix is designed to supplement the coverage of IIS and MSDE in this book, providing extra hints and tips on configuration, and on how to perform common tasks. In this appendix, we'll look at:

❑   Further configuration options for IIS 5.x

❑   Using impersonation when working with ASP.NET and IIS

❑   An introduction to IIS 6.0, and a summary of the most important changes to the environment

❑   Obtaining and installing MSDE

❑   Using MSDE in Visual Studio .NET

Configuration of IIS

In this section, we'll take a tour of the configuration dialogs of the IIS web server. In particular, we'll look at:

❑   Configuring IIS using the IIS management console (also known as the Internet Services Manager)

❑   Securing IIS and the authentication accounts in place for running standard web applications

❑   Locking down IIS to protect against malicious users

Configuring Server-wide Settings

There are many different settings that we can apply to the virtual directories on our system. Server-wide settings configure the 'defaults', and we can then override those settings on a per-directory basis. Let's look at the server-wide settings first, and then examine how to override them.

In the IIS management console, right-click on the node that shows your computer's name (in the left pane), and select Properties. You should see the following dialog box appear:

We are concerned with the **WWW Service** on our machine, so ensure that this option is selected in the drop-down listbox in the **Master Properties** section, and click on the **Edit** button to its right. You should now see the **Master Properties** dialog, with the **Web Site** tab foremost:

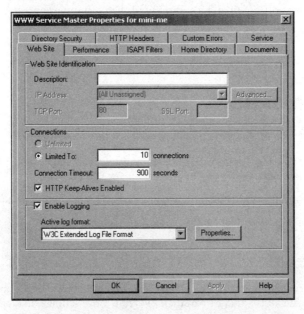

The settings that we apply in this dialog are the default settings for *all* web applications on our web server. As stated above, an individual application can override the defaults, but these settings will provide the starting point.

Connection Settings

The **maximum number of connections** and **connection timeout** properties are as good a pair of settings to begin with as any. The values you can see here are typical for a development machine: it probably will not need to support very many simultaneous connections, but we might like it to keep a connection alive for quite a long time while we're testing.

At the other end of the spectrum, on a machine that serves a production web application with potentially heavy traffic, it is probably better to set a much shorter timeout value here, so that inactive HTTP connections don't sit idly open while other users are unable to connect.

ASP.NET will override the connection timeout setting by using values specified in the `machine.config` file, located in the following folder:

`<drive letter>:\<windows directory>\Microsoft.NET\Framework\v1.0.3705\CONFIG`

The `machine.config` file affects machine-wide settings. For application-specific settings, we can override the `machine.config` value in a `web.config` file in the root of the web application. This means that the setting in IIS for connection timeout only applies to files hosted on the web server that *aren't* an ASP.NET page or web service.

Logging User Activity

The other item to notice on this dialog is the Logging facility. IIS will keep a log of all visits to the web server, unless you configure it not to. Click on the Properties button to the right of the Logging section; this opens up a dialog that allows us to customize the type of information logged, and the frequency of generation of log files:

These logs are stored in the %WinDir%\System32\LogFiles\w3svc1\ folder, and are labeled along the lines of ex*yymmdd*.log. The content of such a log file might look something like this:

```
#Software: Microsoft Internet Information Services 5.0
#Version: 1.0
#Date: 2002-07-31 12:31:54
#Fields: time c-ip cs-method cs-uri-stem sc-status
12:31:54 127.0.0.1 GET /Wrox7329Ch01/helloworld.aspx 200
12:32:05 127.0.0.1 POST /Wrox7329Ch01/helloworld.aspx 200
12:33:01 192.168.202.185 GET /Wrox7329Ch01/helloworld.aspx 200
12:33:08 192.168.202.185 POST /Wrox7329Ch01/helloworld.aspx 200
12:34:50 192.168.0.121 GET /Wrox7329Ch01/helloworld.aspx 200
12:35:00 192.168.0.121 POST /Wrox7329Ch01/helloworld.aspx 200
```

This sample log shows a request for a `HelloWorld.aspx` page originating from the local machine (the request was made by the 127.0.0.1 loop-back IP address). It also shows a couple of other requests for the same page, from other machines on the local network. The IP addresses of all requesting machines are listed, along with the name of the resource that was either requested from the client (HTTP GET) or sent back to the client (HTTP POST). The number 200 at the end of each entry is an HTTP code, which indicates that the transaction was successful.

Logging hits to the web server is a great way to look out for malicious activity, and to track general usage of your site.

Increasing Performance

Move on to the Performance tab of the Master Properties dialog. This tab shows a dialog with a slider, which can help Windows to decide what resources to allocate to IIS. Again, a development machine is unlikely to receive many hits in a day, and for such a machine we would usually move the slider from the default position (in the middle) to the left. That should allow the machine some extra juice for working with Microsoft Word!

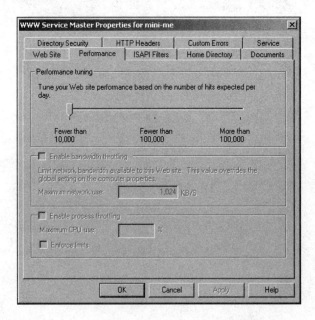

Configuring IIS for optimum performance in a production environment is obviously fairly crucial, but equally important is the impact on performance of the code you've used in your application. For more information on performance issues, you may want to refer back to Chapter 12.

General Security Settings

Now look at the Directory Security tab in the Master Properties dialog; you'll see a section for configuring Anonymous access and authentication on the web server. Click on the Edit... button to bring up a further dialog that we can use to configure access to our web server:

By default, Anonymous access to our web server is enabled; this is a logical choice in an Internet environment, particularly for web applications that are intended to serve web pages to unknown users. When a user accesses the site via "anonymous access", they are still authenticated by the web server; all such users are authenticated under an account defined for that purpose. The default account used for this purpose in IIS is called IUSR_MachineName, and it defines the basic rights assigned to all anonymous access users. We'll look at this account in more detail in just a moment.

Anonymous access is great for public web sites, but it's not always the best solution for an intranet scenario, or for other "restricted area" sites in which we want to control access to our web server. In this case, we can make use of some of the other authentication options available to us. The three options available in this window are Basic authentication, Digest authentication, and Integrated Windows authentication:

❑ **Basic authentication** prompts the user for a valid username and password, and these are transmitted to the server in a base64-encoded, unencrypted format. (Base64 encoding is a standard used for sending binary information over a network.) This isn't a very secure technique, but it is standards-compliant, and it's compatible with almost all browsers. If you're sure that the connection between your server and your client is secure, then basic authentication should be sufficient.

The Secure Sockets Layer (SSL) is commonly used alongside basic authentication to provide a secure method of communication. We'll look at SSL in more detail in just a moment.

❑ **Digest authentication** works in a similar way to basic authentication, except that all transmitted information is encrypted using a hashing technique, which makes it very difficult for a malicious user to intercept the data and decrypt it. This method of authentication can pass data through firewalls and proxy servers, so it's great in an Internet scenario. However, it relies on HTTP version 1.1, which excludes some older browsers, and it's dependent on the server residing in a domain with a Windows 2000 domain controller.

❑ In **Integrated Windows authentication,** user details are encrypted before being transmitted to and from the server, so information exchange is a much more secure process. Users are not prompted for their details, as the current login details for the client machine are sent automatically when requested. If this process fails, the user is prompted to enter a username and password, but the information will still be transmitted using this scheme.

Integrated Windows authentication is dependent on the end user having a compatible browser. It's great for intranet environments in which the clients and server live on the same domain, because it makes it simple for users to log in to a site and gain access to the information they require. The drawback of this method is that it can't reliably pass data through firewalls and routers, so it's best to keep it only for intranets.

If both basic authentication and Windows authentication are selected in this dialog, and the browser supports Windows authentication, it will attempt to use Windows authentication first.

For more information on IIS authentication, you may want to look at http://msdn.microsoft.com/library/en-us/vsent7/html/vxconIISAuthentication.asp.

The Role of Secure Sockets Layer

It's also possible to configure the web server to work with **SSL certificates**, in order to enable secure communication between the server and the client. SSL was created by Netscape, and is designed to run between the root level of communication over the Web (TCP), and the application-level communication (HTTP). An SSL-enabled server and an SSL-enabled client can authenticate each other, and establish a 128-bit encrypted connection.

You may be familiar with this process if you've ever purchased anything online – by default, your browser will warn you whenever you switch between secure and 'unsecure' connections; and when you're in a secure area, you'll see a padlock icon somewhere in the window:

SSL uses **public key cryptography** to establish a secure connection between the client and the server. The server side of the connection must be equipped with an SSL certificate. These are available from various vendors. A good discussion of public key cryptography can be found at http://www.iplanet.com/developer/docs/articles/security/pki.html, and for more information on SSL you may want to read *Professional ASP.NET Security* (Wrox, ISBN 1-86100-620-9).

Authentication Accounts

As suggested earlier, when an unknown user is authenticated by our web server using "anonymous access", it doesn't mean that we are allowing that user to log on to our web server. Anonymous requests are authenticated as the IUSR_*MachineName* user, a special Windows account that we can configure to be used for this purpose. In fact, there are a number of special accounts that you might come across when using IIS:

❑ IUSR_*MachineName* is used for authenticating anonymous users requesting basic web content (not ASP.NET content) on our system. We can affect the permissions available to all anonymous users by altering the permissions available to this user on our system.

❑ IWAM_*MachineName* is an account used when working with older COM or COM+ components with ASP. We'll spend no more time looking at this account in this book, but you may see it mentioned in some areas of the IIS configuration tool.

❑ ASPNET is a user account under which the ASP.NET worker process runs, and the account used for anonymous access to ASP.NET applications. This account has very few privileges on the local machine, and hence ensures that ASP.NET code can't be used for malicious purposes on the server.

Configuring ASP.NET Applications in IIS

We've examined some of the options available for the server-wide configuration of IIS. Now let's expand on the discussion we started in Chapter 1, and look at how we can specify properties that apply to an individual application.

Right-click on the Wrox7329Ch01 virtual directory that we created in Chapter 1 in the management console, and select Properties from the context menu. A dialog like this will pop up:

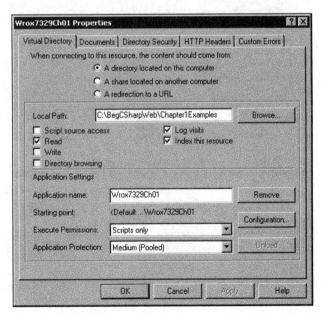

The Virtual Directory tab, shown here, has several settings that we can alter. Let's start by looking at the section that defines the Local Path, which incorporates a series of checkboxes that determine the basic permissions for our application:

❑ Script source access determines whether the client can view the source code for server-side applications. This is normally left unchecked, because it's unlikely that you'll want to allow users to view your source code. Note that this permission can only be set if Read or Write permission is also set.

❑ Read enables browsers to read or download files in the virtual directory. This option should be left checked for published web applications. Unchecking it will mean that clients requesting the page will see an error message.

❑ Write allows users to create or modify files within the directory. In most situations, this should be left turned off.

❑ Directory browsing is a useful feature to use when you're working with an application that contains many files, and you want to allow users to browse the contents of a directory. In most cases, however, it's recommended that you leave this turned off on production sites in order to hide away as much of your site as possible from prying eyes.

The other two options are related to site administration: logging user activity is a good idea when you want to track users (as we mentioned earlier). Indexing your virtual directory speeds up searches on your system.

Moving on to the Application Settings section, you can see that our Application Name is set to Wrox7329Ch01. To the right of this box is a button marked Configuration: click on this button to bring up some options that are specific to this application, including the mappings of file extensions to the ISAPI DLLs that handle each extension. We'll look at ISAPI in a bit more detail in a moment. Looking through this list, you'll see several file extensions that you recognize, but many more that you'll probably never have to worry about:

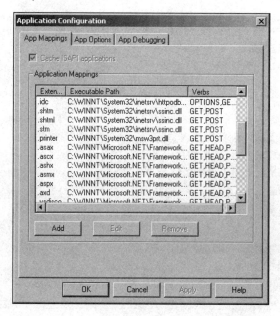

It's actually possible to remove some of these file extensions from IIS (or just from an application), and in some circumstances doing so can aid security. Also in this dialog, we can click on the **App Options** tab to configure session timeout length, which will affect any ASP.NET application that relies on session state:

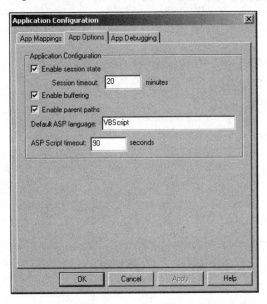

In this dialog, we're overriding the defaults that we specified in the server-wide settings, giving us the ability to work with different timeouts for each application on the server.

We are not going to look at every option available, but it is worth looking through the tabs and dialogs to see what's possible. IIS configuration is something of an art, and balancing performance configuration, security settings, and application load settings is a tricky job for system administrators.

The Role of ISAPI

ISAPI is the acronym for **Internet Server Application Programming Interface**. ISAPI is a low-level interface that resides beneath higher-level abstractions like ASP.NET. In many ways, you can think of ASP.NET as a developer-friendly way of working with ISAPI – it's possible to work with ISAPI directly, but it's much easier if you can find an alternative approach! Every web development technology that's compatible with IIS must be able to communicate with ISAPI, which provides the ability to process page requests and send responses.

An ISAPI module, such as the ASP.NET module, is the go-between that can accept code written in a web programming language, and process it so that it's possible to send an appropriate response to the client browser. IIS has a list of acceptable file extensions that it can handle, and each file extension maps to an ISAPI module designed to handle that type of request.

Our ASP.NET pages have the extension `.aspx`, and our ASP.NET ISAPI module is `aspnet_isapi.dll`, which is located in the `%WinDir%\Microsoft.NET\Framework\v1.0.3705` folder. When IIS receives a request, the file extension will tell IIS which module to pass the request to for processing. This module will then pass the request on to the ASP.NET system process to be processed.

The ASP.NET System Process

The ASP.NET ISAPI module passes requests for ASP.NET pages to `aspnet_wp.exe`, which runs as a system process. The following screenshot shows this process highlighted in the list that's produced by the Windows Task Manager:

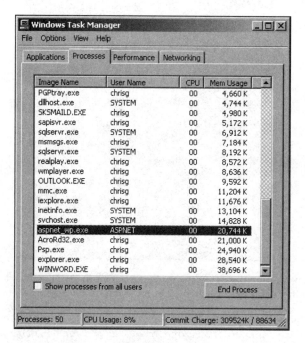

On the first request for a `.aspx` page after the server has been rebooted, this process is started automatically. (This is one reason why the first hit on a `.aspx` page can take so long.) Subsequent hits benefit not only from the fact that there is a cached, compiled version of the page stored on the server, but also from the fact that the ASP.NET process is already active.

> Note that there's also an entry in the list two lines above the `aspnet_wp.exe`, called `inetinfo.exe`. This is the name of the process that IIS runs under, and will appear in the list whenever the web server is up and running.

Locking Down IIS

In general, there are a lot of things that you can do on a day-to-day basis to close down security holes on your IIS server. You can install all the security patches and hotfixes, turn off directory browsing on sites, enable logging, remove IIS samples, and install anti-virus software.

To simplify this process, Microsoft has released a very useful tool that helps to secure IIS 5, called the **IIS Lockdown Tool**. This tool is used to turn off unnecessary features and disable some loopholes in IIS. Furthermore, you should always make sure that your IIS installation is as patched and up-to-date as possible, to prevent newly discovered security holes from affecting your server.

At the time of writing, the Lockdown Tool is available for download from http://www.microsoft.com/downloads/release.asp?ReleaseID=43955. It's recommended the instructions very carefully and understand each step in the process before proceeding if you proceed too hastily then you can end up turning off too many features.

ASP.NET and IIS

When hosting a web application for general consumption, it's usually OK to allow anonymous access to our web server. But what if we wanted to enable more functionality for *certain* users, that would require greater permissions than the anonymous user account can provide? What if certain users need write permissions on a target folder on the web server, or need to write to an event log? ASP.NET can handle this situation by using a technique known as **impersonation**.

Impersonation

In any situation that involves Windows Integrated Security (in an intranet or extranet application, for example), we can enable impersonation on our ASP.NET setup. This means that our users can be authenticated as local accounts that have more privileges than the standard ASPNET account, or the IUSR_MachineName account. By default, all ASP.NET applications access resources using this standard account, even if their users are currently logged on to a Windows domain – authentication occurs at application level, not operating-system level. When we turn impersonation on, we authenticate users under different local accounts, or different Windows domain accounts.

With impersonation turned off, there's an entry in the Machine.config file that determines which account is used for anonymous access. The entry is <processModel>, and the default setting is username="Machine", password="AutoGenerate". Impersonation can be turned on by adding the following to the System.Web element of either the Machine.Config or Web.Config file:

```
<identity impersonate="true" />
```

Using this setting, our anonymous ASP.NET users are now authenticated using the IUSR_MachineName account, instead of the ASPNET account. We can configure this further by adding to this definition:

```
<identity impersonate="true" username="name" password="password"/>
```

Here, the username and password must relate to a valid account on the hosting server. This setting *only* affects the account under which ASP.NET is run, and doesn't affect anonymous access to any other IIS-based application. Implementing impersonation gives users of our application a specific set of permissions for performing tasks that the basic ASPNET user account cannot perform.

Try It Out – Establishing Identity

Let's take a look at how we can use impersonation with a quick example that declares the user account under which ASP.NET is currently authenticated.

1. Open up Visual Studio .NET, and create a new web application called `ImpersonationExample`.

2. Create a new web form in our application by right-clicking on the application in the Solution Explorer and selecting **Add | Add Web Form**. Call the new form `ImpersonateMe.aspx`.

3. Delete `WebForm1.aspx` from the project, right-click on `ImpersonateMe.aspx`, and select **Set as Start Page** from the context menu.

4. View the code-behind file for `ImpersonateMe.aspx`, and enter the following code into the `Page_Load()` event handler:

```
private void Page_Load(object sender, System.EventArgs e)
{
    Response.Write("I am authenticated as: " +
                        WindowsIdentity.GetCurrent().Name);
}
```

5. When you do this, you'll notice that IntelliSense complains about the `WindowsIdentity` bit. This is because we need to tell our web application to reference the classes in the `System.Security` namespace. Add the following line to the top of the code-behind page, before the class definition:

```
using System.Security.Principal;
```

6. Run the project, and view the results:

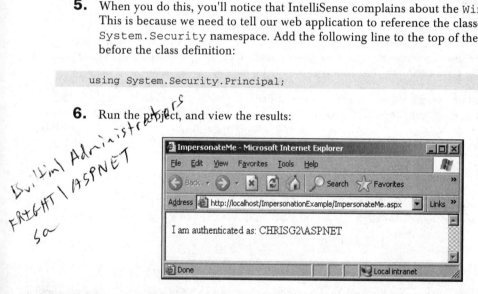

How It Works

So far, we've not done anything too complex – we've just confirmed the fact that ASP.NET pages are run under an account on the web server called `ASPNET`:

```
Response.Write("I am authenticated as: " +
                    WindowsIdentity.GetCurrent().Name);
```

Here, we've output a simple line of text on our browser that gathers information from the local system, using functionality provided by the `System.Security` namespace.

Try It Out – Enabling Impersonation with Anonymous Access

Let's now extend the example to see how we can enable impersonation for anonymous users, and what effect this has on our application.

1. Back in the application, open up the `Web.config` file, and add the following line near the top:

```
<?xml version="1.0" encoding="utf-8" ?>
<configuration>
  <system.web>
    ...
    <identity impersonate="true" />
    ...
  </system.web>
</configuration>
```

2. Run the application again, and you'll see something similar to the following:

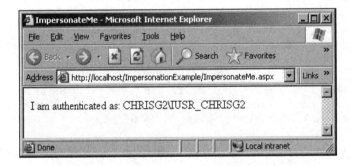

How It Works

The `<identity>` tag that we added to the `Web.config` file has changed the default user account for anonymous access to our ASP.NET application. The application has reverted to the default user account for all IIS anonymous access, which is `IUSR_MachineName` (`IUSR_CHRISG2` in the screenshot above). If we had configured IIS to use a different account for standard anonymous access, then the details of that account would be displayed instead.

To log in as a specific user in this example, we need to have a user account on our local system that we can use. Let's imagine that we've set up a temporary account called `TestUser`, with an eminently hackable password: `letmein`. Let's also imagine this account to be a member of the Power Users group on the local machine. Here's what the line in the `Web.config` file needs to look like:

```
<identity impersonate="true" userName="TestUser" password="letmein" />
```

With all of the above configured, you'd end up with the following result:

Anonymous access

IUSR_FRIGHT

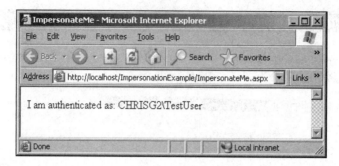

Since this user has more privileges on the local machine than the basic anonymous users, code in ASP.NET applications can now create and modify files as required.

Try It Out – Impersonation and Integrated Windows Authentication

While we've got an example for looking at impersonation and authentication, we can take a quick peek at what happens when Integrated Windows Authentication is switched on for our application.

1. Open up the IIS management console, and right-click and select Properties on the ImpersonationExample virtual directory.

2. In the Directory Security tab, click the Edit button to bring up the anonymous access and authentication control dialog. In here, uncheck the box for Anonymous access, and enable only Integrated Windows Authentication, as shown below:

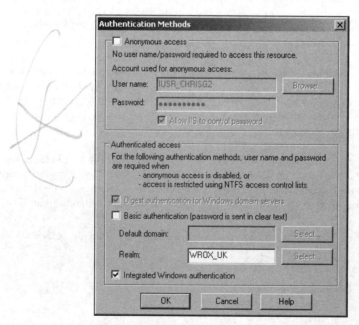

3. Remove the `<identity>` element that we entered in the `Web.config` file, run the application, and you'll find that ASP.NET will revert to using the `ASPNET` account for authentication.

4. Now re-insert the `<identity>` element, as follows, in the `Web.config` file:

```
<identity impersonate="true" />
```

5. Run the application again, and ASP.NET will attempt to use the currently-logged in user's account for authentication:

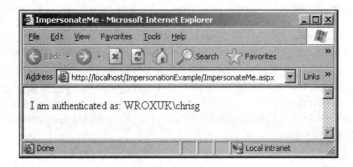

How It Works

As a result of the switch to Integrated Windows Authentication, ASP.NET pages are now running under the current Windows user's account (this Windows user is logged in as chrisg, in the WROXUK domain). Access to our application is now controlled by the Access Control Lists (ACLs) maintained by the operating system, moving the authentication portion of our exchange to the underlying security settings of the system, rather than IIS.

When using impersonation, you should always consider what it is you're trying to achieve. You need to take care to restrict access to the minimum possible privileges for each user, and only rarely will you need to give any user full administrative capacity on your server.

An Introduction to IIS 6

IIS 6 is part of Windows .NET Server, which is, at the time of writing, in Release Candidate 1 phase. The Windows .NET Server family of products is quite different from the Windows 2000 Server family mainly because of the introduction of the Windows .NET Web Server. This product is aimed solely towards hosting web applications, and, as a result, lacks a lot of the functionality contained within the other Windows .NET Server products (the full list is Windows .NET Web Server, Standard Server, Enterprise Server, and Datacenter Server).

IIS 6 is installed by default on Windows .NET Web Server, and is an optional install into the .NET Server family. Windows .NET Web Server is designed to be a cut-down version of the other members of the .NET server family, so it doesn't include functionality to act as a domain controller, and you won't be able to install many server products on it – it's designed to act as a web server, and not much else.

IIS 6 New Features

IIS 6 is designed to be more secure than IIS 5 by default. That is, the default settings you get with an IIS 6 installation have been chosen with security issues foremost, with the potential loopholes disabled (so you have to opt-in, rather than opt-out). ASP, ASP.NET, and technologies such as WebDAV and FrontPage Server Extensions, are disabled in a default IIS 6 installation; if you need them then you need to enable them explicitly. Also, IIS 6 installs security patches automatically by default, so you have to opt *out* of this process if you don't want it.

The major changes and new features of IIS 6 can be summarized as:

❑ **XML Metabase instead of custom metabase.** The current technique for configuring virtual directories in IIS 5 relies on using the custom IIS interface. The new XML-based metabase makes it possible to edit the settings using different tools, and makes it much easier to backup and restore settings. It is even possible to make changes while an application is running and have those changes take place immediately. Changes can be rolled back if necessary.

❑ **Process isolation for web applications without taking a performance hit.** IIS 5 runs in a process called inetinfo.exe. Instead of having a single process for running IIS, IIS 6 hosts applications in a more robust manner by splitting this process into three parts. These parts include the following:

    ❑ The first part is HTTP.sys. This runs in kernel mode and serves the requests. This part alone will give us a performance boost, especially for static or cached content.

    ❑ The second part is the Web Admin Service (WAS – this is *not* the Web Application Stress tool we met in Chapter 12!). This WAS is used to configure HTTP.sys and manage the lifecycle of worker processes. The WAS is what looks after the memory allocation needs of our applications, and detects crashes and protects the server from failure.

    ❑ The last part is the W3 core, which is where our applications actually get loaded. This is where ISAPI extensions and filters are loaded, and it isolates each application in its own process, so if an application crashes, there is less chance that it will take the whole web server down with it.

❑ **Secure by default installation.** Removing security holes and black spots that seemed to plague IIS 5, IIS 6 should help to ensure that hackers who have been used to exploiting vulnerable servers will have a much harder job.

At the time of writing, IIS 6 is available as part of the Windows .NET Server Release Candidate, and is available for download or to order on CD from the Microsoft MSDN web site at http://www.microsoft.com/windows.netserver/preview/default.mspx.

Let's take a quick look at the IIS 6 management console:

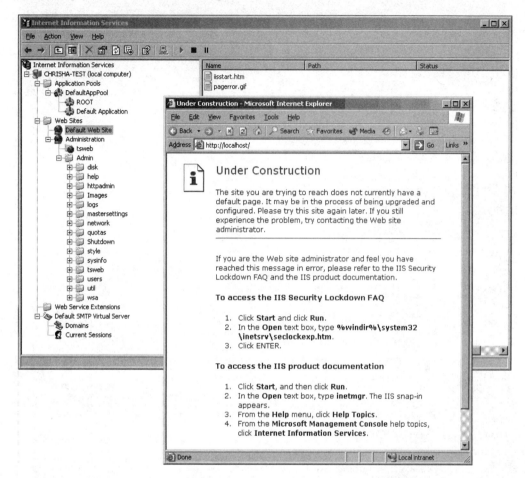

The management console itself has some new nodes in it, notice one called **Application Pools**, which corresponds to the new application process model. Notice also the complete lack of anything under the **Default Web Site** node; this is very different from the default appearance of an IIS 5 server, which has several default directories and virtual directories on first installation. You will also notice that requesting our default page from the web server produces an error instead of a detailed IIS page. These all point to the new "secure by default" aims of IIS 6, as a lot of the functionality that we have seen previously is removed or disabled.

Let's take a quick look at the XML-based Metabase:

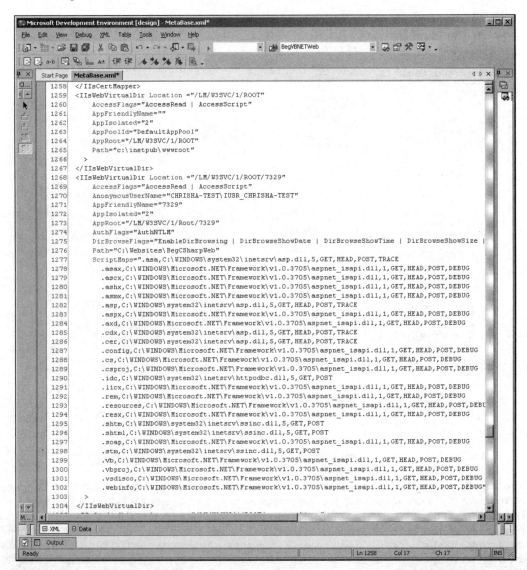

In the screenshot we can see two nodes for <IIsWebVirtualDir ... > that represent the root virtual directory and a custom virtual directory, which I've set up, called 7329. In these sections we can see what our access flags are set to, the name of the account that handles anonymous requests (non-ASP.NET), as well as flags controlling how our application is handled by the web server in terms of process isolation. There are also details of the physical location of each folder, lists of enabled file extensions, which ISAPI module they're handled by, and so on. We could edit this XML file with IIS running, and the changes would be applied without having to stop the web server. This should prove very useful for administrators striving for maximum uptime for their web applications.

The Microsoft SQL Server Desktop Engine

One of most important ingredients of a dynamic web application is the ability to store data in and retrieve data from a database, and several of the examples in the chapters in this book involve this functionality. For that, of course, we need a database, and our choice is to use the Microsoft SQL Server Desktop Engine (MSDE), which is a specialized version of SQL Server 2000. In this section, we'll explain what it is, why we've chosen to use it, and – most important of all – how you can get hold of it and install it.

A Smaller SQL Server

The first thing to say about MSDE is that it's entirely compatible with SQL Server, which is truly an enterprise-class database server. This means that the things you learn while using MSDE will stand you in good stead when you come to use SQL Server itself – it behaves in exactly the same way. From our perspective here, though, the immediate benefits of MSDE are:

❑   It's freely distributable

❑   It's currently sitting on your Visual C# discs, just waiting for you to install it

What this means is that as well as providing the perfect system for us to learn and experiment with, a complete web application can initially be produced and distributed without incurring any costs for the database server. If the system expands at a later date, it can be ported to the commercial distribution of SQL Server with next to no effort. The only features cut down from the full version of SQL Server are that the MSDE is optimized for (but not limited to) up to five connections at a time, that the maximum database size is limited to 2GB, and that some enterprise features are absent.

> *All of the features supported by MSDE are also supported by SQL Server. The converse is not true; some of the richer functionality of SQL Server is not present in MSDE. However, none of this functionality is required by any of the applications in this book.*

Obtaining and Installing MSDE

When Visual C# .NET (or any of the various Visual Studio .NET products) is installed, an item called Microsoft .NET Framework SDK is added to your Start | Programs menu. Beneath this is an item called Samples and QuickStart Tutorials; if you select it, this is what you'll see:

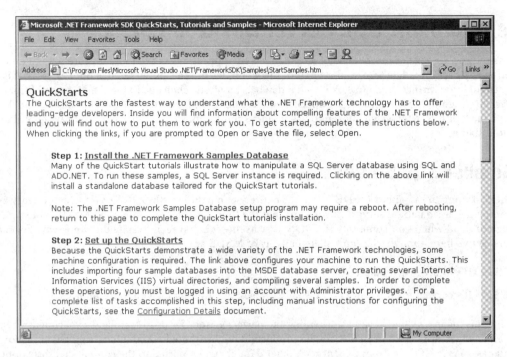

This page is self-explanatory: clicking on the first link will install the MSDE engine; clicking on the second will cause the sample databases to be created.

This page will only appear once, so if you (or someone else) have been here before, you won't see it. Don't worry: you'll find the instmsde.exe *and* configsamples.exe *files that these links invoke beneath the* FrameworkSDK\Samples *folder of your Visual Studio .NET installation.*

Ensure that you're logged on as a user with Administrator privileges on the current machine, and click on the first link (or run the executable). The following dialog will appear:

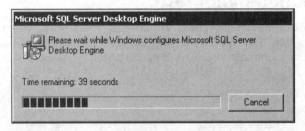

When this has finished, there's no need to restart your machine. You can go straight on to the next step, which will produce another dialog:

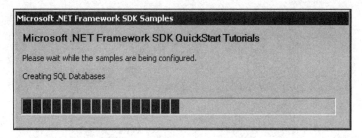

Once again, wait for this step to finish its work, and you can go on the final stage. Before you can run the database samples in this book, you need to enable **mixed-mode authentication**. By default, MSDE is set up only to use a method of authentication called Windows Integrated Security. We need to set up the database so that database users *separate* from the operating system are also allowed to log in.

To this end, we've provided a script that you can run on your machine to configure mixed-mode authentication. It's called `MixedMode.vbs`, and you'll find it in the code download for this appendix. After you've run that, you're all done... but what exactly *have* you done? The best way to understand that is to open up Visual Studio .NET, ready for the quick tour in the next section.

Try It Out – Testing MSDE

In this brief example, we'll use the Visual Studio .NET interface to make sure that our installation of MSDE has worked.

1. Open up Visual Studio .NET, and head for the Server Explorer in the IDE. Click on the button marked Connect to Database, as shown below:

2. Fill in the dialog that appears precisely as follows, test the connection by pressing the Test Connection button, and then click OK.

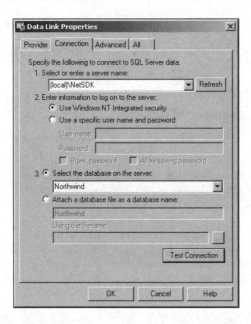

3. Once you've clicked OK, you are returned to the Visual Studio .NET IDE. Expand the new connection in the **Server Explorer**, and double-click on the `Employees` table in the tree to display some sample data:

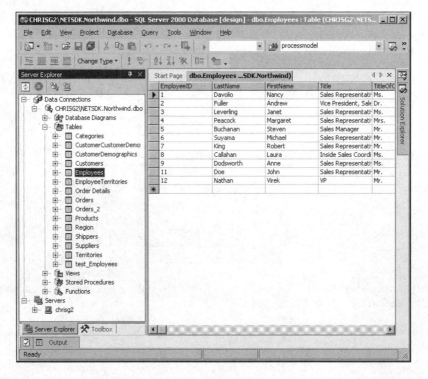

How It Works

We've established a basic connection to our database, and displayed some sample data, simply by clicking some buttons in a Wizard. In the same Wizard, you can select alternative database servers on your network, different databases to connect to, and much more. Working with databases is discussed in detail in Chapters 4 and 5.

Using MSDE via the Server Explorer

Now that we've started to work with data, it's not inconceivable that you might want to check what's going on in the database tables, or edit the data they contain, without having to do it through ADO.NET. For that purpose, we can use the Server Explorer tool that comes with Visual Studio .NET. If you already feel comfortable with this tool, or you'll be using SQL Server's Enterprise Manager to administer the database, feel free to skip the following section. If not, choose the View | Server Explorer menu item and take a look at the Server Explorer window, which will look something like this:

If the Server Explorer hasn't been used before, there may be nothing at all underneath the Data Connections root node. We'll address that right away.

The Data Connections node maintains a list of configured database connections, to which we can add new connections as we see fit. To see how it works, we'll add a connection to the database for the *Friends Reunion* application that we've been working with in this book.

In the code that you've downloaded for this book, you'll find a file called FriendsDB.zip, which contains a detached SQL Server database in a file called Friends_Data.mdf. This latter you should extract to a folder somewhere on your local drive. To attach this file to your MSDE server, right-click on the Server Explorer's Data Connections node and select Add Connection. You will see the following dialog:

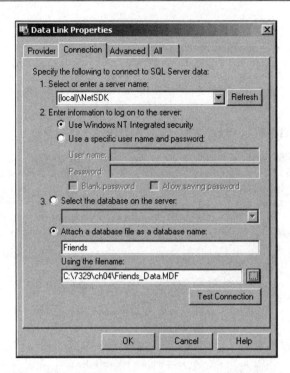

Here, Visual Studio .NET has assumed that you want to make a connection to a SQL Server database (if you need to, you can change this by clicking on the **Provider** tab). As for the specific settings you can see entered in the screenshot, (local)\NetSDK is the name of the MSDE server on your machine, and we are using **Windows NT Integrated security** to log on, which means that we don't need to enter a separate user name or password for the database. Furthermore, we have chosen to attach the Friends database that's contained in Friends_Data.mdf to MSDE, which means that we'll be able to manipulate it from the Visual Studio .NET IDE.

In the Professional and Enterprise versions of Visual Studio .NET, the **Server Explorer** allows us to connect to just about any database we could ever want to manipulate. Once a connection has been established, its node can be expanded, and the features of the database then appear as child nodes. In the version that comes with the Standard Edition of Visual C# .NET, our options are more limited – we can only connect to MSDE and Access databases – but that's more than adequate for our needs here. Let's take a look at how we can use it to edit the data contained in a table.

Try It Out – Changing Data and Performing Queries

In this quick example, we'll use the **Server Explorer** to take a look at the `Friends` database that we just connected to, and perform some simple operations on it through the interface that Visual Studio .NET provides.

1. In the **Server Explorer**, go to the **Friends** connection, and open up the **Tables** node.

2. Right-click on the **User** table, and select **Retrieve Data from Table** (or simply double-click on the **User** table). You should find that the main window displays something like the following, while a new tool bar – the **Query** tool bar – has appeared at the top left of the screen.

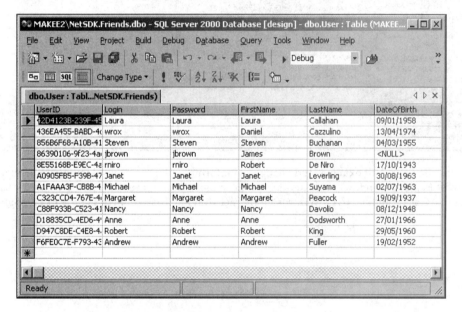

3. At this stage, any change you make to the data will be sent to the database as soon as you move the cursor to another row, just as if you were working in MS Access. For example, locate **James Brown** in the grid, and set his birth date to May 3, 1933. Move the cursor to the next row, and the change will be applied.

4. With the cursor positioned anywhere inside the table, click on the **Show SQL Pane** button to display the SQL code that was executed in order to produce the data you can see.

5. In the new panel, you can write any valid SQL statement, and click the **Run Query** button to show the results. You can also check the validity of the statements you enter by clicking the **Verify SQL Syntax** button.

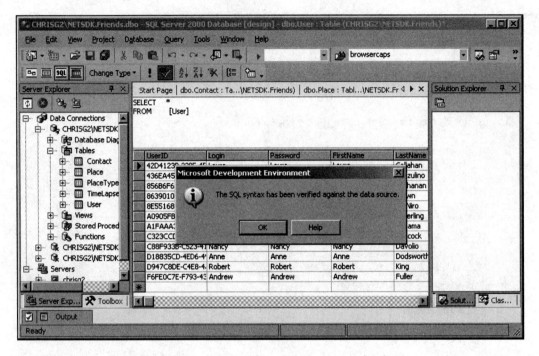

As well as allowing us to examine and change the information in a database, setting up connections in the **Server Explorer** window serves another purpose. Specifically, pre-configuring connections in this way allows Visual Studio .NET's Wizards to interact with databases though the use of components.

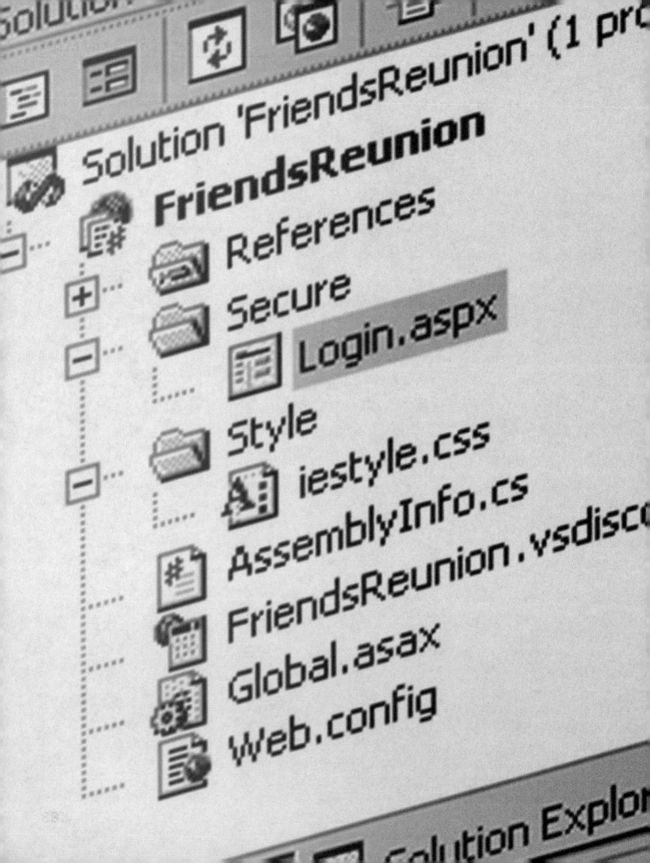

Index

Symbols

I

IComponent interface, System.ComponentModel, 164
identity
see impersonation.
identity objects
.NET concept, 383
FormsIdentity object, 386
Identity property, 384
PassportIdentity object, 386
WindowsIdentity object, 386
IEnumerable interface, System.Collections
binding to sets of data, 179
IIS (Internet Information Server)
administration, 19
configuring, 557
configuring ASP.NET applications in IIS, 563
configuring system for web development, 17, 18
IIS6 introduction and features, 571
impersonation, 567
installing, 18
Internet Services Manager (ISM), 19
locking down IIS, 566
virtual directories, 19
Windows authentication, 390
IIS administration console
custom controls, FriendsReunion example, 114
security, FriendsReunion example, 135
ImageButton class, System.Web.UI.WebControls
CommandName property, 206, 251
Visible property, 211
ImageUrl property, Image class, 194
impersonation
ASP.NET and IIS, 567
enabling impersonation with anonymous access, 569
establishing identity, 567
Integrated Windows authentication and, 570
Inherits attribute, 52
InitForm method, FriendsReunion, 155, 158, 500, 501
initialization
ASP.NET page lifecycle, 62
ASP.NET security, 384
InitializeComponent method, 52
InitPlaces method, FriendsReunion, 153, 158
in-memory storage, session state, 234
InProc mode, state modes, 234
input errors, 414
Insert method, Cache class, 495
FriendsReunion example, 501
InsertUser method, FriendsReunion
debugging, Call Stack window, 440
Install section, User Interface Editor, 534
installation
see also deployment.
custom actions, 540
Launch Conditions Editor, 544
modifying installation user interface, 537
setup projects, Visual Studio .NET, 530
uninstalling projects, 532
Installation Address dialog, Visual Studio .NET, 536
Installation Folder dialog, Visual Studio .NET, 536
Integrated Windows authentication
configuring IIS, 562
impersonation and, 570
IntelliSense, Visual Studio .NET, 74, 104
creating XML documents, 303

Internet Information Server
see IIS.
Internet Server Application Programming Interface
see ISAPI.
interoperability
applications of XML, 275
InvalidOperationException
validating XML from web application, 316
IP (Internet Protocol), 15
IP version 6 (IPv6), 15
IP address
loop-back address, 16
routing requests, 15
IPostBackDataHandler interface, System.Web.UI
LoadPostData method, 244
ISAPI (Internet Server Application Programming Interface)
configuring ASP.NET applications in IIS, 565
ISM (Internet Services Manager)
configuring IIS, 19
IsNull property, SqlString type, 148
IsPostBack property, Page class
adding functionality with code-behind, 54
preserving processing using view state, 246
IsValid property, Page class, 93, 133
Item property
SqlDataReader class, 127
DataRow class, 157, 178
ItemCommand event, DataGrid class, 251
ItemDataBound event
DataGrid class, 251
DataList class, 208
ItemIndex property, DataListItem class, 209
ItemRemovedCallback method, 497
Items property, Context class
postbacks, 258
transient state, 252
ItemTemplate property, DataList class, 199, 203
IUSR_MachineName authentication account
anonymous user account, 561
configuring IIS, 563
IWAM_MachineName authentication account
configuring IIS, 563

J

JIT (Just In Time) compiler
ASP.NET compilation process, 61

L

latency reduction
caching benefit, 484
Launch Conditions Editor, Visual Studio .NET, 522, 544
Launch Conditions node, 545
Search Target Machine node, 544
License Agreement dialog, Visual Studio .NET, 536
<link element>, 77, 89
Load event
ASP.NET page lifecycle, 62
load testing, 473
using tool to load application, 473

591

SQL Server Desktop Engine
  see MSDE.
SqlCommand class, System.Data.SqlClient, 126, 133, 139, 150
  CommandText property, 201
  Connection property, 187, 189
  creating web service, 347
  ExecuteNonQuery method, 126, 134, 179
  ExecuteReader method, 126, 147
  ExecuteScalar method, 126, 140, 241
  Parameters property, 190
SqlConnection class, System.Data.SqlClient, 126, 133, 139, 164
  configuring dynamic ConnectionString, 166
  connection components, 165
  ConnectionString property, 188, 201
  constructor, 134
  creating web service, 347
  Open method, 139
SqlDataAdapter class, System.Data.SqlClient, 149–50, 402
  configuring using Visual Studio .NET, 186, 189, 200
  constructor, 157
  database access performance, 509
  DataMappings property, 187
  Fill method, 150, 157, 177, 193, 212
  SelectCommand property, 157, 187, 189
  Update method, 150, 212
  UpdateCommand property, 212
  using SqlDataAdapter component, 186
SqlDataReader class, System.Data.SqlClient, 126, 147, 148
  database access performance, 510
  FieldCount property, 127
  GetDateTime method, 147
  GetOrdinal method, 127, 147
  GetString method, 147
  GetValues method, 127
  Item property, 127
  Read method, 126, 147
SqlException exception
  rethrowing exceptions, 454
SQLServer mode, state modes, 235
SqlString type, System.Data.SqlTypes, 148
  IsNull property, 148
Src attribute, Register directives, 103
SSL (Secure Sockets Layer)
  configuring IIS, 562
state, 215
  see also session state.
  adding state to web service, 374
  application state, 236
  ASP.NET state utilities, 216
  cookies, 33, 258
  disabling ViewState, 505
  form state, 242
  maintaining state, 32
  scope, 216
  state modes, 234
  stateless protocol, 32, 215
  storage of state information, 216
  transient state, 252
  view state, 242
  viewstate, 33
state modes, 234
state storage, session state, 235
StateServer mode, state modes, 235

static content, web applications, 26
step-by-step execution, Watch windows, 434
stress testing, 473
StringBuilder class
  querying DOM documents, 332
style attribute, 51
Style Builder editor, Visual Studio .NET, 75
style conventions used in this book, 5
styles
  see CSS.
stylesheets
  see CSS.
support
  customer support used in this book, 6
  errata in this book, 6
  p2p.wrox.com, 7
  technical support in this book, 7
syntax errors, 410
System Event log
  exceptions, 458
System Monitor
  configuring, 467
  configuring for key performance counters, 467
  using in PerfMon, 465
System.Diagnostics namespace, 425
  debugging web applications, 414
System.Web namespace, 60
  HttpCookie class, 258
System.Web.Caching namespace
  CacheItemPriority enumeration, 496
  CacheItemRemovedCallback delegate, 497
System.Web.Services namespace, 60
  WebService class, 348
System.Web.UI namespace, 60
  DataBinder class, 170
System.Web.UI.HtmlControls namespace, 60
System.Web.UI.WebControls namespace, 60, 87
  DataListItem class, 209

T

TableMappings property, SqlDataAdapter class, 187
Tables property, DataSet class, 157
tags
  browsers, 46
  nesting, 46
  opening and closing, 46
  Visual Studio .NET, 46
Task Manager, performance-monitoring tool, 465
TCP (Transmission Control Protocol), 15
TCP/IP, 15
technical support in this book, 7
TemplateControl class, System.Web.UI, 122
  LoadControl method, 122
templates, 194
  customized templates, 119–22
  DataList control, 199
  template-only control, 199
test script
  writing, 475
testing
  see under performance testing.
  see also assertions; debugging; tracing.
Textboxes dialog, Visual Studio .NET, 536

595

Notes

p2p.wrox.com
The programmer's resource centre

A unique free service from Wrox Press
With the aim of helping programmers to help each other

Wrox Press aims to provide timely and practical information to today's programmer. P2P is a list server offering a host of targeted mailing lists where you can share knowledge with four fellow programmers and find solutions to your problems. Whatever the level of your programming knowledge, and whatever technology you use P2P can provide you with the information you need.

ASP
Support for beginners and professionals, including a resource page with hundreds of links, and a popular ASP.NET mailing list.

DATABASES
For database programmers, offering support on SQL Server, mySQL, and Oracle.

MOBILE
Software development for the mobile market is growing rapidly. We provide lists for the several current standards, including WAP, Windows CE, and Symbian.

.JAVA
A complete set of Java lists, covering beginners, professionals, and server-side programmers (including JSP, servlets and EJBs)

.NET
Microsoft's new OS platform, covering topics such as ASP.NET, C#, and general .NET discussion.

VISUAL BASIC
Covers all aspects of VB programming, from programming Office macros to creating components for the .NET platform.

WEB DESIGN
As web page requirements become more complex, programmer's are taking a more important role in creating web sites. For these programmers, we offer lists covering technologies such as Flash, Coldfusion, and JavaScript.

XML
Covering all aspects of XML, including XSLT and schemas.

OPEN SOURCE
Many Open Source topics covered including PHP, Apache, Perl, Linux, Python and more.

FOREIGN LANGUAGE
Several lists dedicated to Spanish and German speaking programmers, categories include. NET, Java, XML, PHP and XML

How to subscribe:
Simply visit the P2P site, at http://p2p.wrox.com/

Got more Wrox books than you can carry around?

Wroxbase is the new online service from Wrox Press. Dedicated to providing online access to books published by Wrox Press, helping you and your team find solutions and guidance for all your programming needs.

The key features of this service will be:

- Different libraries based on technologies that you use everyday (ASP 3.0, XML, SQL 2000, etc.). The initial set of libraries will be focused on Microsoft-related technologies.
- You can subscribe to as few or as many libraries as you require, and access all books within those libraries as and when you need to.

- You can add notes (either just for yourself or for anyone to view) and your own bookmarks that will all be stored within your account online, and so will be accessible from any computer.
- You can download the code of any book in your library directly from Wroxbase

Visit the site at: www.wroxbase.com

Register your book on Wrox.com!

When you download this book's code from wrox.com, you will have the option to register.

What are the benefits of registering?

- You will receive updates about your book
- You will be informed of new editions, and will be able to benefit from special offers
- You became a member of the "Wrox Developer Community", giving you exclusive access to free documents from Wrox Press
- You can select from various newsletters you may want to receive

Registration is easy and only needs to be done once. After that, when you download code books after logging in, you will be registered automatically.

Just go to www.wrox.com

wrox

Programmer to Programmer™

Registration Code: 73296AKLKV54B101

Wrox writes books for you. Any suggestions, or ideas about how you want information given in your ideal book will be studied by our team. Your comments are always valued at Wrox.

Free phone in USA 800-USE-WROX
Fax (312) 893 8001

UK Tel.: (0121) 687 4100   Fax: (0121) 687 4101

Beginning C# Web Applications with Visual Studio .NET – Registration Card

Name _____

Address _____

_____

_____

City _____ State/Region _____

Country _____ Postcode/Zip _____

E-Mail _____

Occupation _____

How did you hear about this book?

❏ Book review (name) _____

❏ Advertisement (name) _____

❏ Recommendation

❏ Catalog _____

❏ Other _____

Where did you buy this book?

❏ Bookstore (name) _____ City_____

❏ Computer store (name) _____

❏ Mail order_____

❏ Other

What influenced you in the purchase of this book?

❏ Cover Design ❏ Contents ❏ Other (please specify):

....

How did you rate the overall content of this book?

❏ Excellent ❏ Good ❏ Average ❏ Poor

What did you find most useful about this book? _____

_____

What did you find least useful about this book? _____

_____

Please add any additional comments. _____

_____

What other subjects will you buy a computer book on soon?

_____

What is the best computer book you have used this year?

_____

Note: This information will only be used to keep you updated about new Wrox Press titles and will not be used for any other purpose or passed to any other third party.

wrox

Programmer to Programmer™

Note: If you post the bounce back card below in the UK, please send it to:

Wrox Press Limited, Arden House, 1102 Warwick Road,
Acocks Green, Birmingham B27 6HB. UK.

Computer Book Publishers